THE ROAD OF SCIENCE
AND THE WAYS
TO GOD

The Gifford Lectures
1974–75
and
1975–76

THE ROAD OF SCIENCE
AND THE WAYS
TO GOD

Stanley L. Jaki

The University of Chicago Press

THE UNIVERSITY OF CHICAGO PRESS, CHICAGO 60637
SCOTTISH ACADEMIC PRESS, EDINBURGH EH7 5JX

STANLEY L. JAKI is also the author of *Les tendances nouvelles de l'ecclésiologie; The Relevance of Physics; Brain, Mind and Computers; The Paradox of Olbers' Paradox; The Milky Way: An Elusive Road for Science; Science and Creation: From Eternal Cycles to an Oscillating Universe;* and *Planets and Planetarians: A History of Theories of the Origin of Planetary Systems.* He has translated, with an introduction and notes, Giordano Bruno's *The Ash Wednesday Supper* and J. H. Lambert's *Cosmological Letters on the Arrangement of the World-Edifice.*

Library of Congress Cataloging in Publication Data

Jaki, Stanley L
    The road of science and the ways to God.

    (The Gifford lectures; 1974–75 and 1975–76)
    Includes bibliographical references and index.
    1. Religion and science—Addresses, essays,
lectures.   2. Science—History—Addresses, essays,
lectures.   3. God—Proof—History of doctrines—
Addresses, essays, lectures.   I. Title.   II. Se-
ries.
BL241.J34   215   77-21667
ISBN 0-226-39144-2 (cloth)
ISBN 0-226-39145-0 (paper)

CONTENTS

Preface
vii

PART I TWICE TWENTY CENTURIES
1   Pattern in Blind Alleys   3
2   A Lesson in Greek   19
3   Steps to God As Stepping-Stones to Science   34
4   Empirical Scouting   50
5   Rationalist Road Charting   65
6   Instinctive Middle   80
7   Bricks without Mortar   96
8   Arch without Keystone   112
9   The Illusions of Idealism   128
10   The Price of Positivism   145

PART II THE TWENTIETH CENTURY
11   The Quantum of Science   165
12   The Quantity of the Universe   181
13   The Horns of Complementarity   197
14   The Ravages of Reductionism   214
15   Paradigms or Paradigm   230
16   The Reach of the Mind   246
17   Cosmic Singularity   262
18   Pointers of Purpose   279
19   The Ethos of Science   297
20   Teaching by Examples   314

Notes
333
Index
459

PREFACE

By the stipulation of Adam Lord Gifford, the lectures that for almost a hundred years have been offered by virtue of his bequest are to be aimed at an audience in which scholars active in the lecturer's field form at most a perceptible minority. Presenting a topic in the form of public lectures imposes certain limitations on handling one's material. One such limitation is the need to stress essentials and to paint the intellectual landscape in crisp and bold strokes. Here I have frequently used quotations for this purpose and in every instance have given their provenance in the notes. Explanation and documentation of some secondary claims and details have also had to be relegated to the notes lest development of the principal theme suffer undue interruption. Since the topic discussed in these lectures spans much of cultural history, a selection of highlights was unavoidable.

Writing and delivering twenty lectures over two years is a long road toward a distant goal that could hardly be charted in advance with such accuracy as to make later alterations unnecessary. But apart from the addition of further material in every lecture and minor changes in some, the text printed here is nearly identical with the one delivered at the University of Edinburgh in April and May of 1975 and of 1976. The aim of these lectures is to demonstrate what is intimated in their title, namely, the existence of a single intellectual avenue forming both the road of science and the ways to God. Science found its only viable birth within a cultural matrix permeated by a firm conviction about the mind's ability to find in the realm of things and persons a pointer to their Creator. All great creative advances of science have been made in terms of an epistemology germane to that conviction, and whenever that epistemology was resisted with vigorous consistency, the pursuit of science invariably appears to have been deprived of its solid foundation. Whatever one's reaction to such a thesis, it certainly does justice to the goal set by the founder of this lecture series.

The presentation of this material brought me into lively contact with colleagues, students, and members of the wider academic community in Edinburgh, a city called not without good reason the Athens of the north. The acquaintances I was fortunate to make are among my cherished rewards for the effort expended.

I

TWICE
TWENTY
CENTURIES

One

PATTERN IN BLIND ALLEYS

ON THE TWENTY-FIRST DAY OF AUGUST, 1885, ADAM LORD GIFFORD SIGNED his will providing for a lectureship in natural theology in the four Scottish universities. The core of natural theology consists in tracing out the ways along which reason can ascertain what Lord Gifford called "the knowledge of God, that is, of the All, of the First and Only Cause." He also expressed his wish that the natural theology presented in the lectures should be within the reach of the "whole population" and that it should match the standards of astronomy and chemistry.[1] By "standards" he must have primarily meant exactness, which at that time was more characteristic of astronomy than of chemistry or even of physics. For a historian of science there is more meat in Lord Gifford's poking gentle fun at "whirling vortices" in the ether, which some leading physicists of the time saw as the last word in physical science.[2] Most important, Lord Gifford pleaded for a renewed interest in the metaphysical quest for the reality of God as the only support of that universal intelligibility which alone can satisfy man's inquiring mind and provide a solid basis for his actions. It was a remarkable appeal for the time, when even such a metaphysically minded physicist as Maxwell spoke scornfully of the den of metaphysicians strewn around with dead bones.[3]

The metaphysics of German idealism which Maxwell had in mind certainly deserved the harshest strictures, and these could only enhance admiration for an exact science which lent itself to wide-ranging technological applications. By the 1880s it had become in many quarters a pervasive tone of thought that science was the decisive factor in all aspects of life, a tenet to which Herbert Spencer had already given in 1855 a celebrated phrasing[4] and which he went on to preach with evangelical zeal for the rest of the century. When Lord Gifford signed his will it was not suspected that this very same science, the alleged solution for each and every ill, would soon have to look for new foundations to cope with its own problems. The edifice of science still displayed a timeless quality which made questions about its future as well as its past largely meaningless.

That questions of natural theology were not discussed at that time to any significant extent showed how deserted were its ranks. Such is a chief reason for the custom of offering this lectureship—from its inception on—to scholars whose field of interest has hardly ever been natural theology. Yet the custom expressed awareness that contributions to any branch of natural knowledge can serve as a platform for discourse on a theology not concerned with what is believed to be revealed or supernatural. While the majority of lecturers proceeded at best to within striking distance of natural theology, the presentation of a direct bearing of the history of science, my own field of interest, on natural theology is the unabashed aim of these lectures. Their claim in brief is that the road of science, both historically and philosophically, is a logical access to the ways to God. The study of that road is the historiography of science. Interestingly enough, it came to its most momentous (though for long unrecognized) turning point through the discovery in 1881 of Leonardo's notebooks,[5] only a few years before Lord Gifford signed his will.

Although the best scientists of the nineteenth century were far from agreeing with Spencer and his allies that science was a know-all and cure-all, they were inclined to think that mechanistic science was the last word in exact science and that in a sense science had nothing essentially new in store. Granting perfection to science meant therefore depriving it of future history, and this in turn could but invite an oversimplification of its past. The latter process received justification from reliance on Bacon's and Kant's dicta concerning the proper manner of doing science. Both Bacon and Kant, as will be discussed later, conceived the scientific method and its working in a mechanistic manner, and this could only promote indifference to the question of the origin of science both philosophically and historically.

A hybrid fusion of Bacon and Leibniz (if not of Kant) was the support of William Whewell's History of the Inductive Sciences (1837) and Philosophy of the Inductive Sciences (1840),[6] which served for decades as pattern for most histories and philosophies of science. Part of that pattern was the claim that Bacon and Galileo were each creators of modern science in much the same sense, a delusion which historians and philosophers of science no longer tolerate. Yet they seem to be reluctant to take full stock of the epistemological and methodological differences between the two, differences that affect not only any appraisal of the relatively brief span of modern science but also of its long prehistory. As a result the historiography of science resembles a rudderless ship drifting merrily with each breeze of intellectual fashion. The professional origin of that trouble has been clearly located in the Whewellian provenance of most histories of science written until rather recently.[7] It is still to be realized that the real source of the trouble is that most historians of science, like Whewell, fail to probe into the question of the origin of science. Or if they do so, they don't succeed much better than Spencer, who in 1854 anticipated many present-day efforts to find exclusive enlightenment in psychology concerning the genesis of science.[8] They do this in disregard of the fact that science is an act of understanding and

4

as such demands for its proper interpretation not only the tools of psychology but also those of epistemology.

Reflection, however brief, on the decisive impact of the embryonic stage on future development should make clear that a cursory or defective approach to origins will necessarily affect the handling of all later stages. Historical processes are no exception to this rule. As these lectures try to show, the same myopia about epistemology which prevented a careful weighing of the features of the origin of science also obstructed a proper understanding of the two great phases of modern science, the Newtonian and the Einsteinian. Moreover, the same myopia also supported all the attacks on the traditional proofs of the existence of God, attacks in which it was almost invariably overlooked that the proofs were ultimately the embodiment of reflections on what is the ultimate in intelligibility and being. As with the origin, the ultimate too cannot be wholly dismissed, only redefined. This process of redefinition inevitably affects reflections on science, especially when science is taken for the ultimate in explanation. Consequently, attacks on natural theology could readily become attacks on science whenever their principal presuppositions were rigorously and consistently applied in scientific methodology and historiography. This parallel is supported by a vast array of evidence which it is the burden of these lectures to present first historically and then thematically.

The first of these evidences to be discussed relates to the question of the origin of science, a question about which very little is available in the literature. Indeed, until the publication a few years ago of my *Science and Creation*,[9] the sole monograph on the topic was a now almost two-hundred-year-old book, Jean-Sylvain Bailly's *Lettres sur l'origine des sciences et sur celle des peuples de l'Asie*.[10] It was not the first discourse on that topic by Bailly, an astronomer turned historian of astronomy and called on occasion a *frère illuminé*. (The "illumination" referred to what Rosicrucianism and kindred trends offered to a goodly segment of self-styled rationalists in avid search of a substitute for the mysticism of Christian theism which they had snobbishly rejected).[11] The inner logic that emanates from Bailly's reflections should therefore seem rich in lessons germane to the topic of these lectures, but to grasp those lessons Bailly's sources ought to be considered in some detail. They were either the unwitting heralds or the crusading advocates of an Enlightenment that wanted a theism wholly severed from historic Christianity. Among the former were Jesuits involved in evangelizing China, and among the latter was Voltaire. While the Voltairians (Condorcet is the eloquent witness)[12] were ready to admit that Christianity was most influential in widely implanting such philosophical truths as the existence of God the Creator, the creation out of nothing, the immortality of a soul tuned to

5

moral responsibility, and the like, they were determined to discredit any intrinsic connection of these truths with Christian theism. In that effort they relied heavily on the voluminous reports on China sent by Jesuit missionaries. If not the first, the most notable of those reports was the *Nouveaux mémoires sur l'état présent de la Chine* by Father Louis Lecomte, missionary and "mathematician to the King."[13] The two-volume work, printed and translated half a dozen times in as many years, earned fame if not notoriety by Lecomte's resolve to support the main Jesuit missionary strategy with the claim that during the third and second millennia B.C., the Chinese were possessed of pure monotheism.[14]

The fault a historian of science would find with Lecomte's book concerns not theology, though Lecomte's theological position is what lies at the root of his handling of the backwardness of the Chinese in the sciences. Lecomte contrasted repeatedly the restless European mind with the lack of intellectual curiosity and motivation among the Chinese. In his words, the Chinese in spite of their proverbial diligence "have not produced yet one single person moderately profound in any speculative science," to which he added the remark that the "Chinese have not received the spirit of penetration and subtlety necessary for those who apply themselves to the knowledge of nature."[15] It was in this connection that he referred to the backwardness of the Chinese in geometry. He never tried to explain how the Chinese, short on subtle and penetrating minds, could develop and maintain for many generations an impeccable natural theology. Was their successful cultivation of natural theology, or the metaphysics which it heavily implied, not evidence of a subtle and abstractive mind? But then how could it happen that with such a mind the Chinese did not go beyond ideographic writing? Was it not that same nonabstractive writing in which Lecomte found one cause of the backwardness of the Chinese in the sciences?[16]

That these and similar questions could not for long be evaded can be seen from the correspondence which Jean-Jacques d'Ortous de Mairan, later successor of Fontenelle as perpetual secretary of the Académie des Sciences, began in 1728 with Father Dominique Parrenin, one of the leading Jesuit scientist-missionaries at the imperial court in Peking. The correspondence was predicated on what Mairan called the "strange paradox" of the Chinese, and was given broad publicity in 1734 when Parrenin's long reply containing copious extracts from Mairan's letter saw publication in the widely circulating *Lettres édifiantes.*[17] The first exchange of letters revealed a curious unawareness that Western science, already a briskly advancing giant, had demanded more than a few geniuses and propitious circumstances. To Mairan's wonderment that "chance, variety of nature, and incentives" had failed to produce in China "any extraordinary minds who in turn might have blazed the trail for posterity,"[18] Parrenin could only offer an ambivalent reply, obviously motivated by his missionary strategy, the immediate aim of which was the conversion of leading Chinese circles through re-interpreting their traditions in a light most favorable to the Christian creed. He insisted that there were some scientific geniuses among the Chinese of old, though without successors.[19] Again, while he admitted that speculative sciences were not to the native taste of the Chinese, he extolled their prowess in metaphysics.[20] The latter was evidenced, Parrenin argued, by the fact that he had not met "a single atheist" among the Chinese,[21] although he acknowledged their extremely superstitious bent of mind.

Mairan could be but puzzled by such answers to the paradox, which he further queried in his second letter, written in 1732. His questions forced Parrenin to admit more and more about the less appealing features of the Chinese mind concerning matters scientific. "In my opinion," Parrenin replied in 1735, "the Chinese of those remote times were pretty much of the same character as those now alive—superstitious, indolent, hostile to all innovations—who prefer the actual and tangible interests to what, according to them, is a vain and sterile glory of discovering something new."[22] The rest of Parrenin's letter and also much of his third letter written in 1740[23] was taken up with the question of the interrelation of ancient cultures, especially those of ancient Egypt and China. Neither he nor Mairan perceived the irony of speculating at length on the mutual instruction of two cultures distinctly noninquisitive compared with the "agile" European mind.[24] Why the latter was peculiarly inquisitive was not a problem for them. They took it for granted as one takes the air one breathes.

Yet that air had for some time been subject to a profound change when in 1759 the full text of Mairan's letters to Parrenin saw print. The support which deism derived from the Chinese was foreshadowed in Leibniz's proposal that Chinese missionaries be invited to the Christian West to instruct it in "the aim and practice of natural theology."[25] The same support was bluntly formulated a generation later in Tindal's *Christianity as Old as the Creation*, a work which claimed in its subtitle that *the Gospel* was *a Republication of the Religion of Nature*. There Tindal not only professed to know no difference between "the maxims of Confucius and Jesus Christ," but claimed that "the plain and simple maxims of the former will help illustrate the more obscure ones of the latter."[26] Deism soon became a cover-up for atheism. A good illustration of this was provided by Diderot, who gave away his atheism when in his article on the Chinese in the *Encyclopédie* he took the view that the vagueness of Chinese philosophy permits any interpretation, be it theistic, atheistic, or polytheistic. Diderot's article also illustrates the ease with which technology could be taken for science by advocates of the Enlightenment. Relying heavily on Lecomte's work, Diderot made much of the backwardness of the Chinese in technology (in which only two centuries earlier they were not much behind the West, a fact unsuspected by Diderot) and blamed it on the lack of inventiveness in their mental makeup. Why the Western mind was much more inventive and inquisitive was something Diderot preferred not to explore, although he set great store by it.[27]

For all its biases Diderot's article was instructive, a feature that cannot be said of Voltaire's witty propaganda on behalf of the Chinese, who without any reliance on the supernatural, he claimed, became the embodiment of virtue and enlightenment. In all that propaganda the question of the backwardness of the Chinese of old in the sciences was largely talked away—and in no very consistent manner. Although for Voltaire all people were plagued with superstition, he let it inhibit the Chinese of old more than others in their quest for science. The Chinese also were not alone in being deprived of the warm skies which he saw as a prerequisite for the development of astronomy and of science. He did not ponder why warm skies helped only the Hindus of old, whose land he specified as the cradle of astronomy.[28] None of this was brought up in the salons, nor was exception taken to the fact that in Voltaire's voluminous histories, in which he tried to offer a Newtonian rationale for history, discourse about science—including Copernicus, Galileo, Bacon, and Newton—covered three pages, or one-tenth of one percent of the total output.[29]

Clearly, with such performance roundly applauded, no second thoughts could be prompted by Mairan's questions—questions that are still to be faced by present-day admirers of ancient science, Chinese or other. There were, for instance, the long periods of peace in Chinese history. Why were not they conducive of scientific development? Was not the history of Europe far more turbulent than that of China? Again, why did the repeated besting by Jesuits of Chinese astronomers in public debates fail to prompt the latter to catch up in the sciences? Mairan was not only puzzled, he was indignant: "If this was not a powerful enough motivation and a shock capable of releasing basic talents, I do not know what would help the Chinese!"[30] As Mairan's third letter shows, Parrenin's increasingly frank acknowledgment of the indolence of the Chinese mind clarified, in part at least, what Mairan called again "the paradox," specifying it this time as "the paradox of the ignorance of the Chinese in astronomy and in mathematics compared with the Europeans."[31] Since the Chinese had a different mentality, they could perhaps be excused, but Mairan added: "I do not know whether this will completely free them of all reproach."[32]

The reproach was bluntly spelled out by Bailly in 1775 in the first volume of his history of astronomy, ancient and modern, a work which constitutes a major step toward the historiography of science in the modern sense.[33] That first volume, dealing with astronomy in ancient China, India, Persia, Babylon, Egypt, and pre-Ptolemaic Greece, was introduced with a "Discours préliminaire" in which Bailly set forth his views on the object of astronomy and on its nature, progress, and usefulness. He extolled astronomy as the fundamental science because as the most universal of all sciences it made possible broad generalizations which elevate the investigation of all nature to the level of science. For Bailly, the true astronomer was "the philosopher-astronomer who alone can become the architect of the universe. It is he who combines and connects the facts and grasps their coherence. An explanation generalized in his mind becomes the clue to a great number of phenomena."[34]

This is not to suggest that Bailly advocated a purely theoretical construction of the world. He was fully aware of the interplay which science demands between the data of observation and the perceiving mind. The progress of science was spotty, Bailly remarked, because "the facts were not always available for the genius, and the genius was not always available when the facts were."[35] It was to that interplay that he returned after a detailed discussion of the benefits of astronomy for a great variety of cultural endeavors. The primary benefit was, according to him, a realization of the vastness of the universe. It only remains, he concluded, "that reason should add to that magnificent spectacle knowledge of the simplicity of the laws prescribed for that imposing and vast universe, and then she will arrive at the idea of the extent and power of nature and at the notion of the greatness of the Supreme Being."[36] In uniting scientific methodology and natural theology Bailly was utterly sincere. Sincerity was so ingrained in his character that he refused to take advantage of opportunities to escape the revolutionary court which made him an illustrious scientist-victim of a Terror that formally replaced God with the Supreme Being of a deistic Enlightenment.

As a historian of astronomy Bailly earned, in the short run at least, more barbs than applause. The immediate reason for this was Bailly's disagreement with Voltaire, who placed the origin of science in ancient India on patently flimsy grounds. Bailly took a different and much broader view of the whole question. "When one considers with attention the state of astronomy in Chaldea, in India, and in China, ONE FINDS THERE RATHER THE DEBRIS THAN THE ELEMENTS OF A SCIENCE," he wrote with a measure of conviction expressed in capital letters.[37] The rather exact methods possessed by the ancients to calculate eclipses were in Bailly's eyes only "blind practices with no idea of the principles of such methods, or of the causes of phenomena." For him it was impossible to believe that if any of those ancient peoples were the inventors of astronomy, they could not carry it to perfection during their long history. "Though there may be," he noted, "nations so unfit to march as to be part of the advance of science, would the nation that has once become part of it by the momentum which it imposed on itself ever lose that momentum and come to a halt?"[38]

What Bailly had in mind was a self-sustaining start-up of science, unique in history, and the negative answer he gave to his question must be understood in the light of his statement that "the invention and the progress of science are of the same nature." The phases of progress, Bailly continued in his highly original way, "are but the replay of the original invention, a sequence of similar insights, and perhaps of efforts more or less equal." Thus, "if the ancient Hindus and Chinese made no progress in astronomy, it was only because they did not invent it."[39] Since the debris in all known ancient cultures appeared to him to be remarkably similar and since each of those cultures was enmeshed in intellectual indolence, it was inevitable for Bailly to postulate the existence of an earlier culture marked by scientific and philosophical vigor. He identified this as the first culture after the Deluge, flourishing in a land north of China, somewhere between the fiftieth and sixtieth parallels, during the later part of the fourth millennium B.C.[40]

Nothing was easier than to ridicule this specific conclusion and not to say anything about the incisive reflections preceding it. D'Alembert for one wrote to Voltaire that Bailly had offered possibly the most unsubstantiated idea ever to be proposed, because he had ascertained everything about that ancient culture except its identity and its existence.[41] Voltaire picked on particulars,[42] and on many particulars Bailly was clearly defenseless as he bravely reconstructed not only the astronomy of those mythical descendants of Noah but also the principal features of antedeluvian astronomy![43] Moreover, since Buffon as a geologist was rapidly falling into disrepute, Bailly invited facile objections by his reliance on Buffon's view—which he needed to secure for that coldish area north of China more warmth for the successful practice of astronomy—that formerly the earth's fiery center was more extensive.[44] But Bailly's real failure had its source in his own efforts blindfolded by a deism suspicious of anything Christian in cultural history. It was that suspicion too that made him ultimately prefer climate to genius, not only as he postulated warmer weather north of China, but also as he ascribed the beginning of modern science to "Ptolemy and his school in Alexandria," blessed with favorable skies.[45] This choice of Bailly's has to seem intrinsically suspect if it was also true, as he insisted, that only that birth of science was genuine which was followed by growth. Instead of prompting scientific growth Ptolemy's work enshrined an already old stagnation of science among the Greeks.

10

But not everything was self-defeating and ridiculous in the ten long letters that Bailly nominally addressed to Voltaire and in which he set forth once more and in a far more elaborate and systematic manner his views of the origin of science. The lengths to which he went in discussing the question put him in a different class from Voltaire, as well as from Montesquieu and from many lesser names who claimed to be scientific about cultural history while hardly mentioning science.[46] Voltaire and Montesquieu seem to be the target of the most illuminating pages in Bailly's *Lettres sur l'origine des sciences*. He pointedly asks whether the study of political institutions, wars, social customs, and the like was nearly as important as the study of the evolution of the edifice of knowledge and especially of science. Is it warriors who conquer the world or is it rather knowledge that is the great conqueror? "Can it be that I, a Frenchman, read with interest the history of Rome, which no longer exists, ... and remain insensitive to the history of sciences, to the sequence of the operations and progress of the human mind, which is the most precious part of my being? Why is it that those born to be superior in other centuries did not have the same ideas and did not reach the same truths?" For Bailly there was no mistaking that science put him on a much higher vantage point: "Because of knowledge I am today on a much higher level than many famous men ever attained through their genius. It is my century, raised by them, that puts me above them."[47]

The passage is richly suggestive and strongly incriminating. It not only suggested the tremendous potentialities of the study of the history of science, but also indicted the smug spokesmen of the century of Enlightenment. They not only felt far superior to the previous century—which for science was the century of genius—but viewed through thick filters the workings of the minds of all those geniuses. Thus they were unable to perceive that from Copernicus to Newton it was not deism but Christian theism that served as a principal factor helping the scientific enterprise reach self-sustaining maturity. This should have been evident to any careful reader of their texts even if he still kept swearing by the scientific and intellectual darkness of the Middle Ages. But the smugness of the Enlightenment did not permit an enlightened reading of the classics of the newly born science, a restriction which has begun to be disavowed only recently. Signs of this disavowal ought to be painful to those historians who resent Christian theism as a fact of history while they aim at a respectable level of objectivity. Even with this aim present, few if any questions are yet raised about the "debris" of science scattered across half a dozen blind alleys which the great ancient cultures had become for science.

Indeed, less than twenty years after Bailly's *Lettres sur l'origine des sciences,* his great questions were already ignored in a manner that was

11

to set a pattern. The "Précis de l'histoire de l'astronomie" of Laplace[48] revealed nothing of the intellectual drama embodied in scientific history. The account by Laplace was done in the perspective of his own achievements in celestial mechanics,[49] in which one equation seemed to lead inevitably to the next. Such an approach could hardly cope with details not pertaining to one's own specialty. Thus while Laplace praised the invention of the decimal system by the ancient Hindus as a feat that "escaped [even] the genius of Archimedes and Apollonius, two of the greatest men produced in antiquity,"[50] it did not occur to him that this generous praise generated a question which he as a practicing scientist should have readily perceived. His practice, or researches, would have been inconceivable without the contribution of half a dozen illustrious French geometers living a generation earlier. Clearly, Laplace was part of a sequence, but he failed to ask why no sequence of discoveries and applications followed in ancient India such a great scientific feat as the formulation of the decimal system.

Laplace's later years saw the rise of Hegel in Germany. Hegel's handling of the history of science will be treated later on in its own context and so will Comte's dicta on the history of science. Wherever their influence was felt it strangled rather than promoted the historiography of science, for reasons that were germane to their attitude toward natural theology. Needless to say, they had no eyes for the meaning of the few precious pieces of ancient science invariably locked in blind alleys. Neither were those pieces particularly instructive for Whewell for reasons already mentioned. His brief reminiscences of the Greeks as forerunners of modern science concluded with the momentous remark that the Greeks were unable to match with ideas their observations and experiments.[51] The failure of Whewell, the Kantian, to perceive the implications of that remark is particularly revealing in connection with his comments on Bacon's interpretation of the failure of ancient Greeks in science.[52] The one aspect of that interpretation (which will be discussed later) upon which Whewell, himself a Christian theologian, withheld comment was tied to natural theology as seen through Christian theism.

Since in Bacon's inductivism ideas were epiphenomena and since in Kant's apriorism ideas were ready at hand, the Whewellian historiography of science, resting as it did on Bacon and Kant, could not provide logical room for an appreciative account of the true genesis of scientific ideas. Nor could the uniqueness of the genesis of crucially important sets of scientific ideas be appreciated in the program given to the historiography of science by George Sarton, founder in 1912 of *Isis*, the first professional journal for the history of science. The *Introduction to the History of Sciences*, whose massive volumes were Sarton's own contribution to that program, was based on the claim that science was the slowly accumulating work of all ancient peoples regardless of race, religion, and culture.[53] Sarton himself took up only relatively late in his career the question of the Greeks' failure in science, and he settled the matter with a metaphor, the early burning out of a genius.[54] His facile handling of the matter was all the more startling because he had also stressed that "we shall not be able to understand our own science if we do not succeed in penetrating its genesis and evolution."[55] At any rate, what could be said of individual geniuses was not necessarily true of collective ones, and it was certainly not true that all geniuses burn out early, a point which had to be faced in connection with ancient cultures. They all reached the peak of their scientific creativity within a relatively short period of time.

Sarton is a perfect example of the fact that myopia about the stillbirths of science in ancient cultures easily becomes a myopia about the later, live birth of science, and that the myopia is clearly conditioned by one's attitude toward natural theology. For Sarton this could only be negative, both from the philosophical and historical standpoints, since he disliked metaphysics[56] and was unenthusiastic about the Christian cultural heritage.[57] The latter was never stronger than in the Middle Ages, Sarton's professed area of specialty.[58] This latent conflict in Sarton, the historian of science, can explain why Sarton never probed into the causes of the sudden rise of interest in experimentation during the late Middle Ages, although he extolled the fact itself. Nor did he ask why in this case the genius failed to burn out at an early stage. A curious neglect, because Sarton seized the opportunity to review the first volume of Pierre Duhem's *Le système du monde*,[59] a work that represented a Copernican turn in the historiography of science, but which, like the original Copernican turn, was for long received with silence and unbelief in professional circles, although Duhem did no more than exploit to the full the discovery of Leonardo's notebooks. But Sarton, who insisted that talent ought to be recognized regardless of its provenance, and who could go to enormous lengths in documenting comparatively insignificant achievements, was, for the rest of his life, silent on Duhem.[60]

Clearly Sarton was reluctant to accept Duhem's conclusion that the failure of Greek science was due to the influence of such theological doctrines as the divinity of the heavens and the eternal recurrence of all, an influence which, as Duhem intimated, was operative in other ancient cultures as well.[61] Nor could Sarton have been pleased by Duhem's overwhelming documentation of a solid interest in science from the twelfth century onward, and of the support given that interest by the Christian theism of the medievals. Duhem's scholarly testimonial to that theism could but remain systematically overlooked amid the positivist resurgence of the 1930s. Nobody cared therefore to point out that Duhem had already massively documented Whitehead's famous statement that medieval theism was a crucial factor in the emergence of science.[62] Duhem was at best mentioned as an ally of Mach, whose positivism and historiography were wholly devoid of metaphysics, whereas this was not at all true of Duhem's work.[63] Nor was any genuine attention given to Duhem when, from the 1950s on, the majority of historians of science broke with positivism, largely under the influence of Alexandre Koyré—an influence which, as will be discussed later, meant not an espousal of epistemology but of culturally conditioned epistemologies, none intrinsically more valid than any other. At the international symposium of historians of science held in Oxford in 1961, possibly the most important of such symposia in the past decades, few participants were in sympathy with Henry Guerlac's declaration that Duhem is the "acknowledged teacher of us all."[64] The liveliest topic of that symposium was the paradigm interpretation of scientific history, an interpretation, as will be seen later, unresponsive to the gigantic question of the only successful escape of science from blind alleys in which it repeatedly had lost itself.

What historical scholarship failed to recognize was assured recognition by the march of history. The emergence of China and India on the geopolitical scene meant the entry into modern life of two ancient cultures, the only two that have reached the contemporary scene not as archaeological relics but as political giants. Their future is staked on their successfully solving the problem of assimilating the very same science that never flourished in their ancient soil. The problem clearly implied much more than what could be carried by the smooth rhetoric of Bertrand Russell, who declared in 1922 in his *The Problem of China* that "although Chinese civilization has hitherto been deficient in science, it never contained anything hostile to science."[65] That the problem had deeper and broader dimensions was revealed in the massive volumes of Joseph Needham's *Science and Civilization in China*. As is well known, Needham, in spite of his avowed Marxism, gave prominent place among causes that prevented the escape of science from its blind alley in ancient China to a theological cause, namely, the early vanishing among the Chinese of a belief in a rational Lawgiver or Creator of the world. Lacking that belief, the Chinese could not bring themselves to believe that man was able to trace out at least some of the laws of the physical universe.[66]

Needham did his best to weaken the instructiveness of such a connection between theism and science, a connection that was ascribed to his "Christian meditations"[67] by a Marxist critic who, unlike Needham, did not wish to accord any usefulness to the Judeo-Christian heritage in scientific history. Neither of these tactics can obliterate the fact that the predicament of China, both ancient and modern, is an eloquent though

14

tragic witness to the need of natural theology if science is to flourish. The implicit denial of natural theology in ancient China reached its highest level in the logic-defying aphorisms of Taoism. Today the same insults to the intellect are the daily fare of Chinese minds desperately trying to live with the consistency of science and with the inconsistencies of Taoism resuscitated in the form of Marxist-Maoist dialectic.

The conflict, if not as cruel as in China, is keenly felt in India, where ideas and their impact can be discussed with a fair measure of freedom. It is increasingly realized there that the success of grafting modern technology on a cultural tree conspicuously barren in matters scientific depends largely on the adoption by the whole society of a new outlook on physical nature and human existence. The need for that change has been noted even by Indian intellectuals chiefly concerned with the economic future of their country. Thus, D. K. Rangnekar wrote in 1958 in his *Poverty and Capital Development in India:* "The young Indian ... must be able and willing to tear himself away from his family ties, flout customs and traditions, put economic welfare before cow worship, ... concentrate on material gains rather than dwell on *Kismet* (destiny). These are extremely difficult changes to envisage in the Hindu social structure and ideas. But they seem unavoidable. They may or may not produce the philosophy of *Vedanta,* the literature of *Kalidasa,* or the culture and spiritualism of Buddha or Gandhi. But they will certainly promote the dynamism of Nehru."[68]

Rangnekar's willingness to give up the philosophy of the Vedantas, of Buddha, and of Gandhi for the sake of abolishing poverty may be well-intentioned, but it seems shortsighted. No social, cultural, and economic structure can exist in a philosophical vacuum. Moreover, technological and economic programs of the sort he espouses need a creative science, which is never without deep philosophical roots. Rangnekar's praise of Nehru's dynamism will probably be upheld by some political historians, but a historian of science cannot give Nehru high marks for his way of treating the very same cultural and philosophical problem in which modern India finds itself. Nehru's urging India in his *The Discovery of India* to break with "much of her past," and not let it "dominate the present," is coupled with a romantic evocation of a phase of the national past dominated by "bouyant energy," by "love of life and nature," by "spirit of curiosity," by "mental adventure," by "daring of thought," by "capacity to absorb other people's cultural accomplishments."[69] Such expressions remind one of some nineteenth-century historians poetizing about the Renaissance as the grand opening of the age of science. Nehru, intent on creating the illusion about a great scientific past in India, seized on Laplace's dictum on the invention of the decimal system.[70] Indian historians of science who have tasted real scholarship have no use for such propaganda. One of them, N. R. Dhar, urged nothing less on the part of his colleagues than the cultivation of the spirit of honesty, of a sober respect for the facts of history regardless of whether they support claims of national grandeur or not.[71]

Honesty with historical data should be accompanied by a realistic discrimination of ideas. Since the exact rise of a spirit, scientific or otherwise, is always elusive, a patriotic Hindu like R. C. Majumdar may claim with some impunity that the scientific spirit originated in India five centuries before Thales and Anaximander.[72] It is more of a risk to present the creation hymn in book 10 of the Rig-Veda as the embodiment of scientific spirit—exemplified, Majumdar claims, by the poet's searching inquiry into cosmic origins and in the answer that the original entity was one "who breathed breathless by itself, from whom all creation come into being and that the gods themselves came later into being." According to Majumdar that spirit is also evident in the closing questions of the hymn.[73] But those questions express a deeply skeptical view which cannot be either the first or the last word in science or in philosophy. A creation hymn which ends with asking "Who knows from whence this great creation sprang?" hardly suggests that the ultimate entity from which all came is intelligibility itself and that rationality is thus assured in the created realm. What the hymn actually bespeaks is a failure in natural theology.

"God the One," as he is referred to at one point in the hymn, is not the God of monotheism. The Rig-Veda time and again identifies God with creation (or nature) and describes the coming into being as an inevitable inner development within that pantheistic cosmic entity. As time went on and the further Vedas, the Upanishads, and the Puranas came to be composed, Hindu cosmogony, a form of natural theology, became more and more dominated by grossly animistic details, and fell more and more under the sway of the idea of eternal recurrence in the cosmic unfolding of the Brahma.[74] What all this meant from the psychological viewpoint was poignantly put by King Brihadratha in the *Maitri Upanishad:* "In the cycle of existence I am like a frog in a waterless well."[75] The cycle was the treadmill of the yugas which represented nature not as an inspiration but as a fearsome curse. In the India and China of old the connection between the gradual withering of science and the ascendancy of belief in eternal recurrence stands out in bold relief.[76] The same is also plausibly clear in the cultures of the pyramids, the Egyptian, the Babylonian, and the Maya. The evidence for the same in ancient Greece and among Muslim Arabs has its special instructiveness for any historian of Western science.

This is not to suggest that the philosophy and theology of eternal returns wholly accounts for the failure of science in all great ancient cultures. Yet the philosophy and theology in question seem to be the only factor common to all those cultures. That factor is as much a major cultural pattern as the failure of science is in all of them a monumental fact. That it received so little attention in an age of avid research into far less significant cultural patterns is hardly an accident. The avoidance of the issue seems to be due to that positivist resolve reminiscent of King Lear's reluctance to look in a direction in which madness seemed to lie.[77] While theology in its natural form is not always called madness in positivist circles, it is always looked upon as evidence of intellectual feebleness. Whatever the merit of having keen eyes for the odium theologicum (but not for the odium antitheologicum), the usefulness of this one-way vision in historiography is doubtful. With the rejection of philosophical theology one is left with socioeconomical, geopolitical, and psychological types of explanation. They all appear puny in the gigantic presence of the failure of science in all great ancient cultures. Long periods of peace, economic prosperity, favorable climatic conditions, exchange with other cultures, were not always absent in any of them. None of those ancient cultures lacked individual talents. Nor can it be consistently claimed that each of those cultures had its own special notion of science and that the questions it posed and the answers it permitted were satisfactory within the given psychological framework. On the contrary, the historical record shows in each of them a curious mixture of two attitudes. One is the urge to know more about nature and to use that knowledge more effectively; the other is the saddening sense of defeat in the face of such a lofty goal. Both invite some speculations and impose some directives.

One may for instance speculate what would have happened if King Ashoka had expended his distinctly non-Buddhist activism in the milieu of a different mentality. Science might have surged toward maturity in his court and not in the realm of the Medicis or of the Tudors. Thus India might have become the colonizer of the Mediterranean and even perhaps the political unifier of the British Isles. Or what about the China of the late fifteenth century, which had a navy better than the one at the disposal of Vasco da Gama? Two centuries or so later, Louis XV might have changed the course of history had he not only been willing but also able to spare fifty thousand Frenchmen for his possessions in North America. The China of the fifteenth century had millions of men to spare in addition to having the ships, but she had no navigators with enough will and curiosity to sail to Australia, let alone to the Californian coastlands. The Egyptians of old were clever enough to circumnavigate Africa without a compass and to build pyramids without pulleys. Would the Greeks be remembered today in the way they are had Archimedes been an Egyptian? The weighing of such ifs is not sheer speculation even if one does not look with Parrenin

17

and Mairan at ancient Egyptians as the teachers of the Chinese, or with Voltaire at ancient Hindus as the masters of Pythagoras, or with Bailly at Outer Mongolia as the cradle of science.

As to the directives, the chief of them derives from that pattern which shows science finding in all ancient cultures a blind alley for its promising starts. A principal element of that pattern is the hold which the distinctly theological tenet of eternal cycles had on ancient cultures. It is well known that a very different theological tenet, which implied the linear process from an absolute beginning, or the creation of all, to an absolute end, was the broadly shared view when science at long last found its road to unlimited advance. Therefore the further investigation of a close connection between the road of science and theological tenets should seem a promising directive. Its value will undoubtedly be enhanced when a lesson is taken from the Greeks of old, still the unparalleled teachers by their successes as well as by their failures.

Two

A LESSON IN GREEK

"GREEK MIRACLE" IS BOTH A HALLOWED REFERENCE AND A PROPER credit to achievements which constitute in more than one field marvel itself. In architecture, philosophy, drama, sculpture, and political theory the Greeks of old realized ideals that can hardly be improved upon. In science, their quest for perfection succeeded only in one area, geometry. Their success in physics was in fact limited to the extent to which the phenomena of the physical world readily lent themselves to a geometrical formulation. The phenomena in question ranged in size from Archimedes' bathtub through the dimension of the earth to the planetary orbs. Geometry rightly seemed to the Greeks a saving grace if the inquiring mind was to find coherence and logic in the manifold aspects of the physical world.

Plato's phrase, "to save the phenomena," soon became a shibboleth of Greek reflections on the science of heavenly motions.[1] The phrase also became the center of controversy because it implied a frustrating compromise with deep-seated and long-cherished hopes about a true science of nature which for man meant above all the terrestrial realm. Moreover, true science was to provide full intelligibility about nature, and full intelligibility meant an insight into the cause and purpose of everything that existed and happened. This was an unlimited request in the way of understanding and not surprisingly it made its appearance on the Greek scene with an existential force. The catalyst for that decisive event in Greek intellectual history was the struggle of Socrates with the meaning of explanation.

In that struggle Socrates merely brought some long-standing concerns to a heroic point. Long before him it had been recognized that the question about understanding derives from the experience of change, a point on which any extremist answer could only provoke the other extreme. If there was only change and nothing permanent, as Heraclitus claimed, then any explanation became meaningless. If change was only apparent, as Parmenides insisted, explanation was unnecessary. The Ionians seemed to be more cautious with their solutions, which implied a certain dichotomy. Thales was reported to have stated not only that water was god, but also that everything was full of gods.[2] His first statement was an explanation of change in terms of a purely physical factor, water. His second statement endorsed the traditional approach to change in terms of will and purpose. Of the two explanations suggested by Thales, the first drew the greater attention, in the short run at least. In the universe of Anaxagoras nothing was full of gods; in

19

fact, there was no room in it for considering what the gods represented, namely, will, purpose, and personal determination. In short, in the book in which Anaxagoras ascribed everything to the mind there were regularities, but no mind which regulated, planned, and did so for a purpose.[3]

The rest is well known from Socrates' last dialogue recorded by Plato in the *Phaedo*.[4] It deals with Socrates' rebuttal of his friends' disbelief in the immortality of the soul and in abiding purpose. Their disbelief was groundless, so Socrates argued, because it was based on a purely mechanistic physics, the physics of the Ionians and of Anaxagoras, which dealt only with the succession and configuration of events. From the vantage point secured by classical and modern physics it is clear that physics is not and should not be about purpose. Unfortunately, it is not always realized that physics, classical and modern, is, like all sciences, the product of a most purposeful enterprise, and therefore its methodical disregard of purpose can in no way be taken for a peremptory argument against it. It is hardly remembered at all that what the Greeks from Socrates on tried to achieve in physics was to save purpose for man as well as for the universe. They were wrong, to be sure, but this does not change a fact of enormous historical and cultural consequence. One aspect of this was the failure of the Greeks to escape the pattern of blind alleys in science.

Histories of Greek science are legion. Only a few contain any discussion of the causes of the failure of Greek science, and not one of them does justice to the impact which Socrates' heroic stand had on the remaining long history of Greek thought. The Greeks themselves were fully aware of the magnitude of that impact. Alcibiades anticipated the feeling of the whole of classical posterity when he remarked at the dinner table of Agathon: "When we listen to anyone else talking, however eloquent he is, we don't really care a damn what he says ... I have heard Pericles and all the other great orators ... but they never ... turned my whole soul upside down. But this [Socrates] has often left me in such a state of mind that I have felt that I simply could not go on living the way I did. He makes me admit that while I am spending my time on politics I am neglecting all the things that are crying for attention in myself."[5] Had Alcibiades lived in the years separating Galileo from Newton and had he been a physicist, he could have but wished that, as he put it, Socrates had never lived and that he had never listened to him. By then it was clear that success in physics meant a methodical disregard of questions about purpose. Leibniz, a loner in many respects, was alone among physicists of his time with his speculations about a physics that would do justice to the program given by Socrates to physics in the *Phaedo*.[6] It was that program which put a fateful stamp on each of the three main types of ancient Greek physics, the Aristotelian, the Epicurean or atomistic, and the Stoic. They had the common effect of putting physics into a straitjacket for two thousand years, because their common and overriding aim was not so much to save the phenomena as to save purpose for man as well as for the cosmos.

The resolve to vindicate cosmic purpose clearly commits one to metaphysics and theology. Consequently, if purpose is defined in a perspective which includes a theological vision, and such was certainly the Greek vision of metaphysics, then the success in constructing physics will depend on the theological foundations one has posited. Of the three main types of physics elaborated by the Greeks, the Aristotelian shows, in a far more subtle fashion than do the Epicurean and the Stoic, the impact of a specific view of the ultimate in intelligibility on the viability of physics. Natural motion and natural place are emphatically Aristotelian concepts inasmuch as the emphasis is on the natural, or rather nature, as the embodiment of purpose. The concepts are Aristotelian, but only to the extent to which he articulated the first part of Socrates' argument on behalf of the immortality of the soul. That first part is a contention that motion is unintelligible if it is not for the sake of purpose, that is, for the sake of the better and of the best. The second part of Socrates' argument claimed that there could be no life if there was no absolutely perfect, or immortal, life. It was seized upon by Plato who developed it into his dichotomy between a perfect world of ideas and a shadowy realm of matter. The physics and cosmology that could be had on such a basis was as elusive as shadows are. And just as elusive for Plato was the maker and father of the universe, about whom he remarked that he was "past finding out and even if we found him, to tell of him to all men would be impossible."[7] Along the a priori road charted by Plato neither solid science nor reliable natural theology could be had, and for the same reason. As the *Timaeus*, Plato's last testament, shows, a rudimentary geometrization of the universe in its first part was overshadowed in its far longer concluding part by an account of the universe in terms of the human body, an account both animistic and pantheistic. Plato's universe was the product of a demiurgos (or public contractor, to recall the original meaning of the word) who could not create the world but only fashion it and along the preferences of some fashionable opinion.

Whatever the limitations of the Greek genius, it was not so limited as to accept defeat a priori. Aristotle's approach had a promise of triumph precisely because in it conclusions seemed to be reached in an a posteriori fashion. Actually, Aristotle's discourse about the cosmos was as a priori as it could be. The most notorious example of this is in *On the Heavens* where in a mere hundred words Aristotle explains why the universe is what it actually seems to be.[8] His starting point is the activity of a god which ought to be immortality, that is, eternal life. Socrates would have enjoyed reading it. Here was purpose, carried to its apparently fullest meaning. It was still to be seen what explanation could be extracted from it in respect to the physical world.

Aristotle first explained why everything was not divine and immortal, or why everything was not a god moving forever in a circle, the eternal activity of the gods. His answer was that a circle could not be in motion without its center being at rest. From this followed the dichotomy between celestial and terrestrial matter, the natural motion in a circle of the divine stars, and the natural motion up and down in the perishable sublunary realm. The most disastrous sequel of the latter assertion was the postulating of exactly four elements and of a rate of fall which depended on the "abundance" of nature, which in turn was revealed by the amount of matter embedded in any particular object.[9] Implicit in all this was an unrevisable theory of motion, an unrevisable analysis and classification of matter, in sum an unrevisable framework for physics, chemistry, and cosmology.[10] Within a framework, which could not be revised without being demolished, science was limited to the observation and classification of secondary details. Such was not a negligible task and Aristotle did valuable work in biology, the field best tailored to his method. In connection with the physical sciences the method was not a road but a blind alley.

Because of his premises Aristotle had to deny that wind was air in motion,[11] and he had to claim that stationary and flowing waters were essentially different.[12] By the same token he had to assert that earthquakes and comets were due to the rise of dry exhalation from the bowels of the earth,[13] that the solar heat was ultimately generated by a divinely cool sun,[14] and that the same was true about the light of stars, and that the unchanging contours and hue of the Milky Way could be explained by that most volatile substance, the dry exhalation.[15] Aristotle's theory of the Milky Way as a sublunary phenomenon may be the most stunning case of the extent to which a genius can be blinded by the logic of his initial presuppositions.[16] Genius he certainly was, not only by his ability to systematize, but above all by his realization that some middle road had to be charted between naive realism and dreamy idealism, if the intelligibility of a world of change was to be salvaged. And he built a way of great originality along which the mind was to ascend to the highest form of intelligibility, of purpose, and of being.

Change, Aristotle argued in the famous chapter 6 of book lambda of the *Metaphysics*,[17] is motion in a most general sense, though not a motion which accounts for itself, for any change reveals the potential side of a being and not its actual perfection. Moreover, there would be no movement if there were only a being capable of moving but not actually doing so. This is why Plato's static world of ideas did not find favor with Aristotle.[18] Since he had already argued that regress to infinity was no answer, he could conclude that "there must be a principle such that its very nature is to be in act."[19] Such is a briefest sketch of Aristotle's way to the Prime Mover, a way whose significance lies in the mental effort of putting its phases together and in the features of the target, or the realm of the divine, reached along it. The effort attests Aristotle's trust in the ability of reason to transcend the realm of change. The target, as he formulates it, is significant for three reasons. The first is that in the very same context Aristotle finds it important to note that motion is indicative of purpose.[20] He certainly wanted to be a continuation of Socrates, for whom purpose had on it the stamp of the divine. The second reason should be obvious from Aquinas's utilization of Aristotle's reasoning in the first of his five ways. For Aristotle, too, pure activity is a divine prerogative, for we humans can exercise but intermittently the activity of intellectual vision. The divine, Aristotle states, "is always in that better state." The divine is, therefore, "the eternal best living so that the divine is life unending, continuous, and eternal."[21] This life was, according to Aristotle, the only and supreme source of all intelligibility, and the first principle of nature, order, and beauty. Such a life could seem worlds removed from the cunning and boisterous life of the gods as described only three centuries earlier by Hesiod. On seeing that difference not a few Church Fathers wondered whether Aristotle had not been in debt to Moses and led thereby by truly divine light. Aristotle himself stated that the notion of divine life as pure activity was for him the source of utmost wonder.

He did not suspect that his next statement would be a source of much wonderment but in a very different sense. After declaring that the primary, eternal being cannot have magnitude and parts, since it is separate from all sensible beings, Aristotle raised the question whether the primary motion is one in number or possibly several.[22] Clearly, no sooner had Aristotle risen to unequaled heights than he slid back to a view of the deity which is hardly a cause for wonderment. In that view the primary being is the primary heaven, and this is why Aristotle had to face the questions whether the divine was limited or unlimited and whether it was one or many. His particular problem was to show in what sense the divine was different from the fifty-five celestial motions, and in what sense all those motions were one. At this point the highest form of metaphysics became a purely technical astronomy which saves only phenomena but not purpose and leaves no room for wonderment either about God or about the cosmos.[23]

Is then the concrete target of Aristotle's theology not so much the pure act of the intellect as the eternally revolving heavens? Aristotle corroborates this suspicion when in the next breath he refers to the stars and planets as personal beings in the style of mythological theology for which everything was full of gods.[24] Of this mythological theology Aristotle was willing to retain its glimpse of the divine but not its intent to make the divine also something personal. The pure act of intellect as a definition of the primary being did not prompt Aristotle to see in it any personal trait even when he spoke a page or two later of the order and coherence of the universe.[25] The order of any army is due, he remarked, to its commander, whereas the order of a house is merely due to its being a household, to an impersonal coordination of all within it. Consequently, the universe of Aristotle is a house without a head and the host of stars in it could have no commander. The Aristotelian universe bespoke law and order but not a lawgiver.

While the pure act of intellect, the primary being of Aristotle, constantly thinks itself, it never has the world in mind. It prompts a desire for itself in the stellar realm but the desire is transmitted to lower echelons in a necessary, mechanistic manner. It was through that desire that the saving of purpose was achieved in the cosmos of Aristotle. It was not a saving purpose through free personal acts as Socrates wanted it. The question of free will puzzled Aristotle precisely because his primary being had no such will.[26] The heavens were strictly necessary, and because of this Aristotle's efforts to assert a measure of contingency in the realm of human actions always sounded somewhat hollow. Contingent as he believed himself to be, he certainly did not worship the necessary pure act, divine though it was. His own religious sense attracted him, in a thoroughly unphilosophical manner, to the personal Zeus and Demeter of mythology. In his will he provided for a statue of each. A truly Socratic gesture, though on slightly higher level, for Socrates parted from his life with the wish that a cock be slaughtered on his behalf in honor of Asclepius.[27]

The third reason which gives special significance to Aristotle's specification of the Prime Mover, the target of his way to the ultimate, has to do with science. In warding off the view of a personal deity as expressed in mythologies, Aristotle noted that such views had already been repeatedly developed and lost as many times. This was an echo of his firm belief in the eternal recurrence of all generic things and processes. The sciences formed no exception to this treadmill. According to Aristotle they had repeatedly reached their perfection in previous ages.[28] Even more discouraging should seem the complacency with which he declared that the sciences of his time, together with the crafts and commodities of life, had already risen as high as they possibly could.[29] The statement was a sad prophecy for Greek science. Euclid, Archimedes, Diophantes, and Ptolemy were unable to raise it to a level much higher than where it stood when Aristotle parted from life.

Undue engrossment with one's own system is an ever-present trap, but in Aristotle's case one may go deeper than that. He set forth his theories in a tone suggesting that errors could victimize the mind only in smaller matters, once it was equipped with the proper method.[30] The substance of that method was embodied in Aristotle's way to the pure act which, as we have seen, Aristotle could not keep consistently pure, that is, transcendent to anything sensory, be it the most perfect sphere of stars. Thus the way to the pure act also empowered the mind to ascertain why the world had to be what it was and why it possessed the structure, laws, and principal features it apparently did. This meant that the mind could acquire basic truths about the physical world without undertaking an extensive program of observations and experimentation. A cosmic intelligibility which could be conquered so easily could hardly be illuminating. The Aristotelian universe was necessary and so was its form of intelligibility, but this intelligibility served no real purpose, just as its universe had none, although it seemed to teem with purpose.

The case of Theophrastus, Aristotle's nephew and successor as the head of the Lycaeum, is particularly instructive in this respect. His keenness of mind was certainly in evidence in his realization that science would not profit by explaining every phenomenon in terms of purpose.[31] Yet he failed to see that the problem of purpose in Aristotelian science could not be remedied without touching the very foundations. Much less did he suspect that no meaningful account of science could be based on them. The practice of science as done in the Lycaeum and the Museum went on without ever earning the hallmark of genuine creativity. As Hellenism was succeeded by the Hellenistic age, the creative energies of many a genius were locked in producing further variations on well-known and well-worn themes, an enterprise that could only run aground in the boredom of a dead end.[32]

If the excitement of challenging controversies was not completely absent in Hellenistic science, it was due largely to the influence of Epicurus of Samos and Zeno of Citium. Zeno, the founder of the Stoic school, is known to have been guided by Socrates' life and death as recounted by Xenophon and Plato. Epicurus carried the Socratic detachment for earthly concerns to such a degree that he was honored as a god while still alive. To take such a man for a god shows that ancient Greeks by and large could see in matters divine no higher than Olympus, however ennobled. Historians of science, in their excitement over the insights of Leucippus and Democritus into the structure of matter, mention Epicurus only as an epigone, and epigone he was as an atomist. Yet without him and his ethical philosophy, atomism, so heavily criticized by Aristotle, would have remained on the periphery of interest during the Hellenistic centuries. Lucretius's chief interest was Epicurean ethics, not the science of atoms, and it was no accident that the revival of atomism by Gassendi was tied to his effort to rehabilitate Epicurus, the ethical philosopher.

Epicurus espoused atomism because he perceived the rank necessitarianism lurking behind Aristotelian purposiveness. But was the atomism of Democritus less necessitarian? It certainly was not, but it seemed to Epicurus that, unlike the necessitarianism of Aristotle, that of Democritus might be cured through minor surgery. The operation consisted in attributing to each atom the ability to swerve, however slightly, from the path predetermined by the ironclad laws of mechanical collisions. This was a clever but not very rational procedure, something that did not seem to bother Epicurus. He was not interested in reason and in its urge for consistency. His sole aim was to save a minimum of peace of mind, a minimum of freedom, a minimum of repose for the individual tossed around in the endless flux and reflux of atoms. His only rational contribution to Democritus's atomism consisted in abandoning the latter's dictum according to which atoms of all conceivable shapes existed, even atoms of immense size. Epicurus rightly perceived that if Democritus was right, then even atoms of infinite size had to exist. While Democritus seemed to be a thinker unafraid of the paradoxical consequences implied in his radical materialism, Epicurus wanted no radical confrontation with logic. Nor did his popularizer, Lucretius, face up to the rigor of logic in connection with the puzzle of how material atoms could by definition be "partless" parts.[33] Like Epicurus, he wanted to secure happiness, not explanation.

Early atomism is often described by historians of science as a breakthrough to rationalism. Epicurus himself found no use for the basic rationality of disjunctive statements according to which a proposition is either false or true.[34] Not surprisingly, he was also remembered in antiquity for his hostility to mathematics. He advocated strict empiricism and ended up, as he had to, in naive realism. Both he and Lucretius insisted that the sun and the moon were as large as they appeared to be, a foot in diameter.[35] These and similar propositions of Epicurus were part of a careful strategy aimed at warding off the specter of generalized truths and of a universal causation. This is why Epicurus wanted to have the gods left alone in eternal blessedness and bliss.[36] He sensed that the gods, anthropomorphic as they were, evoked the vista of a universal order of things and principles. Therefore if the gods were to be left alone, the serious study of astronomy and cosmology had also to be avoided.

Epicurus's cosmology, especially his dicta on vortices, may appear prophetic to the ever-misleading wisdom of hindsight and to the chronic unfamiliarity with original contexts. Taken in its context, Epicurus's cosmology served the idea of a purely accidental and disorderly state of things. He warned against attributing strict lawfulness to nature as if nature was ruled by any being "who controls and ordains, or has ordained" such notable regularities as the motion of heavenly bodies, their eclipses, risings, and settings.[37] Neither could nature as such be a source of strict lawfulness. Epicurus insisted that there were several licit explanations for every phenomenon in the sky as well as on the earth. In speaking about celestial vortices, or worlds, he took pains to emphasize that they could be of any shape, even three-cornered,[38] a rather unscientific vortex to be sure. As one would expect, no genuinely scientific idea could be entertained by a thinker who attributed the rising of the sun to the kindling of matter at given positions on the horizon.[39] Particularly distasteful were for him what he called "slavish artifices" of astronomers.[40] No wonder that Epicurus, who could not digest a morsel of science and could not tolerate the idea of one who ordained things as they are, found the myths about the gods palatable after all. The gods would be placated, he said in endorsing the trickery of polytheism and its radical inconsistency, but science "involves a necessity which knows no placation."[41] Once more, the fate of natural theology went hand in hand with the fortunes of science.

The saving reflection that the recognition of scientific necessity was itself the fruit of a most genuinely free act did not occur to Epicurus or to any of his followers. The saving of purpose vis-à-vis science was achieved by the Greeks of old either by preempting purpose of its ultimate meaning, as was done by Aristotle, or by the trick of swerving atoms, as Epicurus would have it, or by the methodical advocacy of a radical schizophrenia, as happened to the Stoics. This had been so ever since Zeno opened his school almost exactly a hundred years after his great idol, Socrates, laid down his life in testimony to an abiding purpose. Those hundred years, or the fourth century B.C., do not offer anything crucial for students of Greek political history. For Greek science, philosophy, and theology the decisive century is the fourth. It was then that the Greeks lost their religion to philosophy and also gave evidence why they were not to have science as a self-sustaining enterprise.

The Stoic quest for purpose was gigantic not only in terms of personal dedication but also in terms of cultural impact. It was a quest that kept its vigor for almost half a millennium, the time that separates Zeno from Marcus Aurelius. Devotees of Stoicism, coming from all walks of life, were animated by a zeal to secure for themselves the conviction that in spite of all appearances to the contrary, their lives and all lives, nay the whole cosmos, were ruled by Providence. Purpose saved by Providence—such was the great message of the Stoics and they urged a most personal gratitude toward that Providence to which they referred as the supreme God. "If we had sense," Epictetus wrote, "we ought to do nothing else, in public and in private, than praise and bless God and pay Him due thanks." With a heroism and serenity reminding one of a saint, Epictetus warned everyone that this gratitude was the supreme duty and fulfillment of man: "If I were a nightingale I should sing as a nightingale, if a swan, as a swan: but as I am a rational creature I must praise God. This is my task, and I do it: and I will not abandon this duty, so long as it is given me: and I invite you all to join in this same song."[42]

To show the rationality of this all-consuming gratitude toward a God of Providence, who beholds man and arranges every detail in the universe for him,[43] was the chief task of Stoic philosophy. To implement that task one only needed, so Epictetus declared, two qualities. They were "a power to see clearly the circumstances of any given particular fact and the spirit of gratitude therewith."[44] Logicians would quickly note that the juxtaposition of these two qualities implied running in a circle, but even worse was in store. As to the circumstances of any given fact, Epictetus advocated naive realism. According to him, the hair on the chin served the noble and important purpose of distinguishing male from female, and proved that everything was carefully arranged by a divine Craftsman.[45]

Of such character was the principal but not the only way constructed by the Stoics to save purpose and to vindicate intelligibility. Other ways were based on the consent of all people about the existence of such a craftsman and on viewing human reason as a participation in a universal reason. All these arguments were soon the target of critics, and the Stoic phraseology was of no small help to them. When Carneades of the Academy objected that the argument from design presupposed the demonstration that the entire universe was a designed product and not a necessary issue of the laws of nature,[46] the Stoics must have admitted that their own words seemed to support the objection. A perfect illustration of this was the celebrated Hymn to Zeus by Cleanthes. The hymn praised God, "the King of Kings whose purpose through ceaseless ages brings to birth whatever on land or in the sea is wrought," but its conclusion called for worshiping "the universal law for evermore."[47]

The one god of the Stoics to whom they professed infinite gratitude was a finite universe, or nature, in which all parts were intimately connected through the good services of the all-pervading pneuma, a very refined form of fire. The scientific insights of the Stoics were inspired by these two great themes, the continuum and the dynamics of fire. Instead of dynamics it has recently become fashionable to speak about the thermodynamics of the Stoics, but this is only a pleasing exaggeration: while the Stoics speculated about physical processes, they had no physics, let alone thermodynamics. Like the Aristotelians and the Epicurean atomists, they achieved nothing more in science than

28

to guide it into an interesting blind alley from which escape was impossible. Interesting it certainly was. The Stoic emphasis on the continuum and its application to certain geometrical problems provided the ground on which ancient Greek mathematicians made halting steps toward infinitesimal calculus.[48] The same preoccupation with the continuum inspired the Stoic speculation on circular and spherical waves as the carriers of physical influences such as sound and light. Equally Stoic in origin was Poseidonius's claim that tides were due to some physical interconnectedness between the moon and the earth.[49]

The interest of Stoics in fire produced results that were scientifically less interesting but philosophically much more revealing. In fire, or in its very refined form, the pneuma, the Stoics saw the essence of reason and intelligibility. Ultimately consisting of fire, Providence then could hardly be a benevolent ordinance of a supreme and personal being. The "only god" of the Stoics was a schizophrenic metaphor and so was their contention about the rationality of the universe. It was rationality only in the sense that man could implement knowingly his inevitable fate, determined as it was by the inexorable dynamics of fire. To be burnt to ashes and to rise from it like a phoenix and to do so in an endless sequence through infinite ages—this was fate, and quiet resignation to it was all that one could have in the way of purpose. To take some of the sting out of that vicious circle, Aristotle admitted only a generic recurrence, but Eudemus, a pupil of his, and the author of the first history of astronomy, admitted that logic was on the side of the Pythagoreans, who advocated individual returns. Or as Eudemus warned his pupil: "I shall converse with you staff in hand and you will sit as you are sitting now, and so it will be in everything else."[50]

It was the sad but logical privilege of the Stoics to turn this mesmerizing world view into a broadly shared conviction. Within that logic not even Socrates, the sacred idol of the Stoics, could be an exception. The assertion that he would argue about physics and immortality with his friends and drink the hemlock again and again, became the touchstone of proclaiming the Stoic doctrine in its fullness.[51] To live with that vision of an eternal treadmill and have peace of mind in it was one thing. To have an intelligently argued sense of purpose was another. Moreover, when fire was the ultimate in intelligibility, there could be no vital spark for science. This is not to suggest that Stoic thought was yet seen in this light by Cicero in his *De natura deorum*.[52] But the academic skepticism of Cotta, who evaluated for Cicero the theologies of the Epicurean Velleius and of the Stoic Balbus, was certainly effective in showing that for the Stoics the one God was nothing but the one world, and that such a world could not be an intelligent being. It was not truly intelligible either and certainly not in a scientific sense. It was in the context of such confusion about intellect and nature that the antiquarian and raconteur M. Terentius Varro, an acquaintance of Cicero, coined the term 'natural theology'.[53]

The Stoic ways to supreme intelligibility rested on two principal assertions. One was that whatever perfection, such as intelligence, existed in man, it had to exist in whatever was superior to man. The second principal assertion was that nothing was superior to the world. Consequently, the world had to be intelligent. In that case it was also necessary to say that the world could read a book and knew how to play the flute.[54] It was no problem for Cotta to turn this reasoning into a reductio ad absurdum, a rather negative technique. On the positive side, Cotta made the point that it was a sign of wisdom to recognize that while man was intelligent, constellations like Orion and Canicula were not.[55] But Cotta, the skeptic, could not be of more help along the road of positive construction. While he claimed against the Stoics that nothing proved that the world was built as a house, he also boasted that he could show that the world was merely built by nature. At this point the text comes to an end with a note by the editor: "The passage here anticipated is lost."[56] One wonders if it was ever written.

Writing that passage could have hardly been done by Cotta. This can be seen from the very next section, which opens with the argument of Socrates about the immortality of his conscience and mind. Strangely enough, Cotta has Socrates ask with the Stoics: "If the world contains no rational soul, where did we pick ours?" As a negative critic Cotta replied, and effectively so, that had the world possessed an intelligent soul we should picture the sun holding conversation with the moon.[57] Cotta carried his positive task only to the extent of a broad hint. Yet he said enough to make one feel perplexed. On the one hand he agreed with Zeno and the Stoics that the parts of the world were so carefully interconnected as to resemble a clockwork.[58] On the other hand, Cotta claimed that the more there is of that order in the world, the more it is to be attributed to the forces of nature, "and the less possible is it to suppose that it was created by divine reason."[59] Cotta's reason for saying this was curiously conditional: no divine power was needed for the explanation of that interconnectedness if one was willing to view it as spontaneous growth.

Whether intelligibility can be rigorously deposited in the idea of spontaneous growth largely depends on one's definition of the spontaneous. The same is true of the idea of a creation by divine reason as advocated by the Stoics. After two thousand years of Christianity, it may be difficult to realize that words like creation, God, and divine reason can be used in a sense very different from that which Christian theists assign to them. Certainly, Cotta did not suggest Christian notions when he noted in criticizing the Epicurean Velleius, who rejected the Stoic effort to conclude from nature's order, "that there must exist some supreme and transcendent being who had created these things and who imparted motion to them and guided and governed them."[60]

Neither Cotta nor Velleius nor the Stoics had in mind a transcendental Creator. The idea of creation out of nothing was rejected by all who were known as dogmatists in late antiquity, namely, the Aristotelians, the Atomists, and the Stoics. As to the academic skeptics, they were, as they are now, the very last ones to favor a creation out of nothing. The ways constructed by any of the dogmatic schools to reach God, that is, the ultimate in intelligibility and being, did not lead to anything transcending the world. The claim that the world itself was intelligent could be and was mercilessly held up to ridicule. What could not be slighted was the quest for understanding, for the ultimate in intelligibility. With no transcendent intellect emerging on the horizon, with the world proved to be without intellect, all that remained was to fall back on the human mind, for which nothing was more natural than to settle with the customary. Such a mind could hardly be alert to deeper perspectives, to patterns of intelligibility very different from those it was accustomed to.

Ways to God that were not utilized to their ontological fullness could only become paths to skepticism, and this is the theme on which the *De natura deorum* comes to an end. One of its final paragraphs deals with theatrical pieces in which the role of wisdom is on equal footing with the role of unwisdom. This farce on the human mind was made complete in the next major appearance in antique literature of the mind's ways to God. In his voluminous teaching of skepticism, Sextus Empiricus reached the conclusion that no difference between teacher and pupil could be rigorously demonstrated. Such a conclusion (which skeptical professors nowadays would not entertain for fear of losing their jobs) reflects well on the consistency of Sextus Empiricus. It is well to recall that his starting point was a survey of not one but of a dozen ways that supposedly could carry the mind to God. He demolished all of them in due order.[61] Of course the notion of final intelligibility and being as contained in those ways was as narrowly confined as was the human mind when deprived of transcendental vision.

That limited intelligibility could not sustain science either. Between Sextus Empiricus's scoffing at God and his doubting the difference between teacher and pupil, there lies a long series of chapters casting doubt on every major aspect of science. Not even the science of numbers was an exception. In this wholesale attack on knowledge Sextus Empiricus was not the first. Pyrrho of Elis appeared on the scene almost simultaneously with Zeno and Epicurus. At that time Pyrrho's systematic abdication of purpose and understanding was a weak dissenting voice and a distant echo of the Sophists, one of whom, Gorgias, wrote a book "on that which does not really exist, or nature."[62] A quarter of a

31

millennium later the dominating and pragmatic Romans eagerly espoused skepticism and looked down on the remaining few Greeks concerned with theoretical knowledge, especially mathematics, about which Cicero disparagingly remarked that for all its arcane character many had made much progress in it without having applied themselves seriously.[63] Half a millennium after Pyrrho, the voice of skepticism was dominant among the theorizing Greeks as well. The time was 140 or so A.D., the time of Ptolemy. He saw no inconsistency, let alone contradiction, in treating the planets as geometrical points sliding along a maze of epicycles, or as dancers instinctively watching one another's steps, or as divine beings, harbingers of all good and evil.[64] Acceptance of such a mixture of viewpoints could only obscure, not illuminate. It suggested no new, creative horizons for science.

Actually Greek science had already lost its creativity by the time the Museum opened in Alexandria. By then the association of Greek city-states, always a fragile enterprise, was dispersing its cultural achievements into the vast lands conquered by Alexander the Great. A feat of fantastic prodigality, but also a heavy drain on a source that was no longer being replenished. Greece was already on a downhill course about which no illusions could be entertained once Hellas and Athens fell to the Romans. Typically enough, Polybius, the chief Greek sage of those times, could find comfort only in conjuring up for the Romans the same fate since nothing was exempt, Polybius believed, from the inexorable fate of eternal cycles.[65]

Although Christians became a force to reckon with only half a millennium later, the decline of Greek science and learning has often been charged to Christianity. Little needs to be said about the cliché which conjures up the destruction by Christian mobs of the Museum in Alexandria, a feat strangely repeated two hundred years later by Muslim conquerors. Less obvious is the fallacy of remarks that contrast the erstwhile self-confidence of Hellenic spirit with its seeking comfort in otherworldly or religious perspectives during Hellenistic times. A little reflection might, however, reveal that Christianity can hardly be responsible for that "failure of nerve" if it hit the Greeks, as it did indeed, in the period 300 B.C.–100 A.D. Yet, is not Christianity implicated by a description of that failure which includes a "rise in asceticism . . . a loss of hope in this life . . . a cry for infallible revelation . . . a conversion of the soul to God"?[66] Christianity is less covertly incriminated in that remark of Sir Thomas Heath, the renowned historian of Greek mathematics and astronomy, who assigned the scientific creativity of the Greeks to the fact that they were "untrammeled by any Bible" and "by organized priesthood."[67] One could only wish that he had recalled that Paul Tannery, his own great master in the history of Greek geometry, had a very different explanation. Tannery, whom Sarton once referred to as "the scholar who deserves perhaps more than any other to be called the father of our studies,"[68] pointed to the domination of Hellenistic thought by Stoic philosophy, which, because of its fundamentally utilitarian character, was hostile to science.[69]

The rise of Stoicism marks the burning out of that flame of scientific creativity that was alive only for a few generations. Its short duration was possibly the most tantalizing event in intellectual history. The ancient Greeks came far closer than any other culture to formulating a viable science. Without achieving it, they provided some justification for saying that "thinking about the world in the Greek way" is an "adequate description of science."[70] Their glimpse of a viable science was as momentary as was their glimpse of the one, eternal, infinite, absolute Act. No sooner had the human mind risen to such heights than it slumped back upon itself. Compared with the natural theology of other ancient cultures, the one produced by the Greeks should seem perfection itself and so should their science. But like their science, their natural theology too halted just before reaching its proper objective. Assertions of monotheism and of a creation out of nothing were among the Greeks of old sporadic at best,[71] like bursts of a fire never to become a broadly shared light. Something of this is acknowledged when a book of a rationalist on Greek rationality ends with the rueful remark that unlike Christianity, the Greeks "did not succeed in imposing any body of philosophical doctrine on the population as a whole."[72] Yet, as it turned out, the rise of science needed the broad and persistent sharing by the whole population, that is, an entire culture, of a very specific body of doctrines relating the universe to a universal and absolute intelligibility embodied in the tenet about a personal God, the Creator of all.

That the scientific genius of the Greeks burnt out quickly is therefore a correct statement but no explanation of the fact it was meant to explain. The explanation should be sought in the manner in which the Greeks of old built ways to the ultimate in intelligibility, only to find themselves at the end of those ways. The failure of the Greeks in natural theology might be readily ignored in an age of science, but their failure in science will keep haunting historians of science wary of theology. Once they muster enough intellectual courage to look straight in the face of that tantalizing failure, the physiognomy of the problem, and therefore its solution too, will appear in its plain theological nature. Such seems to be the most timely lesson that the Greeks of old can offer to a new age steeped and perhaps over-steeped, in science.

Three

STEPS TO GOD AS STEPPING-STONES
TO SCIENCE

To possess oneself is a fine thing, but to find only one's sole self at the end of the quest for the ultimate in intelligibility is in essence to lose hold of oneself. This at least seems to be one of the lessons science provides through its history. Science failed to become an open-ended avenue in the great ancient cultures just as their quest for the ultimate in intelligibility, which is the quest for God, failed to go convincingly beyond man's own self and its cosmic extrapolation, an animated and self-contained nature. The ultimate in intelligibility was first placed firmly on a level transcending both man and nature during the Middle Ages and in a way that constituted a cultural matrix. It manifested a broadly shared conviction that a personal, rational, and provident Being, absolute and eternal, is the ultimate source of intelligibility insofar as he is the Creator of all things visible and invisible. Conviction it was and not merely an intellectual fashion. Its most articulate spokesmen were mendicant friars committed to an evangelical vision of man and world, a vision in which the order, beauty, and peace of nature were a shining reflection of the Creator and Father of all.[1]

The vision was not a sentimental gaze. It had to prove itself in many ways, among them by a full-scale scrutiny of the respective roles of supernatural faith and natural reason. Supernatural faith meant a commitment to a long series of historical facts stretching from the call of Abraham to the call issued to all nations on the first Pentecost to become, through faith in Christ, the beneficiaries of God's covenant with Abraham. Those historical facts and the message perceived in them were believed to be of supernatural origin; they were seen as the stepping into history of a transcendent God who identified himself as existence itself, that is, the One Who Is,[2] in respect to whom the existence of all that is visible and invisible is a gift of creative largeness.

To be sure, faith was meant to be a "rationabile obsequium,"[3] a service in which reason had to play its reasonable part. The continual relapse of many among the chosen people into idolatry and the engrossment of pagan nations in nature worship amply showed the readiness of reason to be unreasonable. Appeals to reason repeatedly occur in the pages of the Old and New Testaments, both in reference to the miraculous interventions of God in history and to the evidence given by nature about God.[4] The emphasis, however, is on the miraculous events of the history of salvation. The pattern was similar throughout patristic times. Christian authors offered proofs of the existence of God as soon as they began to address themselves to the pagan society of the

Roman Empire,[5] but the proofs played no more than an introductory role in that strategy. Salvation could only be had through being included in the covenant mediated by Christ, in whom God fully revealed himself.

The paganism of classical antiquity had collapsed under its own weight, together with its culture, intellectual and social, some time before Christianity began to dominate the public scene with its message of salvation. Saint Augustine's *De civitate Dei* was not an argument between two live contenders but a query about the point whether the only live contender, Christianity, should be blamed for the demise of the other, the pagan Roman Empire.[6] Less than a thousand years later there were no pagans in the oikoumene. Monotheism was an unquestioned tenet in Cordova as well as in Constantinople, in Baghdad as well as in Rome, in Cairo as well as in Paris. But Rome and Paris, or western Christendom, still had to meet a test which Byzantium and Islam had already met in their own ways. The test was posed by the claims of faith in the face of the demands of reason.

In the medieval context reason meant Aristotle. Byzantium largely skirted the issue by withdrawing its orthodoxy into a lofty supernaturalism steeped in Neoplatonism.[7] In such a framework there was no room either for science or for natural theology. The followers of Muhammad broke into two unequal camps.[8] The larger, or theological, camp recognized that the will if not willfulness of Allah, as posited in the Koran, was incompatible with Aristotelian necessitarianism. The smaller, or philosophical, camp opted for a dichotomy. It consisted in paying lip service to revealed truth as given in the Koran, while surrendering at the same time to Aristotle, as was done especially by Averroës. The essentially negative attitude,[9] which Muslim theologians displayed toward the natural ability of reason, should appear all the more frustrating as philosophical insights of tremendous significance originated within Muslim ambience prior to its breaking into the two camps of Mutazalites and Mutakallimun. In view of the sharp contrast drawn in the Koran between Allah and all other beings,[10] al-Farabi declared that with the exception of Allah all actually existing beings, and not only those merely possible with respect to existence, were contingent.[11] But powerful as it was, the Koran, in one crucial respect at least, did not prove itself stronger than Aristotle for al-Farabi. The heavens, al-Farabi declared, existed necessarily,[12] an Aristotelian proviso that discredited the Creator and nipped in the bud the prospects of science in the Muslim world. What could seem but a momentary weakness in al-Farabi's case, became two centuries later a rigid stance for Averroës and for his followers. For them the world was strictly eternal and in no need of a creation. Their natural theology followed closely, though shrewdly, Aristotle's pantheistic natural theology, or its Neoplatonic version, known as the "theology of Aristotle."[13] That theology was as barren of unambiguous words about God as a transcendent being as Aristotle's physics was barren of meaningful science.

It suggests the strange if not mysterious ways of history that Aristotle and his Muslim admirers provided much of the material for Aquinas, author of a classically concise phrasing of the proofs of the existence of God.[14] As given almost at the very beginning of the *Summa theologica*,[15] the proofs were not his first try on the topic. Nor was his longer version of the proofs in the *Summa contra gentiles* their first appearance in medieval philosophy and theology. Anselm's famed ontological argument could hardly have been formulated except in an intellectual atmosphere in which the challenge was not the demonstration of the existence of God, but finding its most perfect form.[16] Other forms of that demonstration had routinely been given some time before Aquinas. For example, the *Sententiae* of Peter Lombard, which Aquinas himself commented upon and which until the sixteenth century served as the standard textbook on theology, provided clear evidence of the conviction that the existence of God could be demonstrated rationally. But since the conviction was generally shared, there was no compelling reason to elaborate on the proofs in great detail. Even in the *Summa contra gentiles* the length of the proofs is puny in comparison with the total length of a work of apologetics which hardly carries conviction if the existence of God has not been demonstrated rationally.[17]

To help reconcile oneself to the brevity of those proofs it might be useful to recall that on inertial motion, the basis of all physics, one finds only a paragraph or two even in the best textbooks. The assumption is, and rightly so, that those who cannot grasp the truth of inertial motion within five lines will not be helped by five hundred. Much the same holds true of Aquinas and his medieval colleagues in proving the existence of God. Lengthy discourse on the topic was unnecessary because only a few disagreed and, even more importantly, because the proofs were believed to be simple in substance. Conviction about that simplicity was of biblical origin. The Bible's inference from nature to God is as brief as a healthy leap.[18] Extended reasoning clearly made no sense if a fool was he who said in his heart that there was no God.[19] The Book of Wisdom added to this the indictment of those students of nature who failed to recognize its true Maker.[20] In his Letter to the Romans Saint Paul made that indictment universal on the basis that "whatever can be known about God is plain to them; he himself made it so. Since the creation of the world, invisible realities, God's eternal power and divinity, have become visible, recognized through the things he has made."[21] Paul's address on the Areopagus showed that it was right to appeal without any specifics to God as the one "who made the world and all that is in it," for "he is not really far from any one of us."[22] It is not philosophical flippancy but this biblical brevity that shines through the proofs as formulated by Aquinas, who was convinced that "all knowing beings implicitly know God in any and every thing they know."[23]

The proofs as they stand in the *Summa theologica* may appear disturbingly brief, even sketchy, if one approaches them by way of logical analysis or in the light of some modern scientific notions. On the basis of the former the proofs will at best appear a shorthand notation,[24] an unlikely possibility in view of Aquinas's concern for the conclusiveness of proofs on behalf of tenets that lie at the basis of Christian faith.[25] If one is led by such modern scientific notions as inertial motion and transfer of momentum by impact, one may easily misinterpret Aquinas's reliance in the first proof on the principle "omne quod movetur ab alio movetur." It is well to recall that the same principle was used by other medieval philosophers, Muslims as well as Christians, whose metaphysics differed from or simply ran counter to that of Aquinas. This point was overlooked by Sir Edmund Whittaker in his well-known dismissal of the first proof.[26] The same oversight underlies Anthony Kenny's onslaught on the proofs, especially on the first based on the reality of motion.[27] Moreover, he failed to note an important fact, fully aired five years prior to the publication of his essay. The fact relates to the handling of the foregoing principle by modern historians of medieval physics, a handling which, as James A. Weisheipl has convincingly shown, [28] is nothing short of confusion, for it implies that Aquinas lined himself up with Averroës on a pivotal point!

A misrepresentation of Aquinas, like the one by d'Alembert, who boasted that he had never read the *Summa* and yet claimed that Aquinas was absorbed in debating such questions as whether Asmodeus was consubstantial with Beelzebub,[29] is not so misleading as one that is wrapped in an apparent study of his thought. A good illustration of the latter is Russell's claim that Aquinas's "appeal to reason is, in a sense, insincere, since the conclusion to be reached is fixed in advance."[30] At any rate, for a historian of science it should seem to be of secondary importance whether the proofs as formulated by Aquinas are conclusive or not. Nor should he be concerned with the question of whether Aquinas meant to offer five varieties of one proof or whether the five proofs are distinct. The important point for the historian of science is that Aquinas gave to a broadly shared rational conviction a concise formulation which had symbolic power. More specifically, the historian of science should keep in mind that the proofs embodied a stance in epistemology which, as further events were to show, contained a directive instinctively obeyed by the scientific movement. About that stance the first main point to be noted is that for Aquinas it is natural for man to be in a cognitive unity with nature. Naturalness stands for ease nowadays, but for Aquinas it implied intense work done by one's cognitive nature. The character of his stance in epistemology was to reveal even more of its value after Descartes became trapped in presumption and Hume in despair so far as knowledge was concerned. The second main point within the stance embodied in the proofs of Aquinas is that the idea of the universe, as the totality of contingent but rationally coherent and ordered beings, is a notion of utmost import. The contingency of the universe obviates an a priori discourse about it, while its rationality makes it accessible to the mind though only in an a posteriori manner. Hence the need for empirical investigations. The contingency of the universe as a whole serves in turn as a pointer to an ultimate in intelligibility which though outside the universe in a metaphysical sense, is within the inferential power of man's intellect.

The further implications of those points were many, of which Aquinas articulated some but not all. He showed, for instance, keen awareness of the psychological obstacles against admitting the conclusiveness of the proofs of the existence of God.[31] Certainly not a psychologist, he was not even a philosopher in the purist sense. His concern as a philosopher was that of a theologian committed to a bold new concept of Christian philosophy. He wanted to protect it both from the sheer rationality of the logicians and from the piety of those who wanted to reduce it to theology.[32] He paid little attention to the manner in which the validity of the notion of the universe, as the totality of contingent and rationally ordered beings, was tied to the notion of God as the ultimate in intelligibility. The tie was certainly intimate, for, as subsequent developments showed, rejection of the proofs went hand in hand with distrust in cosmology, or the scientific and philosophical study of the universe as a whole, a study which underlies, implicitly at least, any nontrivial scientific proposition.

Aquinas can readily be faulted because of his apparent lack of concern for a posteriori empirical investigations. His endorsing of almost all the details of Aristotelian science may seem a facile attitude, but not more so than Roger Bacon's vision of fabulous mechanical inventions with which he hoped to overcome the infidels. That Aquinas made no memorable steps along the road of science is a fact, and for us moderns it sharply contrasts with his unquestioned genius. Some of his contemporaries were so impressed by his acumen as to see in him a new Moses whose face and words shone with a light that could only be had from communing with God.[33] Such a comparison provides at least a symbolic explanation of Aquinas's relation to science, which may seem baffling to historians of science who have some inkling of his stature as a philosopher. It was no small matter to lead, as a new Moses, the mind out of its Averroist enslavement to Aristotle by correcting the Stagirite on at least three crucial issues, the existence of a transcendent God, the creation out of nothing, and the freedom of man rooted in the immortality of his soul. To Moses of old it was not given to enter the promised land. Nor did Aquinas put his foot inside the gates of a science better than that of Aristotle.[34] But he certainly pioneered a crucial phase of the march toward those gates, a fact proved by future developments, or more specifically by two particularly creative phases of exact science largely connected with the work of Newton and Einstein. As the analysis of those phases will show, they were steeped in an epistemology akin to the one implied in Aquinas's natural theology. In the second or Einsteinian phase an already mature science achieved unexpectedly broader vistas. In the first or Newtonian phase science reached maturity while asserting its formal distinctness from theology, both natural and revealed.

Such self-assertion could only be achieved by a sufficiently mature science, and this was still far away when Aquinas lived. It was more unfortunate that his theological times lacked a well articulated and historically developed biblical theology. While Aquinas quoted the Bible often and with great piety, the style of his Christian philosophy was a far cry from the dynamism of biblical parlance, to which the Augustinians and later the Reformers did more justice than he did. Yet dynamism, however vigorous and biblical, was not necessarily a good philosophy either then or afterwards. Though appreciative of the historical growth of theological understanding,[35] Aquinas, as a child of his time, knew, for instance, of Philoponus only as one suspect of monophysitism and not as the seminal critic of Aristotle's cosmology and physics. Aquinas was also a child of his time in the way he couched his disagreements with Aristotle in most polite terms, even on fundamental issues.

Not all contemporaries of Aquinas, some of whose theses were condemned by the decree of March 7, 1277, of Etienne Tempier, bishop of Paris,[36] were paragons of intellectual discernment, including Tempier himself. Aquinas never taught that the superlunary material could only be incorruptible, that it was intrinsically impossible for planets and stars to move in straight lines, that the first matter could only be produced from the celestial stuff, and so forth. He endorsed these points not as of intrinsic necessity but as factuality suggested by the science of his time. Instructive as such distinction could be, it was not enough to save many minds from Aristotelian necessitarianism. To counter its destructiveness to faith the decree did not rely on philosophy. The basis of the decree was that faith which derives its strength from a steady vision of the great acts and words of the history of salvation. In that perspective the nations and the world itself were but a drop on the rim of a bucket. Obviously then, countless other drops and buckets were possible. If such was the case, the enshrining of the science of the day, Aristotelian or other, could only appear ill-advised to say the least.

The decree of 1277 was a jolt, the effects of which reverberated long after it had lost its canonical validity, which was at no time universal.[37] The jolt was to keep one mentally on one's toes in an anxious awareness of the inconceivably numerous ways in which the Creator could go about his work. The jolt could but increase the awareness of created contingent intellects about the impropriety of specifying with ease the actual decrees of the Creator. Standing on one's toes is not a posture easy to maintain. Nor is it a posture that guarantees quick success in spotting hitherto unsuspected aspects of nature. Human nature is notoriously unsteady both individually and collectively, a fact which breeds and traps utopian revivalism. The Middle Ages, like other Christian ages, had their ample share of these utopians, who in one way or another felt themselves to be possessed of the Holy Spirit. One of them was William Ockham. He ended by becoming engulfed in the always self-destructive effort of bringing heaven to earth by political strategy. Long before that he turned the first tenet of the Creed, "I believe in God, the Father Almighty," into a utopian motto for the intellect.[38]

Ockham's specific and overriding concern was to vindicate the world of miracles and the miraculous world of sacraments. Since a miracle is an especially unique event and has for its source a most singular act of God, Ockham felt that unless all reality was restricted to individual events, neither miracles nor effectual sacraments were conceivable. Within such an outlook there could remain no ontological content in the universals. Since universals are indispensable in the construction of any rational proof of the existence of God, it followed from Ockham's position that God's existence could be the object of supernatural faith alone. Ockham's dismissal of the proofs of the existence of God came to an end with the statement that not even the unicity of God could be made obvious to reason. Reasonings like this have peculiar features of which Ockham gave a revealing glimpse as he remarked: "It cannot be demonstratively proved that the stars make up an even number, nor can the Trinity of Persons be demonstrated."[39] Both these propositions were undoubtedly true, but for very different reasons. It made no sense to utter them in the same breath. The utopian supernaturalism of Ockham hardly helped the world of miracles and mysteries, of which that of the Trinity is the deepest, but what should be of concern here is the logic which made natural theology meaningless, as well as any natural discourse about the stars.

The course of that logic need not be recalled here in detail. Its starting point was a claim for the exclusive validity of intuitive knowledge, which Ockham also called *notitia scientifica* or *experimentalis*. It was a knowledge which referred to single empirical data. It escaped Ockham that no verbal reference could be made to any such data without involving some generalizations, that is, universals. He perceived, however, that universals even as psychological experiences presented problems. He tried to save universals as mere signs but then he had to answer the question of why there were such individual entities in nature which produced identical effects in the mind. He invoked the unfathomable will of God who wanted, for reasons never to be known, the effects in question to be produced in the mind. As shown by some of his penetrating remarks, Ockham might have made a name for himself in the description of perceptions as psychic states. But on the basis of his nominalism Ockham would not have been consistent in giving descriptions of the realm of the psyche, as any instructive description implies more than the listing of names. While not even entitled to compose books on psychography, geography, and cosmography, Ockham was certainly barred by his own premises from discoursing on psychology, geology, and cosmology, or science in short.

Limiting reality to what was conveyed by direct sensory perception, Ockham not only banished the soul of science, which always implies generalization in terms of universals, he also excised its very heart, the search for causes embedded in a layer beneath the immediately experienced surface. For Ockham the notion of atoms would have been anathema, both because they implied universals and because they could not be directly experienced. At any rate, he was very explicit on the point that phenomena conveyed by direct sensory impressions were not to be explained by reference to a deeper layer of entities not obvious to the senses.[40] Such is the true provenance of Ockham's razor—which makes one wonder how Ockham could be turned by so many historians and philosophers of science into the enlightened prophet of modern scientific method. Worse even, they seldom hint of the grim resolve by which Ockham unfolded certain implications of his *notitia intuitiva*, that is, the *notitia experimentalis* or *scientifica*. One of these was the assertion that God himself produced a negative intuition of things that one no longer intuited, of things that ceased to exist, and even of things that never existed. But, then, could man muster natural assurance about the reality of phenomena he actually and positively intuited? That the answer to this question could hardly be affirmative may be inferred from the fact that Ockham once more resorted to the omnipotence of God, to whom anything that did not involve contradiction had to be attributed. Thus, from the perspective of natural reason, as defined by Ockham, a nature intrinsically coordinated through the mutual causality of things could not be preferred to a world in which each appearance of coherence demanded a miraculous act on the part of the Father Almighty. As Ockham illustrated this all-important point, since the light of stars and

41

the stars themselves could be conceived as existing independently of one another, reason was powerless to decide whether the light of stars had a real connection with the stars themselves.[41] For the purposes of science the starry sky could not have been enveloped in a deeper darkness.

The only way of knowing that the world was ordered, or, to be specific, that the starlight was due to stars, must therefore come from relevation about the ordained power of God, to use Ockham's favorite expression. Some admirers of Ockham saw in this a redeeming feature because it witnessed to his resolve to do justice to the voluntaristic aspect of the God of the Bible.[42] Whatever that aspect, the feature in question is neither redeeming nor biblical, and it certainly does not redeem Ockham the philosopher. It was to soften the shock of his epistemology that he resorted to a distinction between the absolute and the ordered will of the Creator, a distinction which, by implying an ordered state for all created things, furtively brought the universals back into the real world. Typically, Ockham never tried to develop an epistemology based on knowing things as existing through the ordered will of God. More importantly, the distinction in question does not do justice to the biblical notion of God. It is nowhere hinted in the Bible that when God wills, he does so capriciously, that is, independently of the consistency of his intellect. Will and intellect are never separated in the God of the Bible. On the contrary, Yahweh is always a reasonable God, indeed the supreme meaning and reason in every aspect. Unfathomable as Yahweh's choice may be for the human intellect in many an instance, Yahweh is not Allah. In fact, time and again the Bible predicates the faithfulness of Yahweh on the steadiness of his created work as evidenced by the consistent flow of the processes of nature.[43]

Ockham's version of the absolute will of God, which he grafted on biblical revelation, corresponded to viewing the world as a set of disconnected entities closely resembling what had been proposed by the great Muslim mystic, al-Ashari. What could be argued on the basis of the Koran had no justification in the Bible. Nothing was more contrary to its spirit than arguing from the absolute will of God to the possibility of several worlds so independent of one another in existence and in character as to have their own separate first causes, or "first conservers," to recall Ockham's expression.[44] In Ockham's account of the intellect, the light diffusing in the world was not necessarily coherent with the stars, nor did the same light bespeak a universe in which all stars and material units, small and big, were intrinsically interconnected. Clearly, if the unicity of God was not accessible to the mind unaided by revelation, then the recognition of the unity of material beings, or a unitary vision of the universe so indispensable for science, was also beyond the mind's powers. This was the logic of Ockham, but not the logic of the Bible and of science.

Ockham's significance in the history of science lies in a factor far more penetrating than his utopian razor ever could be. The factor was that almost miraculous instinct by which his contagious influence was resisted in crucial instances. In an atmosphere of growing uncertainty and skepticism, what would have been more natural than having recourse to a magic formula such as Ockham's motto? Did it not promise the solace of faith, did it not sweep away all cumbersome intellectual questions, and did it not clear the way to a strictly evangelical vision and understanding of the world? The contagiousness of such a prospect certainly failed to infect Buridan and Oresme, two chief figures of science in Ockham's century and principal forerunners of Galileo. Whatever their nominalism, they were not Ockhamists. Their epistemology could hardly be derived from Ockham, since in their commentaries on Aristotle's *On the Heavens* they referred time and again to the order and motion in the world as proofs of the Creator.[45] It was that perspective that led them to focus not on motion itself but on its source, which is indicated on the purely physical level by the fact of acceleration. Their theory of impetus had its origin in their openness to the metaphysics of motion, a metaphysics intimately tied to natural theology concerned with the ultimate source of motion. This is still to be recognized by those who, like J. R. Oppenheimer, acknowledge the medieval roots of Newtonian mechanics but gloss over the Christian theism that prompted both the challenge to Aristotle and the insight that to have a viable physics "we did not need to explain motion but we needed to explain acceleration."[46]

Contrary to Oppenheimer, Buridan and Oresme were not mere thinkers. Their theory of impetus contained all the observational details that could be gathered at that time. Their interest in observations was not something sparked by Ockham. Well before Ockham the investigation of particulars was emphasized by Albertus Magnus, Roger Bacon, Witelo, Theodoric of Freiberg, and others. Some of what Ockham said certainly helped reinforce that trend, but he was not accepted as guide either by Buridan or by Oresme. Their skepticism was the caution of men aware of the limitations of the mind and not Ockham's despair of the mind's abilities. Ockham's despair, however, reasserted itself in those who really took him for master. Among them were John Mirecourt and Nicholas Autrecourt, who certainly never became masters in science. Happily for the scientific enterprise, no general credence had been given to Autrecourt's genuinely Ockhamist claim that by putting one's hand repeatedly into fire nothing would be learned about an objective connection between fire and burning.[47]

One did not have to be a follower of Ockham, however, to grow oblivious to Aquinas's firm though cautious attitude in philosophy. Facile trust and nagging skepticism were indeed the two main attitudes toward reason among many who, unlike Mirecourt and Autrecourt, had no reservations on points of faith. The facile trust received, tellingly enough, a classic expression in the very first book to be called *theologia naturalis*.[48] It now owes its fame to its "rediscovery" by Montaigne,[49] a skeptic in respect to revealed religion. For its author, Raymond de Sabunde, natural theology meant the rational demonstration of even such revealed mysteries as the trinity of persons in God. As one might suspect, such efforts presupposed a mind given to allegories, moralizing, and poetic similes, not to hard reasoning. Of the latter there is little if any trace in Sabunde's book, which is also conspicuously void of whatever could be known scientifically at that time about the order and singularity of nature.

As to a skepticism that did not extend to points of faith, the most renowned document from those times is Nicholas of Cusa's *De docta ignorantia*, or *Of Learned Ignorance*.[50] At the time of its publication the last strongholds of Byzantine Christendom were about to be engulfed by the Crescent, a fearful warning to the West suffering the aftereffects of Avignon. Partly under such stress, Nicholas, the future cardinal, pleaded for faith in Christian mysteries on the basis that mere knowledge could not come up with anything strictly certain. The scientific illustrations of this claim were such gems as Nicholas's advocacy of the uncertainty, that is, of the relativity of all motion and the imprecision of geometrical figures. The latter was evidenced for him by the possibility of transforming a straight line into a circle through infinitesimally small alterations. To emphasize the same uncertainty Nicholas argued against the existence of well-defined contours in the universe. Its circumference, to recall his famous words, was nowhere, and its center everywhere.[51] But he was no Einstein. In producing all these gems he cultivated his skeptical philosophy, not science. Cosmology did not profit from his glossing over the difference between planets and stars. Only skepticism, not science, was to gain by his placing the earth inside the watery layer of the moon.[52]

Nicholas of Cusa's real contributions to science are in some of his opuscula, in which he time and again ties the need for quantitative accuracy to the words of the Book of Wisdom about the Creator having arranged everything according to weight, measure, and number.[53] The *Learned Ignorance* of Nicholas had beneficial effects for science only when its scientific gems were appraised by a Christian faith urging intellectual confidence and not pietistic skepticism. When piety and faith were completely absent, those gems became the vehicle of a program which for all its appeals to science only turned it into a tool of obscurantist pantheism. Giordano Bruno's dicta on the relativity of motion, as we find them in his first scientific publication, *La cena de le ceneri*, or *The Ash Wednesday Supper*,[54] owed their lucidity to being a borrowing from Nicholas's *Learned Ignorance. The Ash Wednesday Supper*, the first book on Copernicus, is by and large a virulent case of counterscience, prompted by Bruno's pantheism. For Bruno, the stars and planets (he did his best to gloss over their difference), were the chief embodiments of a divine world, which, because of its divinity, had to be infinite. Apart from that, all of Bruno's cosmological dicta meant to emphasize the perennial and wholly unpredictable transformation of all into all. He was a prophet not of science but of the idea of eternal returns, an idea which led the scientific enterprise into a blind alley in all ancient cultures.

Bruno was burnt at the stake on the morning following Ash Wednesday, 1600, not because of his cosmology but because of a pantheism which systematically preempted of meaning every tenet of the Christian faith. He certainly was not a martyr on behalf of Copernicus, to whose science he paid only lip service. Of its spirit Bruno possessed little if any. The briefest proof of this is in *The Ash Wednesday Supper,* where Bruno decries reliance on what he so tellingly called the "file of geometry."[55] His hostility to geometry and his self-defeating dabbling in it, as displayed in the diagrams of the same work, bespeak his instinctive realization that the clarity and precision of geometry were irreconcilable with the obscurantist vagueness of his pantheistic cosmology. He claimed, for instance, that the orbit of celestial bodies could not correspond to any given geometrical figure, circle or whatever else, because this would put a constraint on their divine freedom and lively instincts. Bruno's interpretation of the last two of the four motions attributed by Copernicus to the earth can only produce utter dismay in any competent reader. The foremost living expert on Bruno, Frances Yates, put the matter bluntly: "Copernicus might well have bought up and destroyed all copies [of *The Ash Wednesday Supper*] . . . had he been alive."[56]

In his better-known cosmological work, *De l'infinito universo e mondi,* also published in 1584, Bruno made no brazen misrepresentation of Copernicus,[57] but this did not improve much Bruno's self-declared status as Copernicus's intellectual heir. It can, of course, be recalled that Bruno championed an infinite universe of stars, whereas for Copernicus the stars hardly existed. Yet, unlike Bruno, Copernicus offered a structure in which it was meaningful to stay for a while in order to prepare further advance. The reason for this lies in the fact that Copernicus firmly believed in what Bruno could only contemplate with revulsion, namely, the notion that the Creator arranged everything according to weight, measure, and number.

Putting this notion into practice meant great expertise in geometry and a genuine attention to its file, that is, to the cutting edge of its quantitative precision. It was not enough to be a Platonist. Ficino was certainly one, but the cause of science only suffered from his and his school's worshipful attitude toward Plato. Plato's few applications of geometry to the real world were playful conjectures, a good pastime if one was indeed condemned to sit with one's back to the light and to learn about things only through their shadows cast on the dark and uneven vault of a huge cave. One could base on Plato one's admiration for the perfection of a circle, and for the even greater perfection of a system of concentric circles, but that was not enough to make a Copernicus. One could believe with Pythagoras in the excellence of fire and in its central position, but that was still not enough to convince one that the flaming sun was indeed in the center. Plato, Pythagoras, and geometry could at best produce an Aristarchus of Samos and his biting rebuttal by Ptolemy and by the whole Platonist antiquity. What was needed to make a Copernicus was an insight and a faith.

The insight was that in the heliocentric ordering of planets their retrograde motions and their relative distances were a consequence of of that ordering, a consequence which gave conceptual (though not computational) simplicity to the new theory. It was now to be decided whether this conceptual simplicity should be given more weight than the enormous weight of the earth now to be set in motion. The physics familiar to Copernicus was of no help in persuading one about the motion of the earth. Sensory evidence, if Copernicus had ever been tempted to look at the matter with the eyes of Ockham, proclaimed the stability of the earth as absolute verity. As Galileo put it a century later, Copernicus was faced with the prospect of committing a rape of his senses.[58] A rape it was and he did commit it. He did so because, as he explicitly put it, the most weighty objection to heliocentrism, the Aristotelian doctrine of light and heavy, could be overcome with faith in the Creator's power and simplicity. He, the Creator, could arrange that each celestial body should have (to anticipate a modern term) its own gravitational field.

On the basis of Ockhamism, Copernicus's action was sheer foolishness. It was logical that an admirer of Ockham, Martin Luther, should be the first to call Copernicus a fool.[59] Because of his Ockhamism Luther failed to see that Copernicus's foolishness was quite biblical. Beneath that foolishness lay the biblical faith that the ways of God are simplicity itself, for in God will and mind are fused in the simplest unity. The same faith also instructed Copernicus that God, unlike the god of Plato, was an all-powerful being for whom nothing was easier than to have the earth move. A good Christian, Copernicus knew that man could not dictate to his Creator. The simple system of heliocentrism had to match the data of observation with the exactness demanded by the file of geometry. To recall, after all this, that in the preface and the first book of his immortal work Copernicus saw a proof of the existence of God in the simple ordering of the cosmos should seem almost unnecessary.[60]

Yet a reminder of this inner logic, which connects the road of science and the ways to God, is more needed than ever. Of the various reasons for this need, one is the always present need for integrity in historical scholarship. This integrity suffers badly when, for instance, a sustained effort is made to present Copernicus, Kepler, and Galileo, chief figures of the astronomical revolution, as students of Plato, while saying practically nothing of their Christian faith. They certainly admired Plato, but they were also good Christians, and this made the enormous difference which there is between Platonism and Christian Platonism. The role played by that Christian Platonism from Grosseteste to Galileo can only baffle historians of science who have never experienced what it means to look at the world as the product of a personal, rational Creator. But if they wish to function as discriminating historical scholars, they must make a sustained effort to describe the mental world of a Copernicus, a Kepler, or a Galileo, not in terms of twentieth-century unbelief but in terms of a belief that was an integral and fundamental part of their mental physiognomy. One need not be a Buddhist to be a good historian of Buddhist thought and culture, but nothing can dispense the historian from a thorough effort to understand what it means for a Buddhist to be a Buddhist and to achieve things by virtue of that Buddhism. The theistic contribution to science and to history, and the Christian concreteness of that theism demand no less in the way of scholarly treatment and integrity. It is, for example, inconsistent to resolve the dispute about whether Copernicus was a German or a Pole with the passing remark that he was simply a "good Catholic" and at the same time to keep silent about the crucial role which his Christian faith played in his Platonism and in his science.[61]

That another historian of science could draw praise for presenting Galileo as an agnostic positivist,[62] and that Einstein was not taken to task by historians of science for speaking of Kepler as a freethinker,[63] illustrate the negative attitude toward Christian theism which prevails in influential scholarly circles nowadays. Little if any effort is made, for instance, to recall the role played in Galileo's scientific methodology by his repeated endorsements of the naturalness of perceiving the existence of God from the study of the book of nature.[64] Much the same silent treatment is given to Galileo's view of the human mind as a most excellent and most special product of the Creator.[65] Again, only brief and imperceptive remarks can be read on something of overriding concern for both Galileo and Kepler—the distinctness of natural and supernatural truths in the Bible, a topic which both handled in detail and with a skill that bested the best of contemporary theologians.[66]

There are, of course, traces of positivism and perhaps even of agnosticism in Galileo and of freethinking in Kepler. There is hardly a believer without moments of doubt and without utterances of disbelief. But it is one thing to lurch and another to sink. The difference should seem all the more important as there have rarely been more opportunities to sink than in the period called Renaissance. Astrology, magic, cabbala, and skepticism, of which Renaissance literature had an unusually large share, were as many illusory stars to lure the fragile ship of science into deadly shallows and to prevent it from reaching waters sufficiently deep for clear sailing and real advance. During that perilous phase the stable star providing safe navigation was neither Plato nor Aristotle nor Ockham, and not even Archimedes. The star was the conviction of Christian theism that nature bespeaks an intelligibility that derives from a transcendental source.

That conviction could not be sparked by Archimedes, possibly the most impressive in a long list of candidates for the role of catalyst in the rise of modern science. Actually, the more light shed on his presence in medieval thought,[67] the more the question arises about the contrast between two approaches to him. One is the rather muted reception of his ideas in late antiquity. In an age which readily deified its heroes, Archimedes never earned the reputation of being the head of a school as Plato and Aristotle did. The other is Archimedes' enthusiastic reception in Western Christendom from the moment when William Moerbeke, best remembered as Aquinas's personal translator, rendered into Latin almost all of Archimedes' works. Long before Galileo referred to the "divus Archimedes," his name was on almost every page of Galileo's forerunners. Unlike Archimedes, they applied, from almost the very start, geometry to problems of motion. Such a contrast will not be understood unless one keeps in mind the contrast between Plato's god, who merely cultivated geometry, and the God of Christian theism, who created everything according to weight, measure, and number even in a world of motion.

Reluctance to face up to this contrast leaves one with no more than pleasing metaphors. Some of them, like the one of self-ignition,[68] appear particularly convincing because of their technological connotations, readily taken as self-explanatory in this age of technology. Although unnoticed by its proponent, the metaphor of self-ignition implies a steady accumulation of material capable of self-igniting, and such was precisely the development of scientific ideas from the High Middle Ages until the time of Galileo. If that metaphor is not used simply as a foil to ward off the perspective of Christian theism, there is no need to slight the possibility of a spark jumping from the Middle Ages across the Renaissance to the scientific revolution of the seventeenth century.[69] Indeed, the metaphor of self-ignition, left unspoiled, can easily answer the long-disputed question about the true nature of the connection between medieval and modern science.[70] The answer will be forthcoming all the more naturally if one keeps in mind that the accumulation in question was not an unconscious process. Long before Descartes set forth his method to enable man to become master and possessor of nature, Hugh of Saint Victor emphatically declared in a widely read work—with an eye on Genesis—that God created man "to be the owner and master of the world."[71] Hugh of Saint Victor was one of the many who kept their eyes fixed on Genesis as on a guiding star. It was a star also in the sense that its light did not burn and blind. It merely twinkled but did so unfailingly in the manner of genuine stars. Such a star still could be ignored, or disputed, or confused with other stars, some of which, to recall Ockham, were accompanied by a light not necessarily their own. Yet, by and large, and this is the marvel and great contribution of the Middle Ages, the star was faithfully kept within sight. It was beheld as the target of the quest for the ultimate in intelligibility which is Someone infinitely greater than one's own self. This was the reason why the steps to God functioned as stepping-stones to science.

Four

EMPIRICAL SCOUTING

IN A CHRONOLOGICAL SENSE THE STEPS TO GOD SERVED AS STEPPING-stones to science by leading to the seventeenth century, the century of genius.[1] Much of that genius was spent turning science from a still insecure child into a self-assured adult. Growing up is a complicated process and is always worth careful study. This is particularly true of the maturing of science as recorded by seventeenth-century philosophers and scientists. The record is astonishingly rich. One of its most valuable (and by historians of science hardly appreciated) aspects is the manner in which positions taken in natural theology became indices of the measure of success concerning formulations of scientific method. This is not to suggest that natural theology provided success for the maturing of science in a manner in which coin-operated machines work. In the nonmechanizable world of philosophical insight and scientific discovery mutual impacts operate in subtler though still recognizable modes. The impact of natural theology on the fortunes of scientific methodology can be recognized all the more easily from the seventeenth-century record as it offers three variations on one theme.

The first of these, the empiricist movement, is usually tied to the name of Francis Bacon, but Hobbes and Mersenne are also very instructive representatives of it. Bacon entered the scene in 1605, at the then rather advanced age of forty-four. His fare of entry was a book, *Of the Proficience and Advancement of Learning, Divine and Human*, generally referred to as the *Advancement*.[2] It was neither his first publication, nor the product of many years of reflection, although this is what one would expect from a title so ambitious. Being overambitious usually presupposes an inordinate measure of self-esteem, and this was certainly not lacking in Bacon. To graduate from Trinity College at the age of fifteen after only twenty months of study would today be the mark of precocious genius, but in 1576 it was merely unusual. Bacon left Trinity with an ample stock of phrases from classical authors and with a penchant for sweeping utterances. Young Bacon had hardly arrived at Trinity when the nova of 1572 appeared in the sky and the twelve-year-old freshman promptly declared that the new star proved both Aristotle and the pope wrong. The not-yet-teenager Bacon might have gathered his words of wisdom from older boys and younger faculty. At any rate, Bacon was already in his sixties when he spoke to Rawley, his personal chaplain, about his youthful evaluation of the meaning of the nova.[3] By then it was no secret that Bacon felt himself superior to any and all. As is well known, he first sought to prove his superiority in public office, but

50

his efforts and his intrigues were not followed with results that satisfied him. Indeed from his early thirties on, he was seized time and again with the feeling that his greatness lay not in politics but in philosophy.

As usual, frustration gave rise to the urge to compensate. Bacon was thirty-one when he wrote about formulating a new philosophy that would surpass all before it, provide power over nature, and lead "to a happy match between the mind of man and the nature of things."[4] The phrase "happy match" could not have been more felicitous in view of the overriding importance of the match in question. Its implementation by Bacon was another matter. Two years later, in 1594, in another essay which also remained unpublished until 1870, Bacon addressed an imaginary hero as if speaking to himself: "You will be a Trismegistus, and because of your philosophy all marvels will cease; for you will be the only miracle and wonder of the world through your knowledge of natural causes."[5] The next year he dreamed about a philosophy that would keep man, as he put it, "on the ridge of the wave."[6]

All these phrases were parts of brief sketches. While involved in politics, Bacon could compose but a small volume of essays published hastily in 1597. Then came his at first glamorous, but ultimately most troublesome attachment to the earl of Essex. Although Bacon assumed the role of crown witness against his former patron, rewards from Elizabeth fell far short of his expectations. His overtures to her successor, James I, met with no better success. The year was 1603; Bacon was forty-two and crestfallen. It was in such a state of mind that he composed an essay, a preface to a planned work on the interpretation of nature. In that preface, a must for historians of science and a gold mine for psychoanalysts, Bacon struck a note of pure altruism as he declared that the inventor is the greatest benefactor of mankind. In contrast to the confinement of political skill to a specific place and time, the art of inventing appeared to him to be more germane to universality and eternity. After the shattering of his political dreams, he should have now frankly stated that his turning to science was due to the urge to compensate for the primary loss. Instead, he spoke of his compunction for having pursued politics rather than science. As a matter of fact he remained a politician while becoming a theoretician of science, and he knew it. He knew that to become the universal inventor was to become the universal politician. Or as Bacon put it in the same preface: the universal inventor would be a "propagator of the empire of man over the universe, a defender of liberty, a conqueror of necessities."[7]

Clearly, there was no reason to be really sorry for having cultivated politics instead of science. Science and politics were so little different for Bacon that almost immediately he got himself elected to Parliament. As luck would have it, Parliament was not in session from December 1604 until November 1605. During those ten months Bacon wrote and published that most ambitious work, the *Advancement*. It was written in the spirit of that preface in which he had already described himself as a being constructed more for the contemplation of truth than for anything else. In the same breath he also declared that his own nature had a "kind of familiarity and relationship with truth."[8] Such a nature could not be that fallen nature of which Bacon had amply read in Calvin's *Institutions*.

Bacon, a Calvinist, wrote on occasion (his essay "Of Atheism" is a case in point) as if Calvin had never existed.[9] It was not with Calvin that Bacon asserted in the *Advancement* that knowledge, namely, natural knowledge, had three main objects, God, nature, and man. Curiously, he offered scores of pages on the manner in which knowledge could be had about nature and man, but only two pages on knowledge about God, that is, on natural theology. It may very well be that Bacon here, too, acted as a politician. James I, to whom the *Advancement* was dedicated, prided himself on being a theologian and a markedly traditional one. It was therefore a well-calculated strategy on Bacon's part to restrict the first book of the *Advancement* to rhetoric on the new knowledge as an art most befitting kings and statesmen. But in the second book the specifics had to be spelled out and Bacon had to tread carefully. He could not alienate the king by voicing Calvin's antagonism to natural theology and perhaps did not even perceive that he was forced by his own logic to reject natural theology. Yet even some kings and statesmen might have wondered whether Bacon's offering on natural theology had really been grounded on natural reasoning. After all, Bacon filled much of his scant two pages on natural theology with a paraphrase of the warning: "Out of the contemplation of nature, or [on the] ground of human knowledges, to induce any verity or persuasion concerning points of faith, is in my judgment not safe: *Da fidei quae fidei sunt*" (Render to faith those things that are of faith).[10] Words once referring to Caesar were now paraphrased to fit a king for whom Bacon's dicta were like the peace of God that passeth all understanding.

To declare that one should discourse of faith on the basis of faith was not an unsound or novel principle and had not been since Aquinas fought the logicians who tried to reduce theology to philosophy. By fighting also the opposite extreme, namely, the reduction of philosophy to theology, Aquinas displayed a consistency that was conspicuously missing in the context containing Bacon's warning. He failed to explain how in view of his warning it was still possible to recognize from nature the power of the Creator. Was not this point also a point of faith? Clearly, one could not have it both ways, not even the future Lord Chancellor. How Lord Verulam would have handled points that belonged to faith one can only guess. His emphatic assertion of the difference between the power and the image of God probably echoed a favorite theme of Calvin's *Institutions*.[11] As to Bacon's handling of the question of man's natural knowledge of God, one can make more than mere guesses. Although his utterances on this topic are very brief, he spoke at some length on the problem of knowledge in general. The principles and views he expounded in that connection make it clear that Bacon could not proceed from contemplating nature to recognizing the power and wisdom of God. From the modern viewpoint, heavily tinged with operationism, logical positivism, and behaviorism, this might not seem to be a defect. But to moderns blessed with the perspective of three more centuries it should be clear that the very same Baconian theory of knowledge that barred the road of mind to God also barred the mind's access to a sound scientific method. Bacon even failed to find his way to the best scientists among his contemporaries. Harvey's name was conspicuously missing from the list of those students of nature whom Bacon thought able to implement his grandiose plan.[12] The plan was the raising of a recently born science into a full-grown adult, or in Bacon's words, the bringing about of the "masculine birth of time."[13]

To see the reason for Bacon's failure as a *paidagogos,* or upbringer of science, one need not even leave the page on which he boasted, "Natural theology which heretofore hath been handled confusedly with Metaphysic, I have inclosed and bounded by itself." He should have written not that he had bounded but that he had impounded natural theology. The very narrow confines within which Baconian science became "inclosed" were due to the same procedure. Natural theology "bound by itself"[14] meant a natural theology without metaphysics, a commodity still to be delivered. To discredit metaphysics Bacon spent half of his two-page-long natural theology on some monstrous aspects of belief in angels.[15] While angels may not have a rightful place either in metaphysics or in natural theology, this is hardly an argument for the possibility of natural theology without metaphysics.

It must be admitted, however, that Bacon was, consciously or not, consistent in his attempt to have natural theology without metaphysics. The metaphysics he advocated was such only in name. First, it was to be distinguished from "summary philosophy" and from physics, of which the former dealt with general rules of reasoning. While this could be readily conceded, Bacon's list of rules, all with some affinity to quantitative relationships, should seem ominous. As to physics, Bacon assigned to it efficient and material causality. The formal and final causes were the domain of metaphysics.[16] Bacon therefore could and did banish from physics the study of final causes as barren virgins,[17] and he rightly insisted on the disastrous effect of their study in the physics of Aristotle. While he retained the study of final causes in human affairs, he looked upon final causality as a state of consciousness and not as something that could have a genuinely ontological aspect. Ontology, or the study of being, did not exist for Bacon, in spite of his assigning to metaphysics the study of formal causes.

For Aristotle the formal cause was the most ontological of the four causes. It gave any being its actuality. For Bacon it meant something very different. According to him formal cause was "law" insofar as it indicated sequence or coordination.[18] With the old definition of formal cause banished, out went also the notion of substance. With the notion of substance abandoned, there disappeared the ontological substratum of change and the logical ground for making judgments about change, the subject matter (in terms of material and efficient cause) of Baconian physics. Clearly, if there was no substance, the starting and ending points of change had no connecting bridge, either ontological or logical. What meaning could then remain in Bacon's idea of formal cause as law or regular sequence? A little more than a hundred years later David Hume gave to this question the answer which unfolded fully the implications of Bacon's stance.

What Bacon called metaphysics was in complete subservience to science. What such metaphysics could do would hardly be of any profit to investigate. What it could not do is very clear from Bacon's efforts in his last ten years. They were largely spent implementing his dream of a definitive encyclopedia of useful knowledge, that is, of science. The effort was a monumental waste of energy on the part of one who did not lack acumen and whose writings are full of sparkling gems. Perhaps the finest of them is the remark, and a very original one, on the failure of Greek science.[19] Being very conscious of the need of a novel conception of science if it was to provide power, Bacon was pushed almost by necessity to the analysis of that failure. He placed the blame for it on the pantheism and a priorism of the approach of the Greeks of old to nature. The approach showed Nature as the image of their own nature in which they were lost as if it were the ultimate in intelligibility.

Bacon now had both his moment of greatness and his moment of failure. Nothing would have been more natural than to say that the world was not the image of man but an image of its Creator. After all, did not the world show his power and wisdom? Bacon was most reluctant to take that route. His reluctance might have had something to do with the biblical emphasis on man as an image of God and with Calvin's continual return to that theme. But the deeper reason seems to have been philosophical. If man, a creature, could be called the image of God, then analogy had to be taken into account. Obviously, man could not be a mirror image, that is, a univocal replica of God. Nor could the phrase "image of God" be a sheer play upon words, a meaningless equivocation. Between the two extremes was the realm of analogy. There could, however, be no resort to analogy in Bacon's system for the simple reason that it had no metaphysics. It was discarded as he excoriated the pantheism of Plato and Aristotle.

No more felicitous was the encomium he heaped on the purely mechanical approach taken to nature in Democritus's atomism.[20] It certainly had the advantage of being free of final causes, perhaps too free. Bacon should have also realized that for Democritus the atoms were the ultimate in intelligibility and being, a tenet not a whit more theistic than the animism underlying Platonic and Aristotelian pantheism. But before Bacon's turn to the purely mechanical world of Democritus defeated itself on the level of theology, it had already been revenged by metaphysics. Nature, or *physis*, is nowhere closer to metaphysics than at its deepest level, the level where the atoms are located. As further developments were to show, no one resentful of the world of metaphysics could really love the world of atoms, that is, cherish thoughts about the ultimate or even provisionally ultimate layer of the world of matter, a layer which is always elusive to the senses. The logic that forced Mach to reject atoms had already been operative in Bacon.[21]

Such reflections on Bacon's predicament are not to be taken as an argument on behalf of a specific metaphysics, let alone of a specific interpretation of the analogy of being. But his case reveals something, though negatively, of the inevitable reliance on a nonextremist position in epistemology whenever science achieves a creative advance. Of course, once a median position is taken in epistemology, a demonstration of the existence of God becomes possible, nay, well-nigh inevitable to any lover of consistency. The median position, which Bacon looked for and illustrated with a reference to bees embodying qualities that neither ants nor spiders possessed,[22] was not far from the truth, but its real nature remained hidden to him. In the digesting of facts, as conceived by Bacon, the intellect played no part appropriate to its very powers that generate discoveries.[23] By failing to find the median position Bacon missed the means, the all-important conceptual filament, that would have tied his gemlike phrases into an organic whole. While Sir Edward Coke, chief justice during Bacon's later years, overshot the mark by calling the *New Organon* an instrument "fit only for the Ship of Fools,"[24] it was as empty of unifying organic force as the *Advancement of Learning*. In both, a metaphysics was claimed which was such only in name.

To see this, it is enough to take a brief look at Bacon's division of sciences that relate to the knowledge of nature. He listed four such sciences, of which he called two, physics and metaphysics, speculative and the other two, mechanics and "magic," or chemistry, operative.[25] According to Bacon, metaphysics was to provide rules and principles for true "magic" so that the transformation of metals into gold might become a reality,[26] and presumably in a few years.[27] Bacon claimed the *New Organon* to be a storehouse of foolproof gold-making rules that his metaphysics provided. The rules were foolproof in that they worked, in Bacon's words, like a machine,[28] and with the certainty of a compass tracing out a circle.[29] The method was so foolproof that even fools could use it, and profitably so. For this exaggeration Bacon's own words are the excuse. His method, he wrote, put all wits "nearly on a level."[30] Did not this imply somehow that geniuses were just as unnecessary (Bacon of course excepted) as fools were useful? Did not Bacon invite everybody to make experiments?

Out of such democracy in scientific research there could emerge only a scientifically coated anarchy, a true replica of the lack of orientation often evident in Bacon's account of the science of nature. The painful artificiality of his "instances" is a case in point. In drawing them up he relied heavily on medieval compilations about winds, waters, materials, and qualities of all kinds. All of them echoed the specious distinctions of Aristotle. Right or wrong, Aristotle was certainly within his right to classify, but Bacon, who poked fun at him, was not. Classification is a leaning on ideas, but on what ground could they enter into Bacon's system? Did he not claim that all our traditional notions were unsound?[31] If so, would it not have been logical to ask the question how one had notions at all, before giving long sets of unsound rules about the art of having sound notions? Logical he was but in a roundabout and self-defeating way. He did not elaborate on the ability of mind to see from nature the wisdom and power of God, because he accepted that ability on other than sound philosophical grounds. He endorsed a theory of the soul which suggested that the soul was subtly material.[32] Now if the soul could not be known to be strictly nonmaterial, how could one have ideas and classifications that had to transcend the sensory, concrete, material particulars?

In the subtly materialistic system of Bacon, ideas could only be immaterial when it came to science. According to him, empirical evidence about magnetism showed it to be a surface phenomenon and, therefore, he described as a "very light fancy" Gilbert's idea that the whole earth was a magnet.[33] Agricola, the mining engineer, seemed to him of greater importance than Galileo.[34] He certainly had no eyes for the greatness and truth of Copernicus.[35] No wonder. Copernicus was possessed of a metaphysical vision of mathematics as well as of nature. For Bacon, mathematics was an appendix of a metaphysics that could not even touch on nature, let alone transcend it. Thus in the Baconian system mathematics played no creative part.[36] It could not because the system was not creative. Its most celebrated detail, the idea of *instantia crucis*,[37] was no source of positive insight. It was merely meant to lay bare wrongly assumed connections among phenomena.

Bacon tried to gain that insight from artisanship, even from tinkering and puttering. Intent on "squeezing and moulding" nature,[38] he failed to realize that this was constructive only when done intelligently. Only then could it cope with the subtlety of nature. Bacon referred to that subtlety time and again.[39] He did not perceive the irony when he declared that the empiricist school could not win over that subtlety.[40] His inductive method remained markedly unproductive precisely because it was but bare empiricism. He at most suspected that the science of know-how depended on the science of how to know. He organized that knowledge regardless, to the point of dreaming up his *New Atlantis*. One wonders whether the scientific geniuses of the century would have found their natural place in its almost mechanized schema of research.[41] There would have hardly been a place there for Galileo, an indomitable individual and an admirer of Copernicus for his courage to disregard the evidence of the senses. The author of the *New Atlantis* showed no readiness to part with his senses in the sense of bravely looking beyond their immediate witness. To do so would have meant the admission of a study of *physis* not only scientifically creative but also genuinely metaphysical. The particular aspects of the connection between Bacon's rejecting metaphysics and his impounding natural theology can be the subject of endless disputes because of his brevity on the matter. But the connection itself is indisputable and logical.[42] And so is its disastrous impact on Bacon's legislation in science.

One thing, however, cannot be denied to Bacon. He sensed, and with an elemental force, that his cause, the advancement of knowledge, had the deepest ties with the world of the senses. He saw himself as performing the "office of the true priest of the sense,"[43] but his orations had few inspired phrases. These struck a responsive chord a generation later when he was hailed as *buccinator novi temporis*, an outcome that should seem all the more appropriate as Bacon had described himself a "trumpeter, not a combatant."[44] The creative battles of science he neither waged nor was he able to outline their strategy. He excelled as trumpeter, a performance more appropriate to a scout than to a priest. It was not without irony that the trumpeter was enshrined as a patron saint in the nascent Royal Society. Only its least creative members acted according to Bacon's precepts,[45] and not one of them adopted the procedure by which he "inclosed and bounded natural theology by itself." Revealingly enough, Thomas Hobbes, who displayed strongly anti-metaphysical traits in the Baconian sense, was denied membership there.

Hobbes, like Bacon, was already in his early forties when he cast his lot with science and philosophy. What prompted him to do so was not his personal encounter with Bacon. The latter had already been dead for three years when Hobbes, during his first visit to Paris, got a taste of

Euclid's geometry. For another twenty-five years he mulled over his find, which at first had put him in a state of ecstasy. Then, in his late sixties, he began to publish treatises in geometry and kept doing so for the next dozen years. Although he made some acute remarks on principles,[46] he developed none of them into a noteworthy set of propositions, despite the sense of superiority suggested by the titles of his geometrical treatises.[47] At the age of eighty, Hobbes returned to his first love, classical literature. In view of what he wrote on geometry one cannot help asking whether he should not have spent his enormous energy on the classics. But Hobbes was also a philosopher with astonishing loyalty to his first principles. From that loyalty nothing could shake him, not even a good exposure to Descartes's ideas, or a personal visit to Galileo. Seeing at close range the gentle Father Mersenne's continual suspensions of judgment in matters philosophical and scientific did not make the slightest dent on Hobbes's single-mindedness. He spent his most productive years showing that on the basis of his principles one could have only one philosophy, the one expounded in the *De corpore*, in the *De cive*, and in the *Leviathan*. In his spelling out all the consequences of those principles lies Hobbes's perennial instructiveness.

The instructiveness is also Baconian, for Lord Verulam aptly noted that truth comes out sooner from a specific error than from speaking confusedly or not at all.[48] But Hobbes's errors are instructive also because they are monumental. To secure truth, political and theological, Hobbes ultimately had to rest his case with the factor most prone to error, the political ruler with absolute power. Undoubtedly, Hobbes wanted to serve mankind and to produce useful knowledge in a spirit that mirrored Baconian empiricism. As in a true mirror image, right and left were reversed. Bacon's empiricism was tied to induction, which Hobbes hardly mentioned. According to Hobbes, once the ultimate truth of sensory perception had been recognized, everything else followed by that strict deductive logic which he found in Euclid's *Elements*. He did not suspect that the parallel postulate, from which everything else followed there, was neither a sensory nor an ultimate truth. Nor was Euclid's geometry a proof that ratiocination was a simple juxtaposition, a sheer computation, or physically speaking, a straightforward mechanical push and pull.

He justified this view with a rigid, if not primitively empiricist theory with room for only two kinds of knowledge, that of fact and that of consequence. Thus the perceiving of a given circle was a "phantasm," a knowledge of fact; the recognition that any line passing through its center divides it into two equal parts was a knowledge of consequence, or scientific knowledge. As an empiricist, Hobbes was at a loss to explain the universal notion of a circle, and the universal validity of notions of consequence. But he had some even more instructive problems. The knowledge of consequence suggested the idea of a knowledge that imposed itself as if by necessity. This had to be the case in the conceptual world of an empiricist who saw no marvel in the workings of the mind but only a replay of the inevitable processes of nature. The most general form of those inevitable processes was motion, in which Hobbes saw the evidence of coming into being. But since he had already accepted as valid knowledge only geometrical reasoning with its apparent inevitability of consequences, valid or scientific knowledge could be had only about such motion that was inevitably necessary, that is, noncontingent in its innermost nature. This reasoning betrayed itself almost immediately.

Since Hobbes held that all sensory motion was strictly necessary, he had to attribute a noncontingent, necessary existence to the world, the totality of such motions. That the world, as the philosopher in Hobbes pictured it, was in no need of a Creator, was just another side of the fact that Hobbes felt no need whatever of natural theology. There was indeed no room for natural theology in an outlook in which religion had four natural seeds, to recall a statement in the *Leviathan*. The four were the "opinion of ghosts, ignorance of second causes, devotion towards what men fear, and taking of things causal for prognostics."[49] If the only valid knowledge was about necessary coming-into-being, or generation, as he called it, then there could be no valid knowledge either about the world as a whole, which did not come into being, or about God, who by definition could not come into being. Hobbes had not yet reached the end of the first chapter of the first book of his lengthy *Elements of Philosophy*, of which the first section was entitled "Concerning Body," when he reached the conclusion, "where there is no generation ... there is no philosophy. Therefore it excludes *Theology* ... the doctrine of God, eternal, ingenerable, incomprehensible, and in whom there is nothing neither to divide nor compound, nor any generation to be conceived."[50] Hobbes, the grim executioner of natural theology, was perfectly consistent, as will be seen shortly, when he went on to decapitate cosmology. He was also consistent in his rejection of history, both natural and political, as part of valid knowledge, that is, philosophy, but he could claim only with the most glaring inconsistency a place in philosophy for the science of the body politic.

A most natural feature of normal political life is the exercise of freedom of the will, but science was an equally big question mark in Hobbes's mechanistic world of ironclad necessity. With history banished as a rational topic Hobbes could not even try to understand science, which is inextricably a historic event. The question is not about that often childish amateurism in matters scientific on the part of Hobbes, who nowadays is accorded greatness (even by his admirers) only as a political philosopher.[51] The question is about the logic which had already eliminated God from the ken of reasoning. What was that very same logic to legislate about the method of science, and what was it to say about the unmistakable emergence of science, an event of which Hobbes was an eyewitness? Unlike Bacon, who pleaded for a broad, though haphazard, scouting across the experimental field, Hobbes left no room for observations and for experiments. He blandly declared that if experimentation were of any importance, pharmacists would be the best physicists.[52] Again, if valid or scientific reasoning was a mechanical push and pull, how could scientific discovery appear in its true nature as an intricate mental process with an elusively creative component? Kepler's works were a gold mine in this respect, but Hobbes did not base his discourse on science on its classics, which his century, the century of genius, was already producing in unusually large numbers. Not even his visit to the blind Galileo could give Hobbes an inkling of the great mental drama of scientific breakthroughs, let alone of their pitfalls. Several years later, when Hobbes took to task Thomas White, a Catholic priest and author of a cosmological work patterned on the *Dialogues* of Galileo,[53] Hobbes defended Galileo's wrong explanation of tides with a heavy recourse to Aristotelian physics.[54]

The scientific chapters in Hobbes's *De corpore*, or *On the Body*, are as drab and pedestrian as a commonplace mechanism. Nothing of what he said in lengthy chapters on motion, sound, heat, light, winds, and rivers has ever been recalled by those historians of science who exhaust themselves in tracking down every little advance. The last scientific chapter in *On the Body* is on gravity, and any admirer of Hobbes might only wish that he had never touched the topic. In his mechanical world everything amounted to a primitive push and pull. Lifting a body meant either or both. But what about the free fall of bodies? Hobbes had no choice but to declare that it was also the result of a push and a pull. Deduction this was, but not from anything empirical.

One chapter in *On the Body*, entitled "Of the World and of the Stars,"[55] deserves special mention. There Hobbes provides a clear example of the fact that an epistemology that obstructs the ways to God also blocks advance on the road of science. The example touches on science in its most sensitive and fundamental area, cosmology. Without cosmology one can be a good repairman, a good technician, nay an inventor, even a Nobel laureate. But without cherishing thoughts germane to cosmology one cannot have creative science. In a most real sense all science is cosmology, and nothing was made more obvious by the history of science than the cosmological provenance and relevance of all major scientific discoveries. The cosmos as such is, of course, not an empirically given fact; it is an inference from empirical data. The inference is not, however, a necessary one in the sense of Hobbes's knowledge of consequence. The inference in question is always a bold leap by the intellect.

Such a leap could not be to the liking of Hobbes, who, most appropriately for an empiricist, described the mind as a "slippery thing."[56] The hallmark of his reasoning was not boldness but grim determination. Much of his chapter on cosmology, the one on the world and the stars, is wasted by his resolve to discredit the notion of void supported by Torricelli's and Pascal's experiments.[57] The resolve of Hobbes, the push-pull mechanist, was that of a scout watching all his steps and catching no glimpse of the scenery, let alone of distant horizons. The last of the five suppositions with which he summed up the astronomy and cosmology of the mid-1600s is a case in point.[58] It referred to the ratio of the distances from the sun to the earth and from the moon to the earth as given by Kepler. There Hobbes wrote: "As for the magnitude of the circles, and the times in which they are described by the bodies which are in them, I will suppose them to be such as shall seem most agreeable to the phenomena in question."[59]

The phrase was as strong in empiricism as it was weak in science. To begin with, the circles were ellipses and Hobbes knew it, but his sole interest in the eccentricities of the orbits lay in his labors to explain them mechanically. The explanation on which his cosmological chapter came to a close produced no echo whatever. Neither did the century of genius see anyone espouse the contentions that opened the same chapter. According to Hobbes, concerning the world as a whole one could ask only about its size, duration, and number. He claimed that none of these questions could be given a definite answer, nor did it matter whether the world was finite or infinite, full or void, eternal or temporal, one or many.[60] In either of these alternatives the appearances could be such as actually observed. The justification of this position was certainly not scientific. At any rate, on the basis of Hobbes's empiricism one could not talk about the world as a whole. It was not a knowledge of fact, nor was it a knowledge of consequence derivable from a phantasm. He noted with some affectation of piety that making a definitive choice among these cosmological alternatives was reserved to those who "are lawfully authorized to order the worship of God."[61] This meant ultimately not the Church or her theologians but the absolute political ruler, hardly a cheerful prospect for cosmology.

In an admirable display of consistency Hobbes offered a rebuttal of the proof of the existence of God from motion in the very same context in which he manhandled the three permissible cosmological questions. His attributing to God an infinitely extended spiritual body was another matter.[62] He failed to correlate his dictum with his famous declaration in the *Leviathan* that what is not the material universe is nothing.[63] What this proved was not only that such an idea of God could not be got from revelation, but not even from his own philosophy, one of the basic propositions of which was that it was "impossible for a man or any other creature to have any conception of infinite."[64] Behind such inconsistencies there must have lain some of the self-delusion betrayed by his writings on geometry. Thus, he brought his discourse on the three cosmological questions to an end with the baffling remark that solutions to them should be appraised with an eye on the true nature of geometry. Geometry, he wrote, "has in it somewhat like wine, which when new, is windy; but afterwards though less pleasant, yet more wholesome."[65] The same was true, he added, of the difference between young and mature geometers. As a geometer Hobbes was neither young nor mature, but largely a plagiarizer, a point made clear in no uncertain terms by John Wallis, the foremost geometer of the time.[66]

Father Marin Mersenne's reasonableness in geometry widely separates him from Hobbes, and his enthusiasm for it places him equally far from Bacon. Lord Verulam, the skilled politician, promoted natural theology to a lofty but carefully isolated spot to let it die a natural death. Hobbes summarily executed it in the manner of his absolutist ruler. Mersenne, the devout monk, was an enthusiast for natural theology. Such is certainly the impression one gains from his thirty-six proofs of the existence of God for which he reserved two hundred columns, or about one-fifth of his famed folio, *Quaestiones celeberrimae in Genesim.*[67] He found material for the proofs not only in philosophy, but in all the sciences, theoretical as well as practical, in music, medicine, rhetoric, natural magic or chemistry, and (not least) in navigation. Mersenne spent his late twenties and early thirties teaching philosophy and theology in the spirit, as he claimed, of Thomas Aquinas, but to expound his texts did not necessarily mean to assimilate his grasp on fundamental viewpoints. Aquinas received but few and cursory mentions as Mersenne gave the philosophical arguments, covering hardly a dozen columns.

The philosophical proof that appealed most to Mersenne was the ontological proof, of which he spoke almost ecstatically. He described it as *excellens doctrina, admodum pia, acuta demonstratio,* and *ratio acutissima.* In fact he gave it in two forms. One was *ex veritate,* the other *ex bonitate,* and he referred to Anselm as well as to Augustine.[68] A good friend of Mersenne, Descartes almost certainly read the celebration of the ontological proof in Mersenne's folio before reinventing it. Mersenne's prolific treatment of the argument from design was too short on philosophical considerations to endear the idea of purposiveness to Descartes. Twenty-five of the thirty-six proofs were variations of the argument from design, for which Mersenne found more than two hundred illustrations from the quantitative aspects of things, small and large, concrete and abstract. The next-to-last argument was *ex architectura,* by which he meant the structure of the solar system as well as of all parts of the human body, all built for a purpose. The one evidenced by the knee was that man may genuflect before God.[69] The last argument was *ex nautica,* or the art of navigation. There he compared the world to a ship because the earth behaved like a magnet. Thus the two hundred folio columns dedicated to the proofs came to a close with a table of the sun's declinations, undoubtedly an important tool for sailing, but also an unwitting symbol that such proofs of God's existence formed the shallows on which the ship of natural theology was to run aground.

Mersenne's was an elementary mistake in philosophical tactics, and it revealed something of his unphilosophical mind. This may seem an unjust remark about Mersenne, who early in his literary career fired a broadside against the skeptics by holding up geometry as the embodiment of incontestable certainty.[70] Was not a campaign against skepticism a most genuinely philosophical attitude? But as Mersenne's intellectual odyssey was to show, his faith in philosophical certainty had a ground only in theology, or rather faith, not in philosophy. His faith and piety were more than enough to save his soul, but they could not save his natural theology and his science. Logic exacted its due from the devout monk no less than it did from Bacon and Hobbes. The logic in question worked not without some touch of drama in Mersenne's case. In 1645, only a year before he died, and only two decades after he had lined up his battery of thirty-six proofs of the existence of God, Mersenne was begging for only one proof, but a proof which, as he put it, would convince each and every reader. He was not only begging, but begging a heretic, Florianus Crusius, a well-known Socinian. In his letter to Crusius, [71] Mersenne noted that the proof should lead to some affirmation about God's essence. To this he added that the notion of God as *ens a se* was not a good starting point because geometers had recently taken the view that the sun and other stars might be considered as entities that always existed.

The geometers were Descartes and the admirers of his *Principes,* of which the third part dealt with the sun and the stars, and in which creation in time, nay creation itself, was not endorsed with great conviction. Mersenne, a lifelong friend of Descartes, never became a Cartesian. He died a skeptic with regard to both philosophy and science. His was the logical fate of an empiricist. In less than a decade Mersenne tired of apologetics and of crusading against the skeptics. There followed a few years of feverish publication on scientific method in a markedly empiricist style. Because of empirical difficulties Mersenne could not bring himself to see the truth of the law of free fall as derived by Galileo. Mersenne's final publications were on inventions and technology. His whole faith in science narrowed to an appreciation of the usefulness of the gadgets it produced. Science still retained for him theological value, but only because it evidenced a provident God through its production of gadgets that made life more pleasant and comfortable.

Mechanical gadgets were not, however, the key to understanding. One could produce them without ever having a touch of that craving for understanding which is the very soul of science and which is the hallmark of all creative scientists. Mersenne, the clearinghouse of the science of his day, moved farther and farther away from science as a quest for understanding and as a method of how to know. At the same time he became more and more preoccupied with inventions, that is, with the art of know-how. One of his last reports was about a machine that could fly from Paris to Constantinople in a day's time.[72] The planned contraption, the brainchild of a mechanic in Paris, was to carry half a dozen men and four or five, as Mersenne reported it, major instruments of war. He must have meant small cannon. The fact that he eagerly reported the project in spite of his express disbelief in its feasibility betrayed his great interest in such lore. Interest concentrated along these lines might have secured entry into the fearful capital of the Crescent and even into the kingdoms of *New Atlantis* and of *Leviathan*. It could not secure entry into the kingdom of science. It was not a kingdom to be opened up by empirical scouting. The blindness of that empiricism in natural theology was of a piece with its myopia in science.

Five

RATIONALIST ROAD CHARTING

THE EMPIRICISTS STAKED ALL THEIR FORTUNES ON FINDING THE ART OF know-how. Equally extreme was Descartes's hope that once the art of how to know had been found the art of know-how would almost mechanically yield its riches. Descartes was not the first rationalist to have such a hope, but his hope had a special magnitude and an unmistakable ring of modernity. The modernity consisted in Descartes's preoccupation with theoretical science. The magnitude can be sensed from that experience which was aptly called by Archbishop Temple "the most disastrous moment in the history of Europe."[1] The experience of having three dreams in one night can easily signal disaster if preceded by one's staying for a whole day "shut-up alone in a stove-heated room."[2] Happily for Descartes, he did not remain, as Archbishop Temple would have it, "shut-up in a stove."[3] Thus the experience did not become a disaster for Descartes's physique but only for his physics. More than a hundred years later, d'Alembert put the blame squarely on Descartes for that stagnation in which physical science remained for some time in France while it advanced rapidly in England.[4]

This may seem an unjust remark on the part of d'Alembert, one of the most illustrious geometers of the eighteenth century. Was not analytical geometry born in that stove-heated room? In a sense, yes, but it was no less true that d'Alembert was a geometer in a way that could not be achieved along the road charted in Descartes's *Discourse on the Method*. Pascal, one of Descartes's early admirers, soon perceived that Descartes was "useless and uncertain," and he planned with an eye on Descartes a critique of those who made "too profound a study of science."[5] As far as physical science was concerned, Descartes's method, or road charting, could only lead to a dream and are not all novels essentially dreams? Descartes was still alive when young Huygens was already on the road to recognizing that the wondrous explanation of the world, the whole physics and cosmology as given in Descartes's *Principes de la philosophie*, was not science but only a great novel.[6]

Clearly, something must have gone wrong in that stove-heated room. Descartes closeted himself there in 1619, on the eve of the feast of Saint Martin, a time of great merrymaking in the France of his day. He pointedly recalled that he had abstained from wine for some time. But he also disclosed that prior to that evening he had felt for several days a steady rise of temperature in his head.[7] It made him suddenly see the magic significance of a clue to a project which he had already described as "unbelievably ambitious." The clue was a beacon of light which

65

would enable him to "dissipate even the densest darkness in the chaos of that science."[8] The science in question was geometry. In the reduction of it to algebra—analytical geometry—Descartes perceived the vista of a general and exclusive method for reasoning with certainty and clarity. As he put it seventeen years later in his *Rules for the Direction of the Mind:* "One conclusion now emerges ... namely, that in our search for the direct road towards the truth we should busy ourselves with no object about which we cannot attain a certitude equal to that of the demonstration of Arithmetic and Geometry."[9]

Here was reductionism, which always buys clarity and certitude at the price of mutilating reality, in a sophisticatedly seductive way of course. Thus Descartes held high the ideal of clear and certain knowledge and of its unlimited universality. He first thought that it was enough to make all problems similar to those of mathematics, and he believed he had succeeded in making some problems of physics and medicine "almost similar to those of mathematics."[10] Like other reductionists to come he did not perceive how ominous was the word "almost." Moreover, there were fields where the subject matter revealed no quantitative aspects. But was not quantity, Descartes reasoned, expressive of more general features, namely, of relation, order, and succession? With an affirmative answer to this question Descartes reached the conclusion that the method in any field was independent of the specificity of the subject matter.

Such a method was unlimited in its fearful potentialities. Indeed, in 1630, only eleven years after that night of three dreams in a stove-heated room, Descartes reported to Mersenne that he had worked out a demonstration of God's existence more certain than the propositions of geometry.[11] This effort went hand in hand with a search for a medicine based on "infallible demonstrations."[12] Ultimately, in Descartes's system of medicine there emerged only one infallible truth, the inevitability of death and the wisdom of facing it with calm resignation.[13] This was excellent medicine but not scientific. As for Descartes's physics, which was thrown in for good measure with his carefree reporting on infallibility, it was not even fallible, that is, permitting a choice between failure and success. With it, one could only fail with deductions about the physical universe. The basic reason for this Cartesian debacle in physics lies in Descartes's "infallible" demonstration of the existence of God. Descartes's original infatuation with geometry first made him work his way toward what is universal in knowledge. Geometry, an obvious embodiment of certainties, also sparked his drive for incontrovertible evidence of certainty. He found it in the reflection of the mind on its own act of thinking. Taking the view that the proposition "I think, therefore I am" withstood "all the extravagant suppositions" of the skeptics, he espoused it "without scruple,"[14] as the first truth of the philosophy which he was seeking.

Whatever the certainty of one's own existence as a thinking being, the fact that the evidence of that certainty implied the act of doubting made the situation uneasy. Descartes found the remedy in the notion of God as the absolute being. His intoxication with his first truth prevented him, however, from seeing that he had got the idea of God, the absolute being, from his Christian upbringing. He rather claimed that the thinking soul inevitably and therefore always possessed that idea. It was innate to the soul which, however, could not help realizing that its own existence was not inconceivable. Therefore, the thinking mind cried out for a being whose idea necessarily implied existence.[15] If Descartes did not learn about the ontological proof from his Jesuit teachers at La Flèche, he could have read it in Mersenne's two long lists of proofs of the existence of God.[16] An independent discovery is, of course, not improbable in view of Descartes's own bent of mind and genius. It was the genius in him that gave an unusual twist to old proofs and phrases. Such was the geometrical garb in which he dressed the ontological proof. The notion of God, he wrote, implied his existence in the same manner in which "the equality of its three angles to two right angles is implied in the idea of a triangle." That geometry could not be a road to God should have now been clear from Descartes's very words. From geometry he could learn that one idea implied another idea, and perhaps that an imperfect geometrical figure suggested another more perfect one, but from geometry he could not learn that any idea implied the very existence of what it referred to. Descartes also recast the hallowed phrase that the external world was the mark of a divine craftsman. He was fully aware of the novelty of his tactic and he voiced it with a touch of apology: "One certainly ought not to find it strange that God, in creating me, placed this idea [the innate idea of an absolute being] within me to be like the mark of the workman imprinted on his work."[17] Until Descartes not ideas but beings were considered marks of the divine craftsman, for although some beings could act like monsters, they could never turn into chimeras, that is, into mere ideas of which not even human craftsmen could be particularly proud.

Before long many a first-rate intellect came to the conclusion that Descartes's proof of the existence of God was valid and that—for such was its rigorous implication—the classical a posteriori proofs could not be valid.[18] Wherever Cartesianism ruled during the rest of the seventeenth century, traditional natural theology went into decline. But once the a posteriori access of reason to God was made impossible by allowing to reason only the road of the ontological proof, the advance of science along the road charted by Descartes also became illusory. The supreme proof of this was Descartes's physics, with its built-in inability to lead anyone, either himself or his disciples, to become "master and possessor of nature,"[19] the shining promise of his method. Descartes perceived nothing of that inability. It even remained hidden to him that the demonstrations of geometry, whose certainty he now extended to the ontological proof,[20] were not proofs in the sense in which the traditional proofs of the existence of God were meant to be proofs. The latter were proofs that implied a cogent but bold leap on the part of the intellect. In its period of maturing, science had already provided ample evidence that its basic proofs rested on similar leaps. On the contrary, the proofs of geometry were the sheer unfolding of the conceptual contents of postulates and propositions. Far more important, while it was sufficient for Euclidean geometry merely to exist in the thinking mind, this was certainly not enough in connection with the absolute being. This elementary difference could hardly be perceived by Descartes, who looked upon geometry as if it were a god. Once raised to that exalted status, geometry had to behave like God, that is, forgo any change. Typically, Descartes frowned on new efforts in geometry in line with his erstwhile conviction that hardly anything new remained to be discovered there.[21] Perhaps the new developments were not to Descartes's liking because they were not rigorous. But should they have been postponed for lack of rigor? It is well to recall that the clearing up of the theory of limit, the cornerstone of infinitesimal calculus, by Cauchy in 1821, was preceded by the exhortation of d'Alembert to his students: "Have faith, the proof will come."[22] By the time it did, four generations of scientists had already taken it on faith.

There seemed to be no need for anything to be cleared up in the geometry of Descartes. It was the embodiment of clarity, and what is clarity if not distinct, precise contours? In addition to the quest for universality and certitude, the quest for distinctness was the third inspiration which Descartes derived from his admiration for geometry.[23] Since distinctness seemed to be an essential feature of geometrical figures, the conclusion seemed to be logical that certainty could not be had without distinctness. This also meant that the entity, or the thinking soul, in which Descartes found certainty, had to be distinct in a rigorous sense. That the soul was distinct from God was for Descartes a certainty, but it rested not so much on his philosophy as on his Christian upbringing. Had he lacked that upbringing, his principles would have readily landed him in the misty realm of pantheism. This was soon to happen to a Cartesian who had lost faith in the God of biblical revelation.

In addition to being distinct from God, the thinking soul also had to be distinct from the world of matter, including that living human body without which there was no experienced certainty about the reality of thinking. To secure the rigorous distinctness of soul from body, or of thinking from anything sensuous, required major surgery, and for this Descartes found the magic tool in the geometrical concept of extension.[24] The basic activities of the mind did not seem to include that concept. On the other hand, everything sensual and material was something extended. Descartes realized that a notion like extension could not logically be generated from that very thinking in which no essential activity implied extension. To generate the notion of extension Descartes relied, not unnaturally, on something akin to generation. The notion of extension was born in the soul, it was innate to it, so Descartes declared.[25] The declaration could be made all the more easily if the infinitely more fundamental notion of absolute being was also an innate notion.

An innate notion of extension could, however, imply that the existence of bodies and their totality, the universe, was nothing but an illusion. Trying to escape the clutches of skepticism by a foolproof method, Descartes was led by that very road back to the edge of skepticism in clear indication that the road charted by him was not a straight advance but a circle. He was so agitated by this possibility as to think that he might have been victimized by an evil genius, very powerful and very cunning, who employed all his powers to deceive him.[26] To save himself from a potentially total debacle of his own making, Descartes, as if by instinct (Christian instinct to be sure), turned to the God of his religion. Such a God, whom Descartes still believed to be the God of his philosophy, was certainly not a deceiver, let alone a creator of global illusions.[27]

The God of Descartes's upbringing was certainly the ever-faithful Creator whose faithfulness was proclaimed in the faithful—that is, regular and rational—course of nature. But Descartes the philosopher could not move to the God of his philosophy along ways cherished in the mainstream of Christian tradition, that is, along ways based on the contemplation of nature. The God whom he reached through geometry and the ontological proof might have been a safeguard against global deception, but that very same God lacked one thing. He lacked the power to permit Descartes to go to the world through the evidence of his senses. That God was not the uncreated absolute being, but the creation of a philosophy which prohibited its devotees to go to the external world unburdened by a heavy load of a priori precepts. The prohibition was the hallmark of science as conceived and legislated by Descartes. It was a matching counterpart of the prohibition issued by him against going to God from the evidence of the senses. No wonder that science, world, God, and soul—all appeared to be illusory after logic had proceeded for some time along the road charted by Descartes.

The world of Descartes was his science and his science was his world.

Such an identity, even its sheer possibility, should alert any scientist, nay anyone with a modicum of knowledge about science. According to that knowledge science keeps developing because there is no strict identity between any actual form of science and the full intelligibility of nature. Quite different is the case with Descartes's science. His science is the world as it supposedly should be, and such a world stands in a one-to-one correspondence to his science. Unfortunately, the real value of the particular world of that specific correspondence was well-nigh zero. Still, from Descartes's errors, which are very specific, one can learn a great deal. Indeed, learning from those errors was very helpful during the seventeenth-century that saw the scientific enterprise reach its maturity.

This is not to suggest that all dicta of Descartes on science and the world are sheer errors. There are some gems there, but they could not be developed within the system itself, nor could its grave errors be corrected within that system. One of the gems was the emphatic assertion of linear inertia.[28] It is almost natural to make the generalization about inertial movement as the advance of a body along a straight line of indefinite if not infinite length. But the world of Descartes could only be full, and in such a world inertial movement could have no convincing meaning because of the impossibility of truly unimpeded motion. Moreover, the only kind of world that could be derived from the Cartesian notion of extension was an indefinite extension of homogeneous matter, an entity suggesting supreme monotony. Obviously, the actual world was not such monotonous, inert body, and the task of coping with this discrepancy forced Descartes to make some references to the Creator's power and freedom. This he did both in the *Principes*[29] and in its stillborn anticipation, *Le Monde, ou Traité de la lumière*.[30]

The Creator's freedom seemed, however, to be undermined by the doctrine of innate ideas, a point which Descartes tried to clear up as early as 1630 in a letter to Mersenne.[31] There Descartes urged Mersenne to state unhesitatingly that God was a sovereign king who freely imposed his laws upon the universe. The true God was not a king like "Jupiter, or Saturn, subject to the Styx, or destiny."[32] The real contrast between the God of biblical revelation and the gods of classical antiquity was largely lost on Descartes. He insisted in the same breath that the essential truths about the world, such as extension, which stood for geometry, were as innate as the notion of God. God's freedom amounted to imposing on the world Euclidean geometry, hardly a freedom if Euclid's postulates were a necessary form of truth and science. Indeed, the God of Descartes the philosopher had no choice but to let the actual world develop from the original chaos in the manner outlined by Descartes.

Complete chaos meant perfect homogeneity,[33] and such was the original form of the world which God, following Descartes's precepts, created out of nothing. Such a homogeneity bore only the faintest mark of contingency. Moreover, Descartes made his reader feel time and again that the development of the world from that absolutely homogeneous primordial state was a necessary and not a contingent development. The problem why anything nonhomogeneous should develop from something perfectly homogeneous should have given pause to Descartes, but his mind was bent on geometry, not on metaphysics. The loss for philosophy once more went hand in hand with loss for science. The idea of the homogeneity of matter, that is, of one kind of matter as emphasized by Descartes, was certainly a great advance over Aristotle. But the gain was immediately dissipated in Descartes's arbitrary effort to differentiate his absolutely homogeneous matter into a given, obviously nonhomogeneous world. First came the subdivision of infinite homogeneous matter into domains whose diameters corresponded to the average distance between stars. Revealingly, Descartes let not philosophy but the Creator perform that cosmic parceling, admitting thereby that only observation and not a priori reasoning could inform us about the size of the domains into which the heavens were to be divided.[34]

Once the stellar domains were established, Descartes had the Creator give to the matter contained within each domain a rotational motion around its center,[35] a tactic which revealed the precious little that Descartes was willing to concede to God. Among other things, he should have also ascribed to God the actual setting up of the direction of the axis of each and every domain. And he should have realized that rotational motion, if it was a genuine motion, was not compatible with his emphasis on the notion of linear extension. When Pascal remarked that Descartes would have been quite willing to dispense with God, and that beyond letting God give each domain a fillip Descartes had no use for God,[36] he was more to the point than he seemed to realize. The fillip did not produce a typically Cartesian motion, which being inertial, had to be linear. The illogical presence of a circular but creative twist in the Cartesian system was, however, a most logical revelation of the fact that the Cartesian God, hardly more than a step in abstract conceptual analysis, could not secure real motion. He could not, because he was not reached by the mind through reflection on what is most real in a world of motion.

Although a detailed analysis of the Cartesian idea of motion would be instructive, there are more striking illustrations of the connection between Descartes's natural theology, on the one hand, and his world and science—his cosmology—on the other. About the a priori character of Descartes's natural theology not much can be done, and there is not much merit either in attempting to play down the a priori features of his world building and science.[37] True, the *Principes* came to a close with the protestation that the world could have been produced by God in countless other ways,[38] but even in that context Descartes claimed on the basis of principles that he started with—and they were entirely a priori—that the development of the world into its present form had to follow inevitably. He had no eyes for the depth of the world's contingency, and as a result his science remained as shallow as any application of the a priori method in science is bound to be. It is well to recall that in the opening section of the third book of the *Principes* Descartes subtly hinted at the a priori character of the world building which was to follow.[39] In the freedom of private communication he sounded very categorical on this point. In a letter to Mersenne, Descartes took the view that his system could be overthrown in only two ways. One was the refutation of his a priori principles, the other was the demonstration of non sequiturs in what he presented as inevitable consequences from those principles.[40]

That experiments and observations could be of no decisive value against his system was Descartes's most considered view. Not that he did not speak profusely of experiments—or rather of their usefulness. At one point he even claimed that he had performed almost as many as he had written lines,[41] and he wrote lines by the tens of thousands. He certainly experimented to a modest extent, but there was no modesty in the manner in which he thought of himself as the sole interpreter of experiments, which he hoped to get from any and all.[42] This was no mere rhetoric. He lectured Harvey, who both discovered the circulation of blood and gave its correct explanation, on what the correct explanation ought to be.[43] The really destructive part of his views on experiments lay not in such incidentals but in general precepts. The first of these was that no experiment could bear on the foundations of physics because those foundations had been established once and for all by pure cogitation. The second precept acknowledged the usefulness of experiments for the clearing up of particulars. This was an acknowledgement that Descartes did not take seriously.[44] Perhaps he sensed that all worthy experiments somehow touched on the fundamentals.

A case in point was Descartes's reaction to experimental difficulties concerning his laws on the collision of bodies. He brushed aside objections with reference to the difference between the ideal and the real world.[45] The difference certainly existed, but not in Cartesian physics for which the ideal was real. Similar was the situation with vortical motion, the all-purpose agent and deus ex machina of Cartesian physics. Rotating pans filled with water carrying around globules of different specific weights did not match his claims about the characteristics he assigned to celestial vortices. His reply was that his theory could not be explained in a few words.[46] Once more the experiments involved fundamentals, and Descartes had to take refuge in generalities and even in an appeal to imagination. The latter could have no logical place in a system based on deductions by an abstractive mind. The Cartesian mind could think but not imagine, and certainly not in that picturesque manner which Descartes constantly demanded from his reader. His success largely depended on the perennial and universal human longing to imagine and on that equally pervasive temptation to fancy that if one could have true science by imagining hard, why was one to bother with hard studies? Indeed, the brightest champion of Descartes, Malebranche, found it important to rebut those who objected to Descartes's cosmology on the ground that it was so simple that even women could understand it.[47] Have not women always excelled in the art of imagining?

The imaginative power of all men and women was in demand when Descartes outlined that colossal grinding process through which the evolution of the universe was achieved. His famous diagram of it reveals an ill-concealed effort to make it appear plausible that contiguous polyhedrons, his stellar domains, could all rotate on their axes without greatly interfering with one another. He failed to warn that if any polyhedron was made to approximate a sphere, the ones contiguous with it had to depart from the spherical form in the same degree. The simultaneous, smooth rotation of celestial vortices, as imagined by Descartes, was a most implausible affair. A similar, equally implausible rotation was to produce Descartes's second kind of matter, the perfectly spherical and transparent globules filling all interstellar spaces.[48] His first kind of matter was made of the very fine filings which, due to their fast motion, were the source of heat and light throughout the universe. The third kind of matter came from the rude chunks, the primary fallout from the cosmic chiseling process. There was nothing inherently impossible in all this as long as demand for exactness yielded to imagination. The process could be imagined, and that was all Descartes needed.

Actually, he needed and used something far more convincing, but he glossed over its true implication. The division of infinite extension into stellar domains was needed by a particularity of nature, the average distance among stars, which could in no way be derived from Descartes's a priori generalities. In attributing that particularity to a direct action of the Creator, Descartes sounded as cursory as possible.[49] Descartes was again very brief, almost surreptitiously so, as he noted that in order to account for the existence of the transparent globules, another cosmic parceling had to be done by the Creator. These particularities, or radical singularities of nature, were not to become for Descartes a path to the Creator of nature. They were not and could not become such, because his philosophy, and therefore his system of the world too, would have immediately crumbled. Both implied the ontological proof as the only admissible road to the recognition of the ultimate in intelligibility and being, that is, God. Once nature was forbidden to proclaim its Creator, he had to be allowed to reenter the scientific explanation of the world through the back door, in unguarded moments and very often in disguise. In the case of Descartes this inconsistency flew in the face of his natural theology as well as of his science. Descartes, who because of his initial assumptions had to deny the existence of atoms,[50] was forced to bring them back in the form of globules, the size of which was not man-made, not even nature-made, but plainly God-made.

Allowing God back, and surreptitiously at that, into the scientific explanation of the world could profit neither natural theology nor science. Surreptitious moves are usually accompanied by studied vagueness, and such was the manner in which Descartes let the Creator perform the original parceling of the infinite into stellar domains. Unlike the parceling on the microscopic level, that on the macroscopic level was not to produce strictly equal parts. In this unspecified inequality lay the trigger and the demise of a self-constructing world whose evolution Descartes painted in bold strokes. Only a genius could be so bold, so original, and also so oblivious to the obvious. The inequality of domains assured the possibility that a large domain with a star in its center might absorb a smaller one, turning the star of the latter into its planet. Such was the essence of the Cartesian mechanism of the formation of planetary systems, a great first in the history of cosmology[51]— and also one of its first great illusions.

As the author of a thoroughly mechanistic cosmogony, Descartes should have paid some attention to the fact that he had already postulated the axes of rotation of neighboring vortices in markedly different directions. This meant that when one vortex engulfed another, their respective senses of rotation would oppose each other, with inevitable diminution of the resulting total rotation. Moreover, it should not necessarily have been beyond Descartes's ken to recognize that in his universe the total amount of rotation had to be zero.[52] While such a criticism may seem to fault Descartes for not anticipating future scientific insight, he may rightfully be taken to task for overlooking the fact that his postulated inequality of domains implied one apocalyptic consequence. On the basis of that inequality the absorbing of one domain by another had to go on until there remained but one star with an infinite number of crusted or dead stars, that is, planets, in its now infinitely large vortex. Ultimately that star too was to be encrusted, with the result that the universe, of which Descartes originally discoursed with a "Treatise on Light," would find its demise in complete darkness.

Darkness had to be the all-engulfing characteristic of the Cartesian universe for another and typically Cartesian reason. Descartes had no choice but to define light as a mechanical pressure acting instantly from any distance, as does the pressure exerted by the end of a perfectly rigid stick, however long. From each stellar surface pencils of pressure extended in every direction, the pencils acting across the boundary layers of vortices. Since in the infinite Cartesian universe the number of such pencils of pressure was infinite, and since they extended in every direction, the resulting pressure at each point had to be zero, that is, complete darkness. Clearly, there was something basically wrong with the idea of a universe consisting of an infinite number of stars homogeneously distributed. Descartes should not perhaps be faulted for not perceiving the paradox designated since the late 1940s as Olbers' paradox.[53] Still, the recognition of the paradox was not intrinsically beyond Descartes's mental horizon. Indeed, two generations after him the recognition saw print with the hint that it had already been widely discussed. Whoever may have discussed it before Halley,[54] Descartes had only to look at the sky on any moonless night to see the strikingly nonuniform distribution of stars.

This marked departure from uniformity should have given second thoughts to Descartes about the truth of his claim that the unfolding of his philosophical principles meant the production of a world as actually observed. Had he been an interested observer of the skies, he might have been led from first- to second- to third-magnitude stars and to their increasingly uneven distribution. Moreover, the telescope revealed an immensely large number of stars in one clearly defined belt of the sky, the Milky Way. Such unevenness was a powerful pointer to the world's singularity, a feature which had no logical place in Descartes's system of thought. He knew God by introspection and not by inspection of the world. It was therefore natural that Descartes should keep silent on the Milky Way,[55] although he must have seen its hosts of stars through the telescope. Of the mounting of the telescope he gave an elaborate though largely useless diagram.[56] What he said of the telescope itself contained nothing essentially new, not even the fact that Kepler, Galileo, and others had much to do with it.

Acknowledgments of the merits of others rarely issued from the pen of Descartes. Rather, he penned variations of the claim that in his physics there was only mathematics.[57] Descartes's discussions of rainbows and of snowflakes were lonely exceptions to his consistently nonmathematical treatment of physics.[58] In both cases he followed an already well-trodden path. Most curious should seem his attitude toward another mathematical detail, the elliptical orbits of planets. He discussed the properties of ellipses with great ingenuity in his analytical geometry.[59] He knew of Kepler's work on the elliptical orbit of Mars,[60] and he seemed to recognize its natural extension to all planetary orbits.[61] In the *Principes* the earth's and the moon's orbits appeared as ellipses on one and the same diagram.[62] But Descartes never acknowledged in words that planets had geometrically distinct and well-defined orbits. His was the ironic choice between having either the elliptical orbits, that is, geometry with its distinct entities, or keeping his artfully vague and variable vortices. He kept the latter. The geometrical reductionism that ruined Descartes's natural theology was to discredit his science as well.

These details of the history of science have been marshaled here in part because of the specific receptivity of our age. In this age of science a well-informed natural theology must make extensive use of some outstanding lessons of science and of its history. But one need not retrace the course of Cartesian physics to the very end to see the source of its debacle in the initial error made by Descartes in natural theology. It is enough to turn to Spinoza, the first great thinker to cast his lot with Descartes's geometrical reductionism. Spinoza showed no interest in Cartesian science and showed very little interest in science in general, although he might by nature have been inclined to science. He eked out a meager living for himself by grinding lenses, yet he never spoke of the science of lenses, a most geometrical topic. This should seem curious on the part of the celebrated author of an ethics patterned on geometry. Again, although a mystic, he was attracted to reality, historical and political, though hardly to the scientific.[63]

The answer to this puzzle lies precisely in Spinoza's acutely Cartesian mind. Since it was Cartesian, he largely accepted Descartes's initial assumptions. But because of the acuteness of his mind Spinoza quickly perceived that there was no stringent need to assert with Descartes the fundamental distinctness of mind, God, and extension. Their intimate coexistence in the mind was for Spinoza a proof that they were essentially one and the same. Such was the brief genesis of Spinoza's philosophical pantheism.[64] Although it became his religion, it could not dispose of questions which a world, however pantheistic, kept posing because of its undeniable composition of finite entities, the very feature of reality that makes science possible. Spinoza, who could spiritedly defend the Cartesian logic of his pantheism, was at a loss for words when pressed for the provenance of finite beings. Partly responsible for this priceless detail was von Tschirnhausen, a gentleman-philosopher from Heidelberg, attracted by his Teutonic mysticism to Spinoza's thought, but not a mystic to the point of parting with commonsense evidence. "Dear Sir," reads Tschirnhausen's letter of June 26, 1676, to Spinoza, "I wish you would gratify me . . . by pointing out how, from the conception of the extension, as you gave it, the variety of the universe can be shown a priori." In his reply, Spinoza confessed that the derivation in question was not possible and he blamed Descartes's definition of matter as extension.[65] Spinoza correctly saw part of the trouble. Matter was far more than the reflection of abstract extension. But being a Cartesian trapped in his own mind, Spinoza could not see that matter was richly varied reality. He looked for the solution in the notion of a homogeneously infinite and eternal essence, a form of pantheism. He granted, however, that he had not been able to put the matter "in due order," though he hoped to succeed were he to live long enough. Less than a year later he died at the age of forty-five.

Malebranche, the other star of the Cartesian heaven, lived nearly twice as long as Spinoza. Legend has it that his death was brought about by an emotional upheaval caused by the visit of a young Irish philosopher, George Berkeley.[66] Their heated dispute must have turned on whether there was any point of maintaining with Malebranche the reality of the world, if one claimed with him that all our ideas were given us by God. Malebranche, a devout priest, could not follow Spinoza into pantheism, or even Berkeley, the future bishop, into emptying the Incarnation of all its flesh-and-blood reality. But being a Cartesian, like Spinoza, and having an equally acute mind, Malebranche also perceived the arbitrariness of the Cartesian trinity—mind, God, extension. As a Cartesian philosopher, but also having a deep commitment to the Christian creed, Malebranche could do only one thing, namely, give away the mind—we know everything in God, he claimed—and assert on faith the existence of an external world.[67] Such a position could contain no logical room, let alone real encouragement, for science. This was tragic in the case of Malebranche, whose writings show many sparkling evidences of scientific ability.[68] They could only remain underdeveloped in a mental world in which natural theology, like all other knowledge, was denied its basis in sensory evidence.

Berkeley's categorical denial of the existence of an external world is often presented as the necessary end point of Cartesian logic. Yet there is equal justification for seeing that end in mid-eighteenth-century French materialism. De la Mettrie, Helvetius, and d'Holbach certainly saw themselves as the logical heirs to Descartes.[69] Their campaign for materialism started with an appeal to Descartes at a time when d'Alembert called on his countrymen, and in particular on the scientifically minded among them, to shake off their infatuation with Descartes. Speaking of d'Alembert, one cannot help thinking of Diderot, as the two were for years in closest collaboration on the *Encyclopédie*. Their break is usually ascribed to d'Alembert's ill-advised article on the city of Geneva, which almost brought the *Encyclopédie* to an end. But the roots of difference between Diderot and d'Alembert were much deeper. The latter was a pure scientist, the former not even a scientist but only a propagandist of technical know-how. For Diderot science was not so much a tool for theoretical understanding as a means for providing tools of practicality. The kind of progress he saw for science matched this misconception of his all too well. It was a progress of technology, not of theory. As to mathematics, Diderot claimed that it had already run its whole course, and tellingly enough he deplored the support it gave to metaphysics.[70] As to physical science, he prophesied that within a century or two it would reach its limits, determined solely by standards of everyday utility.[71] Ironically, he found only recalcitrant allies in those very artisans who, according to him, were to be sedulously consulted by members of the Académie des Sciences.[72] But after a few visits with those "naturally inventive" artisans Diderot found out that, as he put it, only a dozen in a thousand had a vague notion of what they and their machines were doing.[73] It was the "unskilled" academicians who had to provide the explanation and understanding after all!

The art of understanding, or how to know, could hardly be mastered within the context of that materialism of which Diderot was a zealous apostle. His crusade certainly ran counter to the perspectives of d'Alembert's famed Preliminary Discourse to the *Encyclopédie*, a discourse conceived if not in a theistic at least in a deistic spirit. The first salvo in Diderot's campaign on behalf of materialism was his *Lettre sur les aveugles* in which he claimed on the basis of sensationism that the world did not need to be conceived as regulated by reason throughout. Even worse, Diderot put this claim in the mouth of Nicholas Saunderson, who although blind from birth became the occupant of Newton's Lucasian chair.[74] Diderot's last salvo was his libelous script, *Le rêve de d'Alembert*, written in 1769 though published only in 1830. In line with his consummate cunning Diderot took d'Alembert to task for subscribing in part to sensationism. On its basis, and this was the very point on which Diderot, the materialist, wanted to discredit the deist in d'Alembert, one could not logically maintain the truth of any metaphysical proposition, and certainly not the truth of the existence of God.[75]

In less than twenty years Diderot and d'Alembert, once close allies, moved worlds apart. Their parting was foreshadowed in their respective ways in which they treated natural theology and science in the years of their collaboration. For both of them natural theology had cosmology for its basis. "The principal profit," d'Alembert wrote in the *Encyclopédie*, "we should derive from cosmology is to raise ourselves through the general laws of nature to the knowledge of its Author, whose wisdom has established these laws. . . . Thus, cosmology is the science of the universe inasmuch as the universe is a composite entity and yet simple because of the unity and harmony of its parts, and whose basic factors are combined, set in motion, and modified by that supreme intelligence."[76]

Diderot was distinctly unenthusiastic on the subject as he touched on it in his Prospectus to the *Encyclopédie*.[77] His few words showed the direction in which he was already gravitating. To be sure, his *Pensées sur l'interprétation de la nature* started with the declaration that nothing was further from its main thesis than that nature was God and that man was but a machine, claims made respectively by Spinoza and de la Mettrie.[78] In fact, at the end of the *Pensées* he brilliantly warned the skeptics that the crucial aspect of the question why the universe existed was the query why the universe was what it actually was.[79] But in making this penetrating remark about the baffling specificity of the universe Diderot had already been more intent on scoring points in debate than on defending truth. Otherwise he would not have described the question, why does the world exist, as the "most embarrassing question" that can be raised in philosophy.[80] He had already lacked inner strength to see in that question the most enlightening and encouraging question that can be asked by philosophers and even by philosophes.

Tellingly enough he had no longer possessed even that weak affiliation with theoretical science which he had once cultivated. In securing d'Alembert for the *Encyclopédie* Diderot looked for d'Alembert's renown as a scientist but not for his undying devotion to science. Five years before the Prospectus for the *Encyclopédie* was printed, Diderot, still in his mid-thirties, had spoken of Newton's science as a dream long out of date with him.[81] Historical development once more testified to that inner logic which so many intellects find it impossible to gather from plain logic alone. Something of that logic of intellectual history was sighted by Voltaire as he reminded the generation of Diderot about the drift of many Cartesians into Spinozist pantheism, which he never rated higher than rank atheism.[82] Voltaire also reminded his age that the ultimate source of the collapse of Cartesian science lay in Descartes's playing the role of God.[83] What Voltaire, a deist, could not perceive was that far more than deism was needed to account for what he spiritedly championed, the science of Newton.

Six

INSTINCTIVE MIDDLE

IN 1722, THE *Philosophical Transactions* CARRIED TWO PAPERS WITH THE same objective, namely, a refutation of Leibniz's notion of the force of moving bodies. The simultaneous publication could hardly have been done without the approval of Sir Isaac Newton, anonymous author of one of the papers. The other was penned by Henry Pemberton, a physician more than fifty years Newton's junior. Newton was so impressed by Pemberton's paper that, as a contemporary observer put it, he "condescended to visit the doctor at his lodgings." Before long Pemberton was Newton's confidant and in charge of the two-year-long work of seeing the third edition of the *Principia* through the press. A year after its publication it was Pemberton who announced Newton's death in the *New Memoirs of Literature,* where he also served notice of the imminent publication of his own work, *A View of Sir Isaac Newton's Philosophy.*[1]

On reading its preface one cannot help being struck that almost all references there, sometimes three or four to the page, are to the author of the *New Organon.*[2] Pemberton did not have to apologize for giving such prominence to Bacon in a work on Newton. The full title of Newton's immortal work, *Philosophiae naturalis principia mathematica,* was a disavowal of the *Principia philosophiae* of Descartes, who had no real praise for Bacon.[3] If another subtle proof was needed on behalf of Newton's presumed Baconianism, there was the imprimatur running in bold capitals across the title page of the first edition of the *Principia.* By granting the imprimatur, Samuel Pepys, president of the Royal Society, was stating that the author of the *Principia* lived up to the aim of the Society, the promotion of useful knowledge. The expression "useful knowledge" was an endorsement of Bacon, whose ideas regained prestige through the founding members of the Society. For them Bacon was the "thrice excellent Verulam," as Hooke referred to him in his *Micrographia,*[4] the first book of great importance published by one of their number.

On one crucial point Bacon was not the guide of Hooke and his associates in the Royal Society. Their works were a continual celebration of purposeful arrangements in nature and by implication of that very same final cause for which Bacon found no use in science. Cudworth indeed went so far as to charge Bacon implicitly with "promoting atheism" through his negative attitude toward teleology.[5] But even Hooke, perhaps the most Baconian in the Royal Society, spoke readily, and in tacit defiance of Bacon, of the "Grand Oeconomy of the Universe."[6] Bacon was unwittingly needled by Hooke in the very first observation described in the *Micrographia*, the observation under microscope "of the Point of a sharp smalle Needle."[7] It provided for Hooke the material of a teleological proof of the existence of God. Many of the works written by the early members of the Royal Society were plain natural theology, a discipline which Bacon promoted to an exalted lonely level, his strategy being "promoveatur ut amoveatur," that is, demotion by promotion.

One wonders what Bacon might have thought had he lived to read the preface of the catalog of rarities in the Museum of the Royal Society. The catalog was compiled by Nehemiah Grew, who stressed that all those rarities showed the "Providence of Nature."[8] Grew was also the author of *Cosmologia sacra*,[9] which, although it dealt mainly with sacred history, contained an elaborate presentation of the various forms in which purposiveness manifested itself in nature. The prolific ease with which Grew went about his task resembled Mersenne's presentation of hundreds of cases mostly taken from geometry and mechanics. Grew, a physician, took his material from biology, and everything there was grist to his mill. He did not suspect that at times his very reasoning could be turned against him. That no two women had exactly the same face was for him a providential safeguard against any man falling in love with several, let alone with all women.[10] Yet one could just as well argue, with an eye on the fate of Buridan's ass, that with the faces of all women being exactly alike no man would fall in love at all. One of Grew's general claims was that through God's providence animals that were most numerous were also the most useful for man.[11] Such an animal was the horse, and its purposiveness included everything it produced: its breath and foam, Grew declared, were sweet and so were its urine and dung.[12]

This was one of many coarse instances in Grew's book, instances that would alienate any modern reader who retained any sympathy for the proof from design. But their coarseness was indicative of the unreserved acceptance by Grew of a purpose present in every nook and cranny of the cosmos. Moreover, the *Cosmologia sacra* was only one of a great many similar works written in England during the closing decades of the seventeenth century. For a historian of science the most important among these works is the *Confutation of Atheism*, or the Boyle Lectures given in 1692–93 by the Reverend Richard Bentley,[13] the future Master of Newton's Trinity College. The spirited campaign against atheists in late seventeenth-century England, a campaign culminating in the foundation by Boyle of the lecture series, took some "village atheists" too seriously. Although the contemporary slogan "ubi tres medici, duo athei" was a veritable "scandal" for Joseph Glanvill, he failed to list those, physicians or others, giving rise to it.[14] Very few atheists were ever mentioned by name by the Boyle lecturers. They usually denounced Epicureanism as the harbinger of atheism. Epicureanism meant for them a world view in which things, configurations, patterns, and contrivances owed their existence to the blind, mechanical interaction of matter and its forces. Hobbes was suspected of atheism precisely because he advocated such a mechanistic view. It was considered atheistic because of its denial of the possibility of recognizing purposeful arrangements in nature on the basis of natural, that is, scientific considerations.

The question of blind mechanism versus purposeful mechanism could not be explored in a fruitful way as long as those arguing on behalf of purposeful mechanism saw only one way of proving the existence of God, the way based on nature's purposefulness. True, John Wilkins offered four proofs of the existence of God in his The Principles and Duties of Natural Religion (1678),[15] of which two, based on the universal assent of men in all times and places and on the finite age of the world, were obviously not susceptible to rigorous formulation. The other two, based on the skillful arrangements in nature and on their providential character, were thought to demonstrate rigorously the existence of an all-pervading purpose established by the Creator. This was the kind of argument that particularly appealed to Boyle. In his Disquisition about the Final Causes of Natural Things he firmly held, against Descartes and the Epicureans, that final causes could be observed and that they were evidence of a provident Creator.[16] Not surprisingly, Boyle found the most convincing occurrences of purposive design in the biological realm. He recalled with special pleasure his only conversation with Harvey. There Harvey disclosed to the young Boyle that he had been led to accept the idea of the circulation of blood because this alone assured purpose for the valves in the heart.[17] Boyle also set great store by the complicated structure of the eye, which for him could exist only for the purpose of seeing.[18] There was much truth in this but, as it turned out, in order to keep this metaphysical view of the eye in focus, one needed a vision reaching deeper than the level at which patterns and contrivances made their visual appeal. Boyle, in fact, naively equated what he called physico-theological proofs with Bacon's definition of final causes and of metaphysics.

Four years after the publication of the Disquisition and three years after Boyle's death, the first Boyle Lectures were delivered by Bentley, who fully lived up to the Boylean exclusiveness of the proof based on purpose. Bentley's lectures would today be largely forgotten had he not utilized Newton's Principia. Bentley certainly grasped the covert thrust of a book which until then had been perused only by a select few.[19] More importantly, he solicited and obtained Newton's approval.[20] The four letters written by Newton to Bentley owe their principal interest to Newton's refusal to agree with Bentley that the notion of a world consisting of an infinite number of homogeneously distributed stars entailed a gravitational paradox.[21] Newton haughtily lectured Bentley on the addition and subtraction of infinities,[22] but in this case Bentley was the master teacher who instinctively perceived the contradictoriness of such a universe. Bentley's interest in a finite universe concerned the cosmic pattern from which he inferred a cosmic designer.[23] That the finiteness or singularity of material existence bespoke its radical contingency did not emerge clearly on Bentley's philosophical horizon.

As Query 28, added to the first Latin edition of the *Opticks*, revealed a dozen or so years later, Newton's advocacy of the infinity of the world rested not on the addition and subtraction of infinities but on his natural theology, in which infinite space was the sensorium of an infinite God.[24] Apart from that, Newton's natural theology was largely exhausted, as with the virtuosi, in an insistence on the teleological proof based on patterns.[25] To safeguard the pattern of the arrangement of planets Newton also postulated a periodic intervention by the Creator. On the basis of Newton's calculations it had to appear a very rare intervention,[26] but intervention it certainly was. Yet if Newton made palatable a recourse to the divine arm in six different aspects of the solar system,[27] intervention by God at intervals of millions of years could appear tolerable. It appeared intolerable to some on the grounds of natural theology and of science. It has often been claimed that Laplace had scientifically disposed of those interventions and, by implication, of God.[28] It seems certain, however, that had Newton been in possession of Laplace's results about the limits of perturbations he would still have asserted that the solar system, or the system of the world, was a specific pattern pointing to a divine Designer.[29] Newton's demonstration of the existence of God was only superficially based on the gaps of knowledge. What he said on atoms makes it very clear that he was fully aware of the need to base all patterns on an ultimate pattern of which science itself could give no satisfactory account.[30] This was also what he meant in the General Scholium when he insisted on the need of a nonmechanical ultimate cause of mechanical patterns.[31] What he failed to perceive was that looking at patterns in such a way implied much more philosophically than a recognition of the purposeful design in the manifold patterns of nature.

Anyone committed as Newton was to the teleological proof could not be considered a Baconian without major qualification.[32] Newton, who proceeded most methodically in constructing the first reflecting telescope, was not a Baconian tinkerer. While his firm espousal of the existence of atoms hardly made a Baconian out of him, it certainly separated him from Descartes. But to speak approvingly of atoms was to make a hypothesis. Did not Newton thereby become a Cartesian and guilty of that hideous error from which he tried to dissociate himself with the famous phrase, *hypotheses non fingo*?[33] In justification of this Newton could have proudly pointed to the *Principia*, in which there were no atoms, no ether, no animal spirits, no effluvia of any sort. There were not even forces in a sense that transcended the general notion of interaction among bodies.[34] Moreover, and this was the epoch-making value of the book, Newton's account of the motion of bodies in free space and of their gravitational interaction even at planetary distances was such as to convey nothing hypothetical, in the sense of being vague, as Cartesian physics was. The value of the moon's acceleration was derived there with as much if not greater precision than the rate of fall of an apple. But as the early Cartesian readers of the *Principia* quickly recognized, there was no physics there in the traditional sense, let alone the Cartesian sense.[35] The Newtonian account of intricate details of the moon's motion, of tides, of the precession of the equinoxes, of the equivalence of gravitational and inertial mass were given with no reference to mechanisms and physical essences.

The mathematization of material processes and insistence on the agreement of conclusions with observational data apparently formed the sole support of Newton's physics, and are often taken as the whole Newtonian method. The method is clearly at variance with Bacon's method and its lip service to mathematics, and is also at variance with Descartes's glossing over the question of precision. The historian of science, especially if he has an eye on natural theology, cannot settle matters so quickly when it comes to the claim that Newton was a prophet of positivism.[36] The claim is not without some semblance of truth. Did Newton not speak as a thoroughgoing positivist when he remarked in the *Principia* at the very outset that in speaking of forces he implied nothing about their "physical causes and seats"?[37] Did he not warn in almost the same breath that his reader "is not to imagine" that words like attraction, impulse, and propensity were used by him "to define the kind or the manner of any action, the causes or the physical reasons thereof"?[38] Did he not insist that his propositions about the mutual attraction of bodies were to be considered "not physically but mathematically"?[39] And did he not seem to turn the tables on the realists when he noted that to "consider one body as attracting, another as attracted" was to make a distinction "more mathematical than natural"?[40]

Yet this last phrase reveals in Newton's mental physiognomy an urge that asserted itself at the most unexpected moments. He was inextricably in its grip but could never make a clear picture of it for himself. There is something compelling in the manner in which he asserted his faith in the gradual conquest of truth about nature through repeated and ever more reliable inductions. His Fourth Rule of Reasoning, in which he states this faith of his, comes to a close with the warning that this rule ought to be followed so "that the argument of induction may not be evaded by hypothesis."[41] In a modern perspective, what he meant to say was that he had no use for that outlook in which the objective truth of a given explanatory device, or hypothesis, was as much—or rather as little—as that of any other hypothesis. Did he not thereby disavow almost prophetically theories of science fostered by positivism and resuscitated in our days under such names as operationism and relationism?

Science for Newton was a struggle, a gigantic struggle for truth about physical reality. While he engaged in this struggle with the genius of a born strategist, his account of the stratagem was baffling.[42] The stratagem concerned the method of gaining valid knowledge, epistemology. But Newton's most explicit statement on the specific problem of epistemology in science runs to a bare half dozen lines. It starts with a most confusing juxtaposition of mathematics and natural philosophy: "As in mathematics," reads Query 31 of the *Opticks*, "so in natural philosophy, the investigation of difficult things by the method of analysis, ought ever to precede the method of composition. This analysis consists in making experiments and observations, and in drawing general conclusions from them by induction, and admitting of no objections against the conclusions, but such as are taken from experiments, or other certain truths."[43]

One can only wish that Newton had revealed something of what he held to be "other certain truths." Nor did he delve into the problem of induction. Not that he shared the facile trust in the power of induction which prompted Bacon to speak of an almost mechanical formulation of a final set of truths about nature in a few years. Newton's brief recollection on the manner in which he discovered the law of gravitation was that he had been thinking on the matter long and hard. This was typical of a man possessing creative power of the mind in so great a measure. At Trinity he often remained shut up in his room, but there the comparison with Descartes ends. The highly speculative Newton wanted to retain the closest contact with empirical data about reality. His advance toward truth as embodied in nature was along a road that put him somewhere in the middle between the two extremes which Bacon and Descartes respectively tried but which led them nowhere.

The case is much more tantalizing and unexpected than it might appear at first. To think and speak like a Baconian would have been for Newton the most natural and fashionable thing to do, but he did not. His failure ever to refer in print to Bacon, indeed, cannot be noted without surprise.[44] Moreover, the aging Newton did not mind wasting his time by erasing references to Descartes in his manuscripts. Was not this overanxious disclaimer evidence that Newton was a covert Cartesian? Indeed, had Newton been consistent with his dicta on the brain-mind relationship, he should have endorsed the Cartesian method and offered a retraction of at least the more philosophical parts of the *Principia*. In a truly Cartesian manner Newton reserved a direct view of objects to God himself.[45] From what Newton said it did not even appear whether vision was mere eyesight or rather a perception, that is, a sensory experience filled with intelligible content. His rhetorical question resembled a cake with a Baconian frosting and a Cartesian filling: "Is not Vision perform'd chiefly by the Vibrations of this [ethereal] Medium, excited in the bottom of the Eye by the Rays of Light, and propagated through . . . optick Nerves into the place of Sensation?"[46] The exact measure he meant by the adverb *chiefly* might be subject to dispute. The fact is that while he let the power of will excite that medium in the brain, so that one could move his limbs at will,[47] he offered no clues on the role of the mind in the act of seeing and hearing. Hobbled with a narrow, Cartesian view of the mind, Newton subscribed without hesitation to the distinction between primary and secondary qualities.[48] He caught no glimpse whatever of the possibility that the very reasons marshaled against the objective reality of secondary qualities could and were soon to be used by Berkeley against the reality of primary qualities.

Unlike the *Opticks*, the *Principia* contained no patent inconsistencies between scientific creativity and philosophy of knowledge. In the *Principia* Newton rejected the Cartesian view that it was from pure reason that we knew that bodies are extended and therefore impenetrable. He also upheld the validity of inference from common sense. From the common-sense evidence that bodies are extended, hard, and movable in an inertial way, we conclude rightfully, he argued, that all bodies, and even their smallest parts, the atoms, have the same properties.[49] Implied in such an inference was the recognition that the mind is an intellective principle in the closest and most creative contact with external reality. Yet Newton, a most creative scientist, never reflected on the creativity of mind. It did not occur to him that it was his scientific creativity that kept him, as if by instinct, in closest touch with external reality, which, partly because he was so creative, was eminently intelligible to him.

In fact, it appeared so intelligible to him that he made subtle adjustments in the values of data relating to gravity. This was the tactic of producing a "cloud of exquisitely powdered fudge factor blown in the eyes of . . . scientific opponents."[50] One wonders whether Newton would have resorted to such a technique had his mind not been dominated by the grand vision of truth about nature, a truth which was as incarnate in the realm of matter as mind was in the body. Within such a vision of truth nothing was more natural than to leap beyond the range rigorously justified by empirical data. The inverse-square law of gravitation could in no case be verified with perfect rigor. The vision of the world it embodied was ultimately a creation of the mind, a leap from sensory data far beyond the range of the senses. But because that vision was rooted in data provided by nature, the vision could become a vigorous science. It was so vigorous and fruitful that the physical science of the next two centuries became an ordinary science busy with unfolding the potentialities of the creative science of the *Principia*.

Historians and philosophers of science who confine their interest in the past only to what may corroborate the gossip of the present will not find that middle road significant which Newton, the eminently creative scientist, instinctively followed in epistemology. That it was a middle road can be gathered from none other than Pemberton, who, after foisting Bacon and his inductive method on Newton in the preface of his *View of Sir Isaac Newton's Philosophy*, declared that in natural philosophy as exemplified by Newton's *Principia* one has "to steer a just course between the conjectural method of proceeding," and the method of "demonstrating so rigorous a proof, as will reduce all philosophy to mere skepticism, and exclude all prospect of making any progress in the knowledge of nature."[51] Although it wholly escaped Pemberton, the "conjectural method" perfectly fitted the undirected inductivism of Bacon. The method of rigorous proof was advocated by Descartes and the Cartesians. It generated no true progress in physical science but it was to generate the skepticism of Hume. The art of steering that middle course Newton could not learn from the Cambridge Platonists. He could trace it back *nullius in verba* in the Royal Society. He was not a philosopher or a historian of science to spot that middle road subtly present in the writings of his major scientific forebears. The fact that he flirted with Cartesianism in his nonscientific hours also reveals something of the power of the instinct that kept him, a most creative scientist, on an epistemological middle road.

This middle road to which Newton was driven back again and again by his scientific creativity was of a piece with his explicit conviction about the validity of going mentally from the realm of phenomena to the existence of God. Such a mental process was for him not a hackneyed exercise in syllogisms but an unquenchable urge to secure a consistent basis for intelligibility and being. The mechanical design of material beings prompted the mind, so Newton believed, to postulate a cause which was nonmechanical, that is, spiritual. Such was an infinitely perfect mind, the source of all mechanical designs.[52] This inference was a mental leap, and it revealed a broader aspect of the leap which Newton the creative scientist practiced in postulating a perfectly exact physical world on the basis of data not in perfect agreement with the laws he formulated. The coexistence of these two leaps will hardly be of interest to historians of science who in their effort to overcome its Marxist interpretation ascend merely to the plateau of conceptualization lying well below the peaks of truth. The significance of the Newtonian synthesis is not that it replaced, as Koyré wanted us to believe, the world of "more or less," or the world of qualities, with the world of precision, or the world of quantities,[53] but in the fact that it reasserted the validity of the world of qualities through a scientific creativity which from the epistemological viewpoint patently transcends the realm of quantities.

Indeed, it transcends the whole world of accidents, be they quantities, qualities, or relations. The universe of Newton is not a universe of relations but of interrelated things, ranging from impenetrable hard bodies to subtly ethereal fluids. A forceful reminder about Newton the essentialist was given to our times by Popper in his effort to show (not without a Popperian twist) that Newton was not altogether an "obscurantist essentialist."[54] While one can be an obscurantist in many ways, within the Popperian perspective the obscurantist par excellence is the one who thinks he has the final explanations. On the level of essences this means the identification of irreducible essences. Undoubtedly the modern reader, Popperian or not, sees utter obscurantism in the declaration that "the Evidence from the Phaenomena is much stronger in Favor of the Existence of the Aether, than it is in Favour of the Existence of the Air." Made in 1743 by Bryan Robinson in the preface of his *A Dissertation on the Aether of Sir Isaac Newton*,[55] the declaration was typical of the self-assurance of some of Newton's epigones. Although Newton himself would hardly have expressed himself as Robinson did, his conviction about the existence of the ether and of indivisible hard particles of matter was complete. This might make an obscurantist of him in the Popperian sense, but not in any real sense. He would have been truly obscurantist if in the manner of many modern philosophers of science he had been oblivious to the principle that the essence or substance is never a phenomenon. Were it a phenomenon, it could always be better observed and described to the sheer delight of those revelling in endless falsification. When relativity made meaningless the notion of the ether as an absolute, all-pervading essence, it did not disprove the doctrine of essences, just as the splitting of atoms left wide open the possibility of truly fundamental particles. More importantly, while it may be claimed that the superstructure of Newtonian science could function without essences, Newton the creative scientist found them indispensable. For it is essences that secure to a world of change the coherence and permanence needed for its scientific investigation and philosophical interpretation.

In view of this it will not appear a rank obscurantism to state that the traditional ways to God rest on the recognition of the existence of contingent essences. Their contingency points to a noncontingent existence, whereas their being essences indicates unlimited coherence and consistency in the Being whose essence is existence itself. Newton was hardly the paragon of perfection as he philosophized on such matters, but there can be no doubt that the main thrust of his philosophizing was most germane to natural theology and that he was fully aware of this.[56] That the same thrust and awareness occur again during the early twentieth century in another unusually creative phase of science presents its historian with a challenge which he can ignore only if truth means no more than relatively useful concepts. The epistemological predicament of Newton and his espousing the classical, a posteriori way to God have at least one more aspect to which the historian of science must pay serious attention. It is most memorably revealed in a section of the General Scholium which has a distinctly biblical ring. The Pantokrator of the Scholium is anything but the withdrawn God of the deists, whose number in England increased steadily after Lord Herbert of Cherbury appeared on the scene. Concerning Christian mysteries, the secretly unitarian Newton might have endorsed John Toland's *Christianity Not Mysterious,* a book which gained notoriety by being burnt in Dublin in 1697, a year after its publication. But in addition to very unorthodox theological views, Newton also had a biblical, Puritan upbringing from which he retained a feeling of awe for the Creator and Ruler of all. He would hardly have kept that feeling had he not seen a rational basis for it. What he did not see was the historically intimate tie of that conviction about the Creator with the salient facts of biblical history and with their proclamation by historic Christianity. Biblical history was for him mere chronology, the meaning of which he sought in figures, not in facts.[57]

His myopia with respect to historical revelation was pronounced but not isolated. Writings of other members of the Royal Society revealed the same trend away from a supernaturally conceived Christianity toward a Christianity merely natural. What the deeply devout Boyle said of "seraphick love"[58] had a tone very different from the utterances of Francis, the seraphic saint. While trying to adjust the great biblical miracles to mechanistic science, Boyle frowned upon postbiblical miracles as unworthy of God, the supreme clockmaker.[59] But this was more a temptation than a hardened attitude. Boyle and the virtuosi who paved the way to Newton still shared something of that outburst of Christian faith which occurred a century earlier. The outburst produced reformers and saints alike. They were like so many volcanoes, whose principal interests could easily be mistaken in the thunder, flame, and smoke that go with such outbursts. They aimed above all at a powerful reassertion of the contingency of man and world as proclaimed through the history of salvation. The outburst split Western Christendom, partly because the contending sides tried to decide points of doctrinal history with no historical perspective in theology, either revealed or natural. Both sides failed to see that the real issue concerned not polemical points but the principal message of Renaissance Neoplatonism. It consisted in the ancient Greek and pagan belief that the world was an uncreated whole and therefore a noncontingent entity.[60] While resistance to that paganism demanded a firm reliance on the supernatural, the resistance itself could not ignore the natural level. To a large extent the resistance had therefore been an exercise in natural theology—in which Protestant divines showed much interest once the first wave of supernatural re-affirmation was over. This is a point which one historian of science implicitly recognized by giving much credit to "moderate Puritans" for the rise of science in the century of genius.[61] Being moderate, however, meant adopting an epistemological median, the common basis of the road of science and of the ways to God.

The impact of that resistance on the fortunes of the fledgling scientific enterprise was decisive. Science owed to it a renewed awareness of the contingency of the world. From this contingency there followed the logical need of painstaking, experimental investigations. They could not be justified within Cartesian a priorism rooted in a spurious natural theology. Baconian empiricism could be of no use either, because research had to be directed in order to be fruitful. This direction could only come from a conception of the mind's role which transcended empiricism without being trapped in a priorism. This conception had its most cogent and consistent expression in the classical proofs of the existence of God. They represented an epistemological middle road which Newton followed by instinct. Part of that instinct was rooted in Newton's remote connection with the sixteenth-century Christian re-vival. The other part was rooted in Newton's scientific creativity. Both parts pushed Newton toward the same middle road. The identical epistemological relevance of these two parts is the best guarantee against any real conflict between science and natural theology, as understood within its historical, Christian matrix.

It is in this light that one should view the absence of any reference to God, let alone to Christian religion, in the first edition of Newton's *Principia*. In earlier scientific works, references to a theistic view were constantly in evidence in proof of the fact that the same view acted as a womb for the only successful birth of science and as a tutor for its coming to maturity. That maturity was achieved in the *Principia*. With it science had beyond doubt become a self-sustaining enterprise. As such, science could rightly look for a formal definition of its own nature. In this formal definition there could be no room for natural theology. But as long as creative science was the object of that definition, it had to imply an epistemology which only natural theology embodied in full consistency. This also meant that insofar as science, creative science, demanded an epistemological middle road, natural theology, and even its Christian matrix, had received the most important contribution they could expect from natural science.

Nothing of this was perceived at that time or even shortly afterwards when a "sacrum connubium" between science and theology was celebrated within Christian Wolff's version of Cartesianism.[62] The complete clarity, or Enlightenment, emulated by Wolff, was a light not illuminating but blinding. Such a light could not reveal the epistemological middle road that Newton followed, not so much in his formal statements as in his actual procedures. Those, like Clarke, Leibniz, and Locke, who were much closer to Newton, were no more fortunate in their efforts to fathom the relevance of Newton's *Principia* to philosophy in general and to natural theology in particular. Their failure was due to the same source, their subscribing, however covertly, to the natural theology of Descartes. This was the reason why the metaphysical dispute between Clarke and Leibniz culminated in the covertly mechanical question of whether God constructed a perfect or an imperfect cosmic clock. For the very same reason Locke's *Essay concerning Human Understanding*, instead of becoming the metaphysical equivalent of Newton's physics, became an invitation for attacks on metaphysics.

Such a charge may seem surprising, especially in the case of Clarke and Locke. Clarke started his career at the age of twenty-two, when he published Rohault's famed Cartesian physics textbook in a new Latin translation with many Newtonian notes. Seven years later, in 1704, Clarke had the honor of delivering a series of Boyle Lectures under the title, *A Demonstration of the Being and Attributes of God.*[63] Clarke's starting point was the urge common to all men to find a fully satisfactory account of intelligibility and being. Sincere atheists, Clarke insisted, had therefore to look forward to the demonstration of the existence of God. The proof offered by Clarke gave the impression that he was deriving God's existence from the notion of the self-existing or eternal being. Since the procedure was distinctly Cartesian, Clarke was anxious to dispel the appearance of any affiliation with Descartes. In a letter to a critic he claimed that the "Universal Prevalency of *Cartes's* absurd Notions ... hath incredibly blinded the eyes of *Common Reason*, and prevented Men from discerning *Him in whom they live and move and have their Being.*"[64] The remark and its Pauline coda could only mean that Clarke accepted only the a posteriori road to God. But Clarke's reply to another critic stated that in addition to the a posteriori proof there was the a priori proof: "The Proof *a priori* is ... strictly *demonstrative; but ... capable of being understood by only a few attentive Minds; because 'tis of Use, only against Learned and Metaphysical Difficulties.*"[65]

Implicit in this reply was also the hint that since Clarke's Boyle Lectures were for a general audience, he was entitled to present there only the a posteriori proof. His version of it started with the proposition that if there was something, then something must have existed since eternity. While Clarke meant it to be an argument a posteriori, it prompted some apparently serious critics to remark that it was really an a priori proof. In trying to explain himself, Clarke unwittingly revealed that he could conceive the proof of God's existence only in an a priori framework. Only a Cartesian unaware of being a Cartesian could write as Clarke did: "Though the bare proof by Ratiocination, that *there cannot but exist such a* [self-existing] *Being; does not* indeed give us any distinct *Notion* of *Self-existence,* but only shows the *Certainty* of the thing: yet when once a thing is known, by reasoning *a posteriori,* to be *certain; it unavoidably follows* that there *Is in Nature* a Reason *a priori,* (whether we can discover it or no,) of the Existence of That which we know cannot but exist."[66] The passage, a stylistic muddle, shows something of that muddle which is generated by staking one's philosophical, scientific, and theological fortunes on the a priori proof.

A few illustrations of the muddle Clarke created for himself may not be amiss. It was the Cartesian craving for clear, distinct ideas that prompted him to write in reply to the same critic: "Infinite *Space* is infinite *Extension;* and *Eternity,* is infinite *Duration.* They are the Two first and most obvious simple ideas that every Man has in his mind."[67] Descartes would also have felt highly gratified by the manner in which Clarke lumped together and dismissed the scholastics. But the schoolmen, whom Clarke ridiculed for having said that God's infinity was a point and his eternity an instant,[68] were less unintelligible than the infinite space as God's sensorium endorsed by Clarke. And contrary to Clarke, if there was anything amusing, it was not the *actus purus* of the scholastics,[69] but his own claim that the "Scholastick way of proving the Existence of the Self-existent Being, from *the Absolute Perfection of his Nature;* is hysteron proteron,"[70] that is, putting the cart before the horse. This was of course true of the scholasticism that existed in Descartes's mind and of which Clarke was a facile critic because he knew not even one of the best scholastics.

How central the a priori proof was to Clarke's natural theology can also be seen from his very reluctant utilization of the singular order in nature,[71] of which Newton had unfolded such an arresting vision. Clarke invoked that singularity but briefly when he countered Hobbes's contention that matter existed necessarily.[72] It did not dawn on Clarke that he was now touching the very bedrock of the mind's road to God, namely, the radical contingency of any existence engraved in its singularity. The word contingency occurred only once in the sixty or so pages occupied by Clarke's proof of the existence of God and some of his properties.[73]

The question of contingency played no significant role in Clarke's famous dispute with Leibniz, a fact that throws an equally revealing light on Leibniz. He could live only with a world that was the best of all possible worlds, and such a world would not impress with whatever contingency it might have had. True, Leibniz said elsewhere some memorable things about contingency, such as why there is something rather than nothing,[74] but even Clarke could ask this and leave it at that.[75] Leibniz could also give some graphic presentation of the mind's ascent to God, the noncontingent being, from a contingent entity like a single, particular book.[76] But the deeper drive of his mind was in the direction of the cosmology of his "monadology" and there the world could only be what it actually was. Leibniz was clearly in bondage to Descartes and this turned his affirmation of the creation of the world out of nothing into an unconvincing proposition.

Details like these are recalled here only to illustrate the interplay between the fortunes of science and positions taken in natural theology. In the case of Leibniz one can always wonder why such a genius, the constructor of the first calculating machine that multiplied and divided, the independent discoverer of infinitesimal calculus, and the bold theorist of a universal language, produced so little in physics.[77] That he was overburdened with writing the diplomatic history of the House of Brunswick is no explanation. He could have easily found some other post and plenty of time, if he really wanted to do physics. It may very well be that, as with Descartes, the basic position taken in epistemology as reflected in natural theology thwarted potentially creative energies for physical science.

Scientific creativity was not the factor that kept John Locke from running visibly aground on the shallows either of Baconian empiricism or of Cartesian rationalism. The factor was a healthy mistrust about claims of knowing too readily and too clearly. Locke gave an excellent account of the natural history of the mind, singling out with uncanny instinct the more monstrous weeds, such as the innate idea of God as advocated by Descartes. Locke also said much of great originality about the thriving of mental plants, that is, of the psychological context of ideas. But his *Essay*, which began by routing Descartes's innate ideas and his a priori proof of the existence of God, came to a close with a book on knowledge that showed him being tossed from Descartes to Bacon and back. Like Clarke, Locke also voiced statements that sounded as though uttered by Descartes. Such was Locke's claim that "there is no truth more evident than that something must be from eternity."[78] The Cartesian ring was also unmistakable in Locke's dictum that in order to become "certain that there is a God ... we need go no further than *ourselves*."[79]

Since the errors of Descartes's a priorism were most evident with respect to external nature, it was not difficult for anyone with Locke's common sense to keep himself clear of those errors. But lacking a firm philosophical rudder, Locke could only drift to Baconian empiricism when discussing the merits of our knowledge of the world at large. In an age suffocated with fantasies about denizens on other planets there was great merit in Locke's warning that "if we narrow our contemplations, and confine our thoughts to this little canton" (the solar system), we have no knowledge of "the several sorts of vegetables, animals, and intellectual corporeal beings" that may exist throughout that system.[80] Again, in view of what Charleton and Hooke, for instance, pretended to know about atoms, Locke's pointing out the absence of anything positive in such claims was greatly overdue. Also, in view of the widespread illusion that the *Principia* represented the ultimate in science, Locke's insistence on the limitations and uncertainties of knowledge, including scientific knowledge, provided a welcome balance.

But Locke was more uncertain than the interests of science would have demanded. Science needed a certainty, a trust in certainty, that could not be provided by an empiricism tied to nominalism.[81] Creative science, and Newton was the evidence, rose high on that trust in certainty, and on its basis science reached out confidently beyond the realm immediately evident to the senses. On that basis science built models of the world both on the scale of the very large and of the very small. Moreover, science could learn, contrary to Locke and to Bacon, some valuable points about the world as a whole. Such a point was the impossibility of an infinite homogeneous universe, an impossibility proclaimed by the darkness of the night sky. Halley spoke of this in 1720 to the Royal Society with Newton in the chair. But speaker, chairman, and members were too certain of infinity to perceive the obvious.[82]

This certainty of theirs could be based on Locke's *Essay*, in which the validity of Cartesian epistemology was endorsed with respect to mathematics and geometry.[83] Clearly, Locke, the Baconian, had traits that were Cartesian, not of course with respect to innate ideas relating to beings, including the Supreme Being. The proofs which "our own existence and the sensible parts of the universe offer so clearly and cogently" on behalf of the existence of God owed their strength in Locke's case more to his Christian theism than to his empiricism, for he invoked in the same breath Saint Paul's famous declaration in his epistle to the Romans.[84] Divorced from that theism, empiricism was unable to support conviction in the existence of God, a fact which in the century that followed the century of genius was laid bare by geniuses who lacked not only scientific creativity but also real competence about matters scientific. Tired of rationalism, they found that empiricism could not provide rational certainty about the existence of anything. No wonder that the resounding blows they aimed at natural theology were potentially destructive of science as well. Its creative practice did not cease to demand a middle position, to be taken if not by choice at least by instinct.

Seven

BRICKS WITHOUT MORTAR

DAVID HUME DID NOT GET THE RECOGNITION HE SO DESIRED FOR MORE than a hundred years after his *Treatise of Human Nature* "fell dead born from the press"[1] in 1741. Hume, the philosopher, came into his own with the rise of a philosophy of science of which the younger Mill and Ernst Mach were the chief originators. About science Hume himself wrote little. When he touched on it he seemed careful not to go beyond generalities, although he was not reluctant to make the sweeping generalization that elasticity, gravity, cohesion, and transfer of motion by impulse were probably the only "ultimate causes and principles" that would ever be discovered.[2] He was not the first or the last to be trapped into seeing in the science of the day its ultimate phase of development. On points that to specialists appeared laden with great conceptual perplexities he could offer drastic simplifications. Thus he denounced, and in the name of common sense, the pomposity of geometers who all insisted on the infinite divisibility of extension.[3]

Such self-assuredness may seem strange in one who was not a geometer, much less a physical scientist, and not even a philosopher of science. In philosophy, Hume's professed main interest lay in the moral sciences. Still, Hume offered the *Treatise* as the fulfillment of the project of treating moral topics with the scientific, or experimental, method. In fact, in his own eyes, Hume was the Copernicus of moral science.[4] Whatever the merit of that self-evaluation, it makes a similar boast by Kant appear not too original. Without the prompting of some critics, Hume soon took the safer view that moral sciences could not after all be readily treated in the molds of exact science. But he continued to maintain that "politics may be reduced to a science."[5] By science he meant the mathematical sciences, and these certainly included Newtonian physics. While his dictum about the reduction of politics to science contained the saving proviso "almost,"[6] the word did not occur in the *Enquiry* where he listed the "sciences which treat of general facts" as "politics, natural philosophy, physics, chemistry, etc."[7] The moral sciences he now based on "taste and sentiment," which was still reductionism, namely, a reduction to Hume's own nature, dominated as it was by that instinct in which taste and sentiment are deeply rooted.

Such a nature was hardly tuned to living in the sober and often very dry atmosphere of hard, exact science. Nor did Hume spend any notable amount of time in that atmosphere. His expertise in science, especially in Newtonian physics, remained at the level of general courses he took as a candidate for the baccalaureate.[8] For three years following his graduation he read so voraciously as to suffer a nervous breakdown, but this was not caused by his trying to read physics and nothing else. Soon after his recovery he established himself in France, hardly a place in the 1730s to study Newtonian physics. At any rate, writing the *Treatise* left him with no time to raise his scientific expertise to a level much higher than where it was at his graduation at the age of fifteen.

The instant success that greeted the appearance of the first volume of Hume's *History of England* might suggest that he could have gained immediate acclaim as a historian of science had science been his true love. He certainly was a good political historian. As long as human feelings, plans, and interactions were his topic, his mind readily found the principal thread. It was the lucidity of Hume the historian, and his originality in noticing new aspects of political interactions, that prompted Boswell to speak of him as "the greatest writer in Britain."[9] From "greatest writer" to "greatest intellect" there is but a short step, especially in circles where history is the furthest one would go from the concreteness of stories in the direction of abstract reasoning. It was in those circles, in the facile literary skepticism of the rococo salons in Paris, that Hume was first idolized. It is no coincidence that among the leading figures of the Enlightenment Hume found the closest ties with the highly emotional and instinctive Rousseau. As an empiricist and scoffer at religion, Hume made a deep impression on Diderot, but his friendship with d'Alembert, whom he admired for his conduct, did not include what Hume called d'Alembert's "superior parts," or the outstanding geometer in him.[10] Neither d'Alembert nor Condorcet, the other most incisive mind of the French Enlightenment, could conceivably have any sympathy for Hume's radical rejection of any knowledge smacking of metaphysics.

In all likelihood, both d'Alembert and Condorcet were familiar with Hume's *History of England*, of which a French translation began publication in 1760. Being deeply committed to completing the shift of French allegiance from Descartes to Newton, d'Alembert and Condorcet might have first turned to the sections in Hume's *History of England* on the role of science. That his work contained such sections would secure it the luster of originality in the eyes of those unaware of *Le siècle de Louis XIV* in which Voltaire had pleaded the cause of intellectual history. At any rate, there already flourished in the 1760s the myth which two centuries later the *Encyclopaedia Britannica* still propagated in the following words: Hume's *History of England* "saw in the nation the mental interests of the educated citizens as well as the deeds of kings and statesmen, as may be seen for instance in the pages on literature and science at the end of ch. iii under the Commonwealth and at the end of ch. ii under James II."[11]

The passage would have come closer to the record if its references had been to Hume's treatment of sciences under James I and James II. As to the period of James I, or the age of Bacon, Hume's discussion of the sciences runs to less than one page;[12] as to the period of James II, or the age of the publication of Newton's *Principia,* the discussion covers less than two pages.[13] The total, not even three full pages, comprises a mere one-thousandth of the six-volume work. So much for the length of Hume's discussion of the sciences. The discussion is also very shallow. Not only did Hume say more of Bacon's style than of his philosophy of science, but he presented Bacon's science as of the same direction as the science of Galileo. Galileo's superiority over Bacon consisted, so Hume claimed, merely in the fact that Galileo not only proclaimed the truth of experimental philosophy but also implemented it with experiments and with concrete applications of geometry. In registering Bacon's dislike of geometry Hume seemed to be wholly unaware of its intimate relations with the radical inadequacy of Bacon's empiricism. Of that inadequacy Hume perceived not even the faintest trace.

In the picture which Hume painted of the principal members of the Royal Society during the age of James II, half of the attention was given to the king's mistresses, who siphoned off the money that should have gone to supporting science. In the remaining half of the picture, or about one page, Hume, not surprisingly, first praised the empirical method of Boyle and Hooke, giving no hint that their writings also contained some far-fetched speculations. The sixteen-line paragraph which Hume offered on Newton reveals even more of the distorting and darkening glasses of Hume's own making through which he read scientific history.[14] According to Hume, "in Newton this island may boast of having produced the greatest genius that ever rose for the ornament and instruction of the species." Such a phrase was proper only as long as it was sheer metaphor and not an explanation. Strictly speaking, geniuses are not produced by islands, by geography, by economy, not even by selective breeding or carefully planned education. A genius is a genius, a striking evidence of the miracle of the mind. But miracle was a word which Hume did not wish to consider even in the form of a genius. So the greatest genius of the human species was simply ascribed to an island in good demonstration of something very insular in Hume's bent of mind. He was never to step off the island of sensory impressions ruled by instinctive beliefs. The rest of Hume's dicta on Newton are even more revealing, not of Newton, of course, but of Hume. According to him "Newton was cautious in admitting to principles but such as were founded on experiment, but resolute to adopt every such principle however new or unusual." Such a phrase when found in run-of-the-mill histories of science may be left without comment. But with Hume the case is different. Had not the author of the *History of England* already legislated on the art of knowing as exactly in the humanities as we do in the exact sciences? Is it not Hume the philosopher who is looked upon by many today, in this age of science, as the only pre-twentieth-century philosopher still worth reading?

Before taking Hume the philosopher of science to task, Hume the historian of science must give an account of himself. If Hume wanted to paint a moderately good portrait of Newton the scientist, he could have learned much from Colin Maclaurin's *Account of Sir Isaac Newton's Philosophical Discoveries*, of which three editions appeared in Edinburgh between 1748 and 1775. Hume could have easily found out that "the boldness and temerity," for the absence of which he praised Boyle and Hooke, were a principal trait of the mental physiognomy of Newton the genius. In the England of the 1750s, when Hume was composing his *History*, it was also common knowledge that there were some dark points in Newton's character which Hume presented in shining white.[15] Those readers of Hume who accepted his apotheosis of Newton uncritically would hardly notice the central tenet of Hume's philosophy, which was now brought in on Sir Isaac's coattails: "While Newton seemed to draw off the veil from some of the mysteries of nature, he showed at the same time the imperfections of the mechanical philosophy, and thereby restored [nature's] ultimate secrets to that obscurity in which they ever did and ever will remain." The phrase certainly clashed with Pope's famous epigram, according to which "God said, let Newton be, and all was light." If then some readers of Hume's *History* gasped on finding Hume describe Newton as the greatest of all mystery-mongers, they were right in their indignation, historically at least. Rightly or wrongly the consensus was that Newton made all clear. Hume the historian of Newton was certainly wrong, and the reason for this lies with Hume the philosopher, who turned philosophy into mystery-mongering. He did so by reaching the conclusion at the very outset of his *Treatise* that reason and world were inextricably enveloped in obscurity.[16]

Another aspect of this connection between Hume the historian and Hume the philosopher can be seen when one turns to the *Essays*, which are nowadays read only by Hume scholars, among whom, understandably enough, there are no historians of science. Yet historians of science might have found much food for thought in Essay 17, "Of the Rise and Progress of the Arts and Sciences," an essay which—its two other improved versions within seven years are a telling indication—must have been very close to Hume's heart.[17] Study of that essay might have prompted historians of science to speculate on the greatest question of scientific history, the stillbirths of science in all ancient great cultures and its one viable birth within the matrix of Western Christendom. Needless to say, Hume's essay did not in any sense credit Christendom with science. He does not even seem to have been particularly aware of the only viable rise of science in Western Europe and of its rapid growth to full maturity during the century of genius. He knew that geniuses played a part in that process but he was uneasy about their role. Geniuses, he noted, were few.[18] This was true enough. It was another thing to say, as Hume did, that ascribing something to a few factors, even to a few men of great genius, is tantamount to ascribing it to chance. There was more merit in his claim that explanation by chance was not philosophical.

In Essay 17 Hume listed four factors underlying the flourishing of the scientific enterprise. The first, a negative one, stated the impossibility of science arising "among any people unless that people enjoy the blessing of a free government."[19] This was certainly well said, but Hume's third factor declared monarchy to be the most favorable form of government to the arts and a republic to be the best suited for the sciences. As a historian he should have reflected on the lack of substantial freedom in Galileo's Florence, in Kepler's Austria, and in Pascal's France. Nor would a brief look at Cromwell's Commonwealth and at Hobbes's Leviathan have been amiss. Hume merely noted that monarchies have "commonly abridged the liberty of reasoning, with regard to religion, and politics, and consequently metaphysics and morals."[20] If such was the case, then history and the Humean theory of the rise and flourishing of science were in conflict, but worse was still to come. This happened when Hume declared in the same breath that theology, politics, metaphysics, and morals "are the most considerable branches of science. Mathematics and natural philosophy [physics] . . . are not half so valuable." Such a remark should leave one breathless regardless of Hume, but the shock should be particularly sharp for anyone with an eye on him. If sciences were not even half so valuable as philosophy, why was it then so important to introduce into that more valuable domain the spirit of Copernicus?

Hume's second factor would delight, in part at least, some moderate Marxists, for he said that nothing is more favorable to the rise of learning than a number "of neighbouring and independent states connected together by commerce and policy."[21] The fourth factor is worthy of more consideration, for it reveals that Hume had no inkling that a generation or two before him science had become, for the first time in history, a self-sustaining enterprise. While only a generation or two earlier the new scientific method was praised as something "never to be overthrown" and as a sure road to paradise on earth,[22] Hume wrote with studied indifference: "When the arts and science come to perfection in any state, from that moment they naturally, or rather necessarily, decline and seldom or never revive in that nation, where they formerly flourished."[23] While long before Hume it was recognized that all nations are like the grass that is burnt in the oven, Hume could hardly envisage that the England of Newton would be continued in the England of Faraday, Maxwell, Rutherford, and Dirac.

Since Hume referred to various nations and cultures, present and past, he must have realized that science had not reached the same level of perfection in all those places and times. How well he knew this is clear from what he said on China. "In China," he wrote, "there seems to be a pretty considerable stock of politeness [social refinement] and science, which in the course of so many centuries might naturally be expected to ripen into something more perfect and finished, than what has yet arisen from them."[24] Hume should at this point have been somewhat puzzled. But his socioeconomical and geopolitical factors gave him an easy clue to the riddle. "China is one vast empire, speaking one language, governed by one law, and sympathizing in the same manners. The authority of any teacher, such as Confucius, was propagated easily from one corner of the empire to the other. None had courage to resist the torrent of popular opinion. And posterity was not bold enough to dispute what had been universally received by their ancestors. This seems to be one natural reason, why the sciences have made so slow a progress in that mighty empire."[25]

Hume himself felt that the explanation might not be satisfactory. "How can we reconcile," he asked in a footnote, "to the foregoing principles the happiness, the riches and police [social refinement] of the Chinese?"[26] His answer was that the absolute monarchy of the Chinese was not really absolute, and therefore insurrections could assert themselves at any time and in any place in that vast empire. This was certainly true. The history of China is a long history of internal warfare including the horrendous bloodshed of the so-called cultural revolution of the 1960s. There has always been plenty of "police" there in the very modern sense of this word. It could not, therefore, be true at the same time what Hume said about the persistence of the riches of politeness and police, in the sense of social grace, in China.

The most revealing phrase in Essay 17 has nothing to do with Hume's four factors or with his bogging down in the question of the stillbirth of science in China. Before Hume got to these particulars he pondered the role of genius. According to him anyone who would ask why Homer existed at a given place and time "would throw himself headlong into a chimera."[27] A chimera—a fire-breathing animal with a lion's head, a goat's body, and a serpent's tail—can exist only through some supernatural means, a point which must have been in Hume's mind, for he had already insisted that "there is not anything supernatural" in the appearance of a genius. The fire of a genius, he wrote, "is not kindled from heaven. It only runs along the earth; is caught from one breast to another; and burns brightest, where the materials are best prepared, and most happily disposed."[28]

This was most poetically said and contained some truth. But it is also true that no amount of kindling is a fire, and only poets, some geneticists, and some Freudian historians of science would say that Newton sucked his science from his mother's breast. Geniuses like Newton clearly point far beyond their ancestors. They are gigantic facts, rising here and there as lonely peaks. Their uniqueness attests more powerfully than anything else the fact that this existence of which we are a part is a closely interwoven texture of singularities. For those singularities, intellectual and physical, Hume had no use—and for a very simple reason. Considering them to any extent would have made him face up to the radical contingency of existence, a vista which bordered on natural theology and on a theology dealing with the supernatural.

He was not an impartial student of either of them. He first developed hatred for the supernatural, a point amply treated by his better biographers. Nor have they left unnoticed the subsequent presence of that hatred in Hume the historian. No notice has yet been given to his leaving out any reference to the supernatural, or Christianity, in his treatment in Essay 17 of the problem of science in China. At any rate, Hume was not original in that connection. His obvious source, Parrenin's replies to Mairan, widely available in print for almost a decade but not mentioned by Hume, had already set a pattern. But Hume originated a crudely hostile evaluation of the supernatural by his "Natural History of Religion" written around 1750.[29] The title rings like an echo of Buffon's famed *Histoire naturelle,* a work which became the sensation of the decade from the moment its first three volumes were sold out in two weeks' time in September 1749. But with the title, the similarity ends between the two works. Natural history as presented by Buffon meant a painstaking collection of facts—of all plants and animals— regardless of whether they were pleasing to the eye or not. Of such a painstaking, impartial collection of facts there is not even the faintest trace in Hume's natural history of religion. In Hume's rendering, paganism is the embodiment of tolerance, of freedom of thought, and the fostering of man's good instincts. Christianity, with its commitment to a transcendent personal God, is the hotbed of fanaticism, the fountainhead of debasing asceticism, and the mainspring of the enslavement of the mind.[30]

This lopsidedness certainly belied the facts of history, though not the instincts of Hume. Those instincts might have been seen to play havoc with science as well, had Hume not decided at the last minute to call back from the printer an essay scheduled to go to press with his "Natural History of Religion." Almost twenty years later Hume referred to it as "an essay in the metaphysical principles of geometry." At the last minute the manuscript of the essay (which no longer exists) was read by Lord Stanhope, whom Lalande called the best geometer in England at that time. His Lordship, Hume recalled, "convinc'd me that either there was some Defect in the Argument or in its perspicuity."[31] It should not seem surprising that geometry did not remain unharmed in its Humean miscegenation with metaphysics.

Hume's life shows another instance in which the advisability of printing was at issue. In the early 1750s he had completed a book-length essay in dialogue form, a thinly disguised debunking of natural theology. On the advice of friends, however, he refrained from publishing the essay for the rest of his life. His friends recalled to him his unsuccessful tries to gain a professorship, in Edinburgh and in Glasgow, and pointed out that his rejection in both instances was based on the atheism visible between the lines of the *Treatise on Human Nature*. It would have been more reasonable to let Hume teach philosophy and take him to task not for his atheism but for his theory of knowledge, as the real threat of an iceberg is not in its visible peak. In the case of the *Dialogues concerning Natural Religion*[32] the threat is not in the superficial battle set up by Hume among a lackluster divine, a liberal theist, and a leery skeptic. The threat to natural theology is in the philosophical foundations of the platform on which the skullduggery of skepticism is acted out. The numerous victims of that threat all make the fatal mistake of letting Hume control the epistemological foundation on top of which the skirmish is to be fought.

On the battleground of Hume's choosing only Hume could be victorious. But any lover of truth—and Hume wanted to confront only lovers of truth—must then be shown the intrinsic merit, or rather constructiveness, of Hume's victory. In other words, the Humean lover of truth must be shown in full the kind of edifice that can be constructed on the ground that secured victory for Philo of the *Dialogues* speaking for Hume. The ground chosen was sensationism, the extreme form of empiricism, and the bricks he used for construction were sensory impressions. Merely stacking bricks together never produces an edifice, let alone an edifice that is supposed to be the reasoned edifice of knowledge arching over the widest area of logic, metaphysics, morals, and politics. In addition to being so vast, the edifice was also meant by Hume to be so reasoned, exact, and forceful as to give mental comfort even to Copernicus.

Hume's first act in carrying out this program, namely, his decision to use only the bricks of sensory impressions, made it clear that the final result would be no real edifice of knowledge but a castle in the air—or better, perhaps, a heap of bricks. To construct an edifice worthy of Copernicus one certainly needed to rely on reason. But Hume relied on reason only when he felt the need to disrupt. For construction proper he relied on instinct, from the very start. It was most un-Copernican to begin, as Hume did, with the distinction between impressions and ideas as vivid and nonvivid sensory experiences respectively.[33] Again, it was thoroughly un-Copernican to say as Hume did that the rise of impressions was mysterious.[34] There is certainly a mystery in that fundamental form of knowledge. But if for Hume it was a dark mystery, for Copernicus's Christian Neoplatonism it was a mystery diffused with the light of reason, originating in the Creator's reason, in short, a lucid marvel.

Starting with a dark mystery, Hume went on stumbling from mystery to mystery, because he had radically separated at the very outset sense from mind and mind from sense. The rise of sensory impressions then became one unfathomable mystery, the association of impressions another. By ascribing it to some "gentle force,"[35] to an instinctive inclination, Hume only made the mystery even more mysterious. More mystery arose when Hume tried to reduce that instinct to the "original qualities" of mind.[36] The mystery was now so dense that Hume did not pretend to "explain that origin."[37] But Hume could have even that thick mystery only at the price of evoking a vision of mind as a substance capable of having qualities. A little honest reflection on Hume's part might have shown him that man's experience of having a mind consists precisely in experiencing across the range of mental events a peculiar unity which gives them intelligibility and order. Instead, Hume ended up advocating a notion of mind which in his description could easily evoke the image of a heap of bricks. To assume that the heap formed through some all-pervading mortar a genuine unity was an illusion: "What we call a *mind*, is nothing but a heap or collection of different perceptions, united together by certain relations and supposed, though falsely, to be endowed with a perfect simplicity and identity."[38]

For Hume reason was a welcome ally only when its sharp thrust served his purposes. From the fact that sensory impressions could be distinguished from one another, "it evidently follows," he declared, "that there is no absurdity in separating any particular perception from the mind; that is, in breaking off all its relations with that connected mass of perceptions which constitute a thinking being."[39] The rigorous implication of this was that there were mental states but no mind. Hume himself spelled out this consequence in comparing the situation with an endless sequence of scenes in a theater. He cautioned his reader against assuming some identity or simple relationship connecting the variety of scenes: "The comparison of the theatre should not mislead us. There are the successive perceptions only, that constitute the mind."[40] It is well to recall that in the *Treatise* Hume had admitted a sense of fright and confusion arising "from that forlorn solitude"[41] into which his philosophy of the mind placed him. In the same context he spoke of the despair, melancholy, and delirium of his philosophy.[42] It is also well known that as time went on, Hume admitted that his statements on personal identity put him in a labyrinth from which he did not know how to escape.[43] Reflections on this point tormented him in his philosophical hours.[44] Apart from them he was a charming individual, giving all the appearance of complete balance.

This contrast, almost a split, might be worth exploring. When the *Treatise* was completed, its author was twenty-seven. Writing a work like the *Treatise* demanded a very deep motivation. Was Hume really consumed by interest in discovering a new kind of knowledge, a knowledge as rigorous as that which he believed Copernicus opened up in the sciences? This does not seem to be the case because his knowledge of Copernicus, Galileo, and Newton always remained very superficial. It may very well be that the *Treatise* and its subsequent variations were born from a subtle escapism. It is well known that Hume detested supernatural vistas[45] and that he was not at ease even with the natural reflections of a supernatural deity. He wanted peace of mind above all, he wanted a complete freedom from eternal, transcendental constraints. He was unable to live with the vision opened up by a thorough look at man's own radical contingency. In a sudden flash of light Hume might have perceived, possibly by reading Epicurus and Lucretius, that empiricism, if carried out rigorously, would discredit all objective universal truths and would make the transcendental realm go up in smoke. Hume's predicament seems to have been like that of Epicurus, whom he admired and who in the *Enquiry* delivered a speech in his name.[46] Epicurus opted for a philosophy of atomism because it seemed to destroy domination by nature as well as by gods. Once these two universal constraints had been eliminated, Epicurus felt he had secured a peace of mind which consisted in being left alone.

Hume certainly wanted to be left alone by deity, natural no less than supernatural. Once deity was out of the way, one could safely enjoy playing backgammon or anything else. Such escape to safety is impregnable to any argumentation, however rigorous. Yet a theist can at least point out one thing to those who with Hume are ready to consider only sensory impressions and their own instincts. The point is the logic of the *Dialogues* which shows that any systematic attack on metaphysics in general and natural theology in particular will be an attack on science, especially on creative science. This is not to suggest that the author of the *Dialogues* wanted to be guilty of attacking science while attacking natural theology. On the contrary, in the first flare-up in the *Dialogues*, when Cleanthes, the traditional but lackluster theologian, tries to turn the table on empiricism on the ground that Copernicanism, which is universally accepted, has no support in sensory evidence, Philo, the sensory skeptic, is eager to act as the logical defender of Copernicus.[47] But Copernicus and Galileo were never abused as subtly as when interpreted by Philo. Worse even, the halo which so many philosophers and historians of science placed around Hume's head distracted even Norman K. Smith, as a commentator of Hume's *Dialogues*, from perceiving that Hume's defense of Copernicus was a rank effrontery.

For factual proofs of the earth's motion Hume referred to our seeing the moon turn on its axis, and added that "we observe the same" about Venus. Contrary to Hume's claim, no evidence existed at the time of the rotation of Venus.[48] Hume was, of course, correct when he mentioned the rotation of the sun, the revolution of the planets, and the revolution of moons around Jupiter and Saturn. But he now put in Philo's mouth a subtly misleading phrase: "Those analogies and resemblances with others, which I have not mentioned, are the sole proofs of the Copernican system."[49] By "sole proofs" Hume meant exclusive reliance on sensory evidence, for "analogies and resemblances" could hardly for Hume be given the Neoplatonist construction and extrapolation they receive in Galileo's *Dialogue*, a work which Philo strongly recommends to Cleanthes. Reading that great classic of science with Hume's eyes would have certainly kept Cleanthes from seeing (as it did so many Humeans) that the use of analogy was valid in Galileo's eyes because he added the eyes of the mind to the witness of the senses. In fact, the addition was so important that Galileo saw Copernicus's greatness in his courage to ignore what his senses told him.[50] Clearly, Hume's posturing as a champion of Copernicus's and Galileo's way of thinking was an imposture. A perusal of Galileo's *Dialogue* should make it clear, except to close-minded Humeans, that the creative science of Galileo was anchored in his belief in the full rationality of the universe as the product of the fully rational Creator, whose finest product was the human mind, which shared in the rationality of its Creator.[51]

Hume, the alleged champion of the clarity and exactness of Copernican and Galilean thought, had a most un-Copernican and un-Galilean program in mind. First, by emphasizing the finiteness of the human mind, he forced the hapless Cleanthes to rely with Copernicus on the use of analogy and accept the finiteness of the divine mind. Hume kept silent on the fact that for Copernicus the analogy meant a step from the finite to the infinite and not a step from one finite to another finite. From that finiteness of the divine mind, only one step was needed to the possibility of error in God, and another step to his possible plurality, and a mere third step to his pantheistic unity with the universe. With the fourth step Hume reached the idea of an eternal world and with the fifth the notion of a world-god that could go on fumbling forever in producing half-aborted universes.[52] Such were the main steps of Hume's attack on natural theology, an attack which he was not ashamed to present as one for which Copernicus and Galileo were the effective stepping-stones.

106

Hume's *Dialogues* certainly show that the argument from purpose is ineffective when isolated from the other proofs and from the epistemology and metaphysics implied in them. Fragments of the other proofs turn up here and there in the *Dialogues*,[53] in clear evidence of the fragmentary attention paid to them during the seventeenth and eighteenth centuries. While in the *Dialogues* one finds God referred to as He Who Is,[54] and one finds reference to the puzzle of to be rather than not to be,[55] it is clear that the contingency of empirical existence and the notion of God as existence itself made no real impression on the minds of theologians of those times. Being Cartesians in a more or less overt way, they could admire only their own minds and were unable to marvel at their own existence or at the existence of the world. The battle fought in the *Dialogues* is in its ultimate analysis a battle between sheer empiricism lost in complete skepsis and a natural theology weaned by Cartesians from its metaphysical basis.

The instructiveness of the battle is greatly enhanced by the fact that it deeply involves science and especially its most fundamental and most comprehensive branch, cosmology. Hume's first statement in cosmology was antiscience in its most genuine form. As soon as he had declared for a sort of pantheism, he conjured up the endless cycles of the Great Year to which that pantheistic entity was necessarily subjected.[56] Hume was unaware of the historical connection of belief in the Great Year and the historic stillbirths of science. He was led to that connection by the inner logic of his most unscientific thinking. By much the same logic Hume espoused the notion of cosmos as an animal,[57] a notion which historically always had a close tie with the pantheistic concept of the world, and which was equally counterproductive for the fortunes of science.[58] The blindness of that logic was unwittingly revealed by Hume himself as he suggested that the universe should be viewed not as a machine but as a vegetable.[59] The suggestion was a strange echo of the jubilation of the virtuosi over seeing science reach maturity through the paradigm of the machine.[60] The paradigm was not a perfect one, but it greatly facilitated a rational, objective look at nature, a look which permitted a quantitative handling of big and small processes in the universe. With Hume, advocate of a vegetable cosmos, this immense gain was readily expendable. He delighted in the vision of new worlds emerging as the sprouting of vegetable seeds, or as the hatching of eggs left in the sand by ostriches.[61] For Hume the cosmos could just as well be an agglomerate of "botched up universes," or "the first rude essay of an infant Deity," or "the production of old age and dotage in some superannuated Deity."[62]

Like one's God, so one's universe, should have now been the comment of Smith, Hume's chief modern interpreter. Instead, he shook his head in disbelief. Hume's reveling in aborted universes seemed to him to be worlds removed from the central theme of Hume's philosophy, which he saw in a notion of Nature embodying an authority which "man has neither the right nor the power to challenge." Contrary to Smith, it did not follow from Hume's philosophy that through "natural beliefs Nature has determined the scope and character and the very possibility of our theoretical thinking,"[63] because with Hume one could not advance to Nature as such. Had Smith been more attentive to Hume's tenuous ties with science, he might have perceived that Hume was very Humean in singing his swan song on the theme of an irrational universe. Indeed, Hume listed reason, instinct, generation, and vegetation as explanatory principles in cosmology, and he could not imagine why reason should be given preference.[64] Hume wrote his own indictment as an unwitting advocate of antiscience in terms that could not have been more to the point. Long before Buddhism became popular in Europe, Hume, again by the inner logic of his stance, turned to an analogy which historically was an epitome of antiscience. With reference to the Brahmins' doctrine that the universe had been spun in the belly of an infinite spider, Hume spoke of the earth being full of spiders and suggested their bellies as the place where cosmogonies were being spun.[65]

True, some cosmogonies of the seventeenth and eighteenth centuries might have appeared to have originated in a spider's belly. But Hume probably did not know much of them anyhow,[66] nor was he interested in any effort to contribute to a reasoned, scientific cosmology.[67] He wanted a universe of instincts, devoid of objective laws as well as of objective facts. Once more the author of the *Dialogues* showed his resolve to go the full length of the road of his choice. In the closing section of the *Dialogues* the now Humean Cleanthes voices doubt over the possibility of demonstrating matters of fact.[68] Hume must have been smiling as he put in Cleanthes' mouth the voice of skepticism not only about laws but also about facts. But with this explicit doubting about matters of fact Hume now removed all doubt concerning the sense of the famous last words of the *Enquiry* about what should and what should not be kept in libraries. Books not to be burnt could only contain quantities and matters of fact.[69] He had already made it known that quantities, or geometry, were rooted in paradoxes justifying skepticism.[70] He now admitted that matters of fact could not be subject to demonstration either.

The result was the abolition of God as well as of science, for the existence of both God and science could be justified only if the world were demonstrably ordered. For showing this mutual inner logic one has to be grateful to Hume. His starting point was empiricism carried to its extreme, that is, sensationism in which sensations stood as lonely data with no intrinsic relation to mind and world. No wonder that whatever Hume said of mind and world was a mirror image of what he said of sensations. They were like a heap of bricks not cemented into a permanent pattern or order. The instinctive beliefs that Hume advocated as a binding force or mortar could not secure a world suitable for scientific study.

That it could not secure a world needed by a viable natural theology may be a point of little interest to many, but it is a point of considerable importance within the perspective of these lectures. Hume's *Dialogues* reveal their deepest logic if looked at from the standpoint that Joseph Butler chose in his *Analogy,* one of the most famous natural theologies ever written.[71] Butler, whose ultimate aim was to create credibility for belief in supernatural revelation, confined his discourse to belief in general and to the fairly universal belief in God, soul, and eternal reward. Such a propaedeutics to supernatural faith might have pleased those already well-disposed toward it but tired of the omniscience of rationalism and of a rationalist theology still very much in vogue when Butler's *Analogy* was published in 1736. But skeptics could only be made more skeptical by Butler's emphasis on belief. Hume, who sent a copy of his *Treatise* to Butler (who failed to respond),[72] could without any difficulty perceive that the strategy of Butler, a thinker not particularly sensitive to basic philosophical questions, was not at all removed from the strategy of the *Treatise,* a work with a covertly atheistic objective. Butler's demonstration of the existence of God, which systematically eschewed the a posteriori road, if it did not serve Hume as a model, at least served as an invitation to him to compose the most renowned and most seductive attack on rational demonstrations of the existence of God. Belief in God, supernatural or natural, when severed from reason, gave Hume no sleepless nights.

While Hume's admirers rejoice in seeing the logic in this, they are not to be awakened from their Humean slumber by the fact that the world as conceived by Hume is not suitable for science. Hume's admirers can only be as Hume was, persons of instinctive beliefs and of logic but not of reason capable of touching on objective reality, even be it the objective reality of science. Typically enough, among Hume's admirers there have been many philosophers of science and even some scientists, but no great creative scientist has ever been a consistent and persistent Humean. This fact is an uncanny fulfillment of a prophecy by Hume, who noted in the *Treatise* that it would expose him to "the enmity of all metaphysicians, logicians, mathematicians, and even theologians."[73] By mathematicians he must have meant physicists as well. Very few of them became Hume's sworn enemies, but most of them and certainly the great creative physicists gave no lasting allegiance to him.[74] Hume's admirers are not impressed by this fact or by any similar, stubborn facts of scientific history, precisely because in their hearts they know that with Hume no matter of fact is strictly demonstrable and demonstrative.

When Hume died, one of those great stubborn facts of scientific history was already in the making. In his free hours, William Herschel, organist at Bath, busied himself with grinding parabolic reflecting mirrors the like of which the world of science had not seen before. Only eight years after Hume's death Herschel submitted to the Royal Society two epoch-making papers on what he saw with his giant telescopes.[75] It is well to recall that to see and register thousands of galaxies of most varied forms in a manner useful for science meant a superhuman expenditure of physical and mental energy. To sit through countless cold nights, to be ready whenever the sky cleared up, to repolish easily corrodible metal mirrors, to make unusual demands on one's eyesight, was hardly a feat for which one could get inspiration from Hume. He could pour cold water on the conviction of anyone, astronomer or not, that the night sky reveals immensely distant stars as it provides material for man's sensory imagination. Although Hume did not explicitly address himself to astronomers, they fitted best the scenario painted by him: "Let us fix our attention out of ourselves as much as possible: let us chace our imagination to the heavens, or to the utmost limits of the universe; we never really advance a step beyond ourselves, nor can we conceive any kind of existence, but those perceptions which have appear'd in that narrow compass. This is the universe of the imagination, nor have we any idea but what is there produc'd."[76]

That the universe was but the universe of man's sensory imagination has since been a cherished tenet of Humean philosophers. Only a few astronomers have ever subscribed to it, and never while watching the stars and galaxies.[77] Herschel was certainly not given to such schizophrenia. He was not enough of a philosopher to see that Locke's *Essay*, which he admired, was no sound foundation for vindicating one's grasp of reality and the reasonableness of speculations about it. But he displayed a sound philosophical instinct as he challenged a colleague in the Philosophical Society of Bath who claimed in an unmistakably Humean vein that any metaphysician was "a dancing master who came in with a fine bow, and after having amused you a while with his various hops and skips, left you with another very fine bow, no wiser than you were before."[78] To the Humean claim that certainty was restricted to matters of fact, in strict exclusion of reasoning and ideas, Herschel answered with a phrase which brought witness to a basic pattern of scientific practice and revealed the radically unscientific character of the empiricist boasting about matters of fact: "Half a dozen experiments made with judgment by a person who reasons well, are worth a thousand random observations of insignificant matters of fact." Clearly, to do science was to make rational judgments about facts, that is, to do

110

metaphysics. But metaphysics had an even more important role to play than to make science possible. Those of us, Herschel continued, who love wisdom, "by metaphysics ... are enabled to prove the existence of a first cause, the infinite author of all dependent beings."[79]

Although, after advancing from the Philosophical Society of Bath to the Royal Society, Herschel abstained from discussing in print philosophical issues, philosophical asides in his papers kept witnessing the same philosophy of science and philosophical theism which he had already defended in Bath. Adding to Herschel's rebuttal of Hume was the fact that he saw himself as a natural historian registering a tremendous variety of celestial specimens—double stars, clusters, nebulae—which, like as many plants, seemed to grow and decay.[80] Yet Herschel never suggested a vegetable cosmos. He was the type of natural historian which creative scientists ought to be and can only be. No wonder that the tremendous cosmic order and singularity which Herschel unfolded were for him the evidence of the Creator. Of his theism Herschel spoke so little that after his death his son, Sir John F. W. Herschel, had to defend, possibly against some Humeans, his father's firm and reasoned belief in God. But it was part of the written record of the older Herschel that of two errors, speculating too much or speculating too little, he preferred to be guilty of the former.[81] By speculating he meant the use of reason, not of instinct. Science, creative science, testified once more that its conceptual paths were not of the making of Hume but of a make leading to the Maker of all.

Eight

ARCH WITHOUT KEYSTONE

IN THE 1790s, WHEN GERMAN ACADEMIC CIRCLES SUDDENLY BEGAN looking upon Kant as a national hero, nothing was more tempting than to present him as the one who anticipated the observations of Herschel. To justify this new luster in Kant's glory, some admirers of Kant seemed to think one only had to exhume a long-forgotten work of the master, the *Allgemeine Naturgeschichte und Theorie des Himmels,* or *Universal Natural History and Theory of the Heavens.* [1] The several reissues of the work in the 1790s betray the conviction of Kant's admirers that while a telescope was a good thing to have, it was not absolutely indispensable if one had the mental eyes of Copernicus as pictured by Kant. [2] The sudden enthusiasm for Kant's cosmology was evidence that the a priorism of the postcritical Kant had its roots in his precritical phase.

Transition from precritical to postcritical phase would suggest to twentieth-century minds a shift from mental revelry to reverence of hard empirical data. Nothing could be less true of Kant. When, in 1756, a year after his brief venture into cosmogony, he was awakened from his slumber by reading Hume's *Enquiry,* he merely perceived that the idealistic metaphysics of Wolff and Baumgarten was untenable. Hume's empiricism did not push Kant to the empirical world and to empirical studies. The reason for this lies in part with Hume and in part with Kant. Hume's empiricism was sensationism. Instincts, not reason, formed the bridge for Hume from sensations to a coherent account of the external world. As to Kant, his expertise in mathematics, physics, and astronomy always remained at an elementary level. The claim that he learned advanced mathematics and physics in private visits with Martin Knutzen is not supported by hard evidence, although it is submitted again and again in telltale variations. Knutzen did not teach mathematics and physics at the University of Königsberg, nor were respectable courses offered there in either subject in the 1740s. Knutzen's small booklet on the famous comet of 1743, his only publication relating to exact science, is hardly a proof of profound expertise in it. He wrote mostly on philosophy and natural theology. [3] It was only sixty years after those private visits that Bronowski, one of Kant's first biographers, referred briefly to Knutzen as the one who instilled scientific expertise in Kant, but Bronowski did so in that very section of his biography which was not checked by Kant for accuracy. The very recent claim that Knutzen instructed young Kant in the various conflicts between "the two great natural philosophers, Newton and Leibniz," [4] is sheer rhetoric.

Once Kant's meager preparation in science is kept in mind it will be easy to notice the pretentious tone of his introduction to the *Universal Natural History*. His protestations of diffidence were carefully planted devices to let the reader believe that he was a second Newton. Sir Isaac had completed only the mathematical part of cosmology, Kant remarked, adding that he had now worked out the physical part with a "degree of thoroughness" which the "rules of credibility and correct reasoning" permitted in the subject.[5] Only some minor details of his cosmogony could be subject to doubt.[6] In his own estimate only "something less than dubitable"[7] was the third part of the book, which contained his derivations of the physical, intellectual, and emotional characteristics of the denizens of the planets, from Mercury to Saturn.

Kant's cosmogony of two hundred small octavo pages was not without merit. In two or three pages of it Kant presented an account of the Milky Way which was the first fully correct explanation of its visual image to appear in print. He was also the first to describe as Milky Ways the small nebulous patches being observed in increasing numbers, though in this connection he merely unfolded the full implication of a felicitous remark of Maupertuis.[8] Kant's real pride lay in other features of his *Universal Natural History*. One of these was his alleged demonstration that the universe was an infinite, hierarchically ordered system of stars and galaxies. That he was not completely ignorant of matters geometrical is shown by the fact that he had immediately realized that while an infinite Euclidean space could not have an absolute center, his notion of an ever more inclusive hierarchy of galaxies implied it. That he did not have the genuine spirit of a physicist was evident in the same stroke. In the style of an a priori thinker he refused to part with his preconception of the universe. On the plane of geometry an absolute center was a contradiction, but was it, Kant asked with affectation of profundity, on the plane of physical reality?[9]

That center was so much a reality for him that he saw it as the absolute starting point of the mechanical making of the world. It was there that the first stars and galaxy formed through condensation following the creation of homogeneous infinite matter by God. As time went on, this condensation took place further and further away from the center. Kant's universe looked, therefore, like a system of concentric spherical waves. The crests represented galaxies in completely developed shape, whereas the troughs were areas where galaxies had already returned to cosmic ashes out of which new galaxies were to be born again through condensation.[10] Such a universe was, therefore, subject to a great cycle, a cosmic Great Year, at each and every point. In view of the pantheism germane to the idea of the Great Year it should not seem surprising that fifty years later Kant did indeed espouse pantheism.[11] This may be one explanation of the fact that in his last sickness Kant flatly refused to utter a word of prayer.[12] The thirty-year-old Kant still spoke with apparent reverence of the Creator.[13] But his were mere words. The author of the *Universal Natural History* needed only his misleadingly creative mind, not a Creator. Thus he imposed a continuous creation of matter on God,[14] who went on with his work according to Kant's specifications. He did his best to make them appear a priori necessities.

These a priori necessities he particularly needed for his other and even greater pride in cosmogony, a theory of the evolution of planetary systems. According to Kant it was most natural and therefore necessary to assume that the variety of elements or substances depended on the possible range of specific densities. An enormous range it was, for he compared it to the difference between the radius of the solar system and one-thousandth of a line.[15] The upper limit of densities was dictated by the need to have points of condensation separated by the average distance of stars, each to be endowed with a system of planets. In order to keep the equality and, in some sense, the homogeneity of various substances, Kant postulated that atoms of substances of higher specific weight occurred in smaller numbers than atoms of substances of lower specific weight. He did not notice that the manner in which he had specified this inverse ratio led to the self-defeating result that all particles were attracted with the same force from all sides. Kant also failed to notice that in order to have galaxies and supergalaxies of ever higher rank ad infinitum, the range of specific weights and kinds of substances also had to be extended ad infinitum in an infinite universe. Finally, he made no mention of the fact that in the General Scholium Newton had already mentioned and rejected the idea of the formation of the planetary system from a chaos of particles attracting one another. Thus, Kant's theory was not merely a theory based on purely natural processes, to dispense with Newton's recourse to God's arm, but a theory based on the very same process which Newton had already found wholly insufficient to explain the almost circular orbits of planets, an insufficiency which, because of its connection with the distribution of angular momentum, still plagues all theories of the origin of the planetary system.[16]

In dealing with the actual world Kant the cosmogonist had to face up to a large set of singularities which should have given pause to any careful thinker. His careless logic could only produce a carefree cosmogony. When it was rediscovered in the 1790s, nothing was said of its faults by those who in the plain interest of truth should have brought them to full light. The only one who took Kant to task for the science of his cosmogony was J. C. Schwab,[17] mathematician from Halle and collaborator of J. A. Eberhard, founder of the short-lived *Philosophisches Archiv*. Eberhard, an almost archaic Wolffian, could hardly counter the euphoria which suddenly diffused around the author of the *Critique of*

Pure Reason following the publication of ten long letters on its contents by K. L. Reinhold.[18] Once Reinhold spoke, the rest of academe joined in the chorus of accolades. Kant himself grew bold, and in the preface to the second edition of the *Critique* he described himself as the second Copernicus and as the one who perceived the true nature of the flash of light produced by Galileo and Stahl.[19] Those who even today find nothing strange in Kant's equating himself with Copernicus, might reflect on Kant's putting a giant and a dwarf, Galileo and Stahl, on the same pedestal. The incongruity of this was not even suspected when suddenly the *Critique* appeared to many to be above any and all criticism. Before long, Kant was elected to the Berlin Academy as a national hero. It was part of that process that some of his admirers decided that if he was as incisive as Copernicus, he could have been just as far-sighted as Herschel, and without a telescope.

The rash of new editions of Kant's cosmogony provided wide and easy access to what he had said forty years earlier on the physical, moral, and intellectual characteristics of the inhabitants of each and every planet. Starting from the centripetal force which would bring coarser matter closer to the center and leave more refined substances at the periphery of the solar system, Kant went on to build an edifice of sheer fantasy. He claimed, for instance, that the finest intellectual on Mercury was far inferior to a Hottentot on earth, while our own Newton was but an ape in comparison with an ordinary citizen of Saturn. The seventy-year-old Kant should then have stated clearly that the third part of his *Universal Natural History*, dealing with the denizens of planets,[20] was only a youthful vagary, but he never so much as suggested that a retraction was in order. He was still the same a priori philosopher, and he could provide instances of this in the most unexpected contexts. In 1791 he laid it down in writing that Napoleon must land in Portugal and nowhere else. When the official word came about his landing in Egypt, Kant refused to concede. He rather claimed that the official news was political camouflage.[21] For the previous thirty years he had been lecturing on cultural and political geography with an air of certitude, although he had never traveled farther than fifty miles from Königsberg. Such details might suggest the general reason for Kant's refusal to take a critical view of his cosmology. The specific reason, unknown to all but him, was piling up in the drawer of his desk in the form of a manuscript later called the *Opus postumum*.

It was an open secret, however, that Kant retained a very high regard for his cosmogony during the long decades that preceded its triumphant reentry on Herschel's coattails. Between 1763 and the 1790s there appeared four editions of Kant's long essay, "On the Only Possible Proof of the Existence of God."[22] His principal illustration of the proof from design was a lengthy summary of his cosmology. But between the

115

publication of the *Universal Natural History* and the "Only Possible Proof" Kant read Hume's *Enquiry*. Under its impact Kant took the Humean view that cosmic design, even if it existed, proved at best the existence of a designer but not of a Creator.[23] Kant's parting with the proof from design had less to do with Hume than with inner logic. The logic was that an a priori cosmology or science did not need God. It was another aspect of the same logic that science could at best use some minor details of such a priori cosmologies but never their method, or road to truth.

In 1763 Kant still insisted that God's existence could be proved rigorously. The way he went about it was unmistakably a prioristic with a touch of Descartes. Proofs of the existence of God could only be based, Kant declared, either on conceptual possibility or on the empirical notion of existence. He endorsed one of the two conceptual possibilities without seeing that it was a disguised form of the ontological proof.[24] Clearly, he was more Cartesian than he appeared to most of his readers, let alone to himself. This was not without some irony, because Kant did not wish to be related to Descartes. But if God was still needed, there was, on the basis of the "Only Possible Proof," room only for the ontological proof—which did not lead to a really existing God. Concerning that logic, nothing changed substantially when Kant moved from his precritical to his postcritical stage. The only change consisted in the further growth of the consistency and explicitness of Kant's thoughts on God and science. The reality of both were proved to be an intellectual illusion. As to God, the full blossoming of Kant's Cartesianism and of its inner logic is embodied in the *Critique*. As to science, the appalling evidence is in the *Opus postumum*. There Kant tried to present the only permissible form of physics, permissible in terms of the conceptual legislation of the *Critique*.

The distinctive feature of Kant's Cartesianism derives from the fact that in the hundred years that intervened between him and Descartes there lived Newton and Hume. Long before the *Prolegomena* Kant had spoken of the impact of Newton and Hume on his thought. The evidence is all the more instructive because it is contained in Kant's "Enquiry concerning the Clarity of the Principles of Natural Theology and Ethics," written in 1763.[25] Natural theology, metaphysics, and physics once more appeared at a crucial juncture as the three graces, with their fates and fortunes inseparable. Concerning metaphysics, Kant stated a great truth and an equally great untruth when he wrote that "metaphysics is without doubt the most difficult of all human inquiries; but one has never yet been written."[26] In the *Critique* Kant repeated this evaluation of metaphysics in flowery and mournful phrasing. The *Critique* was again anticipated when Kant said that the only way of having sound metaphysics was to have it along the method of

116

Newtonian physics.[27] Kant defined the Newtonian method as a mixture of geometry and experiments.[28] About experiments, in particular about their Newtonian kind, Kant, infected with Hume and with an a priori bent of mind, never acquired a notion in depth. His meager sensitivity for the singularity of the experimental world was soon swallowed up in an a priorism fashioned on the apparent nonsingularity of Euclidean geometry.

So it happened that Kant's essay contradicted a remark in it, a remark of which Kant should have been proud. The remark was that nothing caused so much damage in philosophy as the imitation by philosophers of the method of geometry. This was a wonderful insight, but there were two flaws it it. One was that Kant attributed the remark to Bishop Warburton, though without giving any further reference. Warburton was best known in Germany for his book *Julian*, published in German translation in 1756. What Warburton said there in the way of philosophy was his warning in the preface that in order to see a divine intervention behind Emperor Julian's failure to restore the Temple in Jerusalem, one needed an appreciation of historical proofs, very different from those of geometry.[29] Apparently the remark set off further reflections in Kant's mind, and he unwittingly credited Warburton with his own deep philosophical insight. Unfortunately, and this is the second flaw, no sooner had Kant put that insight in writing than he parted with it. He went on to propose that instead of geometry, physics—Newtonian physics, to be sure—should be the basis of philosophy. It was a counsel to jump from the frying pan into the fire, where philosophy could only burn to ashes.

To fashion philosophy after physics was just as destructive of philosophy as it was to fashion it after geometry, because both were equally Cartesian procedures. In 1763 Kant did not suspect that the inner logic of his newly elected stance was to force him many years later into drawing up a lengthy and disastrous legislation for physics. Nor did he yet suspect a disastrous outcome for natural theology. Yet his claim that natural theology, which he still meant in a traditional sense, had solid footing had a Cartesian touch to it. In Kant's words the notion of God's being unique differentiated it from everything else with the greatest clarity.[30] Long before Kant, Descartes saw in such a clear differentiation the mark of truth. But there was no evading the inner logic of Kant's Cartesian claim that the properties of God could be seen "much more clearly and much more definitely"[31] than those belonging to the totality of things, the universe in short. In the *Critique* this clarity was denied to God as well as to the universe. The consequences were patently disastrous for a scientific study of the world when attempted on such a basis.

In all probability little will be said of this inner logic in 1981, the

117

two-hundredth anniversary of the *Critique*. Rather, there will be further repetitions of statements that Kant was a brilliant interpreter of Newtonian science,[32] that he had the potentiality of becoming a great scientist,[33] and that he was one of the greatest cosmologists—an encomium heaped by Popper on Kant on the occasion of the one-hundred-fiftieth anniversary of his death.[34] Popper would have done better service had he recalled the conclusion which Carl V. L. Charlier, the well-known mathematician and cosmologist, reached a generation earlier: "Evidently the author [of the *Allgemeine Naturgeschichte*] has not himself studied even the first sections of Newton's *Principia* . . . . I mean that the *Naturgeschichte* is scientifically of very small value. . . . I consider the *Naturgeschichte* of Kant unsuitable and even dangerous as inviting feeble minds and minds uninstructed in natural philosophy to vain and fruitless speculations."[35] Charlier spoke, of course, of Kant's chief boast as a cosmogonist, his theory of the evolution of the planetary system.

While the *Naturgeschichte* contains, as pointed out above, two scientific gems, the *Critique* is wholly void of scientific merit. Its thoroughly un-Newtonian and un-Copernican character will not, of course, be spotted by anyone willing to see with Popper in relativistic cosmologies a "confirmation of Kant's bold predictions." In the *De revolutionibus* and the *Principia* one is faced with works which in their whole content are an interlocking set of proofs about the validity of the initial presuppositions. The proofs of the existence of valid a priori synthetic statements, the heart (though not the vindication) of Kant's lengthy *Critique*, cover only a page or two;[36] the rest is amplification and deduction, not a further corroboration of those proofs. Such was indeed a rather un-Newtonian way to secure metaphysical validity (Kant's professed aim) for the science of Newton. Needless to say, the validity of a proof does not depend on its length. Still, when a Copernican turn in thought is claimed to have been achieved, one can clearly expect more than two brief and questionable illustrations of the proposition that there are a priori synthetic truths. The Copernican turn did not consist in merely seeing things in a new perspective,[37] but also in giving a detailed and interlocking account of what was seen in the new perspective. Most importantly, while Copernicus's new perspective meant a physical shift in man's cosmic position, it did not imply a shift in man's epistemological perspective. That shift was grafted on Copernicus's perspective by Kant, the high priest of epistemological geocentrism, an error far more destructive for science than physical geocentrism could ever be. For if the imagined structure of the mind determines the structure of things that are outside the mind, then the raison d'être for experimenting and observation will hardly ever become a compelling reason. Having been infected with Hume's sensationism, Kant could not consider the possibility of the mind's being instructed by the external world. Kant's way of stating this was that the noumenon or Ding an sich was inaccessible to the intellect. This Humean statement was followed by the un-Humean affirmation that noumena existed independently of the thinking subject.[38] Clearly, Kant wanted to retain some intelligible touch with reality. For an Aristotelian, or moderate realist, this touch could be secured through the naturalness of knowing things of the external world, but for Kant this possibility could not exist. The Kantian knowledge of things was a construction by the mind of the semblance of things and not a natural grasp of intelligibility embodied in them. As a result, whatever Kant's longing for an intellectual touch with things other than his own mind, the Kantian impossibility of being in touch with the Ding an sich meant being trapped within one's mind.

Kant was far from willing to admit this consequence. He was not only a Humean but also a Newtonian, at least to the extent that he realized that the success of Newtonian physics was somehow a proof of the intellect's contact with external reality.[39] Being an amateurish Newtonian, Kant accepted, along with Newton's science about which he knew little, that hard dogmatic shell which had grown around it. His familiarity with Clarke's criticism of Leibniz shows that Kant had a fair knowledge of that hard shell. Its most distinctive feature was the concept of infinite space and time as real entities. It was through that fallacy that Kant tried to maintain contact with the realm at the very core of which was the Ding an sich in absolute inaccessibility as far as epistemology was concerned.

In view of the absolute isolation of the Ding an sich, Kant had no right to speak of it at all. Equally inconsistent was his attempt to join the Humean and the Newtonian elements. The trouble with his effort was that Newtonian science was not merely a vast storage of sensory impressions filtered through the categories of space and time. Newtonian science was a true science, that is, the product of a truly inventive intellect pondering the witness of the senses. What Kant saw of Newtonian science was only the surface with its apparently definitive contours. If, however, that surface was so definitive as to represent the only valid form of knowledge, then Kant could only have a philosophy of mind according to which the mind, insofar as it was correct in its operations, conformed to the categories of Euclidean space and time in which all sensory impressions were stored.

Kant can be taken to task on this point even without the wisdom of twentieth-century relativistic cosmology. Kant knew, if not of non-Euclidean geometries, at least of the possibility of more than three dimensions. Some thirty years before the *Critique* he stated that if those multidimensions were possible, then they were physically realized if not in this world in some other worlds.[40] He based this reasoning on the principle that it was demanded by the Creator's plenitude that he should bring into existence all conceivable possibilities. A strange Creator and a strange infinity of worlds which could only destroy the possibility of a logically consistent cosmology. It was a most logical proposition, however, for an a priori thinker such as Kant. It was therefore with some inconsistency that Kant canonized infinite Euclidean space and time in the *Critique*.[41] In doing so he provided the *Critique* with its most obviously a priori and unscientific part. A much less remembered though equally unscientific a priori process was Kant's effort to construct a mind that could do its thinking only by being Newtonian in the sense imagined by Kant. Since the phenomena showed a very rich variety, complexity had to characterize Kant's efforts to trace out the structure of mind capable of coping with that richness. His desperate predicament and his flair for systematization were nowhere more in evidence than in his resort to the twelve Aristotelian categories, which he grouped in four units of triads, each a thesis-antithesis-synthesis sequence.[42] The originality of Hegel was indeed very Kantian. From these already systematized categories Kant produced a schematism of categories. His increasingly more involved speculations were as many stones added to an arch under construction. The two sides of that arch were becoming top-heavy without really approaching each other, an observation with no pretense to originality. In the early part of this century Edward Craig remarked that Kant "started from both ends of the road at once, but he never met himself."[43]

Behind all these efforts of Kant there was only one sensible guideline. It consisted in his recognition of the significance of the unity of consciousness. This unity supported Kant's conviction that the unity of mind with the phenomena was not a dream after all. It certainly was not, though not on a Kantian basis. It must have been with secret despair that at long last Kant credited the unity of mind and phenomena to the faculty of imagination.[44] Imagination was hardly the concise, scientific, logical factor which, to all expectation, should have served as the keystone of the arch representing the structure and genesis of valid knowledge. The impropriety of the situation was first noticed by Fichte, who took the view that the faculty of will should be given the role of keystone in the Kantian arch of understanding.[45] Reinhold agreed with enthusiasm.[46] His endorsement of Fichte had one thing in common with his accolades of the *Critique* ten years earlier. In both cases Reinhold said hardly a word about Newton and science.

To Kant's great displeasure the new keystone proposed by Fichte soon loomed as large as a giant meteor. Kant knew all too well that there could only be one such meteor at a time in the philosophical sky. Of his own philosophy it now became true what he said of all philosophies in

1763 in his *Enquiry*: "Philosophical knowledge ... is like the meteors whose blaze is no promise of their perseverance. They disappear, but mathematics remains."[47] Mathematics, and science with it, survived the *Critique*. This remark may be taken as a suggestion that the *Critique* is a threat to science. This point will be considered, but first some comments may be in order about the more obvious fact that in its heyday and ever since, the *Critique* was seen as a deadly threat to natural theology. As to the heyday, it should suffice here to recall Herder's break with Kant, a break all the more telling because of Herder's long-standing friendship with Kant, and because Herder's famed *Ideas on the Philosophy of the History of Mankind*[48] started with a very brief cosmogony, the cosmogony of Kant. But then Herder became chief examiner in the court of Weimar of candidates for Lutheran ministry, and he could not endure their interpreting all tenets of Christian faith in terms of Kant's *Critique*.

In Herder's time and long after, it was not known that the *Critique* posed no threat to the heart of natural theology, the cosmological argument. Kant's criticism of it shows him both a poorly informed and a poorly reasoning philosopher.[49] If not from Scotus (a paradigm of obscurantism in Kant's time), at least from Leibniz he might easily have learned that the weakness of the ontological argument, in which he saw the basis of the cosmological, is not in its major premise—if God (perfect being) is possible, he exists—but in its minor—but God is possible. The latter can securely be asserted only if the existence of God has already been established a posteriori. Kant's two objections to the ontological argument show him a poor reasoner. They are based on his failure to perceive the conceptual difference between infinite and finite being. Concerning the latter, be it Kant's hundred thalers or the perfect island of Gaunilo (Anselm's first critic), the existence of a thing is wholly extrinsic to the concept of it, but not in the case of an infinite, that is, infinitely perfect being.

The poor reasoner in Kant is once more revealed by his objection to the cosmological argument on the ground that it rests on the ontological. He overlooked the fact that the existence of a necessary being has been proved from the existence of things not necessary by the time the argument turns to the infinite perfection of that necessary being. The fallacy of Kant's criticism of the cosmological argument has not only been noted for some time, but is even recognized by some leading critics of all proofs of the existence of God.[50] At any rate, Kant might have spared himself a debacle had he not been overzealous. Once he had declared that all valid knowledge had to be directed to actual sensory data, that is, to the phenomena, he should have refrained from making any statement about God, soul, and the world as a whole, since none of these three were phenomena. But he was obviously uncertain.

121

It was not enough for him to remark that metaphysics persisted in man as an ineradicable urge, irresistibly producing three transcendental ideas: substance, or soul; cause, or God; and community of things, or the universe as a whole.[51] He went on to exorcise that urge by filling the pages of the *Critique* with words that were as many floggings of a dead horse, the presumed dead horse of traditional metaphysics, which included natural theology and cosmology in addition to a treatise on soul.

Kant's lengthy exorcism of the stubbornly returning ghosts of God, soul, and universe could only expose the illusory nature of his victory over them. The way Kant went about exorcising the notion of the universe consisted in presenting the principal propositions about it as pairs of opposites, of which neither was more valid than its counterpart. In other words, statements about the world's extent, structure, causation, and necessity were antinomies. While Kant's exorcism of the cosmological argument was vitiated by fallacy in logic, the presentation of the antinomies was a flagrant display of inconsistencies. The most general of these was that while the theses—the finiteness of the world, its temporal beginning, its infinite divisibility, the existence of freedom, and the nonnecessity of the world—were presented in terms of Wolffian idealism, or dogmatic rationalism, the antitheses were steeped in empiricism. When discussing the question of freedom and necessity, Kant spoke now of human, now of divine freedom.[52] It was a glaring example of the muddle he was capable of creating. Bertrand Russell, a great master in coining memorable phrases, was not far off the mark when he remarked that in the history of philosophy Kant was a mere muddle.[53] The aspect of that Kantian muddle, which ought to be of interest to a historian of science, is all the more instructive because Kant's specific purpose in discussing the antinomies was to show that the concept of the totality of phenomena was unsuitable for scientific purposes.

A brief look at twentieth-century cosmology might show that the idea of the totality of consistently interacting things is indispensable in a meaningful scientific discourse about the universe of galaxies. Modern science is equally committed to the atomicity of matter and energy. While even a Thomist may agree with a Kantian that the beginning of the universe in time cannot be decided in philosophy,[54] all the modern scientific evidence (as distinguished from flights of fancy) suggests a finite energy reservoir and time span for physical processes. But as in the case of Kant's dicta on the absolute validity of Euclidean space and time, evaluation of the merits of Kant's antinomies can be carried back into the context of the science of Kant's time. Bentley's Boyle Lectures were well known not only in England, a country about which Kant was eager to be well informed, but also in Germany, where they were available in translation[55] and were being quoted in philosophical and theological literature by the time Kant was born. From those lectures Kant could have easily learned that there was something seriously wrong with an infinite universe of stars. The decisive period of chemistry, running from Lavoisier to Dalton and covering Kant's last thirty years, made it clear that belief in the atomic structure of matter was the intellectual commitment that carried forward the science of matter. As to Kant's third antinomy, concerning free actions, he should have pondered whether any scientific discoveries, including those of Copernicus and Galileo, could be considered necessary events. For even if one insisted on the deterministic way in which the muscles of Galileo constructed that inclined plane and set some balls rolling, could science still be meaningful if the flash of that sudden intellectual insight of Galileo was an inevitable outcome?

Obviously, if it was not indifferent for science whether one considered the universe finite or not, atomistic or not, devoid of evidence of freedom or not, then it was not indifferent whether one considered the universe contingent or not, the alternative which constituted the fourth antinomy. Indeed, the whole rise of science depended on considering the universe as a contingent construct which, since it was a free creation, was a natural abode for beings who pursued freely the scientific quest. Had Kant read carefully the great creative documents of science from Copernicus to Newton, he might have spared himself not only the scientific debacle of the antinomies but something far worse and equally significant for science.

That "far worse" had been in the making since Kant conceived the plan and thrust of the *Critique*. Once the Copernican turn in the theory of valid knowledge had been achieved, it became logical to let particular branches of learning benefit from the epoch-making breakthrough. Metaphysics itself was now firmly and permanently established; its few details not yet discussed in the *Critique* could, so Kant believed, be worked out within a few years.[56] In his own eyes Kant was in a sense the end of metaphysics and of metaphysicians. Had his metaphysics succeeded in imposing itself on physicists, physics too would have come to an end. He certainly wanted to give physics its final structure. If adopted, that structure would have become a straitjacket for physics, a possibility that he was unable to suspect. The task of completing physics soon appeared to Kant a problem far more complex than completing metaphysics. In this matter-of-fact world of ours, tampering with material facts reveals its risks much sooner than tampering with concepts and ideas. Something of the dangers of the Kantian turn which physics was to be given seemed to have been already perceived by Kant in the *Prolegomena*. There he was wrestling with the question whether the recasting of physics in the molds of the *Critique* was to bear only on general notions or also on specifics.[57] It would be tempting to suppose that because of his inability to resolve this dilemma Kant laid aside the whole matter and turned to recasting the philosophy of morals, esthetics, and religion. Such an assumption would certainly be generous to Kant but would do no justice to Kantian logic. The *Critique* made it clear that a science of ethics, of esthetics, and of religion could not be had. While these topics could be handled in the framework of some basic presuppositions, these in turn could not have strict, scientific validity as far as critical, that is, Kantian philosophy was concerned.

About Kant's ethics let it be recalled briefly that its autonomy heavily prompted autocracy not only on the theoretical but also on the political level.[58] As to Kant's theory of religion, especially his evaluation of Christian religion, the theory declared well in advance the purely natural character of its origins.[59] The procedure had little in common with the scientific custom of first carefully weighing the facts and claims before pronouncing on them dogmatically. As to Kant's esthetics, it was based on a principle voiced in the *Emile* of Rousseau, whom Kant considered a very cognate soul, a circumstance that should reveal something of the depths of Kant's subjectivism. Equally removed from the professed objectivity of the *Critique* were Kant's efforts to vindicate purpose for mankind. They revealed his lifelong loyalty to the principle of plenitude, a principle as void of basis in reality as Kant's examples of purposefulness in nature were astonishing by their naiveté.[60]

A consistent application of the spirit and letter of the *Critique* could only be had in physics, the science which by definition dealt with the phenomena produced and stored in the categories of space and time. That application is embodied in the several thousand handwritten sheets known since their publication almost a hundred years after Kant's death as the *Opus postumum*.[61] It represents Kant's chief preoccupation during his last seven years. Few were given any hint of what his thoughts were centered on, but those few might have formed a good idea of the kind of physics to be produced by Kant on the basis of what he had already published on questions touching on physics since the publication of the *Critique*. What he published—two smallish essays—was not much, but it revealed much of the debilitating impact that Kantian epistemology and dialectic would have on the handling of scientific questions. The first of these essays, published in 1785, was a discussion of a minor controversy touched off by Herschel's discovery of what he believed to be volcanic fire on the moon.[62] Reluctant to admit with Aepinus the volcanic origin of that fire and even more reluctant to dispute Herschel, Kant sought refuge in the distinction between the idea and the fact of volcanic fire. By conceding to Herschel the demonstration of the "idea" of volcanoes in the moon (Herschel, Kant remarked, could not observe volcanic craters, always very small in diameter) he felt at liberty to assign the lunar craters to aquatic erosion and to the explosion of elastic vapors from the interior of the moon like the bursting of so many great bladders. Since the explosion had something to do with heat, Kant elaborated on its nature, which he identified with matter. This might have explained the hotness of the sun, but it forced Kant to credit the larger planets with a heat source compensating for the meager amount of sunshine they receive.

The straitjacket of Kantian dialectic and uncritical speculation were just as evident in the other essay, "Something on the Moon's Influence on the Air's Temperature,"[63] published in 1794. The essay was certainly to the letter of the *Critique* in presenting the problem in a thesis-antithesis-synthesis form. The thesis-antithesis was provided by a statement of Georg Lichtenberg, professor of physics in Göttingen, that the moon should not have any influence on the weather—though it does. In support of the thesis Kant submitted that the moon's light and gravity—factors, beyond which, Kant warned, one was not to look for hidden powers in that connection—had no influence on the air. The moon's gravity affected the air only in conjunction with the sun, and as evidence of this Kant reported that in Bengal deaths due to fevers were more frequent when the moon eclipsed the sun![64] His treatment of the antithesis rested on his introduction of two aspects of the temperature of the air, of which the wind was one and weather the other. The latter he discounted on the basis that various kinds of weather could produce the same barometric pressure. As for the wind, he spoke of its resurgence with every new moon and of a shift of the prevailing wind every three months as if these were indisputable facts. Since he had already admitted that the position of the moon did not influence barometric pressure, he had to base the synthesis, or the solution of the dilemma, on postulating the existence above the atmosphere of an imponderable matter susceptible to lunar influence and capable of influencing by chemical affinity the atmosphere. The objection that the solution relied on something about which nothing was known, namely, the imponderable matter, was countered by Kant with a reference to de Luc's recent conclusion on cloud formation. The conclusion, Kant remarked, by disposing of long-accepted views left one in a status of ignorance, although no one would doubt the fact of cloud formation.[65] Such was Kant's handling of a concrete scientific question after he had installed "pure reason" on the throne of science.

None of the sections of the *Opus postumum* are as systematically developed as the foregoing lucubration on the moon's influence on the temperature of the air. Yet, they clearly evidence the muddle which Kant was preparing for physics and the epistemological source of that muddle. Drawing on that source, Kant produced not only a parody of physics but also a rank pantheism. Indeed he spoke of himself in the *Opus postumum* as being God.[66] Both these traits were noted by E.

125

Adickes, whose two-volume monograph on Kant the scientist has still to make its proper impact more than half a century after publication. Adickes should, of course, have used stronger expressions than "starkly monistic" and "Schellingian" to describe respectively the theology and physics of the *Opus postumum*.[67] While Kant might have tolerated the former, he would have flown into a frenzy on hearing that his physics was equivalent, as Adickes put it, to Schelling's Naturphilosophie. Clearly, Kant would not have been willing to see himself the originator of the Naturphilosophe movement which posed a grave threat to German science during the first half of the nineteenth century. Yet he was the originator of that threat, and ultimately, by taking the epistemological stance of the *Critique*, preempted the possibility of natural theology and of science by the same logic.

The case for natural theology is well known. The case for science is all too well attested by the laborious pages of the *Opus postumum*. Yet even a brief look at the names of the many scientists mentioned there by Kant should be convincing.[68] Of a total of about 350 references almost one-third are to Newton, which in view of the un-Newtonian character of Kant's dicta on science, will impress only the unwary. Second in the list is Spinoza, with thirty-two mentions, a revealing fact in view of Spinoza's effusiveness on pantheism and careful silence on matters scientific. Galileo is mentioned only eight times, a discreditingly low number, since such nonentities in the history of science as de Luc and Wallerius are referred to ten and eight times respectively. It should be even more revealing that Zoroaster too is in that relatively high category of eight references. One wonders what Zoroaster could contribute to the task of giving a final form to physics. The only scientists of stature who are high in that tabulation are Huygens and Kepler, the former with twenty-one, the latter with fifteen references. Both of them, and certainly Kepler, were figures of the remote past by 1800. Also, as with Kepler, it may have been his Teutonic penchant for the arcane that had appeal for Kant.

Equally revealing is the *Opus postumum*'s nomenclature of contemporary scientists. Lichtenberg, a romantic mind who made no noteworthy contribution to physics, is referred to fifteen times, whereas Laplace is referred to only five times. One would look in vain in that nomenclature for d'Alembert, Euler, Franklin, Lavoisier, Herschel, Lagrange, Gauss, and a host of others who should have been mentioned if Kant's Copernican recasting of physics on the basis of the *Critique* had any scientific merit. Copernicus is not mentioned at all. The absence of his name is a symbolic proof of the un-Copernican character of Kant's final and fateful venture into the world of hard, exact science. It was a venture which he instinctively tried to delay but could not avoid. In view of its intimate connection with the reasoning of the *Critique*, the venture

126

showed that a systematic departure from the ways to God would readily prevent one from traveling on the road of science.

This is a truth that admirers of Kant still have to learn. One of them, Paul Deussen, the great Sanskritist, once noted that "it is a great pity that children in the first two years of their life cannot talk, for if they could, they probably would talk Kantian philosophy."[69] Children being what they are, they would not talk science, a topic that demands maturity of mind. Or if they talked science it would be as amateurish as the science of a pretentious footnote in the *Critique*, where Kant credited the equatorial bulge of the earth with preventing continental elevations and volcanic eruptions from changing the direction of the earth's axis of rotation![70] Unquestionably, Kant was right in stating in the *Prolegomena* that for anyone who had grasped the principles of the *Critique* (or rather who was grasped by them), the relation of its doctrine to traditional metaphysics would appear as the relation of chemistry to alchemy or that of astronomy to astrology.[71] What Kant had actually proved was that on the basis of the *Critique* one could only write a science which would hardly transcend the level of alchemy and astrology, both childish performances when compared with the science of chemistry and astronomy. The principal heirs to his thought vastly increased that evidence.

Nine

THE ILLUSIONS OF IDEALISM

IN MODERN TIMES NO PHILOSOPHERS HAVE DISCOURSED SO MUCH ABOUT God as Fichte, Schelling, and Hegel, the chief representatives of German idealism. The harm done by them to natural theology was matched by the threat they posed to natural science. On a cursory look Fichte may not seem to fit this parallel. He spoke but sporadically of science and when he did he was conspicously brief. But the paucity of his words on science is only the negative mirror image of his verbosity about God. Today, interest in Fichte centers on what he said on law, social organization, and political history. Fichte, however, considered himself above all a pure philosopher. He fell in love with philosophy at the age of eighteen through an encounter with Spinoza's *Ethics,* a work reasoned "in the manner of geometry." It was recommended to him by a Lutheran minister to whom Fichte turned with his perplexity about determinism and the freedom of the will. Fichte, himself a candidate for Lutheran ministry, was immediately taken by the sweep of Spinoza's rationalism and determinism.

Fichte was not the first of Spinoza's victims, nor was he the first to realize that the freedom of the will was not something Spinoza could account for. The problem was felt by Fichte all the more keenly because impetuosity of will was his principal personal characteristic. Such was the Fichte who wrote a decade or so later to his fiancée: "Personally, I have exceedingly little inclination to become a professional scholar. I do not wish merely to think, I want to act."[1] By then he had already found the long-sought support for freedom of the will in a book which, curiously enough, gave it no solid endorsement—Kant's *Critique of Pure Reason.*[2] The real support of the freedom of the will is not, of course, reason, especially when "purified," but plain common sense, a commodity not highly valued around 1790, after two centuries of rationalism.

That Kant's *Critique* nevertheless contained for Fichte the key to the vindication of the freedom of the will reveals something of Fichte's philosophical genius. He correctly saw that the *Critique of Pure Reason* was ultimately the gospel of pure subjectivism. Once Fichte had perceived this he assumed a condescending attitude toward Kant, whom he had approached only two years earlier with hat in hand. "My conviction," Fichte wrote in October 1793, "is that Kant has only indicated the truth but neither unfolded nor proved it. This singular man has a power of divining truth, without being himself conscious of the grounds on which he rests."[3] The ground was subjectivism, which certainly could dissipate the specter of Spinoza's ironclad determinism, but from which it was but one short step to the claim that will is the ultimate datum—the real keystone that Kant vainly sought in his quest to unify the arch of knowledge. Fichte was so convincing in interpreting Kant that by 1797 even Reinhold, once the source of fame for Kant, declared allegiance to Fichte. Kant now could muse over his statement that there could be only one bright meteor in the philosophical sky at a time.

But Spinoza and his geometrical reasoning were not to be forgotten completely. As Fichte wrote in December 1793: "I have discovered a new principle from which all philosophy can easily be deduced. . . . In a couple of years we shall have a philosophy with all the clearness of geometrical demonstrations."[4] As is well known the philosophy in question centered on the notion of absolute ego and will. It should now seem a foregone conclusion that a philosophy of will expounded with the precision of geometry could only be imprecise and willful. Geometry is a particularly impersonal branch of scientific thought which always leads away from the personal and subjective, let alone willful, toward the nonpersonal, the abstract, and the objective. For a historian of science there is therefore nothing surprising in Fichte's shying away from scientific topics, although he had more than one excellent occasion to face up to the phenomenon of science.

One of those occasions presented itself while he was writing the book that he considered his most cogently argued work, *The Closed Commercial State*, published in 1800. It contains much grist for the mill of scholars specializing in Fichte the economist and social theorist. It contains, too, plenty of ammunition for anyone who wishes to make fun of him. Even in 1800 and even in the still heavily agricultural Germany it must have appeared an agrarian anachronism that Fichte defined the absolute unit of economic value as one bushel of grain and proposed the replacement of silver coins with "grain money" to be printed on leather with a technique to be held in closest secrecy. But Fichte, the son of a poor farmer, knew that agriculture could be helped greatly by technical inventions. He was emphatic on the point that there should be no barriers to the importation of inventions, machinery, and the like. While his ideal state was supposed to profit from technical inventions, it made no explicit provision for educating technicians and scientists. The main groups in Fichte's state were farmers, artisans, and merchants. They were in turn ruled by bureaucrats, teachers, and soldiers. Scientists and technicians, whom Fichte did not mention, could, of course, be implied among teachers and artisans, and he hoped that in his state newspapers would contain only reports about inventions and the progress of the sciences.[5] More revealing was his lack of reference to scientists in his famous lectures *On the Nature of the Scholar*, in which he somewhat unenthusiastically acknowledged that for the unfolding of will it was necessary that men learn to calculate future events and secure thereby domination over nature.[6]

This slighting of science and scientists was particularly curious for Fichte, an avowed admirer of the French Revolution. He was a Jacobite who supported the revolution with an anonymous pamphlet whose authorship was an open secret. He did not see the close ideological and practical connection of revolutionary France with the eagerness to organize and exploit science and technology to the full. Fichte, who loathed the empirical given in nature,[7] showed no sympathy for the objective embodied in science. How could he, dedicated as he was to the notion and experience of will? In his view, history was the unfolding of the absolute will and ego in five epochs.[8] The first was the age of innocence, which he equated with the age of reason as instinct. The second was the age of progressive sin, in which instinct was replaced by external authority. The third epoch corresponded to the age of complete sinfulness. The fourth was the age of progressive justification through advance toward knowledge as truth. The fifth consisted in bringing about complete justification and sanctification, as reason turned into art. According to him, mankind was then living in the third epoch, the age of complete sinfulness. Such a designation of the times was perhaps not altogether incorrect, but Fichte attributed much of that sinfulness to engrossment with empiricism. Of course by this he did not mean science as such, but he often seemed to be dangerously close to indicting science itself. Yet closely linked to that science was the Europe to which Fichte assigned the cultural leadership of the future.[9] He was a convinced and spirited European, but curiously he could not see that a most tangible evidence of the uniqueness of Europe was the unique birth of science on European soil.

Being tuned to the will, he could not be tuned to science. Nor could he see anything creative and perennially vital in it. For him science had been completed in its essential structure, and this was strictly a priori. All that remained was to make practical applications.[10] The completion of science was due to the completion of the self-unfolding of the intellect, which was always an aspect of the absolute will. Obviously, once the a posteriori approach was preempted, science too was deprived of its fertile soil. The same heavy reliance on will and a priorism showed in full its self-defeating logic when Fichte took up the proofs of the existence of God. He did it in an essay on "The Basis of Our Belief in a Divine Government of the Universe,"[11] the publication of which brought his career in Jena to an end. While the students chanted that "there is only one Fichte and there is only one God,"[12] Fichte was dismissed on charges of atheism. The essay contained the declaration that "an explanation of the world and of its forms from the purpose of an intelligence . . . is complete madness."[13] Such was Fichte's summary dismissal of the traditional proofs of the existence of God. The essay ended by defining true religious feeling as that measure of being possessed by one's own will which bars any and all sense of reproach.[14] The true source of one's belief in God was one's own consciousness of being "free of all influence of the world of sense, absolutely active within my own self, and through myself, that is, like a power raised above all the sensory."[15] Whatever the value of such an experience for reaching God, it was certainly not germane to science. At any rate, Fichte's dictum could easily be taken as an open invitation to engage in rank willfulness, and it was indeed taken by many as such. Fichte himself was an avowed admirer of Machiavelli.[16]

The Machiavellianism of Fichte was as idealistic and soft as the music that was to open the Sunday service in the Church of General Christianity, which in Fichte's vision would embrace all Germans of the twenty-second century.[17] Inspired by that music the congregation proceeded to a reverent inspection of the community's armory stored in the church building. That the field libraries of German armies in World War II were heavily stocked with Fichte's works was not perhaps a complete misinterpretation of his trend of thought. As to the baptismal rite, it promised eternal life through insertion "into the entire Fatherland of the German Nation."[18] That such a Church still had the New Testament as her official prayer book shows something of the measure of inconsistency of which German idealists were capable. A good example of it is Fichte's "Critique of All Revelations." First published anonymously, the book created the impression that Kant was its author. Fichte soon learned that Kant himself was working on the application of the *Critique* to the question of religion. It was in the spirit of that work, *Religion within the Limits of Reason,* that Kant advised Fichte about the publication of his essay. In that advice Kant approved of Fichte's claim that "true religion can imply only such articles of faith as likewise belong to the province of Pure Reason."[19] Historically, Kant continued, there might have existed a subjective reason for miracles and revelation to teach mankind articles of faith that can now be apprehended by reason, but such a position, Kant warned Fichte, would not satisfy the censor.

The censor was not indeed satisfied, and rightly so, even if he could not see the right reason why Fichte and Kant were wrong. They were wrong because they were inconsistent. If miracles and revelation could not be right on the level of objective reason, how could they be acceptable subjectively if truth was one and absolute? But the truth of idealism derived from an illusion. It corresponded to a stark dichotomy between the objective and the subjective, and in all such dichotomies it is the subjective that is going to have the last word. This inner logic could not help affecting attitudes toward scientific method and work, both strongly marked with impersonal features. No wonder that German idealism found itself locked in a warfare with science and scientists as soon as its logic was further articulated by Schelling.

Schelling was a youthful genius. What he published during the last forty years of his life was merely a variation on the prodigious outburst of his late teens and early twenties. The outburst resembled a volcano, with no consideration for the limits set by the initial moves. One of those initial moves was Schelling's doctoral dissertation, presented at the age of seventeen, "On Myths, Historical Legends, and Speculations of Most Remote Antiquity" (1793), together with two other works that also saw print before he was out of his teens.[20] They dealt with the problem of the ultimate ground of being and of the true form of philosophy in that self-centered perspective that also dominated at the time the thinking of both Kant and Fichte. What Schelling said in those works of his tender youth made it illogical for him to spend much of the remaining half-century of his life maintaining the illusion that in his concept of the ultimate ground of being he was giving the proper rendering of what had traditionally been known as Creator and creation. The other initial move was Schelling's resolve to supply the Kantian arch of knowledge with a workable keystone. Schelling was only twenty-three when there appeared in 1800 his "System of Transcendental Idealism," a book in which he proposed artistic experience, or rather its allegedly infinite satisfaction, as the keystone of that arch.[21]

Schelling's claim about the "infinity" of artistic experience entitled him to talk about nature, but not in the sense in which science deals with nature. There is, of course, a very proper sense in which one can have a reasoned discourse about nature—a science—without donning the gown of a scientist. One need not be a scientist to see with Schelling that the chief task of philosophy is to shed light on nature as something existing. Schelling formulated this task most emphatically in his "Philosophical Letters on Dogmatism and Criticism."[22] There he tried to steer a middle course between Spinoza's apersonal pantheism and Fichte's pantheistic personalism. With his effort Schelling merely served notice that within the framework of pantheism all extremes are middle courses and all attempted middle courses are extremes. Since Fichte was alive and nearby, a rapprochement with his position would have meant playing the epigone. The semblance of a new path could be maintained only by rephrasing the distant Spinoza, and this is what Schelling did.

The way Schelling went about this crucial business in his philosophical venture can best be seen in the seventh letter of his "Philosophical Letters on Dogmatism and Criticism." The letter opens, not unexpectedly, with a recall of Lessing's question to Jacobi about the most characteristic trait of Spinoza's thought.[23] According to Jacobi's reply the trait in question was the principle of *ex nihilo nihil fit*, taken, of course, in the sense that not even a Creator can bridge the gap between nonexistence and existence. Whatever exists, exists by itself without any limit, either in space and in time, or in energy and activity. As already mentioned, the only objection to which Spinoza had no answer was the problem of going from infinite to finite existence within his own conception of the infinite as a pantheistic entity. The bridging of that gap as attempted either by what Schelling called Spinozist dogmatism or Kantian criticism found no favor with him. Schelling clearly aimed at Kant's recourse to imagination as the "Mittelglied" (a term analogous to *keystone*), when he said that the intellect was incapable of finding that middle factor.[24] But, according to Schelling, this did not mean that the intellect was thereby giving up its uppermost interest, the unity of knowledge. The intellect merely recognized that it did not need that middle factor as a strictly intellectual one. The unity of knowledge referred to the unity between mind and phenomena, or in the ultimate perspective of idealism, to the unity between infinite mind and phenomena that were finite in all appearance. The eternal drive in man from the finite to the infinite could only be *felt*, so Schelling declared, and felt most genuinely in the esthetic experience.[25]

Schelling now proceeded to the reinterpretation of Spinoza, or more specifically, to the solution of the problem to which Spinoza had no answer. According to Schelling, the solution was that finite causality differed from infinite not in principle but only in extent.[26] He did not explain how this solution was free of contradiction. This was hardly a problem if one had already gone along with Schelling on the point that the finite could only be seen in the infinite, the act of seeing being essentially an act of esthetic experience. Logically speaking, this was submerging if not suppressing a major metaphysical problem in the fluidity of esthetics. This was not a logical thing to do, but philosophers are not always logical. They are, however, bound by inexorable logic to their own inclinations. Once a philosopher tips the balance of proportion between mind and sense, between infinite and finite, between necessary and contingent, his inclination is bound to lower him into a labyrinth.

Not all philosophers try to escape from labyrinths of their own making, but most of them do. Their predicament is like that of Icarus of old. To fly out of his own labyrinth Icarus made use of wings, a scientific enterprise in itself. There was, however, a major fault in the way he used them. He thought he could fly with them to any height. But when he flew too close to the sun, the wax in his wings melted and he crashed into the sea. The extensive writings of Schelling on science and nature were as many soaring flights out of the labyrinth of his pantheistic transcendentalism. All those flights followed an illusory course with wings that had at best the strength of wax. In a sense, Schelling was an innovator. While Kant was constructing in complete privacy his scientific wings, composed of thousands of sheets of the *Opus postumum*, and while Fichte kept silent on science and flew on the wings of will, Schelling came into the open with his scientific gear, the first transcendental philosopher to do so.

As soon as Schelling came into close touch with the sunshine of real nature, as evidenced in its stubborn facts and singular laws, his wings began to melt, ending his flight in a crash landing. Plato, Aristotle, Plotinus, and Descartes could maintain for a long time the credibility of their illusory flights out of the labyrinths of their own making. Around 1800 the situation was wholly different. For more than a hundred years science had already been a robust, cogent, tightly interlocked exercise of the mind. The end of the eighteenth century was the age of Lavoisier, Herschel, Laplace, Coulomb, Lagrange, Dalton, and Davy. While in former times philosophers like Aristotle and Descartes were avidly studied by scientists, this was not true of Schelling's voluminous philosophical production on science. First came, in 1797— Schelling was then twenty-one—his "Ideas for a Philosophy of Nature."[27] It was sheer Naturphilosophie. On its heels came a work entitled "On the World Soul," its subtitle being a "Hypothesis of Higher Physics for the Elucidation of the Universal Organism."[28] Such a physics could only be very unusual coming as it did from the pen of a nonphysicist. The next year, 1799, saw the publication of Schelling's "Introduction to the Plan of a System of Naturphilosophie." The bold appearance in the title of "Naturphilosophie," which Schelling described in the third page as "the Spinozism of physics," was as ominous as the subtitle which stated that the work was about "the concept of speculative physics and the inner organization of a system of this science."[29]

Rarely was a subtitle chosen more appropriately. The physics of Schelling, a philosopher uninstructed in Newton, Euler, and Laplace, could be neither theoretical, nor experimental, but only speculative. The basis of his speculation was a generalized esthetics giving rise to a travesty of mechanistic physics in his "General Deduction of Dynamic Processes,"[30] published in 1800. The first year of the new century witnessed the publication of Schelling's "On the True Concept of Naturphilosophie and the Correct Method to Resolve Its Problems."[31] With an ironic logic the ends of a chain whose links were world, soul, speculative physics, and Naturphilosophie were being joined with a link that Schelling called "Bruno, or a Conversation on the Divine and Natural Principle of Things."[32] The Bruno was none other than Giordano Bruno, the Hermetic magus, who for the first time was presented as a respectable philosopher and scientist. The book reveals much of the systematic obscurantism which pervades the lengthy manuscript composed by Schelling shortly afterwards under the title, "The System of the Entire Philosophy and of Naturphilosophie in Particular."[33] Heaping encomiums on Bruno could be done with some impunity in the elusive categories of transcendental idealism, but when it came to the hard facts of science there was no way of being elusive. Dynamics and optics could not be eluded by calling gravitation an expression of poverty and light a manifestation of abundance.[34] That the human body was the prototype of the organization of planets still could be explained away with some skill in poetry,[35] but only a trickster could infer their elliptical orbits from mere words about polarities.[36] The trickster, who claimed to have given physics its wings, was a new Icarus, and no physicist of any consequence took him for a pilot. Indeed, how could a scientist take meaningful direction from the one for whom man was "the most perfect and most successfully executed cube,"[37] and for whom the number of celestial bodies in the planetary system had to correspond to the sacred number twelve, and for whom those bodies were intelligent, living animals?[38]

This last expression, indicative of animistic pantheism, might have been taken from Giordano Bruno's *Ash Wednesday Supper* or from his *Infinite Universe and Worlds*.[39] The similarity between Schelling's Bruno and Giordano Bruno was equally strong in their giving lip service to experiments and mathematics. To rely on either or both was unnecessary if it was true, as Schelling put it in Giordano Bruno's fashion, that "man was the center of the universe" and that "man was in immediate, inner communion and identity with all things he was to know."[40] Again, Giordano Bruno was echoed when Schelling declared that "man was the fulness of infinite substance on a small scale, that is, the integrated being, man become God."[41]

Man become God, such was the true course and very essence of the illusion of idealism. It was an illusion not only about man and God but also about the world. A world from which the contingency of createdness had been eliminated was as useless for natural science as it was for natural theology. What Schelling offered was, therefore, a striking vindication of the sanity and fruitfulness of the opposite course, the course in which God became man. According to Christian faith God became man because man as a free created being made use of his ability to fall in a moral sense. The fall had cosmic relevance but not in the sense of destroying the investigability of a rationally ordered contingent nature. The Schellingian account of the biblical fall first eliminated the distinction between creation and fall by turning creation into a universal fall. Furthermore, the creation could only be an emanation, a centrifugal movement to be matched by an equally necessary centripetal motion. Such were some of the principal ideas in Schelling's "Philosophy and Religion,"[42] which brought to a conclusion in 1804—he was only twenty-eight—his activity as a philosophical volcano. Eleven years earlier he had started by considering the biblical doctrine of genesis and fall as one of many such myths. He was now writing his own version of the genesis of the world, the only kind permitted by transcendental idealism. The world produced in that genesis was a myth, an illusion, and so was its science as given by Schelling.

In his time he was not taken to task for that science, but he had to explain himself on the question of freedom in the world he had created. According to Schelling the production of the world was a cyclic process, the interplay of centrifugal and centripetal tendencies, a process that was bound to repeat itself. Schelling spelled out this consequence in a work, *The Ages of the World*, [43] which he refrained from publishing. Had he let it be printed, all his endorsements of freedom would have appeared hollow and repulsive. Curiously, the very example that Schelling had already used to explain himself on freedom was the necessary yet free betrayal of Christ by Judas, [44] an act casting even in its stark singularity enough doubt on freedom. But what could be the meaning of freedom if Judas was to betray Christ an infinite number of times in an infinite number of successively emanating worlds? The prospect of Christ's suffering an infinite number of times was in the eyes of the Church Fathers the most blasphemous implication of the doctrine of the Great Year dominating pagan cosmologies. [45] The contrast between what the facts of salvation meant for the Church Fathers and what they meant for Schelling and the idealists could not have been greater. The Fathers kept alive a faith that ultimately triggered the rise of science, the idealists made both faith and knowledge meaningless. Had Schelling and others like him had their way, they might have succeeded in ushering in the twilight of science.

How this twilight would have come about can be best seen in Goethe's long and bitter campaign against Newton's theory of colors. The ultimate roots of that campaign lay in Goethe's commitment to the pantheistic monism of German idealism. It prevented Goethe from seeing the difference between a mechanistic science of physics and a mechanistic philosophy, or physicalism. As a result, one of the greatest poets of all times fell prey to the illusion that whatever he had achieved as a poet was inferior to what he had done as a physicist. [46] Another telling aspect of the antiscience of German idealism and Naturphilosophie was the manner in which idealist philosophers went about implementing the program of their "higher" physics or science in the German academic world. The bitterness of the clash was registered by Helmholtz, who in 1862 could look at it as a thing of the past: "The philosophers accused scientific men of narrowness, the scientific men retorted that the philosophers were crazy." [47] Fortunately, scientists saw deeper than the level of academic politics. Reared in the spirit of reverence for facts, they were keenly perceptive about philosophical statements which related to facts, especially to the facts of science. It was most natural that Gauss, one of the cofounders of non-Euclidean geometries, should be one of the first to attack Kantian philosophy at its apparently invincible cornerstone, the distinction between analytic and synthetic propositions. The distinction, in Gauss's terse statement, was "one of those things that run out on triviality or are false."[48] Equally perceptive was the remark of Maxwell, who wrote with an eye on German idealists: "Taking metaphysicians singly we find ... that as is their physics, so is their metaphysics."[49]

The whole history of metaphysics shows that metaphysical systems were to be discredited in the measure in which they were grafted on a particular form of physics. When the physics in question was simply a parody of physics, as a so-called "higher" physics had to be, then the force of logic asserted itself with fearful rapidity. Hegel is a perfect case. In 1800, at the age of thirty, he presented at Jena a Habilitationschrift on planetary orbits. There he claimed that nature must conform to reason if science is to be successful. To illustrate this brazenly aprioristic and crudely antiscientific statement he argued that it was insane to search for a planet between Mars and Jupiter.[50] According to Hegel the search was mistaken because it was based on the arithmetical progression suggested by planetary distances, and not on the Pythagorean or geometrical progression which alone could generate reality. To make the irony of all this complete, Hegel not only manipulated the geometrical series,[51] but published his Habilitationschrift only months after the discovery of Ceres on January 1, 1801. No wonder that Ernest of Saxa-Gotha, princely patron of the astronomer F. X. von Zach, editor of the *Astronomische Monatschrift,* called Hegel's essay "the monument of the madness of the nineteenth century."[52]

The true madness of that century was still to be printed. It appeared in the pages of Hegel's *Enzyklopädie der Naturwissenschaften.* This work is hardly ever referred to by Hegel's admirers, but when they occasionally discourse on it they are not reluctant to present it as genuine science.[53] Hegel himself not only gave constant attention to it by bringing it out in three "improved" editions,[54] but with exemplary consistency took it for the concrete truth of his abstract dialectic. In its basic form the dialectic was the continual oscillation of all between the polarities of coming into being and passing out of being, an oscillation in which Hegel found eternal repose, though he acknowledged that it was the repose of "Bacchic delirium in which not one of its components is not drunk; and since each becomes immediately dissolved when the others withdraw, that delirium is also simple and transparent repose."[55] Croce, who found the "highest wisdom" reflected in that Bacchic-Hegelian delirium,[56] saw it also reflected in what Nietzsche fondly called the "Dionysiac."[57] Those who were terrified by it were in Croce's eyes "timid thinkers," of whom he singled out Rosmini, a thinker unable to understand why any being should inevitably experience the urge to go out of existence. Rosmini was unable to do so because he clearly saw that the urge was madness itself: "The system of Hegel," he wrote, "does nothing less than to make being go mad and introduce madness into all things. . . . I do not know if a similar effort was ever made in the world to make all things, even being itself, go mad."[58]

That a Rosmini, who was courageous to the point of writing a book entitled *Cinque piaghe della Chiesa* (five wounds of the church), for which he was quickly put on the Index, is qualified a "timid thinker," demands a dialectic in which words can go out of, if not their being, their plain meaning. Rosmini refused to be sucked into the vortex of Hegelian dialectic not because he was timid but because he realized that it made no sense to accord the same dignity to madness as to sense. This realization derived from his conviction that all beings owed their existence to an absolutely transcendental and absolutely rational being, the Creator of all. This conviction, the foremost fruit and expression of Christian theism, was the source of his unwavering commitment to the nondialectical stability and rationality of all beings, a source which obviously could not be resorted to even by a "critical" Hegelian like Croce. With a Hegelian twist he found it meaningful to oscillate between the living and the nonliving as he gave his famed evaluation of Hegel's system, the *What Is Living and What Is Dead of the Philosophy of Hegel*, in which he admitted that "it sometimes seems as if Hegel was not in full possession of his thought," a Hegelian's euphemism for being out of one's mind.[59]

That Hegel's system is living, though in a sense not foreseen by Croce, will easily be realized by all those who are not too timid to keep firmly in mind that the Right *and* Left issuing from Hegel's system achieved their maddening distinction through the numbers of cruel deaths they produced. Tracing those deaths back to Hegel will not fail to arouse the indignation of many well-meaning Hegelians, who see Hegel as a prophet of intellectual and spiritual liberation, his apotheosis of war notwithstanding. Yet all those deaths remain an attack on liberty in its deepest sense, a point which will be readily overlooked under the impulse of a subtly Hegelian dialectic. It helps one recall the Nazi holocausts, but it makes one turn a deaf ear on the data presented by Solzhenitsyn with an arithmetic precision that would have thrown Hegel into a frenzy. According to those data, during the eighty years of repeated attempts on the Czar's life seventeen persons a year were executed in prerevolutionary Russia. At its height, the Spanish Inquisition destroyed about ten persons every month. However, during the first two years of Lenin's revolution more than one thousand persons per month were executed without trial, still a puny number compared with the forty thousand executed every month during the height of Stalin's terror.[60] To improve on these figures became, logically enough, the privilege of the Chinese Cultural Revolution, another genuine form of the madness of which Hegelian dialectic is the theoretical wellspring.

The theoretically deepest form of that madness is the instability of the mind with respect to the difference between being and nonbeing, a difference which on the intellectual level can appear in such innocent-looking versions as Croce's proposal that Hegel's philosophy, in order to reveal its greatness, should be read as poetry.[61] Whatever the merit of abolishing the difference between poetry and philosophy, the madness of it becomes brazenly evident when one turns the philosophy of nature, or science, into poetry—the most benevolent evaluation that can be given of the performance embodied in the *Enzyklopädie*. Croce himself remained trapped in his Hegelianism when he insisted, on the one hand, that the "false sciences" of the *Enzyklopädie* must be constantly kept in mind in all their details and, on the other, gave but vague glimpses of them.[62] Another tactic typical of Hegelians is also evident in Croce's claim that as one goes from the exact mathematical sciences toward the biological and psychological sciences, one finds an increasing merit in works like the *Enzyklopädie*,[63] a claim that he failed to illustrate with concrete examples. Clearly, a Croce who felt that Engels succeeded in finding valuable and seminal details in Hegel's discourse on the sciences could hardly realize the true measure of its falsity.[64]

The wise will find food for thought in a few details which might be best introduced by Hegel's brushing aside Schelling's Naturphilosophie as "humbug," as "philosophizing without knowledge of fact," as a set of "mere fancies, even imbecile fancies," and producing a systematic parody of science while boasting of his expertise in differential calculus and chemistry.[65] For was it any better than humbug to say with Hegel that magnetism was "nature's naiveté" and that electricity was "the angry self of the body"?[66] The only rational (or rather, consistent) aspect of such utterances—and a great many of them were made by Hegel—was the logic generating them. Because of that logic he could approach the finite and singular facts of nature only from his idea of the infinite, the absolute, and the universal. Reflecting on the idea of the absolute was for him a communing with infinite ontological richness and universal dynamics. But this communing as done by Hegel could only unfold his own subjective mind. Its contents with respect to the facts of nature were exceedingly meager and often plainly ridiculous, a logic that could not be escaped by such critics of Hegel who similarly opted for the primacy of the subjective.[67]

This is not to suggest that Hegel was not attracted to facts, objective finite facts. He certainly was. He had a tremendous interest in the facts of history, and he let his fury descend on theologians who wanted Christianity without its historical facts and foundations. Had he not possessed a genuine interest in finite facts, he could have simply refrained, as did Spinoza, from writing thick volumes about them. Yet all that interest was misplaced through Hegel's interest in God. He had much of deep Lutheran piety, but nothing of traditional Christian faith. Like Boehme and other German pietists, he wanted the absolute with no mediation whatever. The result was that he ended up claiming that the philosopher's knowledge of God is God's knowledge of himself.[68] Nothing in one of Hegel's last lecture series, which was on the proofs of the existence of God, reduced the measure of this confusion. There Hegel noted the devastating impact of Kant's criticism of the proofs,[69] and he deplored the prejudice created against them.[70] Hegel declared Kant's criticism of the proofs to be inconclusive,[71] and he charged him with starting the process of a "complete maiming of reason."[72] Hegel was also a valuable witness of the predicament of theologians who, because of Kant, were ashamed of the proofs.[73] According to Hegel there were even some, obviously younger theologians, unaware of the fact that such proofs had ever been formulated.[74] In Hegel's words they wanted to base faith exclusively on religious experience.[75]

The most informative aspect of Hegel's lectures lies in his account of the two main traditional proofs, the cosmological and the teleological. His phrasing of them shows the inability of the idealist to give a reliable account of the train of thought of a realist. Not that he did not try, but his tongue slipped at the crucial juncture. Since he had devoted the first eight of fifteen lectures to the idealist framework, within which, he claimed, the only good perspective of the proofs could be had, the slip of the tongue was bound to occur as he turned to the proofs themselves. According to Hegel, one class of the proofs, the cosmological and the teleological, proceeds "from the Being to the thought of God." The other class, formed by the ontological proof, "proceeds from the thought of God, from truth itself, to the Being of this truth."[76] That thought was equal to truth was flagrant idealism and a gross injustice to what was meant by Saint Anselm, whom Hegel recalled admiringly.[77] Hegel's phrase, the move "from the Being to the thought of God," was neither idealism nor realism, but sheer fantasy. The same was true of the phrase which he added as an explanation: "from the Being to the thought of God, that is, to put it more definitely, from determinate Being to the true Being as representing the Being of God."[78]

That for Hegel the second part of the phrase could be identical with the first betrayed the idealist for whom thought was being. The idealist in question was the Hegelian kind, as it was Hegel who proposed that the keystone in the arch which Kant built should be thought itself, to secure for that arch a cohesion which neither Kant's imagination, nor

Fichte's will, nor Schelling's esthetic experience could provide. On the plane of logic it could be argued that if thought was equal to being, then it was the going from infinite to finite that alone made sense. But on the plane of being the situation was very different. Thus, because of the true logic of Hegel's position, what he had said on God and world proved equally illusory. His passionate reaffirmation of God and historic Christianity made him in the long run not an ally of theists in general and of Christians in particular but "an enemy in disguise, the least evident, and the most dangerous." Such was the astute remark of J. M. E. McTaggart,[79] not a Christian, not even a theist, but an acute and surprisingly sober idealist, and certainly an expert on Hegelian thought.

As to the illusory character of Hegel's profuse dicta about the world, it should not be forgotten that to his credit he took the world as the totality of physical as well as of historical facts. History was for him the unfolding of the absolute Thought, or Spirit, in the fine arts, in religion, and in philosophy. The historical unfolding of that spirit in religion and in philosophy furnished him countless occasions to speak about science, but when he touched on it he demonstrated clearly the insensitivity of the idealist to what matters in science as historical fact. In his *Philosophy of History* Copernicus and Galileo are mentioned only as targets of Rome.[80] Newton was not found worthy of being mentioned at all. Copernicus was not referred to in the *Phenomenology of Mind*, in unwitting evidence of the wholly un-Copernican character of that turn concerning the mind's position and nature which Kant initiated and which culminated in Hegel. A relatively long part of the *Phenomenology of Mind* is taken up by Hegel's attack on Gall's phrenology.[81] Clearly, Hegel could not tolerate any attempt, even a misguided one, to infer the features of mind from phenomena. Of course, with Hegel it was not on experimental grounds that phrenology was to be refuted. His concluding words on the subject contrasted the infinite depths of a self-unfolding mind with the abject lowliness of the same mind when intent on sensory information. On the biological level, Hegel added, the same contrast was displayed by nature in using the same organ for what is the highest function, procreation, and for what is the lowest, urination.[82]

Hegelian thought was not always so self-revealing. Unwary historians of science, familiar with the role of geometrical apriorism in Galileo's derivation of the law of free fall, might even be impressed by Hegel, who in the *Phenomenology of Mind* ascribed the law of free fall to the urge of the intellect able to transcend contradictory experiments.[83] Here was a Hegelian error beautifully packaged in half-truths. First, the urge in question was not a mystical proclivity but a lucid commitment to clearly definable and testable propositions. Second, while experiments could appear contradictory up to a point, they could be gradually improved by approaching the ideal situation with the aid of analogy. It was that judicious use of analogy which Hegel rejected in the same breath. Hegelian historians of science would find it difficult to explain that Galileo's proposition had to go through the cauldron of experimental testing in order to become a law.

In speaking of the universal laws of nature in his *Philosophy of History* Hegel once more could dazzle the unadvised. There he ascribed the tracing out of those laws to experimental science and gave the creativity of the intellect its due as he wrote of the rise of science in the early seventeenth century: "It seemed to men as if God had but just created the moon and stars, plants and animals, as if the laws of the universe were now established for the first time, for only then did they feel a real interest in the universe, when they recognized their own Reason in the Reason which pervades it."[84] This was as beautiful as it was erroneous, historically at least. Copernicus, Galileo, and Newton might have been unfortunate in having been born before Hegel, but the historical fact is that in making their discoveries they saw in the newly unfolding lawfulness of nature not the traces of their own minds but the vestiges of the Creator's mind. For them the world was an objective entity, and they would have had only scorn for Hegel's seeing in their feats the triumph of "the independent authority of Subjectivity."[85] Contemporary science was equally distorted through Hegel's perspective. All that happened a few decades earlier to the caloric and to the phlogiston should have given Hegel ample food for thought about that cutting edge which no subjectivity could ever have. It was not subjectivity that gave Newton the stepping-stone to a wholly new view of the laws of planetary motions. The view subjectivity could provide was perfectly illustrated in Hegel's a priori legislation on planets. It started with the remark that Newton's physics was "merely a mechanistic physics, but not a *true* physics."[86]

Mechanistic physics could be, and had to be, improved to become a truer physics but in the process Hegel would prove not an ally but an enemy in disguise and the worst enemy at that. This became a painful reality as soon as the Hegelian Right and Left had come of age in the Hegelian sense by becoming political entities, the culminating phase of Hegelian dialectic. The trials of exact science in Nazi Germany and the Soviet Union have been carefully documented, a status still to be achieved with respect to Communist China. Those researchers, however, should also pay attention to the virulent hostility of those regimes to Christian theism, an inquiry that might seem valuable even to those of the so-called rationalist tradition. It was its respected spokesman, Sir Karl Popper, who traced the resolve of Fichte, Schelling, and Hegel to part with "any kind of rational argument" to "Kant's criticism of all attempts to prove the existence of God."[87] Other implications of his remark—whether a rationalist still can believe in God, whether Kant's criticism is valid, and whether Kant should carry a large share of the blame for the irrational illusions of idealism—are, of course, secondary to the main point of these lectures which deal with the historical connection between theism and rationality as science. Staying within the historical context of that connection let one more detail, by way of conclusion, be recalled about it. The detail is the passionate endorsement of the idea of eternal recurrence, or the Great Year, by Blanqui as well as by Nietzsche.[88] Blanqui was not the only Marxist to do so. From Engels on, the idea of eternal cosmic cycles has been a dogma with orthodox Marxist philosophers and with intimidated Soviet cosmologists. Blanqui, for a while a rival of Marx for the leadership of the international proletariat, endorsed the idea of the Great Year in a book which culminates in a passionate rejection of man's craving for explanation. What Blanqui advocated as a remedy was an assimilation of man with the blind forces of the cosmos, an attitude which is the very denial of what has been the best and most creative element in the whole history of science.

Of Nietzsche's philosophy there have been many interpretations, some of which curiously neglect Nietzsche's repeated and emphatic assertions that the idea of eternal recurrence formed the very essence and soul of his philosophy. It is generally agreed that Nietzsche had close ties with German idealism and was not altogether unfit for the role in which he was resurrected by the Nazis, never friendly to science. Not surprisingly, almost everything that Nietzsche said on science is a travesty of it. But he provides more than general evidence of the interconnection between idealism and eternal recurrence, on the one side, and antiscience, on the other. His was a unique sensitivity for interconnections, and to his credit he spelled them out with an elemental force. The force bordered on hatred when Nietzsche spoke of the Judeo-Christian notion of Creation. Faith in the biblical notion of creation was for him the most fatal aberration of the human mind, and he identified the moment of scientific truth with the rejection of the doctrine of creation. At the same time he designated his advocacy of eternal recurrence as the "European form of Buddhism."[89] Logic has seldom been so consistent and so misleading at the same time. Within the logic of Nietzsche one could only espouse Buddhism. What was wrong with that logic was not only the antiscientific impact of Buddhism wherever it made itself felt, but also the fact that historically the belief in creation and the Creator was the moment of truth for science. This belief formed the bedrock on which science rose. It is a telling reflection on the tragic instability of human thought that, a century or two after the rise of science, its true origins could be ignored or fiercely attacked by so many gifted minds. The tragedy was their yielding to the illusion of idealism in which only the mind—not the stubborn, finite, contingent facts of nature and history—had true existence. That the most articulate spokesman of the nineteenth-century positivism, the very opposite of idealism, was to drift into Buddhism, shows that extremes have the same logic and much the same consequences, boding ill for science no less than for theism.

Ten

THE PRICE OF POSITIVISM

IN HIS CAPACITY AS FOUNDER AND FIRST HIGH PRIEST OF THE POSITIVIST Church, Auguste Comte composed in 1852 a liturgical calendar of thirteen lunar months.[1] The twenty-eight days of the eleventh month, called "Descartes," were devoted to the saints of modern philosophy. Among the fourth week's philosopher-saints, Kant, Fichte, and Hegel form a prominent group, a fact which might suggest that Comte was an eager student of the German idealists. Their names he certainly knew, but hardly their thought.[2] The positivism of Comte was not a reaction to German idealism. But like the German idealists, Comte too was indebted to Hume, whom he greatly admired and to whom he reserved in the month "Descartes" the fourth or last "humanidi," or "man day," the positivist substitute for the Lord's day.

Comte liked Hume not as a student but as a congenial soul. He found in Hume the same kind of commitment to facts and to facts alone which he had already chosen as his own philosophical creed. This choice of Comte was undoubtedly influenced by his admission to the Ecole Polytechnique, where sciences were almost exclusively cultivated with a rigid emphasis on factual, that is, technical, applications. The Polytechnique was also a hotbed of republican politics and social reformism. Comte's short-lived career at the Polytechnique was followed by half a dozen years of sociological pamphleteering. Its highlight was the "Plan for Scientific Studies Demanded by the Reorganization of Society," published in 1822 and reprinted three years later under the title, "System of Positive Policy."[3] The six volumes of the *Cours de philosophie positive* and the four even heavier volumes of the *Système de politique positive* added only details, very instructive to be sure, to what had already been set forth in the "Plan."

On one very essential point, the "law of three states,"[4] Comte had never added anything substantive. According to that law all processes of thought start with the theological stage, and, after going through the metaphysical stage, they advance to the stage where they retain only their positive core. In speaking in the "Plan" about the theological stage, Comte presented the Alexandrian school, or Clement and Origen, both philosopher-theologians, as the ones who laid the groundwork for Christianity, as the culmination of that very stage.[5] Eight years later, in the first lecture of the *Cours*, Comte had in mind natural theology as elaborated within the Christian matrix when he wrote that "the theological system reached the highest perfection of which it is capable when it substituted the providential action of a unique being for the varied play of numerous independent deities that had been imagined primitively."[6] In eleven more years, there appeared the fifth volume of the *Cours*, with two-thirds of its six hundred pages taken up by long lectures on the three phases of the theological stage: fetishism, polytheism, and monotheism.[7]

Those long lectures were part of the section called social physics. The intellectual content of the development of philosophical theology, as Comte called natural theology, seemed to him to be completely valueless. In the proofs of the existence of God Comte saw an implicit admission of doubts and a steady support for the skeptic.[8] His approving presentation of Pascal as the only Christian thinker who perceived the grave pitfalls of relying on the proofs was a poor rendering of a detail of intellectual history. But there could hardly be much need of thorough historical research if the positivist philosophers were right in contending that the facts themselves inevitably imposed the only truthful conceptual system. The particular trouble with this was that according to Comte the truth of positivism rested on two historical proofs. One was provided by history as generally understood, the other by one's own personal history. As Comte stated, everybody starts as a theologian, grows into a metaphysician, and ends as a "physicien," that is, a physicist.[9] Comte the historian and Comte the individual were a plain rebuttal of both proofs.

Comte's flat dismissal of natural theology matched the manner in which he made short shrift of metaphysics. It was to be abandoned because the progress of biological science made it clear that, as Comte quoted with approval a contemporary author, "ideology was a part of zoology."[10] Animal instinct rose, therefore, to the level of intelligence and intelligence sank to the level of instinct. The only essential difference between animality and humanity was the degree of development of this or that faculty common to the whole living realm.[11] Consequently, Comte declared that the "famous scholastic definition of man as a rational animal is veritable nonsense, because no animal can live without being reasonable up to a certain point."[12] It made no positivist sense to have recourse at a critical juncture to expressions such as "up to a point." It was nonsense, not scholastic but positivist, to declare with Comte that "although the moral nature of animals has so far been very little and very poorly explored, it can nevertheless be recognized without the slightest uncertainty" that in animals there is a use of language, a display of altruism, an experiencing of boredom, and even the readiness to do what apparently only man can do, namely, to commit suicide.[13] At the end of this sentence, which in its original phrasing runs to twenty-four lines, any rational animal could indeed wonder what to take, a long pause or his own life.

Here let the fact merely be registered that Comte dismissed

metaphysics, and let attention be turned to the connection of this with his reading of the history of science. To see that connection one does not even have to turn more than a few pages. In debunking metaphysics Comte relied heavily on biology, a procedure that could be given a semblance of reliability. Quite different is his reliance on the work of Gall, whom he considered the most advanced and most enlightened biologist of the early nineteenth century.[14] No wonder that Comte desperately tried to exonerate Gall from the vagaries of phrenology. Fourteen years later Gall was given in the *Catéchisme positiviste* equal honors with such giants of science as Galileo, Newton, and Lavoisier.[15] But the most revealing aspect of Comte's esteem for Gall lies in his efforts to create the impression that Gall's appearance in science was an inevitability.[16] Beneath that eagerness of Comte lies the very soul of the Comtean view of history in general and of scientific history in particular. In this view, science is not so much discovered by scientists as scientists are successively uncovered by science in a mechanistic fashion. By the time Comte came to discuss biology in the *Cours*, he had already claimed in its first two volumes that this was indeed what had happened in astronomy, physics, and chemistry. Biology, however, in all its branches, presented a far more complicated case. Since the best biologists of the day refused to consider life as sheer mechanism, Comte had no choice but to build up those biologists, however insignificant, who seemed to share his definition of "positive" knowledge.

This arbitrary evaluation of contemporary scientists was not the only or even the heaviest price Comte had to pay for the kind of positivism that radically excluded metaphysics, together with its reference to the first cause, and indeed to any other cause. Since, according to the law of three states, science, positivist science to be sure, was an inevitable outcome, scientific discoveries, big and small, formed a necessary sequence. That a discovery was sometimes akin to the miraculous never occurred to Comte, who wanted to become the first professor of the history of science and at such an illustrious place as the Collège de France.[17] As a historian of science Comte failed to see the gigantic singularity of the rise of science. If that rise was so inevitable, why did it not come about at half a dozen other times, in half a dozen great cultures other than Western Christendom? Comte never asked why it was that fetishism and polytheism were transcended by monotheism only in one culture and in such a way as to make monotheism an effective stepping-stone to positive science. All these and similar questions should have been raised and faced by the very logic of the law of three states.

That Comte did not face and answer these questions might suggest that his real interest was neither in the law of three states nor in the history of science. Comte's true ambition lay in the scientific organization of society, the bringing about of a scientific heaven on earth—and what is a heaven if not a perfect and definitive order of things and conditions? In Comte's perspective, perfect meant exact, and he saw himself as the Galileo of a sociology the laws of which were as exact as the law of free fall.[18] The soundness of Comte's ambition depended, therefore, on the demonstration that science, and biology in particular, had reached the definitive, or perfect, that is, exact, stage. If the claim was not true, the positivist reorganization of society, the most inclusive biological system, could only be a dream. To declare in the 1830s that the biology of the 1820s was the final form of biology, in its essentials at least, must appear even to nonspecialists as bordering on the pathetic. The same pathetic aspect can be seen, and without bringing in much specialized material, if one turns to Comte's handling of astronomy, physics, and chemistry, as they stood in the early part of the nineteenth century. As could be expected, Comte made much of the stability of the solar system as established by Laplace. While the discovery of Uranus in 1783 by Herschel did not invalidate Laplace's conclusions, it certainly made evident that knowledge of the solar system was anything but complete.

The prospect of that incompleteness loomed for Comte as a bad omen, which he was resolved to exorcize. Since exorcism is not a procedure practiced in science, the result could only be an invitation to Mephistopheles. He came into full view as Comte spoke of the "insane enthusiasm" that greeted the sighting of Neptune.[19] Comte frowned on efforts to go much beyond Saturn, for fear that new discoveries would undermine the ultimate truth of the stability of the solar system and with that the foundations of the positivist heaven on earth. Without the demonstration of the stability of the solar system, Comte wrote, "social physics would be an impossible science," and added that "if astronomical conditions were liable to indefinite variations, human existence which depends upon them could never be reduced to laws."[20] Twenty years later he unfolded the true meaning of this odd claim when he declared in the *Système de politique positive* that social usefulness was the only justification of science.[21]

In a manner that could not have been more emphatic, Comte also asserted that positive science could extend only as far as the naked eye carried one's vision,[22] and the practical limit was the orbit of Saturn. What he said on the future tasks of astronomy amounted to a positive and positivist abolition of solar physics,[23] astrophysics,[24] and cosmology,[25] in the age of Fraunhofer, Bessel, and of the two Herschels—a supreme irony in view of the very Comtean phrase that the "history of science is science itself."[26] The irony was the logical price for Comte's holding with utmost consistency that the heavens declared no longer the glory of God, but of Hipparchus, Kepler, and Newton, that real science was "in radical opposition to all theology,"[27] that "the whole notion of creation, properly so-called, must be radically avoided,"[28] and that astronomy "succeeded in emancipating the human mind of all theological and metaphysical tutelage."[29] A radical exclusion of God, that is, Cause in the deepest sense, led through the exclusion of causes in any real sense, to the exclusion of the study of a causally interconnected cosmos,[30] the only cosmos worthy of the name. In all this, as if to make a mockery of Copernicus, Comte contrasted the solar and cosmical views of the universe as properly useful and largely useless views, respectively.[31] The solar viewpoint advocated by Comte was a return to philosophical geocentrism, a move that abolished the glory of God and of Copernicus by the same stroke. A philosophy of astronomy in which planets ultimately became sensitive living beings could only bespeak the tragically hollow glory of Auguste Comte, the philosopher of science.

Of physics, too, Comte decreed that it was in complete opposition to any theological perspective, though he felt that unlike the laws of astronomy, the laws of physics had not yet been formulated in their final form in every detail. This relative imperfection of physics could give rise, Comte warned, to the illusion fostered by scholastic subtlety that the laws of physics were not necessary but contingent, a distinction which "directly tends to throw an artificial uncertainty on the true definition of that science."[32] He was not the first or the last to look for a physics that was necessarily what it was and could not be anything else. Comte's special place among these misguided minds is due to the fact that he did not recoil from applying this precept in great detail to the physics of the day. The application was nothing short of putting physics, as well as astronomy and chemistry, into a straitjacket.

The maddening evidence of all this is in the *Cours de philosophie positive*, and as a result the even more maddening series of precepts which Comte issued from the completion of the *Cours* in 1842 until his death in 1857 cannot be simply brushed aside as the result of an emotional breakdown. Long before Comte solicitously limited the length of the three daily meditations enjoined on members of the Positivist Church,[33] he had blandly curtailed the extent to which man was permitted to penetrate the cosmos. Long before Comte decreed that in his world-state no province should be smaller or greater than Tuscany,[34] he had set equally arbitrary limits to astronomy and physics. Long before Comte declared in his *Catéchisme* that the science of cosmology was equivalent to the study of the earth,[35] he had abolished a cosmology competent to deal with anything beyond the orbit of Saturn. Long before he declined to include the classics of science in the "library of positivist instruction for the benefit of the proletariat," he had spoken and written of science as if he had never read its great classics. Comte's list contained no Copernicus, no Galileo, no Kepler, no Newton, no Euler, no Herschel, no Faraday.[36] The clue to such selectivity lies in Comte's philosophical authors, a mere five. The chief of them were Francis Bacon and David Hume. The latter, Comte noted, was his "principal forerunner in philosophy."[37] Obviously, Bacon and Hume had to make up practically all the philosophy that the proletariat, that is, the new society, was to learn, if indeed science was made by facts alone and not by scientists as well. Once the library had been universally studied, society was perfect and could devote all its time to worshiping itself as the Great Being in the Positivist Church, which sanctified its members by nine sacraments. Such was the ultimate price to be paid for the positivist rejection of the truly ultimate in Being and in Intelligibility.

Comte's most distinguished ally, John Stuart Mill, was not to enter the Positivist Church. He gave his reasons in a book, *August Comte and Positivism*,[38] a storehouse of revealing information about the older Comte. But Mill never disavowed the younger Comte, the apparent paragon of a positivism untainted by mystical cravings. After all, Mill's *System of Logic* was, in that purely positivist fashion, an effort on behalf of a society which, to recall the words of Mill's *Autobiography*, was to derive its health from eschewing the metaphysical mischiefs that plagued morals, politics, and even religion! For Mill metaphysics was equivalent to the contention of German idealism that "truths external to the mind may be known by intuition or consciousness, independently of observations and experience." Such a metaphysics was certainly full of mischiefs, mainly because it was wholly beyond physics. The realm of the physical was not for it that springboard which alone can assure reality to the soarings of the mind. Mill could not have been more mistaken in stating that this mischievous metaphysics had its stronghold in its "appeal to the evidence of mathematics and of cognate branches of physical science."[39]

By discrediting this appeal with a radically empiricist notion of scientific laws, the author of the *System of Logic* certainly did not wish to rescue religion in general or natural theology in particular. It was, of course, true that the notion of a universe of laws had always been the stronghold of traditional natural theology, but this could hardly be noticed when idealism loomed so large. In attacking idealism Mill was drawn into a campaign worthy of Sancho Panza. Mill wrote as if he were unmasking the products of the windmills of idealism, but he seemed to end up legislating about the wind. To suggest that the wind blew only there, where it was felt, could do credit to a Sancho Panza, but not to a philosopher bent on speaking the language of science. Yet the suggestion in question was implied in Mill's interpretation of the validity of induction. It reached only as far as the instances of enumeration. To assign uniform lawfulness and rationality to the universe beyond its actually explored portion was, in Mill's words, "an idle attempt."[40] In fact he went so far (and let credit be given to him for being so consistent) as to declare it to be a "folly to affirm confidently" that in distant parts of the stellar regions "the law of causation prevails any more than do specific physical laws that have been found to hold universally on our own planet."[41]

Logicians will continue with their quarrels over Mill's definition of induction. For a historian of science it is enough to register the historical fact that creative physicists, astronomers, and cosmologists have always asserted confidently, nay with the utmost assurance, the validity of the same laws throughout the whole universe, not just within its "explored portion." When Mill was writing the *System of Logic*, the most hotly debated question in science was whether the nebulae seen through the telescopes of the two Herschels and of Lord Rosse were part of the Milky Way or were independent systems called island universes. Nowhere in the scientific literature was it even indirectly hinted that those island universes, if there were any, were ruled by laws different from the ones so far established, let alone ruled by random sequences of events to the exclusion of any law. This most unscientific possibility had in Mill's eyes scientific support in nebulae as so many island universes.[42]

The firmness of his views on this point can best be seen from the fact that twenty-two years later he claimed that worlds were possible where two and two would make not four but five for minds produced and conditioned there.[43] Such worlds were realms where atoms, to give modernity to the implications of Mill's stance, could behave like Humpty Dumptys, while the king's horses could act on occasion as if they were atoms. In such worlds, devoid of consistency, one could even revel in the possibility of putting Humpty Dumpty together again, though not in the possibility of splitting the atom on the basis that neutrons had the same properties in each and every atom everywhere in the universe. While the possibility of such worlds cannot be strictly excluded on the basis of Mill's empiricist logic, such a logic, when its full implications are kept in mind, excludes science, for science is possible only on the basis of unrestricted consistency. Once this destructiveness of Mill's empiricist logic for science is remembered, the threat of the same logic to natural theology will lose much of its force and almost all of its intellectual respectability.

Mill knew something of the common threat of empiricism to natural theology and to science, a threat which in the England of the 1830s was noted in his own way by none other than Coleridge. Since natural theology was not equivalent to religious experience, Mill in his essay on Coleridge, written in 1840, could concede to religionists that the posi-

151

tions of mysticism and of empiricism were mutually impregnable.[44] There was some truth in this, and all the more so because the natural theology of German idealism, which Coleridge championed, could for very good reasons be taken for plain mysticism. But it was one thing to describe idealism as mystical, and another to equate empiricism with reason and science. Revealingly, Mill did not try to evaluate idealism and empiricism against the standards of science but in relation to political and social theory. It was a curious bypassing of the principal issue, a tactic paralleled by Mill's treatment in the *Logic* of the true features of science as it grew into full maturity during the century following Copernicus. Mill was not willing to see in that process any trace of metaphysics, a fact which should nowadays discredit his logic in the eyes of those historians of science who cultivate their discipline on the basis of reading the original sources. According to Mill, Kepler's establishing the ellipticity of planetary orbits was not even a case of induction by enumeration. Since astronomers long before Kepler had observed that "planets periodically returned to the same places" (so Mill presented his reading of scientific history) "there was no induction left for Kepler to make, nor did he make any further induction."[45] Clearly, Mill did not bother to plod through the laborious pages of Kepler's *Astronomia nova de stella Martis.* There he would have met face to face the heroic groping of a great man of science with facts, with ideas, with perspectives, and not least with the need to arrive at a law which enabled the prediction of planetary positions with the greatest possible accuracy. Nothing of this was intimated in Mill's account of what had happened. The account had actuality only in Mill's positivism in which even the most complex and herculean inductions performed by the mind had to appear as simple, matter-of-fact self-organization of observations.

Those who applauded Mill's handling of the proofs of the existence of God never noticed that the limited God which Mill allowed was the counterpart of Mill's equally limited concepts of science and of the universe. Whether the case was that of God or of science or of the universe, the cause of the debilitating limitation was the same, namely, the positivist clipping of the wings of the mind. The idealists equipped the mind with illusory wings to enable it to leave forever the realm of the sensory. The positivists confined its flights to within that realm. The wings of the mind could perhaps be clipped, but the urges of its nature could in no way be denied. While it could be disputed that it was man's nature to be a rational animal, neither Comte nor Mill disputed, in the deeds of their very human nature, that man was a worshiping animal. The former died worshiping society, the latter died acknowledging a demiurge, or more specifically, a Manichean ultimate composed of good and evil halves.[46] Given the choice of worshiping a

Manichean god or human society, one wonders whether it was not Mill rather than Comte who paid the higher price in a disastrous deal.

For a historian of science an important detail in Mill's reflections on natural theology is his assertion that a strong, universal conviction in the lawfulness of nature had to precede the rise of monotheism.[47] The assertion is historical and therefore its truth is a question of the historical record. As was the case with Mill's reading of Kepler, here, too, a historian of science is allowed only the conclusion that Mill's positivist claim is at variance with the record written by history. While biblical monotheism owed nothing to Greek science, that science could develop into a true science only within a monotheistic matrix, which happened to be biblical through the mediation of Christianity.

This point of history could not be perceived at a time which simply took the century of genius as the rise of rationalism, which took the Renaissance for the herald of science, and which conceded to the Middle Ages only a longing for something which later became known as Romanticism. Mill's blindness on such points of history will appear less shocking if one recalls that William Whewell, a scientist, a theologian, a philosopher and historian of science in one, and a critic of Mill's Logic, also failed to perceive the contribution of historic monotheism to the rise of science, a fact strongly suggestive of the intimate epistemological connection of natural theology with scientific methodology.[48] The logic of that connection was, however, all too evident in Mill's Logic and was revealed in a dramatically factual way before the century was over. It was also revealed simultaneously that George Romanes was the true author of A Candid Examination of Theism, a book that created a sensation when published in 1878 under the pen name Physicus.[49] Romanes, whose work on natural selection earned him Darwin's generous praise, surveyed and rejected such formulations of the proof of the existence of God that only indirectly involved the question of the contingency of existence as such. They were the arguments from the human mind, from design, and from general laws. Romanes's rebuttal of these arguments was largely based on Mill's Logic, in which the question of contingency was unanswerable. No wonder that Romanes's final position with respect to existence was an insistence on its unfathomable mysteriousness.[50] But on the basis of the same logic not only the existence of mind, order, and general laws remained unanswerable, but their consistent meaning too became doubtful, a point which Romanes came to recognize only some time after he had left Edinburgh, where between 1886 and 1890 he was the occupant of a special chair in biology.

His untimely death, at the age of forty-six in 1894, did not permit him to publish a lengthy essay, entitled "A Candid Examination of Religion," which was to appear under the pen name Metaphysicus. In that work he wrote: "Of all philosophical theories of causality the most repugnant to reason must be those of Hume, Kant and Mill which ... attribute the principle of causality to a creation of our own minds, or in other words deny that there is anything objective in the relations of cause and effect, i.e. in the very thing which all physical science is engaged in discovering particular cases of it."[51] It was not philosophical, Romanes argued, to state the perception of the fact of causality and to refuse at the same time to inquire about the origin of the fact itself. Once the ontological, factual content of causality was vindicated, the objective rationality of the universe was secured, and with that both science and natural theology were justified. Such was the conclusion which Romanes reached under the impact of his reflection on science as actually practiced. In the second part of his work, which, however, dealt not so much with science as with questions of ethics, he even perceived the intimate connection between intellectual history and historical theism concrete in Christianity.

Neither Romanes nor Mill was or professed to be a historian, and therefore their oversight of the historical connection between theism and science can to some extent be excused. Such an excuse cannot be offered for Ernst Mach, who saw in historical studies a means to judge more competently current aspirations in science.[52] All his historical studies did not open his eyes to the value of atomism, a shortsightedness all the more strange because he was an uncompromising advocate of psychological atomism.[53] Yet psychological atomism entitled him neither historically nor conceptually to endorse psychic determinism. In Mach's words the hands of a beggar reached out for a penny with as much necessity as a fly kept coming back to one's face.[54] Had Mach equated the movement of the fly not with the action of a beggar, of which he had no experience, but, say, with the reaching out of a writer for his pen or his wallet, he might perhaps have realized that the experimental evidence of psychological determinism was not obvious at all. At any rate, there was no logical need for such a test because in Mach's perspective mental processes were part of the behavioral complex and therefore could only be strictly determined. The success of cogitation depended on the principle of the least expenditure of energy. A further and very important aspect of Mach's biological view of knowledge was that man as a biological mechanism had already completed his adaptation. On the level of cogitation this meant that man's knowledge of the world was in its ultimate stage.[55]

Standing on such a height easily generates smugness about the process leading to it. Mach, as historian of science, is a perfect illustration. In his history of mechanics, which was in a sense the history of science in its very foundations, there was no real history but only a series of anticipations of the final truth in physics. It corresponded to Newtonian mechanics with Mach as its first genuine interpreter. No wonder that in such an outlook on scientific history there was no way of perceiving anything of the drama in which the ancient Greeks failed to secure science in spite of almost having it in their hands. Oversight of that drama should have brought into even bolder relief the rise of modern science, especially if it was true, as Mach contended, that modern "scientific enlightenment" stood in "full independence" of classical antiquity. For Mach, a historian, was not reluctant to claim that "the traces of ancient ideas, still to be found in philosophy, law, art, and science act adversely rather than constructively, and will become untenable in the long run."[56]

This rude slighting of Greek ideas in every form, including Greek science, may rightly create some suspicion about the connection with science of that "scientific enlightenment" which Mach held high. Indeed, the enlightenment in question was not derived from science but from sensationism, the brand of positivism Mach advocated. Moreover, the enlightenment in Mach's case was not so much positivistic as mystical. According to Mach's own recollection the most decisive event in his life was an experience he had at the age of eighteen. Its mystical vividness was felt by him even half a century later: "On a bright summer day in the open air, the world with my ego appeared to me as *one* coherent mass of sensations, only more strongly coherent in the ego. Although the actual working out of this did not occur until a later period, yet this moment was decisive for my whole view."[57] Three years before that experience, Mach, then a mere fifteen, read Kant's *Critique of Pure Reason*. The book, to quote his words, made "a powerful and ineffaceable impression on me, the like of which I never afterwards experienced in any of my philosophical reading."[58] Mach traced to that impression his resolve "to adopt in physics a point of view that need not be changed the moment our glance is carried over into the domain of another science; for, ultimately, all must form one whole."[59]

There was more in these words than the superficial urge of bland reductionism. Mach's urge was mystical that made him take lightly the intellectual labors of scientific discovery. Already in his first major publication, a study on the discovery and meaning of the conservation of energy, Mach declared: "If all the individual facts ... were immediately accessible to us, science would have never arisen."[60] An extraordinary phrase, which suggests that it is not scientists who create science with the eyes of their minds fixed on sensory data, but these very data give rise to science, and automatically so. The experience in our own times of the overthrow of parity in the 1950s is a major proof that it was not enough to see in the 1930s the asymmetric emission of beta rays on nuclear emulsion plates. By studying without prejudice the case history of any major scientific discovery Mach could easily have perceived that there was something seriously wrong with his sen-

155

sationism, but he was blinded by its mystical light. A small but striking illustration of this blindness is his praise of the ideographic script of the Chinese. He saw in it the genuinely sensationist and economic recording of ideas.[61] If such was the case, the Chinese could logically have been expected to be the first to formulate a viable science. That their failure in science was not a question that appealed to Mach shows something of the lack of logic in his sensationism, which hardly entitled him to point out how little the development of science takes place in a logical and systematic manner.

Clearly, it was not logical to reject Newton's ideas on space and time as absolute containers and to accept at the same time Euclidean space and time as fundamental forms of perception. It was not logical to wish with elemental force for an experience of the totality of things and then to frown on cosmology, the science of the totality of things. Mach let the visible stars play the role of reference points, but he was most reluctant to take up questions about the interaction of the totality of stars. The so-called Mach's principle of modern relativistic cosmology has at best tenuous ties with Mach.[62] It is rather the brainchild of those who tried to be enthusiastic about both Einstein and Mach, an effort tenable only as long as one does not read either Mach or Einstein carefully. Mach, an eager student of the writings of Wilhelm Wundt, creator of psychophysics, must have known about that debilitating feature of an infinite, homogeneous universe of stars, known as Olbers' paradox, on which Wundt wrote a long essay.[63] Yet Mach never mentioned the paradox, possibly because it would have put him in direct touch with that metaphysical subject matter of cosmology, the totality of consistently interacting things. It was mere rhetoric when Mach asserted, in a most genuinely cosmological context, the otherwise very sound precept that consideration of the particular should alternate with that of the total.[64]

Since in its basic nature science is cosmology, disdain of cosmology cannot help affecting one's science. Mach's crusade against atoms and relativity can give a revealing glimpse even to a layman of the manner in which Mach hampered himself as a physicist. He shifted his position on atoms only when a colleague brought to his sickbed a capsule of radium and a scintillation screen. Relativity he fought to the bitter end. But here it is not so much Mach the scientist as Mach the historian of science who is at issue. As a scientist Mach could give silent treatment to metaphysics and especially to natural theology, but as a historian of science he could not. In particular, as a historian of mechanics Mach could not ignore the fact that from Descartes to Maupertuis the foundations of mechanics were anchored in natural theology, that is, in the philosophical study of the ultimate in intelligibility and being.

How Mach was to handle this question was clear from the opening remark of his chapter "Theological, Animistic, and Mystical Points of View in Mechanics," in *The Science of Mechanics*. There he suggested that no chance reference to a living scientist would be a reference to a real believer.[65] Had Mach been attentive to the facts, he would have had to note that believers even in his time still outnumbered unbelievers among scientists and the more so the higher the quality of their science. The massive evidence for this was available in the pages of a German theological periodical and also in book form.[66] It could have been utilized in the last three editions of *The Science of Mechanics*, but Mach could hardly be factual in these matters, as he abhorred belief in God and nourished hatred for Christianity, the most positive form of that belief.[67] Hatred it was if self-contradictions are a sign of anything. The self-declared champion of liberalism was a chief opponent of Austrian Catholics trying to set up a university free of state interference, while, though a professed freethinker, he calmly administered as rector of the University of Prague the oath of Catholic orthodoxy to newly appointed professors. Nor could Mach, allegedly wholly indifferent to matters of faith, refrain from calling on all Catholics to leave the Church following the publication of the Syllabus of Pius X.[68]

The same double standard that determined his evaluation of the present also set the tone of his discussion of the past concerning the relation of science and natural theology. The bias, therefore, posed for him the problem of explaining the coming forth of good results from a bad source. The good results were practically all the basic laws of mechanics. Inertia, momentum, conservation of matter and motion, the indestructibility of work and energy, or to continue with Mach's words, "conceptions which completely dominate modern physics, all arose under the influence of theological ideas."[69] How could then theology, the source, be bad? Mach's solution to this problem was very simple. He denied that theology, or, to be more specific, faith, was the real source. Theology and faith were in their apparently crucial relation to science not a source but merely the improper garb of the proper source. The garb of Jewish and Christian monotheism was useless and deserved to be discarded. About Jewish monotheism all Mach could say was that it was by no means free from belief in demons, sorcerers, and witches; about Christian monotheism his sole remark was that in medieval times it was "even richer in these pagan conceptions."[70] Mach sounded distinctly benevolent to paganism, which he presented as deeply permeated with the "conception of a will and intelligence active in nature."[71]

Monotheism could then be readily presented by Mach as a mistaken form of man's urge to have a more comprehensive view of nature and to feel his oneness and sameness with it. In Mach's estimate this urge was the real root of science. Why that root, so widespread and strong in paganism, failed to assert itself in a scientifically sound manner in so many pagan cultures, but only in Christian Europe, was then an obvious problem which a thinker burdened as Mach was with heavy blinders could hardly perceive. The indications are that he was not entirely unaware of a problem which he seemed to prefer to keep, as it were an ominous skeleton, in a closet. That the moment of truth, which came for the historiography of science with the discovery in 1881 of Leonardo's notebooks, could not make itself felt in the first edition of Mach's *Science of Mechanics* published in 1883, is understandable. That Mach was really alerted to the significance of that discovery only a quarter of a century later, following the publication of Duhem's *Les origines de la statique* in 1905, is another matter. Not even his professed admiration for Duhem[72] made him recognize the crucial importance of those publications of Duhem on Leonardo which by 1906,[73] or seven full years before the sixth edition of the *Science of Mechanics*, had begun to shed strong light on medieval anticipations of the science of dynamics. The most Mach was willing to concede was the continuity between the Greek science of statics and its Galilean form, a continuation effected by some whom Mach refused to call medievals.[74] Not even a mere token of intellectual respectability was to be accorded to the Middle Ages and medievals by the one who left unchanged through six editions and over almost three decades a chapter on the "theological, mystical and animistic points of view of mechanics," replete with a crisp dose of agnostic propaganda.

Propagandists usually work with blinders on, and in Mach's case the blinders were neither philosophical nor scientific but plainly mystical. There is nothing wrong with being steeped in a mystical experience, provided one does not want to be known as a rationalist or empiricist all the time. The price to be paid for this self-deception, if not the deception of others, is that what is mystical will be called rational, and what is rational will be called mystical in the sense of being irrational. To see this logic at work one need not even leave Mach's discussion of the connection between science and natural theology. Mach, who saw in the splendid rationality of Judeo-Christian monotheism only the evidence of superstitious mysticism, said almost in the same breath that, once physics has been reduced to the analysis of sensations, we shall find our hunger not so essentially different from the tendency of sulfuric acid toward zinc, our will not so essentially different from the pressure of stone, and then we shall feel ourselves nearer to nature and free of the necessity to "resolve ourselves into a nebulous and mystical mass of molecules."[75] Once monotheism was no longer considered rational, molecules became mystical. Mach, who envisaged a reduction of physics to the analysis of sensations, had no right to speak about the tendency of sulfuric acid toward zinc. This tendency might have been a sensation for sulfuric acid and for zinc, and perhaps for both, but certainly not for Mach or for anyone else, however hungry to have the sensation of that tendency. Of course Mach, who had lived on that experience of everything being united in his ego, had an escape from the dilemma, but it could be used by others only if they had the same privilege of being mystics in the sense in which he was one.

The sense in question was distinctly Buddhist. Buddhism was one of the two dominating factors of Mach's last ten or so years. He was criticized for it in print as early as 1903.[76] The other dominating factor of those years was Mach's feverish effort to discredit Einstein's relativity on theoretical as well as on experimental grounds. He clearly perceived that the epistemological presuppositions of relativity and its world view struck at the root of an empiricism which he carried to its logical extreme in Buddhism. Of that extreme Mach left a priceless description in a note sent to W. Ostwald, which both agreed to withhold from publication: "After I recognized that Kant's 'thing in itself' was nonsense, I also had to acknowledge that the 'unchanging ego' was also a deception. I can scarcely confess how happy I felt, on thus becoming free from every tormenting, foolish notion of personal immortality, and seeing myself introduced into the understanding of Buddhism, a good fortune which the European is rarely able to share."[77] Kant might have mused that precisely his view of reality as based on the Ding an sich had undermined that unity of consciousness which he looked to as the rational basis of thought and science.

That the rationalism in question was akin to Buddhism and that therefore it had no kinship with science must have awakened anyone not yet wholly in the grip of Mach's sensationism. Being wholly in its grip, Mach could even speak of Buddhism as a religion most germane to science. Mach, the historian of science, cared not to reconcile his evaluation of Buddhism with the fate of science in Buddhist India. The fate was a drift into a monumental blind alley, a fact that escapes only a few Buddhists. Mach was one of them. His philosophy was in fact so much of Buddhist coinage as to prompt Philipp Frank, once a close associate of Mach, to emphasize its close resemblance to the view of Nietzsche, a chief advocate of Buddhism and of its classic doctrine of eternal returns. Frank indeed caught a glimpse of the very core of Mach's thinking, himself very fond of asserting the slow but gradual advance of science,[78] when, in speaking of the importance of Mach's philosophy for our times, he declared that "the progress of science takes place in eternal circles."[79] What Frank should have recalled in this connection was Mach's turning to Buddhism, which had again been aired shortly after he died in 1916.[80] The printed evidence, however, was not remembered by those, and Frank was one of them, who in the 1920s formed the Verein Mach, transformed afterwards into the Vienna Circle. The image they painted of Mach, an image which gained wide currency in the academe,[81] had many defects. The most glaring of these was the lack of any reference to his espousal of Buddhism. Whether its recent and amply documented exposure will effectively correct that spurious image of Mach as a positivist purist is not to be taken for granted.[82] Myths in the history of science have an unusually high endurance value.

Mach's Buddhism is not merely the mark of a full circle in the inner logic that guided him personally. It is also the mark of that full circle which science could possibly have run in a span of twice twenty centuries, starting with the first evidences of science recorded a little beyond 2000 B.C. More than the first three thousand years of that span were a pattern of historical blind alleys, a pattern of repeated stillbirths for science. The birth of science came only when the seeds of science were planted in a soil which Christian faith in God made receptive to natural theology and to the epistemology implied in it. The transition from that first viable birth to maturity was made neither in the name of Baconian empiricism nor in the name of Cartesian rationalism. The transition was made in a perspective which was germane to natural theology and which was instinctively adopted by Newton, chiefly responsible for completing that transition. The next two centuries saw the rise of philosophical movements, all hostile to natural theology. Whatever their lip service to science, they all posed a threat to it. The blows they aimed at man's knowledge of God were as many blows at knowledge, at science, and at the rationality of the universe. All those philosophical movements from Hume to Mach also meant an explicit endorsement of the idea of eternal returns, an idea which from the viewpoint of science acted as the chief road into its great historical blind alleys.

In modern times, the logic of those blind alleys has nowhere revealed its tragic frustration more keenly than in Mach, a man of great scientific and philosophical talent, a recognition which Planck and Einstein readily accorded to him. Mach's failure should appear all the more tantalizing as his most active years coincided with decades which produced cryptic evidences that classical physics was not as coherent as it appeared to be. To give physics its final coherence was Mach's great ambition. By not having real use for its future, he misinterpreted its past and missed the great opportunity of its present. His achievement as a physicist and philosopher-historian of science helped no physicist of any consequence to go forward with his task.[83] That look into the future, that decisive breakthrough for physics, was reserved to two scientific geniuses who had completed their historic feats while Mach was still alive. Their appearance on the scene was in a sense the breaking out of a circle which seemed to close upon itself and trap science within its apparent perfection. Those were the years that were marked not only by the belief of many a scientist that only two small clouds remained to be banished from the bright skies of science,[84] but also by the far more dangerous and carefully cultivated conviction that science was a mere empiricist economy of sensations. It was an economy that fed on its capital instead of being fed by it. Such "economy" in thinking about science would only lead first to the slowing down of its momentum, followed by its gradual coming to a halt, and finally to its slow demise. Sad prospects like these, if carefully thought out at that time, could have served as a retrospect into what characterized much of those twice-twenty centuries of the scientific enterprise. In the absence of seeing that prospect and of having that retrospect it was very tempting for Lord Gifford and others to look for a science of natural theology as perfect as the science of nature appeared to be. Planck and Einstein, who perceived more keenly than others that exact natural science around 1900 had very serious defects, had no professed concern for natural theology. Yet they diagnosed the situation and found the cure with the help of an epistemology which unknown to them was the common foundation of the forward road of science and of the only reliable ways for the mind to God. The evidence of this seems therefore the logical starting point of lectures that deal with science and natural theology in the twentieth century.

II

THE
TWENTIETH
CENTURY

Eleven

THE QUANTUM OF SCIENCE

THE SURVEY BY MAX PLANCK OF THE STEPS THAT LED TO HIS DIS-
covery of the quantum of action was the last major publication he saw
through print. Although written in 1943, when he was eighty-four, the
survey showed an undiminished mental vigor and a lifelong consistency in aims. Details of events long past were now spelled out by him
with a crispness suggesting the depth to which they were inscribed
in the memory of the great old man of German science. Many of
those details referred to Planck's student years. He recalled that the one
professor of physics and the two professors of mathematics to whom
he owed the foundations of his scientific training at the University
of Munich, and who in 1879 judged his doctoral dissertation, had no
appreciation for and possibly no grasp of its contents. They approved
it, Planck added, because they knew of his diligent work in the physics
laboratory and in the mathematics seminars.[1] Planck also noted that
his dissertation, which dealt with entropy in reversible and irreversible
processes, was ignored by precisely those physicists in Germany
who should have found it germane to their own researches. Helmholtz
did not read the dissertation, Kirchoff rejected it, Neumann remained
noncommittal, and Clausius turned out to be unavailable when Planck
traveled from Munich to Bonn to see him. This negative attitude must
have left an enduring and painful impression on Planck, who also
remembered in another context that he had gone to Berlin during the
winter of 1877–78 to attend Helmholtz's lectures. But as Planck was
to find out, Helmholtz was invariably unprepared, fumbling for data
in a little notebook, and making one mistake after another on the
blackboard. Within a few weeks the overflow audience of Helmholtz's
course had dwindled to a mere three. One of the faithful remnant
was the nineteen-year-old Planck, who went to Berlin to find an in-
spiring teacher worthy of his own mind, full of the highest aspirations.
So did Planck unburden himself in 1947, at the age of eighty-eight.[2]

Fifty-three years earlier, in giving his Antrittsrede at the Berlin
Academy of Sciences in 1894, Planck could not, of course, speak so
freely, and certainly not of Helmholtz. The undisputed leader of the
German scientific establishment, Helmholtz was privately referred to
as Reichskanzler of German physics, and he certainly acted as such.
Planck therefore merely noted, though not without some asperity, that
he had not had the good fortune of ever being exposed to the influence
of an outstanding teacher.[3] Planck was, intellectually at least, a lonely
young man both in choosing physics for a career and in concentrating

on theoretical physics, especially on thermodynamics. As for physics as a career, Philipp von Jolly, who held the only chair for physics, experimental physics, at the University of Munich and who was a colleague of Planck's father, told the seventeen-year-old Planck not to choose physics because hardly anything more could be done there.[4] The advice might have been fateful in the case of any other young man gifted, as Planck was, not only in the sciences but also in the classics, in music, and in mathematics. Whatever other field Planck might have chosen, he would have pursued it with the intensity of his idealism and with his unmistakable sense of future greatness, qualities that are strikingly evident in the photographs taken of him during his student years.[5]

Planck entered the University of Munich with no definite plans. "I could have become," he reminisced in 1930, "just as well a classical philologist or a historian. What led me to the exact sciences was an external circumstance, namely, a mathematics seminar given by Professor G. Bauer, which... I attended and which satisfied me within and served as stimulus; that I did not side with pure mathematics but went over to physics was due to my deep interest in questions of Weltanschauung, which could not, of course, be solved on a purely mathematical basis."[6] A deep-seated interest in Weltanschauung, that is, in a world view steeped in scientific, metaphysical, religious, and moral interests, was the leaven that produced Max Planck, one of the two outstandingly creative physicists of this century, the century of physicists.

This interest in Weltanschauung was hardly surprising in a grandson and great-grandson of Lutheran ministers and theologians. The rational justification of Planck's otherwise wholly liberal religious orientation was Neo-Kantianism, increasingly popular since Planck's student days but into which he never waded deeply. Had he done so, he would have most likely read into the *Critique* his own Weltanschauung. Its core was his belief in the objective existence of a rational, wholly harmonious cosmos in which everything was united through a single, ultimate law. That such would have been Planck's reading of Kant can safely be guessed from what he read among the works of such disparate thinkers as Rudolph Clausius and Ernst Mach. The *Abhandlungen* of Clausius fell into Planck's hands during that disappointing winter in Berlin and the impact was enormous.[7] From Clausius, Planck learned the precise notions of the first and second laws of thermodynamics, the conservation and dissipation of energy, or its entropy, and also their sharp distinctness. In his scientific autobiography Planck made it indirectly clear that his reading of Clausius had given him the conviction that Kirchoff's law of radiation implied something universal and absolute about the physical realm,[8] precisely because, according to that law, the relation of radiation and absorption of thermal energy by a body was independent of its physical properties. Radiation was a thermal process which, if it revealed something universal or absolute, could only be one of a kind. Illuminating as the law of entropy could be, it seemed to introduce into the physical absolute a duality which was hardly to Planck's liking. Indeed, his doctoral dissertation was an effort to unite the first and second laws by trying to derive both from a more general, theoretical consideration. Planck's Habilitationschrift written a year later, in 1880, was an application of his dissertation to various physicochemical phenomena. As Planck himself recalled, the impression it made on the scientific public was "gleich Null,"[9] that is, exactly zero.

With his intense commitment to an absolute embedded somehow in the physical,[10] an ontological topic he was unequipped to handle philosophically, young Planck could become an easy prey to any soaring diction on the unity of nature and of our knowledge of it once the wording was scientifically coated. Such a coating was certainly heavy in Mach's writings on the process of knowledge, and Planck himself recalled that he was a convinced Machist during his stay in Kiel,[11] where he held his first professorship from 1885 to 1889. He became an admirer of Mach without suspecting that Mach's soaring phrases guaranteed neither an objective nature nor a reliable knowledge of it. Planck's awakening from his love affair with Mach's philosophy was to come precisely through his longing for the physical absolute as something existing objectively and knowable as such. The eighty-eight-year-old Planck still felt the ardor of a young lover when he recalled the first steps of his approach through science to the absolute: "What has led me to science and made me since youth enthusiastic for it is the not at all obvious fact that the laws of our thoughts coincide with the regularity of the flow of impressions which we receive from the external world, [and] that it is therefore possible for man to reach conclusions through pure speculation about those regularities. Here it is of essential significance that the external world represents something independent of us, something absolute which we confront, and the search for the laws valid for this absolute appeared to me the most beautiful scientific task in life."[12] The first part of the statement was a subtle endorsement both of Mach and of the Kantian a priori which might have permanently trapped a mind with less genuine scientific sense. It was Planck's being possessed by that sense in an extraordinary degree that made it possible for him to escape from Mach, the scientist-philosopher, and to achieve one of the greatest creative breakthroughs in science. The two processes unfolded slowly but simultaneously, and this was also true of Planck's awareness of what was actually taking place in the innermost recesses of his mind. That both processes implied the endorsement of philosophical views pointing toward traditional natural theology remained hidden to him.

167

During the last forty years of his life he spoke as often on religion, philosophy, and ethics—Weltanschauung, in short—as on science, but he did so always with a touch of pantheism reminiscent of the old Kant. His influence Planck could never wholly escape. Neo-Kantianism was part of the cultural milieu in which Planck grew up. His reverence for that milieu—it was also the mainspring of his ardent patriotism and marked conservatism—was for him an absolute value never to be betrayed.

Planck was thirty-six when membership in the Berlin Academy was extended to him, following his promotion from extraordinarius to ordinarius at the University of Berlin a year earlier, in 1893. As with the appointment in Kiel, the invitation to Berlin was due more to external circumstances than to achievement. Planck candidly recalled that his appointment in Kiel had much to do with the fact that Gustav Karsten, professor of physics there, was a close friend of his father, who had gone from Kiel to Munich as professor of law: "I therefore considered it a matter of pride to justify the trust placed in me."[13] Of the eight papers he produced in Kiel three were on the increase of entropy and four on the thermodynamics of chemical processes. None of them was outstanding, not even the eighth, a paper on the constancy of energy, although it received the prize of the faculty in Göttingen. The chair in Berlin, the most prestigious in the First Reich, came to Planck by default when Heinrich Hertz, to whom the chair had originally been offered, opted for the University of Bonn. The ten or so papers which Planck published in Berlin as extraordinarius witnessed his continued concentration on thermodynamics. They earned him the status of ordinarius which in turn assured him of membership in the academy. The great feat, however, on which he had set his sights was still to be achieved. All these details should be kept in mind if the significance of the major points of his brief and carefully phrased Antrittsrede is to be appreciated, as the work provides a priceless insight into Planck's intellectual development and the nature and intensity of his motivation.

At the very outset Planck named the theoretical investigations in which he hoped to make useful contributions. He was, however, quick to point out that the only basis for these theoretical investigations was the principle of energy, not mechanics. "Mechanics," he stated, "proved to be inadequate. Instead of one mechanical model there are today a great number of such models [concerning basic physical processes]."[14] While the successes of the kinetic theory of gases, the principal form of atomic theory, were undeniable, Planck felt that advance along those lines had come to a standstill characterized by keen dissatisfaction. "The deeper the problem [of physics] is seen, the more complex it appears."[15] From this impasse Planck saw only one way out, the study of the two laws of energy, or thermodynamics, which appear to be wholly independent of the mechanical nature of the processes themselves: "As a firm starting point we are left with only a few principles, among them the universal law of energy."[16] This shift from mechanics to thermodynamics as a basic form of physics was seen by Planck not as an aim in itself, but a strategy "in pursuit of the ultimate, of the ever-remote goal, which consists in the presentation of all forces of nature in one single interconnection."[17]

Since he insisted that the innermost form of this connection lay in the identity of all forces, it was only natural for him to state that the role of the theoretician in pursuing this lofty goal will be indispensable though limited. The limitation was due not only to the fact that theory was useless without observational data, but also to the vastness of the problem involved. "The times are long gone when the general and the special can normally be cultivated in a single individual. Already today a gigantic intellect would be needed in that respect . . . and the miracle of such an intellect can only appear greater in the future."[18] By the gigantic intellect "in whom our academy takes its greatest pride" Planck meant Leibniz, the founder of the Berlin Academy.[19] Since Leibniz was a spokesman for scientific cooperation, Planck's remark on the need for all colleagues, theoreticians and experimentalists alike, to play confidently into each other's hands was very Leibnizian.[20] His trusting candidness earned him the generous cooperation of precisely those experimentalists, Rubens and Kurlbaum, who were doing the best work in measuring black-body radiation. By then they were impressed not only by Planck's character but also by his scientific creativity.

The unfolding of that creativity during the years 1894–1900 meant intense work, being prepared for the unexpected, and unswerving commitment to the notion of an objective, absolute truth embodied in the physical universe. The intense work was evidenced by the five papers he presented to the academy between 1897 and 1899 on the irreversible character of radiation. They showed Planck gradually approaching a lofty goal although without so much as suspecting its specific form. Another evidence of Planck's groping in the dark was the character of his first critical study on energeticism,[21] the physics of Ostwald and Mach. While they spoke profusely of energy, they shied away from the topic of its dissipation. Planck, for whom that dissipation, or entropy, had now become the cornerstone of speculation, decried energeticism without seeing the epistemological cause that made the energeticists ignore entropy. As to being prepared for the unexpected, Planck quickly sensed that in the displacement law, which Wilhelm Wien proposed in 1894 in connection with the energy distribution of black-body radiation, there was something of fundamental importance. In fact, Wien's law put the experimentally obtained curve of energy distribution in a new light for Planck, the light of the absolute.

As Planck recalled it in his scientific autobiography: "This so-called normal energy distribution represents something absolute, and since the quest for the absolute always appeared to me as the most beautiful research task, I eagerly set myself to work."[22]

Planck felt he had caught a glimpse of the absolute in the fact that the equilibrium state of black-body radiation could apparently be derived by assuming that the radiation damping of charged oscillators was conservative in contrast to their damping by ordinary resistance. This held out to him the all-important prospect that irreversible processes might be explained by conservative forces. The explanation, if successful, would dispense once and for all with the need, implied by statistical methods, of assigning a fundamental role to discontinuities and probabilities. The vagaries of Ostwald's energeticism, to which Planck was just awakening, would have received a peremptory rebuttal by the same stroke.[23] No wonder that he characterized that prospect as the task which confronted "theoretical physics more urgently every day."[24] This of course had to be the case if the survival of physics was really tied to the continuum implied by conservative forces. Planck hardly expected that the very first installment of his contribution to that task, the first of his five papers published between 1897 and 1899, would contain the switch that was to shift his train of thought in the opposite direction.

The switch was an error pointed out by Boltzmann, and under the impact of his criticism[25] Planck introduced in 1898 the notion of "natural radiation,"[26] which, by being analogous to Boltzmann's molecular chaos, could be taken as the very rebuttal of how nature appeared to Planck. On the basis of that "natural radiation" Planck was able to show by the middle of the next year[27] that the relation of the spectral distribution of equilibrium radiation to the average energy of an oscillator depended on the specific form of the dependence of the entropy of an oscillator on its energy. The determination of that specific form could be obtained by making use of Wien's recently proposed empirical formula for the frequency dependence of black-body radiation, but at the same time Wien's displacement law too had to be satisfied. This meant the appearance in that specific form of two constants. One of them, the value of which he gave as 6.885×10^{-27} erg-sec, made history under the label h given to it by Planck a year later. Something of its significance was unfolded by Planck without delay. The constant made possible the derivation of units for mass, length, time, and temperature which are "independent of specific bodies and substances, and necessarily keep their meaning for all times and for all cultures, even for extraterrestrial and extrahuman cultures, and which can be designated as 'natural units.' "[28]

This was an achievement of which Planck could rightly be proud. He did not suspect that the crucial test of his creativity still lay ahead of him. In March 1900 he still spoke with satisfaction about the explanation on the basis of his work of the "apparent paradox" of Wien's formula,[29] according to which the intensity of radiation did not indefinitely increase with decreasing wavelength. But while the formula worked for short wavelengths, there were already indications that it was unsatisfactory at the other end of the spectrum. A better formula had to be found, and all the more so as others too became interested in that "apparent paradox." One of them was Thiesen, whose work was known to Planck; another was Rayleigh, whose formula published in June 1900 remained unknown to Planck for another year. Planck spoke of nothing less than a sense of desperation, meaning dire urgency, as he recalled his feelings many years later. "Briefly summarized, what I did can be described as simply an act of desperation," he wrote on October 7, 1931, to R. W. Wood in Cambridge. In the same letter he referred to his "peaceful inclinations wary of all doubtful adventures."[30] Planck, a conservative in almost every respect and often in the best sense, did not wish to become a scientific revolutionary in the sense in which revolutions are an invitation to chaos.

Indeed, as late as 1910 he insisted that in introducing the quantum of action into physical theory "one should proceed as conservatively as possible" and make "only those changes in existing theory that proved to be absolutely necessary."[31] The existing theory was the wave theory or rather electromagnetic theory of light, belonging among, as Planck put it, "the proudest successes of physics, nay of all science," and for Planck still incompatible with the quantum of action. He was most reluctant to see the propagated light as a bundle of quanta. The remark was all the more revealing of Planck, fittingly called "the most reluctant revolutionary of all time,"[32] because he had already known for five years that the incompatibility was more a burden on classical electromagnetism than on the quantum of action. The latter's dimensions were the same as the square of electric charge divided by the speed of light,[33] a circumstance immensely strengthening the case of the quantum of electric charge, which had no natural place in classical electromagnetic theory. It is therefore very likely that Planck did not suspect the full truth of his statement made in 1911 before the German Physical Society that not only "the hypothesis of quanta will never vanish from the world," but that "with this hypothesis a new foundation is laid for the construction of a theory which one day is destined to permeate the swift and delicate events of the molecular world with a new light."[34] The first major step in the fulfillment of that prophecy was made within two years with Bohr's presentation of his theory of the hydrogen atom.

Planck accepted the role of a revolutionary only because he felt free to stick to his conviction that in spite of all appearances to the contrary the constant h would not play havoc with the consistent interaction of bodies and therefore would pose no threat to the objective, absolute character of scientific truth. In a perfectly good sense he worshiped scientific truth, which for him was the reflection of something absolute. Such is the background of a statement in his letter to Wood: "A theoretical interpretation *had* therefore to be found at any cost no matter how high."[35] What he referred to was his search for the derivation of the formula that he had found by early October 1900, a formula that satisfied both ends of the energy spectrum with an astonishing accuracy. About that search he later said that it meant for him the most intense work he had ever been burdened with.[36] The measure of that intensity even prompted him to part with his usual reserve to the extent of speaking to his seven-year-old son, Erwin, about what was going on in his mind. Erwin was his favorite child, and in later years his confidant. It was from Erwin Planck that two scientists learned during the 1930s that his father had spoken to him during walks in the woods near their house of his immediate prospect of making a discovery comparable only to those of Copernicus and Newton.[37] Both the intensity of Planck's feelings and the integrity of Erwin Planck are sufficient guarantee that we are not faced here with a legend similar to the words *eppùr se muove*, put in the mouth of Galileo a hundred years after his death.

To what extent and in what form the derivation of his formula was to put things in motion was not suspected by Planck when on December 14, 1900, he presented his epoch-making paper to the Deutsche Physikalische Gesellschaft. Actually, Planck saw his derivation of the formula in terms of discontinuous energy packets as a major corroboration of the faith of science in absolute truth and order. The only philosophical reflection in his two papers of October and December 1900 was a reiteration of the absolute as the perennial objective of science. In October he argued in support of his formula on the basis of its simplicity.[38] In December he added to the consideration of simplicity the prospect which his formula held out in a far greater measure than did other formulas for a general interpretation of fundamental questions of physics.[39] But his real pride lay with that constant which he now called h. "We consider," he declared, "E [the radiated energy] to be composed of a well-defined number of equal parts and we use thereto the constant of nature $h = 6.55 \times 10^{-27}$ erg-sec." This, he noted, "is the most essential point of the whole calculation."[40]

What made him supremely satisfied was his success in establishing the existence of basic constants and in vindicating through their interconnectedness the absolute constancy of nature. The last part of his paper presented quantitatively this interconnectedness stretching from Loschmidt's number through Boltzmann's constant to the value of the charge of the electron. "If the theory is at all correct," was his next to last remark, "all these relations should be not approximately but absolutely valid."[41] Clearly, what Planck believed he had found was not so much the quantum of action, but in and through it a supreme piece of evidence on behalf of an unbreakable bedrock: an objectively existing nature as embodiment of absolute truths which formed the very core or quantum of science, not to be fragmented in any way. This was his own interpretation of what he had achieved: "I was ready to sacrifice every one of my previous convictions about physical laws," but the core of physics was not to be sacrificed. This core was represented to him by the two great laws of thermodynamics. They, he wrote, "must be upheld under all circumstances."[42] Needless to say, his choice of those two laws was no shallow act of favoring one's own specialty. The rigorous validity of those laws implied an outlook on nature that had already vindicated itself by its enormous fruitfulness in science during the century of genius, the century of Galileo and Newton. This was indeed the point which Planck succeeded in articulating better than any other point as he was drawn deeper and deeper into defending not so much the quantum of energy as the quantum of science and the philosophy, or Weltanschauung, connected with it.

Sons often turn against their fathers, and this happened also to the father of the quantum of energy. That it could pose a threat to the quantum of science was not something entirely illogical. In his opposition to Democritus's atomism Aristotle had already warned that with the demonstration of the existence of a minimum quantity everything in science and philosophy could be subverted.[43] In identifying science and philosophy with his own system, implying the physical continuum, Aristotle patently overstated the magnitude of the threat. His exaggerated fear of atomism was a consequence of narrowness in philosophical outlook. Atomism, instead of destroying science, turned out to be a most useful tool for it, a point which Planck himself had to learn the hard way. For six years, he recalled, "I had been wrestling unsuccessfully with the problem of equilibrium between radiation and matter."[44] It could hardly escape the eyes of a candid thinker like Planck that the magic thread that led him out of the labyrinth was the atomism of kinetic theory advocated by Boltzmann, which he had opposed during the very years when he most needed it. Was it not Boltzmann's just criticism that made him adopt the notion of "natural radiation," a notion which opened his eyes to the usefulness of Boltzmann's statistical derivation of entropy on the basis that energy was the multiple of a finite number of identical quantities? Was it not that derivation that during those very strenuous weeks of late 1900 made him perceive the exponential structure underlying the successful formula of black-body radiation? Was it not that exponential structure that suggested to him a mathematical technique in which the sum of energy under the black-body radiation curve was obtained not by integration but by summation? Was not this summation the very key to the feat that crowned his effort of two decades to say something very novel and very fundamental about the absolute truth embedded in nature? Had he not learned at the very start of his university education the enormous difference between integration and summation? Did not integration deal with infinitesimally small quantities that fused into a continuum at the limit, and did not summation mean working with very small quantities, equal and permanently distinct from one another, and thus foreclosing the possibility of going to the limit?

Such reflections, which might have emerged naturally in his mind and in this very same sequence, could only make him look for the cause of the shortsightedness that had kept him from spotting the promised land and might have deprived him of the privilege of being the first to enter there. After all, his correction of Wien's formula might have conceivably been achieved by anyone skilled in the mathematical art of curve fitting. His twenty years' study of thermodynamics was not indispensable to his success. Of course, Planck knew that the study was far from being wasted. Through it he had eliminated one by one the possibilities of classical theory to cope with entropy in general and blackbody radiation in particular. But he also knew the haste required to come up in two months with the derivation of the correct formula. While he was far better prepared than anyone else to take the radically new approach, he could also muse on how close he had come to seeing someone else carry away those laurels that appeared to him most worthy of human effort.

Planck would not have been human if he had not seen this, but he was also human enough to resent the cause of the near shipwreck in his quest of a major discovery. He was not, however, human to the point of being vindictive or carrying on a personal vendetta. What mattered to him above all was the cause of science, a cause that was not to be hurried in the manner in which humans hurry. But the cause could be threatened, and threatened it was. Still it took a very human event, the suicide of Boltzmann, to trigger (and even then not hastily) a move by Planck which sent shock waves around the world of science. It was an open secret that a principal factor in the despondency that led to Boltzmann's suicide in 1906 was the influence that Mach's antiatomism exercised in Germany and even beyond.[45] Already aware of the inhibitory character of Mach's influence on his own scientific creativity, Planck could now see in Boltzmann's fate a tragic instance of that influence. By 1906 it had for several years been clear to Planck that Boltzmann was a genius, and thus the loss resulting for science from his untimely death must have appeared enormous. Planck also knew that Mach's contribution as a physicist was negligible compared with that of Boltzmann.[46] Such was the background of that ringing phrase "By their fruits ye shall know them" with which Planck closed his first (and best) public lecture on the Weltanschauung without which, he believed, science could not exist.

The lecture, delivered on December 9, 1908, in Leiden, was all the more momentous as Lorentz, the grand old man of physics at that time, had just conceded victory to Planck on the validity of the derivation of his formula, following a several-year-long dispute of international repercussions.[47] Planck's lecture consisted of four parts. Their tightly knit sequence was indicative of a composition on which much effort and time had been spent. Behind the drive of logic evident through the whole lecture there could be felt Planck's own drive for preeminence in physics, a drive which started with his choosing physics at the age of seventeen as the study most germane to the cultivation of Weltanschauung. It was no accident that his lecture was "On the Unity of the World Picture of Physics."[48] The ever-recurring theme of the lecture was the question as to what conception of the world was most profitable to physical science. The answer to the question was a matter of value judgment, an evaluation of the past and future of physics, to see whether the palm should be given to that conception of the world in which all processes, forces, and factors in nature reflected one basic unchangeable law, independent of the scientist's culture and habitat. The world presupposed by science had to be one, consistent throughout, and objectively existing. Such was the genuine foundation of the continual drive in physics toward a conceptual unification of its subject matter.[49]

It was easy for Planck to show that physics made a great step forward whenever two or more of its branches became unified. It could also be demonstrated that whatever the physicist's dependence on his various senses, he had to ignore progressively the anthropomorphic or sensory specificity of heat, sound, and tactile forces in order to work out a general mechanics based on the notion of energy. As for the future, Planck held out the hope of an eventual unification of mechanics and electrodynamics, or as he put it, of matter and of ether, in terms of energy. He had now reached the second part of his lecture, in which he pointed out the nonanthropomorphic, or objective character of the two laws of energy. The physics of the future was to have two branches, one dealing with reversible, the other with irreversible processes. While the irreversibility of heat radiation could at first be taken as a "predilection" of nature, through the "life-work of Boltzmann," Planck noted, it was elevated to the rank of a real law.[50] But Planck also insisted, and this was the climax of the third part of his lecture, that since the law in question was real, it had to be fully objective and causal. He had therefore to show that neither causality nor objectivity were preempted by Boltzmann's "life-work" based on the statistical method of kinetic theory. True, the theory permitted Boltzmann to conjure up cosmic processes running backward, but, as Planck pointed out, they were not scientifically meaningful because they could not refer to *our* universe taken as a whole and in the broadest sense. Science had its consistent unity, Planck remarked, because the universe was one and could only be one if it was truly a universe.[51] The radiation of heat with its objective and invariable dissipation was ruled, as Planck put it, by constants valid no less for physics if cultivated by denizens of Mars than for physics written by terrestrial beings.[52]

From what had been said of the conceptual road leading Planck to his great discovery of the quantum of energy, it can easily be seen that he, now exactly fifty years of age, had compressed into his lecture more than three decades of his own quest for creativity in physics. He was still to give a most personal glimpse into that quest. It came in the fourth part, where he contrasted the unity and objectivity of a world view needed by physics with the disconnected miniatures provided by the less advanced stages of physical science.[53] A return to these earlier stages was, in Planck's judgment, implied in Mach's program for science. Had Mach not been so popular, Planck could simply have ignored his claim that a scientific world picture was merely an "economic adaptation of our ideas to our perceptions to which we are driven by the fight for existence."[54] Partly because of the Darwinian and Spencerian roots of his views, Mach was immensely popular, and thus in a lecture in which the recurring theme was the question of the world picture most useful to science, Mach could not be ignored.

Planck traced Mach's popularity with physicists to the disillusion that had set in a generation earlier about mechanism.[55] Mechanical models of the ether and of the atom, absolute space and time, action at a distance, and the like, had turned out to be blind alleys, and Mach could find a favorable echo for his insistence on a return to the evidence of the senses as a starting point for striking a new path in physical inquiry. But, as Planck warned, Mach's program implied a subtle return to that anthropomorphism from which physics had to extricate itself in order to make progress. According to Planck the anthropomorphism consisted in Mach's case in his mistaking mechanics for physics,[56] a mistake rooted in the apparent ease by which Mach's sensationism could be grafted on mechanics. Sensationism implied, however, radical subjectivism, the very opposite of the world view which sustained science in its creatively best, progressive sense. That world view implied commitment to objective reality and to its unity and consistency. The objectivity in question presupposed a mental leap beyond direct sense perceptions, and as a proof Planck invoked the rapidly accumulating indirect evidence on behalf of the existence of atoms. "Atoms," he declared, "little as we know about their actual properties, are as real as the heavenly bodies, or as earthly objects around us."[57] Although the weight of a hydrogen atom and the weight of the moon were separated by forty-nine orders of magnitude, one weight involved, in Planck's words, "as much learning" as the other.[58] More pointedly, Planck referred to the "weighing" of Neptune long before it was seen, a scientific procedure that made no logical sense within Mach's sensationism. "There is not in existence," Planck added in his most momentous phrase, "a method of physical measurement in which all knowledge dependent on induction is eliminated."[59] While Mach's philosophy was no match for the marvel of induction, Planck's Neo-Kantianism could not handle it either, at least in a satisfactory manner. It was his creativity in science that kept Planck confident about the validity of induction concerning the reality of a single, objective universe.

Had Planck said nothing more on the subject, his lecture would have already contained much food for thought both for contemporaries and for posterity. As to contemporaries, steeped in philosophies ranging from Neo-Kantianism through positivism to sensationism, they could hardly see the philosophical thrust of Planck's evaluation of the most valuable form of scientific philosophy. The evaluation, sound in itself, was couched in an unconvincing philosophical diction about objective reality. Hardly more could be expected from Planck, an amateur student of Kant and a disillusioned disciple of Mach. It was of a piece with that philosophical myopia of Planck and of most of Planck's contemporaries that those who took exception to his criticism of Mach decried it as something unprofessional and unwarranted by the theme of Planck's lecture![60] As to posterity, we are still to do justice to the two concluding pages of Planck's lecture which relate to the history of science and to natural theology.

Planck's bringing in the history of science should not appear strange. No small part of Mach's fame rested on his interpretation of the history of mechanics, the apparent core of exact physical science. As the various editions of Mach's *Science of Mechanics* saw print, exception was seldom taken either to his scholarship as a historian or to his way of interpreting the facts of scientific history. Whatever erudition there was in the *Science of Mechanics* came in a large measure from the long historical essay which graced Lagrange's *Traité de mécanique analytique*.[61] As for the interpretation of facts, Mach curiously slighted some of the outstanding interpretations brought into focus, as noted in the preceding chapter, either by historical or by theoretical research. Among the former was pre-Galilean dynamics, among the latter, entropy. Though not a historian of mechanics, Planck might have spotted Mach's indebtedness to Lagrange. But what he noticed with the sure instinct of a creative scientist was that economy of thought was not the leading motivation of such great creators of modern science as Copernicus,

Kepler, Huygens, Newton, and Faraday. What moved them, Planck declared, was "their firm belief in the reality of their picture [of the world] whether founded on an intellectual or a religious basis."[62] Moreover, Planck continued, this belief of theirs did not so much refer to their *own* picture of the world as to *the* world, or nature itself.

Planck did not expect to turn the tide. He knew that much more would be written on these questions, because, as he put it, "theorists are numerous and paper is patient."[63] But he urged three points of view to be kept in focus in all future discussion. One was scrupulous self-criticism, another was respect for the personality of scientific adversaries, the third was the test of theories on the basis of the fruits they produced. On all these points Mach would readily have nodded in agreement. But the third point was phrased by Planck in a way which cut Mach to the quick. For Planck not only spoke of the trust in judging a proposition by its consequences or fruits. He spoke of a "lasting confidence in the force of the Word, which for more than 1900 years has given us ultimate, infallible test for distinguishing false prophets from true—'By their fruits ye shall know them'."[64]

A thinker deserves to be called great either because of his positive achievement or because of his consistency in building systems or because of his sensitivity to the presence of anything he is resolved to oppose. In this third respect Mach undoubtedly is a great thinker. He rightly sensed that Planck's third point had a theological overtone. It was, therefore, wholly logical for Mach to let his rejoinder reach its climax in a remark equally theological though with a sarcastic overtone. Planck's use of biblical phrases, "prophets" and "fruits," was for Mach evidence that what Planck really advocated with his epistemology was to turn the community of physicists into a church. "My answer is simple: If belief in the reality of atoms is for you so essential, I will separate myself from the way of thinking appropriate for physics, I will be no true physicist, I will renounce every scientific claim—such in short is my 'thanks' to the community of believers. Freedom of thought is dearer to me."[65]

Planck's rejoinder,[66] like his Leiden lecture, was remembered, if at all, only for some of its incidentals. That Planck was right in pressing Mach on the meaning of "economy of thought" was true, but this was not the real issue between them. Nor was there anything crucial in Mach's contradicting himself by declaring every form of thought relative and yet presenting his own "economy" as something absolutely superior to all other systems of thought.[67] Modern cosmologists, however frequent their references to the so-called Mach's principle, do not remember a devastating though not central remark of Planck's: that on the basis of Mach's notion of relative motion it made no difference whether the stars had an infinitely large angular momentum or none at all.[68] Historians of science have failed in their turn to notice that if a principal aspect of Mach's reading of the history of mechanics could be so illogical, then perhaps there was something seriously wrong with the logic of the whole reading. Planck's reliance on a biblical phrase has been recalled only in a small farce on Planck as father confessor trying to convert Mach, the sinner.[69]

Planck himself seemed to be apologetic about phrases behind which, as he admitted, "Christianity could be smelled in disguise."[70] But the phrase about fruits, however Christian, could not be improved upon, Planck insisted, and certainly not within the outlook of Mach's economy of thought.[71] Economy without fruits was no economy. Planck certainly did not want Christianity to enter the scene even in disguise, nor did he wish to be known as a Christian. His Christianity never went beyond mere formalities such as reciting prayers before and after meals when courtesy demanded, or acting when good manners required as elder in the Lutheran church near his home in Grünewald.[72] When toward the end of his life a newspaper reported that he had been converted to Catholicism, a professed atheist in Germany quickly asked him about his reasons for doing so. Planck, already near death, cared to send a reply which, if it had been made public immediately, would have quashed rumors about his conversion: "While from youth on I was deeply attuned to the religious, I do not believe in a personal God, let alone in a Christian God."[73]

The God Planck professed to believe in was as pale an entity as Spinoza's God, a God toward whom one could not, logically speaking, have a relation of existential dependence. But the fact was that Planck not only did what a Spinozist was not supposed to do, namely, acknowledge his dependence on God; he even expressed trust in his goodness, thereby ascribing to God that very personal trait which Spinoza's God could not have under any circumstance. The circumstance that demolished Planck's carefully cultivated pretension about his Spinozist religiosity was the tragic death of his son, Erwin. Word of his execution in late 1944 came to Planck when everything else—home, country, science—seemed to have fallen in ruins around him. What nothing could demolish within him was his long-ignored faith in God. A Spinoza would never have written what Planck now wrote to a friend: "What helps me is that I consider it a favor of heaven that since childhood a faith is planted deep in my innermost being, a faith in the Almighty and All-good not to be shattered by anything. Of course his ways are not our ways, but trust in him helps us through the darkest trials."[74]

Planck did not seem to realize that such words were logical only if God was in some mysterious way a personal God, a notion which, even in its vaguest form, was a remnant of Planck's heritage from Christian

179

theism. He never perceived the measure of his debt to that heritage. To the end he waged a spirited crusade on behalf of a world view distinctly metaphysical and ethical,[75] without seeing that it made logical sense only if the world was the product of a rational, personal Creator, a notion maintained by historic Christianity and from which the republic of science received crucial benefit. He repeatedly uttered memorable phrases about the faith needed by science and scientists,[76] again without seeing that this faith in the enduring rationality of the cosmos made sense only as long as the world, its laws, and (not least) its constants, were *given* in the deepest ontological sense. Was it not Planck who insisted on that *givenness*, especially with reference to those natural constants wholly independent of race, time, and even of cosmic habitat? The universality of all those constants was tied through his own constant into a fundamental facet expressive of the manner in which the universe operated through the communication of energy from atom to atom. It had to appear a most peculiarly tailored communication to any observer capable of a little reflection. While entities determined by the constants provided the material of the fabric of the universe, the h was the label of the manner in which they were knit together into a superbly working unit.

Planck, an avowed admirer of Spinoza, might have profited by reflecting on Spinoza's puzzlement at the existence of finite entities.[77] In addition to finite entities, such as atoms, electric charges, and the like, there was their peculiarly specific interaction. Neither the entities themselves nor their interaction could be conceived as necessary. Their peculiarity rather suggested that they were contingent, the very opposite of necessary. That peculiarity was nowhere condensed and embodied more tellingly than in the constant which he christened h. Together with its bafflingly peculiar numerical magnitude, it was to be the only decoration on the tombstone of Max Planck, who had chosen physics because it was particularly akin to Weltanschauung. Although he never perceived the full logic of the fact that his creativity in science kept him attached to a world view laden with genuine metaphysics, great creative advance once more showed—now through Planck's work—that the world needed and interpreted by science meant advancing toward a realm beyond.

Twelve

THE QUANTITY OF THE UNIVERSE

HAD PLANCK AND EINSTEIN NOT BEEN THE TWO DECISIVELY CREATIVE minds in twentieth-century science, they would still represent so much in common as to make it almost impossible not to discuss Einstein immediately after speaking of Planck. Their creativity was, of course, the ultimate reason why their careers ran side by side for two full decades in the Berlin Academy. But long before coming to Berlin on Planck's pressing invitation, Einstein, twenty years Planck's junior, joined forces with him by becoming the first to see the immense potentialities of Planck's discovery of the quantum of action, which until 1905 was but rarely mentioned in scientific circles, and never with a hint of its far-reaching significance. In 1905, in three months of extraordinary concentration accompanied by threats of mental breakdown, Einstein completed three papers, any one of which would have inscribed his name in the annals of physics. The first was on light as consisting of quanta; the second on particles of atomic size responsible for the Brownian motion; the third on the electrodynamics of moving bodies in terms of what later became known as the theory of special relativity.[1] It was six more years before Planck came around to seeing light, as Einstein did, in the light of his own quantum of action. But the creative character of Einstein's paper on special relativity was immediately clear to Planck. It was he who accepted it for the *Annalen der Physik* and he was the first to hold a seminar on it.[2]

Nothing shows better the measure of Planck's esteem for Einstein than Planck's referring in 1909 to him as the Copernicus of the twentieth century.[3] It was in that year that Planck and Einstein first met at the annual congress of German scientists where Planck still cautioned any and all against Einstein's theory of light based on the quantum of action. But two years later, at the first Solvay conference, Einstein succeeded in convincing Planck and wrote to a friend about the outcome: "Planck is an utterly honest man. He handles arguments with no consideration of his own personal views."[4] This second meeting between Planck and Einstein triggered Planck's plan to bring Einstein to Berlin. The plan, which took two years to implement, was a challenge most appropriate for Planck. An unabashed patriot, Planck wanted to secure Einstein for German science by creating for him a position which involved only rights and benefits, although ultimately it was science and a special Weltanschauung based on it that Planck wanted to promote. The proof of this was Planck's memorandum to the Prussian government in which he argued that Einstein's scientific contributions should be viewed also in their bearing on epistemology,[5] and who was there to recognize better than Planck, by then Mach's chief antagonist, the crucial role of epistemology for science and Weltanschauung!

On a cursory look it could appear almost contrary to present Einstein in 1912 as a champion of epistemology in the sense in which Planck intended. In the same year Einstein failed to protest when Joseph Petzold, Mach's most industrious ally, declared that relativity was a victory over metaphysical absolutes.[6] Worse still, Einstein signed the same year an antimetaphysical manifesto.[7] It was possibly a run of good luck both for Planck and Einstein that Planck had no information about those declarations of loyalty which Einstein made to Mach during 1909–13. They were all the more striking as Einstein used Planck for a dark background. In a letter written on August 9, 1909, to Mach, Einstein praised the influence of Mach's *Science of Mechanics*, adding that thirty years earlier even Planck would have been considered a Machist by all physicists.[8] A few days later Einstein acknowledged in effusive terms Mach's immediate reply and signed his letter: "Your respectful student, Einstein."[9] Two years later, during a visit with Mach, Einstein declared that their views on atoms were much the same.[10] In 1913, Einstein sent a reprint of his paper on gravitation and the equivalence of accelerated frames of reference to Mach,[11] together with a letter in which he referred to the eventual observation of the bending of light rays around the sun. Through such an eventuality, Einstein added, "your inspired investigation into the foundation of mechanics—despite Planck's unjust criticism—will receive a splendid confirmation fully in the sense of your critique of Newton's bucket experiment."[12] In writing this, Einstein could not be unaware of Planck's well-known, incisive criticism of that critique, which implied, as noted in the last chapter, the patently absurd consequence that, according to Mach's position, it made no difference whether the stars had an infinitely large angular momentum or none at all.[13]

All that Planck could know at this point about the ties between Mach and Einstein was Mach's endorsement of the theory of relativity in 1909 in the second edition of his book on *The History and Root of the Principle of the Conservation of Energy*. Curiously, neither Planck nor Einstein were surprised to find Mach saying there in a freshly added note that the latest advances in physics were turning into a reality his often expressed view that the "foundations of physics may be thermal or electric."[14] Such a view, or rather self-imposed myopia, revealed what Mach had really always been, not a physicist or a historian of physics but a philosopher of sensations. The indisputable evidence of this had already been drawn up by him, though neither Planck nor Einstein could know about it in 1913. In that year Mach wrote a preface to his book on physical optics[15]—to appear in print only eight years later—a preface which proved, if proof was needed at all, that in 1913 the genuine interpreter of Einstein's relativity was not Albert Einstein, but Max Planck and Ernst Mach: Planck, by perceiving and enthusiastically endorsing its absolutist character, Mach by repudiating it for being precisely such.

Planck knew, of course, of that telltale reaction of Einstein, who in 1907 brushed aside the relevance of data which Kaufmann presented against the increase of the mass of electrons with velocity, a prime consequence and criterion of special relativity. According to Einstein, Kaufmann's data, the correctness of which he did not dispute, were of no consequence because they supported no theory even remotely as broad in its assumptions as the theory of special relativity.[16] Such was a remark that no genuine Machist could make. Far more important for Planck than such particulars was his general standard—by their fruits ye shall know them—to evaluate science and the creativity of scientists. Long before Einstein began to suspect the real physiognomy of his own mind, Planck had already diagnosed it correctly. Around 1913, when general relativity was still to be formulated in full, there was no question in Planck's mind that if a physical theory ever witnessed the absolute in the physical world, the theory of general relativity did so. Ten years after Einstein had arrived in Berlin, Planck became the first to put general relativity in that light in a widely publicized lecture, the title of which, revealingly enough, was "From the Relative to the Absolute."[17] Planck brought his lecture to a climax with a reference to the absolute value of the metric in the four-dimensional space-time manifold. This was one of the four evidences marshaled by Planck in support of his theme. Another evidence, the absolute value of energy in terms of mass, was also of Einsteinian provenance, and Planck drew special attention to what he called the "paradox" of relativity: instead of relativizing everything, it unfolded absolute, objective aspects of the physical world.[18]

A far more important reason for bringing in Planck at this point lies in the fact that at about the same time Einstein was beginning to present his philosophy of science along lines that at a cursory view could appear to be mere replicas of Planck's principal themes. Einstein, of course, was no echo of anyone. He spoke his mind with a verve and abandon which went more directly to the heart of the matter than Planck's often laborious and always solemnly meticulous utterances. As a philosopher of science, and above all as a philosopher of his own creative science, Einstein from the 1920s on spoke with that touch of originality which also characterized even the style of his scientific papers from almost the very start.[19] Once Mach's preface to his book on optics awakened Einstein from his Machist slumber, he made statements on Mach which in their sharpness revealed more of Mach's philosophy than did methodical arguments. The sharpness of those statements was due less to a personal disenchantment than to seeing his own mental physiognomy for the first time in its true nature, and not masked by a Machist crust. Once this crust was removed, Einstein's reflections upon himself bubbled forth in the unabashed freedom of one who at long last had discovered himself.

Einstein could now see that although like Mach he had read Kant's *Critique* as a teen-ager,[20] unlike Mach he did not remain its captive. It had also become clear to Einstein that his youthful enthrallment with cosmic vistas had a character diametrically opposed to that of the young Mach. In Mach's case the cosmos was reduced to his own ego and sensations. In Einstein's case the cosmos loomed large in its own right and in its least sensory aspects. There was little if anything sensory in the way in which the sixteen-year-old Einstein wondered—as the sixty-six-year-old Einstein recalled—whether one could have a time-independent light wave if one followed it with the speed of light.[21] The question was as far from the sensory as it was close to that objective core of physical reality which was of paramount importance for physics. Einstein might also have recalled that in a letter written in 1901 he had commented on intermolecular forces, the theme of his first scientific paper published in the same year, in the following words: "As regards science I have got a few wonderful ideas in my head which have to be worked out in due course. I am now almost sure that my theory of the power of attraction of atoms can be extended to gases and that the characteristic constants for nearly all elements could be specified without undue difficulty.... It is a magnificent feeling to recognize the unity of a complex of phenomena which appear to be things quite apart from the direct visible truth."[22] How un-Machist, and one may add, un-Ostwaldian a statement for the twenty-three-year-old graduate of the Zurich Polytechnique who in the same year had begged Ostwald to take him as assistant! Einstein's high regard for Ostwald was well known to Einstein's father, who, when no reply came from Ostwald, wrote to Ostwald that of all living scientists he was esteemed most by his son.[23]

This Ostwaldian and Machist crust was completely removed from Einstein by 1922. The chief event in that year for Einstein was his visit to Paris, where he was in part admired because of his refusal in October 1914 to sign a statement in which ninety-three German scientists rejected the charge that Germany was responsible for the war.[24] In Paris Einstein provoked not only admiration but also some surprise, especially during his discussion of the philosophical problems of relativity with a blue-ribbon panel of French philosophers. To Léon Brunschvicg, who queried him on his relation to Kant, Einstein replied that he had differed from Kant's philosophy precisely on the question of the a priori, a necessary category for Kant.[25] To Emile Meyerson, who brought up Einstein's relation to Mach, Einstein characterized the potentiality of Mach's method as one which would provide a catalog but not a system.[26] To underscore his statement Einstein added that "in the measure Mach was a 'bon méchanicien' he was a 'déplorable philosophe'."[27] Once more, it must be emphasized, these first public disavowals by Einstein of Mach, the philosopher of science, had motivations which were not only deeper than personal resentment, but also antedated the publication of Mach's preface to his book on optics. True, in 1916 Einstein warmly eulogized Mach as one who under more favorable circumstances might have very well discovered the theory of relativity precisely because of his interest in epistemology.[28] But a year later, in a letter to his close friend, Michel Besso, Einstein wrote of an essay of Adler, a protagonist of Mach, that Adler "rides Mach's poor horse to exhaustion." In his reply the astonished Besso, an admirer of Mach, pictured Einstein, the relativist, as a latter-day Don Quixote riding Mach's horse. Einstein, as if cut to the quick, replied: "I do not inveigh against Mach's little horse; but if you wish to know, this is what I think of it: it cannot give birth to anything living, it can only exterminate harmful vermin."[29]

In the measure to which Einstein realized the extent of his disagreement with Mach, he perceived the similarity of his intellectual motivations to those of Planck. This change in Einstein's self-evaluation had been fairly well known by the late 1920s. It was only his Machist and positivist admirers who failed to see the evidence. Philipp Frank, for instance, had to learn at the congress of German physicists in Prague in 1929 from a "well known German physicist" that "Einstein was entirely in accord with Planck's view that physical laws describe a reality in space and time that is independent of ourselves." Moreover, Frank had to learn of this shortly after he had warned German physicists against metaphysics and urged them to embrace Mach's intellectual bequest.[30] In 1930, Moritz Schlick, already the founder of the Vienna Circle, received from Einstein himself the hardly pleasant news that he had found Schlick's "whole presentation [of physical theory] too positivistic." In the same letter Einstein described himself as "the metaphysicist Einstein," adding that "every four- and two-legged animal is de facto ... a metaphysicist."[31] Schlick never came to notice the fact, let alone the depth, of what Einstein had published a year earlier on physical theory. Such a theory, according to Einstein, not only had to find out how nature's transactions were carried out but also why nature was exactly the way it was and not otherwise. In fathoming that latter point, Einstein wrote, the scientist experiences the deepest, nay the religious motivation of his work to the point of perceiving that God himself could not have arranged connections between things in any other way than the actually existing one.[32]

Such a formulation of the very core of scientific work was wholly nonpositivist, although it does not do full justice to Einstein's views. He was not an idealist sold on an a priori clarification of the mysteries of the universe. An a priori approach was at most a temptation to him but not a program, let alone a creed. Certainly the one who expressly endorsed Planck's conception of the epistemological status of physical laws and his belief in the metaphysical quest of science could not be the champion of a priorism.[33] The a priori ring of Einstein's foregoing statement on the scientist's religious motivation was an accidental byproduct of the vehemence with which he dismissed positivism. Indeed, his endorsement of Planck on epistemology was meant to be an introduction to Planck's broadside against positivism.[34] It also signaled the beginning of Einstein's asserting in unmistakable terms the nonpositivist roots of his own creativity in science. First came, in January 1931, an address at the California Institute of Technology in which Einstein, while praising Michelson for his experiment on ether drift, carefully avoided seeing in that experiment the experimentum crucis, or trigger, for his theory of relativity.[35] With this Einstein dissociated himself from an already stereotyped claim of positivist historians and philosophers of modern physics, but they took no notice of this.[36] Even more specific was Einstein's contribution to the commemorative volume on Maxwell. The opening phrase of that essay might have been written by Planck himself: "The belief in an external world independent of the perceiving subject is the basis of all natural science."[37]

The strong disavowal of positivism contained in that phrase should seem all the more precious because in the next breath Einstein made it very clear that he was not the prisoner of a prioristic cravings. Appealing as could a physical theory seem by doing justice "to perceived facts in the most logically perfect way," it could not be final because "sense perception gives information of the external world or physical reality indirectly." What Einstein meant to say was that since sense perceptions are an ongoing process, the possibility of new information about the physical world remains ever present, an obvious source of incompleteness in physical theory. This meaning was not, however, strengthened by his remarks that we can grasp physical reality only by speculative means and that our notions of physical reality can never be final. The remarks, which implied a subtle relapse into Kantianism and an oversight of the fact that physical theory was not a notion about physical reality but merely implied it, still revealed his instinctive groping for a median position in epistemology. On its basis it logically followed that the status of final truth could not be accorded even to a theory like that of Maxwell's, although it embodied two characteristics most desirable in physical theory. One was the inclusive character which accounted for all that was then known in electromagnetics. The other was Maxwell's effort to justify those equations by abstract or general considerations.[38] Einstein found his own mind reflected in Maxwell's basic motivations, according to which the value of a physical theory was to be measured by its inclusiveness or universality concerning phenomena, and by the generality of its intellectual justification. This generality in turn implied for Einstein the notion of continuity, and thus his essay came to a close with his voicing the hope—it was the first time he had done so in a prominent context—that physicists would not satisfy themselves, in the long run at least, with the discontinuities and indirectness built into the epistemology of quantum mechanics.[39]

Two years later, in giving his famous Herbert Spencer Memorial Lecture in Oxford, Einstein provided further evidence that he viewed the whole development of science through his own creative experience, which entailed a realistic metaphysics and epistemology occupying a middle position between idealism and positivism. He was offering a key to his own mental odyssey and to the whole history of exact science in that phrase which opened his speech and which has since become a classic: "If you want to find out anything from the theoretical physicists about the methods they use, I advise you to stick closely to one principle: don't listen to their words, fix your attention on their deeds."[40] The deeds he had in mind were the deeds of a mind working intellectual miracles and setting an example to be emulated forever. As one might expect, Einstein evoked ancient Greece as the cradle of Western science, where "for the first time the world witnessed the miracle of a logical system," Euclid's geometry.[41] As a genuine scientist, however, Einstein had to be wary of trusting unconditionally his or any mind, even that of Euclid. Scientific discourse about physical reality had to be controlled by physical facts, a precept which he learned through his instincts as a genuine physicist and not through his reading of Euclid's abstractions.

Neither his being a physicist nor his reading of Euclid made him sensitive enough to the control which the facts of the history of science ought to exercise on remarks about it. It was hardly a factual reading of scientific history when Einstein summarily credited Kepler and Galileo with being the fathers of modern science through their insistence that "experience is the alpha and omega of all our knowledge of reality."[42] Einstein could have easily seen the decisive role that Galileo gave to theory (with even a heavy touch of the a priori) by reading Galileo's *Dialogue* as he was writing a foreword to its English translation.[43] As he graced a translation of Kepler's letters with a foreword Einstein remained equally blind to the heuristic role which Kepler attributed to geometry.[44] Remarks like these may indicate the extent to which Einstein remained a captive of Mach the historian of science, whom he had always held in high esteem.[45] It was only while watching himself that Einstein was able to see the true nature of his own creative deeds in science, and this he did with increasing clarity.

From his Spencer Lecture on, Einstein took more and more frequently a look at his own creative steps, and whenever he spoke of this to the world it was a variation on the same theme, the marvelous inventiveness of the human mind. This inventiveness was not, however, caprice in any sense. The avenues to its marvels, though not securing automatic progress, were clearly recognizable in a broad sense. The chief of those avenues was steeped in the invariable, absolute, geometrical beauty of nature. If this was the case with nature, true scientific knowledge of it had to reflect that beauty. Such was the avenue along which Einstein proceeded in formulating both special and general relativity. In the first case he did so instinctively, but in the second case with full awareness of what he was doing. His two theories were in a sense mislabeled with the word *relative*, because both the special and general theories of relativity were more absolutist in character and content than any other scientific theory.[46] Their starting point was not a positivist aggravation with experimental incongruities, but a burning desire to safeguard the beauty of nature and of laws which reflected that beauty. Such laws were Maxwell's equations. To protect their simple beauty from deformation, to which they were subject while being referred from one inertial system to another, Einstein preferred to part with the simple rules of correlating inertial frames of reference. Such was the birth of special relativity in that classic paper on the electrodynamics of moving bodies. A paradoxical birth indeed. The simple beauty of Maxwell's equations was safeguarded by according to them the utmost generality, which in turn imposed a most specific singularity, the invariable constancy of the speed of light. The measure of that speed, the same regardless of the motion of light-emitting bodies, was a powerful indication that the beauty of nature was most singular in its utmost generality.[47]

The fruitfulness of special relativity was an invitation to Einstein to unfold even more of the constant beauty of nature and of the exact science of that beauty. It was an undertaking far more taxing than the working out of special relativity, which had taken not even a year's intellectual labor. The theory of general relativity was in the making for about ten years. To formulate the interrelation of accelerated frames of reference in a way satisfying their covariance was one thing. To fill them with physical content was another. The most universal case of constant acceleration was provided by gravity, but no branch of physics was in a sense less explored than gravitation. Until Einstein, the innumerable cases of gravitational acceleration had been studied as examples of the inverse square law in connection with inertial frames of reference. In the theory of general relativity that same acceleration was to stand for all similar accelerations and for any and all accelerated frames of reference. Being a scientific law, this generalization had to have not only an inherent beauty, but also an ability to predict unsuspected effects of gravitation. The first of these new effects, the bending of light in a strong gravitational field, was perceived by Einstein as early as 1907,[48] but it was only in 1911 that he realized that it might be detected during a full solar eclipse.[49] It took four more years before he was able to draw two other consequences of general relativity. They were the gravitational red shift of light and the advance of the perihelion of planets, detectable only in the case of Mercury.[50] He now had for his theory three supports which were all the more priceless because they were not dependent on one another and showed that Newton's great synthesis of gravitation was but a limiting case of general relativity. The latter took four more years to be worked out to Einstein's satisfaction. Einstein could then rightly feel, as he wrote to Sommerfeld on November 28, 1915, that "I have just lived through the most exacting period of my life; and it would be true to say that it has also been the most fruitful."[51] He no longer had to fear, as he put it, that "my field equations of gravitation had been entirely devoid of foundation."[52]

The crowning feat of Einstein's work was still to be achieved. Here, too, the achievement was similar to that of Newton but on a much higher level and in a far more general sense. Newton's *Principia* ended with a discussion of the "system of the world," the world meaning the solar system, a puny part of the cosmos. In fact, on the basis of Newtonian gravitation one could only speak of relatively puny parts of the cosmos and never of the whole of it. The homogeneous distribution of an infinite number of stars, the accepted picture of the cosmos from Newton's time on, implied an infinitely large gravitational force on the basis of the inverse square law of gravitation.[53] Scientific meaning could not therefore be secured for the cosmos as a whole in a Newtonian outlook and on a Newtonian basis. Newton, however, never entertained the idea held by Seeliger, an older contemporary of Einstein, who in order to save the Newtonian cosmos from the teeth of its gravitational paradox, postulated a zero density of matter at infinity.[54] Einstein, almost invariably defective on details of scientific history, seemed to ascribe Seeliger's procedure to Newton in his memoir on the "Cosmological Consequences of the General Theory of Relativity," published in 1917,[55] a memoir which was to be the first chapter of truly scientific cosmology. It was easy for Einstein to show that the procedure in question was self-defeating because, if Boltzmann's gas theory was right, zero density at infinity meant zero density everywhere.[56] This, however, meant turning the whole cosmos into sheer nothingness. A universe of infinite mass could be freed of this contradiction by giving it, for instance, a cylindrical structure through a modification of Poisson's equation, but, as Einstein himself noted about this device of his own, it "does not in itself claim to be taken seriously, it merely serves as a foil for what is to follow."[57]

What followed was the specification of boundary conditions for the cosmos according to the general theory of relativity, and this meant that the universe was unbounded but finite. The space, or rather the set of lines of motion generated by the finite mass of the cosmos was curving back on itself. Thus it was possible for the first time to speak of the whole cosmos to the point of sizing it up in a strictly quantitative manner, and without suggesting that there were limits to the cosmos in an anthropomorphic sense. Such a cosmos, as Einstein put it, was not "running the risk of wasting away"[58] in spite of the fact that the total mass M of the universe was finite and could be exactly calculated.[59] Such was the reward of traveling on a "rough and winding road," as Einstein characterized in retrospect his intellectual journey.[60] It was a creative journey to the new science of cosmology, a science about the quantity and quantitative structure of the universe. It was a science which could only be had as a whole, as an indivisible quantum of science, or not to be had at all. Such was the deepest aspect of the identity between the two creative giants of modern physics, Planck and Einstein, and between the culminating points of their creative labors, the quantum of action and the quantity of the universe.

The cosmos now roughly approximated a spherical space, but in a consistent four-dimensional sense. This spherical space corresponded to a positive curvature, and this gave Einstein great satisfaction. About spherical space he hastened to point out two things. One was that this positive result could possibly be safeguarded even without the so-called cosmological constant,[61] which two years later he had decided to eliminate.[62] His motivation for this was that the constant was "gravely detrimental to the formal beauty of the theory."[63] This reference to the role of beauty in scientific considerations was only one of his many such references, but its presence here in the crucial context of the birth of scientific cosmology cannot be emphasized strongly enough. The other point was that the consistent scientific notion of the cosmos was achieved by giving "an extension to the field equations of gravitation which is not justified by our actual knowledge of gravitation."[64]

Positivists, especially those of the virulent Machist strain, could only gasp as they watched relativity make headlines after the observation at Recife of the bending of starlight around the sun during its eclipse in 1919. Had World War I not prevented using the solar eclipse in 1914 for the same purpose, Mach himself might have seen that scientific expeditions could be motivated not only by curiosity about sensory evidence to be collected, but with the anticipation of specific results having their sole basis in theory. Special and general relativity were not born out of consideration for sensory evidence but out of thoughtful reflection on what ought to be the proper approach to any such evidence. "A great adventure in thought had at length come safe to shore," Whitehead commented six years after the announcement of the Astronomer Royal to the Royal Society concerning the evaluation of photographic plates taken during that eclipse of 1919. The comment brought out forcefully the nonpositivist core of Einstein's achievement, already celebrated in a remark of Whitehead's which immediately preceded. This was about a drama which no facts but only intellectual insight could produce: "There was dramatic quality in the very staging—the traditional cere- monial, and in the background the picture of Newton to remind us that the greatest scientific generalisation was now, after more than two cen- turies, to receive its first modification."[65] Such great generalizations are a feat of the intellect probing the rational content of matters of fact, a feat to which positivists simply blind themselves. All their comments on general relativity—and how authoritatively they often were handed down—failed to come even within striking distance of what Bernard Shaw, an outsider to science, grasped unerringly when he remarked that "Einstein has not challenged the facts of science but the axioms of science and science has surrendered to the challenge."[66]

The best thing that could be done by a positivist was to praise Ein- stein's theory and to talk away its metaphysical stings. Of these the most conspicuous was the cosmological part, in which Einstein em- phatically called attention to the finiteness of the mass composing the universe.[67] Contrary to Einstein's original model, the mass had a uni- formly expanding movement, but this fact could bring comfort to the infinitists only in that the expansion did not necessarily have to be con- ceived as a once-and-for-all process. Indeed, in 1945, when Einstein gave his last written comment on the cosmological question,[68] the data of galactic counts seemed to leave this question open. But in all cases a scientific cosmology, which could consistently be constructed on gen- eral relativity, bespoke a most singular universe. Positivists could not help sensing that in achieving for the first time in the history of cosmol- ogy a scientifically meaningful formulation of it could mean the reopen- ing of the long-discredited book of natural theology. The validity of scientific cosmology implied the validity of our notion of the universe as the totality of all material entities interacting with one another. The universe of general relativity was such a universe, and validly so in the scientific sense. This had to be a deadly blow at Kant's hallowed claim that our notion of the totality of things, or the universe, was not valid knowledge—the claim on which Kant based his contention that no way to God starting from the universe was reliable. Positivists and operationists must have sensed this implication, or else one is at a loss to understand their tactics of silence, of diversion, and of evasion concerning the touchstone of scientific cosmology, the subtle limitedness of the universe.[69]

Einstein himself had a vivid realization of the broader vistas of his cosmology. For him genuine scientific knowledge about the cosmos was not sensory evidence, but a cosmic leap beyond the sensory. The scientific reliability of that leap filled him with the greatest wonder, an intellectual stance repeatedly discredited since Descartes. Whatever philosophy Einstein had inherited, it cautioned him against marveling. Nor did he have any religion to attune him to wonderment. It was his creative scientific instinct which made him marvel at the mind as well as at the world, and to perceive thereby new vistas for science. For him the comprehensibility of the world was a miracle,[70] and so was science. His best statement about the history of science came when he viewed it as a universal problem in epistemology. In that outlook the ultimate problem was not why the Chinese of old failed in science, but rather why science was born at all.[71] Moreover, if it was true that there was no logical (that is, mechanical) road to discovery, as Einstein repeatedly, emphatically, and most correctly, emphasized,[72] science could not develop in a mechanistic way along the empiricist road specified by Mach's sensationism, Einstein's endorsement of Mach the historian of science notwithstanding.

The superficial and uninformed agreement between Einstein, never a historian of science, and Mach, the somewhat informed but always tendentious historian of science, should not conceal the enormous difference between Einstein and Mach concerning epistemology and cosmos. Mach would have labeled Einstein a Trojan horse for theology had he lived to read some of Einstein's letters to his old Machist friend, Maurice Solovine. Mach, who claimed that there would be no need for science if all sensations were available to us, could only have disagreed violently with Einstein, who in his letter of January 1, 1951, to Solovine spoke of the miraculous character of man's ability to comprehend the world.[73] If there was any project dear to Mach it consisted in showing that nothing was miraculous in the act of knowledge and precisely because of this there was no reason whatever to look beyond our sensations in an ontological sense. Ontology, as Mach unerringly sensed, smacked of metaphysics and of theology. Moreover, the fragmentary character of our sensations barred within the Machist context the possibility of knowing something about the cosmos as a whole. No wonder that Solovine, the Machist, fell to wondering about his friend Einstein. His reply to Einstein provoked Einstein not to a retraction but to something akin to a theological profession of faith: "You find it surprising," he wrote to Solovine, on March 30, 1952, "that I think of the comprehensibility of the world (insofar as we are entitled to speak of such world) as a miracle or an eternal mystery. But surely, a priori, one should expect the world to be chaotic, not to be grasped by thought in any way. One might (indeed one *should*) expect that the world evidenced itself as lawful only so far as we grasp it in an orderly fashion. This would be a sort of order like the alphabetical order of words. On the other hand, the kind of order created, for example, by Newton's gravitational theory is of a very different character. Even if the axioms of the theory are posited by man, the success of such a procedure supposes in the objective world a high degree of order, which we are in no way entitled to expect a priori. Therein lies the 'miracle' which becomes more and more evident as our knowledge develops." To this Einstein added the even more revealing remark: "And here is the weak point of positivists and of professional atheists, who feel happy because they think that they have preempted not only the world of the divine but also of the miraculous. Curiously, we have to be resigned to recognizing the 'miracle' without having any legitimate way of getting any further. I have to add the last point explicitly, lest you think that weakened by age I have fallen into the hands of priests."[74]

Einstein was then seventy-three, still in full command of his mental powers and still pursuing vigorously his ultimate scientific aim, the unified field theory, a theory in which gravitation and electrodynamics were but different aspects of a more general law. He failed, but there was an Einsteinian greatness in his failure. It was not unclear to him that success demanded more than simplicity of equations. He tried many of them, often making the comment that they were so beautifully simple that God himself would not have passed them over.[75] But he also knew that beyond simplicity of forms there was need for a simplicity of principles, like the ones that guided him in connection with special and general relativity. Far more important, he knew in the measure in which the true physiognomy of his creative science had become clear to him that those principles had to relate to an objectively existing totality of things, or the universe. Such a universe was not the creation of the mind, nor could its high degree of order be expected a priori. The orderly world was something given. Moreover, Einstein, the scientist, knew that the specific form of that order could not be derived a priori if the need for experimental verification was to retain any meaning. Finally, Einstein, the philosopher-scientist, perceived that such a train of thought was not only a road of science but it also came dangerously close to turning at the end into a way to God. No wonder that he hastened to make it clear that he had not fallen into the hands of priests.

Like all such slightly nervous disclaimers, his was a tacit admission of an insecurity of which he most likely was not aware. His disclaimer was based on his falling back on one leg of the cliché argument of Kant that there was no legitimate ground for going from the world to its Creator.

To balance oneself on one leg is always a precarious act, and in this case it was certainly a most un-Kantian performance. For, according to Kant, the illegitimacy of arguing from the existence of the world to the existence of God rested on the illegitimacy of our notion of the world as a whole. That notion was, according to Kant, a bastard product of the metaphysical urge of the mind. At the age of thirteen, Einstein read the *Critique* and felt that everything in it was clear to him, a statement worthy of a teen-ager, however precocious. Years later, science taught him how mistaken Kant was on the a priori. To the end Einstein failed to perceive that according to the very same science, which created scientific cosmology, Kant's dictum on the world as a whole was wholly fallacious.

If such is the case, however, the case for natural theology must be reopened, and for a scientific reason at that. The student of natural theology should not feel uneasy because of Einstein's rejection "of getting any further." This refusal of his was rooted in the basic inconsistency of his views on religion as he gave them in their most detailed and matured form in 1939 and in 1941. On the one hand he urged teachers of religion "to give up the doctrine of a personal God" and promote "emancipation from the shackles of personal hopes and desires." That emancipation was for him the road to "the humble attitude of mind towards the grandeur of reason incarnate in existence."[76] But in addition to advocating surrender to an apersonal cosmic order as the highest form of religion, Einstein also held high moral ideals, with an authoritative content. Their source was not in reason. Rather they existed "in a healthy society as powerful traditions." Their highest form was according to him deposited in the "Jewish-Christian religious tradition." It was no secret to Einstein that such traditions, especially the Jewish-Christian, came into existence not through rational demonstrations, as he put it, but "through revelation, through the medium of powerful personalities."[77] Since all those personalities in the Jewish-Christian tradition derived their inspiration from belief in a personal God, nay considered themselves his inspired spokesmen, it would have been logical to ask how the highest ethical values could originate in a belief which was not only an illusion but the source "of incalculable harm to human progress." Again, could the idea of a personal supreme being be summarily declared an illusion if that very same notion was, as Einstein admitted, "accessible by virtue of its simplicity to the most undeveloped mind"?[78] Finally, how could the human person be the embodiment of an unconditionally binding moral value in a cosmos which as such was strictly apersonal in its quality as the ultimate in existence?

For all his myopia about the baffling emergence of personal beings with absolute moral values in a radically amoral and apersonal cosmic existence, for all his espousal of the "religious" tied to his dismissal of religion,[79] for all his occasional eagerness to play the role of scientific advisor to a nonexistent God,[80] for all his effort to justify himself as a "deeply religious unbeliever,"[81] Einstein the scientist-philosopher is an invaluable witness on behalf of natural theology. A Carnap, a Neurath, a Russell, a Reichenbach, a Bridgman, in sum all the positivists and operationists who have set the tone of philosophy and of philosophy of science for the last half century, were fully aware of the unabashedly metaphysical character of Einstein's science. Some of them begged him—almost put words in his mouth—to state that experimental data were the trigger of his speculations and achievements.[82] He refused to give them any comfort, although aware that in return they were to charge him with what he had called "being guilty of the original sin of metaphysics."[83] He was fully aware of the fact that most contemporary scientists were giving allegiance to Mach's philosophy or to one or another of its versions,[84] but he kept telling them that every true theorist was a tamed metaphysician no matter how pure a positivist he fancied himself.[85] Nothing was clearer to him than the fact that what most memorably separated him from the vast majority of his colleagues was not a disagreement on technicalities of quantum mechanics but a disagreement concerning their efforts to see the ultimate word for science in the positivist and agnostic roots of the Copenhagen theory. After Planck's death Einstein's dissenting voice became even more a voice crying in the wilderness. His resolute opposition to the Copenhagen theory was a classic proof of the dictum that arguments are not counted but weighed. And weigh he did on the minds of his antagonists. After a long debate with Einstein at the Institute for Advanced Study in Princeton, Bohr, the chief protagonist of the Copenhagen school, could do no better than to walk around the table, move to the window, and stare out of it while muttering the words: "Einstein ... Einstein ... Einstein."[86]

Students and lovers of natural theology might reflect with profit on the inability of so many scientists of our times to extricate themselves from the snares of positivism, in spite of the monumental lessons provided by the creative science of Planck and of Einstein. These two, whom Harnack in 1918 had called the two great philosophers of our times,[87] were like all genuine prophets, rejected by their own. Clearly, the failure to see the logic and evidence is not merely a phenomenon connected with discourse on the ways to God, that is, on natural theology. It can plague also those who wish to speak only of the road of natural science. Their case shows that discourse about that road will suffer as long as one has no sympathetic consideration for the inexorably metaphysical destination of that road. The bold extension in our century of the road of science through the work of Planck and

Einstein is indeed very much in the direction of the point toward which that road has tended from its inception. The point is its junction with the ways to God.

Thirteen

THE HORNS OF COMPLEMENTARITY

PLANCK AND EINSTEIN SIGHTED A NEW LAND OF SCIENCE, A LAND STRETCH-
ing incomparably farther than the one known before. In their footsteps
came a generation of unusually gifted younger physicists eager to take
possession of the new land but also reluctant to share the vision of its
discoverers. These younger men made within a few years an apparently
complete survey of the new land and concluded that it was all the land
science could have and that the land itself could not be any other than
the one just discovered. The very same professionals, who smiled at the
belief widely shared within their profession a generation earlier that
nothing really new could be learned in physics, now claimed that they
had disclosed such features of physics as made the physics of the day
the last word in physics. The physics of the day was quantum mechanics. As it was developed into quantum electrodynamics, the conviction
became general that one needed only more powerful mathematical
techniques to derive from first principles all data listed in the hand-
books of physics and chemistry. So was the matter put in 1959 by
Robert B. Leighton, of the California Institute of Technology, author of
an advanced and widely used textbook on modern physics.[1]

Leighton acknowledged that quantum electrodynamics could not
cope with phenomena that directly involved nuclear forces, weak interactions, and gravitation. For all that, quantum mechanics seemed to
him to hold the key to all physics. "With the rapid advances that are
being made in particle physics," wrote Leighton, "perhaps it is not too
much to expect that in a few more decades all physical phenomena will
be equally well understood."[2] A generation earlier, C. P. Snow, the
future novelist-laureate of the scientific community, had already diagnosed the same conviction as he let scientists speak of what had just
been achieved by the discoverers of quantum mechanics: "They had
found the boundary of knowledge, something would remain unknown
forever."[3] What this implied for all men of science, of those times and of
all times to come, was put in their mouths by Snow as follows: "One of
the results of this new representation of matter was to tell us what we
could not know as well as what we could. We were in sight of the end."
To be in sight of the end can easily provoke a peculiar feeling, especially
in moderns who had replaced God, the infinite, with an endless search
in an allegedly infinite universe, and who had grown accustomed to
setting (with Lessing's Nathan) a higher value on the search for truth
than on the possession of truth itself. No wonder that they were deeply
perplexed by being in sight of the end. As Snow voiced the feeling of

197

one of them: "It seemed incredible to me, brought up in the tradition of limitless searching." This limitless search meant a distrust of limits, an uneasiness about the limited field, however vast. Commitment to the infinite implied the absence of agoraphobia, the very opposite of fear of the circumscribed, the only fear with intellectual, or rather scientific, respectability. As Snow's scientist mused of that limitless search: "I resented leaving it."[4]

Snow's scientist spoke in the name of practically all his colleagues in theoretical physics, but they certainly did not include Einstein. The ones Einstein could count as his allies were few and far between, though hardly negligible. In addition to Planck, there was Schrödinger, one of the architects of quantum theory. In a letter of August 8, 1939, to Schrödinger, Einstein spoke to him of his viewpoint which, as Einstein put it, "has driven me into a deep solitude."[5] The viewpoint related above all to the question of whether reality existed independently of the observer, a question which most cultivators of quantum mechanics answered in the negative. Schrödinger had them and their often arcane formulas in mind when a decade or so later he remarked in a lecture dealing with the modern, scientific notion of material reality: "A widely accepted school of thought maintains that an objective picture of reality—in any traditional meaning of that term—cannot exist at all. Only the optimists among us (and I consider myself one of them) look upon this view as a philosophical extravagance born of despair in face of a grave crisis. We hope that the fluctuations of concepts and opinions only indicate a violent process of transformation which in the end will lead to something better than the mess of formulas that to-day surrounds our subject."[6]

In its original form the crisis consisted in the inability to accomplish anything more than an ad hoc systematization of some of tens of thousands of spectral lines carefully measured during the decades straddling the turn of the century. In 1913 Bohr's atom model brought some relief, but it promised more than it immediately delivered. Once it was applied beyond the simplest lines of the hydrogen atom, an increasing number of arbitrary corrections had to be grafted onto it to make it work. The situation appeared so unsatisfactory as to prompt Ehrenfest to remark that teaching mathematical physics in its present confusion gave him insight into Hegelian dialectics, "a succession of leaps from one lie to another by way of intermediate falsehoods."[7] About the same time Pauli wrote: "At the moment physics is again terribly confused. In any case, it is difficult for me, and I wish I had been a movie comedian or something of the sort and had never heard of physics."[8] A few months later, after the publication in 1925 of Heisenberg's paper on matrix mechanics, Pauli wrote: "Heisenberg's type of mechanics has again given me hope and joy in life. To be sure, it does not supply the solution to the riddle, but I believe it is again possible to march forward."[9] Pauli by then was famous through his contribution of the fourth quantum number, later known as spin, which permitted the derivation of the periodicity in the table of elements. But the spin was still an ad hoc device, however successful. When something of its logic was unfolded in 1929 through the work of Dirac, the perspective of Einstein was once more vindicated, but this was noted only many years later and by Dirac himself.[10]

The true aspect of a major advance in theoretical physics could not be perceived at a time when a young Heisenberg could retort to Einstein with a reference to what he had been taught by Bohr, almost as if truth in physics depended on one's choice of teachers. The incident took place shortly after the publication of Heisenberg's paper which earned him an invitation to deliver a lecture before the Akademie der Wissenschaften in Berlin presenting his theory in full detail. Far more important than this appearance before that august body for Heisenberg, not yet twenty-five, was the walk he was invited to take with Einstein following the lecture. Hardly a word of their conversation, which continued in Einstein's home, was lost on him. The conversation, reconstructed by Heisenberg in great detail many years later,[11] reveals another reason why Einstein felt more and more isolated. Heisenberg's matrix mechanics—and Heisenberg argued persuasively a year later that Schrödinger's wave mechanics was equivalent to it—rested on the principle that physical theory concerns itself only with what is directly observable. Within the context of quantum mechanics this meant the very opposite of espousing naïve realism or even moderate realism. It rather meant the radical abandonment of all ordinary notions of space and time, and especially of causality, because strictly speaking they were not observable. "Bohr has taught me this," Heisenberg told Einstein as he backed up his argument with reference to the authority of his venerated teacher.[12]

Bohr has turned into an authority for most younger physicists, the best of whom spent a year or two with him in Copenhagen. The success of his atom model was undeniable. Upon learning of it in 1913 Einstein called it one of the great discoveries.[13] But Bohr's discovery, however great, was far from being as original as the work of Planck and Einstein. By 1912 all the pieces were ready for Bohr's atom model. Indeed some of the pieces were already in place.[14] It was the final touch that Bohr supplied. Lately, some psychoanalytical historians of science have seen philosophical hedonism with a special Danish flavor behind Bohr's magic move,[15] but the evidence is rather forced. It is far better to credit the sense of a mathematically minded physicist who was led as if by instinct toward the correct formula, a process of which the history of physics contains many an example.[16] The philosophy was added by

Bohr only after the mathematical structure was ready and was added to it a decade or so later.[17] The structure itself resembled a racetrack partitioned by concentric rings of high hedges between which the electrons, like so many horses, were running. The horses as such were not observable. The only observable data were occasional flashes from the racetrack, and these were interpreted as the jumping of horses from one track to another. The theory of Bohr's atom model had nothing to do with such questions as why a horse jumped from one track to another, and at a particular time, and why to one track rather than to another,[18] and whether identity was maintained by any horse. Indeed, the theory was impervious to such questions. In an age in which Mach's influence was felt everywhere among physicists, nothing was more natural than to declare, as Heisenberg did to Einstein, that the atom exemplified Mach's tenet that only what was directly observable had a place in physical theory.[19] This was the tenet which Bohr instilled in Heisenberg and in many others while they were in Copenhagen. He never did it with philosophical profundity, but always with a charming plausibility and from the pedestal of his atom model, which steadily rose in esteem. The measure of his persuasiveness kept rising at the same rate. Thus young Heisenberg found nothing wrong in arguing *ex auctoritate*, a type of argument one should always avoid in physics.

To be sure, this was not his sole argument. He was ready to turn the tables on Einstein by telling him that his own special relativity was an implementation of Mach's tenet about restricting physical theory to what was directly observable. To young Heisenberg's consternation Einstein's reply was a flat repudiation of Mach: "Possibly I did use this kind of reasoning but it is nonsense all the same."[20] Much of what has been said in the last chapter makes it superfluous to explain why and how Einstein had come to consider Mach's program nonsense. As to Heisenberg's consternation, it merely indicated that Einstein's characterization in Paris in 1922 of Mach as a "déplorable philosophe"[21] had not yet reached most physics departments, in spite of their proverbial capacity to spread scientific gossip with almost the speed of light. Yet, that Mach's philosophy was deplorable was unwittingly voiced by Heisenberg himself. After referring to what Bohr had taught him about our inability to describe processes in time and space with our traditional concepts, Heisenberg added: "With that, of course, we have said very little, no more in fact than that we do not know."[22]

This phrase, far from revealing a Socratic depth,[23] was an anticipation of Bohr's shallow resorts to the limitations of human knowledge as he turned to expounding the philosophy of quantum mechanics. The first major presentation by Bohr of that philosophy took place at the International Congress of Physics held in Como in September 1927. The presentation was also a vast one, running to forty printed pages. For a historian of science its most telling aspect is the manner in which Bohr tried to make it appear that the "general point of view" which he advocated put him and his followers "on the very path taken by Einstein of adapting our modes of perception borrowed from the sensations to the gradually deepening knowledge of the laws of nature."[24] The phrase was a classic in studied vagueness, for Bohr must have already known that there was no real moving away from sensations on the basis of a philosophy of physics which allowed only for observables a role in physical theory. Nor could Bohr in 1927, for years at the center of the latest cross-currents in physical theories and of their epistemological interpretation, be unaware that Einstein had been growing more and more impatient with the customary presentation of his theory of relativity as ultimately resting on Mach's precepts about sensations. And who in that congress of physicists could be unaware of the crusade which Planck had launched in the name of science against Mach in Leiden in 1908, a crusade which he had been waging ever since!

At the very outset of his lecture Bohr referred to Planck, himself present at the Congress, as "the venerated originator of the [quantum] theory,"[25] but the reference was mainly a matter of politeness. Bohr was not yet through the first page of his long lecture when he specified two essential features of his chief message which he described as a "certain general point of view." He believed it to be "suited to give an impression of the general trend of the development of the theory from its very beginning and . . . will be helpful in order to harmonize the apparently conflicting views taken by different scientists."[26] One of the two features was the very opposite of what Planck primarily stood for, namely, the assertion of a rationally ordered nature existing objectively, that is, independently of the observer. Since, as Bohr put it, the quantum postulate implied that every observation of atomic phenomena was equivalent to influencing them, it followed that, to quote Bohr, "an independent reality in the ordinary physical sense can neither be ascribed to the phenomena nor to the agencies of observation."[27] Of course, this had to be true if objective knowledge could only be had through exact measurement, but Bohr was not enough of a philosopher to see this obvious condition of the truth of his statement. It is an equally poor reflection on Bohr, the philosopher-physicist, that while speaking in the presence of Planck, he did not feel the need to explain himself as he referred in the same context to the "inherent 'irrationality' of the quantum postulate."[28] This "irrationality" was reasserted by him as he reached the midpoint of his lecture[29] and the "inevitability of the feature of irrationality" was his next to last remark.[30]

While this celebration by Bohr of irrationality in nature was diametrically opposed to the principal concern of Planck, it was a logical consequence not of quantum theory but of the Machist and pragmatist epistemology which Bohr grafted on it. As could be expected, Bohr, the pragmatist, was not to renounce reason in a consistent manner. He was neither the first nor the last on the long list of more recent philosophers and scientists who believed it possible to save something of reason while espousing ultimate irrationality. The possibility for Bohr consisted in restricting discourse to *aspects* of reality while barring questions about reality itself, and especially about its objective existence. In Bohr's case this was all the more laden with further problems because the *aspects* in question were more opposite, nay mutually exclusive, than merely distinct. He tried to hold them together by offering the idea of complementarity, which he believed was "suited to characterize the situation, which bears a deep-going analogy to the general difficulty in the formation of human ideas, inherent in the distribution between subject and object."[31] Like Höffding, his philosophical mentor, Bohr never pondered the logical implications of the complementary presence of both the rational and of the irrational in knowledge.

Although Bohr took up in detail the relation of subject and object only two years later, his lecture at Como gave unmistakable clues to the real character of the ultimate results of his answer to the question. Quantum mechanics demanded, according to Bohr, a "fundamental renunciation regarding the space-time description"[32] in the interpretation of observations. One could have either space or time, but not both together. To Bohr's credit, he clearly perceived that this implied "a radical departure from the causal description of Nature,"[33] and it meant also that stationary states and individual transition processes on the atomic level have, as he put it, "as much or as little 'reality' as the very idea of individual particles."[34] Bohr, and again let credit be given to him for his consistency, spelled out before long the full logic of his epistemological interpretation of quantum mechanics. In an "Introductory Survey" written in 1929 for the publication of his lecture given at Como together with some other lectures of his, he admitted that the consequence of this state of affairs was that "even words like 'to be' and 'to know' lose their unambiguous meaning."[35]

One need only be modestly familiar with the inexorability of logic to realize that such an admission had a devastating potential. Indeed, it was a bomb that exploded almost immediately in Bohr's own hands. Again, in view of the inherent sweep of logic it could be of no surprise that as the fuse of that bomb was burning in Bohr's hands, natural theology—which is rational concern about the ultimate—appeared in its ominous light for a brief but illuminating moment. Following his declaration that words like "to be" and "to know" no longer had unambiguous meaning, Bohr offered an example from quantum mechanics about the manner in which ambiguity enveloped everything in nature.

Renunciation of causality, Bohr remarked, gave rise to a new use of words in which "one speaks of a free choice on the part of nature."[36] Bohr was more than eager to keep the phrase ambiguous. For if one spoke unambiguously, Bohr added, the phrase implied "the idea of an external chooser."[37] Since the chooser in question was external with respect to nature as a whole, it could most naturally evoke the notion of God. Bohr, never sympathetic to anything genuinely transcendental, let alone supernatural and Christian, was most careful not to give unwitting respectability to the idea of a God who can choose with respect to nature. Much less would Bohr have tolerated the reintroduction of God into rational discourse through the mediation of quantum mechanics. The haste with which he tried to dispel the indirect appearance of God on the scene spoke for itself. Moreover, when it came to dispelling the remote flicker of God, Bohr was ready to forget that his own premises permitted him to perform only ambiguously a feat which he meant to be an unambiguous philosophical exorcism. There was not even a trace of ambiguity in the manner in which Bohr now set up the idea of nature against the beckoning of the notion of God. For Bohr, nature was *unambiguously* the totality of things, and thus the possibility of an external chooser from among the many conceivable possibilities inherent in nature was denied by Bohr in a manner which he meant to be strictly unambiguous. Unlike philosophers who can easily be ruined by their science, scientists cannot ruin their science by their philosophies, but they can easily give themselves away as dilettante philosophers, forgetful of consistency, the first rule in the art of philosophizing.

In addition to his inconsistency in using the word *nature* unambiguously, Bohr also seemed to forget that since no expert in quantum mechanics could ever claim to have observed nature as such, let alone nature as a whole, it could not be part of any discourse on quantum mechanics as long as its Copenhagen interpretation was true. But there was a far greater problem, a sinister trap, in Bohr's unfolding of the ultimate consequences of his interpretation of quantum mechanics. "We here come," he declared, "upon a fundamental feature in the general problem of knowledge, and we must realize that by the very nature of the matter, we shall always have last recourse to a word picture, in which the words themselves are not further analyzed."[38] Astonishingly, Bohr did not seem to suspect the self-defeating nature of his utterance. For if words were impervious to further rational probing, then the end of philosophy was not merely in sight but on hand. It should seem equally astonishing that so many physicists and philosophers of modern physics, who have read Bohr's lecture for the past fifty years as if it were holy writ, fail to see that Bohr's words, if taken seriously, could mean the end not only of philosophy but also of natural philosophy or physics. But how could this fateful end be suspected by those who felt convinced that with the Copenhagen theory physics had entered its final glory!

This philosophical myopia of most cultivators of quantum mechanics has both an aggravating and a mitigating aspect. The former has to do with the fact that many centuries earlier it had already been recognized by all but the sophists that words are neither the first nor the last in the process of understanding. The first and the last in understanding is understanding itself. This is why it has become an axiom since ancient times that the man of wisdom, or the philosopher who understands, is not interested in mere names and words—de nominibus non curat sapiens—an axiom which carries far more understanding than the whole Copenhagen epistemology of quantum mechanics. The mitigating circumstance derives from the fact that parallel to the rise of the Copenhagen school of epistemology a far more rigorously articulated formulation was given to the same epistemological presuppositions in the hands of those who banded together as the Vienna Circle. The credibility which Schlick, Carnap, and others enjoyed for over a generation could easily strengthen the assurance of the physicist-philosophers of the Copenhagen school that they were on the safest possible ground. But the ground provided by the Vienna Circle, as will be discussed later, contained only words, hardly a foundation for sound philosophy.

Long before this was scathingly laid bare by none other than Bertrand Russell,[39] a flood of words, well-meaning to be sure, was generated within the Copenhagen school. It was the flow of complementarity, and its main wellspring was Bohr himself.[40] Unquestionably, subject and object complement each other in the process of understanding. The same can also be stated of such pairs of aspects as the physical and the mental, the animate and the inanimate, the freedom of the will and mechanical necessity, associative thinking and identity of personality, concepts and their applications, phenomena and the means to observe them, and not least, the celebrated twofold roles of being "both onlookers and actors in the great drama of existence."[41] That drama is nowhere more spectacular than in the rise and clash of cultures. The well-known divison of a circle into two complementary parts, known as yin and yang, was chosen by Bohr as his coat of arms, a choice which showed that the Copenhagen theory implied a shift from Western thought to Eastern cultural mentality. True, late in life, Bohr warned that complementarity with respect to cultures could not be taken as strictly as in connection with atomic science and psychological analysis,[42] as if to take the edge off the symbolism of his coat of arms. His warning was a classic case of trying to save health by fostering disease. The health, or at least science, was a distinct product of Western culture. The disease was Bohr's equating problems of physics with problems of psychology, an equation legitimate on the basis of Bohr's epistemology but not on the basis of the epistemology that gave rise to physical science. To be sure, Bohr offered the equation somewhat ambiguously. He defined his program as giving "an *impression* of the general epistemological attitude which we have been forced to adopt in a field as far from human passions as the analysis of simple physical experiments" (emphasis added).[43]

Whatever the distance of human passions from atomic physics, the real question was whether one's epistemological attitude was truly general, that is, consistent, or not. The impression Bohr gave was that one was to have two kinds of epistemology, one for atomic phenomena, another for everything else, but it was still to be explained whether the understanding, or *episteme*, could be split in two. On this decisive point Bohr gave at best an impression which was vague and superficial. Staying with superficial impressions means staying on the surface, and this in turn implies the avoidance of deep questions. Typically enough, Bohr completed the final review of his epistemological conflict with Einstein with the remark that "through a singularly fruitful cooperation of a whole generation of physicists we are nearing the goal where logical order to a large extent allows us to avoid deep truth."[44] The most obvious of such deep truths should have been for Bohr the truth of the complementarity of matter and light, waves and particles, atomic stability and indeterminacy. The truth that they were complementary to one another was not a matter of observation, but an inference, and a genuinely metaphysical one, which had no justification in the Copenhagen theory. The truth in question was about the truth of a reality which had complementary aspects. These aspects could *really* complement one another only if they inhered in a deeper reality, about which Bohr could only be agnostic. A harmony of relations or aspects, complementing one another, such was Bohr's epistemological message, a message void of reference to the ontological reality of anything harmonious. About the entity which embodied the harmony of relations he was not permitted by his own premises to make any claim and he carefully avoided doing so. In a truly pragmatist way, which he learned from Höffding, a forerunner of William James, Bohr could speak of fruits, though not of their harmony (which is never a matter of direct observation), and certainly not of the tree that produced the fruits, to say nothing of the soil which supported and nourished the tree. For Bohr the deepest aspect of existence was pragmatic fruitfulness, the rather shallow perspective in which he saw physics itself: "Perhaps the most distinguishing characteristic of the present position of physics is that almost all the ideas which have ever proved to be fruitful in the investigating of nature have found their right place in a common harmony without thereby having diminished their fruitfulness."[45]

As will be seen shortly, this was not even true of quantum mechanics, a fact which should surprise no one. The really creative elements of quantum mechanics are not the data observed by the eyes of physicists, but the marvelous ideas formed in their heads. Of those heads few were as impressive and persuasive as that of Bohr, who for many was the twentieth-century Moses with two flaming horns on his forehead. The horns were the horns of complementarity, but as interpreted by Bohr they could not secure *reality* to the atomic realm, to say nothing of Moses or Bohr himself. Bohr's pairs of complementarity resembled pairs of horns from which one could not even infer unambiguously either that they were rooted in the same head and were thereby truly complementary or that the head itself was real, and even more fundamentally real than the horns themselves.

Such pairs of horns, or complementarities, had one advantage. Neither their proponents nor their opponents could be impaled on them in any real sense. But the philosophy of complementarity had a pair of horns on which science itself could be impaled. Those horns first raised their threatening aspect at the Solvay Congress of 1927. In the philosophically facile atmosphere of the conference, however, their logical threat was not appreciated, although they gave expression to the debilitating dilemma created for physics by Bohr's doctrine of complementarity, a dilemma which has been left intact by the immense literature produced by his followers. One of the horns was traced out by Dirac.[46] He took as a starting point the experiments of W. Bothe and H. Geiger, who showed in 1924 that the coincidence of scattered X-rays and recoil electrons was such as to make wholly untenable a theory proposed by Bohr, Kramers, and Slater.[47] According to that theory, atomic processes were purely statistical, and therefore the principles of the conservation of energy and of momentum were not valid on the atomic level. The nonchalant abandonment of these principles in the Bohr-Kramers-Slater theory anticipated much of what had emerged at that Solvay Congress as the Copenhagen epistemology.[48] In recalling the Bohr-Kramers-Slater theory, Dirac, one of the youngest participants at the congress, kept strictly to the facts of physics. None of those facts were more obvious and more indispensable at that time for atomic physicists than the ionization tracks shown in cloud chambers. Any such track consists of millions of ionized atoms, each serving as a nucleus of condensation for suddenly cooled water vapor. Nothing therefore could be more natural than to look for a function which generated the sequence of nuclei in a coherent manner, that is, permitting a causal transition of the process of condensation from one nucleus to another. But on the quantum-mechanical basis the function, the famous ψ-function, permitted only a statistical sequence in which the string of nuclei was not the causal product of a single process. On such a basis the invariable appearance of well-defined tracks in cloud chambers had to appear a great puzzle. It could in no way be resolved by considering nature as a series of disconnected events, a prospect which like the specter of a fearful horn was conjured up by the Copenhagen theory of quantum mechanics. To avoid being impaled on that horn, Dirac demanded nothing less than assigning to nature the ability to choose from among an infinite number of possibilities, all equally probable, the one that appeared to produce a coherent set of events.[49]

Physics, it may be recalled, saw its growth to maturity in the century of Galileo and Newton following the renunciation by physicists of any concern in physics with teleology, which, in a sense, is a brand of animism. Originally, the banning of teleology from physics was meant to be a method not a dogma. Once that ban had been turned by the Copenhagen theory into a dogma, the consistency of the work of physicists could not be saved except by assigning to nature the ability to choose, and purposively at that. Such was one of the fearful horns to be faced by physics severed from a realistic epistemology. The other horn, which Heisenberg traced out at the same congress, also had its root in the Copenhagen epistemology of quantum mechanics. The two horns meant the abandonment of all philosophy except its extreme forms. In Dirac's case nature became endowed with the ability to choose; in Heisenberg's case, it was the physicist who constituted nature through the choice of his observations. Heisenberg's brief but revealing reasoning must be given in his own words: "I am not in agreement with Mr. Dirac when he says that in the experiment in question nature makes a choice; . . . this choice of nature can never be known before the decisive experiment has been made; . . . I would rather say . . . that the *observer himself* makes the choice, because it is only in the moment when the observation is made that the 'choice' has become a physical reality."[50] Obviously, once the physicist had departed from that philosophical middle road in which expressions like "to be" and "to know" can have unambiguous meaning, he could not remain immune to the inner logic that was to toss him from one unscientific extreme to another. One extreme was unmistakably similar to the position of animistic physics in which nature made choices and acted for the best, to recall Socrates's dictum and his program for physics implemented by Aristotle;[51] the other extreme was closely akin to Hegel's position in which nature was constituted by one's thought.[52]

No sooner had this fateful pair of horns appeared on the scene than it was forgotten. Nobody at the Solvay Congress was roused to action by seeing Dirac and Heisenberg lock horns in a somewhat facetious manner about a hardly facetious problem for physics and for philosophy. Einstein himself figured in the official *procès verbaux* of the congress with only a brief remark[53] which did not relate to this issue. It is from a different source, from Bohr's final review of his dispute with Einstein, that we know something of Einstein's reaction—which ought to be of importance both to historians of quantum mechanics and to students of natural theology. It was at that congress that Einstein was first noted for voicing his conviction about an orderly nature in the phrase that God does not play dice.[54] As Bohr recalled it, "Einstein mockingly asked us whether we could really believe that the providential authorities took recourse to dice-playing." Such was Bohr's rendering of Einstein's words which Bohr quoted in parentheses in the original German—*ob der liebe Gott würfelt.* "To which I replied," Bohr continued, "by pointing at the great caution, already called for by ancient thinkers, in ascribing attributes to Providence in everyday language."[55] This locking of theological horns by Einstein and Bohr tells a great deal even in its mocking brevity. Bohr's reply, a covert allusion to a warning by the skeptic Cotta in Cicero's *De natura deorum*,[56] made it evident that Bohr considered natural theology, if he considered it at all, only within its pagan context. His answer to Einstein, may have appeared solemn, but the whole discussion, as Bohr pointedly recalled, was in a humorous vein. Bohr's rendering of Einstein's reference to "der liebe Gott," a phrase of undeniably Christian provenance, as "providential authorities" should seem equally revealing. Of course, for Einstein the phrase "der liebe Gott" did not even mean "providential authorities" but only "traditional" ones that were no better than any tradition. But between the contents of the two phrases there was an abyss as vast as there is between a providential Creator and a cursory phrase. To overlook this fact was most natural both with Bohr and with Einstein because of their views on historical religions in general and on Christianity in particular. Nor could one expect of most participants of that Solvay Congress more than a gently mocking attitude toward natural theology. It was possibly there that Pauli, who later turned to mysticism, characterized Dirac as follows: "Dirac says there is no God and Dirac is His prophet."[57]

A scientific congress is hardly the best means to bring out the best in its participants, but at congresses or not, it was impossible to give more than mocking thought to natural theology on the basis of the Copenhagen epistemology of quantum mechanics. An epistemology which blocks questions about the problem of being can provide no eyes for metaphysics, the very foundation of natural theology. Such an epistemology blinds the eyes even about physics, and for the very same reason, provides one more instance of the subtly but inevitably common fate of natural theology and natural science. To see the scientific side of that instance one need not leave the Solvay Congress of 1927. As Bohr's survey of his disputes with Einstein informs us, it was there that he and Einstein first locked horns on the question whether it was possible to devise thought experiments which would show that explanations of atomic phenomena included factors that were nonobservable.[58] For several years Einstein kept devising such thought experiments without seeing the futility of his strategy. First, not much could be done if one was faced with extremely self-satisfied opponents, about whom Einstein himself complained in 1928 to Schrödinger: "The Heisenberg-Bohr tranquilizing philosophy—or religion?—is so delicately contrived that, for the time being, it provides a gentle pillow for the believer from which he cannot very easily be aroused."[59] Second, Einstein took the view that in order to overthrow the Copenhagen interpretation of quantum mechanics one had to discredit its hallowed shibboleth according to which quantum mechanics (and physics by implication) was in no need of hidden variables.[60] By asserting the need for hidden variables in physical theory Einstein wanted to vindicate the objective, fully determined causal layer of entities underlying the surface level of measurements where everything seemed to be indeterminate and therefore statistical.

The year of that Solvay Congress was, it is well to recall, the year in which Heisenberg gave his derivation of the principle of indeterminacy concerning measurements in physics. One can therefore in a sense understand Einstein's tactics in taking on the Copenhagen interpretation at its nerve center, which consisted in the insistence that measurements were inconceivable without someone doing them. Thus it would be argued that the act of measurement, which in one way or another implied pointer readings and therefore a reliance on light quanta, deprived the measurement of absolute precision. Such insistence when elevated into a first principle became equivalent to withdrawing into a citadel. Once confined to measurements within that citadel, one could declare that physical theory was limited to the measurable and therefore had no need of hidden variables. Withdrawal into that citadel also meant the viewing of anything outside it as unreal. It was such a citadel that Einstein wanted to conquer from within, by trying to devise a thought experiment in which absolute precision was in principle possible. He was bound to fail for the very reason that no measurement is possible without observation. But it did not follow from this that knowledge of reality was equivalent to measuring it, let alone measuring it with absolute precision. Philosophically the citadel in question did not represent the full range of man's knowing reality, and it certainly did not represent the full range of modern physics. Einstein's own theory of relativity was a case in point, and all members of the Copenhagen school could have been forced to admit that it was a telling case.

Having won his Nobel Prize not for relativity but for the theory of light as a stream of quanta, Einstein, who during the first twenty years of quantum theory did more for its development than anyone else, would have been in an excellent position to remind his younger colleagues about the presence in quantum mechanics of assumptions which even if they did not constitute hidden variables were not deducible from measurements and from the mathematical techniques of matrix and wave mechanics. Such assumptions were the strict, nonstatistical equality of all quanta, of all electrons, of all fundamental particles within a given class, to say nothing of the invariability of the laws of electrodynamics in all atomic processes and measurements. There were in addition some curious features of the historical development of quantum mechanics which, if carefully recalled, might have cast immediate doubt on the validity of the Copenhagen interpretation of quantum mechanics. To begin with, the very backbone of matrix mechanics, the universal validity for atomic physics of a noncommutative algebra, was not at all a derivative of observation. Heisenberg first merely found that for several families of spectral lines there appeared a strange, noncommutative method of calculating their relative spacings. Strange it was also in the sense that on seeing it Born had to rack his brains to realize its identity with that matrix calculus he had learned some twenty years earlier.[61] Nobody at that time cared to ponder the question why nature favored one of the many algebraic schemes devised by pure mathematicians long before the advent of atomic physics. In the late 1920s all those jubilant with matrix mechanics merely took it for granted that some mathematical techniques were marvelously successful in dealing with nature. Some spoke of the revival of the Pythagorean idea of nature, but no thought was given to the philosophical implications of the success by which esoteric mathematical theories could be applied to nature.[62] At any rate, no observation indicated that there was a universal truth in the proposition that, unlike nature's behavior on the macroscopic level, where it obeyed commutative algebra, on the atomic level it preferred a noncommutative algebra. The recognition of this was a feat of the mind, the very same mind whose creativity could not be handled by the Copenhagen interpretation of physics. No wonder that in the whole account by Bohr of his dispute with Einstein and in all his references to relativity, there is not a hint about the creativity of mind by which Einstein had set so great a store.[63] Whatever the merits of Bohr's epistemology, his account of the conceptual history of modern science, especially of the one created by Einstein, was curious to say the least. One wonders how Bohr hoped with such an approach to win over Einstein, a hope which strongly motivated his epistemological reflections.[64]

In view of this it may safely be said that a close study of the immediate historical record might have helped both Einstein and Bohr to see a way out of their inconclusive struggle, if a word is allowed in favor of the usefulness of historical studies in science. But historical perspective and wisdom are always a step or two behind actual development. A case in point is the explanation given by Dirac in 1964 of Schrödinger's failure to be the first to sight the realm of antimatter. As Dirac recalled it, Schrödinger, in formulating his wave mechanics, did not have enough trust in the heuristic value of the principle of symmetry, and as a result he left his famous equation "unbalanced."[65] Led by faith in nature's obeisance to mathematical symmetry, Dirac in 1929 "balanced" Schrödinger's equation and obtained not only a natural explanation of the spin quantum number but also negative values for kinetic energy which could be explained only if one assumed the existence of matter with a negative sign.[66] Later successes of quantum mechanics in the field of fundamental particles had a more or less similar character. The genesis and success of the so-called eightfold way is one example among many such.[67] Also, on the basis of the Copenhagen epistemology it made no sense that after the overthrow of the conservation of parity, leading theoretical physicists turned as a man and as if by instinct to finding means of restoring full parity, that is, symmetry for all subatomic interactions, a feature which neither is demanded by measurements nor is noncommutative.[68]

It was not given to Einstein to learn of any of these startling advances, made almost invariably by people who at the same time gave generous lipservice to the ultimate validity of the Copenhagen epistemology. A few years before he died, Einstein could count only Schrödinger and Max von Laue as his allies among physicists concerning the proposition that no one can get around the question of reality as long as one is intellectually honest.[69] Einstein retired more and more into solitude. He felt the epistemological truth in his bones but the feeling, however vital, was only enough to make him wag his little finger in defense of objective reality.[70] His Humean and Machist background robbed him of the ability to articulate consistently and from its very foundations the epistemological common-sense truth about reality. Yet his whole being resonated when he found this truth presented in its plainest form. One of these instances was unwittingly provided by Bohr, and it fascinated Einstein for the rest of his life.[71] For only common sense could decide unambiguously whether a cat in a box was there only when observed or also immediately before and after the act of observation. The Copenhagen people, Einstein wrote to Schrödinger on December 22, 1950, "believe that the quantum theory provides a description of reality, and even a *complete* description; this interpretation is, however, refuted most elegantly by your system of radioactive atom + Geiger counter + amplifier + charge of gun-powder + cat in a box, in which the ψ-function of the system contains the cat both alive and blown to bits. Is the state of the cat to be created only when a physicist investigates the

211

situation at some definite time? Nobody really doubts that the presence or absence of the cat is something independent of the act of observation. But then the description by means of the ψ-function is certainly incomplete, and there must be a more complete description."[72]

Such was the plain truth concerning the Copenhagen epistemology. To grasp that truth it was enough to have a cat in addition to a basic trust in that much-discredited and ridiculed ability of ours to grasp reality on a common-sense basis. Such a grasp was ruled out of court by Bohr and so uncompromisingly and consistently as to prompt Clifford A. Hooker, author of the vastest (and still fairly recent) study of the nature of quantum mechanical reality, to conclude: "*It is precisely* the hardness of his refusal to bridge the gap between complementary situations that guarantees that consistency. Difficulties arise in quantum theory only when we try to construct a model of reality common to complementary situations."[73] The most fundamental, though in a sense the least discussed, of those complementary situations or relations is the one between the atomic and ordinary levels, or rather between knowledge on those two levels. It was that complementarity that provided Bohr with an escape hatch from Schrödinger's thought experiment about a cat in a box. Bohr insisted that Schrödinger mixed up the two levels instead of considering the case either on the atomic or on the ordinary or common-sense level. Had Bohr remembered Eddington's sagacious remark that "molar physics has always the last word in observation, for the observer himself is molar,"[74] he might have perceived the epistemological fallacy in that fundamental complementarity as interpreted by him. The two levels are not on an equal footing. Knowledge on the ordinary level can be corrected by what one learns on the atomic level, but is not inconceivable without it. On the other hand, knowledge on the atomic level is always a function of knowing on the ordinary or common-sense level.

Even more important, one's knowing is meaningless unless one knows something, that is, unless one's knowledge touches on reality. Elementary as this truth may appear, it has been stolen from Western rationality ever since Kant made his mark. Being heirs to that intellectual larceny, Bohr and his followers tried to understand not reality but only our understanding of reality and in the process Bohr was driven, as Hooker aptly remarked, "toward the twilight zone of mere appearances."[75] A world of appearances is most germane to oriental mysticism, and Bohr's categorical rejection of ontology was rightly seen as a telltale aspect of his basic sympathies with that mysticism.[76] Once ontology based on the common-sense grasp of reality is rejected, natural theology can easily be blown to pieces by any talk about knowledge even without having recourse to Geiger counters and explosives. But the same can also be done to Geiger counters and to ψ-functions, that is, to science. But how could this be perceived by those whom Einstein, in his letter of December 22, 1950, to Schrödinger, pitied as the ones who were unable to see what a risky game they played with reality?[77] Playing such a game takes overconfident people, people who feel they know everything, even what cannot be known—people who think that the glorious end is in sight. At the end of the same letter Einstein noted, not without a touch of sadness: "It is rough to see that as far as science is concerned we are still in the stage of wearing swaddling clothes and it is not surprising that the [Copenhagen] fellows struggle against admitting this even to themselves."[78] While it is never pleasant to be impaled on the horns of a dilemma, it must be positively uncomfortable to be dangling on horns when one's protective gear amounts to swaddling clothes. But if the true scientific spirit can demand humility enough to admit that even on that last and glorious leg of the road of science one's gown is but swaddling clothes, it will not perhaps be too much to ask for some intellectual humility when it comes to trying out once more the ways leading to God.

Fourteen

THE RAVAGES OF REDUCTIONISM

QUANTUM MECHANICS IS THE MOST RECENT PHASE OF THE LONG ROAD which science has so far traveled. Such a phase can be taken by the unwary and self-satisfied for the final stage, and this is what was done by not a few cultivators of quantum mechanics. A hundred years from now, and perhaps sooner, historians of science may have much fun with the inference that since quantum mechanics needs no recourse to variables hidden behind its magnificent façade, exact science has indeed reached the final stage of its road. The specifics to be learned by science in the century to come are anybody's guess. Predictions drawn up around 1850, 1900, and 1950 about future progress in astronomy turned out to be obsolete within a decade or so.[1] There lies a similar truth beneath the nomenclature of fundamental particles. The particle christened alpha around 1900 is still a name with historical pathos. Its discovery meant a heroic beginning. The name omega given to a particle in the 1950s is already the story of a pathetic presumption. Whatever the role of alphas in science, the omegas in it are like so many good watches that faithfully mark the advent of new times. The end of the road of science is always momentary, like the end of a day or of a year, a purely chronological convenience.

Having reached the end of that road in a chronological sense, we are now at the moment of turning more systematically to the ways to God, the other main part of the subject matter of these lectures. No longer are these ways, as in former times, the object of broadly shared discourse. They are mostly taken for trails reserved for dreamers in search of a brief escape from hard reality. In the intellectual climate of our times respectability is reserved to such avenues of reason as are meticulously free not only of theological connotations but of even the least touch of metaphysics. What is novel in that climate is not its antitheological and antimetaphysical character. The novelty lies in the resolve to restrict rational discourse to the pattern set by the method of physics. This is the essence of present-day reductionism. Its protagonists are physicalists known by such names as operationists, behaviorists, and logical positivists.

The intellectual avenues advertised by them have made their appeal by features like those of superhighways: straight direction, absence of steep rise, and deep embedding in the ground. Compared with such features, the ways to God ought to appear as misty trails, and all the more so as those admirable features are generally conceded to the avenues in question. Willingness to make this concession has become so general as to constitute a climate of opinion. But even a brief retrospect into intellectual history can make one realize that a specific climate of thought, however pervasive, is not necessarily a healthy and lasting condition. At any rate, in a physicalist perspective a climate of opinion is best discussed in terms of the properties of the atmosphere, one of which is atmospheric distortion. The heavier the air the stronger the distortion. Thus the possibility ought to be explored whether the un-appealing appearance of the ways to God might not be due to the presence of a medium which conceals to the eyes of reason the true nature of some of its uses.

In the creation of that medium, or atmosphere, the chief triggering role was played by the Wiener Kreis, or Vienna Circle, an outgrowth of the Verein Ernst Mach.[2] The Manifesto of the Vienna Circle issued in 1929[3] was followed by a rash of publications and conferences all des-tined to play the role of a trigger.[4] To use atmospheric physics as a comparison, the enterprise was like the seeding of clouds to produce rainfall. The clouds were present everywhere. They had for some time been generated by Wittgenstein's logical atomism, by Watson's behav-iorism, by Dewey's pragmatism, and by Mach's sensationism. Now the seeds, like so many shining iodine crystals, streamed forth from the splashy balloons floated by the Vienna Circle and soon the precipitation was felt all over the intellectual world.

As can easily be guessed, a sudden academic chain reaction is never a purely intellectual process. Indeed, the Vienna Circle functioned from the start in a manner that at times suggested the activities of missionary headquarters[5] and not those of a debating society. Some, like Popper, were attracted to its meetings solely because of their interest in the logical structure of knowledge. Popper, in fact, soon earned the reputa-tion of being the "offizielle Opposition."[6] There can be no doubt, how-ever, that Neurath, Carnap, and Frank fully shared the aim of Moritz Schlick, the galvanizer of the Circle.[7] What Schlick wanted to achieve far transcended the distinterested search of a typical scientist for par-ticular results. Schlick had originally been such a scientist, a physicist who earned his doctorate under Max Planck in 1904. His dissertation, a study of the refraction of light in nonhomogeneous medium, had no unusual merits, but most dissertations are such even when produced under the guidance of distinguished mentors. Actually, Schlick looked for far more than what physics could provide. Before long he was earn-ing his degree in philosophy, and it was as a professor of philosophy that he spent the almost two decades of his academic career. It led him from Rostock through Kiel to Vienna, where in 1922 he became the occupant of the prestigious chair originally established for Ernst Mach.

According to stereotype accounts, Schlick's philosophical activity stood in the exclusive service of resolving purely intellectual questions.

One would not expect such a philosopher to present his first book under the furtively emotional title of *Lebensweisheit* and find him arguing that the deepest meaning of existence consists in retaining the spirit of youth and joy.[8] Such a theme suits poets far better than philosophers, and good poets as a rule fare better with it than even the best philosophers. Schlick is not to be ranked among these even when such a classification is based on the philosopher's ability to perceive the ultimate implications of his basic propositions. They could hardly be clear to Schlick in 1918, when he published his *Allgemeine Erkenntnislehre*,[9] his sole major work on philosophy. Even the second edition in 1925[10] gave a picture of Schlick as one who wanted to retain something of realism. Only one with an instinct for realism could state as Schlick did that the entire world in its endless abundance of forms can be expressed in a single conceptual system since "the world itself is a unified whole, because everywhere within it the same is found in the different."[11] In view of this, Schlick's subsequent definition of knowledge as the reduction of conceptual signs to a minimum still could be read without hearing in it the ominous ring of reductionism. Yet that ominous ring was already there and indicated that Schlick's balance, to use a physicalist simile, was an unstable balance which had to turn into a precipitous course once given the proper impact. The impact, represented by Wittgenstein and (especially) Carnap, found little resistance in Schlick, who had already failed to perceive the irony in his profession of faith in an objectively existing rational world being preceded by his declaration of loyalty to Hume. He qualified his position on induction as being basically that of Hume, adding that he did not believe it "possible to move essentially beyond him."[12]

However far Schlick seemed at times to move away from Hume, he invariably gravitated back to him. Like Hume, Schlick too wanted to be "scientific" in epistemology, and as for Hume, the connection of epistemology with science as proposed by Schlick revealed a superficial grasp of it. To emphasize the "scientific" character of his epistemology, Schlick expressed deep satisfaction in the preface of his *Erkenntnislehre* that it was accepted in a series devoted to the sciences. The validity of knowledge, so Schlick justified his satisfaction, increased in the measure in which knowledge approached the kind of knowledge embodied in the exact sciences. The truth of such a phrase depended on the depth of one's knowledge of exact science. If grasp of technicalities was the proper gauge of that depth, Schlick with his doctorate in physics should have possessed it. But the proper gauge was much more refined, and it could not be had from Hume, Kant, Avenarius, and Mach, the authors most frequently quoted by Schlick. He referred to Einstein only twice and almost forgot his famous mentor, Planck.[13] Schlick, the philosopher of modern scientific knowledge, never caught a glimpse of the philosophy of knowledge underlying the science of Planck and Einstein. This was all the more baffling because Schlick became in 1919 the first philosopher to write on the significance of Einstein's general theory of relativity, which had received its capstone in its cosmological part only a year earlier.[14] But even here Schlick's interest in realism could be seen to be undermined by the intrusion of a very different interest. It made its cryptic appearance in the garb of Giordano Bruno, whose inspiration concerning the cosmos Schlick found exemplified in Einstein's cosmology![15]

Small details like this can at times convey more information on one's grasp of a situation than can long treatises. In fact, it was a very short treatise that revealed for the first time the full logic of Schlick's trend of thought. His brief essay on experience, knowledge, and metaphysics, published in the *Kantstudien* in 1926, was less a repudiation of Kant, the metaphysician, than an unveiling of Schlick, the reductionist or physicalist. The starting point of that essay was Gorgias's dictum that no knowledge was communicable. The chief claim of the essay was the other extreme: only that was knowledge which was strictly and unambiguously communicable.[16] On that basis external forms and logical relations always had the right to be called knowledge (Erkenntnis), while its experienced content (Erlebnis) had to be viewed as strictly ineffable. Clearly then, metaphysics, which is concerned not with the form of knowledge but with its content as touching on reality, loses its validity because that content can only be grasped through an assertion which is inseparable from that experienced element. Schlick should at least have realized that his banning of metaphysics could not be logically secured on the basis of the opposition he had set up between Erlebnis and Erkenntnis. The opposition, if logical, could only deal with the notion of Erlebnis and never with the content of any Erlebnis in which reality is experienced. If, however, the notion was not severed from its content, the opposition as conceived by Schlick defeated its own logic, to say nothing of the fact that logic as such could not even touch on the experienced reality of communicating logic itself!

Not seeing this, Schlick could claim without misgiving that the rationality of knowledge was best realized when forms, relations, and sequences were expressed in a mathematical mould.[17] This was as much a Procrustean bed for knowledge as it was for the history of science, especially for its very recent phase. For Schlick Einstein's relativity remained a proof that valid discourse is only about relations, forms, and structures, but never about a meaning referring to the reality in which they are embedded. For Schlick the deepest of Einstein's insights was his realization of the impossibility of giving an operational definition of simultaneity. Although Einstein unfolded far deeper insights about his scientific work, and did so years before Schlick's tragic death in 1936, this was never noticed by Schlick or other members of the Vienna Circle during its decade-long official existence. The way they spoke and wrote of Einstein at that time and even later gave the impression that Einstein as a philosopher was but an echo of Mach and that Mach as a physicist was a herald of Einstein. The reason for this myopia lies in the scientism professed by all members of the Vienna Circle. Scientism is never a genuine reverence for science but a harnessing of science for a nonscientific purpose. Since that purpose is fixed, science can only serve it by remaining fixed, namely, by remaining in its supposedly final stage. Taking that final stage of science as being wholly free of metaphysics, members of the Vienna Circle could freely devote themselves to their vivid Erlebnis, which propelled them to prune all rationally valid knowledge of any Erlebnis. It was a program as self-revealing and self-defeating as any effort to discredit utopia with more utopias, or as any strategy to disarm crusaders by engaging more crusaders.

Utopian crusaders they all were at heart. On occasion they sounded more like evangelists than philosophers. Only the style, not the substance, of their message was a far cry from the diction of d'Holbach, of Condorcet, and of Saint-Simon, the prophets of Paris. Yet, Neurath sounded more like a prophet of Paris than a prophet of Vienna when he declared that universal happiness would arrive through the systematic replacement of the priest with the physiological physician and with the sociological organizer.[18] In a less "Parisian" tone the promise of happiness was always an essential part of the message of the Vienna Circle. The message was about a scientific philosophy which stood in the service of life, a remark which brought to a close the Manifesto of the Circle drawn up by Hans Hahn, a physicist, Otto Neurath, a sociologist, and Rudolf Carnap, a logician.[19] The Manifesto was dedicated to Schlick in gratitude for his decision not to exchange his position in Vienna for one in Bonn. Schlick had then just completed a visiting professorship at Stanford University and felt like one carrying far and wide the all-important good news. The readers of the first page of the first issue of *Erkenntnis,* the freshly acquired quarterly of the Circle, were left in no doubt about Schlick's certitude concerning the onset of final deliverance. Descartes and Kant might easily have recognized the ring of their own futile hopes in Schlick's sanguine declaration: "I am convinced that we now find ourselves at an altogether decisive turning point in philosophy, and that we are objectively justified in considering that an end has come to the fruitless conflict of systems."[20] What gave Schlick this unlimited confidence was the possession of a method that made the conflict of philosophical systems unnecessary by making the conflict impossible through the elimination of philosophy itself.

The elimination of philosophy (in its traditional sense) was the consequence of the radical distinction between form and content, a distinction which was in essence identical to the distinction between Erkenntnis and Erlebnis.[21] Whatever meaning words carried, it could relate only to relations and not to a content tied to one's experiencing reality in any form. Such an experience was ineffable, that is, communicable not by words but only by deeds.[22] It is doubtful whether Schlick had in mind the deed of Samuel Johnson, who kicked a stone to demonstrate external reality,[23] or the deed of Diogenes, who walked across the hall to dispose of one of Zeno's sophisms. In both instances actions were used, presumably to no avail, against those who admitted only relations. If philosophy was henceforth to be concerned only with relations, then a radical change in the use of the word philosophy had been introduced, a point which Schlick acknowledged and emphasized. In particular he claimed that the whole development could only be understood in that perspective. Greatness was achieved by scientists—and Schlick singled out Einstein[24]—in the measure to which they turned their field of investigation into a study of relations. While the task had been completed in physics, the deliverance of ethics, esthetics, and psychology still had to be completed. Schlick did not expect quick conversion of all, but the final outcome was for him a foregone conclusion: "Rear-guard defenders of old philosophy will go on for centuries with their pseudo-questions, but in the end they would no longer be listened to; they will come to resemble actors who continue to play for some time before noticing that the audience has slowly departed."[25] A generation later a founding member of the Circle, disturbed by the rapid thinning out of the ranks of logical positivists, comforted himself with having once caught the bus of fashionable philosophy, and with the further thought that buses usually come around again.[26]

The planned and promised elimination of philosophy is, in principle at least, the chief and most fundamental of all ravages which reductionism is capable of perpetrating. The prospect of such ravage can but deeply disturb the natural theologian hopeful of keeping functional his ways to God, be it in the form of narrow trails. The demise of philosophy will much less disturb those who denounce it while making ample though furtive use of it. They, mostly men of science, can be alerted to the seriousness of that ravage only by being reminded of its impact on such branches of intellectual discourse as come under the heading of science. Concerning the well-established exact sciences, mathematics and physics, the ravages can hardly become more than hypothetical. Modern mathematicians, who achieved their greatest breakthroughs by relying heavily and explicitly on intuition, have not for a moment taken the advice of Hahn, who urged them to forgo intuition and limit themselves to strict logic.[27] As for physics, once its modern form had been created by Planck and Einstein, and through their thinking steeped in metaphysics, it was of no consequence that Hahn urged the "physicalisation of physics."[28] Younger colleagues of Planck and Einstein, eager to emulate their creativity, did not mind thinking metaphysically for the sake of success while professing the tenets of logical positivism. Ravages could, however, be easily inflicted upon younger branches of science, about which it is still highly doubtful that they can ever become exact, like physics. It was two such branches, psychology and sociology, that were selected by members of the Circle as ripe targets for deliverance from old philosophy, that is, metaphysics.

As to psychology, the program of deliverance was set forth by Carnap in publications that could not have had more outspoken titles, "Psychology in Physical Language,"[29] and "The Language of Physics as the Universal Language of Science."[30] Carnap's reduction of psychology to physics had no more merit than his effort to put it into a historical perspective. Not unexpectedly, he voiced the claim typical of the Vienna Circle that through the joint efforts of Mach and Einstein physics had become practically free of metaphysics.[31] This misleading evaluation of the present was of a piece with the propagandistic strokes wherewith Carnap listed in a physicalist spirit the major past developments of science. According to him Copernicus ousted man from his central position in the universe, Darwin deprived him of any supra-animal distinction, Marx reduced his history to the interplay of material factors, Nietzsche stripped his ethics of any transcendental halo, and Freud located the source of his ideas in his "nether regions."[32] To take Freud in 1932 for the last word on the origin of man's ideas was an intellectual Gleichschaltung, and not even a Carnap could live with it consistently. He conspicuously failed to ask whether Freud's theory of ideas was but the product of Freud's libido, to say nothing of Carnap's own libido as the possible source of Carnap's logic and physicalism. The same inconsistency and the same Gleichschaltung of scientific history was lurking behind what Carnap stated on Nietzsche, Marx, and Darwin. As to Copernicus, Carnap seemed to follow the hallowed pattern of speaking of Copernicus without having read what he wrote on God, man, and the universe.[33]

The Gleichschaltung of scientific history, which Carnap could do in a few lines without blinking an eye, was equivalent to compressing the thick and rich volumes of history into thin layers of playing cards. The procedure was certainly germane to the dictates of logical positivism and was also typical of its devotees. A generation later a leader of logical positivism in the United States confessed to "inexcusable conduct," namely, "that a few of us, though proud of our empiricism, for some time rather unashamedly 'made up' some phases of the history of science in a quite a priori manner."[34] Long before the facts of science were on hand, the physicalists could safely predict what they had to be. A classic case was the straitjacket which Carnap imposed on the problem of the reducibility of biology to physics. While he acknowledged that biological research was not yet able to settle the issue between vitalism and mechanism, he claimed that since the results of research did not touch upon the universality of physicalist language, the reducibility of biology to physics had to be granted in principle at least.[35] But if this were true, then an empirical question could be settled in advance, a procedure bound to produce its ravages in any field, like biology, with strong ties to the empirical.

The reductionist cultivation of psychology, which in Carnap's program ranged from the exclusion of all introspection to the glorification of graphology,[36] could only lead to a state of affairs which a generation later provoked the biting remark: "Psychology having first bargained away its soul, and then gone out of its mind, seems now, as it faces an untimely end, to have lost all consciousness."[37] Consciousness was eliminated from psychology by Carnap by simply ignoring it, and in a most conscious manner at that. Physicalism equally discredited its own logic with respect to the so-called physicalist language. By definition it was to be the language of physics, and by logic it had to be the language of the most developed forms of physics, general relativity and quantum mechanics. The language of physics used by the physicalists of the Vienna Circle was not even a distant cousin to either of them. Both general relativity and quantum mechanics were based on renouncing efforts to visualize,[38] that is, to stay within direct contact with ordinary experience. In neither of them could a decisive role be played by protocol sentences (sentences containing only sense data), which Carnap presented as the ultimate reference points of scientific discourse. Concerning those sentences it was not logically permissible to use in them even such modestly abstract words as copper and wire. According to Carnap, they were to be replaced with the primitive expression "long thin brown body" in order to conform parlance with immediate experience. In the same context Carnap did not, however, offer a primitive substitute for the smell of ozone connected with some electrical phenomena.[39] One wonders what that primitive substitute would have been when selected from the not too wide range of odors. Was the smell of ozone more primitive than the sight of copper wire from the viewpoint of sensory evidence? More important, was the expression "long thin brown body" free not only of ambiguities, but free from being a generalization steeped, as are all generalizations about sense data, in metaphysics?

Clearly, it was not possible to carry the logic of protocol sentences to its very end, because then reality would have obviously slipped through that nominalist net by which logical positivists tried, illogically enough, to catch reality. The full logic had to be avoided, and the half-way house of unconvincing protocol sentences had to be retained or else the semblance of remaining empirical had to be given up. This is why the language of physicalism as cultivated within the Vienna Circle remained that of the physics of Ernst Mach, a physics which for all its critique of classical physics remained naïvely classical in more than one respect. The situation was all the more reprehensible because it was clear to Schlick that Mach's position had to be transcended if the physicist was to reach the level of mathematical formalism. But once the reductionist approach reached that level, it fell into the predicament of the proverbial owner of a goat and of a field of cabbages. If the cabbages representing reality were so many relations, they could only disappear in the belly of the goat, the ever voracious mathematics, without leaving a trace of that reality which they represented.

Long before the Vienna Circle came into existence, it was known that the most varied physical phenomena could be reduced to the same mathematical formalism.[40] The attraction of electric charges, the attraction of masses, the intensity of light, all diminished according to the inverse square law, but no physicist of any consequence drew the conclusion that the diversity of such phenomena was therefore an illusion, a conclusion that is inevitable on the basis of logical positivism. It had other problems too concerning the relation of mathematics to reality. The Vienna Circle was only a few years old when Whitehead found it necessary to call attention in his never trivial diction to the trivial truth that while mathematics could count the number of atoms in an apple, it could not provide the apple itself.[41] Four years before the formation of the Vienna Circle Eddington made a remark on music which for all its brevity unveiled in advance the true consequences of Carnap's ambitious article on the "Elimination of Metaphysics through the Logical Analysis of Language." The article culminated in Carnap's reference to metaphysicians as "musicians without musical ability."[42] Many metaphysicians might have been bad musicians in more than one sense, but they never thought of abolishing discourse about music. Several members of the Vienna Circle were well known for their fondness for music, but they never realized that their premises barred them from speaking of music as such. The only aspects of music that could be discussed on the basis of logical positivism were either the physicality of instruments or the frequency of notes. In the former case music was equivalent to scraping horsetails on the intestines of cats, in the latter case one had to be reminded by Eddington that the sequence of frequencies was not the tune itself.[43] Thus while a logical positivist could be a musician of great ability, he was not entitled to speak of what music really was because this implied going beyond instruments and numbers. Within the physicalism of logical positivism music enjoyed no higher logical status than did cabbages: one could enjoy both without the right to say anything meaningfully communicative about one's enjoyment.

The situation was akin to the head-scratching which brings to a close a Viennese story about two neighbors who decided to submit their dispute to a rabbi renowned for his Solomonic wisdom. The source of the dispute was a cat, which, as one of the neighbors contended, had gobbled up her five-pound piece of butter. Her opponent, the owner of the cat, claimed that cats did not eat butter. After hearing both sides, the rabbi called for the cat, put it on a scale, the needle of which moved exactly to the five-pound mark on the dial. Looking intently at the dial, the rabbi said "We have found the butter," but he was clearly perplexed. Scratching his head he asked with a sigh: "But now where is the cat?"[44] The story might have brought home many an elementary truth to the members of the Vienna Circle, but the same could have been achieved by any story provoking the laughter of which Vienna never runs short. While laughter is a strikingly special part of human psychology, Carnap passed it over in silence. Laughter is, of course, no small problem even for a psychologist who works without the blinders of physicalism. One of the relatively few to tackle the psychology of laughter was T. A. Ribot, whose conclusion, now fourscore years old, is still worth recalling: "Laughter manifests itself in circumstances so numerous and heterogeneous—physical sensations, joy, contrast, surprise, oddity, strangeness, baseness, etc.—that the reduction of all these causes to a single remains very problematical. In spite of all the work devoted to so trivial a matter, the question is far from being completely elucidated."[45]

Three generations after Ribot, laughter is still a source of exasperation for a consistent physicalist. He can hardly rely on Bergson's somewhat dejected conclusion that "the philosopher who reaches out for too much hilarity will find on occasion in any measure of it a certain dose of bitterness."[46] Nor is the physicalist, or anyone else, helped by Freud's conclusion that the comical derives its satisfaction from being equivalent to an economy of thought surging from the subconscious.[47] The depths of the subconscious should certainly prove unfathomable to anyone fond of the doctrine of protocol sentences which easily leaves one stranded in the shallows of equivocation. An unwitting example of this was provided by Helmuth Plessner, a lifelong student of the problem of laughter, who in a way reminiscent of logical positivists wanted to keep the deeper perspectives wholly out of sight. Believing that equivocal relations were the way out of the problem, he proposed the relation of "Leib" (organic body) to "Körper" (plain body) as a clue to the explanation of laughter.[48] Equivocation is, of course, not absent in jokes producing laughter, but puns are their most superficial form. Not far removed from that superficiality is the famous claim of the Manifesto of the Vienna Circle: "We strive for order and clarity, reject all dim vistas and fathomless depths, for in science there are no "depths," all is on the surface."[49] Such claim deserves only the comment with which Niels Bohr once disposed of the counterarguments of his son who reminded him of consistency: "You are not thinking, you are merely logical."[50] Logic gives a very superficial view of science, indeed so superficial a view as to leave one unsure whether the proper reaction to it is to burst out in laughter or in tears.

Ample reasons are provided for both in the reduction of sociology to physics, a project which had Neurath as its chief champion in the Vienna Circle.[51] Neurath was not, of course, the first to advocate the use of quantitative method in sociology, but he was the first to try to give logical basis to the claim that only quantitative procedures were admissible in the study of society. His influence could only reinforce the already widespread preference among sociologists for quantitative discourse, which received in 1956 its well-deserved lampooning in Sorokin's *Fads and Foibles in Modern Sociology*.[52] That even a Sorokin could not stem the tide can easily be gathered from a book published in 1972 under the title *Social Sciences as Sorcery*,[53] the sorcery being largely equivalent to the fad of peppering the sociological brew with mathematical symbols. The tide of that fad flushed ashore the hilarious and the tragic in mighty splashes. One can only be amused at differential equations purporting to represent and predict the ups and downs of the American-Soviet arms race.[54] Apart from bemoaning the waste of taxpayers' money, one can still smile at the project of that historian of the American Civil War who claimed that its true causes will remain hidden unless the complete voting record of Congress between 1830 and 1860 is analyzed by computers.[55] Hilarious as the project may appear, it brings out the tragic pattern that in order to have the light of physicalism, all light deriving from common sense must first be extinguished. It is this systematically enforced oversight of the primordial importance of plain evidence which reveals the tragic dimension of the ravages of reductionism in sociology, which is usually hiding between the lines. A case in point is the massive collection of data on the time spent on a wide range of activities in twelve countries divided almost equally by the Iron Curtain.[56] The data show that the amount of time spent on sleeping, eating, working, sports, movies, reading, and the like, is essentially the same on both sides. From this a physicalist sociologist must conclude, and undoubtedly there are some who did conclude, that life is much the same on both sides of the Curtain, a conclusion which explains everything except the Curtain and especially those sections of it which are equipped with automatic devices spreading a curtain of bullets on man or beast stirring in its vicinity.

What Neurath's reaction would have been to the grim reality of such a curtain, made either of iron or of bamboo, had he lived to see it, is a secondary matter. As a convinced Marxist, he might have even been willing to justify it, since for a good Marxist the end always justifies the means. At any rate, on the basis of his physicalism emotional reactions would have come under the heading of experience or Erlebnis, which is ineffable in the sense that it can form no part of rational discourse. Uncounted experiences connected with the Curtain are ineffable in the sense of being beyond the pale, if not of physicalist, of ordinary reason. All those experiences are connected with the question of freedom, which is, however, a pseudoproblem within any sociology or psychology based on logical positivism. It should not therefore be surprising that Neurath found the mechanistic determinism of Marxist materialism very much akin to the spirit of logical positivism[57] and that Carnap's sundry dicta were found curiously reminiscent of that very same materialism.[58] It is no coincidence that the behaviorist author of *Beyond Freedom and Dignity*[59] was applauded by physicalist sociologists and psychologists unconcerned about the loss of either freedom or dignity, except of course when their own freedom, if not their dignity, is at stake. That loss will be classified as a ravage only by those who have not yet come, either politically or ideologically, under the fearful sway of the physicalist tenet that man is but a bundle of relations, each reducible to a stimulus and response.

When Neurath saw behaviorism as a natural ally of physicalism, he merely served evidence of his talent to articulate the Manifesto of the Vienna Circle in its full consistency. No one gave him more credit on that score than Carnap, who felt it important to note in 1932 in his long essay on physicalism as a universal language that it was Neurath who insisted from the start and with unflinching constancy both in discussions and publications sponsored by the Circle that the distinction between form and content must be observed rigorously. Such was in Carnap's words Neurath's definition "of physicalism in its most radical form." Concerning his own work, Carnap added: "I have arrived at results which wholly confirm Neurath's views."[60] Those results stated nothing less than that all statements which meant to convey anything but relations conveyed nothing but pseudoproblems.

Carnap, Neurath, and all founders of the Vienna Circle were convinced that one had only to cultivate metaphysics and natural theology to be lost in the meaninglessness of pseudoproblems. Conviction on this point was not the result of their work but a basic assumption of it. The essence of the evangelism of the Vienna Circle was the intention of depriving statements made on behalf of a transcendental outlook on cosmic and human existence of all rationality. Of all members of the Circle no one worked so long and so methodically as Carnap to validate this motivation. Yet the subsequent phases of his philosophical development were so many proofs that any systematic exclusion of metaphysics and of natural theology meant the exclusion of science as well. As Popper noted in retrospect in his classic summary of Carnap's work: "In all its variants demarcation by meaninglessness has tended to be at the same too narrow and too wide: as against all intentions and all claims, it has tended to exclude scientific theories as meaningless while failing to exclude even that part of metaphysics which is known as 'rational theology.'"[61] Such a phrase, coming as it does from a champion of the rationalist tradition, ought to be of no small comfort to anyone interested in the logic that connects the road of science and the ways to God.

Long before the foregoing statement of Popper was published in 1964 and long before it became public knowledge that Popper had urged against the publication of the *Encyclopedia of Unified Knowledge* as amounting not to a codification of truths secured by logical positivism but to a mere exercise in tautology,[62] the self-defeating character of Neurath's position was laid bare by none other than Bertrand Russell, one of the original inspirations of the Vienna Circle. In view of Carnap's endorsement of that position, Russell's criticism of it therefore affects logical positivism as a whole, Russell's protestations notwithstanding. His criticism saw print in his *An Enquiry into Meaning and Truth,* which marked one of the most unexpected and also most skillfully camouflaged turnabouts of any intellectual odyssey.[63] Russell, who had earned popular fame with his witty but shallow preaching of logical atomism in books that covered all major topics from science to religion, was deep enough to turn at long last to the question of meaning. "Neurath's doctrine, if taken seriously," he declared, "deprives empirical propositions of all meaning. When I say 'the sun is shining,' I do not mean that this is one of a number of sentences between which there is no contradiction: I mean something which is not verbal, and for the sake of which such words as 'sun' and 'shining' were invented. The purpose of words, though philosophers seem to forget this simple fact, is to deal with matters other than words." Since there were philosophers even at that time very much aware of that "simple fact," Russell should have declared them to be the only good philosophers. Instead, as if to cover himself, he hit Neurath with a broadside by declaring his doctrine to be a "neo-neo-Platonic mysticism."[64] Russell did not so much as hint that for almost three decades he had served that very same mysticism as one of its chief purveyors. Without a touch of guilt feeling he took the judgment seat and issued the otherwise impeccable sentence: "Some modern philosophers hold that we know much about language, but nothing about anything else. This view forgets that language is an empirical phenomenon like another, and that a man who is metaphysically agnostic must deny that he knows when he uses a word."[65] On reading this Einstein could only comment: "I am particularly pleased to note that, in the last chapter of the book, it finally crops out that one can, after all, not get along without 'metaphysics.' The only thing to which I take exception there is the bad intellectual conscience which shines through between the lines."[66]

The charge that logical positivism amounts in ultimate analysis to neo-neo-Platonic mysticism is both stinging and well founded. Those still asserting the reliability of words making up the ways to God need not therefore worry that those ways seemed to shrink to narrow trails in contrast to the apparent grandeur of the road laid by logical positivism. Its grandeur never surpassed the greatness of mere words. The place of final deliverance from metaphysics, where words cannot function as roads to reality, is a never-never land. It was in such a land that Schlick, Carnap, Neurath, and their many allies did their glittering work as surveyors of the terrain of intellectual discourse. They have made it abundantly clear that their sole concern was with conceptual relations divested of reference to reality. For such was the gist of Carnap's famous reminder to potential critics among supporters of any of the old philosophical "isms": "We pursue Logical Analysis, but no Philosophy."[67] On such a basis it was already illogical to try to bring reality back through references to statements that were admissible in science. But even when this backdoor procedure was overlooked, there was little resemblance between a reality which the best form of science asserted, and a reality which logical positivists allowed science to work with. While Einstein's general relativity was inconceivable without a realist notion of the world, while the universal validity of Planck's quantum made sense only within a world really quantized in some of its basic aspects, the logical positivists had to look at the notion of the world as being nonscientific. It was Ernst Mach who spoke through Neurath when he proposed that the caption, "Vienna Circle for the Dissemination of the Scientific World Outlook," be replaced with the phrase, "Vienna Circle for Physicalism," for, as Neurath added, "world" was a term which does not occur in the language of science.[68]

Anyone familiar with the central role which the notion of a rationally ordered world held in the work of all great scientists from Copernicus to Einstein can easily guess the true measure of distance which separates Neurath's dictum from science and especially from its part known as physics, to which all other sciences were to be reduced according to the program of the Vienna Circle. Revealingly, only a few physicists tried to work according to its definition of reality. When a major appeal was made to all physicists to do so, the dimension of potential ravage for science loomed large indeed. In 1936, when Bridgman made that appeal,[69] he had already established himself as the most consistent scientist-spokesman in the United States of a radically empiricist cultivation of physics.[70] He practiced what he preached, as shown by his famous series of papers concerned with the techniques of producing high pressures. In none of them did Bridgman try to connect his valuable data with atomic theory or with theories of stellar evolution, topics very germane to the physics of high pressures.[71] He had been well known for his empiricist assault on scientific cosmology, which he tried to discredit both with respect to theory and to observational extrapolations.[72] For his readiness to label and dismiss as metaphysical the assumption that nature obeys mathematical simplicity[73] he received his due share of criticism from fellow scientists but he remained undaunted. Three years after his empiricist evaluation and dismissal of modern cosmology as a branch of metaphysics, he urged all physicists fond of the cosmology of general relativity to consider the essential difference between laboratory physics and cosmology. The difference between the two was the difference between science and nonscience. Shift of interest from cosmology to "ordinary experimental physics" was to occur, Bridgman hoped, "once the realization of that difference of meaning has actually got under one's skin."[74]

Any branch of science can be stifled in various ways. Around 1936 the whole school of cosmology was liquidated in the Soviet Union because the topic smacked of bourgeois metaphysics. Bridgman, a staunch opponent of political totalitarianism, certainly had no such brutal course in mind, but he could not be completely unaware of the consequences for scientific cosmology of his totalitarian empiricism. Historians, who know how much depends in science on prevailing moods of thought, will admit that the shift of interest advocated by Bridgman could be, if heeded, very fatal to scientific cosmology. Although not a member of the Vienna Circle, Bridgman advocated principles that were characteristic of its program. Bridgman is now history and so is the Vienna Circle. It has even been suggested that to question further the verifiability theory of meaning, the touchstone of logical positivism, would be tantamount to flogging a dead horse, "because there are no longer any logical positivists."[75] Yet, ten years after this premature obituary was issued, Professor Ayer, a still very vigorous proponent of logical positivism, was given the prestigious opportunity of a Gifford lectureship to apply his sharp dissecting tools to natural theology.[76]

Since the tools were suited for definitions and not for the intellectual act of grasping reality, the whole of natural theology was treated by Professor Ayer as a set of definitions, which natural theology, by and large, was never meant to be. If the ways to God rested on a definition of God, then it was clearly appropriate to introduce them, as Professor Ayer did, with the anecdote, already a century old, about that theist who admitted that once he had given his definition of God any atheist could dissect it.[77] Of course, when it came to the moral argument steeped in the freedom of the will, definitions appeared strangely disparate from a reality as close to anyone as one's ability to choose freely and responsibly. On Professor Ayer's premises there could be no objection to inducing a good choice with drugs, a procedure which he confessed he was unable to disqualify, although he himself did not like it.[78] His dissecting the other proofs was, if not self-defeating, at least very dated. Hume's formulation of the proof from teleology, which he took as its standard form, is an old distortion of it. Kant's reduction of the cosmological argument to the ontological is so inconclusive as to be recognized as such even by some leading logical positivists, another fact of which Professor Ayer seemed to be unaware.[79] That it could be clear to him that religion does not contribute in a significant way to morality, even though he admitted that he knew of no historical studies of this question,[80] should be of no interest to scholars still appreciative of positive data. What he offered as a whole illustrated Popper's remark that "there is no such a thing as a logical method of having new ideas."[81] Presumably, many looked with glee at Professor Ayer's performance as a splendid ravaging worthy of a Roman holiday. The BBC, which carried his last lecture, which dealt with natural theology, found it appropriate to grace its text in *The Listener* with a cartoon of the devil declaring: "If Professor Ayer did not exist, it would be necessary to invent him."[82] No such inventiveness is needed to note that in connection with Professor Ayer's performance no one cared, publicly at least, to reflect on the ravages which the tools of logical positivism are capable of when applied not only to natural theology but to any branch of science. Such a lack of reflection is neither positive nor logical, but is highly characteristic of logical positivism, that chief modern breeding place of the ravages of reductionism. Once those ravages, potential and actual, are firmly kept in focus, the proud avenues of logical positivism will appear for what they really are, blind alleys. Therefore, just because of logical positivism one certainly need not take for misty trails the roads which lead man to God.

Fifteen

PARADIGMS OR PARADIGM

IT IS AN OLD TRUTH THAT SINS OF OMISSION CAN BE AS SERIOUS AS SINS OF positive action, if not more so. The same is true of ravages. Studied neglect can be the source of a ravage as fateful as any ravage actively inflicted. Neglect is particularly productive of ravages when camouflaged as careful attention. Logical positivists professed so much admiration for science as to give it a "timeless" quality. With this they reduced science to pure logic and also severed it from its real history. Within such an approach to science it was most natural to continue with the old cliché according to which science suddenly emerged when Galileo dropped weights from the Tower of Pisa and let balls roll down an inclined plane. This hallowed picture of Galileo, the empirico-logician, might have fitted some cubbyholes of logic, but certainly not the empirical facts of history. Had logical positivists been possessed of sincere interest in those facts, they would have been rudely jolted when in the late 1930s it was carefully pointed out that Galileo never dropped weights from any tower and that he had derived the time-squared law of free fall long before he experimented with balls and inclined planes.

Of these two jolts the first could conceivably be minimized.[1] No such maneuver was possible with the second jolt, administered in 1939 through the publication of Alexandre Koyré's *Etudes galiléennes.* Galileo's own words, if read without the color filters of positivism, often indicate that for him it was enough to rely on the eyes of the mind in order to reach portentous scientific conclusions about the physical world.[2] One can, of course, be easily carried away in unfolding the obvious meaning of classic but long-misinterpreted texts. Koyré went indeed too far in claiming that Galileo could not have carried out the inclined-plane experiment with the success demanded by the empiricist school,[3] and that, anyhow, for him experiments were almost always thought experiments.[4] Had Koyré's *Etudes* not proved themselves extremely influential and had he not offered during the following decades further variants of his claim,[5] it would hardly have provoked a primitive though ingenious rebuttal. This consisted in the experimental demonstration that Galileo could easily have carried out the inclined-plane experiment in such a way as to obtain data embodying with significant precision the time-squared law.[6] Consequently, it had to be considered that this symbolic starting point of classical physics might have been due to a Galileo who, contrary to Koyré, was more than a mere Platonist. When this unexpected turn presented itself in the early 1960s, Koyré's influence was at its zenith. A younger generation of historians of science, who for the first time were numerous enough to be recognized as a separate profession, looked upon the *Etudes* as a "revelation of what exciting interest their newly found subject might hold."[7]

It may indeed be repeated (with some reservation) that the *Etudes* were "no arid tally of discoveries and obsolete technicalities, nor a sentimental glorification of the wonders of the scientific spirit, nor yet (despite the author's Platonism) a stalking horse for some philosophical system whether referring to science like the positivist outlook, or to history like the Marxist."[8] The author of a book so highly regarded deserves all the more attention because during his whole career and especially in its first half Koyré showed keen interest in natural theology. His first book was on the formulation of the ontological proof by Descartes,[9] the second on the original propounding of that proof by Saint Anselm, in which Koyré even defended its validity against Kant's objections![10] Whatever the character of Koyré's theism in 1923, the following ten or so years found him absorbed in a study of three thinkers well known for their pantheism. They were Boehme,[11] Tchaadaev,[12] and Spinoza.[13] That is hardly a negligible list if a scholar's choice of research topics is any evidence of his intellectual sympathies. In fact, Koyré was always thinking in such a way as to let ultimate reasons, as he held them, make their presence subtly felt in whatever he wrote. Consequently, his interpretation of the history of science cannot be isolated from his views on natural theology, the area of widest possible concern for the ultimate implications of one's basic postulates. In view of Koyré's influence on that new generation of historians of science, such an isolation might even deprive one of an important clue as to why a principal branch of the present-day historiography of science has grown in a very specific direction.

In the late 1930s Koyré was also putting on paper his most cherished reflections of Plato,[14] which are so many clues to understanding why Koyré had eyes for spotting the Platonic trait in Galileo, but no eyes for another, equally important trait in Galileo's mental physiognomy. That other trait shows Galileo a Christian Platonist, and partly because of this he was a genuinely modern scientist for whom a close agreement of theory with facts was not as secondary as Koyré wanted us to believe.[15] Some food for thought can also be found in Koyré's attitude toward Bacon and Pascal. Obviously, Bacon's empiricism hostile to geometry was not the right diet for a Platonist who had no misgivings about Plato's apotheosis of geometry. But precisely because of this, Koyré could hardly warm to Pascal,[16] although Pascal was a renowned geometer and an Archimedean as far as science was concerned. The God of Pascal was above all the God of history, and Pascal made no secret about the immense superiority of that God over the God of geometry, let alone over geometry turned into a god. That Koyré felt no sympathy for Pascal, too incisively Christian for him, sheds therefore also some light on the narrowing of horizons which is bound to occur in the perspectives of a Platonizing historian not far from being a pantheist. Thus no perplexity was shown by Koyré, the historian, as he singled out Archimedes for the role of catalyst in bringing about the scientific revolution.[17] Koyré never pondered why Archimedes himself could not bring about that very same revolution if Galileo needed but Archimedes to bring it about.[18] The impact of Archimedes was, according to Koyré, the vehicle of return from the Aristotelian concept of motion as concrete process to its Platonist version as abstract state. In that return Koyré saw the watershed separating the ancient from the modern, the nonscientific from the scientific, nay he spoke of it as the most decisive event in intellectual history.[19] Koyré would certainly not have agreed with Whitehead, a Platonist not entirely severed from Christianity, who recognized that only the biblical faith in God centered on the babe born in Bethlehem made in that history a stir even greater than science did.[20]

In its concreteness that intellectual and scientific history is the very opposite of the abstract immobility of the Platonic realm of ideas. Not even geometry was in the 1930s the steady affair that it was in Plato's days. Since Koyré was not so much of a Platonist as to identify any given form of thought as absolute and eternal, he had to descend from the heights of Platonist metaphysics to the much lower level of Platonizing psychology, and from there it was but a short step to the labyrinths of experimental psychology. There any sudden and major shift, especially if it related to science, qualified if not for absolute enlightenment then at least for a relative, time-conditioned phase of it. Koyré, therefore, could not only retain the notion of thought as a subtly pantheistic participation in eternity,[21] but he could also revel in the succession of enlightenments which, being sudden, could just as well be labeled revolutions, a term self-explanatory to modern ears deafened by the din of revolutions. Thus it happened that Koyré, the Platonist reader of the seventeenth-century scientific revolution, became the dean of historians of scientific revolutions,[22] who cared for psychology and revolutions, hardly for Plato, and certainly not for metaphysics.

Few if any of them studied Koyré's early interest in the ontological argument, often a convenient stalking horse for pantheism. Even fewer cared to look into his monograph on Boehme, a rank pantheist, or to look up his glowing comments on Tchaadaev, the first champion in Russia of the pantheist Schelling.[23] Koyré's translation of Spinoza's treatise on the reformation of the intellect made its way to the United States, the home of most of Koyré's admirers, in only a few copies. Koyré's introduction to it, therefore, went unnoticed, as did the possibility that his new translation might have been born of some inner need governing his trend of thought and not of the unavailability of an older translation. Koyré's book on Plato's dialogues, however, was widely available and should have raised a question or two about Koyré's tacit endorsement of relativism on the pretext that Socrates never meant to teach truth but only enlightenment.[24] None of these factors, and certainly not the subtly theological ones, were hinted at by Koyré when in 1961, in the presence of a large gathering of historians of science in Oxford, he declared on behalf of himself and his followers: "Our 'idealism' is nothing else than a reaction against the attempts to interpret, or misinterpret, modern science . . . as an extension of technology."[25] A curious declaration, since until very recently the so-called "internalist" historians of science simply ignored the "externalists," hardly an attitude of reaction.[26]

That the "idealism" advocated by Koyré had less to do with metaphysics than with psychology and sociology was evident on the first page of the *Etudes*, where conceptual evolutions were identified with conceptual revolutions.[27] There Koyré echoed with sympathy Gaston Bachelard's account of those revolutions as sudden mutations of the intellect.[28] In the same *Etudes*, devoted to the seventeenth-century scientific revolution, the second page carried a reference to another revolution that had taken place in physics in the early part of the twentieth century. Insofar as repeated revolutions might have implied a fragmentation of the Platonic archetype of science into pieces that could not be interpreted as so many stepping-stones toward the apex of a single pyramid representing science, Koyré did not seem to mind it. Actually, his notion of the rise of scientific revolutions could be likened to the sudden breakthrough of shafts of sunlight from behind dark clouds. This is one of the reasons why Koyré showed no sympathy for Duhem's thesis about the long medieval preparation of the seventeenth-century scientific revolution. This is also why he failed to be attracted to studying the fact that the shift from Aristotle back to Plato contained the seed of an epistemological development which in the long run was to contradict the scientific enterprise. But if evolution was a chain of revolutions, then contradictions hardly needed to seem upsetting. This carefree and "revolutionary" attitude toward deeper contradictions was, however, clearly contradictory if there was any truth in Koyré's admirable claim that the primary justification of the study of the history of science lay in the philosophical lessons it contained.[29] The same contradictoriness was particularly evident at the end of the *Etudes* where Koyré spoke of the victory of Galilean and Cartesian science as implying also the loss of "cosmic value" in the notion of space and physical law. He noted with a touch of pathos that no higher price had ever been paid for a victory.[30] One can only guess what Koyré really had in mind by that price. In a historicist fashion he suspended inquiry at the very moment he arrived at the most momentous question raised by his investigation of the scientific revolution. Had he delved into that question he might have perceived that his rendering of Galileo's "ontology" failed to include crucial clarifications about ontology. Keeping in focus such clarifications might have led him to probe the meaning of intellectual revolutions in such depth as to do proper justice both to science and to the human mind capable of doing science. Had this happened, the new historiography of science might have steered clear of the shallows of historicism and would not have provoked the feeling that many recent studies of the history of science should be rated X for students of science.[31]

Historicism is a study of history which derives philosophical conclusions from the facts and trends of history without taking stock of philosophy itself. The logical result is the claim already formulated by Dilthey that "the relativity of all human concepts is the last word of the historical vision of the world."[32] Being an obviously nonrelativist proposition, the relativity of all concepts can give away even a relativism mindful of philosophy. When philosophy is largely ignored, as is usually the case within historicism, a brand of positivism, the basic concepts used as tools of interpretation will turn potentially deep statements, such as Comte's words that "no concept can be really known except through its history,"[33] into historicist slogans. Those tools, if sharpened by logic but used with no recourse to the light of philosophy, will at best produce precision but no enlightenment. Such a consequence is not readily apparent within a historicism which is "externalist" in the sense of relying on external factors—economic, social, political, and technical—as tools of interpretation. But the same consequence can become rapidly evident within the "internalist" position advocated by Koyré and his followers. Since the internalists explain intellectual history in general and scientific history in particular in terms of ideas, it would seem to be their logical task to pay close attention to the question of whether intellectual development, philosophical or scientific, can be understood in terms of its conceptual history, with no questions raised about the nature of intellects—which presumably are the producers of ideas and the carriers of their development. Once intellects are methodically overlooked, the concepts can be expected to do the thinking, with the result that the act of understanding becomes a subjective enlightenment and not an objectively valid clarification. The manner in which Koyré presented the lesson given by Plato in the *Meno* and the reformation of the intellect proposed by Spinoza were votes cast for that subjective enlightenment which lends itself to proliferation and not to consolidation and coherence.

The proof of this is the wide and at times wild variety of present-day interpretations of science derived from its history. An important role in that process was played also by the publication in English of Popper's *Logic of Scientific Discovery*, a chief claim of which was that there was no logic in the act of scientific discovery, but only in the finished scientific theory.[34] Such a claim suited all too well the subjectivism of the trend originated by Koyré, a subtle subjectivism to be sure, because it was apparently restricted to the very few fundamental questions of epistemology. Concerning secondary questions or the whole superstructure of knowledge, the claim to objectivity was retained. The situation could be compared to a relatively stable surface hiding foundations where everything was in flux. Such was the background of the phrase "science in flux," to recall an idea of Popper popularized by Joseph Agassi.[35] Having been declared impervious to a logic standing for epistemology, the flux was to be treated in the framework of phenomenology. The procedure had more than one advantage. It could be molded to historical relativism, it could be dressed in the scientific garb of experimental psychology, and, not least, it could create the illusion that questions about objective truth were thereby answered. Such was the mechanism of the proliferation of "scientific" explanations of science derived from its history. In all those explanations the data of scientific history serve as a façade for the historicist philosophy wrapped in the jargon of psychology and sociology.

While the pedestal on which science as objective truth was formerly placed might have been too exalted, historicism could knock science down only in such a way as to make it suffer the fate of Humpty Dumpty. This is not to suggest that all those participating in the act were happy with the result. Norwood R. Hanson's "patterns of discovery" represented an effort to put rationality or coherence back into science. But since he postulated for discovery a "modal" logic irreducible to normal logic,[36] he retained in a sense as many logics as there were discoveries, leaving science in its fragmented status. Because of his insistence on an inherently subjective logic, Hanson failed to give a rational answer to the question why man was able to make discoveries and through discoveries, science, and why he acquired science at a specific juncture in history. Yet unless these and similar questions are answered, the patterns offered as explanations will remain sophisticated but disconnected descriptions. As such, they will easily create the impression that science has only patterns but that science itself is not a pattern. Breaking science down into "research programmes"[37] is an artful way of begging the question of why there is any research at all, a point which becomes evident as soon as the word research is replaced by science, a replacement clearly justified because science is inconceivable without research. Trying to understand science through its "images" is not much help either,[38] unless one faces up to the question of whether those various images are merely subjective states of the scientist's imaginative powers, or objective aspects of one and the same science. Identifying "themata" running through the scientific enterprise can be very illuminating,[39] but they assume the existence of that enterprise instead of coping with it as a problem for epistemology. As to the reduction of scientific theories, or knowledge, to myths,[40] it should be enough to ask whether that reduction is itself objective knowledge or merely a myth.

The careful avoidance of basic epistemological questions in these "explanations" of science is the main feature common to all of them. That avoidance is present even when a "happy ignorance" is claimed about the demarcation line between philosophical and scientific ideas.[41] Obliteration of that demarcation is just as unphilosophical as any overemphasis of it. Understandably enough, when captions like "paradigms," "images of science," "research programs," "patterns," "themata," "myths," and the like are preempted of epistemological rigor, they will, as was aptly remarked, "threaten to deteriorate into little more than vogue words and vogue concepts."[42] Of such concepts or captions none enjoyed greater vogue than Thomas Kuhn's paradigms gracing almost every page of his *The Structure of Scientific Revolutions*.[43] The vogue was, however, well merited. For unlike authors of other captions, Kuhn made the term "paradigm" carry a train of thought developed to its ultimate implications concerning the interpretation of the history of science. It is precisely because of this that the historicism advocated by Kuhn brought into focus basic questions about the history of science and threw a brief flash on its connection with natural theology.

Historicism it was, as can be seen from Kuhn's early exposure at Harvard to Conant's "strategy of science," a strategy notoriously short on philosophy,[44] but in which Kuhn saw great merits.[45] Historicism was also implied in that list given by Kuhn of historians of science, who (Koyré was prominently mentioned) seemed to offer most of what Kuhn was groping for.[46] Historicism was also clearly evident in Kuhn's claim that the place of philosophy as supreme interpreter was to be filled by logical analysis, linguistic studies, and above all by sociology and psychology.[47] It was indeed during a year spent among behavioral scientists that Kuhn received both the stimulus and the insight, to each of which he attributed a crucial role in his intellectual development. The stimulus was his reading of a fairly recent though hardly noticed book, Ludwik Fleck's monograph dealing with the resistance to Wassermann's discovery in 1906 of blood tests as means of detecting syphilis.[48] The book convinced Kuhn that scientific ideas must be put in their sociological context to let their meaning be revealed. A rather inflated inference if one keeps in mind that scientific ideas are a personal matter in a sense very different from the one in which problems of syphilis and related woes can become personal and sociological inhibitions. The insight Kuhn gained through his association with sociologists related to the ease with which physicists could achieve consensus in contrast to the disagreements plaguing sociologists and psychologists.[49] To attribute that ease to something in the subject matter of physics might have seemed natural, but this would have implied a specific concept of nature and a specific epistemology. Since these were not to be considered, a recourse to sociology and psychology was inevitable. From the viewpoint of sociology the consensus was a state of political normalcy, whereas its emergence, or formation, was a political revolution. From the viewpoint of psychology the state of consensus was interpreted as the fixation of mind on a Gestalt, and the emergence of the consensus as a Gestalt switch.[50]

Condensing all this into the expressions paradigm and paradigm change proved to be a mixed blessing for Kuhn's theory. The word paradigm certainly did not have the unpleasant overtones of the word dogma, which Kuhn originally used side by side with paradigm.[51] The word paradigm, which Hanson had already used very sparingly,[52] unlike the grammarians to whom it really belonged,[53] had its signification extended by Kuhn so much as to require quite a few words to suggest what the new meaning really was.[54] This was not necessarily a drawback in an age given to catchwords with very pliable basic meanings. While Kuhn himself admitted that he used the word as a substitute for "a variety of familiar notions,"[55] minor consternation was felt when it was pointed out that he had attached to the word at least twenty-one different meanings[56] within the covers of a not very long book. Although this variety of meanings could be subsumed in three main groups,[57] the remaining variety still left not much room for rigorous debate, while it certainly left Kuhn with always handy escape routes from the grasp of his critics.

They paid less attention to the lack of rigor in Kuhn's use of the word revolution, which played an equally important role in his theory. He had hardly passed the midpoint of his book when he declared that its remainder served to demonstrate the striking similarity of paradigm changes to political crises resolved by revolutions. This sociological perspective was so fundamental as to play the role of final arbiter: "As in political revolutions, so in paradigm choice—there is no standard higher than the assent of the relevant community."[58] This was a phrase not only pivotal but also very fragile because of the philosophical burden it carried. While concerning scientific questions the scientific community could perhaps claim exclusive relevance, the relevance of philosophical questions was far broader. Was their relevant community the body of philosophers haughtily rejecting common sense, or rather the mass of plain folk sticking to it, to say nothing of revolutionaries throwing common sense to the wind as well as philosophy? Kuhn seems to have parted momentarily with philosophy, for his endorsement of the role to be played by the notion of political revolutions came on the heels of his admitting the existence of "vast and essential differences between political and scientific development."[59] If such was the case, what was the rationale for vindicating the notion of revolution as a metaphor that alone could cope with the dynamic, that is, historical reality of science? Failure to face up to this question is one source of those ambiguities which repeatedly show Kuhn trying to resolve problems by recognizing their existence and then going on with his project as if it could be carried out satisfactorily without taking up those problems—almost invariably epistemological and even metaphysical in character.

Such tactics were unjustified even within Kuhn's own perspectives, for what could be the point of registering the impact of nature and of logic on scientific debates[60] if that impact was not to be investigated in detail? Worse even, any detailed presentation of that impact could only be preempted of its significance if it was true that "an apparently arbitrary element, compounded of personal and historical accident, is always a formative ingredient" in the paradigm.[61] That arbitrariness was so far from being only apparent as to prompt Kuhn's declaration that "the competition between paradigms is not the sort of battle that can be resolved by proofs."[62] Intellectual battles that are not resolved by proofs must qualify as irrational, made so by the maddening resolve to concede nothing good to the other side. The major battles of science therefore become revolutions which "close with a total victory for one of the two opposing camps."[63]

Typically enough, the many references made by Kuhn to scientists concern not so much their reasonings as their states of mind, implying much more than rigorous arguments. States of mind or shared paradigms, to use Kuhn's idiom, may be good subject matter for a psychology not concerned with thinking as such. It is another matter to hypostatize those states. There is more than poetical metaphor in Kuhn's phrase that if a particular paradigm "is destined to win its fight, the number and strength of the persuasive arguments in its favor will increase."[64] What this shows is that once the thinking man is removed from the center stage, thought itself will be invested with functions reserved for him. The personified thoughts or paradigms will then be seen as contending with one another in accordance with Darwin's concept of evolution. Such is Kuhn's "resolution" of scientific revolutions, about which he emphatically stated that "it is the selection by conflict within the scientific community of the fittest way to practice future science."[65]

That there is no place in Darwin's theory for goal-directed process is well known. Kuhn undoubtedly assumed the unquestionable truth of that theory as he declared that "even such marvelously adapted organs as the eye and hand of man—organs whose design had previously provided powerful arguments for the existence of a supreme artificer and an advance plan—were products of a process that moved steadily *from* primitive beginnings but *toward* no goal."[66] This indirect but very logical dismissal of natural theology should not distract from a more immediate aspect of Kuhn's theory, which is also its culminating point. The succession of paradigms is like the successive emergence of species: an increasingly more adapted "set of instruments which we call modern scientific knowledge."[67] Critics of ˏKuhn had immediately noted that if one denies cumulative progress to science because successive paradigms are irreconcilable,[68] one cannot without contradiction claim also that stages of that succession constitute a "developmental process" and that they are marked "by an increase in articulation and specialization."[69] For the same reason it also becomes contradictory to speak of the structure of scientific revolutions as long as the structure is meant to transcend the parts and give coherence to the whole, in conformity both with the obvious meaning of the word structure and with the astonishing coherence of science as it has existed for the past four hundred years. This coherence is not something to be taken lightly. Actually, it was its magnitude that forced Kuhn to make his most telling retraction, by weakening, however slightly, the rigorous incommensurability of successive paradigms.[70] In doing so, he could but seriously weaken the appeal of Gestalt switches and revolutions as the explanation of science.

Although now a largely closed episode, Kuhn's theory is very useful and instructive for a historian of science intent on unfolding the relevance of his field to natural theology. Kuhn's incidental though hardly accidental reference to natural theology is a clear indication that in the perspective of historicism natural theology cannot be what it is and wants to be. It can at best be a Gestalt that has outlived its usefulness, or a revolution that has already been wiped out by revolutions of very different nature. At any rate, natural theology cannot exist without the possibility of answering and in a specific way the question: "What must nature, including man, be like in order that science be possible at all?"[71] This question of Kuhn, the first of a series of questions bringing his essay to a close, is a question that is patently metaphysical. The answer to a metaphysical question, assuming that it is not declared in advance to be a pseudoquestion, ought to be metaphysical, and if one does not want to hear such an answer one should refrain from raising any such question. If, however, the question "What must the world be like in order that man may know it"—a variation by Kuhn of his former question—is valid, but, as Kuhn put it, "remains unanswered,"[72] then an explanation must be given about the manner in which psychology and sociology can answer this and other metaphysical questions on Kuhn's list. One looks in vain for that explanation in Kuhn's essay, unless one is willing to take the jargon of sociology and psychology for epistemology and metaphysics.

Psychology and sociology, cast by Kuhn in the role of epistemology and metaphysics, are the sources of all the basic defects of his frequently very interesting essay. This is why he could give but incomplete answers to the questions remaining on his list: "Why should scientific communities be able to reach a firm consensus unattainable in other fields? Why should consensus endure across one paradigm change after another? And why should paradigm change invariably produce an instrument more perfect in any sense than those known before?"[73] The answers given by Kuhn are not only incomplete but create a deep sense of puzzlement, mainly because of his failure to come to grips with a disproportion of his own making, the existence of which was not hidden to him. In much the same way as he developed only the similarities and not also the admittedly vast and essential differences between political and scientific "revolution," he cared not to probe into the grounds and consequences of his assertion that the world remains the same even after it is seen in a totally different perspective following the paradigm shift.[74] But how can the world remain the same if it is true, as Kuhn also claimed, that his incommensurable paradigms are constitutive not only of science but of nature as well?[75]

Since the longest chapter in Kuhn's book is devoted to this claim,[76] his failure to do the probing mentioned above should seem all the stranger. While a psychologist can reasonably claim the overwhelming preconditioning in the world views of some individuals, the case is quite different when such a preconditioning is presented as an always valid predicament. Then not only the world's objective endurance in the teeth of shifting paradigms remains unanswerable, but the suspicion may also arise that what is being advocated is a kind of subjective idealism.[77] This suspicion is strengthened when a look is taken at the consequences resulting for science both from idealism and from Kuhn's psychologism. Both are a form of subjectivism destructive of a science claiming any measure of objectivity. The sad record of idealism vis-à-vis science is so clear that only idealists uninformed about science try to create the contrary impression.[78] As for Kuhn's paradigms being constitutive of nature, they proved to be unacceptable precisely because of their intrinsic threat to the objectivity of science and of nature. The brief, negative reference in Kuhn's essay to natural theology should therefore cause no surprise. It is a consequence of the subjective idealism implied in his paradigms. The destructiveness of idealism for science and for natural theology alike is once more seen.

While this symptom forms a basic lesson in the context of these lectures, it is only the philosophical part of the lesson which is provided by the psychologism and sociologism adopted as basic platforms in Kuhn's essay. The historical part of that lesson derives from the same absence of evenhandedness which has already been observed in connection with the applicability of the concepts of revolution and paradigm. Kuhn's is a heavily tilting balance when he acknowledges that world views and metaphysical beliefs are essential ingredients in any paradigm constitutive of science[79] and pays no further attention to them. Yet if it is true that paradigms constitutive of science and of its revolutions emerge in a few select minds before they become widely shared by the scientific community,[80] it would have been easy to recall the history of world views and metaphysical beliefs which animated the great creative figures of science from Copernicus to Einstein.

The world views reveal a remarkable similarity. Copernicus's message is incomprehensible if the world of which he spoke is not assumed to be objectively real and ordered. Again, what could be of greater significance to a historian of scientific revolutions than the case of Planck and Einstein, the last two in the relatively short list of great scientific revolutionaries? Was it not science that drove them away from Mach's sensationism toward the emphatic defense of a view for which the world was objective and orderly? If, however, the great scientific revolutions were sustained by this belief in an objective world and in an objective account of nature, can a historian raise the question: "Does it really help to imagine that there is some one full, objective, true account of nature and that the proper measure of scientific achievement is the extent to which it brings us closer to that ultimate goal?"[81] While to imagine this may not help a historian who plays the philosopher in the cloak of historicism, all scientists who not only imagined that account of nature but firmly believed in it were immensely helped, and through them science was helped in a crucial manner. Not of course that ordinary or "normal" science, about which Kuhn traced out a gripping bundle of characteristics, but that science which displays through its major advances or revolutions its creative nature. About that help, a most logical topic for Kuhn's essay, one would look there in vain for anything tangible.

If, however, creative science drove an Einstein toward a world view which in its very core was identical to the one held by Maxwell, Faraday, Euler, Newton, Galileo, Kepler, and Copernicus insofar as objectivity and order were concerned, then one may suspect with good reason a fair measure of identity to be present in science throughout its cultivation from Copernicus to Einstein. To dispute that identity Kuhn presented the Newtonian and Einsteinian concepts of mass as being radically different, on the basis that in the former mass is conserved whereas in the latter it is convertible with energy.[82] Yet if the two concepts are radically different how can one be the limiting case of the other, a point acknowledged even by Kuhn? Nor should one forget that the notion of inertia, which lurks behind both Newton's and Einstein's concepts of mass, obviously establishes some identity between the two. The question of this partial identity is philosophical and will never be answered by Gestalts and by revolutions. The philosophy which allows the notion of partial identity must steer a middle course between nominalism, in which no two valid notions can overlap ever so slightly, and idealism, in which the overlapping of all is well-nigh complete.[83] Neither of these extremes is germane to science. Indeed, the most successful cultivators of science were driven toward that epistemological middle road, another pattern which gives a striking measure of identity to the whole scientific enterprise and casts one more doubt on the parceling of it into as many sciences as there are "scientific revolutions."

To find the metaphysical beliefs, the other major constituent of paradigms, would have been equally easy and revealing. Indeed, instead of metaphysical beliefs, it would have been enough to speak of one belief, the belief in a personal rational Creator. It was this belief, as cultivated especially within a Christian matrix, which supported the view for which the world was an objective and orderly entity investigable by the mind because the mind too was an orderly and objective product of the same rational, that is, perfectly consistent Creator.[84] Even the nineteenth century saw only one major scientist, Darwin, part with that metaphysical belief as he drifted from a poorly informed Christian faith to an uneasy agnosticism. If one adds to this Einstein's uncanny realization that his advocacy of an objective, orderly, and contingent world could suggest that he had fallen into the hands of priests, then the case is almost complete for a major puzzle running through the historicism now in vogue in the historiography of science. The puzzle is posed by the consistent reluctance to take that metaphysical belief for what it is, a major propellant of intellectual and scientific history.

For such a reluctance a price is to be paid sooner or later. It usually consists in being forced to have a recourse to circumlocutions. In Kuhn's book two such devices keep under cover the role played by Christian faith in the Creator in the emergence and development of science. They appear at that critical juncture where the role might have naturally come to the fore. The juncture is Kuhn's reference to the single emergence of science as a viable enterprise in the course of recorded history. It took place, as Kuhn remarks, only "in civilizations that descend from Hellenic Greece," which alone "possessed more than the most rudimentary science."[85] This statement first ignores the question why the Greeks themselves stopped short of developing a viable science. Second, there is the predicament of the Arabs, for centuries in possession of the entire Greek scientific corpus but not advancing it to a viable stage. Finally, there is Byzantium, certainly an heir to Hellenic Greece, but never a part of that Europe about which Kuhn now declares: "The bulk of scientific knowledge is a product of Europe in the last four centuries. No other place and time has supported that very special community from which scientific productivity comes."[86] It is certainly a circumlocution in sociology when it is declared about a small, very special society or community that it finds its support not in a more extensive community or social matrix but "in place and time." Had Kuhn spoken of that matrix directly it would have been possible for him to speak not merely of Europe but also of that Christian faith which turned that Europe into a most specific place and time, certainly so far as science is concerned.

Had this fact not been covered by circumlocutions, it would have been easy to recognize that before science could go through revolutions, it had tò have its evolution, and prior to this it had to be born. With the recognition of this birth it would have been possible to sight the fundamental paradigm of science: its invariable stillbirths in all ancient cultures and its only viable birth in a Europe which Christian faith in the Creator had helped to form.[87] With the notion of a unique birth in mind, the specter of revolutions bringing ever new entities to the scene would have immediately lost its cogency and appeal. Birth is followed by a growth in which the organism remains essentially identical throughout its development. Painful as some phases of the process of growing up may be, they are not a threat to the identity and continuity underlying the whole process. The so-called scientific revolutions also show patterns which make them different from those sudden and complete transformations attributed to political revolutions not so much by reputable historians as by novelists and by the growing number of activists with messianic consciousness.[88] Among those patterns is the gradualness evident both in the personal intellectual evolution of "revolutionary" scientists and in the spreading of their "revolutions." Were this not the case, the history of science would have long been pivoted on a few eurekas, a couple of apples, and some sudden conversions.[89] Instead, one witnesses the painful groping of extraordinary minds for more light, a process which has more similarity with organic growth than with very large mutations, which, it may be noted, are not useful even for the purposes of Darwinian evolution.

Growth it is, however, and not mechanically assured accretion. The latter is a cliché fabricated by nineteenth-century rationalism and empiricism, contemptuous of the past—intellectual, religious, and social. That cliché determined until very recently much of what has been written about science as an intellectual enterprise and has become part and parcel of every textbook on science. Kuhn's book will certainly be remembered as a spirited challenge to it. The challenge was acted out against a backdrop that is the most valuable part of the scenario presented by Kuhn. While his dramatis personae, the paradigms and revolutions, are incoherent characters, the backdrop, or "normal" science, is most enlightening. Not of course for rationalists and empiricists, who must feel cut to the quick by Kuhn's portrayal of that "normalcy." Compared with the glories of scientific revolutions, the normal phases separating them must appear a drab affair, hardly pleasant news to that rationalist-empiricist tradition which cultivated a view of science as a gloriously automatic breeding place of ever-wider verities. It was, in fact, philosophers of science from that tradition who first turned against Kuhn's thesis, a somewhat illogical act for them. In their theory of science, known as the hypothetico-deductive theory, science is a two-tiered enterprise consisting of the psychological genesis of scientific hypotheses on the lower, unfathomable level, and of conclusions derived from them verifiable on the upper, or logico-empirical level. Such a theory is not greatly different from Kuhn's thesis.[90] Just as in the latter the revolutionary emergence of a new paradigm is beyond the control of reason, the genesis of scientific ideas or hypotheses at the deeper level of the two-tiered theory is also outside the realm of rational justification.

This parallel went unnoticed by Kuhn's rationalist critics, for whom the notion of science devoid of continuity and stability was unacceptable. Yet the rationalists' disdain of conceptual origins reflected the same myopia about reason, or rather mind, as did the theory of Kuhn, who took refuge in the unfathomable emergence of paradigm-Gestalts. In both cases one stands in the presence of a distrust in the ability of mind, a distrust that has plagued Western thought since Ockham reduced truth to names. That distrust could only increase after the failure of the Cartesians and idealists to secure full confidence in abstract cogitation. That this distrust in the ability, particularly the creative ability, of the mind asserts itself in theories about science should seem paradoxical, because science embodies stunning evidences of the mind's coherence even in its creativity.

What this paradox attests is that science, a triumph of the mind, can only be treated properly with the proper study of the mind—which is metaphysics. Psychology, biology, and sociology can be of help in shedding light on the conditions under which the mind works, but even Polanyi, who did more in a constructive way than anyone else in our times to emphasize the role of those disciplines in a coherent theory of knowledge, spoke of questions which were left unanswered by Kuhn and which, if left permanently unanswered, could be disastrous in their consequences.[91] Those questions are obviously neither psychological nor biological and sociological: they belong to epistemology and metaphysics. Since these questions are never absent in science as it lives through history, this history cannot be done justice by a reliance on psychology, biology, and sociology which excludes or abuses metaphysics. The road of science as a road of the exercise of the mind's creative abilities is a metaphysical road and in no lesser degree than are the ways to God. The reliability of what one says either of that road or of those ways will therefore largely depend on what one says about the mind. If the road of science is presented as an essentially disconnected succession of paradigms, science will become the victim of the same relativism that allows to religious thought, including its philosophical branch, natural theology, a validity of meaning only within specific cultural and temporal contexts. Such relativism, as Kuhn advocated it with so much ardor, can splinter science too into contexts or paradigms having only relative significance, a significance unworthy of that marvel which only a mind unfettered by relativism can appreciate. Concerning the road of science, it should now seem obvious that nothing marvelous can be said of it without doing justice to the big and small marvels of the mind. If, however, one renders to the mind those things that are of the mind, the ways to God will appear quite marvelous in their very naturalness.

Sixteen

THE REACH OF THE MIND

IN ORDER TO DO JUSTICE TO SCIENCE ONE HAS TO RENDER TO THE MIND what is of the mind, a lesson suggested by the two preceding chapters. Their topics were two very different efforts aimed at coming to grips with the rationale of the scientific enterprise. One was reductionism as a manifestation of logical positivism, for which science is a definitive and therefore static conceptual construct; the other was historicism, which by its own logic is restricted to the temporal or dynamic aspect of science. Widely differing as these two efforts are, their patently unsatisfactory accounts of science have a common source. It consists in the methodical avoidance of taking a long look at the working of minds responsible for great scientific discoveries. When Hans Reichenbach stated that "the philosopher of science is not much interested in the thought processes which lead to scientific discoveries,"[1] he voiced an attitude typical of most logical positivists and reductionists. Apart from the fact that the greatest appeal of logic has always been in its unrestricted consistency and sweep, the restriction endorsed by Reichenbach is obviously self-defeating in science, the field par excellence of discovery. Reichenbach himself acknowledged defeat as he admitted in another context: "The critical attitude may make a man incapable of discovery; and as long as he is successful, the creative physicist may very well prefer his creed to the logic of the analytic philosopher."[2] All truly creative physicists have had a creed very different from the dogmas of logical positivism concerning the ability and role of the mind, and all of them acted, that is, made their discoveries, by living up to the tenets of that creed of theirs.

Much the same can be said about that creed in relation to a consistently developed historicism. Since it renders the notion of scientific progress meaningless, it can hardly have a genuine appeal to great scientific discoverers. Indeed, no great scientist has ever hoped to make a discovery incommensurable with all that had previously been discovered in science. Kuhn, who gave the most consistently historicist account of science, was not consistent to the extent of suggesting that creative scientists should not stick to their creed, but rather have their creativity mesmerized by a vision in which science becomes a chain of disconnected visions or Gestalts. But through a slip of the tongue Kuhn revealed that he was not wholly unaware of the crucial role which the mind—an active mind and not merely the locus of suddenly emerging Gestalts—plays in the scientific enterprise. In speaking of Galileo's discovery of the isochronism of pendulums Kuhn presented it in line with his basic contention, namely, that the discovery was a shift of vision, and then he asked why the shift of vision had taken place. His answer was that it came "through Galileo's individual genius, of course."[3] This is an answer in the right direction, for, as Kuhn took pains to note, the Aristotelian perception of pendulum motion could descriptively be just as accurate as the one given by Galileo. Clearly, observation of pendulums was in itself not enough to induce automatically the perception of a new truth about them. "Rather," Kuhn added, "what seems to have been involved was the exploitation by genius of perceptual possibilities."[4] About that genius, which through its intellectual exploits makes discoveries and through discoveries, science, not a word more was said in *The Structure of Scientific Revolutions.* No wonder that in Kuhn's hands science finds itself deprived of a structure tying all its parts into a coherent whole, while at the same time revolutions are invested with a scientific character they never possessed.

Discovery is the soul of science, a truism badly needed in an age in which so much influence can be exercised by philosophical and historical interpretations of science that have no use for the intellectual reality of discoveries. That scientific discoveries are the fruit of the painstaking self-exertion of geniuses is also worth emphasizing in an age in which approval is given to claims that the mind is merely a concept[5] and that philosophy is but talk about talk,[6] and not an investigation of that understanding which bespeaks a mind. It is even more important to note that the finest scientific discoveries, including above all the bold new generalizations, are at best pragmatic conveniences if one takes seriously the empiricist logic concerning the possibility and validity of inductions. According to that logic, to recall a candid utterance of Bertrand Russell, no matter how many meals one had eaten and no matter how many sunrises one had observed, a fully rational man could never be sure whether his next meal would nourish him and whether the sun was going to rise again. Russell did not wish to be known as a fully rational man in either respect,[7] and he was certainly not one if his longevity was a witness to the sun's reliability and to the nourishing value of meals. At any rate, no scientist of any consequence has ever considered it less than rational to hold it as a verity that regardless of one's meals the sun will indeed rise.

The deeds if not always the words of scientists show that they have always held a fairly steady set of propositions as verities,[8] of which two are of fundamental importance for the scientific enterprise. One is the existence of a world intrinsically ordered in all its parts and consistent in all its interactions. The other is the existence of a human mind capable of understanding such a world in an ever more comprehensive manner. While a philosopher of science may fancy that objective truth as embodied in the universe is merely a regulative principle for scientists, the historian of science will easily find a stumbling block in that view. Scientists have always done their work in the belief that, to recall a remark of Popper, the very idea of error is inconceivable without the idea of truth.[9] This belief of theirs must have its basis (if their experiments are to make sense) in the strict interconnectedness of things, that is, in a universe existing independently of their own ideas. Once this is admitted, it will seem questionable that the idea of ultimate truth is (contrary to Popper) a purely regulative principle. Precisely because of the ontological reality of the universe the idea of ultimate truth will appear to posses an ontological content, a fact which makes itself felt even in the comparison offered by Popper to illustrate his point. Undoubtedly a mountain climber will not always know his exact relation to the summit, owing to interference by subsidiary peaks and overhanging walls. More often than not he may follow the wrong route toward the summit. But unless there is objective reality in his vision of that summit, he cannot claim for his climbing a status higher than the efforts of Sisyphus, and the truth he pursues cannot be compared to a mountain peak which is "permanently or almost permanently wrapped in clouds."[10] The need for that qualifying phrase, "almost permanently," gives away the intended meaning of the comparison—which anyhow is incompatible with a salient fact of scientific history. All great scientists have always professed, if not in words at least in deeds, the existence of that summit, standing for the objective truth embodied in the universe. The same is true of their convictions about the ability of the mind to grasp that truth ever more comprehensively. Emphatic endorsement of these two tenets was in evidence when science rose to maturity three to four hundred years ago and again when it made a spectacular advance around the beginning of this century. While the objectivity of nature and the ability of the mind to grasp it ever more comprehensively are assertions that conflict with rigorous empiricism, their fruitfulness for the creative scientific mind suggests a natural alliance between science and natural theology. Even more is revealed of that alliance by a close look at the working of the scientific mind, especially as it is being caught up in the process of groping toward the specification of a more comprehensive vision of the physical world. Once that closer look is achieved, it is easy to see that it is not respect for science but dislike of metaphysics that prevents the logical positivist and the historicist historian of science from considering discoveries as acts of understanding, showing reason at its best.

To see this dislike for what it is, is to make an illuminating discovery, one that can be made far more readily today than half a century, let alone a full century, ago. For that greater ease much credit should go to studies generated within the new historiography of science. They disclosed that big and small classics of science contain many informative passages in addition to those which are useful for empiricism. Actually, recent studies in the history of science have shown beyond the possibility of doubt that none of the giants of science from Copernicus to Einstein and beyond did their science in such a manner as to fit the precepts of empiricism. Nor could it be welcome news for empiricists that new developments in scientific technology added only further pages to the old story that the mind, scientific or not, does not work in the manner of sophisticated mechanisms developed by science.[11] Studies of the great scientific discoveries also showed that minds responsible for them always had to cope with the absence of important empirical details, an absence which from an empiricist viewpoint could only invalidate what was perceived as a broader and deeper truth about nature.

To what has already been said about Copernicus, Kepler, Galileo, Newton, Planck, and Einstein, or rather about the manner in which they pressed forward toward their great discoveries and held fast to them, one could add many other examples, each a rebuttal of the empiricist slighting of the mind. Unlike two generations ago, it is no longer without risk to present Oersted, Faraday, Helmholtz, Clausius, Maxwell, and Hertz as discoverers going about their business in an empiricist fashion. Enough is known about the puzzlements of such professedly nonmetaphysicist physicists, like Bohr, Born, Heisenberg, and Dirac, to permit one to shrug off the empiricists' interpretation of twentieth-century physics—which also has on its roster Schrödinger, de Broglie, Compton, and others whose votes were never cast in favor of empiricism. All these great figures of exact science gave the lie, if not with their words at least with their deeds, to an empiricism restricting the reach of the mind to what is directly observable. Whether they peered into the realm of the very small or of the very large, they were led by the conviction that greater than what is seen through an instrument is the act of looking through it.[12] It was their confidence in the act of looking, in which the sensory reveals the rationality of its objectivity, that made them follow a Copernicus in reaching out for the vistas of a coherent universe, a target which empiricism cannot secure. Like Copernicus, they had fear only of those willing to use but their physical eyes. Theirs has always been that assurance about the ability of the mind to find an ever-deeper rationality in the physical universe which can be felt on every page of the introduction to Copernicus's *De revolutionibus*—an assurance they had to have if they were to succeed in unfolding that deeper rationality. Its objectivity was one side of a coin and the other side was their personal commitment to it. Separated from the physical universe, that commitment would turn into a mere urge; without that commitment the physical realm could never appear a universe, that is, a totality of coherent things and processes.

Science can therefore be called personal knowledge,[13] provided it is remembered that personal intellectual commitment is not enough to make science. That commitment must have a target, an objectively existing physical world whose notion is capable of indefinite development by the intellect. The four hundred years of modern science are the first major installment of that development. Development it is, but not mechanical. Often it gives the appearance of being a desperate groping in the dark, a tacit knowledge, to recall another felicitous phrase of Polanyi,[14] and this too tells something of the bafflingly nonempiricist way in which the mind reaches out into the unknown. The plethora of details which Kepler offered about that groping in the dark has unfortunately no replica in the annals of the history of science. Even Faraday's extensive diaries of his scientific work are a mere skeleton compared with Kepler's offering. Most scientists gave at most a glimpse of their groping, and usually only years after they had achieved success. The pattern was well exemplified by Helmholtz, who in referring to his solution in 1891 of some long-standing problem of mathematical physics compared himself to a mountain climber who had to retrace his steps time and again. "In my works," he added, "I naturally said nothing about my mistakes to the reader, but only described the actual path by which he may now reach the same heights without difficulty."[15] Making many mistakes before achieving success must, however, have a deep epistemological relevance if it can spur the intensity of Einstein's words relating to the years preceding the formulation of general relativity: "In the light of knowledge attained, the happy achievement seems almost a matter of course, and any intelligent student can grasp it without too much trouble. But the years of anxious searching in the dark, with their intense longing, their alternations of confidence and exhaustion, and the final emergence into the light—only those who experienced it can understand that."[16]

Fortunately, the new historiography of science implemented in no small measure a request made almost a century ago by Maxwell that the history of science ought "not to be restricted to the enumeration of successful investigations." It also has, Maxwell warned, the duty "to tell of unsuccessful inquiries and to explain why some of the ablest men have failed to find the key of knowledge, and how the reputation of others has only given a firmer footing to the errors into which they fell."[17] Indeed, partly under the impact of Popper's interpretation of science, it has become fashionable to heap such praises on making errors as to create the impression of a decrease of interest in truth on the part of our best scientists. Actually, it was a burning desire for truth about the universe as a whole which prompted a distinguished cosmologist's statement that "our whole problem is to make the mistakes as fast as possible."[18] The same desire is the source of relief expressed by a leading investigator of the brain-mind relationship that he "can now rejoice even in the falsification of a cherished theory, because even this is a scientific success."[19] Whether such desire can have solid support in Popper's theory of science as a falsification of hypotheses, and whether that theory is compatible with his later groping for objective reality,[20] is a debatable matter.

What is undeniable and ought to seem really important is the growing documentation by historiographers of science that making errors has always been an integral part of the scientific quest for truth and that indulging in hypotheses is an equally indispensable, though hardly empiricist, feature of the same quest. Moreover, when a historian of science unfolds Galileo's reluctant abandoning of his empiricist theory of the tides for one bordering on number mysticism,[21] or when he points out how Newton continually contradicted his empiricist motto, "hypotheses non fingo," he is faced with telltale signs of the mind's inexorable trust in the existence of an ultimate truth embodied in an objectively existing universe.[22] That so many informative lessons, which the history of science gives about the urges and abilities of the mind, fail to impress the empiricists should be of no surprise in view of the myopia shown toward that very same history by such empiricist cultivators of it as Comte and Mach. Tellingly enough, they show as little sensitivity toward the empirical present of scientific history. Einstein had already repeated verbally and in print for at least two decades that belief in the objective rationality of the universe was indispensable for doing creative science when Milton K. Munitz traveled to Princeton to query him on that very score. Yet Munitz remained skeptical even after Einstein reiterated this point to him in a most emphatic manner.[23] Such philosophers of science will show even more reluctance to find anything worthwhile in statements of great scientists about the workings of their minds, which from the vantage point of empiricism seem to border on the irrational or savor of metaphysics. The latter are largely connected with the end results of the workings of the scientist's mind, namely, with their firmly assertive inferences about the universe, a point to be taken up in the next chapter. The former have to do with their mental steps to discovery, steps that cannot be accommodated in narrow-minded logical schemes about the workings of the mind, scientific or otherwise.

While the road to discovery cannot be charted by the simplistic means of empiricism and logical positivism, it can become a preparation for the ways to God only if discourse about it is not left to philosophers of science who in the name of a philosophy reduced to mere exercises in logic let the jargon of psychology turn that discourse into sophisticated mystery mongering. For what more could be expected from empirical psychology, to which Popper confined legitimate interest in the mental act of discovery, if he was correct in claiming that the manner in which a "new idea occurs to man—whether it is a musical theme, a dramatic conflict, or a scientific theory—. . . is irrelevant to the logical analysis of scientific knowledge"?[24] Is not this a tacit claim that logical analysis alone provides the "scientific" or valid knowledge? But if the road to discovery is carefully broken down into its phases, the mystery of discovery will not be greater than the mystery present in the generalization embodied in each and every word, indispensable even to the logician intent on living without any mystery. Moreover, once justice is done to the fact that scientific discovery is not merely the perceiving of a relevant fact but also of the relevance of theories, the mind will appear neither an empiricist slave nor an idealist lawgiver with respect to nature, but a partner which teaches about nature by learning from it.

Teacher and learner are distinct though intimately interrelated entities in constant interaction with each other. Their interrelation is very complex in the case of a genuine teacher and learner but not at all mysterious, unless complexity is taken for mystery, an expedient often resorted to by logicians content only with conceptual streamlining. That mind and nature should be viewed as similarly relational entities ought to be clear to anyone with serious concern for science and with clear awareness of the mishaps of disregard of that special interrelation in some philosophical interpretations of science. The mishaps have been most strikingly instanced by empiricism and idealism. The former assumes a complete identity between nature and mind. The latter is based on assuming a complete independence of the mind with respect to nature.Thus as Richard J. Blackwell, author of the only major discussion of the epistemology of discovery,[25] points out, the relational aspect in the reality of mind and nature will appear paradoxical only as long as empiricism and idealism are taken as exclusive alternatives for dealing with mind and nature.

Since science is divested of its nature when it ceases to be about nature, it is but logical to start with the facts of nature in staking out the epistemological phases of the road to discovery.[26] The most immediate feature of those facts is their complexity, a complexity, however, that is far from chaotic. Regularities in those facts are obvious even to a cursory look, but so are departures from them. It is these departures or anomalies that spark curiosity in the mind, a feature which is mysterious only to those who are busy with the task of clearing up the process of understanding without admitting their curiosity about the task itself. Curiosity is not an automatic reaction, and much less automatic is the urge to look for the more meaningful curiosa presented by nature. Such a look involves a patient sorting-out process, which in turn implies the isolation of special factors operative in nature, giving rise to more and more specialized or abstractive notions of it. The interrelation of those

252

factors into sets and the integration of the sets themselves are further steps along the road to discovery of so-called fact laws, which are obtained when a complete generalization is achieved in the act of induction.

In all these steps it is the facts of nature that dominate the mind, in the sense of holding it to a steady diet of facts, data, and observations which the mind must digest into an increasingly more abstractive nourishment. The mind, however, is able to assert a kind of superiority over nature when it comes to the discovery of theories. As laid out in Blackwell's meticulous analysis,[27] the discovery of theories consists of two main steps, both having at first but indirect connection with facts. One is the process of idealization, the other, creative postulation. The crowning feature of the former is the thought experiment, whereas the latter's finest fruit is the theoretical prediction of entities hitherto unsuspected in nature. Of course none of those steps is mechanical. Reichenbach is therefore correct in claiming that "there are no logical rules in terms of which a 'discovery-machine' could be constructed that would take over the creative function of the genius."[28] But from this it does not follow that the act of discovery is beyond the realm of rational analysis, unless reason is restricted to that kind of logic which is unwilling to take consistently into account the chief modern discovery about logic, namely, that it cannot derive its consistency from itself. That Gödel's two theories of incompleteness failed to make a proper impression on most members of the Vienna Circle, in spite of Carnap's constantly reminding them of their enormous import,[29] should be enough of a proof that their minds too were anything but logic machines.

The mind which alone can cope with an understanding of its own discoveries is neither a machine nor a mere appendage to that machine which is the human body. Such understanding is reserved for a mind whose nature is conceived in terms of its intimate interrelatedness with the body which teaches the mind and is in turn instructed by it. Precisely because of an interaction that is not mechanical, man is not only capable of making errors, including scientific errors, but it is natural for him to make them—a truth hardly conceivable within empiricism and idealism. Only an epistemological middle road between these two can lead man through errors to the truth hidden in discoveries, a fact which is a reflection on man's nature, for which there is still no better label than that of a "rational animal."[30]

For some time that label has been branded as an outdated resolve to make room for hybrid beings in the supposedly one-level realm of existence. Such a notion of existence was the product of the mistaken urge, fostered by the rise of classical physics, to picture the mind in terms of its most dazzling product, the quantities. Yet the mind not only produces knowledge other than quantitative, but the mind itself, or the knower, cannot be comprehended in terms of mathematics. The scientific methodology of Descartes and Galileo could not resolve this puzzle.[31] Indeed, the picture of the mind which Descartes was the first to paint, on a "scientific" basis and on a grand scale, was a caricature of the mind, a ghost, and, as is usually the case with ghosts, it could only invite even more ghastly portrayals of the mind. In Spinoza's hands the Cartesian ghost-soul turned into an apersonal universal spirit, while in the hands of materialists (the Cartesian Left) it was transformed into plain matter. The German idealists, who turned everything into thought, merely provided a variation on Spinoza's procedure or, if one prefers, a dialectic response to materialist empiricism. They also served evidence of the jarring mishaps in store for those who want to be "scientific" while discoursing about the mind.

Materialists and idealists represented the two chief possible options of a monistic approach to the question of the mind-body relationship, an approach which was one of the alternatives within the perspectives of realism. The other was dualism, of which the Cartesian version was meant to be "scientific," whereas the Aristotelian-Thomistic version remained content being plainly philosophical. Since hardly anything was known during the eighteenth century of that philosophical approach untainted by scientism, the limitations of the scientific method could all the less readily be recognized by that age which loved to hear a d'Holbach and a Condorcet declare that all errors of man were errors made in science.[32] It took another hundred years before classical physics revealed itself as a possible source of grave errors concerning material reality, to say nothing of the spiritual.

As is well known, the typical reaction to the "failure" of classical physics was the declaration that science had nothing to say about reality, a principal contention of the operationist approach which in our century has set the tone of much of the philosophy of science. With science still being taken for the last word in understanding, this meant that nothing at all could be said about reality. As a result, solutions of the mind-body problem which have been proposed on a "scientific" basis in our century have almost invariably been conceptualist. Since interest in reality can hardly be exorcised completely, some of these conceptualist theories can be described as "weak," because of their subtle relapse into attaching a realistic hue to what are allegedly mere conceptualizations about the mind. Of these "weak" theories the one known as the identity theory of the mind has earned most favor in our times.[33] A similarly "weak" version of the conceptualist approach, and also tied furtively to a monistic ontology, is the one in which rationality is a mere epiphenomenon of man's animality.[34] It seems debatable, however, that the shadowiness characterizing epiphenomena can be responsible for that overpowering impact which the scientific mind can exercise on matter. A brief look at modern technology may make one wonder whether it is not matter that is the epiphenomenon. But long before man's mind produced modern wonders with matter, he worked even greater wonders by putting his mind into matter in a wide variety of forms, which as a class attracted new interest through Popper's theory of the brain-mind relationship.[35] It is the best representative of what may be called the "strong" kind of mere conceptualizations about the mind. Popper introduced his theory in 1967 with the remark that he was a realist,[36] but an epistemology which professedly has no room for the "knowing subject"[37] (World Two) cannot, in spite of ingenious efforts, secure access either to the reality of the material world (World One) or to the world of the objective content of thought (World Three). Those aware of the mishaps of scientism will not be surprised to find Popper defining epistemology as the "theory of *scientific* knowledge"[38] (emphasis added).

The major faults of such an epistemology are easily apparent. First, it can treat science only as a finished product, that is, with a radical disregard for the making of science in and through discoveries. Second, World One and World Three as conceived by Popper cannot be consistently tied to World Two, or the reality of consciousness. Needless to say, a hundred or so years after Darwin, World Three as conceived by Popper could not be a simple reconstruction of the immobile world of Plato's ideas. Popper himself insisted on the understanding of World Three in terms of biological evolution.[39] Others with an equally strong desire to escape the metaphysical grip of dualism also sought relief in a conceptualization based on the science of biology, with the invariable result that once metaphysics is shunned, reality slips through one's fingers. For what is the lasting reality of a person if he is, as Marjorie Grene contended, merely an "achievement of a human organism mediated by participation in a culture"?[40] Indeed, there is nothing really lasting in such an "achievement," for, as Grene stated in conclusion, "our nature demands for its completion . . . also the unreal," although "we are like other things, physico-chemical systems," and therefore "our making is also an unmaking."[41] Obviously, in such paradoxical reasoning the so-called "negative theology" is referred to as an illustration, in confirmation of the logic that if one once departs from the metaphysics and epistemology of moderate realism, one will end by dialectically negating any and all achievement.

That the departure in question is made in the name of science does not make the end result less disastrously antiscientific. Actually, what is initially wrong with that departure is the conviction that science is omniscience. It matters little whether omniscience is conceived in terms of physics or biology. The intrusion of inconsistency is glaring and inescapable in both cases. Laplace had hardly meant to include the

255

mental acts of his own discoveries, and at times willful theorizing,[42] to say nothing of his schemes and bungling in politics, when he conjured up that omniscient spirit foreseeing everything through a complete mastery of initial conditions.[43] That one's own "thoughtful" propositions are just as unaccountable in terms of a "non-physicalist" biology is clear when the effort to shun the metaphysical leads to the declaration that "man's so called rationality resides not in his grasp of some transcendent truths, but in his power to doubt, to criticize, to ignore or deny the actual in favor of the barely possible, if not the impossible . . . . We are such stuff as dreams are made on."[44] Obviously, such a proposition was not meant to be a dream but a truth transcending all possibilities and impossibilities.

In addition to the sad fate of ending in debilitating inconsistencies as long as one is resolved to escape the reality of a mind transcending the level of a body, taken physically, biologically, or even "culturally," it is well to recall the inconsistency implied in the major difficulties raised against dualism. One is the so-called puzzle of psychophysical causality. While it is a puzzle for scientistic schemes, it is an indispensable resource even for scientistic writers on the mind-brain relationship. Or are they willing to deny that something other than the mind causes their fingers to move the pen so as to record thoughts that are not mechanically necessary and are utterly incommensurable on the energy scale with physical acts recording them? Again, one can object to the "isolation" of individual minds implied in dualism only if one admits merely the scientistically univocal meaning of "isolation." Is it not the scientific enterprise that provides the most telling instances of the meeting of great creative minds, all invariably committed to the belief in a material world existing independently of their minds?

To ignore such points demands a motivation more than scientific, and one ought to be grateful for finding it spelled out in such form that one can account for the mind "without returning or even longing to return to the tidy theocentric cosmos of earlier centuries."[45] Whatever the tidiness of the theocentric cosmos of earlier centuries, a cosmos which is conceived as theocentric will at least be tidied up of inconsistencies in one's interpretation of cosmic existence. But in order to achieve this one ought not to try to save the mind by losing the cosmos, a point which tells much of the peculiar interrelation between mind and body and tells it through a major lesson of scientific history. It consists in the persistent failure to establish a priori the shape and structure of the cosmos. Failures of that kind range from the amateurish to the sophisticated. That the gestation periods of some quadrupeds can be expressed as multiples of π is interesting enough,[46] but the readiness to see there scientific significance is suggestive of seeing pies in the scientific sky. The same may also be true of expressing, however ingeniously, atomic constants and ratios in terms of the same irrational number.[47]

This is not to deny, to recall a pregnant phrase of Eugene P. Wigner, that one is confronted time and again with an "unreasonable effectiveness of mathematics" while investigating the physical world.[48] Yet, although some mathematical formalisms proposed a century ago proved themselves to be extremely efficient for twentieth-century physics, mathematics provides no clues as to which of its formalisms is most useful for the physicist. Again, aiming at complete mathematical symmetry in theoretical physics can be so fruitful as to prompt a Dirac to declare that it puts one "on a sure line of progress."[49] But one can hardly devise equations a priori so as to convey a symmetry far more profitable for physics. Einstein's fruitless struggle for a unified theory is a case in point. Unlike his work on special and general relativity, where the basis was a profound reflection on physical laws and reality, his work on unified theory required him to rely mainly on mathematical formalisms which proved to be unsatisfactory in spite of their symmetry. Einstein would not have been human had he not been tempted to demonstrate in a subtly a priori fashion that the world could only be what it actually is, but he never elevated this temptation into "an enduring hope to find a few simple general laws that would explain why nature with all its seeming complexity and variety, is the way it is."[50]

Much less did Einstein entertain sympathy for Eddington's effort to derive from epistemological considerations the number of fundamental particles and the numerical magnitudes of atomic constants. The effort was that of an idealist who was forced by his own logic to say of man's scientific effort that ultimately it shows him not the world but only his own footprints.[51] A surprising result, though hardly provoking that wonderment which is a hallmark of the scientist's attitude toward nature and which is unaccountable for the empiricist no less than for the idealist, both equally distant from the epistemological middle road. The avid collection of facts in Bacon's empiricism is a largely mechanical procedure, never a source of wonderment. Taking the other extreme, Descartes left no room for wonderment by trying to make everything clear to reason. Malebranche and Berkeley had no occasion to marvel because they turned every occasion into a miracle. There was nothing to marvel at in Hume's conclusion that empiricism entitled one only to intellectual despair, which Kant wanted to escape. He failed because he recognized only such knowledge that in its certainty could not accommodate marvel. His successors marveled, as all idealists do, only at themselves, a predicament which prompted William James's remark to his colleague, the absolutist idealist Josiah Royce of Harvard: "The Absolute must have fun being out of you, Josh."[52] The unintended message of that remark was that only fun but no wonder could be had as long as the mind was allowed to make fun of the contingency of being. This insensitivity to the marvel of the mind and to its ability to marvel received its "scientific" sanctioning when Mach declared that with all sensations present science would no longer be necessary. One should therefore admire all the more the strength of genuine scientific mentality which kept Einstein's mind, in spite of its Machist and Kantian preconditioning, firmly attached to the intellectual soundness of wonderment.

Einstein was not the only giant among modern physicists to recognize that wonderment was the heart of scientific understanding and that no wonderment was meaningful if that understanding did not carry one to an objectively existing physical reality. Nor was Einstein the only one among those giants to lapse back on occasion into Kantianism while reflecting on that wonderment. He spoke not simply of the world but of "the world of our sense experiences" as he declared that "the fact that it is comprehensible is a miracle." Nay, in the very same context he credited Kant "with the great realization" that "the setting up of a real external world would be senseless without that comprehensibility."[53] On Einstein's part this implied a curious lapse of memory, for he had already dismissed Kant's a priori categories of comprehensibility sixteen years earlier, during his famous visit in Paris in 1922.[54] Voicing his wonderment about the comprehensibility of the world, and about the same time as Einstein did, de Broglie similarly fell back on Kantianism as he noted that "the great wonder in the progress of science is that it has revealed to us a certain agreement between our thought and things, a certain possibility of grasping, with the assistance of the resources of our intelligence and the rules of our reason, the profound relations existing between phenomena."[55] What is Kantian here is the implicit belief that the mind has rules which it can know without knowing the world. Moreover, modern science made it clear that the true resource of reason is to be in intimate union with reality and not to impose itself, à la Kant, on reality. A reason which tries to act in terms of Kant's precepts deprives itself of the right to remark with de Broglie: "We are not sufficiently astonished by the fact that any science may be possible."[56]

Such a wonder is not something that can be understood in terms of science itself because, to recall an incisive remark of Gilson, "the question posed about the possibility of science in general is not susceptible of a scientific answer because this implies the existence of science for its own justification."[57] The answer to the possibility of science can therefore come only from metaphysics, though only from a metaphysics not yet detached by Kant from its moderate touch with reality and not yet divested of itself, under Hume's guidance, by a purely instinctive, naive reveling in the flow of sensory data. Of course, if a physicist does not wish to consider the possibility that the mind is capable of understanding reality because both mind and reality are the products of the One who disposed everything according to "weight, measure, and number," then the very same physicist must rest satisfied with what Gilson called "the paradoxical experience of the unintelligibility of intelligibility."[58] Einstein, who was resolved "not to fall into the hands of priests," was indeed forced to claim that "the very fact that the totality of our sense experiences is such that by means of thinking ... it can be put in order ... is a fact which leaves us in awe, but which we shall never understand."[59] The real flaw in this attempt to escape the Ultimate is that it vitiates the reasonableness of the awe in question. Clearly, if one does not wish to hear the highest answer of metaphysics, one should not delight in raising its deepest question.[60]

Any resort to Kantian epistemology in order to escape the full logic of a realist metaphysics is discredited not only by the marvel which modern science provokes about the mind's understanding of the world in general. Modern science also served notice that contrary to Kant's precepts the mind's success with reality has a far greater measure of selectivity than the one permitted by Kant's a priori categories. Mention may also be made of the insights provided by studies about the strategy of master chess players, studies prompted by the sanguine expectations placed in chess-playing computers. To the no small surprise of advocates of thinking machines, it was found that master chess players rely on a relatively few moves applied in successive phases of the game, which cannot be foreseen because of the unpredictability of the opponent's moves. Herein lies the source of that chronic inability of programming computers to play chess with even moderate success, not in the staggering number of moves to be taken into account.[61] If, however, mind and machines work in a fashion so dissimilar, the mind-body problem should appear anything but a pseudoproblem. In fact the problem should loom very large to anyone who cares to understand science in its deepest ramifications. Or as Wolfgang Köhler, whose greatness as experimental psychologist needs no pointing out, noted in 1959: "Recent advances in philosophical thinking and in experimental research had made the problem even more challenging than it was, say, thirty years ago. For now we have begun to realize that almost any imaginable solution is likely to affect our interpretation of what we call the physical world."[62]

Any interpretation of that world can only be incomplete if it does not include physics, and physics is not completely understood without a careful look at the presuppositions, or more generally at the workings of the mind, on which it rests. Long considered a worn-out warhorse of backward philosophers, the mind-body problem remains therefore a central problem for a physics which is a quest for understanding the universe. The problem should certainly be central for those who claim that on the basis of quantum mechanics the observer cannot be abstracted from the process under observation. Whatever the merit of the claim that the physics of the future ought to include the mind as its object,[63] one would still need to have a mind first before one could have physics, especially if it is to be a physics of the mind. The mind in question ought to be more than a brain machine, but it cannot be so much more as to be "an angel driving a machine,"[64] or what is much less, a "ghost in the machine."[65] For the mind cannot reach so far beyond the senses as to be wholly independent of them. When Einstein declared that the great advances in science are the fruits of the free creations of the mind,[66] he certainly did not wish to resuscitate Descartes's innate ideas laid to rest by Locke, or Kant's a priori categories of space and time shattered by non-Euclidean geometries. Much as some ideas may appear to be free creations of the mind, Einstein knew that they had to be continually referred back to the empirical for at least an indirect verification. Without that verification even his general relativity could turn, as he put it in 1920, "into mere dust and ashes."[67]

By reaching back to the empirical the mind retains its sense of reality threatened by logicism, keeps its sanity endangered by idealism, and readies itself for a new soaring above the flatlands of empiricism. Such is the gist of the meaning of the long road of science for natural theology, which is so largely a concern about the ways to God. Those ways, starting as they do from the sensory, are soon blocked if the mind is but a machine. Nor are those ways needed if the mind is a disembodied spirit, trapped in the body. But the same fate is in store for the road on which science travels if the mind is either a machine or a ghost in the machine. Clearly, both science and natural theology demand a view of the mind in which justice is done both to the mind's essential dependence on the body and to the mind's ability to reach not only beyond its own body but also beyond the totality of bodies, or the universe. For the conceptualization of such a view of the mind no single word, be it "soul" or something else, can do full justice. It can only be grasped by an unreserved commitment to that very richness which nature displays in man alone. Once this commitment is unhampered by empiricist and rationalist phobias, the thinking man will appear that slender reed[68] which for all its fragility is stronger than all the matter making up the universe. While the universe does not know man, man is able to know the universe, witnessing in more than one sense the truth of the phrase that knowledge is power.

Respect for the one who knows is the very respect on which science rests, a point still to be learned by rationalists who are empiricists in disguise. The ethical motivation they attribute to Mach for his reverence for facts[69] (although it was his sensations he revered), they should accord to those who stand in awe of the act of knowing, inasmuch as knowing is a comprehension of reality. Science is inseparable from that process of comprehending which is a conscious experience tying the real world and the knower into a unity. Once this tie is slighted, one is left either with solipsism or with physicalism. On the basis of the former one can build up oneself but not a world,[70] on the basis of physicalism one will not have a physics which is a *comprehension* of the world. In unfolding this dilemma, Popper noted that "theologians or metaphysicians might be very pleased to learn that statements such as 'God exists' or 'The Soul exists' are precisely on the same level as [the phrase] "I have conscious experiences."[71] Since some theologians and some metaphysicians have always known this, they should be amused to find that such a distinguished representative of the rationalist tradition as Popper ties consciousness to natural theology, while trying to secure—without taking proper stock of consciousness—that very same tradition and its alleged superstructure, science.

What is still to be learned by these rationalists, fearful of the slightest trace of "rational theology" even as a historical part of rationalism, is a little lesson in consistency. It means the recognition first, that the "facts" of nature by which they rightly set so great a store will have no coherence unless they are rooted in an objectively coherent universe; and second, that the "acts" of knowledge, including the bold conjectures so necessary for science,[72] will issue in disconnected refutations unless those acts reveal the actor to be that "hybrid" essence which a rational animal appears to be. Whether his rationality is called soul, mind, or genius, is largely irrelevant. What is important to remember is that this being can, for all his materiality, transcend all matter and achieve an intricate grasp of its totality, a grasp not material though rooted in material data. This should reveal at once that there is something very wrong with Kant's claim that universe and soul are bastard products of the metaphysical cravings of the mind.

If Kant was so wrong about universe and soul, his claim that God too was a bastard product of the same cravings can only be suspect. Since what misled Kant in the first place was his misleading notion of scientific knowledge, the true manner in which man as a thinker comprehends the world can be suspected to serve not only as a ground for science but also as a ground for gaining a glimpse of God. With God emerging on one's mental horizon, soul and universe alike will be seen in their deepest perspective. Soul, universe, and God have a common fate as objects of man's understanding, but a very promising fate as long as there is no threat, intellectual or social, to the genuine understanding of science. By setting the scientific record straight in many places, the new historiography of science did much to facilitate that understanding. It takes more than historiography, however, to produce minds ready to look straight at the record, especially when all its main lines run parallel and as such can only meet at infinity.

Seventeen

COSMIC SINGULARITY

As SUGGESTED IN THE PREVIOUS CHAPTER, THE UNDERSTANDING OF SCI-
ence is in a sense the grasp of man's ability to reach beyond his own
materiality, nay beyond all matter. Man transcends all matter when he
forms for himself a notion of the universe, or the totality of consistently
interacting material things, and he is assured by what is best in
twentieth-century science that when he does so he is not the victim of a
transcendental illusion. During this century of ours science has not only
discovered the realm of the atom and the realm of galaxies but for the
first time in its history science has become a cosmology, a consistent
discourse about the universe. Today only rigorous positivists disagree
with the dictum that all science is cosmology, or if they agree they will
be forced to resort with Carnap to a "logical construction of the world"
that yields not a universe, but only the illusory world of solipsism.[1]
About such a world one can only say to its proponents, "cherish it"—
the reply of Chesterton to a solipsist who wanted to convince him that
solipsism offered the best of all possible worlds.

Long before rationalists[2] and Marxists[3] began to voice the dictum that
all science is cosmology, theists had already cherished the reality of the
cosmos and its study, cosmology. The basic form of all rational ways
to God is by no accident called the cosmological argument. The first
book to carry the word cosmology in its title was a "sacred cosmology,"
the *Cosmologia sacra* written by Nehemiah Grew in 1701.[4] Christian
Wolff's *Cosmologia generalis,* published in 1731,[5] which made "cosmologia" a household word in academe, was a product of Protestant
scholasticism. After that a course in cosmology became a staple feature
of curricula in scholastic philosophy both Protestant and Catholic. This
happened so quickly that twenty-five years after the publication of
Wolff's *Cosmologia* the principal utility of *cosmologie* was defined by
d'Alembert in the *Encyclopédie* as the demonstration of the existence of
God from the general laws of nature.[6]

Philosophical cosmology is not, of course, the same as scientific cosmology. But those mindful of the wonderment implied in the question
"What is in a name?" will easily suspect something wonderful in the
twentieth-century reinstatement of the word "cosmology" in scientific
parlance. When Lambert published in 1761 his *Cosmologische Briefe,*[7] he
could hardly suspect that for more than a century no major scientific
publication was to carry in its title the words "cosmology" or "cosmological." The absence of these words in Laplace's *Exposition du système du monde,* first published in 1796,[8] will hardly seem unintentional

for anyone mindful of d'Alembert's definition and of Laplace's intentions. Laplace was determined not to treat of ultimate causes,[9] a determination perfectly legitimate in a scientific discourse about the universe, but an always troublesome resolve as long as the discourse is truly about that universe which is the totality of consistently interacting things. Little of that trouble could be felt as long as scientific discourse about the universe conveniently settled with a dichotomy which, as will be seen shortly, restricted, as late as the beginning of this century, the science of cosmology to a tiny part of the universe. But once the whole universe became the object of that discourse, the troublesome specter of philosophical cosmology was again clearly in sight.

It was a realist epistemology demanded by his scientific cosmology that prompted Einstein's disclaimer that he had not fallen into the hands of priests. That priestly discourse, or rather metaphysics, was not to reenter the scene via cosmology should seem therefore a telltale contention in the two major surveys of the history of twentieth-century cosmology. In one of them it is claimed that scientific cosmology should not contain any reference to "creation."[10] The other concludes with an apotheosis of the hydrogen out of which worlds and intellects keep emerging by hazard and necessity. The last two phrases of that book read as follows: "With Voltaire the god of the Bible turned into a clockmaker; with Hoyle the Pan of antiquity becomes the 'potential of creation.' One can still love him and admire that he [god] has become so respectful of mathematics as to let reason return to it to settle accounts concerning [the question of] becoming."[11]

Cosmology became a science in the hands of Einstein who, as already pointed out, created consternation with his emphasis on the finiteness of matter constituting the universe.[12] One should not, however, think that man's scientifically reliable mental grasp of the totality of matter is possible only if that totality is finite. That grasp has for its real target the specificity of matter as it exists, a specificity which is even more striking for an infinite amount of matter conceived in a distribution amenable to scientific treatment. What makes scientific cosmology possible is the coherent singularity of the cosmos, the very same aspect of it which justifies philosophical cosmology and secures its only reliable recourse to scientific findings and conclusions. It was therefore most unfortunate for philosophical cosmology to be born at a time when science began to be dominated by a notion of infinity which heavily distracted from the singularity of the universe. Euclidean infinity, which was taken by Newton to be God's sensorium, was so nondescript or nonsingular as to be soon taken for the only possible way in which the universe could be "sensed."[13] Not surprisingly, the need to move from the universe to God was no longer felt once it was accepted that the universe could only be what it appeared to be, an infinite homogeneous three-dimensional extension. The pale God of deism, capable of creating but a Euclidean world, could readily be replaced with a cosmological infinity showing, on a cursory view, but pale or weak singularities. They were, as will be seen, not at all pale, but to see them for what they were demanded eyes still sensitive to the light of a metaphysics steeped in considerations about the singularity of existence.

As is well known, the infinite universe of Newton replaced a closed spherical universe, largely articulated by the Greeks of old. As was the case with three-dimensional infinity, the sphere too could appear as the embodiment of a perfection that alone was natural for existence. Thus the Greeks, too, failed to appreciate the singularities shown by their cosmos and to realize that their cosmological speculations were indeed centered on cosmic singularities. In close parallel to what happened in the three Newtonian centuries the resulting loss was not only a loss for metaphysical vision, but also for the vision that science needed in order to make progress in cosmology. Since all science is cosmology, failure to make progress in cosmology meant failure to make vital advances in science. This story, by far the most incisive aspect of the history of cosmology—and of science—is still to be written. That it has not been written is obviously due to that positivist and rationalist phobia about metaphysics in which the historiography of science was born and developed until very recently.

Yet even today no audible criticism is provoked by that facile summary of the pre-Socratic cosmological speculations which asserts that their most instructive achievement was the creation of a nondogmatic atmosphere in which the disciples were invited to refute the conjectures of their masters.[14] Pre-Socratic science was rather an effort, however half-hearted at times, to face up to the singularity of the cosmos. Thales derived the universe from water without pondering what a peculiar substance water was. It was so singularly peculiar that Anaximander anchored cosmology in the indefinite, an entity as nondescript as was conceptually possible. That the derivation of the very definite or singular world from the "indefinite" was far from satisfactory can be guessed from the fact that Anaximenes turned to fire, a rather specific "substance," to account for a specific world. Heraclitus could not live long with his "absolute" chaos[15] and the atomists were soon forced to embellish their unspecified atoms with specific hooks and with the most peculiar ability to swerve, however slightly. The Pythagoreans, too, had to discover that even beneath the perfect homogeneity of integers there lurked "irrational" singularities which came into sight as soon as the linear sequence of integers was turned into two and three dimensions in order to build a universe.

Apart from the singularly indefinite or "irrational" character of the number π, the same for all circles and spheres, each circle and sphere carries a singularity in its actual size, including the sphere of the stars, the paragon of all spheres. Although the Greeks made estimates of the size of their finite spherical universe and even computed the number of sand grains that could be accommodated within it,[16] they never asked what made the universe to be of such particular size. But the sphere of stars showed even more peculiar singularities, each obvious enough to prompt further questions. One was the presence in that apparently perfect sphere of half a dozen vagabonds, or planets, the other was the Milky Way. The peculiarity of planets was submerged in a complex of spheres, showing that the sphere, a natural image of perfection, psychologically could not amount to more than a weak singularity which hardly prompts one to raise further questions. As to the Milky Way, the best the Greeks did was to ignore Aristotle's efforts to talk the Milky Way out of the sky.[17] Their best speculation about the Milky Way, that its whitish glow was due to the fusion of the light of many small stars,[18] was never followed up, possibly because it was offered within Democritus's infinitism, in which the universe was denied a meaningful singularity. The Greek passion for understanding could not find anything to understand in a universe in which chance ruled supreme, to the extent of depriving even the atoms of universally valid singular characteristics. In that universe not only the atoms but even the stars could be so uneven as to let Democritus compare the hue of stars forming the Milky Way to the whiteness produced by grains of salt. For a Democritus, who postulated atoms (and worlds) of most unequal sizes,[19] stars could not convincingly constitute a specific class of entities. Within such an outlook the Milky Way was as little a thought-provoking departure from homogeneity as it was in the worshipful admiration of the homogeneity of a cosmic sphere.

Yet the Milky Way remained a markedly singular phenomenon through its ragged and often sharp contours, through its mosaics of white patches, and through its display of the brightest stars. Indeed, the Milky Way could appear so singular on any clear moonless night from any hilltop in Greece as to threaten the sphere of stars with break-up. Theophrastus in fact took the Milky Way as evidence that the heavenly sphere came about by the gluing together of two hemispheres.[20] If such was the case, the heavenly sphere could hardly be the ultimate in the cosmic realm. No such problem was raised by Theophrastus or by those who reported his opinion of the Milky Way in late antiquity. The Greeks' attitude toward the sphere was summed up by Aristophanes in Plato's *Symposium* as he described the sphere as man's original, divine shape.[21] It raised a question only when it was actually cut in two so as to prompt Aristophanes to speak of boys who were concerned about coins only when given but one-half of a piece.[22] In Solon's time, as Plato recalled, the Hellenes were mere children in their views on ancient and cosmic history.[23] Later, as they cultivated cosmology, they proved themselves to be not much more than children by their smugness in the presence of the singularities of their spherical universe. Had they asked questions about those singularities, Greek science would have changed considerably and for the better, but raising such questions would have demanded a natural theology better than the best formulated by the Greeks of old.

The most singular feature of the spherical universe of the Greeks of old was, of course, the sun, an unusually large and bright "planet" compared with the rest. Greek science might have been pulled out of its decline had the anomaly of the sun as a planet been recognized in its true significance. But Aristarchus of Samos, the ancient Copernicus, had become a lonely voice. When three hundred years after him Ptolemy branded it as "absurd" and "ridiculous" to remove the earth from the center,[24] he gave a glimpse of that inner logic which stifles science in the measure in which cosmic singularity is not kept at the focus of attention. Heliocentrism, the crucial advance in turning science into a viable enterprise, could take roots only in a mental atmosphere which provided a logical anchoring of cosmic singularity in a rationale pointing beyond the cosmos. That atmosphere was not the revival of Pythagorean sun worship by Ficino and his school, a somewhat "irrational" claim especially when made by champions of the so-called rationalist tradition.[25] Ptolemy, who worshipped the sun no less than Pythagoras, was more skilled in geometry than Copernicus; yet he fought heliocentrism tooth and nail. The atmosphere needed by heliocentrism was the Christian belief in the Creator, a factor playing a decisive role in the thinking of Copernicus, Kepler, and Galileo. They were not at all disturbed by the removal of the earth from the center; rather, they rejoiced in the fact that with the sun in the center the whole universe looked more singular than ever, in telling evidence of the Creator's design.

While it has been customary to read into some brief remarks of Copernicus an advocacy of an infinite universe of stars,[26] it seems that Kepler made explicit a genuinely Copernican notion when he argued that the world had to be finite because of a great central emptiness surrounding the sun. To this Kepler added another argument, derived from the Milky Way, which he took for a ring.[27] Since it was limited inside, he assumed it to be limited from the outside as well. Kepler's conception of the Milky Way as a ring failed to find an echo partly because the notion of a spherically finite universe was rapidly falling into disrepute, a process in which Descartes's emphasis on homogeneous three-dimensional immensity played an important part. Descartes made a world with no Milky Way in it,[28] in evidence of the extent to which the shift from the finite to the infinite universe was an invitation to ignore basic singularities in the universe.

Until very recently it has been popular to glorify that shift as an unmitigated diffusion of light and, what is worse, to credit it to Giordano Bruno. One can only assign to a fear of metaphysics the failure of so many historians of science to see, first, that Bruno offered not science but a most virulent antiscience and, second, that the mainspring of his antiscience was his resolve to eliminate all specific distinctness from the universe. Like all pantheists, Bruno knew that cosmic singularities attested most effectively the point that instead of being divine the world bespoke its divine Maker. Curiously, even a pantheist like Goethe could perceive about Bruno what many historians of science after him failed to point out, namely, that the few phrases of Bruno that could qualify as scientific gems were hidden in a heap of dung,[29] his prolific discourses steeped in Hermetic mysticism. No wonder that the century of genius, free of an agnosticism which blinds one to the difference between gems and dung, cared not a whit for Bruno's science, a point still to be aired in full.

It is also still to be pointed out in detail that engrossment with infinity could blind even first-rate scientists during that very century, when the much glorified transition was made from the closed Aristotelian world to the infinite Newtonian universe. Alexandre Koyré, who provided much of the historiographic glory to that transition,[30] failed to note that the allegedly infinite homogeneous universe kept its share of perplexing singularities. Among them was, of course, the Milky Way, about which Newton offered a mere half-line, and that only as he discussed the whiteness of the tail of comets.[31] Newton was rudely highhanded about another major singularity of the same universe implied in its gravitational paradox. For that attitude he was certainly not taken to task by Koyré, who provided fresh credibility to the old fallacy that the two chief difficulties voiced by Bentley about the infinite universe, the actually realized infinite number and the gravitational paradox, were indeed paralogisms as Newton claimed them to be.[32] Koyré did not quote Bentley's perfectly sound statement that such a universe represented "an equal attraction on all sides of all matter," which was "equal to no attraction at all."[33] As to the optical paradox unfolded by Halley in Newton's presence, Koyré did not seem to be familiar with it.[34] Koyré was, however, quick to have his readers familiarize themselves with the manner in which scientists eager to foist their scientific postulates on the Creator discredited the Creator himself. Once turned into a "Dieu fainéant,"[35] or "do-nothing-god," God could only depart from the scene, an outcome which Koyré did not seem to mind. For Koyré, a historicist, it was of no professional interest to probe into the further consequences of replacing with a do-nothing-god the God who is the source of all doing and being. Yet, as it turned out, it was infinity that was to become for nineteenth-century scientific cosmology a do-nothing factor, in perfect agreement with the definition given by the schoolboy: "Infinity is where things happen which don't."

Koyré, the consummate tactician of a historicism which lends convenient support to agnosticism, seemed to realize that infinity naturally becomes that weak singularity which the sphere had already proved itself. With the weakening of the Christian matrix of theism during the eighteenth century and even more so during the overtly materialistic nineteenth century, the notion of the infinite universe had become as weak a pointer toward the Creator as the sphere was for the Greeks. Thus, after Kant and especially Laplace had irrevocably grafted the time parameter on cosmology, the question of beginning in a metaphysical sense could be written off conveniently. One who did not do so was Herschel, the first to see galaxies by the thousands in varied shapes that bespoke their evolution. He quietly disagreed when in his presence Laplace insisted to the First Consul that cosmogony did not need the hypothesis of the First Cause.[36] It took another generation before Whewell pointed out that the nebulous start of the universe was not self-explanatory either scientifically or metaphysically because the original nebula was a very singular entity, for only such an entity could give rise to a very specific world such as ours.[37]

Once the universe was considered infinite in space and time, recourse to infinite regress from one singular state to another could easily appear satisfactory with metaphysics already on its way out. Metaphysics was certainly not in Spencer's way as he failed to suspect that in reinstating the idea of eternal cosmic cycles he reinstated the very cosmology which condemned science to a stillbirth in all ancient cultures. The antiscience of a cosmic perpetuum mobile evidenced itself in Spencer's case also by his systematic oversight of the principle of entropy. Rankine's effort to restart the rundown cosmic engine by the refocusing of dissipated energy from concave ether walls[38] only showed that singular problems could only be handled by singular solutions, and his concave ether walls were singular in more than one sense.

While the singularity introduced through entropy into the cosmos compelled the best scientific minds, there prevailed during the closing decades of the nineteenth century a curious acquiescence with the dichotomist view in which the universe was divided into a small, physically meaningful part and an infinite, physically nonmeaningful expanse around it. The former was the Milky Way, supposedly dominating all the nebulae visible through telescopes.[39] That the infinite number of nebulae outside the Milky Way's domain was physically meaningless was urged by Lord Kelvin on the ground that the light coming from the Milky Way was itself insignificant in comparison with the light of the sun. Such was his dismissal of Olbers' paradox,[40] an example of the manner in which so many distinguished scientists were ready to take the infinite homogeneous universe as presenting no problems for science. They were not greatly behind the times, because as late as 1938 a Nobel-laureate physicist still rejected calculations of the age of the universe from radioactivity on the basis that infinity was the very foundation of science.[41]

By the 1930s cosmology had reached a phase of its development much higher than any of its earlier phases, and bespoke cosmic singularities more strongly than ever before. In fact, it did so to an extent that was intensely upsetting to anyone loathing transcendental perspectives. In the cosmology of general relativity Euclidean space as an empty receptacle was replaced by a space consisting of the totality of lines of motion specified by the amount of mass in the universe. While that mass could in principle be infinite, its homogeneous distribution could be conceived only in such a way as was "not to be taken seriously," to recall a phrase of Einstein's.[42] What was to be taken seriously was a universe of finite mass giving rise to a net of lines of motion with a curvature such as to imply a maximum radius for possible paths of motion along which the light went "round" the universe. The universe looked therefore no less specific than a garment on the clothier's rack, carrying a tag on which one could read if not its price at least its main measurements. Just as there was no logical necessity for a given garment to be of a particular size, there was no scientific reason either why the universe had to have the singular measure it possessed.

This measure had become increasingly unbearable for some as the time parameter of the cosmology of general relativity began to be unfolded and the results were confirmed by the observation of the recession of galaxies. Viewing this velocity in reverse was equivalent to coming to a primordial superdense state of the universe and to computing its age from its rate of expansion. To be delighted, or at least not to be disturbed by such singularity, presupposes an absence of hostility toward metaphysics. As long as that hostility was relatively muted, the result was advocacy of an oscillating universe by Jeans and Millikan at a symposium organized in 1931 for cosmologists by the British Association for the Advancement of Science.[43] Later on, with hostility to metaphysics grown virulent, a radical effort to eliminate the strikingly singular age of the universe became inevitable. That for Hoyle the effort was also motivated by a deep dislike of the Christian world view based on a creation once and for all is clear from his own published statements.[44] But whatever the motivations, there was no foundation whatsoever in the claim of the steady-state theorists that a certain cosmic radiation could be evidence of the continual emergence of hydrogen

atoms out of nothing, and at a very specific rate, to secure the ageless-
ness of the universe. Their claim became the epitome of counter-
metaphysics as they specified that this emergence out of nothing was
spontaneous, in no way involving a Creator.[45] To be caught in such
contempt of logic is evidence of that inner logic which cannot be
escaped when one tries to exorcise the prospect of a cosmic beginning.
The force of that logic is such as to make one contemptuous of Ockham's
razor and claim that an infinite number of illogical creations is preferable to one which at least satisfies the laws of logic.[46] That such reveling
in plain contempt of logic and scientific method could gain considerable
popularity among scientists will surprise only those who are unwilling
to consider the mental bias which can be generated by aversion to the
basic tenets of Christian theism. This must have been true of that philosopher of science who in the early 1960s wondered how the steady-
state theory still drew adherents long after the exposure of its fallacies.[47]
He should have also pondered why Munitz, who gave one of the ear-
liest and most incisive rebuttals of the farcical nature of the creation
concept of the steady-state theory, still could claim that "the explanation in terms of a Creator is more difficult to accept than an admission of
failure in trying to resolve the mystery of existence."[48]

The reason for such a claim is not in science, perhaps not even in logic
and metaphysics, but most likely in honest psychoanalysis, if not plain
confession, in which full disclosure is made of the motives which
prompted, for instance, Monod to state: "We would like to think ourselves necessary, inevitable, ordained from all eternity. All religions,
nearly all philosophies, and even a part of science testify to the un-
wearying, heroic effort of mankind desperately denying its own contingency."[49] For the explanation of such statements science can be invoked
only in the measure to which it is mishandled in the desperate effort to
blunt the sharp point of brutally strong cosmic singularities. One such
mishandling is provided by a little-noted dichotomist aspect of the
steady-state theory, according to which an infinite number of hydrogen
atoms have since the infinite past receded into that unobservable infinite universe which surrounds the observable part in which we find
ourselves. Eddington could hardly guess what a sound warning he gave
in 1935 when he remarked: "That queer quantity 'infinity' is the very
mischief, and no rational physicist should have anything to do with
it."[50] The most rational of them in modern times, Einstein, had certainly no use for a dichotomist view of the cosmos when he raised
cosmology to a scientifically rigorous level by making the totality of the
universe the prime subject of cosmological investigations. When asked
during Hoyle's famous lecture series at Princeton in 1952 about the
steady-state theory, he dismissed it as a "romantic speculation," a
generous assessment.[51]

As is well known, orbital satellites in the mid-1960s failed to detect the radiation postulated by the steady-state theory. Neither this negative result nor the improved count of galaxies made by radiotelescopes, however, impressed a cosmologist as antimetaphysical as Hoyle. His famous reassertion of his faith in the steady-state theory in 1968 before the Royal Society[52] is a classic illustration of the hardened stance that antimetaphysics can inspire in the thinking of a scientist. Whereas the original version of the steady-state theory conjured up the creation out of nothing of one hydrogen atom per cubic meter in every 3×10^5 years (hardly a "directly observable process"[53]), in Hoyle's revamped version the continual creation of matter is pictured as a spectacular, gigantic singularity, demanding nothing less than the proverbially unshaken faith of unbelief. For surely, it is nothing short of spectacular if matter is indeed being "poured into the universe" at the center of highly condensed celestial objects such as quasars and Seyfert galaxies. But what is truly spectacular is that Hoyle simply took the unusually large red shift shown by these galaxies as observational evidence that matter is indeed being poured into the universe.[54] Such an inference, which genuinely though most erroneously is a metaphysical inference, can come only from a metaphysical motivation, be it in fact countermetaphysical. That motivation is the resolve to eliminate fundamental cosmic singularities, a motivation easily recognizable in Hoyle's carefully nonmetaphysical phrasing: "Observation shows that the opposite is true, matter emerges from strong gravitational fields, it does not collapse into singularities."[55]

The "opposite" of the opposite is Einstein's general relativity, which implies not only the gravitational collapse of matter into gigantic singularities, but also, as Hoyle admitted, a structural similarity between "the singularity which represents the origin of the Universe in the big-bang cosmologies" and the local singularities.[56] This is an unwitting admission of the closely interwoven character of the truths of cosmology, a fact not at all surprising to those aware of the similar character of some higher truths which have found their classic symbol in a seamless garment. While it would be unwise to take general relativity for the last word in physics, it is certainly the finest aspect of the physics we have. The effort to sacrifice it in order to escape singularities in time resembles an age-old attitude ready to promote counterscience or half-science in order to escape metaphysical perspectives. Hoyle is not the only one committed to such a dubious option. Peter G. Bergmann struck a similar note when he pointed out that general relativity cannot cope with the singularity of the cosmic background radiation produced by the start of the expansion of the universe,[57] because that radiation represents not only a privileged frame of reference but also points to a state of the universe in which its metric was singular, that is, independent of the choice of coordinate systems.[58] That the very same general relativity, which originally had led to a scientifically coherent singular universe, should now be overhauled if not discarded in order to let cosmic singularities dissolve into aprioristic homogeneities is surely a strange wish, even if Einstein himself was lured by it at the very end of his life.[59] Of course, these and similar efforts, among which Gérard H. de Vaucouleurs's pleading for hierarchical cosmology may be an example,[60] succeed in eliminating fundamental singularities from the universe only along the time parameter. But apparently some feel that an eternal universe, however singular in space, is enough to exorcise the specter of a universe created by God.

In the 1970s escape from the cosmic singularity of a beginning is sought chiefly in the idea of an oscillating universe. Although the count of galaxies has increasingly favored the single-expansion model, the idea of a cosmos going through endless cycles of expansion and contraction has exercised its fascination since the 1930s for many a cosmologist of antimetaphysical preferences. Clearly, more than science is at play when a cosmologist characterizes the strong evidence that the universe will keep expanding forever as a "horrible thought," something akin to an inexorable march toward a "graveyard of frozen darkness." This, according to the same cosmologist, "would make the whole universe meaningless. If that were true, I would quit, and spend my life raising roses."[61] That the eventual coming to an end of physical processes makes the universe meaningless is not a scientific statement but a metaphysical one and there should be plenty of food for thought in the fact that escape from metaphysics can readily turn into escape from astronomy, hardly a rosy prospect for anyone who has cast his lot with science.

Should the universe go from expanding into contracting, the cosmologist resentful of metaphysics can but escape again into his rose garden. At the end of that contraction the universe is bound to turn into a gigantic black hole, out of which not even the slightest bit of matter can escape. Since according to the studies of I. D. Novikov and Ya. B. Zel'dovich the thermodynamical possibility for another expansion is well-nigh nil,[62] the prospect of an endless alternation between expanding and contracting phases is at present not something to be asserted as reputable science. There is, however, an impressive amount of science about black holes which are black only from the outside because not even photons can escape their gravitational pull. Were it possible for any sentient being to stand on the surface of such a black hole, the sky all around would look immensely bright, owing to the onrush of all matter and radiation toward it. No wonder that such an extraordinary state of the universe makes some of its best investigators think that somehow they stand on the threshhold of creation. The crisis of gravitational collapse, wrote Charles M. Patton and John A. Wheeler, "brings us into closer confrontation than ever with the greatest question in the books of physics: how did the universe come into being? And what is it made of?"[63]

Inasmuch as the "how" of creation becomes a question for physics, the answer given to it will fall far short of being an answer to the fact of creation, a fact which only metaphysics can handle. That even the "how" of creation cannot be an answer to be had from physics can be seen from the extreme vagueness of that pregeometry out of which Patton and Wheeler see the universe emerge necessarily and uniquely. That such a vision of cosmic emergence is ultimately an idealist a priori vision should be of no surprise.[64] Apart from that inevitable drift into idealism there is much food for thought in the three questions voiced by Patton and Wheeler. In the first two, they ask whether it is "imaginable that the deeper structure of physics should govern how the universe came into being" and whether it is "not more reasonable to believe the converse, that the requirement that the universe should come into being governs the structure of physics?"[65] The latter question, which demands a positive answer, is only one more instance of the proposition that all science is cosmology.

But since the cosmos is most singular, its science, and all science, is most singular, a point which sets the tone of the third question posed by Patton and Wheeler: "Shall we conclude that the only cosmology worse than a universe with a singularity is a universe without a singularity, because then it lacks the power to come alive?"[66] This question certainly reveals the covert realization on the part of the non-metaphysician cosmologist that the product of creation is singularity. That he arrives at this metaphysical conclusion on the basis of his appreciation of science, which is a singularly specific discourse about a bafflingly singular existence, should surprise only those unmindful of the very same logic which directs the road of science no less than the ways to God. The metaphysician knows, of course, that the *totality* of perfections, which entails the exclusion of all singularities, is reserved for the noncreated Being for whom the capability of creating things, that is, concrete singularities, is exclusively reserved. The only being he cannot create is his infinitely perfect being with no trace of those singularities which are always signs of existential limitations that in him alone find their ultimate explanation. The cosmologist disdainful of metaphysics will be left with a formidable if not frightening array of singularities, and the only scientific thing he can do about them is to trace them to another array of singularities, a most satisfactory and safe pastime as long as one remains oblivious to the fallacy of infinite regress.

That the foremost among very recent books on cosmology comes to an end with a chapter on the initial singularity of the universe and with a discussion of the nature and implications of singularities[67] is a subtle forecast of a topic on which the cosmology of the future will be pivoted. Unlike the sphere and Euclidean infinity, the space-time structure of the universe found by modern cosmology shows singularities that are brutally strong. Some of them can only be grasped by specialists, others are within more general reach. In a sense those singularities are basic constants of physics out of which, as Victor F. Weisskopf showed,[68] one can derive the singular size of atoms as well as of stars, the singularly blue color of the sky, and even the singularly limited height of mountains, to mention only a few examples. Even more breathtaking should seem the extremely specific manner in which the interaction of various physical factors had to take place to produce the universe as we know it. The evidence for this derives from the greatly increased precision by which the cosmic background radiation was measured a few years ago by Arno A. Penzias and others at the Bell Telephone Laboratories in Murray Hill, New Jersey. The radiation is a relic of the state of the universe one second after its expansion got under way. The temperature of that radiation controlled the rate of interaction between protons and neutrons in a way that ought to make any cosmologist hold his breath. Or as Sir Bernard Lovell put it not so long ago: "It is an astonishing reflection that if the interaction were only a few percent stronger, then all the hydrogen in the primeval condensate would have turned into helium in the early stages of expansion. No galaxies, no stars, no life would have emerged, it would be a universe forever unknowable by living creatures."[69]

The prospect of this might easily give to the cosmologist averse to metaphysics the feeling which Victor Hugo voiced about creation: "An always imminent end, with no intermediate stage between being and nonbeing, the return to the chasm, the slide possible at every moment, such is the precipice called creation."[70] Creation will appear a reassuring event only if beyond it one is willing to see an existence which is absolute consistency, stability, and reliability, with no trace of caprice whatever. To catch a glimpse of that existence more is needed than skill with the laws of physics. Although those laws are certainly expressive of contingent existence (and in a sense far more consistent than was suspected by Emile Boutroux a century ago[71]), they are as such not a grasp of that existence. Taken in themselves they are, as Emile Meyerson showed half a century ago, mere identity relations that tell nothing about that sequence of events which brings novelty into every new moment and makes reality tangible and palpable.[72] Nor do the laws of physics, as identity relations, tell anything about causality, although every experiment in physics is based on the assumption that any given stage in an experimental set-up will not merely follow the immediately preceding one but will be caused by it. It would hardly be scientific to assume that the pulling of a trigger merely precedes the explosion of gunpowder, that the latter merely precedes the uniting of two non-critical masses of uranium, and that this last event again only precedes the atomic holocaust. Moreover, while all these various events can be related to one another by equations which merely juxtapose entities in identity relations, the events themselves bespeak their drastic differences and bring witness to that reality of nature which escapes scientific explanation.

It is a fundamental shortcoming of science that on its exact and formal level it gives the appearance of being severed from that reality which is a vast network of events standing in causal relation. Yet, while science may and should appear in that sense severed from reality, science becomes an illusion if that apparent severance is declared to be real. These were the obvious implications of Meyerson's classic reflections on exact science, but he never spoke of them. When pressed by friends whether he advocated by implication a realist ontology, he invariably replied with an enigmatic smile and turned to other topics.[73] His personal right to do so should not, however, mean a prohibition against spelling out those implications. The first and most important to note is that the reality of events without which science becomes an illusion cannot be reached by the identity relations of science, but only by one's surrender to that reality through an act of rational judgment.[74] This assertion of reality is not an act derivable from mere logic but an act steeped in metaphysics, albeit not an idealist one. It presupposes a readiness to be filled with wonderment, for which—an old story in philosophy—let Wittgenstein be the spokesman in an age over which logical positivism, contemptuous of wonderment, cast a long shadow. His was on occasion an experience which, to quote his words, "when I have it *I wonder at the existence of the world*. And I am then inclined to use such phrases as 'How extraordinary that anything should exist' or 'How extraordinary that the world should exist.'"[75]

About Wittgenstein it is better remembered that in line with his logical positivism the world for him "was a totality of facts not of things."[76] Yet, if such a statement is taken in its rigor (and was it not Wittgenstein who insisted on utmost rigor?), the totality of facts would never constitute that coherent wholeness which is called the world, a world presupposed by that very science which logical positivism avidly claims to itself. Underlying the facts or events there ought to be some permanence giving rise to things. But precisely because the things are also events, they cannot be absolutely permanent. A thing insofar as it is an event is a happening and whatever happens can be said to exist only in a limited sense. The world as a totality of facts is a totality of such limited things, a notion against which no serious objection can be raised on the basis of science. On the contrary, and precisely because of science, including its historical genesis and growth, things and their totality must appear strikingly singular. The universe, to recall a felicitous phrase of Loren Eiseley, is an "unexpected universe."[77] What is to be expected is the continued failure of an a priori derivation of the singularity of the cosmos. While an eventual fusion of quantum theory and gravitation may greatly narrow the choices open to a physicist,[78] the fusion will leave wholly intact the singularity of the quantum of action. And should it turn out, as Dirac first surmised in 1937, that the value of the basic constants of physics is a function of cosmic evolutionary time,[79] the singularity of the universe along the time parameter will become even more striking.

As has already been noted, the assertion of the reality of events insofar as they are things, and of the reality of things insofar as they are events, is indispensable for securing for science the reality and consistency of its object. The recognition of the contingent reality of all things, precisely because they are events, is not something that one is forced to do by pure logic. But there is no logic that would force one with mathematical rigor to one's next meal. This last remark should remind one of Bertrand Russell and of the beginning of his parting with logical positivism. Almost ten years later, in his famous debate with Father Copleston on the existence of God,[80] he was already so far from logical positivism as to admit the validity of the notion of the world as a whole, nay even as a great brute fact. What he refused to admit was that this brute singularity of the fact of the universe justified any further question about it. He based his refusal on the assertion that the notion of totality implies no logical necessity for asking about its cause, because causes always deal with particulars.[81] Atheists who look at logic as their citadel should remember that it was not by pure logic alone that in our century men of science achieved the vision of the world as an all-inclusive singularly brute fact.

Just as no man can live by bread alone, no cosmologist (a term which includes all genuine scientists) can live without a realist notion of the universe as the totality of all interacting things. This is a major lesson of the history of science. It is therefore most illogical to espouse science and at the same time avoid facing a fundamental question about the world, a question that can be raised only on the basis of a metaphysics which not only is capable of giving the answer but which alone is compatible with science. As shown by the whole history of science, that metaphysics is not idealism. And since it is indeed metaphysics, it cannot be positivism, let alone that logicism which wrote on its banner that "metaphysics is excluded as nonsensical."[82] And since naive realism is not metaphysics either, the metaphysics in question can only be moderate realism. Old and new spokesmen of that school have articulated often and well enough its final question about the universe and its answer to it. Here it was merely shown that the history of science provides a rich background to that answer. This consists in the pattern valid especially for all phases of the history of cosmology. In all those phases the universe appeared markedly singular, invariably raising further scientific questions and showing thereby the built-in inadequacy of scientific answers which are but so many steps from one cosmic singularity to another, none of them self-explanatory. To keep this in mind ought to be very helpful in an age in which science is taken for the basic and universally accepted currency.

Just as this very same science cannot be understood without recognizing the existence of a mind able to hold within its reach the wholeness of nature and be thereby superior to it, the understanding which science gives of nature will fully satisfy the urge to understand only when that urge is allowed to carry one to the recognition of that Existence which is not limited by any singularity. That this inference is strongly resisted by advocates of a so-called rationalist metaphysics merely shows the extent to which even those can remain the captives of positivism who resolutely try to save science from its lethal clutches.[83] Rationalist metaphysics is not the genuine voice of that limited reason which strangely enough cannot find a lasting satisfaction in limited things and not even in their totality, which is always limited with respect to existence, precisely because all of them exist only inasmuch as they *happen*. With an inexorable urge that limited mind reaches out for the unlimited in existence which, precisely because it is genuinely unlimited, cannot *happen* but can only *be* and is therefore most aptly called He Who Is.[84] He is the sole explanation that can be given of limited existence revealed to us by the strong and weak singularities of limited things. Without keeping him in one's mental focus, those singularities will appear as that "inexhaustible queerness" which J. B. S. Haldane once cited as the main characteristic of the universe.[85] Cosmic singularities severed from their Creator turn indeed into queerness, and discourse about them can easily become something akin to that proverbial "mystic chant over an unintelligible universe."[86]

For a theist the universe is never queer, but singular. He does not even absolutely need the brute singular queerness of the universe unfolded by modern cosmology to gain assurance about the Creator. A theist is one who is always aware that anything can appear incredibly singular "if you can skin off the crust of obviousness our habits put on it."[87] But the theist needs the science of cosmology to counter effectively the claim that "the complete extinction of theological superstition" is the precondition of the truth of the otherwise sound statement that "an adequate cosmology will only begin to be written when an adequate philosophy of the mind has appeared."[88] The theist mindful of the idealists' mishandling of science will not be impressed by the idealist ring of such a statement. Idealists can only produce a queer universe in which there is no place for that wonder about queerness which is capable of producing science. The theist also knows that the universe must be queerer than he can imagine, because he knows he can never be privy to the Creator's sovereign choice in creating a world of which man is an equally contingent constituent. The supreme queerness in all this is the ability of the mind to master what is not mind by finding it to be a coherent whole, a universe, queer as it may appear beyond any expectation. By relating that queerness to the ultimate ground of all being, cosmic queerness becomes that cosmic singularity which points to the Ultimate in intelligibility and being. The singularity of the universe is a gigantic springboard which can propel upward anyone ready to exploit its metaphysical resilience and catch thereby a glimpse of the Ultimate and Absolute in the form of a unique inference. Catching that glimpse, or sensing the truth of that inference, is always transitory, nay momentary. Our need of and hunger for the sensory quickly pulls us back to things tangible which, when properly touched, will again propel our minds toward the Absolute as the explanation of what is singular and contingent. The alternative to this continual surging upward is to envelop existence in a never-to-be-resolved mystery.[89] Those who prefer this mystery-mongering to an explanation which is a surrender to the existence of the Creator, are right in stating that no surrender is without agony. As to the agony of surrendering to the Creator, it certainly does not have its source in that cosmology which more than any other branch of science shows nature in her powerfully strong, yet beautifully lucid singularity.

Eighteen

POINTERS OF PURPOSE

THE SINGULARITY WHICH IS THE HALLMARK OF THE COSMOS BOTH IN ITS entirety and in all its details calls, as was argued in the last chapter, for a Being capable of an act which is creative in the strictest sense. Such an act implies a selection demanded by the singularity of the actual cosmos, one of the infinitely many worlds that are conceivable. Singularity diffuses through all things in such a manner as to turn them into a universe of beings that interact with one another in an invariably consistent and most specific manner. Such a singularity is striking enough in inert matter and is plainly astonishing in the realm of the living. What is not astonishing at all is that in our times it fell, as noted before, to a prominent molecular biologist with unabashedly materialistic conviction, to describe intellectual evolution as a struggle by man to dissipate the specter of his own contingency.[1] Of all facets of existence none is more fragile (and therefore palpably contingent) than life, and a materialist biologist is hard put to account for life as if there were nothing deeply contingent in it. If life, as Monod wanted us to believe, is nothing but chance and necessity, the voice of life's contingency can only become muted. Monod's effort, or any similar effort, has certainly not been meant to be a matter of mere chance or of necessity, let alone of both. Indeed, the effort is highly purposeful, though hardly consistent with the perspective in which chance and necessity are the sole explanatory devices. Of course, Monod was careful not to make the superficial among his readers realize the compound fallacy in his claim that just as the initial unconscious choice at the start of biological evolution determined the rest of what followed, "so the choice of scientific practice, an unconscious choice in the beginning, has launched the evolution of culture on a one-way path; onto a track which nineteenth-century scientism saw leading infallibly upward to an empyrean noon hour for mankind, whereas what we see opening before us today is an abyss of darkness."[2]

Concerning Monod's claim about an unconscious beginning of the evolution of culture, in which he undoubtedly included science and possibly science alone, a historian of science can only note that whatever beginnings the scientific record shows, they invariably indicate a high degree of consciousness. Could they be called to the witness stand, a Thales, an Archimedes, an Oresme, a Galileo, or whoever is to be credited with the beginning of scientific culture, would give Monod a resounding denial. As for perceiving the abyss opened up by science, this makes sense only for beings permeated with a sense of purpose, which it was Monod's intention to discredit once and for all. That both scientific history and philosophical sensitivity fare so badly within one sentence is not at all surprising in a book of philosophical biology written with the intention of explaining life with no reference to purpose. The same has been a chief characteristic of all publications of that kind ever since they obtained their modern perspective through the notion of an evolution by natural selection a little over a century ago. Such a situation leaves no choice to a historian of science mindful of philosophy, including its discourse about the Ultimate, but to study that situation in its very origin—which is particularly an origin because of its essential ties with a book called *Origin of Species*.

That the *Origin* quickly gained enormous publicity and applause was due in no small measure to the glowing review of it which appeared in the *Times* on the morning after Christmas, 1859. Writing that review, Thomas Henry Huxley became the first convert to Darwinism, indeed, its most articulate and ardent spokesman for the next three decades.[3] Of all Darwinists, old and new, Huxley showed the greatest willingness to face up to the difficulties of Darwinism, of which, needless to say, the question of purpose is the most fundamental. He even perceived that the singularity present everywhere in the realm of the living was enough to remind one not only of purpose but of a most transcendental and universal kind of purpose. "That it is possible," Huxley observed in 1863, "to arrange all the varied forms of animals into groups, having this sort of singular subordination one to the other, is a very remarkable circumstance."[4] From a singular subordination it is but a short step to assuming a design behind it, and for all we know, the origin of a design is an intelligent act animated by purpose. Huxley would have in no way allowed such inference. As if to nip it in the bud, he quickly added: "But, as Mr. Darwin remarks, this [singular subordination] is a result which is quite to be expected, if the principle which he lays down be correct."[5] The principle which Darwin laid down, the principle of natural selection, would not have in itself preempted the validity of the foregoing inference; it was the manner in which Darwin laid it down that made it appear to him and to most of his followers that the universe, living and nonliving, was void of design and of purpose.

Darwin himself never engaged in speculations about the nonliving world. Among contemporary evolutionists this was the specialty of Herbert Spencer, whom Darwin considered a thinker comparable to Descartes and Leibniz, about whom he admittedly "knew very little."[6] But one did not need to have a particularly speculative mind to perceive that on the basis of Darwin's philosophizing the singularity of the cosmos could not be the reflection of an unconditional rationality and consistency. This was not only a Darwinian but also a Spencerian view, and when Huxley voiced it, he did so, revealingly enough, with a reference to Spencer's greatness as philosopher of evolution. About this universe of ours "of simplest matter and definitely operating energy," Huxley stated—and his statement came very close to conjuring up a basic cosmic singularity—"it is possible to raise the question whether it may not be the product of evolution from a universe of such matter, in which the manifestations of energy were not definite—in which for example our laws of motion held good for some units and not for others, or for the same units at one time and not another."[7] A world of incoherence giving rise to partial worlds of coherence was in Huxley's eyes the perfect realization of an "Epicurean chance-world," which alone was compatible with consistent agnosticism. Huxley failed to note that no great physicist up to his time had found an Epicurean chance world germane to scientific thinking. Had Huxley felt how strongly great scientists were committed to the idea of an intrinsically and unconditionally coherent universe, he might have sensed the extent to which the universe was a design and therefore a pointer for purpose. Lacking a vivid realization of the singular rationality of the universe, he could easily be drawn into the Darwinist program of devoting one's entire career to the purpose of proving that there was no purpose. As Whitehead remarked of all such men of science, they "constitute an interesting subject for study."[8]

Scoffers at purpose, old and new, could therefore be safely left behind were it not for the apparently unassailable scientific evidence piled up in the wake of Darwin's *Origin of Species* against the reality of design and purpose. A hundred years after the *Origin,* the word evolution stands for many as a rebuttal of any argument on behalf of purpose, to say nothing of the argument derived from purpose on behalf of the existence of God. Just as the idea of evolution was in the air in the decades preceding the publication of the *Origin,* so was its exploitation against the argument from purpose. A letter of John Henry Newman written in 1870 sums it all up: "And to tell the truth, though I should not wish to preach on the subject, for forty years I have been unable to see the logical force of the argument myself. I believe in design because I believe in God; not in a God because I see design."[9]

The word "evolution" made its appearance in the *Origin* only in the form "evolved," and only in its sixth edition in 1872. The word became a prophetic counterpoint to that grand conclusion into which Darwin inserted (from the second edition on) a reference to the Creator as the one who "originally breathed life with its several powers into a few forms or into one."[10] Darwin, who stated in his *Autobiography* that he was though not a Christian at least a theist when he wrote the *Origin,*[11] might not by 1872 have reached agnosticism, the final phase in the evolution of his Weltanschauung. Yet the whole evolution of Darwinism shows that the last phrase in the *Origin* about the Creator is

281

out of place in what evolutionary philosophy, or evolutionism, has by and large come to be. A telling anticipation of this was the conflict between the last phrase of the *Origin* and the third of the three mottos introducing it. Through that motto, a quotation from Francis Bacon, Darwin warned against the presumption of believing that one could by contemplating nature be in possession of final truths either in divinity or in philosophy. The *Origin* was a vast offering of one final, more philosophical than scientific, truth based on the contemplation of nature, namely, that all development of life was mechanistic in such a sense as to render unnecessary all philosophy, to say nothing of theology, however natural.

When a great book comes to a close on a note of glaring inconsistency, the first reaction is to attribute it to mannerism of style. Unfortunately, more than style is implied here. Darwin meant the *Origin* to be taken for "one long argument."[12] Long it certainly was, but insofar as the mechanism rather than the fact of evolution was concerned, an argument most uncertain. This is a fact that Darwin suspected at times, but it can hardly be gathered from the writings of present-day Darwinian biologists. Some recent historians of Darwin, unimpressed by the myth created about him, are more instructive in that respect.[13] From them one can also learn that had Darwin thought of his book as one great vision, he would have put it into a more correct but still very scientific perspective. Copernicus prescribed no mechanism for the motion of planets around the sun, and yet his vision of their heliocentric arrangement was persuasive and most scientific, except of course for dyed-in-the-wool empiricists, of whom Francis Bacon was a chief spokesman. Boasting of having worked on the basis of "true Baconian principles,"[14] Darwin, a self-styled Baconian, failed to realize what it meant that (according to his own admission, made only in private) he had no empirical evidence that natural selection had indeed ever produced a new species.[15] He was so unaware of his theory's being a vision that he did not notice that the core of his argument was not inductive but deductive.[16] Thus he had no qualms as he, avowedly unsuited for metaphysics, tried to divest his theory of all metaphysics. This is why his most scientific vision about the fact of evolution and about the instrumentality of one species in the emergence of another was overshadowed by his emphasis on a wrong science, the omniscience of natural selection. It is that omniscience which is suggested, however unwittingly, when the perpetuation of types which are not too well adapted is described as a "kind of selection sub specie aeternitatis,"[17] or when it is declared that "it is certain that if we can see any advantage whatever in a small variation (and sometimes even if we cannot), selection sees more."[18] Such phrases are good only to divert attention from the unsatisfactory character of natural selection as an all-purpose mechanism of evolution. What made that mechanism unsatisfactory did not lie so much in its often ambiguous fit to concrete examples offered by Darwin, as in its lending itself to a philosophical interpretation through which Darwinism quickly became the trade name for Spencerian evolution, a fact which Spencer strongly resented.[19]

Most of Darwin's admirers took the *Origin* as the empirically incontrovertible proof of evolutionism which a starkly materialistic generation was avidly looking for, an expectation quickly registered by friend and foe. The same expectation was still in its full vigor around the centenary of the *Origin*,[20] when the non sequiturs of Darwinian theory were freshly presented by Gertrude Himmelfarb in her *Darwin and the Darwinian Revolution*. As a reviewer of it wrote on July 17, 1959, in the *Manchester Guardian*: "It must have been at a fairly early age that I decided that Mr. Darwin had a better explanation of my existence than God . . . . Dr. Himmelfarb knocks holes in his data and logic, but even if she took the bottom out of him altogether . . . I should still find him satisfying, even if not right."[21]

Old or new enthusiasm for Darwinism should be no cause for alarm to a theist. Nor should he primarily rest his confidence on the shaky condition of the proofs of Darwinism, a theory of evolution radically opposed to any consideration that implies metaphysics in general and teleology in particular. Even if the mechanism offered by Darwinists old and new were a satisfactory explanation of the evolutionary record, a theist still could confidently press his claims. As the whole history of science shows, the more successful a scientific theory becomes, the more it prompts questions about its singular success in respect to a vast array of very singular phenomena and laws. These questions are the ones posed by the reach of the mind and by the singularity of the cosmos, of which the living realm is a most conspicuously singular part. A singularly specific aspect of that realm is that, as Sir Julian Huxley put it, "at first sight the biological sector seems full of purpose. Organisms are built as if purposely designed." Needless to say, Sir Julian quickly added: "As the genius of Darwin showed, the purpose is only an apparent one."[22]

The theist may take some comfort from the fact that, Sir Julian notwithstanding, Darwin failed to show the unreality of purpose. First, there are a great many astonishing cases of mimicry, parasitism, and adaptations of organs, which to account for in terms of natural selection amounts to explaining miracles by magic. The magic resorted to by Darwinians is the implementation of the motto, "let us briefly look at these facts and pass on quickly to others." Tellingly enough, reverence for bothersome facts is, in this connection too, mainly cultivated by those who believe in miracles.[23] All those cases make it easily understandable why purpose is a nightmare in a Darwinian universe in much the same way that freedom is in a mechanistic universe. Second, Darwin failed to exorcise purpose from the universe of the living precisely because his genius was such as to disqualify him for performing feats of metaphysics. Actually, the more the Darwinists argue against purpose and design, the more support they provide to a theist fond of the argument from design, and they do this both by the persistent inconclusiveness of their arguments and by the persistence of their arguing. It is in connection with this persistence that the historian of science is well suited to assist the natural theologian.

Darwin was and still is enormously persuasive in presenting a vast array of data that make evolution appear nothing short of a self-evident fact. But the mechanism of natural selection, by which he tried to explain that fact, could persuade only those who already believed that a rapt contemplation of "blind forces" was the vision of nature required by science. Enthrallment by blind forces can produce blindness, which increasingly plagued the six editions of the *Origin*. Darwin grudgingly attributed more and more to the Lamarckian view of the use and disuse of organs, although his prime objective was to discredit Lamarck for good. Darwin was not so blind as to be wholly unaware of this predicament of his. Yet, while he spoke of it in private correspondence,[24] he left the vast crowd of readers of the *Origin* in the dark about it. Worse yet, from its third edition on, they were offered a Historical Sketch in which Lamarck was all but held up to ridicule and Buffon dismissed as one "who does not enter on the causes or means" of evolution.[25] A telltale phrase not only about a Darwin careless with philosophically crucial differences, such as the one between causes and means, but also about a Darwin unable to see that the shoe was on the other foot. When at the urging of Huxley he took at long last a serious look at Buffon, he remarked: "Whole pages are laughably like mine."[26] It was hardly a laughing matter that some of Darwin's reasonings were strikingly similar to those offered by Buffon a hundred years earlier.

Such oversight of an obviously one-way relation has its explanation in two factors. One was Darwin's single-minded commitment to give a purely mechanistic account of evolution, the other was his inability to grasp what was philosophically implied in a mechanistic account presented as *the explanation*. On the level of explanation it was self-incriminatory to admit as Darwin did in private correspondence shortly after the publication of the *Origin* that he was "not accustomed to metaphysical trains of thought."[27] If that was the case, he should have avoided attributing the kind of exclusiveness to mechanics which turns the latter into a metaphysics in disguise. It forced him to renounce not only his recurring feeling that the universe was not a product of chance but also the conviction that man's universe of thought was reliable.

"With me," Darwin wrote to W. Graham in 1881, "the horrid doubt always arises whether the convictions of man's mind, which has been developed from the mind of lower animals, are of any value or at all trustworthy. Would any one trust in the convictions of a monkey's mind, if there are any convictions in such a mind?"[28]

Darwin was most illogical in trusting his explanation of evolution, a product of the human mind no less than teleology was such a product. His perplexity showed that if one does not trust the existence of design in non-consciously-living beings, one is logically prevented from having confidence in one's own most consciously purposeful activity, of which reasoning is the most revealing and most far-reaching. But the same perplexity also showed that attack on the proofs of the existence of God is an implied attack on science. Darwin, of course, hardly suspected this as he tried to justify the gradual weakening of his trust in the mind's ability to reach firm conclusions about the existence of the Creator. Five years after he wrote to Graham, Darwin spoke in his *Autobiography* in almost identical words about being seized time and again with the conviction that the universe was not a product of chance and asked: "Can the mind of man which has, as I fully believe, been developed from a mind as low as that possessed by the lowest animal, be trusted when it draws such grand conclusions? May not these be the result of the connection between cause and effect which strikes us as a necessary one, but probably depends merely on inherited experience?"[29] Darwin was not enough of a philosopher to realize that if there was merit in his questions, then his claim about natural selection could well be considered merely an effect of hereditary experience, and therefore void of objectively valid intellectual merit.

Such a reflection might have given him pause, but his mind was already beginning to focus on a very personal target. It was his youthful commitment to faith in God—a commitment that extended to taking each statement in the Bible as literal truth.[30] Such commitment can easily turn into resentment, for which pointed evidence was provided by the aging Darwin when in the privacy of his *Autobiography* he felt no need to blunt his remarks. Once more he failed to realize that any blow aimed at natural theology reaches its target by hitting science first. "Nor must we overlook," Darwin wrote, "the probability of the constant inculcation in a belief in God on the brains not yet fully developed, that it would be as difficult for them to throw off their belief in God, as for a monkey to throw off its instinctive fear and hatred of a snake." But if doubt and suspicion could be cast on religious education on such a basis, why could an education geared to the "truth" of natural selection be less suspect? And if it was the best precept for an evolutionist never to consider anything intrinsically higher or lower (a precept laid down

285

by Darwin),[31] on what ground could a theistic outlook, or even a mere belief in design and purpose, be considered intrinsically inferior to agnosticism and atheism?

Most of Darwin's admirers were just as innocent and inept concerning such implications, the sole excuse, for instance, for Tyndall's declaring in 1870 to the British Association that a "mind like that of Darwin can never sin wittingly against either fact or law."[32] Darwin was certainly unaware of his many sins against clarity of thought. He felt no need of philosophical clarification when Huxley specified his "most remarkable service ... to the philosophy [!] of biology" the reconciliation of it with morphology,[33] and when Asa Gray credited him in a similar vein with the restoration of teleology to morphology.[34] No Darwinist cared to ask about the precise meaning of that "perspective much larger and much more coherent" in which, according to Francis Darwin, "evolutionary biologists began to study the destiny and significance of organs thanks to the restoration of teleology by my father."[35] Neither Huxley nor Gray nor the two Darwins suspected that the truly larger and more coherent perspective would be kept alive by a morphology which was to become a continual challenge to Darwinism precisely because of the morphologists' genuine interest in the destiny and significance of organs. Organs, like organisms, betray that wholeness of things which consists of far more than the mere mechanical juxtaposition of parts. It is that perspective of wholeness which reveals purpose and ultimately permits a genuine reference to the Creator, a reference which was wholly out of place in the *Origin*. No Darwinist demurred when John Dewey declared that "the *Origin of Species* foreswears inquiry about absolute origins and absolute finalities."[36] Such an inquiry, let it be noted, not only demands the largest and most coherent perspective about finality but the only perspective in which one can consistently discourse about purpose and design, and explain with a reference to the Creator the emergence of man, an eminently purposive being, hardly the chance product of genuine evolution, let alone the product of an evolution which is purposeless by definition.

That Creator and absolutes had no place in the vision presented in the *Origin* was a key to its tremendous popularity. The *Origin* supplied the already strong craving for the elimination of all metaphysics with a support which through its massive factuality appeared scientifically unassailable. The objective of that craving, as articulated mainly by Spencer for the second half of the century, was repose in the endless flux and reflux, a happy acceptance of the prospect that man and mankind were but bubbles on unfathomable deep and dark waves, bubbles free of eternal purpose and unburdened with eternal responsibilities. Bubbles—racial and individual, commercial and political—could form and burst with the ease of vagueness because evolution was a process insensibly slow. Vagueness exuded also from Darwin's style, another smokescreen to hide the real issue between the old and new teleology. The issue did not consist in the specific creation of each species, and at a proper time at that. The issue was between a divine creation which is inherently specific and a man-made chaos which is intrinsically hazy. The clear recognition of that issue demanded a perspective which only time could provide—in more than one sense.

The teleology of old, with its almost invariable and always unfortunate ties to the fixity of each species, had too many pointers toward purpose, which like so many trees could obliterate the vision of the forest. Yet the chaos itself, if it was to be helpful for science, could not be pictured as rigorously chaotic. The only kinds of chaos which are helpful to science are *forms* embodying singular specifics expressive of a design which in turn points to purpose. Failure to probe deeply into the meaning of the fact that a chaos ought to be a *chaos designed* if it is to serve science, including the science of evolution, has since Darwin been the signal failure of most evolutionists. Actually, even when the specificity of that chaos is recalled, the emphasis is on its alleged purposeless unfolding into purposefully intelligent beings. Once the original properties of matter were given, George G. Simpson declared, evolutionary theory demonstrated that "the whole evolution of life could have well ensued and did probably ensue automatically."[37] Whatever the feasibility of that mechanistic automatism, in its perspective it is the evolving matter which is admired and not its being "but one mask of the many worn by the Great Face behind."[38] True, some perceptive biologists, like George Beadle, argue that there is no conflict between science and religion because in dealing with the primeval universe science has no answer to the question "Whence came the hydrogen?"[39] Yet the thrust of such discourse all too often becomes equivalent to that slight travesty on Genesis which Harlow Shapley offered: "In the beginning was the Word, it has been piously recorded, and I might venture that modern astrophysics suggests that the Word was hydrogen gas."[40] That the hydrogen, or something equivalent, is all too readily declared the ultimate, or "god," should be clear to anyone familiar with the writings of most present-day Darwinists.

Clearly, there is more than science in Darwinism. The chief additional ingredient is a craving for the absence of metaphysical perspectives, a craving which should not be left immune to scrutiny. This craving is the clue to a curious symptom of one sector of recent literature on Darwin and Darwinism. The symptom is the flat declaration that Darwin was right and that mechanistic evolution is an indisputable truth. There is not a hint in Sir Gavin de Beer's recent article on Darwin in the *Dictionary of Scientific Biography* that there were and still are many difficulties with Darwin's theory.[41] Sir Julian Huxley declared not only that Neo-Darwinism "is fully accepted by the great majority of students of evolution" but that a "century after the publication of the *Origin*, Darwin's great discovery, the universal principle of natural selection, is firmly and finally established as the *sole* agency of *major* evolutionary changes"[42] (emphasis added).

Phrases like "great majority" are sufficiently vague to create the illusion that the minority is negligible qualitatively as well. This is far from being the case. Indeed, the persistence over four generations of a minority quantitatively not at all small and qualitatively most respectable, is quite a unique phenomenon in the history of modern science, in which the opposition to the main trend usually dies out with the generation of the original dissenters. Dissenters to Darwinism were so strong during the decade anticipating the centenary of the *Origin* as to prompt Simpson to caution his fellow American students of evolution against "provincial complacency." In referring to basic questions of the evolutionary outlook, including the question of continuity versus saltation, he noted that "the fact is that many European evolutionists just as accomplished as any in America do not consider those questions closed and give quite different answers from those of the American majority."[43] Twenty years earlier the fifth volume of the *Encyclopédie française*, written with the collaboration of all leading French biologists, came to a conclusion almost impossible to believe and just as impossible to find quoted: "It follows from this presentation that the theory of evolution is impossible.... Evolution is a kind of dogma in which its priests no longer believe but which they keep presenting to their people. So much about a matter which it takes courage to spell out so that men of the coming generation may orient their research in a different way."[44]

While present-day Darwinists obviously prefer to ignore such demurrals of the recent past, a historian of science has no such license. Nor is he allowed, if he knows something of the personal and political views of leading French biologists, from Claude Bernard to Lucien Cuénot, to dismiss their resistance to Darwinism, old and new, with easy reference to ecclesiastical pressure or to chauvinism.[45] As history marches on, camouflages are not only unmasked but often quickly replaced, and so the historian of science ought to be sensitive to another, broader consequence of the artful tilting of the balance of evidence. The phrasing of that consequence by the duke of Argyle, a friend of Darwin, seems particularly appropriate: "To accept as a truth that which is not a truth, or to fail in distinguishing the sense in which it is not true, is an evil having consequences which are indeed incalculable. There are subjects in which one mistake of this kind will poison all the wells of truth, and affect with fatal error the whole circle of our thoughts."[46]

In view of the encomiums heaped by Sir Julian and others on Darwin's theory on the occasion of its centenary,[47] it would be reasonable to assume that major breakthroughs had occurred in evolutionary biology between the 1930s and 1950s. Perhaps Sir Julian and others took for such breakthroughs the statistical work done in genetics and the observation of industrial melanism in moths. All this strengthened only the cause of microevolution, not the central point of dispute. Had any real breakthrough occurred in favor of macroevolution, the crucial issue with Darwinism, no self-respecting scientist would have risked his reputation with a statement which Professor James Gray of Cambridge had the courage to make: "No amount of argument, or clever epigram, can disguise the inherent improbability of orthodox [evolutionary] theory; but most biologists feel it is better to think in terms of improbable events than not to think at all."[48] That such a courageous statement had to come from a botanist should surprise only those unaware that botany is the most frustrating field for any Darwinist, because in the plant world macroevolution defies even the proverbial powers of Darwinian imagination.

Even in the animal world the mechanism of macroevolution has remained as hypothetical as ever. The data supporting microevolution show that a large number of factors must be in a very delicate balance if evolution is to occur even on the level of species and genus.[49] Moving beyond genera, the balance must be imagined as enormously more delicate, that is, improbable. This does not mean that it cannot occur, but it certainly means that what may occur is not bound to happen. Indeed, it is so far from being bound to happen as to impose the suspicion that if it happened it did so by some design. What makes the balance most improbable is the rapidity by which it had to establish itself time and again to permit the developmental bursts implied in macroevolution. The most crucial of these bursts relates to the emergence of man. The Darwinian "descent of man" was easily shown by Wallace to be extremely questionable, since primitive man hardly needed a highly evolved brain for his survival,[50] an objection which preceded the publication of *The Descent of Man*—and was not answered there. A hundred years later it is still the problem of having first the egg or the chicken, if one considers Noam Chomsky's findings about the same basic structure implied in every language, however primitive.[51] Language presupposes in the brain a special neuronal network which must exist as a whole to give rise to language embodying integral structures. Its use cannot therefore be invoked for its gradual development from primitive stages by the struggle for survival. About the rapidity of that development the discoveries of the Leakeys and others have provided a paradoxical reminder during this very last decade. With fossils of man found to be older than two million years, the branch representing him on the evolutionary tree may easily appear as a branch hanging in mid air, pictorial representations to the contrary notwithstanding.[52]

It is therefore safe to say that matters with evolutionary theory stand today as they stood in December 1858 when Darwin, writing the concluding chapters of the *Origin,* commented to George Bentham: "You will be greatly disappointed [by my forthcoming book]; it will be grievously too hypothetical. It will very likely be of no other service than collocating some facts; though I myself think I see my way approximately on the origin of species. But, alas, how frequent, how almost universal it is in an author to persuade himself of the truth of his own dogmas. My only hope is that I certainly see very many difficulties of gigantic stature."[53] In a manner which most Darwinists inherited from him, Darwin had no intention of presenting the difficulties in their true weight. As he put it in the Introduction to the *Origin:* "I am well aware that there is scarcely a single point discussed in this volume on which facts cannot be adduced, often apparently leading to conclusions directly opposite to those at which I have arrived. A fair result could be obtained only by fully stating and balancing the facts on both sides of each question, and this cannot possibly be here done."[54] True, Darwin mentioned all difficulties of which he was aware, but the manner in which he verbalized about them shows that he did not suspect how gigantic some of them were. It is difficulties of this kind that saddle any theory with inherent improbability and add an extra burden to the Darwinians' dilemma to think or not to think.

This dilemma is of their own making and is rooted in their narrow thinking about the science of mechanics, a shorthand for the laws of physics and chemistry. Contrary to the illusion of Darwin and Darwinists, the science of mechanics is not that mechanistic science which they want the science of the living to become. The science of mechanics is not about disembodied sequences of push and pull. What makes the study of mechanisms into a science of physical reality is not merely the tracing out of general laws, but the ascertaining of laws within given boundary conditions. Without the boundary conditions set by the quantum of action the law of black-body radiation leads into what is not so much an ultraviolet catastrophe, but the catastrophe of infinity, the vanishing of physical reality in the absence of boundaries. A similar catastrophe is generated in cosmology when the inverse-square law of gravitation is not constrained within the boundaries set by general relativity for a specific average density of matter. What is true of mechanisms of atomic and cosmic dimensions is also true of any and all machines of the intermediate range. They make sense and are useful only because each of them represents a harnessing of the laws of mechanics within given boundary conditions which are not derivable from those very laws.

All boundary conditions embodied in machines attest their design and purpose, a point which is not, of course, a matter of dispute in connection with man-made machines. The dispute is about the living machines of nature, about which there is no reason to suppose that they work consciously toward the implementation of a goal—the chief of which is propagation, or reduplication, a process that appears well-nigh impossible when evaluated by the most advanced methods of exact science.[55] Does the absence of consciousness preempt design and purpose in spite of the fact that the more complex an animal machine is, the more overwhelming is its evidence of working for a purpose? This evidence of working for a purpose is so overwhelming as to be the perennial thorn in the side of all Darwinists. Hardly any of them failed to voice at one time or another the perplexity registered by Lucien Cuénot: "The more one penetrates the [various] determinisms [at work in animal organisms], the more complex the interconnections become; and since that complexity leads to a most specific result, which can be disturbed by the smallest deviation, the idea of a finalist direction is born invincibly; I admit that it is incomprehensible, undemonstrable, that it amounts to explaining the obscure by the more obscure, but it is necessary; it is all the more necessary the more the determinisms become known, because it is not possible to forgo a guideline in the train of [biological] events. It is not daring to believe that the eye is made for seeing."[56]

To explain that the eye is made for a purpose, or that all organs and organisms pursue a purpose, theists have often made the error of espousing some kind of vitalism. The only intrinsic merit of vitalism is that, as Bergson once put it, while "the vital principle may indeed not explain much, it is at least a sort of label affixed to our ignorance, so as to remind us of this occasionally, whereas mechanism invites us to ignore that ignorance."[57] A mechanism inviting ignorance is the mechanical philosophy ignorant of the meaning of boundary conditions. They exist everywhere in nature, indeed they turn nature into a coherent whole. Mechanists preferring to ignore this—T. H. Huxley is their classic forerunner in this respect[58]—are forced to let all of nature's machines share in various degrees in human consciousness. Clearly, neither vitalism nor mechanism are able to safeguard for biology, in a meaningful way, the exclusive validity of the laws of mechanics. That validity can only be safeguarded by a thorough grasp of what is implied in boundary conditions present everywhere in nature. First, the boundary conditions are *given*, they are not derivable from laws. Second, no boundary condition exists separately from the overall boundary con-

291

ditions that constitute nature as a totality of beings. Third, the explanation of a given set of boundary conditions can only be done in terms of a
more general set.[59] These sets form a hierarchical structure in respect of
which the foolhardiness of infinite regress is forbidden not only by
logic but also by the fact that the universe has, in its structure if not in
its extent, an overall boundary condition. Since this overall boundary
condition is not self-explaining, it is legitimate to look for its givenness
in a factor which, since the universe embodies all that is physical, can
only be metaphysical with respect to the whole universe. That factor is
not a super-designer or an engineer-in-chief, and much less a demiurge,
but a Creator who alone is capable of producing a universe with that
true mark of givenness, a contingency implying creation.

A genuinely created thing is always specified by boundary conditions, the sign of its limited perfections. A perfectly unlimited being
cannot be created, for such a being is God himself. The conceptual
content of God reached along such a way is, needless to say, minimal
compared with the notion of God of a theism made into a gigantic
historical reality through a revelation given in history, a point that has
been made often and well enough. In view of the uniqueness of nature
it should not seem surprising either that it gives rise to only one way to
God. It has since long been recognized that the five ways of Aquinas, or
any number of ways based on the contemplation of nature, are
essentially but one way, the way from contingency. The elimination of a
specific way to God based on design and purpose actually strengthens
rather than weakens one's rational hold on any purpose, cosmic or
particular. There is indeed a very deep insight in Newman's disclosure
that he believed in design because he believed in God and not the other
way around. Once the boundary conditions of the universe are anchored in a rational Creator, they will appear as a choice out of an
infinitely large number of conceivable boundary conditions. It is that
rational choice of a rationally coherent set of boundary conditions that
make them appear as a design. Therefore, all the lower echelon boundary conditions will also appear as designs, and this unhindered
metaphysical perspective will at one stroke eliminate anthropomorphic
concerns about cosmic purpose. If the content of the notion of God
provided by the ways of God is minimal, one should expect even less
with regard to fathoming by unaided reason the purpose of his creation.

When the argument of contingency, the form of the basic way from
nature to God, is set in the perspective of design, the temporality of the
universe lends itself to a deeper understanding of the emergence of ever
higher forms as time goes on. With the true God present in the background the biologist will not be forced into the self-defeating dilemma
of thinking à la Darwin or not thinking at all, a dilemma generated by

the false gods of mechanistic philosophizing. What the biologist interested in unfettered thinking has to do is to grasp in depth the meaning of that admirable precept which Darwin had learned in connection with a major error in an early paper of his. "My error," he reflected many years later, "has been a good lesson to me never to trust in science to the principle of exclusion."[60] Had he learned this lesson not in 1862 but ten years before, natural selection would not have been given an exclusive role in the first edition of the *Origin*, and the history of modern biology might now be told with no reference to an inordinate craving to "deify natural selection."[61] Biologists with more sensitivity to metaphysical trains of thought than Darwin displayed might even have rediscovered a truth or two which not only would have resolved the reductionists' dilemma to think in terms of mechanisms or not to think at all, but would have also shown that the road of science was a natural approach to *that* way to God which is staked out by pointers of purpose insofar as contingent designs are suggestive of purpose.

Suspicious as one ought to be about specifying purpose in every nook and cranny of the universe, unrestrained suspicion is as self-defeating as consistent skepticism. The absolute skeptic, as was aptly remarked, can have no mind to doubt with. The deepest source of the scientific knowledge of the universe is a most purposeful commitment to the tenet that the universe is the embodiment of design. One should therefore be on guard against taking lightly the varied phenomena of the animal world which are strongly suggestive of a striving designed for purpose. Qualms about recognizing purpose will quickly lose their scientific coating if one considers that even man's conscious striving for purpose is a metaphysical reality which leaves intact the laws of physics and chemistry. Once that kind of reality is recognized for what it is, its *analogous* realization in the animal world will represent neither an epistemological nor a scientific problem. The problem will be the making of those who think that they must exchange metaphysical reality for science, forgetting at the same time that the barter deprives their science of a grasp of physical reality itself.

Of course, if the notion of purpose is reduced to the notion of naive benefit, one will be trapped in Darwin's problem. The trap can only be avoided by walking both the road of science and the ways to God which are equally based on philosophy. Darwin voiced a basic philosophical truth about that road when he wrote in 1870 to Hooker: "I cannot look at the universe as a result of blind chance." It was the poor philosopher in him reluctant to walk those ways who continued: "Yet I can see no evidence of beneficent design, or indeed design of any kind, in the details."[62] Contrary to him, even in her details nature was full of designs, a fullness about which molecular biology—it is enough to think of the intricately designed world of amino acids[63]—revealed astonish-

293

ing details. To resolve the problem of a no-chance universe apparently void of beneficent design, Darwin would have needed the insight that man as a created being could not dictate to the Creator about beneficial purpose, an insight certainly available to anyone willing to walk the ways to God. But as Darwin confessed in the same letter: "my theology is a simple muddle."[64] Few if any of his followers made such a frank and badly needed confession.

The most they were willing to confess on rare occasion was that, as August Weismann once put it, their adherence to Darwinism was based on grounds other than scientific.[65] Just as rarely did they admit with J. B. S. Haldane that in spite of Darwinism the world remained "full of mysteries," of which "life is one" and "the curious limitations of finite minds are another," and that it was "not the business of evolutionary theory to explain these mysteries."[66] More often than not they proclaimed with T. H. Huxley that they were "prepared to go to the stake if requisite" in support of much of Darwinian theory,[67] because, again with Huxley, they believed that "the alternative is either Darwinism or nothing."[68] Such a preparedness was unfounded even if it was true, as Huxley claimed, that apart from Darwin's theory there is no "rational conception or theory of the organic universe which has any scientific position at all" and that "whatever may be the objections to his views, certainly all other theories are absolutely out of court."[69]

The truth of all this was threatened not so much by the eventual reinstatement into scientific respectability of Lamarck's views,[70] an eventuality which would have certainly left Huxley gasping, but by a chronic oversight by Darwinians of a basic fallacy in Darwin's theory. While he wanted to be scientific in the Galilean-Newtonian sense of eliminating from scientific discourse any consideration of purpose, he also wanted to explain purpose, or rather to explain it away, through the same method. His most purposeful campaign against purpose in nature offered one more startling bit of evidence about man's ability to know design and to act purposively. This ability of man is the perennial stumbling block for efforts that admit but sheer mechanism in life, bring men and animals strictly under the same head, and reduce everything to chance or necessity or both. Chance and necessity do not even explain a book so entitled. Every book is a tangible witness to purpose, to final cause, which is so different from the efficient cause as to never contradict any of the conservation laws of physics. By forgetting that difference one will not only commit the blunder of attributing to Aristotle the view that final causality is efficient causality, but what is worse, getting bogged down in the strategy of replacing the word teleology with the word teleonomy—as if a mere change of words were needed by the evolutionary biologist.[71] What he needs is not new words but a renewed thinking, which would show him that his use of teleology is not merely reflective, regulative, descriptive, operational, but also explanatory in a genuinely ontological sense.[72] Once he has grasped this, he will no longer have to look at teleology as a lady without whom he cannot live but with whom he would not appear in public.[73]

It should be of no surprise that this double standard is evident in the efforts of historians and philosophers of science who try to understand the nature and growth of science in terms of Darwinian theory.[74] That theory is hardly the proper means to a noble end, the vindication of the continuity, identity, and therefore of the purpose of scientific enterprise against its fragmentation in theories of science steeped in the notion of revolutions and looking for their justification in Darwinian theory.[75] Theories of science, which, in order to be faithful to Darwin, purposely avoid talking about purpose in science and scientists, are thoroughly unfit to cope with that relentless and purposeful drive which, to recall the words of Hugh of Saint Victor reinvented by Descartes, aims at becoming masters and possessors of nature.[76] Such theories will meet a stumbling block in every scientific experiment, in every laboratory, in every scientific project, some of which are heroic testimonials to purpose. Witness the comparing of tens of thousands of star images to discover Pluto, the testing of some one hundred thousand soil samples to find streptomycin, and the scanning of millions of unit fields of vision on nuclear emulsion plates to track down the magnetic monopole. That science is a most purposeful activity may be a platitudinous truth to non-Darwinians, but apparently a sorely needed reminder for most admirers of Darwin. They seem to forget that Darwin's work is a classic example of scientific success dependent not so much on mental creativity as on the single-minded devotion to a specific purpose. Darwin himself saw his own achievement in this distinctly teleological perspective.[77]

That the misguided message of his most purposive research was that there was no purpose should not distract from the magnitude of his real achievement, which was his indirect and somewhat muddled message. It was about time, although in Darwinian theory time was a soulless parameter along which events could move indifferently backward and forward, a point already noted by T. H. Huxley.[78] Huxley was a good interpreter of Darwin but a bad interpreter of science when he endorsed the notion of a cyclic universe, now developing, now degenerating, a notion which, it is well to recall, became the blind alley for science in all ancient cultures. In the same way in which, according to Darwinian theory, there could be nothing higher and nothing lower in the realm of living organisms, there could be no truly irreversible time to carry their development, because Darwinian theory banished purpose from time. But as often happened in the history of science, decisive advances once more were made by partly wrong steps. The vast amounts of time which

Darwin's theory needed and the importance which he correctly attributed to the paleontological record were moves that placed our vision of nature irrevocably within the perspective of time. What Darwin and the Darwinians failed to see—and this is why Darwin's theory, though not his vision of evolution, failed—was that time needed a womb, a purpose, if it was to issue ultimately in the most purposeful activity of science and not merely in its stillbirths. For evolution has a direction marked by time's arrow, analogous to the one designed to mark direction, which through its very meaning serves as a pointer of purpose.

Nineteen

THE ETHOS OF SCIENCE

As long as something is obvious, let alone ubiquitous, there is no need for pointers. Arguing the existence of pointers of purpose means therefore the implicit admission that purpose in nature is neither obvious nor to be found in every nook and cranny. Much too well known is the stunning extent to which nature can flout the implementation of ends. Of all seeds only a minute fraction start actual growth. It is in the same lopsided proportion that organisms stifled early in life outnumber the specimens that achieve their end in full maturity. Nature aborts human fetuses in much the same measure as it allows live births. A brief reference to the birth of monsters, animal and human, should be enough to complete a picture that may suggest sheer monstrosity instead of purposeful plan. Bleak as that picture may appear, streaks of light cut across it as so many pointers of purpose. To deny those streaks, stubbornly present in a dark landscape, would be as unreasonable as to despise candles because their flickering light cannot dissipate the cover of night.

The perspective needed here is very similar to what is required for a search into the ultimate reason for nature's rationality. Evidences of it can be secured only if one is receptive to them, an attitude that takes one beyond what is simply revealed to the senses. Water molecules, so many marvels of exact rationality, are never seen by the naked eye. They hide their marvels in the apparent irrationality of muddy puddles, torrential rains, and stormy oceans, so many symbols of the flood of errors by which man can be overwhelmed. That flood flows freely even through that domain, science, which until recently had been taken for the realm of truth itself. Statements akin to Faraday's quiet admission that only one-tenth of one percent of all his ideas were worth pursuing are voiced by today's scientists quite unabashedly.[1] What may seem even worse is that even in science one is urged to rely on the advice of William Blake: "Drive your cart and your plow over the bones of the dead."[2] But just because the quest for truth in science cannot be implemented without turning many a past conclusion into dead bones, the turning up of ever deeper layers does not become thereby a self-defeating enterprise. The thick strata of erroneous conclusions are interrupted by layers of truth, indicating the direction toward the rock bottom consisting only of truth. Of the mining of truth what holds of mining in general is valid: the vast preponderance of waste does not make the enterprise worthless.

Yet both are painful enterprises, part of the human landscape full of pain. While pain is not a human prerogative in nature, it is nature's most painful rule that the more complex a living organism the greater its ability to suffer. For Darwin the suffering of myriads of lower animals, be it the devouring of caterpillars by ichneumons or the playing of cats with mice, was enough to discredit belief in an omnipotent and benevolent God.[3] Even more negative had to appear the case for God when man too was considered, for in man the ability to suffer is part of his self-awareness, a circumstance which provides pain with its least bearable component. But as if consciousness of physical pain were not enough, man's nature is receptive of an even deeper torment, the sense of guilt. It is that sense which until recently was taken as plain evidence of the ethical dimensions of man's nature. The traditional acceptance of that dimension can best be seen from Kant's un-Kantian effort to salvage God, if not for the thinking man, at least for man as an ethical being. But the God and ethics of "practical reason" were bound to become a matter of self-centered practicality in full accord with the self-centeredness imposed by Kant on thinking. This subjective ethical practicality found its supreme sanction in the image which evolutionism paints of man. In that image ethics is reduced to man's practical responses in his struggle for survival.

Anyone moderately aware of the destructiveness inherent in reductionism can easily suspect that its grip had to be fatal for ethics as a set of impersonally binding norms. Almost a century ago T. H. Huxley deplored the "moral flavour" attached to the "survival of the fittest." As he noted, "the thief and the murderer follow nature just as much as the philanthropist,"[4] a point still to be perceived by advocates of sundry varieties of evolutionary ethics. Even if they write with the brilliance of Bertrand Russell,[5] they merely provide variations on the notion of ethics as formulated by Darwin.[6] Such an ethics justifies not the morally right but the physically strong. "A man," Darwin wrote, "who has no assured and no present belief in the existence of a personal God or a future existence with retribution and rewards, can have for his rule of life, as far as I can see, only to follow those impulses and instincts which are the strongest or which seem to him the best ones."[7] What he declared in the next breath, namely, that "a dog acts in this manner," was as unreflective as his failure to perceive that as soon as he returned to man, there emerged also the specter of a philosophy incompatible either with his biologism or with his agnosticism. For how could it be true without a love of wisdom, which is philosophy, that, as Darwin put it, man, who after all does not act blindly as a dog does, will find "in accordance with the verdict of all the wisest men, that the highest satisfaction is derived from following certain impulses, namely, the social instincts"?[8] Such consensus of wisdom, if it ever was a reality, could not, however, become an objective, always valid norm. For, to let Darwin continue, on occasion man's reason can tell him "to act in opposition to the opinion of others, whose approbation he will then not receive; but he will still have the solid satisfaction of knowing that he has followed his innermost judge or conscience."[9]

Conscience, even as depicted by Darwin, was more than social instinct. Herein lay a conflict which he failed to see, although had he seen it he might have but said: "a dog might as well speculate on the mind of Newton." That was his remark on finding himself unable to resolve the conflict between his conviction that all details in nature were produced by chance and his inability to believe that "this wonderful universe and especially the nature of man," were in essence the product of brute forces, that is, forces not designed by a Creator.[10] No aspect of man's nature is more beyond the tools of a naturalist than conscience, unless, of course, those tools include common sense and "some power of reasoning," both of which Darwin emphatically claimed to himself.[11] That his personal reliance as a scientist on the mind and on personal uprightness were unexplainable on the basis of what he wrote on life, mind, and morality should seem obvious. What is less obvious pertains not to philosophy but to sociology. As long as social consciousness implied a firm distinction between good and evil, it could pass for a harmless academic pastime to claim that there were only strong and weak urges, strong and weak individuals. As long as most people professed a difference between ethical good and ethical evil, society could safely live with its margin of evildoers while its pundits theorized that any difference between good and evil was merely a social custom. Had Darwin been asked by his son what should be done by a man who falls in love but cannot marry, he might have referred the matter to his pious wife, or might have brushed his son aside, as did Frederic Harrison, the leading British positivist and an avid Darwinist, who told his own son: "Do what morality prescribes in such circumstances." Unlike Harrison, Darwin might not have risen to theological heights and declared that incontinence was immoral and that it made man a beast. Nor might he have given to the insistent question, "Positivism then takes the theological view about morality?" the reply: "Of course. Even more so . . . . A man who gives way to the flesh is a wrongdoer." But like Harrison, Darwin would have most likely cut off further importuning with the remark: "It is not a subject decent men do discuss."[12]

It was less than a generation before Freud decided that contrary to what Harrison believed, silence on touchy questions was not the mark of intellectual decency. Two generations after Freud we have a society in which not playboys but gentlemen carry the social onus to justify their behavior. About this abolition in the Western world of traditional sexual ethics, an abolition which is now receiving legal sanctioning to a startling degree,[13] it falls upon the Darwinian biologist to answer a question loaded with grave biological consequence. A hundred years after Darwin, biologists are forced to ask whether the rearing of human offspring can still be achieved when monogamous family life has been displaced by free gratification of the sexual urge. The gravity of the question is such as to have forced a Darwinian biologist to urge his colleagues to be less impatient with the "deliberate way in which [the Catholic Church] approached the population question."[14] The counsel appears a remarkable turnabout when one recalls that Huxley saw one of the greatest merits of Darwinism in the fact that "it occupies a position of complete and irreconcilable antagonism to that vigorous and consistent enemy of mankind, the Catholic Church."[15] But the same counsel is also an uncanny echo of the aging Spencer's realization that "a cult of some sort . . . is a constituent in every society which has made any progress" and therefore "the control exercised over men's conduct by theological beliefs and priestly agency" has been indispensable.[16]

Spencer would not have been an evolutionist had he pleaded for application in the present of an antidote useful in the past, although both he and Darwin enjoyed the protection of an ethical shell grown by that very organism in which they did not believe. With that shell being shattered today, evolutionists are beginning to find out that a society which does not believe in angels cannot lay claim to policemen who behave like angels. Few if any of these will be around to man the ramparts when private property, that last bulwark of traditional ethics, is stormed by the underprivileged, free of qualms about implementing the law of the survival of the fittest. They will launch their final assault in the name of an ideology for which Darwin's *Origin* is as much a favorite document as it is for the opposite camp. No sooner had Marx read the *Origin* than he informed Engels and Lassalle about the crucial support it provided "for the class struggle in history."[17] Andrew Carnegie, one of the fiercest of capitalists, derived from Darwin and Spencer that flood of light which, as he put it, made all clear to him.[18] While evolution could be hard for the individual, he wrote in another context, "it is best for the race because it insures the survival of the fittest in every department."[19] According to John D. Rockefeller, Jr., business, by which he obviously meant big business, and Christianity had basic principles in common, such as honesty, industry, persistence, and justice. The latter was equivalent to the golden rule, which led him to speak "of consolidations and of the crowding out of some" as justified by "the greatest good to the greatest number." As an illustration of the latter he pointed out that the "most beautiful rose results from cutting buds," that is, the sacrificing of many for one.[20] Whatever the number of sacrificial victims of both Marxism and capitalism, the number of those sacrificed can only increase as Marxism and capitalism find themselves locked in a life-or-death struggle.

Concerning that confrontation, it is becoming increasingly clear that what inspires the attitude of countries claiming an economic life based on free enterprise is not so much a firm ethical commitment to the ideal of freedom as a pragmatic stalling for time. While such stalling can be part of a strategy of firmness, it can also be a sign of irreversible weakening. The latter possibility can be surmised from the manner in which traditional ethics has been reappraised during the last two decades. The reappraisal not only took place in the name of evolutionary process but imposed on that process, always imperceptibly slow in nature, an artificially accelerated rate. The feverish procedure, which aimed at replacing the self-restraint of liberty by unrestrained licentiousness, revealed something of the symptoms of an organism in the grip of high fever. No wonder that the world of free enterprise finds less and less strength for denouncing, let alone opposing, the growing threat to the freedom of enterprise, to say nothing of deeper aspects of freedom. Clearly, something more than evolutionary or pragmatic ethics, nay something akin to "political theology,"[21] is needed if one is to muster courage and denounce dictatorial regimes for what they are, the systematic warmongers in history. Wars are a staple feature of the Marxist struggle for life, and it is well to recall that those wars, which the Marxists call wars of imperialism and which helped so much the formation of Marxist empires, have been envisioned and endorsed by consistent Darwinists.

Darwin noted in reference to the Civil War in America that "in the long run a million horrid deaths would be amply repaid in the cause of humanity."[22] He registered with glee that "the more civilized so-called Caucasian races have beaten the Turkish hollow in the struggle for existence."[23] It was not the author of *Mein Kampf* but of the *Origin of Species* who wrote: "Looking at the world at no very distant date, what an endless number of the lower races will have been eliminated by the higher civilized races throughout the world."[24] Two generations later the Nazi program of giving military birth to a new Europe found much inspiration in Ernst Haeckel, Darwin's first and foremost apostle in Germany. While Haeckel's role was well displayed in *The Scientific Origins of National Socialism*, its author, Daniel Gassman, did not seem to know of Darwin's foregoing statements or of Darwin's high regard for Haeckel. Worse even, Gassman blamed Haeckel for taking Darwin's work not for "an interesting and possibly fruitful scientific theory," but for "a complete rendering of the nature of the cosmos,"[25] as if Darwin had not meant his theory to be that very rendering.

Haeckel was not at all incorrect in stating in his *Freedom in Science and Teaching*, to which T. H. Huxley wrote an appreciative preface, that the demand of "equal rights, equal duties, equal possessions, equal enjoyments for every citizen alike" had been proved by the theory of descent to be "a pure impossibility."[26] While Haeckel had a point in describing the foregoing demand as "the fathomless absurdity of extravagant socialist levelling,"[27] it was another matter whether its best antidote was the theory of descent, or "this English hypothesis,"[28] as he called it. Actually, the hypothesis was for him the supreme principle that ruled every form of life. Thus one had to resign oneself to the "cruel and merciless struggle for existence which rages throughout all living nature" and to the fact that "only the picked minority of the qualified 'fittest' is in a position to resist that struggle successfully, while the great majority of the competition must necessarily perish miserably."[29] On the human level this meant the acceptance of the inevitable "arrest and destruction of the remaining majority."[30] In Haeckel's words the "kernel of Darwinism" was the survival of the fittest and the victory of the best, a kernel "anything but democratic; on the contrary, aristocratic in the strictest sense of the word."[31] If then the human species too had to be led by an elite, logic demanded that among the races constituting that species there should be an elite, a status which Haeckel assigned to the Nordic race. No wonder that following the outbreak of World War I Haeckel denounced England as a traitor whose arms were covered with noble blood.[32]

Such recrimination was an inevitable consequence of the glorification of war which again was based on Darwinism in the famous lectures delivered in 1897–98 by Heinrich von Treitschke, professor of political history at the University of Berlin. He decried the "blind worshippers of perpetual peace,"[33] declared war to be the sole womb of nationhood,[34] and found "the beauty of history" in the "everlasting for and against of different states."[35] The wish to abolish that bloody rivalry was for him "simply unreason."[36] World War I was still two years away when the English-speaking public could read in its own tongue that General Friedrich von Bernhardi had already justified Germany's role in the next war with ample references to the Darwinian struggle for life.[37] It was therefore highly ironical that V. L. Kellogg, an American biologist working with the American relief mission in occupied France prior to America's entry into war, found it surprising that staff officers of German Great Headquarters constantly referred to Darwin's theory as a justification of waging war on behalf of the fittest.[38] While it would be simplistic to blame the doctrine of Darwin for World War I, it would be equally mistaken to underestimate its role as a justification of war. In his *Heartbreak House*, which the world certainly resembled in 1919, Bernard Shaw saw Darwinism in precisely that light: "We taught Prussia this religion; and Prussia bettered our instructions so effectively that we presently found ourselves confronted with the necessity of destroying Prussia to prevent Prussia destroying us. And that has just ended in each destroying the other to an extent doubtfully reparable in our time."[39]

Help to repair the damage certainly could not come from evolutionary ethics steeped in Darwinism. Consistent Darwinists could only speak as did Sir Arthur Keith, who only two years before World War II declared that while he loved the idea of peace, a peace of five centuries would make the world look like "an orchard that has not known the pruning hook for many an autumn and has rioted in unchecked overgrowth for endless years." Nothing, he added, can surpass war as a means "for the real health of humanity and the building of stronger races."[40] Whatever one's trust in Sir Arthur's claim that he was no champion of war[41] and whatever his claim that Darwin gave "utterance only to the gentlest of judgments,"[42] he can certainly be trusted on the alliance between Darwin's theory and war. Much more so than those Darwinian biologists who do their best to create the illusion that Darwinian science and the cause of peace are natural allies. The price of that misalliance is to make elementary misrepresentations of Darwinian theory. A case in point is Sir Julian Huxley's evaluation of competition within the species in his Romanes Lecture, delivered at a time which Churchill labeled the "hinges of fate." While as an argument for peace Sir Julian noted the harmful effects of such a competition for the species as a whole, he failed to point out that the same kind of competition was a chief aspect of Darwinian natural selection.[43] If one adds to this Gabriel Marcel's consternation on hearing Teilhard de Chardin brush aside the extermination of millions in Soviet slave labor camps as a mere episode in a march toward a glorious future,[44] one may grasp the extent to which evolutionism can act as an ethical blindfold.

It was not science but scientism that made that blindfold seem an eyeshade to protect one's eyes from the glare of ethics and metaphysics. As for ethics, its glare suddenly became too strong to permit it to be taken for a spurious light. The flash of the atomic bomb dispelled the darkness that provided cover for the illusion that science was an ethically neutral enterprise. In the light of that flash it was also revealed that while man as a scientist grew into a giant, as a student of ethics he gradually shrank into a dwarf. And a dwarf he suddenly appeared, especially to those who made and used the bomb. In speaking of its makers John von Neumann remarked: "I know that neither of us were adolescents at that time, but of course we were little children with respect to a situation which had developed, namely, that we suddenly were dealing with something with which one could blow up the world."[45] In his turn, General Omar Bradley drew the following parallel: "We have grasped the mystery of the atom and we rejected the Sermon on the Mount. Ours is a world of nuclear giants and ethical infants."[46]

This ethical infantilism will not be overcome as long as Darwinians and pragmatists set the tone of moral philosophizing on the basis of science. That tone is a shriek of contradictions. It is clearly contradictory to decry dictators, as did the Nobel-laureate biologist A. von Szent-Gyorgyi, and not to decry the view that truth, scientific and ethical, is like claws and fangs, a tool produced by the brain which itself is the product of a blind struggle for survival.[47] It is again contradictory to try, with Bronowski, to overcome positivism by pragmatism and then to fall back on it by creating the impression that there is an ethical sense in the dictum, "This is the scientist's moral: that there is no distinction between ends and means."[48] That such philosophizing will not promote a true "Ascent of Man"[49] can easily be guessed by a brief recall of that maddening resolve by which one nation after another forces its way into the nuclear club, an effort clearly justifiable on the basis of the pragmatist principle that there is no difference between the "ought" and the "is." For once their difference is completely abolished, the circularity remains wholly intact in the "social axiom" of justifying action by action as proclaimed by Bronowski: *"We* OUGHT *to act in such a way that what* IS *true can be verified to be so."*[50] It is that circularity which underlies the subtle transforming by pragmatic action of the hallowed motto *quo Urania ducit,* a noble urging to follow the voice of superior wisdom, into *quo uranium ducit,* the clever though tragic labeling of the runaway course toward the proliferation of nuclear weapons. The course is that of infants who keep playing with the burner even after having badly burnt their fingers.

Examples of unwitting support of that ethical infantilism turn up in every effort in which science is set up as the foundation of values, particularly of ethical values. A case in point is a remark in J. M. Ziman's *Public Knowledge,* a remark which also leads back to the problem with which these lectures began, the problem of blind alleys, or the fate of science in all ancient cultures. Ziman's remark starts with a reference to the consensus about a noncontradictory universe as the foundation of modern science, a consensus which had its source in the religious consensus of the Middle Ages. Ziman also endorsed the view according to which the failure of science in ancient China and India ought to be traced back to the doctrinal permissiveness of their religious systems. An estimate like this can only be reached by rising well above the flatlands of positivism, and it was possibly the fear of higher regions that forced Ziman back to the lowlands of ethical relativism: "Toleration of deviation, and the lack of a very sharp tradition of logical debate may have made the very idea of a consensus of opinion on the Philosophy of

Nature as absurd to them as the idea of absolute agreement on ethical principles would be to us."[51]

The statement is certainly suggestive of the age-old fact that surrender to ethical truths is even more difficult than surrender to general philosophical truths about nature. Unfortunately, Ziman's phrase also suggests that the medieval consensus was absolute only about the rationality of nature but not also about the ethical dimension of man, as if the two had nothing to do with one another. To inform oneself on this question it should be enough to recall Saint Paul's Letter to the Romans, a document more influential than any other in shaping Christian thought. There the cosmological argument, the epitome of rational conviction about the rationality of nature, is followed by the ethical argument, that is, the claim that the moral law is written in the heart of the heathen, all of whom "know God's just decree that all who do such things deserve death."[52]

The list of those "things" could just as well have been drawn up by a morals squad in the 1970s, and there is an equally up-to-date ring in what Saint Paul took for the worst aspect of immorality: the approval of it. Indeed, little seems to stand in the way of defining the new morality as the old immorality. But it is also a fact that while immorality was rampant even in times characterized as Christian, it was at least not systematically talked away, a difference that even today would make a world of a difference. This holds true with particular force of that very science about which we spontaneously speak as the factor that made our modern world different from all previous worlds. Yet it has also become the privilege of this world of science to hear a Fermi allay concern about making the bomb by saying that it was just "superb physics,"[53] and an Oppenheimer declare that when something is found to be "technically sweet," scientists just go ahead with it regardless of the consequences.[54] Superb physics, technically sweet projects, and the like, are phrases which reflect not so much the immorality of our time but, what is worse, its amorality. That is why it may not even occur to a typical modern scientist to suspect that truth and morality are intimately connected.

Yet, and the history of science shows this all too well, it was in the close union of two consensuses, one about truth, another about the morally good, that science was born. Ethical concern about the possible misuse of scientific inventions was conspicuously absent in Archimedes. If he disliked making war machines, the like of which no one had made before him, it was only because artifacts were unworthy of a philosopher called to the Platonic contemplation of geometrical truths. What Archimedes was not concerned with, Roger Bacon felt keenly. Although not reluctant to conjure up the vision of vehicles running at high speed across land and under the seas, Friar Roger saw the chief benefit of experimental science in the possibility of ending warfare with hardly any bloodshed.[55] Forerunner as Leonardo was of modern thought, he did not tailor to it his Christian conscience. As a result, he destroyed the blueprints of an underwater device that could, so he believed, destroy entire seaports.[56] The same kind of ethical concern is also evident in that trumpeter of modern times, Francis Bacon. Enthusiastic as he was about the new science, he knew that it might "open up a fountain, such as it is not easy to discern where the issues and streams thereof will take and fall." This is why he voiced his hope that the practice of the new science would be "governed by sound reason and true religion."[57]

The two Bacons and Leonardo are figures fondly remembered even by that positivist historiography of science which never indicated that science could be anything but an unmitigated blessing and which invariably viewed traditional ethics as irrelevant and outdated. It should be of no surprise that the origins of that historiography closely coincide with the beginnings of efforts to discredit an ethics which in more than one sense is a way to God. The positivist trend away from truth to facts even in connection with ethics was exemplified in Condorcet's effort to seek moral standards in statistics[58] and was carried by Rousseau to its full logic with his idealized picture of natural man. The trend, as Voltaire correctly saw, was the implementation of Descartes's program in which man could play the role of God. "A similar extravaganza," Voltaire wrote, "has infected morals. There are people blind enough to undermine the very foundations of society by hoping to reform it." Not that Voltaire would have been much offended if Rousseau had only preached free love. But Rousseau and others attacked private property as well, the only area of morality which most advocates of immorality like to retain. "There have been some," Voltaire complained, "foolish enough to maintain that *yours* and *mine* are crimes; that one should not benefit by one's work; that not only all men are equal, but that by assembling they had perverted the order of nature."[59]

Voltaire's cherished project was the establishing of an ethics occupying a middle ground between an ethics historically reflecting Christian revelation and no ethics at all. The project was the counterpart of the plan to maintain commitment to nature's and man's rationality without cultivating the historical or Christian matrix of that commitment. Both projects were fraught with the same danger, namely, the threat of social upheaval. Thus Voltaire, who was not at all concerned by the erosion of some aspects of traditional morals, wanted the intellectual propaganda on behalf of atheism to be kept within bounds, and he counseled atheists to play their tunes softly lest the outraged populace break their instruments on their heads.[60] Renan, who wanted no holds barred in the intellectual arena, argued on behalf of great moral restraint. Indeed, the former seminarian of Saint-Sulpice imposed on himself the "moral code of a Protestant pastor" on the basis of the following consideration: "One should never allow oneself two kinds of audacity at the same time. The freethinker must be regulated in his morals. I know of Protestant ministers, very broad-minded, who save everything by their irreproachable white cravat. I myself got away with what human mediocrity considers audacity thanks to a moderate style and grave manners."[61]

The grave manners endorsed by Renan derived from the proverbial insistence of Reformed theologians on the sense of guilt which sinful man ought to feel. A hundred years after Renan, guilt feeling in matters sexual is earmarked for clinical elimination in much the same way in which infectious diseases are slated for being wiped out. Yet other aspects of the sense of moral guilt, an indispensable starting point in the ethical way to God, are as vivid as ever. Curiously, that vividness owes much to that very practice of science which until recently has been looked upon as immune to ethical considerations. The vivid guilt feeling about man's intervention in nature, or the question of ecology, is a case in point and a case particularly relevant for a basic theme of these lectures, namely, the traditional Judeo-Christian theism as matrix of the viability of science. What is true of the epistemological aspect of that viability is also true of its ethical aspect. A roundabout recognition of this is hidden in those recent efforts which lay the blame for the technological ruination of nature on the Christian or biblical urge to dominate nature.[62] It is almost invariably overlooked in those efforts that the moral blame in question makes sense only if merit for the creation of technology and science is also credited to that very same Christian or biblical urge. Furthermore, the blame becomes simply meaningless if the staple claim is true that science and scientists had long ago disavowed Christian theism, to say nothing of its morality.

Clearly, science has an ethical dimension, and if the road of science is leading to the ways to God, this has to be also true of the connection of science with ethics. To see more of that dimension it is enough to recall that "science has flourished under a freedom which it has not created." This statement, made by Edward Conklin in 1937 in his capacity as president of the American Association for the Advancement of Science, can but sound unbelievable to positivist historians of science, but Conklin had in store truths even more unbelievable to them. Today, he said—and was not each day a threat to freedom in 1937?—"as in former centuries, it is left largely to religious bodies to defend freedom of thought and conscience while great scientific organizations stand mute."[63] Curious evidence of this is a very recent appeal on behalf of "refusenik" scientists in the Soviet Union. The appeal made by the

American Federation of Scientists has a motivation stemming not from science but from Jewish religious conscience, a source too honorable to be hidden under a cover name, however scientific.[64]

Regardless of what source is to be credited with the creation of that spirit of freedom, it is a spirit which breathes the spirit of an ethics which cannot be evolutionary in character. Social freedom is the child of the ability of the individual to choose freely, a freedom which from the evolutionary viewpoint must appear as the biggest and most unbelievable quantum jump. Moreover, freedom must be considered an acquisition to be kept for good and not a transitional stage, or else science is not serving the cause of good. Science cannot even serve in the sense of prospering except in an ambience which is spiritually free. While technological exploitation of major scientific discoveries can be achieved even under a cloak of secrecy and even in a closed society, the development of creatively new scientific principles demands openness of mind and of lines of communication. None of this can so much as be intimated in the China of today, but recently leading Soviet scientists began to force considerations to the surface which have long been proclaimed in the West by scientists appreciative of their unique heritage of freedom.[65]

True freedom of research implies far more than the absence of rude constraints, physical or social. Actually, every act of research is a defiance of restraints, and this is what makes man's freedom a nightmare for those who make it a scientific claim that the universe is a sheer mechanism, be it physical, biological, or psychological. Revealingly enough, during the age of classical physics no physicist of any consequence supported the view that the laws of physics, which were then taken to be strictly deterministic, had discredited the freedom of the will.[66] Even since the advent of quantum mechanics only a few physicists have gone so far as to seek an explanation of the freedom of the will in the indeterminacy principle or in the principle of complementarity. Exploiting the former principle for such a purpose can easily lead, as Eddington's efforts showed, to stultifying evaluations of the quantitative amount of freedom.[67] Max Born's reflections are in turn a good illustration of the fact that the principle of complementarity may at best prompt the recognition that there is more in the realm of human experience than ironclad physical mechanism.[68] Arthur Holly Compton got much closer to the heart of the matter when he vindicated the freedom of the will on the basis that his inner conviction about moving his little finger at will carried far greater and far more immediate evidence than all the deterministic laws of physics taken together.[69]

Compton's approach to the problem of free will has the quality of being eminently scientific, philosophical, and ethical. It is scientific because it reveals an unreserved respect for facts, an old hallmark of the scientific enterprise. While in any other area—business, politics, arts, letters—the willful tampering with facts is at times widespread, the history of science knows only a few such cases.[70] Its recent history under totalitarian regimes, well known for their arbitrariness with facts, revealed their deep-seated antagonism toward a science which cannot but be honest with facts. There is indeed a special ethos embodied in the practice of science, an ethos which is far more than usefulness or expediency. It is rather the ethos of an unconditional commitment, a most unreasonable posture unless one assumes that the world of facts is always reasonable, which in turn implies that all facts are bound together through an unfailing consistency. Commitment, nay surrender, to that consistency is that ethos of science which prompted Einstein's remark: "Most people say it is the intellect which makes a great scientist. They are wrong: it is the character."[71]

An honesty which is not a momentary compliance with disconnected data but a free and lasting surrender to their consistency obviously puts on it a philosophical quality which removes to a higher level the apparent conflict between freedom of the will and laws of nature. That higher level cannot be reached with the conceptual tools of cultural relativism. These cannot even cope with the brute historical fact that while there were many cultures, only one culture gave birth to science, and when this science is introduced into cultures that failed to give rise to it, it is not science but those cultures that are faced with the problem of major adjustments. Some of these are philosophical and religious and far transcend the horizon of sociological model making about the spread of Western science into underdeveloped countries.[72] Those adjustments are also ethical in the sense that they imply a resolute break with subjectivist, irrational world views and the acceptance of the consistency of nature and of the consistent exercise of man's freedom.

That exercise has a quality which in addition to being scientific and philosophical is also thoroughly ethical. Clearly, not all consequences of man's free actions are equally desirable. One need not be a believer in metaphysical ethics to perceive the threat of polluted rivers and a smog-laden air. A pragmatic, utilitarian zest for life is enough to insist on the decontamination of spacemen returning from the moon. It takes no special metaphysics but only the metaphysics of common sense to keep in mind the difference between short-range and long-range effects and to refrain from changing the genetic structure of some bacteria lest an uncontrollable chain reaction ensue.[73] It takes more than the "metaphysics" of a utilitarian ethics, however, to justify a conscientious care for gravely defective members of the human species. From the utilitarian viewpoint such care can only appear as a senseless drain on the resources—mental, emotional, and physical—of the human race. On the basis of utilitarian ethics there is no ground for condemning the

309

extermination in Nazi Germany of more than one hundred thousand incurably sick senior citizens.

If the preservation and protection of such members of the human race is claimed on the basis of compassion, it becomes particularly appropriate to recall T. H. Huxley's remark that yielding to compassion is not only not justified by biological evolution but is simply reversing it.[74] A rational justification of compassion implies the attributing of such a value to the individual as to make him superior to the race itself. Such a value cannot be derived from utilitarian ethics or from purely biological considerations without contradicting oneself and without being contradicted by some salient and sobering facts. A good illustration of this is provided in the late Professor Waddington's *Ethical Animal*, a book which was meant to be free of the circularity which vitiated the evolutionary ethics set forth in Julian Huxley's *Evolution in Action*. In referring to Nazism Waddington felt that "the elimination of the whole thing may be advantageous if that rids man of a number of ideas which impede anagenesis, at the expense of only a few potentially valuable ones."[75]

The distinction between ideas that impede anagenesis and which promote it makes sense only if anagenesis is invested with a teleological and ethical meaning, a meaning which cannot be secured within Waddington's theory without committing the error of circularity. The sacrificing of a few valuable ideas through eliminating many harmful ones may seem a commendable procedure as long as it remains on the level of abstraction. At any rate, Waddington's supreme standard and goal, the optimum level of "the Idea Pool of the human species," cannot be realized by relying on biological criteria alone. Those criteria doom to extinction not only the withering elderly but also the retarded young, which might have included Albert Einstein, so late in learning to speak that his parents feared he was subnormal.[76] While Einstein was generous enough to say that relativity would have been discovered even without him, he would have agreed that an artistic feat like Beethoven's C Minor Symphony could be written only by Beethoven and no one else.[77] Actually, had Waddington's ethics based on an "idea pool" been in force two hundred years ago that symphony would have never been composed. A hundred fifty years after its composition a Waddingtonian gynecologist was asked for advice by a colleague faced with the fourth pregnancy of a tuberculous woman, wife of a syphilitic man. Their first child was born blind, the second died in infancy, the third turned out to be deaf and dumb. The unhesitating advice was: terminate the pregnancy. The reply, "Then you would have killed Beethoven,"[78] should at least give pause to unhesitating advocates of an ethics based only on eugenics and expected to improve man's "idea pool."

Whatever the history of eugenics, the history of genetics and the history of any branch of science is the history of that "idea pool" in which Waddington rightly saw the finest result of evolutionary process. Physiological theories and their sociological counterparts, whether evolutionary or not, cannot account either for the emergence of that "idea pool" or for the absolute obligation to protect it. That protection can only be achieved if even the fittest members of society surrender to unconditionally binding ethical norms. Such is at least the lesson of science, biological as well as physical, especially when that science is interrogated about the various phases and aspects of its long road. That still open road did not create its ethical basis, but assumed it all along. By ignoring or slighting that basis scientists will glory in theories which can profit only the strong and doom the weak, be they individuals, nations, or races. The surrender in question ought to be unwavering and invariable, because the chief features of the ethical basis of science are invariable and are tied to an unwavering commitment to a consistent understanding of a rationally coherent universe. Of that coherent universe no theory revealed more than Einstein's relativity. It should therefore seem a sad reflection on our age that a theory so absolutist in character could be presented by so many and so often as the proof that all, especially all ethics, was relative.[79]

While such presentations still can be heard, it can also be heard and with increasing frequency that science as such is no source of ethics.[80] This is certainly true when science is taken as a purely conceptual matrix. But as soon as science is taken as an activity engaging the concrete individual, the ethical foundations of science immediately become evident. To state, as James B. Conant did, that all decent thinkers agree about those foundations but that no reason can be given about that agreement betrays a facile agnosticism and not a serious philosophical and scientific mentality.[81] Science in part owes its existence to the courage of men and women in raising questions regardless of the difficulty of getting proper answers. To account for the unanimity by which commitment to ethics is endorsed is particularly difficult when an "exact" account is requested. Aristotle warned that ethical theory implies a train of thought considerably different from the one embodied in mathematics.[82] Spinoza's *Ethica more geometrico demonstrata* only proved the impossibility of a "scientific" ethics. That a consistent discourse or science about ethics is not "scientific" should be clear from even a brief look at ethical theories offered since the publication of G. E. Moore's *Principia ethica* (1903). Yet all those theories,[83] even the ones more critical than constructive, merely prove that the exact mapping of the contours of ethics is as futile a task as the mapping of all points on the surface of the ocean. From this, however, it would be equally futile to infer that neither the ocean nor the science of ethics should be taken for real.

It is no less futile to slight the validity of ethics with the kind of remark that "possibly the American inventor of anaesthetic has done more for the real happiness of mankind than all the moral philosophers from Socrates to Mill."[84] The better an ethical theory the less it is a pill for happiness. A happy world would always be a world without ethics. Ethics has its source in the sense of guilt, and this is why the true Sisyphus is always the one who tries to turn pain, of which ethical guilt is the most unbearable, into an impassable roadblock on the ways to God. To ignore this is to construct in vain a debilitating paradox out of the reality of evil. The paradox as formulated by Albert Camus deserves to be quoted because of its brevity: "In the presence of God there is less a problem of freedom than a problem of evil. You know the alternative: either we are not free and God the all-powerful is responsible for evil, or we are free and responsible but God is not all-powerful. All the scholastic subtleties have neither added anything to nor subtracted anything from the acuteness of this paradox."[85] Such a formulation of the paradox shows that the ethical proof of the existence of God makes no sense if isolated from the other proofs. Human freedom is not simply a freedom but the freedom of men who, like the rest of nature, are contingent in every respect of their existence, which is, however, not contingent to the point of lacking inner coherence. An existentialist like Camus refuses to admit any coherence in that contingency. That refusal is the source of the existentialist's craving for the moment, asking no questions about the possible coherence of moments and of the ulterior and ultimate consequences of actions that are all in a sense momentary. It should therefore be of no surprise that Camus is not a friend either of ethics or of science, both of which mean coherence in space and time. Contrary to the wish of existentialists, who look for the immobility of the actual moment, science will continue on its coherent road and by its very march will existentially overcome the paradox of Camus in much the same way in which one of Zeno's paradoxes was solved, by *ambulando*. But science will march freely only as long as it marches responsibly. Both that freedom and that responsibility will keep pointing and in a coherent manner beyond science to a realm where its road turns into the ways to God.

That turn must be recognized and cultivated or else a fearful premonition of the existentialists may turn into reality. The premonition was predicated on a false picture of science fostered by the positivist denial of all questions with a metaphysical, let alone with an ethical, flavor. What is, however, more metaphysical than existence itself and especially an existence steeped in ethical responsibility? A soulless positivist image of science must loom large as a threat to existence itself, a point particularly relevant ever since we started living in the Orwellian decade.[86] If the world as pictured in *1984* is so appalling, it is because of its wholly unethical use of a science reduced to sheer technology. That reduction brings about by the same logic the end of the road of science as well as the end of discourse about the ways to God. Such a reduction is inevitable if the road which science traveled has indeed been determined by genetic inheritance, tools of production, and cultural conditioning. But the rise of that road, as history shows, was not determined in advance. Actually, it became an open-ended road not in the cultural ambience of a Democritean ethics,[87] about which one can say with certainty only that its background was the incoherence of Democritus's worlds. That ethics could produce only an "open society" which is without any containment and can only slowly but surely dissipate its contents in the manner of a barrel freed of its hoops, an outcome well exemplified by the long decline of ancient Greek culture, which at first had shown so much promise for science. It was not the "open" society of the Greeks that saw the road of science become open-ended. That event could take place only in a culture steeped in awareness of the transcendental confines of man's freedom and ethical responsibility, a culture strongly though unwittingly endorsed even today by the ethos of science.

Twenty

TEACHING BY EXAMPLES

IN SPEAKING OF THE PROOFS OF THE EXISTENCE OF GOD, PASCAL REMARKED "always to have proofs ready is too much trouble."[1] Coming as it does from a giant of the intellect, the remark might justify the trouble expended in these lectures to reach the stage of taking a look at some of the proofs. Useful as a look can be, a look is never a vision, let alone a fixation of the mind. To quote Pascal again: "The reason acts slowly, with so many examinations, and on so many principles which must be always present, that at every hour it falls asleep, or wanders, through want of having all its principles present."[2] With that insight into the instability of the mind, Pascal could hardly be complacent about the proofs. He knew both that "proofs only convince the mind"[3] and that it is true only of some minds that they find plenty of light by looking at "the heavens and the birds."[4] Pascal also knew that to tell atheists that it is enough to look at the course of the moon and the planets to see God openly is the best means of arousing their contempt for demonstrations of that kind.[5]

Such a reserved attitude concerning the proofs could irritate no one more than Voltaire, who all his life loathed Pascal for seeing man in his fallen reality,[6] the source (among a great many other things) of man's fumbling with the basic reasonings that constitute those proofs. These were always a straightforward matter for Voltaire, whose exposition of Newtonian philosophy started with a facile account of what he believed was Newton's natural theology. Concerning that natural theology and Newton's philosophy of science, to say nothing of Newtonian science itself, Voltaire did better in what he said about the errors of Newton's opponents than in what he offered about Newton. Although Voltaire could understand but relatively few pages of the *Principia*, he had no excuse for claiming, for instance, that according to Newton the world was finite.[7] Yet no one would deny the effectiveness by which Voltaire's book on Newton helped the French, if not to grasp Newton, at least to extricate themselves from the Cartesian bondage that had kept them away from him.

The effective use of a similar strategy in Pascal's *Pensées*—a work which excelled by laying bare the weaknesses of the rationalist and skeptical position—haunted Voltaire so much as to make him the first to congratulate Condorcet on publishing a selection of the *pensées*, obviously to blunt their incisiveness.[8] A rationalist like Voltaire, for whom reason was the sole virtue, must have felt threatened in his very stronghold by Pascal's fundamental proposition that to admit only reason

314

was as much an extreme as to exclude it completely.[9] A scientist of the first rank, Pascal knew what Voltaire, hardly a scientist, failed even to suspect—in connection with science too the truly "scientific" attitude consisted in avoiding those very same extremes. Science, Newtonian physics, was for Voltaire so closely equivalent to reason that he tried to find in universal history the same universal laws that physicists find in nature. In that effort of Voltaire, China, as the apparently oldest culture, provided the primary beacon. The light of that beacon was the light of a purely natural reason which made the Chinese appear the supreme teachers of the art of how to achieve a truly human society guided by reason alone.

That China could not boast of progress in science was therefore a signal problem for Voltaire's science of historiography, a problem which he tried to resolve with references to the varieties displayed by the natural dispositions of various nations,[10] introducing thereby subtle contradictions into his conception of the universality of natural reason. A hundred years earlier, when the first detailed reports about China began to obscure for some the beacon of the Christian West, Pascal did not let himself be trapped in similar contradictions. He emphasized once more the median position as he took up the objection, "but China obscures," an objection which might have as well been phrased by Voltaire himself. "I answer," Pascal wrote, "China obscures, but there is clearness to be found; seek it."[11] Judging by the influence the *Pensées* exercised and still exercise, it is not difficult to imagine the impact Pascal might have made by carrying out the project he suggested concerning the China problem as it appeared around 1660: "All that you say," he addressed his opponent, "makes for one of the views, and not at all against the other. So this serves, and does not harm. We must then see this in detail, we must put the papers on the table."[12]

To put those papers on the table would have been well-nigh impossible even if members of the Society of Jesus, the chief source of information about China, had been a century or two ahead of the times. Had their reports been drawn up with a greater anticipation of modern historical scholarship,[13] Voltaire and his companions, also very much children of their own times, would still have produced a garbled version of those reports, the very thing Voltaire expected Condorcet to do with the *Pensées*. For Voltaire the virulent atheism of Condorcet was less of an irritation than the Christian theism of Pascal. Voltaire's massive universal history either ridiculed historic Christianity or passed over it in silence. Historiography was for Voltaire the apologetics of rationalism. The unscholarly character of Voltaire's account of history can easily be gathered from the fact that he mentioned Christ only once, and by then he was dealing with Constantine's crossing the Milvian

Bridge.[14] Not content with turning Christ into a virtual nonentity, Voltaire was also careful to dissociate Christ from historic Christianity. The fury of his sarcasm would certainly have descended on anyone trying to establish a positive connection between Christian theism and Newtonian science, or science in short.

Such an attempt would have implied above all a look at history which in Voltaire's time would have been difficult to achieve. The main reason for this would not have been the inaccessibility of much of the late medieval material gathering dust in the soon-to-be-dissolved monasteries. The major documents of modern science, from Copernicus to Newton, were available in print, but to read them properly one would have needed eyes not blind to Christian theism as a historical fact. Led by contempt for Christianity, Voltairian historians had to invent history according to their preferences, which all too often led them to accept outright myths about history. The astronomy of the mythical nation which Bailly located in an area corresponding to present-day Mongolia was as much a myth as the science of the denizens of Atlantis, about which Bailly could discourse with equal ease.[15] His lengthy peregrinations into no-man's-land were the fate of one who, like many of the protagonists of the French Enlightenment, exchanged the rationality of Christian theism for the mysticism of Rosicrucianism and of kindred self-deifications.[16] While Voltaire disagreed with Bailly concerning the erstwhile inhabitants of Mongolia, he did not take exception to Condorcet's calling Bailly a "frère illuminé,"[17] an epithet reserved for the mystics of the Enlightenment, or to Bailly's strategy to look for the origin of science in complete disregard of historical Christian theism.

When two generations later Comte turned to the history of science, antagonism to Christian theism was no longer permitted to credit mythical nations with the origin of science, although it was still permissible, nay advisable, to ignore the question of that origin. For a while this had passed for a scholarly attitude, but historical scholarship was not to be denied its day forever. By the 1860s the editing of unpublished source materials had become recognized as a major requisite for making progress in historiography, and the historiography of science came before long to its moment of truth. This arrived in 1881 with the publication of Leonardo's notebooks. These in the long run forced a reluctant parting with the hallowed shibboleths of a positivist and at times militantly agnosticist if not atheistic historiography of science. The grudging recognition that Galileo and his immediate predecessors had read Leonardo led to the admission that Leonardo owed much to the long-despised medievals. Among the results of this development was not only a rise of interest in medieval science, but also a recognition of the need to read the printed classics of science with eyes freed from the scales of positivism. This is not to suggest that there are no diehards left in this respect. Among them are Popperians who, following their leader's procedure,[18] readily jump from the pre-Socratics to Descartes, and if they take a brief stopover in the Middle Ages, they are apt to equate Scholasticism with Talmudism.[19]

With allowance made for such symptoms it may still be said with some assurance that unlike the situation in Pascal's or Voltaire's or Comte's time, it has for some time become possible to put the papers on the table and see whether Christian theism (the only kind of theism which has a major and positive relevance for the history of science) is obscured by science, or whether its light is indispensable to the understanding of the scientific enterprise. An affirmative answer to the second alternative is what has been offered in these lectures, and in a manner akin to putting on the table the papers relevant to the issue. Being Gifford Lectures, they have had to do with natural theology, but even when Lord Gifford signed his will specialists on natural theology were already few and far between. In a century which put the word "progress" on its banner, no criticism could be more devastating than Lord Macaulay's remark that "natural theology is not a progressive science." Its evidences and problems, Macaulay declared, were the same as they have been in the days of Thales and Socrates.[20] Macaulay should have recalled, however, that to the extent to which Thales started progress, Socrates too was the source of a very important development. Thales, who began the progress which led man from water to hydrogen as the ultimate constituent of "god" of all, had also moments in which he saw everything full of gods even when he saw no water. As for Socrates, it is well to remember that the influence which natural theology was to make in intellectual history grew out of his keen disappointment on reading Anaxagoras's purely mechanistic account of nature, an account inspired by Thales. The influence was so great that Leibniz, perplexed by the fallacies of the new mechanistic philosophizing about nature, suggested a broadening of the horizons of physical science in terms laid down by Socrates in the *Phaedo*.[21] Mechanistic accounts of nature progressed immensely between the time of Anaxagoras, even of Leibniz, and the time of Lord Gifford, a span covering twice twenty centuries, but as the nets of those accounts stretched wider and wider, fish ever more telltale could also swim through any and all such nets. Kinds of that fish, or questions slipping through the net of a purely naturalistic frame of explanation, could be found by investigators of almost any field. Thus while natural theologians had almost become an extinct species by Lord Gifford's time, there has always been a fresh supply of specialists ready to discuss questions which, though raised by their specialties, could be answered only by a philosophy akin to natural theology.

This explains the custom, in evidence from the inception of this lecture series, of inviting specialists from various fields to show how their respective fields of study bear on questions of natural theology. This is an eminently sound approach, since a theology that is genuinely natural must be responsive to anything learned about nature, of which man is the most eminent part. As for man, it has become very evident since Pascal's time, and especially since Voltaire's, that what makes man so particularly human is that *Homo sapiens* is the sole species capable of making history. Of that capacity of man the last few centuries, and especially our own, have revealed an entirely new way of making history—through science. That science makes history has become a sad truism for an age which sits on the nuclear powder keg and perhaps on stacks of even more devastating explosives. Until very recently kings, statesmen, politicians, and agitators seemed to be the makers of history, but in the wake of Hiroshima, James F. Byrnes, then U. S. Secretary of State, felt impelled to remark: "In this age it appears every man must have his own physicist."[22]

Once it became obvious that science makes history, curiosity about the inner workings of the new powerhouse grew by leaps and bounds. The proliferation of courses, chairs, institutes, conferences, congresses, and societies concerned with the history of science is a post–World War II phenomenon. Before long it became clear that like other historians, the historian of science is apt to mistake "his story" for history. The source of this error is in the inevitable need to select for one's narrative only the significant facts and their significant connections. This implies an anticipated understanding of what is to be understood, a danger which is equally present when science is made an object of inquiry from the philosophical viewpoint, another field that has been enjoying increasing popularity since World War II. In the postwar historiography and philosophy of science the most characteristic and certainly the most vociferous trends constitute a variation on the two extremes about which Pascal made his pointed warning. The variants are to exclude history and to admit only history.

Needless to say, a philosophy of science oblivious to its history and a history of science devoid of philosophical viewpoints that transcend history can only offer an image of science in which no trace, however faint, of an ultimate metaphysical cause can be found. A history of science in which the metaphysical principles underlying a particular phase of science are assumed to be "phased out" with that phase can only generate agnosticism. A philosophy of science must do the same when interest in logical connections is cultivated to the exclusion of a sense of reality, including a sense of historical reality. Chapters 14 and 15, "Ravages of Reductionism" and "Paradigms or Paradigm," deal with this contemporary exercise in extremes. It represents a problem which should weigh heavily on the mind of a theist aware of the dam-

318

age that can be done to the potential metaphysical openness of those not mature enough to see what is reliable learning in current academic discourse and what is mere agnostic propaganda.

If this agnosticism is to be overcome, both metaphysics and historical reality must be taken seriously and in their entirety. Concerning metaphysics this implies the readiness to keep in mind questions about the ultimate in reason, cause, purpose, and responsibility and to keep in mind these perspectives with unrestricted consistency. As for the history of science, one must show readiness to look for a lesson in all its phases, in the most developed as well as in the most embryonic, and in particular to try to see whether a consistent lesson can be found in the entirety of the historical process. Such a program may appear too systematic in an age which, unlike some previous ages, is not fond of great systematizations. Natural theology has flourished for better or for worse in times when one may have yielded too much to the lure of system building, but one was at least aware that unrestricted consistency is always preferable to being satisfied with hardly any consistency at all. It is well to recall that arithmetic theorems have to be broad enough, that is, have a consistency of more than trivial range, if sweeping lessons like Gödel's theorems are to be obtained.

For a philosophy of science reduced to logic the question of the historical origin of science is no more significant than the account of a single discovery, and equally for a historicist historiography of science, the origins contain no more meaning than any other phase. But the question of origin is paramount when interest is focused on the reality of a thing undergoing a development, an interest which naturally brings into focus the question of coming into being, the classic problem of metaphysics. If such an interest maintains more of the integrity of the subject matter than do other approaches, then it certainly ought to be considered more "scientific"—from the methodological viewpoint at least. At any rate, it seems that there is much more than methodological purism in that careful avoidance by a historicist historiography of the question of the origin of science. The failure of science in great ancient cultures has features that make it appear too metaphysical and theological for historicist historians. The day is still to come when research into that failure, perhaps the most gigantic of all cultural failures, will command at least as large a research grant as did the field study of the ability of Australian aborigines to discriminate among perspiration odors and the investigation of why some children fall off their tricycles.[23] Were research into that cultural failure to be sponsored, the results might make it appear that what aborigines, children, and many of their civilized counterparts need above all is not deodorants, better tricycles, or even science, but a growth in awareness of God's existence.

Something of his existence was grasped on occasion by the greatest

319

philosophers of ancient Greece, where science suffered its most tantalizing failure. The adjective "tantalizing" is appropriate when one falls short of the goal in almost clear sight of it, and such indeed was the case of the Greeks of old with respect to science. More than any other ancient people, the Greeks were profoundly aware of the rationality of nature and of the measure in which consistency gives rationality to reasoning. They were the first to construct formal ways to the ultimate in being, and Aristotle even perceived something of that aspect of the contingency of things which was implied in the fact that not all that was possible did in fact exist.[24] But he was unable to extend that contingency to the heavenly regions. As a result, Aristotle could only give a cosmology, always the fundamental form of science, which was an a priori discourse about the universe. Thus the problem of the failure of ancient Greek science is largely the failure of the Greeks of old to go resolutely one step beyond the prime heavens to a prime mover absolutely superior to it. As a man of religion, Aristotle was unable to go even as far as he did as a philosopher. He worshiped idols, and in the worship of idols there lay hidden that supreme trickery which ultimately triggered among the Greeks of old a pervasive "failure of nerve." Yet, the blame for this is hardly ever placed on the true culprit, idolatry, in an age intent on its own covert idols.

Since Christians were not a force to be reckoned with, even toward the end of those four centuries that started with Alexander the Great and witnessed both the loss of self-confidence among the Greeks and the demise of their scientific creativity, the political turmoils that plagued the Greeks after Alexander might seem to offer a more expedient explanation. But such turmoils were at least as common in medieval Europe, if not more so. Europe, it will be recalled, found itself then in a protracted state of siege due to the Moslem conquest of much of the Mediterranean seacoast. And as for inner turmoils, it might be noted that restricting violence by the *treuga Dei* and the *pax Dei* to certain days of the week was the best that could be hoped for by the way of utopia in early medieval Europe. Yet medieval men of intellect did not despair. Unlike paganism, which failed the Greeks, Christian theism provided the medievals with mental confidence and incentive. Without these the medieval acquisition of Greek science would not have developed into an intellectual enterprise surpassing the science of the Greeks. A proof of this is the sad contrast offered by the failure of medieval Arabs to add anything substantial to the Greek scientific tradition.[25] They failed to make that decisive step beyond the Greeks, a step which was to make science a viable enterprise, for reasons rooted in the Koran's theism.[26] The making of modern science from Grosseteste to Galileo was a long and complex process,[27] but a crucial role was played in it by the Christian medievals' reflections on man's natural knowledge of God, or natural theology.

Natural theology means above all the ascertaining by the light of reason the existence of God, or in short, the proofs. These proofs, as developed and discussed by the medievals, were the core of an epistemology which science embodied in its first phase of maturity, during the three centuries stretching from Galileo to Kelvin. Six chapters are devoted to that phase, most germane to questions of natural theology. In three of these the respective fortunes of Baconian empiricism, Cartesian rationalism, and of Newtonian science were analyzed in the light of their epistemologies. Central importance in that analysis was given to the historical fact that the connection between the proofs of the existence of God and the methodology needed by science was made explicit there and then by Bacon, by Descartes, and by Newton, the chief actors in that intellectual drama. Their respective successes in science represent also the measure of soundness of the stance they took in epistemology, a field most intimately connected with the proofs of the existence of God.

The first three chapters, of course, also deal with this connection as historical fact. But the farther back one goes in history the more difficult it is to document facts, including the fact of that connection. On the contrary, the more one progresses into modern history the more striking the connection becomes. By the time one reaches that century which became the first of centuries to deserve being called the century of science it becomes simply overwhelming. As to the next century, the eighteenth, it is very clear that Hume, Kant, and their nineteenth-century positivist and idealist disciples were fully aware of that inner logic which connects the proofs of the existence of God and the epistemology needed by a successful, creative science. Indeed, precisely because that connection seemed to them very harmful, they did their best to undo the proofs of the existence of God. It is therefore not enough to expose the fallacy of their criticism of the proofs. Since they claimed that their criticism of the proofs makes for a better understanding of science, their interpretative legislation about science must be carefully put in balance. The fact is, although it is still largely to be learned, that when one weighs in such a balance a Hume, a Kant, a Hegel, a Comte, and even a Mach, one will see appear those ominous words which once cut Nebuchadnezzar down to size. In order to reach this conclusion one must, of course, take Hume, Kant, Hegel, Comte, and Mach as they most explicitly wanted to be remembered, as philosopher-saviors of science.

Once these philosopher-saviors are measured against the goal they have set for themselves, the juggernaut of agnosticism into which present-day philosophy and historiography of science are turned time and again appears small indeed. That juggernaut is of no use against those two gigantic figures, Planck and Einstein, who mark the transit from the inland sea of classical physics to the wide ocean of modern physics. Through their achievement the world appeared more singular and more coherent than ever. The unfolding of ever deeper layers of the microcosmos and the grasp of ever farther reaches of the macrocosmos continue to be based on the quantum of action and on general relativity, respectively. Although both of these theories are often presented as supports of positivism, the physical reality they bear witness to calls for an epistemology irreconcilable with positivist legislation on reality as well as on science. Mach had already perceived this, and to such an extent as to part company with both Planck and Einstein—a significant fact to be sure, for both started out as admiring disciples of his. It is also a fact that both Planck and Einstein had come to recognize their own epistemological physiognomy under the impact of their creativity in science. No less is it a fact (though less publicized) that both Planck and Einstein realized that their science had brought them dangerously close to being considered theists.

That both recoiled from the full force of logic in that particular respect shows that even the finest minds of a century can become the victims of its malaise. For the twentieth century that malaise is resolute agnosticism concerning ultimate questions. Lesser minds showing the same surrender to that malaise need cause no undue concern. It is enough to keep in mind their impalement on the horns of complementarity. Offered as a liberation from the mechanism and determinism of classical physics, complementarity achieves that freedom only be the suspension of reasoning at critical junctures, a point which is being increasingly recognized. It is also a sign of progress that in the mid-1970s, unlike the 1930s, the ravages of reductionism are too obvious to make their exposure an academic *lèse majesté*. Historicism in the study of the history of science is also slowly turning, if not into a fact of the past, at least into a questionable stance of the present. What remains a refreshing fact is the marvelous ability of the mind to find ever deeper rationality in the data provided by the senses. Twentieth-century science has furnished telling evidence that no idealized machine can be imagined which can perform all the steps of logic the mind is capable of, to say nothing of operations of the mind implying judgments of existence and of values. Twentieth-century science has also come to the reliable conclusion that the mind can transcend the whole universe by forming a scientifically valid concept of it.

As Kant now would sadly say, if you have the mind, or soul, and the whole universe as valid notions, critical philosophy can no longer prevent you from proceeding to the reality of God. All the less can one be prevented from doing so if the universe appears—and it does so appear with every advance of science—more strikingly singular. Such is a fact of the universe in the face of which a priori thinking must admit defeat. The coherence displayed by singularity throughout the cosmos witnesses that although that singularity pervades the entire cosmos, it comes to the cosmos from without, from the creative choice of an Intellect necessarily acting for a purpose which can, in its specifics, at most be surmised by human intellect. Such a conclusion—even indeed any immanent notion of purposeful design—is of course denied by the standard philosophy of evolution, which tries to discredit purpose by the self-discrediting stratagem of being very purposeful about it. What adds a tragic touch to this farcical game is that without purpose there is no ground for ethics and ethical responsibility. Ethics and responsibility are, however, needed in grand measure if man is to cope with the frightening prospect of the blessings of science turning into a global disaster.

Such are the facts, in brief, as presented in these lectures dealing with the road of science and the ways to God. A very broad topic to be sure and even twenty lectures have permitted putting only the most relevant papers on the table. Such a presentation is obviously made for a purpose, which consists in helping to bring about a reversal of the change once advocated by John Stuart Mill in memorable words: "I am now convinced that no great improvements in the lot of mankind are possible, until a great change takes place in the fundamental constitution of their modes of thought."[28] To help forestall the complete realization of Mill's objective and to help redirect intellectual and cultural energies toward the mode of thought which alone secures a firm foundation for the improvement of mankind, has been the aim pursued throughout these lectures. This mode of thought is the one in which the secular or scientific is not set at cross-purposes with the sacred or philosophical. About the prospects of reinstating that mode of thought through these lectures, no illusions should be entertained. What Nehemiah Grew, author of *Cosmologia sacra*, said in that respect almost three hundred years ago, is particularly appropriate: "The hardest Question I have been asked, is this, Do you think to Damm up the *Thames*? I answer, No: Yet a Bridg may be laid over it. And this too, may be so far from Stemming the Tide; as only to cause it to make a greater Noize. But as the Bridg may not be able to stop the Tide; so, I trust, the Tide shall never be able to beat down the Bridge; but that many will hereby Land themselves, safe from Drowning in the common Stream."[29]

Perhaps these lectures may become a bridge that will help some to walk over that "common stream"; perhaps the piers of that bridge will be grasped by some already carried downstream. Perhaps the papers put on the table will arouse through their factual contents the interest of

323

those who with Huxley confront theists with the call: "Sit down before fact as a little child, be prepared to give up every preconceived notion, follow humbly wherever Nature leads, or you will learn nothing."[30] Perhaps through these lectures they will realize, first, that the facts of nature can lead only insofar as they become the facts of philosophy, and second, that unless one sits down as a little child before the facts of science embodied in its history—prepared to give up preconceived notions about it offered by positivists, idealists, historicists, and agnostics, and ready to retrace in full the actual historical road of science—one will never learn the fundamental truth that real science is the science of a contingent universe.

It should be understandable that in these lectures devoted to the road of science and to the ways to God, the facts about the road were emphasized over the facts pertaining to the ways. A speculative study of natural theology is not my specialty. In any case, the latest trends of natural theology, and clear evidence of its progress, were recently given a splendid exposition by Eric L. Mascall, in a series of Gifford Lectures delivered also at the University of Edinburgh.[31] The reason for the emphasis laid on the road of science, however, goes beyond the fact that the study of that road is my own specialty. Emphasis on science is imperative in an age for which the common currency is made of scientific data and for which the parlance of science is the common idiom. Scientific expressions more and more frequently turn up in discussions that have very little to do with science—and where they often make little sense. But since the expressions are scientific, they are taken to be self-explanatory. Were this age of ours still the age of Euler, an atheist might still be silenced by confronting him with a simple algebraic equation. On being challenged by Euler—*Monsieur, $(a + b^n)/n = x$, donc Dieu existe; répondez!*—Diderot, so the story goes, fell silent and decided to leave at once the court of Catherine the Great where he had been busy spreading the good news of atheism.[32] Like most atheists of his time, Diderot would dispute God but not science, with which his familiarity grew thinner as he grew in age though not in wisdom. Ours is, however, the age in which atheists and agnostics are often superbly versed in the technicalities of science and they are more than eager to bolster their countertheistic cause by scientific expressions. They have not neglected the history of science either. In their reliance on science and on its history they know that in the global battle that is waged for minds it will be of decisive tactical importance which side can make a convincing case for having science as a genuine ally.

Thomas Henry Huxley saw his program of educating everybody in science and in its history in this light. While he made no secret about his hope to have only one culture, the culture of science,[33] a hundred years later it was found more expedient to hope for that one culture by deploring the split between two cultures. To remedy that split, C. P. Snow urged the exposing of everyone to courses in science,[34] hardly an effective procedure to make general that wisdom which Sir Charles later recognized to be of the highest cultural value.[35] A few courses in science give no expertise in it, let alone the wisdom needed for the survival of a culture about which Malraux noted with obvious misgiving that it is the first culture in history which tries to survive without religion.[36] At any rate, though not all educated men can ever become experts in science, they are all being more and more distracted by science from what is truly intellectual but not science. This is largely due to the influence of logical positivists and of Marxists who pursue similarly extreme stratagems. The former permit what is not scientific merely as subjective experience, or *Erlebnis,* but never as an *Erkenntnis,* that is, a knowledge with claim to validity. The Marxists try to make science out of everything, in the belief that dialectical materialism is the universal key to a scientific interpretation of everything.

Regardless of the crusading overemphasis on science in some quarters, science will inevitably claim more and more of mankind's attention. Pressures on human life created by its growing technologization will certainly help condone the increasing disregard for classical studies. When even in Greece teachers of classics face almost empty classrooms, elsewhere the number of "barbarians" (in more than one sense) already provides an easy count for the perfect number visioned by Plato. Whether or not Butterfield's prophecy made at Harvard in 1959 that the study of the history of science will replace the study of classics as a basic framework of education will come true remains to be seen.[37] The change would not necessarily be an unqualified loss if men and women were in general more able to study the history of science than the classics. It seems, however, that less formal ability is needed for a proper study of the classics than for an adequate study of the history of science. A goodly portion of the latter simply cannot be studied without a thorough grounding in the classics, while one can become an excellent classicist without knowing much of science. Clearly, the universal study of the history of science is bound in most cases to become an additional boost to that cultural superficiality which is taking an increasing hold and toll of Western education and civilization.

In that exercise of superficiality not only Homer and Plato are swept under the rug but Shakespeare, Goethe, and Dante as well, to say nothing of the Bible. In the West this is due to foolhardiness, in the East to planning. In the West one can meet university students for whom Sodom and Gomorrah were two brothers,[38] information which they might have as well acquired in homosexual clubs now officially recognized in distinguished universities. In the East, university students of the national literature must now take a special course in the Bible because their elementary and high school teachers are forced to keep them in the dark about a certain Moses, a certain Solomon, and a certain Jonah to which their greatest poets referred in a matter of fact manner a century or two ago.[39] With such appalling instances of the superficiality, if not barbarism, which mark ever greater numbers of educated men and women, the history of science presented to them can at best be a skeleton of the actual historical reality of science, vibrant with metaphysics. Like skeletons in general, a history of science reduced to its skeleton will easily be abused for inferior purposes, among them the furthering of agnosticism and atheism. It is far more difficult to abuse classical studies in the same way. The great masterpieces of literature, classical or recent, are always replete with metaphysical and ethical questions. It is not typical of a man with a taste for the classics to say that ultimate questions cannot be profitably asked. The statement, typically enough, was made by the scientist-author of a book on the completeness of science, that is, on the self-containing character of scientific theories.[40]

The fact that science is an ongoing process is a proof that these theories are not complete even today and that they have never been so in the past. The history of science, however, provides many examples of the fact that the idea of a "complete" theory is a perennial utopia in science. While the unification of quantum theory and of general relativity is still to be achieved, their fusion will not be a *complete* theory. It will contain no explanation of that singularity which is embodied in the universe and which cannot be derived from general considerations. Scientists chase an illusion when they try to establish that the world can only be what it is.[41] Eddington, who was so fond of the number 137 (the reciprocal of the fine-structure constant in atomic physics) that in cloakrooms he preferred to hang his coat on a peg marked with that number, might perhaps have succeeded in pegging the whole of physics on that number, but this would still have left him with the puzzling difference between numbers that are many, nay infinitely numerous, and a universe which is one in number for cultivators of the science of nature.

Although it is not for science to answer the question about the reason for the existence of a unique or singular universe, this is a question that must be asked and answered if one aims at completeness in the way of understanding. The answer, which only metaphysics, or rather natural theology, can give, will not, of course, "profit" the scientist in a narrowly "scientific" sense. But the answer, which is God, will greatly strengthen the scientist's trust in the existence of an objectively existing, rationally ordered universe which can be investigated by the human mind, a pursuit which is man's exclusive privilege and responsibility. This trust, privilege, and responsibility constitute the backbone of the scientific enterprise. Science arose when these three factors became a cultural matrix. It is only the theoretical and experimental techniques of science that can change and increase. The essence, or quantum, of science represented by those factors is an attainment to which nothing can be added. Nothing can be subtracted from them either without undermining the scientific enterprise itself.

To speak of science as a truth that man after many and long trials has grasped and which he either holds or rejects but which he cannot change, will hardly sound attractive. Ours is an age intent only on process, not on what undergoes process in such a way as to save the basis for consistency by retaining its substantial identity during the process. Theologians who were eager to be "scientific" by espousing Whitehead's process philosophy[42] might have spared themselves its shallows by first considering whether it does justice to science, a process that has retained its own "being" or substantial identity ever since it became a viable enterprise. The history of that enterprise reveals the unfolding of one majestic paradigm and not the haphazard succession of sundry paradigms. The persistence of that one single paradigm or matrix means, however, that in a very deep sense science is not progressive. It is anchored in a few basic philosophical, nay metaphysical, propositions about the mind and the universe, just as philosophy is being constantly pushed back to the same fundamentals. Evolutionary biologists grappling with the relation of individuals to the species are forced time and again to return to that often ridiculed philosopher's stone, the question of universals.[43] Fundamental-particle physicists boldly dissolving distinctions among electrons or among photons are still to achieve awareness of the question of universals—a question that gives a basic unity to philosophy as an intellectual experience across time.[44] The same experience also gives basic unity to ultimate scientific questions. From that experience and the position it represents there is no "progress" to be made.

Once this fact is learned about science it will not be possible without risk to dismiss natural theology with the remark that, unlike science, natural theology shows no progress. Being in possession of a basically valid perspective, natural theology is under no obligation to make progress, just as science itself cannot outgrow its metaphysical matrix. This is a fact, illustrated by the entire history of science, and with particular force by its twentieth-century development. That science brings such an unexpected witness to natural theology will only surprise those who tried for so long to ignore the elementary relation between rootstock and fruit. The enduring metaphysical matrix of science is only one of many facts of the history of science that can bring cheer to the student of natural theology. Unfamiliarity with these facts will generate dispiriting efforts to give respectability to theology by refashioning it according to models of science that bear but scant resemblance to the true reality of science.[45] Those facts the student of natural theology must especially know and be able to set forth, if natural theology is to be effective in an age that is not only an age of science but unfortunately an age that has almost lost itself in science—a fact that prompted no less a positivist than Brunetière to admit the bankruptcy of science as an ethical and social guide.[46] That bankruptcy came about because Comte's law of three states, which Brunetière was eager to extend even to the evolution of literature, permitted but a superficial grasp of the facts of scientific history. Once these facts, which it has been the aim of these lectures to recall and document, are firmly kept in mind, the history of science will fully implement the truth of Lord Bolingbroke's priceless phrase: "History is philosophy teaching by examples."[47]

The examples he had in mind were the facts of political history, on which he expected the skillful politician to hone his cleverness. Bolingbroke, the man of intrigue, was too busy to perceive that in his age, the age of Newton, politicians were already being advised that Newtonianism was the best form of government,[48] an uncanny anticipation of the present-day hiring of physicists by politicians. Since science too had, and still has, its politics, some facts of science can serve, unfortunately enough, as patterns for politics. The history of science, however, is rich in facts far more important than those useful for political scheming. Awareness of these facts will certainly be needed to secure a sane polity for mankind. But such facts of scientific history become examples only if they turn us into examples, examples of refusal to yield to fashions and pressures, academic and political, examples of unswerving loyalty to truths which launched science on its creative road and which also keep man on a way that stretches from his intellect and will across the universe to God.

Such examples, examples of commitment to a theistic outlook, we must become not only for our own sakes but also for the sake of future generations. Their connection with us will constitute history which can teach only with examples. The example we give must be such as to serve as inspiration for generations to come and for a very simple reason. They will have far more science than we can even dream of. But the more science they have, which they certainly will in a technological sense, the more inspiration they will need, so that the powerful forces at their disposal may find proper ends. Inspiration the younger generation certainly looks for now, and with an intensity that can be gauged by anyone mindful of the forces that animate the countless captives of varied forms of counterculture. Most of those captives would, if asked for an explanation of their drifting into the realm of the occult, the magical, the astrological, and the psychedelic, point a finger at science, and not without reason.

For the past three hundred years science, or rather the method of science, has been presented as bringing utopia to earth, but it was only during the last generation that utopia seemed to have been delivered to everyone's doorstep in the form of sophisticated gadgets that even the most sanguine scientists never dreamed of half a century before. Yet at the same time, science increased man's destructive capabilities in a measure which brought a sense of horror to every doorstep. The decade of bewilderment, which the 1960s became, was the product of a conflict between a heavenly promise and a hellish threat both coming largely from the very same source. Worshipers of science gladly swallowed J. Bronowski's claim that science was not responsible for Hiroshima,[49] and they applauded the words of the retiring Nobel laureate physicist, I. I. Rabi, that "science is the *only* valid underlying knowledge that gives guidance to the *whole* human adventure [and that] those who are not acquainted with science do not possess the *basic* human values that are necessary in our time"[50] (italics mine). Those who did not worship science, to say nothing of those who were ignorant of it, could only be made antagonistic by such sophomoric encomiums heaped upon it.

Just as science could not serve as a source of inspiration for mastering its promise and threat, prevailing trends in philosophy could not provide that inspiration either. Logical positivists only fostered the soullessness of scientistic reasoning, while existentialists encouraged flirtations with irrationality. Pragmatist pluralists, who tried to steer a middle course, failed more often than not to speak as frankly as did their idol, William James, who at least minced no words about the inner logic of pluralism. Its rejection of the proofs of the existence of God implied the adoption of a mixture of polytheism and pantheism heavily coated with scientific evolutionism.[51] Yet the mixture was in essence so antiscientific as to demand, as James admitted, the renunciation with Hegel of the principle of contradiction and identity.[52] Indeed James himself suggested, and with an eye on the rejection of the traditional proofs of the existence of God, that the word rational be given up altogether.[53]

The inspiration which fashionable psychology could provide was again no match for the tasks of this scientific age, which demanded a commitment to a sense of purpose in a larger measure than such demands have ever been made by any age. That sense of purpose was certainly no part of the picture of man painted by behaviorists. In that picture man's health was predicated on his being cured of preoccupations with a formulation of purpose which transcended him. Had behaviorists reflected with care on Dostoevsky's *The Brothers Karamazov* they might have realized the futility of their program. The book was about the chief question from which, so Dostoevsky himself stated, he had been suffering "consciously or unconsciously all life

329

long: the existence of God."[54] Neither was Dostoevsky the only one to suffer from that question, nor was he able to show how to free from it either one's conscience or what was subconscious in anyone.

If the inspiration in question is to be had only through coming to terms with the existence of God, some recourse to theologians would be most natural, but the most audible of them have lately offered only an inspiration that denied satisfaction to man's rationality about the Ultimate, or God. A case in point is Tillich's proclamation that "it is as atheistic to affirm the existence of God as it is to deny it." He received the well-deserved retort from an agnostic that if belief in the existence of God was the worst form of atheism, he was at least free of that.[55] Rationalists could only smile on seeing rationality handed over to them by theologians blandly declaring that the traditional proofs of the existence of God were "no more significant than the twitchings of a body already dead."[56] Worse even, "modish" theologians departed from transcendental perspectives to the extent of largely ignoring what had been clear to the nontheologian and pantheist Goethe: that "the real, the deepest, the sole theme of the world and of history, to which all other themes are subordinate, remains the conflict of belief and unbelief."[57] If many theologians had no longer any use for such a vision, it was only because they had already lost confidence in rationality as investigated by philosophy and thus failed to recognize the crudity in Kierkegaard's painting natural theology as a harlot who "sits by her window in powder and paint, courting the favour of philosophy and selling her charms."[58] As a result they had neither vision nor courage to remember the elementary truth stated in Gilson's question about the proofs of the existence of God: "Why, to put it bluntly, is the philosophical world divided into two groups: those who believe in Him, and those who, not believing in Him, judge such proofs to be impossible?"[59]

Of course, it would be equally mistaken to look at those proofs as being more than a skeleton of the flesh-and-blood reality which man's relation to God, the Ultimate, ought to be. A skeleton, as was aptly remarked about the proofs, "cannot walk, but you cannot walk without a skeleton."[60] Theism can fulfill its role as the most needed inspiration in this age of science only if it has both flesh and bones. Such a theism is a subject that can be taught only by a living example, living to the extent of being engaged in prayer. A theism without prayer and worship is mere reasoning, which can at most show its rationality and the inconsistency of its critics, who most of the time are unwilling anyway to carry their assumptions to their logical end. To show these ultimate implications demanded a painting of the intellectual landscape in stark colors, almost in black and white. When a culture is so grayish as ours, it will not perhaps appear a crime to make it clear that gray itself is a fusion of black and white, nay all too often their plain confusion. It is this confusion which is fomented by those reluctant to see the ultimate implications of their philosophies and histories of science. Whatever the results of that reluctance, they hardly include constructive inspiration. Such inspiration can only come from unreserved commitment to the very same inner logic which gives life to theism as well as to science. It is our chief cultural task to transmit to the upcoming generation that inspiration which will be theirs in the measure in which they, inspired we hope by our example, will keep in mind about scientific history a fundamental facet: the tie binding the road of science to the ways to God.

NOTES

CHAPTER ONE

1. *Earnest Enquirers after Truth: A Gifford Anthology: Excerpts from Gifford Lectures, 1888–1968,* selected by B. E. Jones (London: George Allen & Unwin, 1970), p. [7].

2. Ibid., p. 12. The occasion was a lecture given by Lord Gifford to the Edinburgh Y.M.C.A. in 1878. His remark reflects both the infatuation of contemporary physicists with whirling vortices in the ether and the perspicacity of an outside observer. It was only a decade or so later that some perceptive physicists began to have doubts, a telling example of which can be found in Fitzgerald's letter of Feb. 4, 1889, to Heaviside: "I am afraid nothing except the complete overthrow of his whole notion of how the functions of the ether are produced will cure Sir W. T. [Lord Kelvin]." See E. Whittaker, *A History of the Theories of Aether and Electricity* (London: T. Nelson and Sons, 1951), 1:148, and chapter 9 ("Models of the Aether," pp. 279–303).

3. In his Address to the Mathematical and Physical Section of the British Association (1870); *The Scientific Papers of James Clerk Maxwell,* ed. W. D. Niven (Cambridge: University Press, 1890), 2:216.

4. The phrasing consisted in giving the word "Science" as a resounding answer to a long list of questions concerned with all basic problems of man. It provided the grand conclusion of Spencer's lecture "What Knowledge Is of Most Worth?" delivered at the Royal Institution of Great Britain and published in the *Westminster Review* 72 (1859): 1–41. In pleading for a general education based overwhelmingly on the study of sciences Spencer anticipated the position taken by Huxley against Matthew Arnold on the respective merits of scientific and humanistic education. For details, see my essay "A Hundred Years of Two Cultures," *University of Windsor Review* 11 (1975): 55–79.

5. For further details, see chapter 10.

6. Whewell's sustained insistence that the key to scientific progress is the matching of observations with proper and specific ideas showed his awareness of the need for a middle road between rationalism and empiricism, but he offered no clue to the epistemology underlying it. For him the rationalist and empiricist positions (he identified the former with Kant and the German idealists but carefully avoided identifying the latter with Bacon) were equally inadequate to deal with the process of understanding, which he graphically described as a "drama in which *Things* are the *Dramatis Personae* and the *Idea* which governs the system is the *Plot* of the drama." For the Kantians the *things* could be only "mute personages," whereas for the empiricists the drama could have no *plot*. See *On the Philosophy of Discovery: Chapters Historical and Critical* (London: John W. Parker and Son, 1860), pp. 312–13.

7. While J. Agassi made a valuable contribution in this respect in his *Towards an Historiography of Science* (The Hague: Mouton, 1963), his Popperian rejection of metaphysics prevented him from spotting the epistemological root of the quandary in which the historiography of science now finds itself.

8. "The Genesis of Science," in H. Spencer, *Recent Discussions in Science, Philosophy and Morals* (New York: D. Appleton, 1871), pp. 155–234. Spencer's chief offense against scholarship did not consist in his taking up the grave question of the genesis of science, though he was no historian of science. He

erred chiefly by promising to give a historical explanation while in the same breath reducing history to psychology. Even if he had used a psychology far better than his own brand, within such an approach history could have no questions, but only answers, a circumstance that vitiated all of Spencer's reflections on ancient science as well as on the revival of scientific spirit, which he sharply identified with Galileo. It is that sudden revival, needless to say, of which genuine historians are invariably suspicious. Part of Spencer's long article was a criticism of the evolutionary classification of sciences given by Hegel and Comte. The criticism could not be based on the fact that both Hegel and Comte knew history before consulting it, because Spencer himself was guilty of the same pretension.

9. Published in 1974 in Edinburgh (Scottish Academic Press) and in New York (Science History Publications). For full title, see note 74.

10. Published in 1777 in London (M. Elmesly) and in Paris (De Bure l'aîné). The following year a German translation was printed in Leipzig (Weygand).

11. The process has been amply aired and analyzed in such classics as C. L. Becker, *The Heavenly City of the Eighteenth-Century Philosophers* (New Haven: Yale University Press, 1932), and R. R. Palmer, *Catholics and Unbelievers in Eighteenth Century France* (Princeton: Princeton University Press, 1939). On the crowding of the supporters of the Enlightenment into Masonic Lodges devoted to the celebration of Rosicrucian mysticism, see E. B. Smith, "Jean-Sylvain Bailly: Astronomer, Mystic, Revolutionary, 1736–1793," *Transactions of the American Philosophical Society* 44, pt. 4 (1954): 465–67.

12. In his *Esquisse d'un tableau historique des progrès de l'esprit humain* (1795); see the English translation by J. Barraclough, *Sketch for a Historical Picture of the Progress of the Human Mind* (New York: Noonday Press, 1955), p. 95. The passage, a whole paragraph, is not from the only surviving manuscript, but its authenticity is not in serious doubt. It is an elaboration on the preceding paragraph in which Condorcet hails scholastic sensitivity to "the most fugitive shades of meaning" as the beginning of our philosophical analysis but also decries it, not without inconsistency, as the cause which retarded the progress of natural sciences in the schools. The naïveté of Condorcet's views on the Middle Ages has been often noted.

13. As he is identified in the title page of his work originally published in 1696 (Paris: Jean Anisson). The work consists of fourteen letters, with the ninth letter opening the second volume as Lettre I.

14. Ibid., 2:134–36. The context is the letter entitled "De la religion ancienne et moderne des Chinois." The claim touched off a new and stormy phase of the rites controversy, the broader ideological background of which is well portrayed, though with no reference to the respective fortunes of science in Europe and in China, in V. Pinot, *La Chine et la formation de l'esprit philosophique en France (1640–1740)* (Paris: Librairie orientaliste Paul Geuthner, 1932).

15. Ibid., 1:442–43. The passage is from Lettre VIII, which deals with the special characteristics of the Chinese mind.

16. Ibid., 1:383.

17. *Lettres édifiantes et curieuses écrites des missions étrangères par quelques missionnaires de la Compagnie de Jésus*, 34 vols. (Paris: Nicolas le Clerc, etc., 1702–76). Publication started under the editorship of P. Charles Le Gobien. For Parrenin's letter, see vol. 21, pp. 77–186.

18. Ibid., p. 86.

19. Ibid., pp. 108 and 113.

20. Ibid., p. 109.

21. Ibid., p. 120.

22. *Lettres édifiantes,* 24 (1739): 1–91; for quotation see pp. 25–26.

23. *Lettres édifiantes,* 26 (1743): 1–85.

24. So agile in Parrenin's case as to make him perceive the long-range significance of Russian penetration into areas lying immediately north of China. Parrenin also conjured up the prospect of Russian soldiers standing one day on the banks of the Rhine (ibid., pp. 26–27 and 81–82).

25. In the preface of his *Novissima sinica historiam nostri temporis illustratura* ... [fol. 8r]. The work did not indicate its having been printed by Förster in Hanover in 1697 and had only the letters G. G. L. for the identification of its author. Actually, Leibniz wrote only the preface to six Jesuit reports from China. Leibniz found it providential that the two extremes of the Eurasian continent were most advanced in culture, because this seemed to assure an effective impact on the less advanced central parts. He felt that China and Europe were at that time on the same level with respect to technical skill, an evaluation contradicted in part by his admission that the Chinese had at best that "empirical knowledge of geometry which was mastered at times even by our workmen" [fol. 3r].

26. The subtitle of this work published in London in 1730 speaks for itself: "or, The Gospel, a Republication of the Religion of Nature." For quotation see p. 342. The last chapter in Tindal's work (pp. 353–432) is a criticism of S. Clarke's claim made in his *Discourse concerning the Unchangeable Obligations of Natural Religion and the Truth and Certainty of the Christian Religion* (1706) that revelation demands something very different from what nature dictates. Tindal's dissolving the perplexity of revelation into the light of nature found its rebuttal in *The Analogy of Religion, Natural and Revealed, to the Constitution and Course of Nature* (1736) of J. Butler, who insisted that nature displayed as much obscurity as did revelation. The potentially self-defeating aspect of Butler's position was unfolded by Hume, who made nature appear so perplexing as to invalidate any inference from nature to nature's God.

27. His article "Chinois (Philosophie des)," in the *Encyclopédie, ou Dictionnaire raisonné des sciences, des arts et des métiers* 3 (1753): 341–48, comes to conclusion with the declaration: "In sum, they [the Chinese] do not have the genius of invention which shines today in Europe; had they had among them superior intellects, their light would have vanquished the obstacles by the sheer impossibility of remaining locked up in them; ... since the sciences and the arts demand a rather restless activity, a curiosity that never ceases searching, a sort of inability to be satisfied, we are better prepared, and therefore it is not surprising that although the Chinese are more ancient, we have so far surpassed them." Diderot, who could not praise highly enough the expertise of Jesuit missionaries in the mechanical arts, even decried the Chinese skill of making porcelain as being tasteless (p. 347). He ascribed Chinese social stability to laziness in thinking, to which he also traced the obscurities of Chinese religion, which, precisely because of their similarities with Spinoza's pantheism, were declared by Diderot to be beyond the pale of clarification (p. 346).

28. *Essai sur les moeurs,* in *Oeuvres complètes de Voltaire* (Paris: Garnier Frères, 1877–83), 11:176 and 186–88. See also note 10 in chapter 20.

29. See the edition quoted above, in which the *Essai sur les moeurs* and its sequels, *Le siècle de Louis XIV* and *Précis du siècle de Louis XV,* comprise about three thousand pages. Even worse, a goodly part of those three pages is devoted to Hevelius's contributions to astronomy!

30. *Lettres de M. de Mairan au R. P. Parrenin, missionnaire de la Compagnie de Jésus à Pekin: Contenant divers questions sur la Chine* (Paris: chez Desaint & Saillant, 1759), p. 42. On the previous, private circulation of these letters, see p.

iii. The three letters (pp. 1–153) are followed by a dissertation on ancient Chinese-Egyptian contacts.

31. Ibid., p.76.

32. Ibid., p. 77. De Mairan also contrasted the situation in Europe, where the growth of astronomical knowledge had eliminated in a hundred years the custom of hiding in caves during eclipses, with the situation still prevailing in China, where "an eclipse is what the approach of enemy is to an army of poltroons. I say that all this, the superstitiousness of the country, the meager talents of its inhabitants for calculus and speculations, and the hardheadedness, well- or ill-founded, to add nothing new to the knowledge of ancestors, forms a picture which perfectly characterizes the nation" (p. 152).

33. The first volume carried the story to the age of Ptolemy, the second, published in 1779, to the year 1730, the third, published in 1785, to the year 1782. In 1787 Bailly published a special volume on ancient Hindu and oriental astronomy. The merits of Bailly's work can best be seen when compared with the diligent but almost wholly unspeculative listing of data and titles in J. F. Weidler's *Historia astronomiae sive de ortu et progressu astronomiae liber singularis* (Wittenberg: sumtibus Gottlieb Heinrici Schwartzii, 1741).

34. *Histoire de l'astronomie ancienne depuis son origine jusqu'à l'établissement de l'École d'Alexandrie* (Paris: chez les Frères Debure, 1775), p. iii.

35. Ibid., p. vi.

36. Ibid., p. xxii. Here Bailly referred to W. Derham's *Astro-theology* (1714) as an illustration of the fact that astronomy, when properly studied, demonstrates the existence of God.

37. Ibid., p. 18.

38. Ibid.

39. Ibid., p. 19.

40. Ibid., p. 105.

41. In a letter of March 25, 1776; see *Voltaire's Correspondence*, ed. Theodore Besterman (Geneva: Institut et Musée de Voltaire, 1953–65), 94:47.

42. See his exchange of letters with Bailly (ibid., 92:170–71; 93:34–35, 95–98; 96:86–87).

43. *Histoire de l'astronomie ancienne depuis son origine*, pp. 61–128.

44. Ibid., p. 103.

45. Obsession with favorable climate placed Bailly in an uncomfortably narrow position in more than one sense. In pondering the problem of why the priest-astronomers of ancient Thebes failed to anticipate Ptolemy's achievements, he argued that, unlike Alexandria, Thebes was close to the "torrid zone" and therefore could not serve as the cradle for speculative thinking. See *Histoire de l'astronomie moderne depuis la fondation de l'École d'Alexandrie jusqu' à l'époque de MDCCXXX* (Paris: chez les Frères de Bure, 1779), 1:7.

46. In Montesquieu's *Esprit des lois* science is merely mentioned as a factor subversive to tyrannical regimes. The slight impression made by Western science on the visitors from Persia in Montesquieu's *Lettres persannes* suggests neither familiarity with nor enthusiasm for science on his part.

47. *Lettres sur l'origine des sciences*, pp. 218–19.

48. In its original form it was book 5 of Laplace's *Exposition du système du monde*, which Laplace saw through five editions between 1796 and 1824. The first separate publication occurred in 1821.

49. Laplace did not aim at presenting the history of what had happened but of what might have happened had the ancients possessed the wisdom of hindsight given him by his attainments in celestial mechanics. In other words, Laplace tried to explain why the actual course of scientific history differed from

a hypothetical, ideal course. This was particularly evident in Laplace's discussion of Kepler's work, which fully revealed the Cartesian strain in Laplace, who as a professed Baconian knew all too well that according to Bacon the two courses should coincide.

50. *Exposition du système du monde*, 5th ed. (Paris: Bachelier, 1824), p. 323.

51. W. Whewell, *History of the Inductive Sciences*, 3d ed. (London: John W. Parker, 1857), 1:54–66.

52. Ibid., pp. 344–46.

53. See especially section 5, "Three Aspects of the Fundamental Unity of Life," in the Introductory Chapter of *Introduction to the History of Sciences* (Baltimore: William and Wilkins, 1927–48), 1:29–32. See also his *The Study of the History of Science* (Cambridge: Harvard University Press, 1936), p. 5. This booklet contains the enlarged text of the lecture that inaugurated, on October 4, 1935, the study of the history of science at Harvard University.

54. See the second of his three Colver Lectures delivered in 1930 at Brown University and published under the title, *The History of Science and the New Humanism* (Bloomington: Indiana University Press, 1962), p. 76. His sole explanation of the metaphor consisted in pointing out the failure of the Greeks to match the level of their science with moral strength and political wisdom.

55. *The Study of the History of Science*, p. 5.

56. In his *Horus: A Guide to the History of Science* (Waltham, Mass.: Chronica botanica Co., 1952) Sarton deplored the persistence of "a perverse desire to transcend experience. Even the greatest men of science are not immune from that weakness" (p. 7).

57. *The History of Science and the New Humanism*, pp. 97–98. While Sarton recognized the importance for the future of science of the eventual fusion of Greek philosophy and Hebrew monotheism, he credited with that fusion the Muslim and not the Christian medievals. He could not therefore say much of the Averroist claim of double truth which set the tone of thought of most Muslim philosphers interested in science. In Sarton's view Christianity merely carried out, and in an unenlightened way at that, the injunction of Christ concerning charity and otherworldliness (ibid., pp. 78 and 83). It should be easy to guess where Christian thinkers were placed in Sarton's simplistic categorization of intellectual history, about which L. Pearce Williams pointedly noted, "Sarton's ... view of history is almost painfully naive. The *dramatis personae* are divided into 'good guys' and 'bad guys' and customs into 'good practices' ... and ... 'bad practices,'" in his review of the second volume of Sarton's *A History of Science* in *British Journal for the Philosophy of Science* 11 (1960): 160.

58. *The History of Science and the New Humanism*, p. 74. This claim of his is certainly in conflict with his statement, "I do not claim to be a mediaevalist," in his *Introduction to the History of Science*, 1:14.

59. He did so less than a year after the publication, in 1913, of that first volume, in the June 1914 issue of *Isis*, where he concluded: "All historians of science await impatiently the publication of the remaining volumes" (p. 204). Although four more volumes were published by 1917, they were conspicuously absent from among the many reviews with which Sarton filled the pages of *Isis* after it resumed publication in September 1919. Duhem's magisterial work was found worth reviewing in *Isis* only when its last five volumes were published in the 1950s.

60. A quick look at the carefully compiled name-index in Sarton's *Introduction to the History of Science* is eye-opening. Although the various parts of the first five volumes of Duhem's *Système du monde*, to say nothing of his other historical studies, should have deserved continual mention, Duhem is referred to only

five times. Many lesser historians of science receive several times as many mentions, a discrepancy that could hardly be unintentional.

61. *Le Système du monde*, 1:65–85. A historian of science, like Sarton, who claimed that Roman Christians hardly understood the Hebrew spirit culminating in monotheism (*The History of Science and the New Humanism*, p. 78) and who was unable to see in the Roman martyrs' refusal to sacrifice to the idols a supreme form of understanding it, could but be resentful on reading Duhem's ringing declaration: "To the construction of this sytem [of the divinity of the heavens revolving in units measured by the Great Year] all the disciples of Greek philosophy, Peripatetics, Stoics, Neoplatonists, have contributed; to this system Abu-Mashar offers the homage of the Arabs; this system has been adopted by the most illustrious rabbis from Philo of Alexandria to Maimonides. To condemn it as a monstruous superstition and to throw it overboard Christianity had to come" (*Le Système du monde*, 2:390). Clearly, this could not be the message which Sarton was eagerly awaiting in the "remaining volumes" of Duhem's magisterial work.

62. *Science and the Modern World* (New York: Macmillan, 1926), p. 10.

63. In his *The Aim and Structure of Physical Theory*, trans. P. P. Wiener (New York: Atheneum, 1962), his programmatic interpretation of the philosophy and history of science, Duhem spoke of the gradual convergence of scientific theories toward an ideal form of thermodynamics in which he saw the definitive scientific explanation of the universe (p. 302). This advocacy of convergence widely separated him from the empiricist "relativism" of Mach and his followers. Because of his firm conviction in that convergence Duhem would not, contrary to M. B. Hesse's claim, "hasten to applaud" the conclusion "as confirming his view that ... scientific knowledge is superficial and transient compared to the revealed truths of a theological metaphysics" ("Duhem, Quine and a New Empiricism," in *Challenges to Empiricism*, ed. H. Morick [Belmont, Cal.: Wadsworth Publishing Company, 1972], p. 227). Precisely because of his belief in the gradual convergence of natural knowledge toward *truth*, Duhem would in no circumstances have seen it in radical isolation from the truths of metaphysics and revelation. He would have been baffled by "revealed truths of a theological metaphysics."

64. "Some Historical Assumptions of the History of Science," in A. C. Crombie, ed., *Scientific Change* (New York: Basic Books, 1963), p. 809.

65. London: George Allen and Unwin, 1922, p. 193. The statement was followed by the remark that in China "the spread of scientific knowledge encounters no such obstacles as the Church put in its way in Europe." Just as Jewish and Christian faith was for Russell a "fanatic belief" (p. 186), Chinese mentality had for him only favorable features. He prophesied that given a stable government China would within thirty years produce "remarkable work in science," nay they "might outstrip us because they come with fresh zest and with all the ardour of a renaissance" (p. 193). This was as pleasing a rhetoric as it was bad historiography—and hardly a good prophecy.

66. In Needham's own words: "It was not that there was no order in Nature for the Chinese, but rather that it was not an order ordained by a rational being, and hence there was no conviction that rational personal beings would be able to spell out in their lesser earthly languages the divine code of laws which he had decreed aforetime" (2:581). The heart of the phrase is "conviction." In various synonyms, such as faith, confidence, trust, and so forth, it appears in the classic documents that mark the rise of science from Copernicus to Newton and in the creative recasting of its foundations in the hands of Planck and Einstein. See on this my articles, "The Role of Faith in Physics," *Zygon* 2 (1967):

187–202, and "Theological Aspects of Creative Science," in *Creation Christ and Culture: Essays in Honour of T. F. Torrance* (Edinburgh: T. & T. Clark, 1976), pp. 149–66.

67. R. S. Cohen, "The Problem of 19 (*k*)" *Journal of Chinese Philosophy* 1 (1973): 117. In the second volume of Needham's *Science and Civilization in China* the problem in question is discussed in section 19(*k*).

68. London: Oxford University Press, 1958, p. 81.

69. New York: Day, 1946, p. 520.

70. Ibid., p. 211.

71. "Progress of Science and the Experimental Method," in *Proceedings of the Symposium on the History of Sciences in India held at Calcutta on August 4 and 5, 1961*, in *Bulletin of the National Institute of Sciences in India No. 21* (New Delhi: National Institute of Sciences in India, 1963), pp. 31–35.

72. My chief reason for referring to Majumdar's article, "Scientific Spirit in Ancient India," originally published in *Journal of World History* 2 (1962): 265–73, is that it has received wide publicity by being reprinted in *The Evolution of Science: Readings from the History of Mankind*, edited for the International Commission for a History of the Scientific and Cultural Development of Mankind by G. S. Métraux and F. Crouzet (New York: New American Library, 1963), pp. 77–87.

73. Ibid., p. 80.

74. For a documentation and discussion of this process, see chapter 1, "The Treadmill of Yugas," in my *Science and Creation: From Eternal Cycles to an Oscillating Universe* (Edinburgh: Scottish Academic Press, 1974).

75. *The Thirteen Principal Upanishads*, translated from the Sanskrit by R. E. Hume, 2d rev. ed. (London: Oxford University Press, 1934), p. 414.

76. For a documentation and discussion of this and of the remaining statements in this paragraph, see the first eight chapters in my *Science and Creation*.

77. *King Lear*, act 3, scene 4.

Chapter Two

1. The classic account is still Pierre Duhem's monograph written in 1908 and available since 1969 in English translation: *To Save the Phenomena: An Essay on the Idea of Physical Theory from Plato to Galileo*, translated by Edmund Dolan and Chaninah Maschler, with an Introduction by Stanley L. Jaki (Chicago: University of Chicago Press, 1969). Duhem's monograph is not quoted in J. Mittelstrass's dissertation, *Die Rettung der Phänomene: Ursprung und Geschichte eines antiken Forschungsprinzips* (Berlin: Walter de Gruyter, 1962), although it does not carry the topic much beyond the chronological range covered by Duhem.

2. This apparent contradiction is pointedly noted in R. K. Hack, *God in Greek Philosophy* (Princeton University Press, 1931), p. 42, and in E. Gilson, *God and Philosophy* (New Haven: Yale University Press, 1941), pp. 1–5.

3. For a very informative systematization and interpretation of Anaxagoras's dicta that survived in direct and indirect form in classical literature, see D. E. Gershenson and D. A. Greenberg, *Anaxagoras and the Birth of Physics* (New York: Blaisdell Publishing Company, 1964).

4. See sections 96–104 in *The Collected Dialogues of Plato including the Letters*, edited by E. Hamilton and H. Cairns (New York: Pantheon Books, 1966), pp. 84–96.

5. *Symposium* 215d–216b, in *The Collected Dialogues of Plato*, p. 567.

6. *Phaedo*, see especially sections 98a and 105e (ibid, pp. 79 and 87).

7. *Timaeus* 28c (ibid., p. 1162). In fact, Plato maintains that the world remembers but briefly "its maker and its father." In a most explicit endorsement

of the idea of the Great Year (*Statesman* 272e–273e, ibid., pp. 1038–39) Plato subjects man's comprehension of God to the pessimistic logic of eternal recurrence in which each cosmic cycle is largely dominated by increasing dissolution. For much of each Great Year neither man nor the world remembers God's instructions because the world is destined by and large to "travel on without God." Needless to say, a world not governed by its divine pilot is a largely irrational world which discourages natural theology and science by the same logic.

8. *On the Heavens* 286a–b. The derivation is predicated on the clearly pantheistic claim that the world must of necessity have that activity of a god which is immortality and which can only be expressed in continuous circular motion.

9. *On the Heavens* 274a. Aristotle in fact specifies that "if the half weight covers the distance in [time] x, the whole weight will cover it in [time] $x/2$." While such rendering of the original in *Aristotle: On the Heavens*, with an English translation by W. K. G. Guthrie (Cambridge: Harvard University Press, 1960), pp. 49–51, smacks of modernity, it does full justice to Aristotle's reasoning. He voiced it in a less "quantitative" manner on several occasions in clear evidence of the inner connection of this very faulty law of free fall with his basic assumptions about "natural" motion. See *On the Heavens* 277b, 294a, 304b, 308b, 309b and 311a. The recognition that the rate of fall is independent of the amount of the falling mass antedates Galileo, but he was the first to give an exact formulation of it.

10. Unrevisable within the system itself. The revision, when achieved by Galileo and Newton, meant the abandonment of the entirety of Aristotle's physics. For a detailed discussion of this, see my *The Relevance of Physics* (University of Chicago Press, 1966), pp. 30–33.

11. *Meteorologica* 349a. Aristotle went as far as to brand as absurdity the view that wind is air in motion (ibid., 360a).

12. *Meteorologica* 363b.

13. *Meteorologica* 344a.

14. *On the Heavens* 289a. Since one glaring error readily breeds another, it should not seem surprising that Aristotle has soon to declare that the motion of the sun, though the source of great friction in the air, is not the cause of any noise (290b). A curious friction indeed.

15. *Meteorologica* 346a.

16. Its analysis is given in chapter 1 of my *The Milky Way: An Elusive Road for Science* (New York: Science History Publications, 1972). During the medieval and Renaissance centuries Aristotle's blindness in connection with the Milky Way was often noted (see chapters 2 and 3).

17. References are to *Aristotle's Metaphysics*, translated by Richard Hope (New York: Columbia University Press, 1952).

18. Ibid., p. 256 (1071b).

19. Ibid.

20. Ibid., p. 257 (1071b).

21. Ibid., p. 260 (1072b).

22. Ibid., p. 261 (1073a).

23. Ibid., p. 265 (1074a). The ultimate result is the preempting of meaning of the Socratic program to "save the purpose" by rendering meaningless the sense of wonderment which is the very beginning of Aristotle's *Metaphysics*. Once purpose and wonderment become mere words, discourse about God also becomes void of any sense of excitement. The dispassionate discourse of Aristotle about God is a matching counterpart of his self-assured reasoning in matters scientific where he professes to know practically everything. On the dis-

passionate tone of Aristotle's natural theology, see A. N. Whitehead, *Science and the Modern World* (New York: Macmillan, 1926), p. 249.

24. *Aristotle's Metaphysics*, p. 265 (1074b).

25. Ibid., p. 267 (1075a).

26. On the one hand he holds that human action is seen to follow necessarily once its appropriate premises are apprehended. On the other hand he also wants to maintain that virtue and vice are in man's power. For further details, see W. D. Ross, *Aristotle*, 5th rev. ed. (London: Methuen, 1949), pp. 197–201.

27. *Phaedo* 118, in *The Collected Dialogues of Plato*, p. 98.

28. *Politics* 1329b. For further details, see my *Science and Creation: From Eternal Cycles to an Oscillating Universe* (Edinburgh: Scottish Academic Press, 1974), pp. 113–14.

29. *Metaphysics* 1074b.

30. Such is the broader perspective of his description of error as "a state of mind more natural to animals than the truth, and in which the mind spends the greater part of its time" (*De anima* 427b).

31. See *Theophrastus: Metaphysics*, translated by W. D. Ross and F. H. Fobes (Oxford: Clarendon Press, 1929), p. 31.

32. Or as Whitehead conjured up the ultimate fate of a Hellenistic civilization spared of barbaric invasions and of the rise of monotheism: "For two thousand years the Greek art-forms lifelessly repeated: The Greek schools of philosophy, Stoic, Epicurean, Aristotelian, Neo-Platonic, arguing with barren formulae: Conventional histories: A stabilized Government with the sanctity of ancient ceremony, supported by habitual pieties: Literature without depth: Science elaborating details by deductions from unquestioned premises: Delicacies of feeling without robustness of adventure" (*Adventures of Ideas* [New York: Macmillan, 1933], p. 331).

33. The metaphysical question derives not only from the "partless" characteristic of units of matter having some extension, but also from the limiting of those units to within a specific magnitude. On Democritus, see G. S. Kirk and J. E. Raven, *The Presocratic Philosophers* (Cambridge University Press, 1962), p. 409; on Epicurus, see his Letter to Herodotus 51, in *Epicurus: The Extant Remains*, with short critical apparatus, translation and notes by C. Bailey (Oxford: Clarendon Press, 1926), pp. 23–25; on Lucretius, see *De rerum natura* 1:625, Latin text with English translation by W. H. D. Rouse (Cambridge: Harvard University Press, 1937), p. 47.

34. Letter to Herodotus 51, in *Epicurus: The Extant Remains*, p. 29.

35. Letter to Pythocles 91, ibid., p. 61; *De rerum natura*, 5:564–65 (Rouse, pp. 379–81).

36. Letter to Pythocles 97 and 113 (Bailey, pp. 65 and 79).

37. Letter to Herodotus 76 (p. 49).

38. Letter to Herodotus 78 (p. 51).

39. Letter to Pythocles 88 (p. 59).

40. Letter to Pythocles 92 (pp. 61–63).

41. Letter to Menoeceus 134 (p. 91).

42. "The Discourses of Epictetus," bk. 1, chap. 16, "On Providence," in *The Stoic and Epicurean Philosophers: The Complete Extant Writings of Epicurus, Epictetus, Lucretius, Marcus Aurelius*, edited with an introduction by Whitney J. Oates (New York: Random House, 1940), p. 253.

43. Ibid.

44. Ibid., chap. 14, "That God Beholds All Men," pp. 250–51.

45. Ibid., chap. 16, "On Providence," p. 253.

46. As reported by Sextus Empiricus in his "Against the Physicists" (1:140–

41); see *Sextus Empiricus*, with an English translation by the Rev. R. G. Bury (London: W. Heinemann, 1933–49), 3:75–77.

47. *The Stoic and Epicurean Philosophers*, pp. 591–92.

48. See the discussion by S. Sambursky, *The Physical World of the Greeks*, translated from the Hebrew by Merton Dagut (London: Routledge and Kegan Paul, 1956), pp. 154–55.

49. Ibid., p. 142.

50. Ibid., p. 202. For further texts evidencing the widespread belief in individual or at least in generic returns during classical antiquity, see chapters 5 and 7 in my *Science and Creation*.

51. In combating the doctrine of eternal returns Origen made much of this aspect of Stoic philosophy. See my *Science and Creation*, pp. 172–75.

52. References will be to *Cicero in Twenty-Eight Volumes: 19, De natura deorum; Academica*, with an English translation by H. Rackham (Cambridge: Harvard University Press, 1933).

53. As reported by Saint Augustine in his *De civitate Dei* (bk. 6, chap. 5), where he quotes Varro's description of natural theology or the discussion of questions of the following type: "Who the gods are, where they are, of what kind and of what character they are; whether they came into being at a certain time, or have always existed; whether they derive their being from fire (the belief of Heraclitus) or from numbers (as Pythagoras thought) or from atoms (as Epicurus alleges). And there are other like questions all of which men's ears can more readily tolerate within the walls of a lecture-room than in the market-place outside" (Augustine, *Concerning the City of God against the Pagans*, a new translation by H. Bettenson with an Introduction by D. Knowles [Harmondsworth: Penguin Books, 1972], pp. 234–35). For Augustine the exclusion by Varro of natural theology from public discourse implies his admission that natural theology as described by him is really not natural, that is, truthful.

54. *De natura deorum* 3:9 (p. 307).

55. Ibid., 3:10 (p. 311).

56. Ibid. (p. 310).

57. Ibid. 3:11 (pp. 311–13).

58. The reference is to an "orrery recently constructed by our friend Posidonius, which at each revolution reproduces the same motions of the sun, the moon and the five planets that take place in the heavens every twenty-four hours" (ibid., 2:34 [pp. 207–9]). Paley was anticipated in the next remark in which it is asked: Were such a machine to be transported to the barbarous regions of Britain or Scythia, "would any single native doubt that this orrery was the work of a rational being?" Somewhat later (2:37; [p. 217]) in an even clearer reference to clockwork mechanisms it is stated: "When we see something moved by machinery, like an orrery or clock or many other such things, we do not doubt that these contrivances are the work of reason." The high level of skill achieved in classical antiquity in the construction of such mechanisms is best illustrated in D. J. de Solla Price, *Gears from the Greeks: The Antikythera Mechanism, a Calendar Computer from ca. 80 B.C.* (Philadelphia: American Philosophical Society, 1974). See also A. G. Drachmann, *The Mechanical Technology of Greek and Roman Antiquity* (Copenhagen: Munksgaard, 1963).

59. Ibid., 3:11 (p. 313).

60. Ibid., 1:36 (pp. 97–99).

61. In his "Against the Physicists" (1:57–125); see *Sextus Empiricus*, 3:35–67.

62. The work survived only in a free rendering by Sextus Empiricus.

63. *Cicero: De oratore*, with an English translation by E. W. Sutton, completed with an Introduction by H. Rackham (Cambridge: Harvard University Press, 1942), 1:9. Cicero also praised the Romans for having restricted the cultivation

of geometry and mathematics "to the practical purposes of measuring and reckoning." See *Cicero: Tusculan Disputations*, with an English translation by J. E. King (Cambridge: Harvard University Press, 1951), p. 7.

64. Of these three views on planets the first is in the *Almagest*, the second in the *Planetary Hypotheses*, the third in the *Tetrabiblos*.

65. *Polybius: The Histories*, with an English translation by W. R. Paton (London: Heinemann, 1923), 3:275–77. In his defeatist outlook Polybius could hardly perceive either the novelty of the whole oikoumenē being under a unified rule, or some possibly lasting benefits, such as the universal impact of Roman law, that might derive from such a new situation.

66. G. Murray, *Four Stages of Greek Religion* (New York: Columbia University Press, 1912), p. 103. Indeed, Murray implicated Christianity in a way which defies both chronology and comparative religion. Christians constituted hardly one-fifth of the population of the Roman Empire as late as the rise of Constantine and were a negligible group at the end of the first century A.D., or four hundred years after the sudden "failure of nerve" had hit the Greeks. The unqualified juxtaposition by Murray of Gnostics, Mithras worshipers, Gospels, Apocalypse, Julian, Plotinus, Gregory, and Jerome deserves no comment.

67. *A History of Greek Mathematics* (Oxford: Clarendon Press, 1921), 1:9.

68. *The Study of the History of Science* (Cambridge: Harvard University Press, 1936), pp. 3–4.

69. "It was the age immediately before that of Constantine and the triumph of Christianity. It has been said with some justification that the major revolution which followed was fatal to science. It is certain that from that time forward mankind was offered a very different ideal from that which Plato and Aristotle had set forth so brilliantly, namely, the life of the man of learning as the contemplation of theory for its own sake. But ... the accusation against Christianity is without foundation. Just as the barbarians experienced no difficulty in bringing about the ruin of Greco-Roman society, which had already collapsed from within, Christianity had only to liquidate the affairs of the bankrupt official philosophy after the century of the Antonines. The Platonic ideal had long since given way to that of the Stoics, which was fundamentally utilitarian and thus opposed to science, in spite of the outward appearances of its lofty moral system" (P. Tannery, *La géométrie grecque* [Paris: Gauthier-Villars, 1887], pp. 10–11).

70. J. Burnet's dictum is best known from his Preface to the third edition of his *Early Greek Philosophy* (London: Adam and Charles Black, 1920), where he remarks that he had already stated this "elsewhere." Most of those who, like E. Schrödinger (*Nature and the Greeks* [Cambridge University Press, 1954], p. 18), quote with approval Burnet's catchy phrase, do not weigh the fact that the Greeks failed in science and so did some people, like the Romans and the Arabs, who came under the influence of the Greeks. In fact, Burnet himself, who saw the Greeks' progress in philosophy as a function of their progress in science (*Greek Philosophy, part I: Thales to Plato* [London: Macmillan, 1914], p. 2), failed to consider this problem.

71. And invariably unconvincing. The "monotheist Xenophanes," as referred to without any qualification by K. R. Popper (*Conjectures and Refutations* [New York: Harper and Row, 1968], p. 145) is a conjecture that does not merit refutation. One wonders, however, why Popper does not view with such benevolence the whole medieval philosophic tradition steeped in genuine monotheism.

72. G. Boas, *Rationalism in Greek Philosophy* (Baltimore: Johns Hopkins Press, 1961), p. 479.

Chapter Three

1. Scoffing at the intellectualism of medieval scholasticism usually goes hand in hand with insensitivity to the religious ideals proclaimed in the rules of Saint Dominic and Saint Francis. Yet, there ought to be food for thought in the fact that intense evangelical fervor was a basic and undisputed characteristic of the foremost scholastics, Albert, Aquinas, Bonaventure, and Scotus. If scholasticism as an intellectual movement spread like wildfire, it was partly because it was carried by the contagiousness of an evangelical spirit of which it could be a natural component. It is in such a perspective that one should look at scholastic intellectualism, which had become a pervasive cultural matrix, a fact grudgingly acknowledged even by some notable antagonists and critics of Christianity in general and scholastic philosophy in particular. Condorcet's statement mentioned in chapter 1 (see n. 12 there) has been the pattern of many similar ones since.

2. The almost twenty printings since 1941 of E. Gilson's *God and Philosophy* (New Haven: Yale University Press) will be enough justification for omitting references to other works that emphasized the uniqueness of the conceptual content of "Yahweh" as a name for the ultimate in intelligibility and being and its impact on the history of philosophy and natural theology.

3. Surely in this Pauline expression (logikē latreia, Rom. 12:1) "logical," or "rational," means far more than what logical positivists have it mean today; it indeed implies full use of all the discernment reason is capable of.

4. These references are usually brief, but not always, as, for instance, in some of the Psalms on the created realm, in Isaiah's denunciation of idolatry, and in the portrayal of the blindness of idolaters in the Book of Wisdom. But even when of some length, those references differ in character from the formal reasoning developed in Greek philosophy. The Hebrew appeal to reason will be lost only on those for whom thinking is no longer a grasp of reality but a game with concepts. The rationality of Hebrew thought might have been given better justice by T. Boman in his *Hebrew Thought Compared with Greek*, trans. J. L. Moreau (London: SCM Press, 1960).

5. For documentation, see E. Gilson, *The Spirit of Mediaeval Philosophy* (Gifford Lectures 1931–32), trans. A. H. C. Downes (New York: Charles Scribner's Sons, 1936), pp. 69–71.

6. As D. Knowles points it out in his Introduction to the translation by H. Bettenson of Augustine's *Concerning the City of God against the Pagans* (Harmondsworth: Penguin Books, 1972), p. xv, in 410, when the capture of Rome by Alaric put an end to all pretensions about the power of imperial Rome, the leading families in Rome and all great cities of the empire were still preponderantly pagan and tried desperately to perpetuate their pagan religion, though it was obviously at its demise.

7. See the perceptive remarks in "Introduction: Two Philosophies of Nature" by D. O'Connor in *Creation: Impact of an Idea*, ed. D. O'Connor and F. Oakley (New York: Charles Scribner's Sons, 1969), pp. 23–24.

8. For further details, see chapter 9, "Delay in Detour," in my *Science and Creation: From Eternal Cycles to an Oscillating Universe* (Edinburgh: Scottish Academic Press, 1974).

9. Its classical formulation is the *Tahafut al-falasifah* of al-Ghazzali, available in English translation by Sabih Ahmud Kamali (Lahore: Pakistan Philosophical Congress, 1958).

10. The most often quoted passage in this connection was verse 88 of Sura 28, "everything shall perish except Himself." See translation by George Sale, *The*

Koran: Commonly Called the Alkoran of Mohammed, with explanatory notes selected by F. M. Cooper (New York: A. L. Burt, n.d.), p. 313.

11. See the German translation by F. H. Dieterici of "The Bezels [Foundations] of Philosophy," in *Al-Farabi Philosophische Abhandlungen* (Leiden: E. J. Brill, 1890), pp. 57, 66.

12. For texts and commentaries, see the essay by E. L. Fackenheim, "The Possibility of the Universe in al-Farabi, Ibn Sina and Maimonides," *Proceedings of the American Academy for Jewish Research,"* 16 (1946–47): 39–70.

13. The work, originally written in Syriac, was translated into Arabic around the middle of the ninth century by Ibn Abdallah Naime, who typically enough ascribed it to Porphyry of Tir, a disciple of Plotinus.

14. In R. Arnou's collection of the most representative of these texts, *De quinque viis sancti Thomae ad demonstrandam Dei existentiam apud antiquos graecos et arabes et judaeos praeformatis vel adumbratis: Textus selecti* (Rome: Gregorian University, 1932), thirty of the eighty pages preceding the texts of Aquinas are taken up by passages from Aristotle and ten from Avicenna. In addition to these the collection contains passages from Plato, Plotinus, Saint John Damascene, Saint Anselm, and Maimonides.

15. Quaestio 2 of part 1. For an English translation, see *St. Thomas Aquinas: Summa theologica,* first complete American edition in three volumes, literally translated by the fathers of the English Dominican Province, vol. 1 (New York: Benziger Brothers, 1947), pp. 11–14.

16. Proofs of the existence of God were given in the *Sententiae* of Peter Lombard, chief textbook of theology from its composition ca. 1150 until the early 1500s. Albertus Magnus taught Aquinas those proofs by commenting on it and Aquinas himself first tried his hand on the proofs by doing the same. A century before Peter Lombard, Anselm of Canterbury created a sensation by his ontological proof. Indeed, no theologian of any consequence, and there were a legion of them during the twelfth and thirteenth centuries, failed to discuss and almost invariably endorse at least some of the proofs. Equally universal was the discussion of the proofs among Jewish philosophers and theologians, of whom Maimonides was held in particularly high esteem by Aquinas.

17. Three-fourths of one percent of the total, as can be seen in any complete edition or translation.

18. A point well known by anyone familiar with the Psalms, and immaterial to anyone unfamiliar with them.

19. Psalm 14:1.

20. Nature worship is held there (13:1–19) less reprehensible than idol worship.

21. Rom. 1:20.

22. Acts 17:27. The subjective difficulties experienced by the gentiles in their quest for God through nature are, however, recognized in the same breath by Paul: "They were to seek God, yes to grope for him and perhaps eventually to find him." The God whom Paul has in mind at this point is the author of nature, intimately close to all who are conscious parts of it. It is only afterwards that Paul turns the topic to the specific man, Christ, appointed by God, in whose death and resurrection the judgment of God becomes a reality for all.

23. *Quaestiones disputatae de veritate,* qu. 22, art. 2 ad 1[am].

24. As argued by V. Preller in his *Divine Science and the Science of God* (Princeton University Press, 1967), p. 24, and with a somewhat different thrust by E. Sillem in his *Ways of Thinking about God: Thomas Aquinas and the Modern World* (New York: Sheed & Ward, 1961), pp. 55–66.

25. As, for instance, in the *Summa theologica*, pt. 1, qu. 46, art. 2: "And it is useful to consider this, lest anyone, presuming to demonstrate what is of faith, should bring forward reasons that are not cogent, so as to give occasion to unbelievers to laugh, and to think that such are the grounds on which we believe things that are of faith." See also E. Gilson, *Reason and Revelation in the Middle Ages* (New York: Charles Scribner's Sons), p. 77.

26. *Space and Spirit: Theories of the Universe and the Arguments for the Existence of God* (Hinsdale, Ill.: Henry Regnery, 1948), pp. 45–46. It reveals something of the usually meager information of a scientist, however brilliant, in matters relating to the history of philosophy that Whittaker found the second and third ways inconclusive because of Kant's claims that the principle of causality was applicable only within the realm of experience and that Aquinas's argument rested on Anselm's ontological argument.

27. *The Five Ways: St. Thomas Aquinas' Proofs of God's Existence* (London: Routledge and Kegan Paul, 1969). For an incisive criticism of Kenny's reasoning, see P. T. Geach's comments in *Philosophical Quarterly* 20 (1970): 311–12.

28. "The Principle *Omne quod movetur ab alio movetur* in Medieval Physics," *Isis* 56 (1965): 26–45. As Weisheipl showed, the 'movetur' and 'motio' have in the first way of Aquinas a meaning which transcends qualitative and quantitative change as well as local motion. In view of Aquinas's resolute criticism of Averroës, who considered form as cause of motion separate from "prime matter," and in view of Aquinas's resolve to reach God along the way in question, the meaning of motion in the first way can only be that of generation or coming into being. It is unfortunate that all major historians of medieval physics failed to note the Averroist provenance of their interpretation of the principle in the light of modern physical science. It cannot be emphasized enough that nature for Aquinas and for Aristotle is not a cause but principle, and that it has the closest connection with the notion of substance as the basis of explanation of the radical oneness of individuals. Typically, rejection of the five ways or of some of them always goes hand in hand with the rejection of the notion of substance, and on occasion even with skepticism about one's personal identity. For a discussion of the problems concerning the exact meaning of the five ways in their historical and speculative perspectives, see E. Gilson, *Elements of Christian Philosophy* (Garden City, N.Y.: Doubleday, 1960), pp. 43–87 and 291–300.

29. For this and similar dismissals by d'Alembert of medieval philosophy, see R. Grimsley, *Jean d'Alembert (1717–83)* (Oxford: Clarendon Press, 1963), p. 226.

30. *A History of Western Philosophy* (New York: Simon and Schuster, 1945), p. 462. The two cases with which Russell illustrated Aquinas's "insincerity" concerned his proofs of the indissolubility of marriage and of the existence of God. Keeping in mind Russell's views on marriage and related matters, one can hardly consider him a disinterested party. As to the proofs of the existence of God, Russell brushed them aside with the remark that every mathematician knows that a series having no first term is not impossible. As a mathematician Russell should rather have pondered the question of the actually realized infinite number, a problem that would have also helped him realize that Aquinas dealt not with notions, mathematical or otherwise, but with the actually existing reality of things.

31. For various texts, see E. Gilson, *Christianity and Philosophy*, trans. R. MacDonald (New York: Sheed & Ward, 1939), pp. 64–67. Indeed, these and similar utterances of Aquinas suggest a healthy measure of agnosticism in his philosophy. See V. White, *God the Unknown and Other Essays* (New York: Harper & Brothers, 1956), pp. 18–25 and 50–52.

32. As unwittingly expressed in the title of one of Bonaventure's short

treatises on mystical theology, *De reductione artium ad theologiam.* See its translation into English with a commentary and introduction by E. T. Healy (St. Bonaventure, N.Y.: Saint Bonaventure College, 1939).

33. See *The Life of Saint Thomas Aquinas: Biographical Documents,* trans. and ed. with an introduction by K. Foster (London: Longmans, Green and Co., 1959), pp. 33–36.

34. As a result, the topic of science and scientific method takes up but three pages in J. A. Weisheipl's authoritative monograph, *Friar Thomas d'Aquino: His Life, Thought and Work* (Garden City, N.Y.: Doubleday, 1974), pp. 134–35. It is also revealing that the article "Thomas Aquinas, Saint," by W. A. Wallace and J. A. Weisheipl in the *New Catholic Encyclopedia* (14:102–15) contains not even an indirect hint of Aquinas's significance for science.

35. For relevant passages, see M. D. Chenu, *Toward Understanding Saint Thomas,* translated with authorized corrections and bibliographical additions by A. M. Dandry and D. Hughes (Chicago: Henry Regnery, 1964), pp. 148–49.

36. For a succinct presentation of this problem, see the article by Wallace and Weisheipl quoted above, especially p. 108.

37. The decree was revoked in 1325.

38. The following paragraphs on Ockham owe much to the incisive exposition of the principal trend of his thought in E. Gilson's *The Unity of Philosophical Experience* (New York: Charles Scribner's Sons, 1937), pp. 67–91. Others reached similar conclusions, independently of him, which, however controversial, must be mentioned by any student of Ockham in view of Gilson's indisputable greatness as a medievalist. Absence of any reference to him is a serious shortcoming in the recently published vast monograph by G. Leff, *William Ockham: The Metamorphosis of Scholastic Discourse* (Manchester: University Press, 1975).

39. *Quodlibeta* 1, qu. 1, in *Ockham: Philosophical Writings,* a selection ed. and trans. by Philotheus Boehner (London: Nelson, 1957), p. 126.

40. Behind this seemingly empiricist stance, which might evoke Mach to the unwary, there is, however, Ockham's infatuation with God's omnipotence which, according to Ockham, cannot be constrained by permanence in things. Herein lies the ultimate reason for Ockham's prohibition against looking for a layer of entities underlying the observed one. See Gilson, *The Unity of Philosophical Experience,* pp. 76–77.

41. *Quodlibeta septem,* Quodlibet 6, qu. 6, "Whether there can be intuitive knowledge of a non-existent object," in *Selections from Medieval Philosophers, vol. 2, Roger Bacon to William Ockham,* ed. and trans. with introductory notes and glossary by R. McKeon (New York: Charles Scribner's Sons, 1930), p. 373.

42. Thus, for instance, F. Oakley in *Creation: The Impact of an Idea,* p. 64. Christian Ockhamists usually fail to ponder how close Ockham's philosophy is to occasionalism, Moslem and Malebranchian, and how little justice it does to biblical utterances declaring God's radical unchangeability.

43. For texts and discussion, see my *Science and Creation,* p. 150.

44. For further details and references, see F. Copleston, *A History of Philosophy, vol. 3, Late Medieval and Renaissance Philosophy, pt. 1, Ockham to the Speculative Mystics* (Garden City, N.Y.: Doubleday, 1963), p. 95.

45. See Buridan's *Quaestiones super libris quattuor de caelo et mundo,* ed. E. A. Moody (Cambridge, Mass.: Medieval Academy of America, 1942), pp. 152 and 164, and Oresme's *Le livre du ciel et du monde,* ed. A. D. Menut and A. J. Denomy, translated with an introduction by A. D. Menut (Madison: University of Wisconsin Press, 1968), p. 283. Buridan's departures from Ockham on some crucial points are carefully noted in E. Gilson, *History of Christian*

Philosophy in the Middle Ages (New York: Random House, 1954), pp. 512–15.

46. See his essay "Physics," in *Listen to Leaders in Science,* ed. A. Love and J. S. Childers (Atlanta: Tupper and Love, 1965), pp. 44–45.

47. For documentation, see E. Gilson, *History of Christian Philosophy in the Middle Ages,* p. 508. Other consistent Ockhamists, like Gregory of Rimini and Robert Holkot, expressed similar views wholly irreconcilable with a scientifically meaningful investigation of the external world. See Gilson, pp. 500–503.

48. Written in the 1430s, the work was printed many times during the sixteenth and seventeenth centuries. A reprint of the edition by J. Sighart (1852) was issued in 1975 in Stuttgart (Friedrich Frommann Verlag) with an introduction and notes by F. Stegmüller. The discussion by C. C. J. Webb (*Studies in the History of Natural Theology* [Oxford: Clarendon Press, 1915], pp. 292–312) of its principal contention and contents is still useful.

49. For a succinct but penetrating portrayal of that discovery as reflecting the skeptical mood of the mid-1500s, see E. Gilson, *The Unity of Philosophical Experience,* pp. 119–20. Montaigne does not seem to have perceived the fundamental inconsistency of Sabunde, who on the one hand claimed that contemplation of nature was an easy and reliable clue to all natural and supernatural mysteries, nay, even the source of man's complete moral healing, and asserted on the other hand that unless one was cleansed of original sin one could not read the open book of nature, and this is why the ancient philosophers failed to find in it the proper enlightenment. See fol. 4r and fol. 6v in the edition of 1635 (Frankfurt: impensis Georgii Thomasini et Octaviani Pulleni).

50. See translation by G. Heron with an introduction by D. J. B. Hawkins (London: Routledge and Kegan Paul, 1954).

51. Ibid., p. 111.

52. Ibid., pp. 112–13.

53. See, for instance, his *De staticis experimentis* where he quotes the passage in question as he argues that study of the weights of various bodies can effectively lead "to a truer grasp of the secret of things and that the same method would also yield much knowledge" (*Nicolai de Cusa: Opera omnia* [Leipzig: Felix Meiner, 1937], 5:120). The same passage is quoted in *Of Learned Ignorance* to support the paradoxical thesis that a boundlessly large world that has no center can still be harmoniously ordered (p. 119).

54. It is curious that the many admirers of Bruno in English-speaking countries shied away from making this book available in English. While the modern German translation by F. Fellmann (Frankfurt: Insel, 1969) takes too many liberties with the text, only one-fourth of the total is available in the French translation by E. Namer (Paris: Gauthier-Villars, 1965), who restricted himself and his readers to the "scientifically relevant" passages. For G. Aquilecchia, the critical editor of Bruno's Italian works, Bruno was too much a hero to let his antiscientific stance become too evident. My translation into English of the *Cena* with introduction and notes, *The Ash Wednesday Supper* (The Hague: Mouton, 1975), appeared two years after the Copernican anniversary, which, strangely enough, did not promote commensurate interest in the first book on Copernicus.

55. *The Ash Wednesday Supper,* p. 165.

56. The work, *Giordano Bruno and the Hermetic Tradition* (Chicago: University of Chicago Press, 1964), p. 297, in which Yates gave that devastating appraisal, is undoubtedly the most enlightening publication that has so far appeared on Bruno.

57. The really valuable part of this book of Bruno, made available by D. W. Singer in her *Giordano Bruno: His Life and Thought: With Annotated Trans-*

lation of His Work *"On the Infinite Universe and Worlds"* (New York: Henry Schuman, 1950), is Bruno's criticism of Aristotle's cosmology. But this was a negative effort already in progress for some time. When it came to the positive side of the program, the outline of a new cosmology, Bruno was immediately lost in pantheistic animism. It made him see deity as an infinite, refined body which he called space. Therefore, according to Bruno, wherever there was space, bodies were also generated. His very philosophy deprived him of the opportunity to reverse the order and say in an unwitting anticipation of Einstein that wherever there were bodies, space was generated.

58. This was not an incidental remark on Galileo's part. The importance he attributed to this aspect of Copernicus's search for truth can be judged from the fact that he twice elaborated on it in the *Dialogue concerning the Two Chief World Systems.* See translation by S. Drake (Berkeley: University of California Press, 1962), pp. 328 and 334.

59. For documentation on Luther's dictum and on its various interpretations, see A. Koyré, *La Révolution astronomique* (Paris: Hermann, 1961), p. 77.

60. There Copernicus discloses that what prompted his investigations was his annoyance with the philosophers, who although they "had made a very careful scrutiny of the least details of the world, had discovered no sure scheme for the movements of the machinery of the world which has been built for us by the Best and Most Orderly Workman of all." Rereading, as he put it, "all the books by philosophers which I could get hold of," led him, through assuming the earth's motion, to that simple correlation of all celestial motions which "binds together so closely the order and magnitudes of all the planets and of their spheres or orbital circles and the heavens themselves that nothing can be shifted around in any part of them without disrupting the remaining parts and the universe as a whole." That this simple and best order should lead man's mind to the recognition and admiring contemplation of the Artificer of all, is the opening theme of book 1, where he emphasizes that scientific knowledge of the world is particularly conducive to that end: "And since a property of all good arts is to draw the mind of man away from the vices and direct it to better things, these [mathematical] arts can do that more plentifully, over and above the unbelievable pleasure of mind [which they furnish]. For who, after applying himself to things which he sees established in the best order and directed by divine ruling, would not through diligent contemplation of them and through a certain habituation be awakened to that which is best and would not wonder at the Artificer of all things, in Whom is all happiness and every good?" In the next breath Copernicus also gives an unmistakable glimpse of the help which he received from his Christian heritage for the cultivation of this outlook on the world: "For the divine Psalmist surely did not say gratuitously that he took pleasure in the workings of God and rejoiced in the works of His hands, unless by means of these things as by some sort of vehicle we are transported to the contemplation of the highest Good." Reference to Plato follows and does not precede this declaration, in clear evidence of the commanding role which Christianity had in Copernicus's Platonism. For quotations, see translation by Charles G. Wallis in *Great Books of the Western World,* vol. 16, *Ptolemy, Copernicus, Kepler* (Chicago: Encyclopaedia Britannica, 1939), pp. 508 and 510.

61. See *La révolution astronomique,* p. 19.

62. The work in question is L. Geymonat's *Galileo Galilei: A Biography and Inquiry into His Philosophy of Science,* translated with additonal notes and appendix by S. Drake (New York: McGraw-Hill, 1965).

63. It is surely inconsistent to claim, as Einstein did in his introduction to *Johannes Kepler: Life and Letters* by C. Baumgardt (London: Victor Gollancz,

1952), pp. 12–13, that while "Kepler was a pious Protestant," his scientific success depended on his "freeing himself to a large extent from the spiritual tradition in which he was born."

64. As amply evidenced both in the *Dialogue Concerning the Two Chief World Systems* (pp. 3, 14, 103–104, 464) and in the "Letter to Grand Duchess Christina." The latter circulated widely in manuscript copies until its printing in 1636, twenty-one years after its original composition. See translation by S. Drake in *Discoveries and Opinions of Galileo* (Garden City, N.Y.: Doubleday, 1957), pp. 183 and 196.

65. *Dialogue Concerning the Two Chief World Systems,* p. 104.

66. After I succeeded in persuading a world-famous biblical scholar to read Galileo's "Letter to Grand Duchess Christina," I heard him exclaim: "He was three hundred years ahead of his time!" Kepler displayed his acumen in biblical exegesis in the preface to his epoch-making work on the orbit of Mars (*Astronomia nova,* 1609). The importance attributed to that preface during the seventeenth century can be seen by its publication in English translation by T. Salusbury in his *Mathematical Collections and Translations in Two Parts* (London: printed by William Laybourn, 1667), reprinted with an introduction by S. Drake (London: Dawsons of Pall Mall, 1967), pp. 461–67 of part 1.

67. For an authoritative survey of that research, see M. Clagett, "Archimedes" in *Dictionary of Scientific Biography* (New York: Charles Scribner's Sons, 1970–), 1:213–31. Clearly, Archimedes' name was a household word among the learned for at least two centuries before Galileo mentioned him more than a hundred times in his *Dialogue.*

68. Proposed by S. Bochner in his article, "Infinity," in *Dictionary of the History of Ideas* (New York: Charles Scribner's Sons, 1968–74), 2:609. The ineptitude of that simile matches the grave shortcomings of the historical scholarship of Bochner, who in patent disregard of documentary evidence wrote: "Among cosmological models of the universe that are presently under active study there are hardly any that are as completely infinite as was the universe of Giordano Bruno, which played a considerable role in philosophy between 1700 and 1900" (ibid., p. 607).

69. The effort was made by Bochner whose tendentiousness can easily be seen in his contrasting the "voluminous work" of Pierre Duhem with the "well-reasoned works" by Anneliese Maier. See Bochner's "Infinity" p. 609.

70. The dispute seems to have peaked in the mid-1960s and is well surveyed in E. McMullin, "Medieval and Modern Science: Continuity or Discontinuity?" *International Philosophical Quarterly* 5 (1965): 103–29.

71. *De sacramentis fidei christianae,* liber 2, pars 1 (Migne, *Patrologia Latina,* vol. 176, col. 205). One need not be a medievalist: it is enough to recall the vigor of the technological quest during the High Middle Ages, to make one realize the risk of writing off this phrase as untypical of medieval mentality, as done by R. Gruner, who found the phrase quoted by K. Löwith (*Gott, Mensch und Welt in der Metaphysik von Descartes bis Nietzsche* [Göttingen: Vandenhoeck and Ruprecht, 1967], p. 37) and who in his essay "Science, Nature and Christianity" (*Journal of Theological Studies* 26 [1975]: 55–81) came to the conclusion that Christianity neither helped nor impeded the rise of science. Of course, as long as one uncritically follows Löwith, not seeing the enormous difference between the sovereign Creator of the medieval Christians and the pantheistic "God" of Schelling, belief in the Creator will not appear as a special factor with an impact of its own worth pondering. Again, if that belief is kept in the background by a studied agnosticism, the results will not be better than lip service to medieval theology, as can be seen in *The Cultural Context of Medieval Learning: Proceedings*

of the First International Colloquium on Philosophy, Science, and Theology in the Middle Ages, September 1973, ed. with an introduction by J. E. Murdoch and E. D. Sylla (Dordrecht: D. Reidel, 1973).

Chapter Four

1. As aptly labeled by A. N. Whitehead in chapter 3 of his *Science and the Modern World* (New York: Macmillan, 1926).

2. References will be to the text in *The Works of Francis Bacon*, collected and edited by J. Spedding, R. L. Ellis and D. D. Heath in 14 vols. (London: Longmans, 1857–74; reprinted New York: Garrett Press, 1968), 3:261–491.

3. In view of the tone of Bacon's words to Rawley, Spedding characterized that event as the most important in Bacon's life (*Works*, 8:4), but it is rather to be viewed as a subconscious effort on Bacon's part to find an early support of his self-evaluation as a genius. The event did not prompt him to delve into the study of astronomy and cosmology.

4. In his "Praise of Knowledge" (1592); in *Works*, 8:125.

5. In an essay entitled "The Second Counsellor: Advising the Study of Philosophy" (1594); in *Works*, 8:335.

6. "The Hermit's Speech" (1595); in *Works*, 8:379. In surveying Bacon's correspondence, E. A. Abbott could not help being struck by frequently recurring instances of his megalomania: "Plain Mr. Francis Bacon not only felt himself superior to the world . . . but also took no trouble to disguise his sense of superiority" (*Francis Bacon: An Account of his Life and Work* [London: Macmillan, 1885], p. 32). It is well to recall that when Bacon left Trinity at the age of fourteen, he had spent no more than twenty months in college. But ten years later, in 1585, he felt himself qualified to write his "Advice to Queen Elizabeth," in which he had counsel for the queen on all points of policy, including the extremely intricate problem of dealing with Catholic dissenters. Burdened with such an inflated ego, Bacon could hardly perceive the genuine meaning of his felicitous phrase in which he likened access to man's kingdom founded on science to "entrance into the kingdom of heaven, whereinto none may enter except as a little child" (*New Organon*, bk. 1, aph. 68; in *Works*, 4:69).

7. "Proemium de interpretatione naturae," in *Works*, 3:518.

8. Ibid.

9. It was a far cry from the position on natural theology taken by Calvin in his *Institutiones* when Bacon declared in that essay that "God never wrought miracles to convince atheism, because his ordinary works convince it"; that "depth in philosophy bringeth men's minds about to religion"; and that when the mind of man "beholdeth the chain of them [secondary causes], confederate and linked together, it must needs fly to Providence and Deity." The extreme naturalness and cogency of the recognition of the God of nature implied in these statements is further corroborated by Bacon's insistence that atheists merely pretend not to know God, because such a stance is more in accordance with their moral depravity. In the same essay, a gold mine of memorable statements, Bacon extols atomic theory as more germane to theology than the Aristotelian system of four elements, because the order resulting from "an army of infinite small portions or seeds implaced" obviously indicates the existence of a "divine marshal." To this facile exercise in natural theology, hardly to Calvin's liking, Bacon added remarks, equally non-Calvinistic, on the history of philosophy and ethnography. He insisted that Epicurus was not an atheist at all, and that even "the Indians of the West, . . . those barbarous people, . . . have the notion [of God], though they have not the latitude and extent of it" (*Works*, 6:413–14).

10. *Advancement*, in *Works*, 3:350.

11. See chapters 11 and 12 in T. F. Torrance, *Calvin's Doctrine of Man* (new ed.; Grand Rapids, Mich.: W. B. Eerdmans Publishing Co., 1957).

12. Missing possibly because of Harvey's devastating opinion of Bacon ("he writes philosophy like a Lord Chancellor," quoted by Spedding from *Aubrey's Lives* in *Works*, 3:515), but the roster of those selected by Bacon to build Bensalem, the science state, dismayed even such a grim admirer of Bacon as B. Farrington. See his *Francis Bacon: Philosopher of Industrial Science* (1949; New York: Collier Books, 1961), pp. 121–22.

13. The title of this frontal attack on Plato and Aristotle, originally drafted in Latin, is "Temporis partus masculus," a fragment probably written in 1609. See *Works*, 3:528–39.

14. *Advancement*, in *Works*, 3:353.

15. Ibid., 3:350–51.

16. Ibid., 3:356.

17. See the *De augmentis scientiarum*, or the considerable rewriting in Latin of the *Advancement*, where he stated: "Finalium inquisitio sterilis est, et tamquam virgo Deo consecrata nihil parit" (*Works*, 1:571). There is some truth in the remark made by Ellis in a footnote that no saying of Bacon has been more consistently misquoted than this, because Bacon in the immediately preceding page accepts evidence on behalf of purposiveness. It still remains a fact that within Bacon's philosophical perspective it was impossible to justify the commonsense evaluation of purposiveness, as was amply shown by subsequent developments within the empiricist movement.

18. *Advancement*, in *Works*, 3:357.

19. Ibid., 3:358. More emphatic and explicit on this point is the wording in *De augmentis* where Bacon catches a glimpse of the danger of pursuing the search for final causes with no firm grasp on the ultimate final cause, God: "And in this Aristotle is more to be blamed than Plato, seeing that he left out the fountain of final causes, namely God, and substituted Nature for God." According to Bacon, Aristotle "had no further need of God," because he saw nature too replete with purposiveness. The antiteleological position of atomists allowed at least the investigation of correlations (laws) in the physical realm, a project unappealing within the Aristotelian obsession with teleology. See *Works*, 1:570–71 and 4:364–65.

20. *Advancement*, in *Works*, 3:358.

21. According to Bacon the doctrine of atoms implied the hypotheses of the vacuum and of the immutability of matter, both of which he viewed as "false assumptions" (*New Organon*, bk. 2, aph. 8, in *Works*, 4:126).

22. "Those who have handled sciences have been either men of experiment or men of dogmas. The men of experiment are like the ant, they only collect and use; the reasoners resemble spiders, who make cobwebs out of their own substance. But the bee takes a middle course: it gathers its material from the flowers of the garden and of the field, but transforms and digests it by a power of its own" (*New Organon*, bk. 1, aph. 95, in *Works*, 4:92).

23. In the succinct phrasing of Augustus de Morgan: "What are large collections of facts for? To make theories *from*, says Bacon; to try ready-made theories *by*, says the history of discovery" (*A Budget of Paradoxes*, 2d ed., ed. D. E. Smith [Chicago: Open Court, 1915], 1:88).

24. See *Brief Lives Chiefly of Contemporaries Set Down by John Aubrey between the Years 1669 and 1696*, ed. A. Clark (Oxford: Clarendon Press, 1898), 1:299.

25. *Advancement*, in *Works*, 3:351.

26. Ibid., 3:362.

27. *New Organon*, bk. 1, aph. 112, in *Works*, 4:102.

28. Ibid., preface, in *Works*, 4:40. "I have provided the machine," Bacon noted in the Epistle Dedicatory (4:12), and had the same in mind when he re-marked that "in the mathematics it is easy to follow the demonstration when you have a machine beside you" ("Plan of the Work," 4:31).

29. Ibid., bk. 1, aph. 61, in *Works*, 4:63.

30. Ibid.

31. Ibid., bk. 1, aph. 15, in *Works*, 4:49.

32. Bacon's brief dicta on the soul, which he held to be partly rational (divine) and partly sensitive (animal) (see *De augmentis*, in *Works*, 1:604) can be traced to Telesius of Cozensa, whom he recommended as "the best of novellists," or reformers of philosophy. The eclecticism of Telesius was of as little concern for Bacon as the dubious value of his notion of the soul, a notion that had long before been the subject of heated debates and was found unacceptable by Aquinas.

33. Bacon's reason for stating this revealed in him an instinctive and ever-present nonempiricist component of reasoning: "It is impossible," he argued in his "De fluxu et refluxu maris," against Gilbert's view, "that things in the interior of the earth can be like any substance exposed to the eye of man" (*Works*, 3:58 and 5:455). Such was a genuinely rationalist argument, which he disavowed as vehemently as he did the "Empiricist school of philosophy." The latter, according to him, "gives birth to dogmas more deformed and monstrous than the Sophistical or Rational School." He recalled as past instances of such dogmas those of the alchemists, adding that they are "hardly to be found elsewhere in these times, except perhaps in the philosophy of Gilbert" (*New Organon*, bk. 1, aph. 64, in *Works*, 4:65). Another instance of Bacon's frustrating search for a middle road in epistemology.

34. A fact which caused even Farrington some perplexity (see his *Francis Bacon*, p. 122). Typically enough, Bacon's encomium on Agricola (*Works*, 1:572) follows closely his decrying final causes as barren virgins, whereas he was distinctly unenthusiastic about Galileo's reports that Jupiter had four satellites, that the Milky Way could be resolved into myriads of stars, and that the moon's material was similar to that of the earth ("Descriptio globi intellectualis" in *Works*, 3:746–47, 760–61). These comments of Bacon on Galileo published only posthumously reflect the "suspicion" which Bacon had already voiced in the *New Organon* about Galileo's telescopic observations (bk. 2, aph. 39, in *Works*, 4:193).

35. Enthusiasm is hardly the hallmark of such remarks of Bacon that Coper-nicus's theory should be corrected by "natural philosophy" ("Valerius Ter-minus" in *Works*, 3:229), that Copernicus deprived nature "of quiet or im-mobility" ("Descriptio globi intellectualis" in *Works*, 3:738), and that although Copernicus's system cannot be refuted, it "may be corrected" (English transla-tion of *De augmentis* in *Works*, 4:373). While Bacon was keen on referring to the inconveniences of Copernicus's system, he was reticent about its great advan-tages ("Descriptio globi intellectualis" in *Works*, 3:740–41).

36. That Bacon's empiricism could lead nowhere should be clear to anyone familiar with the creative role played by mathematics in physical science from Galileo to Einstein and beyond on reading Bacon's dictum: "Inquiries into nature have the best result when they begin with physics and end in mathemat-ics" (*New Organon*, bk. 2, aph. 8, in *Works*, 4:125). Tellingly enough, even in that sympathetic exposition of Bacon's scientific method in *Theories of Scientific Method: The Renaissance through the Nineteenth Century*, by R. M. Blake and others (Seattle: University of Washington Press, 1960), it was admitted that in spite of Bacon's repeated endorsements of the desirability of quantitative de-

terminations, he "wholly failed to realize the importance of mathematics in scientific investigations, and this failure constituted one of the gravest *lacunae* in his doctrine" (p. 298).

37. In *New Organon* (bk. 2, aph. 36, in *Works*, 4:183) the rendering is "decisive instance." On Hooke's coining with a reference to Bacon the phrase "experimentum crucis" in the *Micrographia* and on its appearance in Newton's *Theory of Light and Colours*, see J. A. Lohne, "*Experimentum crucis*," in *Notes and Records of the Royal Society of London* 23 (1968): 169–99.

38. See the "Great Instauration," or the introductory part of *New Organon* (*Works*, 4:29).

39. Ibid., "Great Instauration" and bk. 1, aph. 10, in *Works*, 4:16 and 48.

40. Ibid., bk. 1, aph. 64, in *Works*, 4:65.

41. The schema consists of seven hierarchically subordinated classes of scholars, of which only the last class, that of the "interpreters of nature," is supposed to theorize in a more or less genuine sense (see *Works*, 3:164–65). As A. de Morgan aptly noted in his *A Budget of Paradoxes* (1:79), the schema reveals (in accordance with Bacon's lifework as a lawyer) the mentality of a judge who is not supposed to form an opinion, let alone to pass judgment, on a case before *all* the facts have been surveyed.

42. Only a few of Bacon's admirers went as far as Voltaire, who claimed in his "Lettres sur les Anglais" that "nobody before Chancellor Bacon had been familiar with experimental philosophy" and that "of all experiments in physics performed after him there is hardly one that had not been indicated in his book [*New Organon*]." See *Lettres philosophiques* in *Oeuvres de Voltaire* (Paris: Garnier, 1877–83): 22:119. But almost all recent critics of Bacon have followed Voltaire in his failure to see the impact of Bacon's natural theology on his legislation about science. With his characteristic superficiality Voltaire even failed to perceive the contradiction between his two claims, namely, that Newtonian science was a logical unfolding of Baconian principles and that Newtonian science was connatural with natural theology—which Bacon rejected. A brief and pointed reference to the wider implications of Bacon's position in natural theology can be found in the Gifford Lectures of C. E. Raven, *Natural Religion and Christian Theology* (Cambridge University Press, 1953), 1:107–8.

43. In the "Great Instauration" in *Works*, 4:26.

44. In his letter to Dr. Playfere (1608) in *Works*, 10:301.

45. For a somewhat different interpretation, see H. G. Van Leeuwen, *The Problem of Certainty in English Thought: 1630–1690* (The Hague: Martinus Nijhoff, 1963), pp. 1 and 12.

46. A claim of A. de Morgan (*A Budget of Paradoxes*, 1:110), who, however, failed to list those insightful remarks.

47. That sense should seem particularly reprehensible in view of Hobbes's obsession with topics, such as the squaring of the circle, the duplication of the cube, the cubing of the sphere, which in his time failed to attract properly trained geometers. He refused to heed the criticism of Wallis, Savilian professor of mathematics at Oxford, decried Descartes's effort to "arithmetise" geometry, and had for Wallis's contributions to analytical geometry only such comments as "scab of symbols" and of a hen's "scrapping on the pages." Some of these comments were reported in Wallis's scathing criticism of Hobbes's geometry discussed below.

48. See *New Organon*, bk. 2, aph. 20, in *Works*, 4:149.

49. In book 1, chapter 12, "Of Religion," in *The English Works of Thomas Hobbes*, ed. W. Molesworth (London: John Bohn, 1839), 3:98.

50. *The English Works*, 1:10.

51. As noted by M. Oakeshott in the introduction to his edition of *Leviathan*, in Blackwell's Political Texts Series (Oxford: Blackwell, 1946), p. liii. Being called "the greatest British political philosopher," in *Hobbes Studies*, ed. K. C. Brown (Oxford: Blackwell, 1965), p. 168, would have hardly satisfied Hobbes, *the* philosopher!

52. In his "Examinatio et emendatio mathematicae hodiernae," in *Opera philosophica quae Latine scripsit*, ed. W. Molesworth (London: J. Bohn, 1839–45), 4:179.

53. In his *De mundo dialogi tres* (Paris: apud Dyonisium Moreau, 1642), he proposed a finite, homogeneous world of stars and planets centered on the sun and allowed the existence of animals and plants on other globes. In contrast to the three interlocutors in Galileo's work, White's had four.

54. See pp. 236–37 in *Thomas Hobbes: Critique de "De mundo" de Thomas White*, ed. J. Jacquot and H. W. Jones (Paris: Vrin, 1973). White's explanation of tides as the effect of ethereal emanation from the sun was a development of Kepler's explanation of the orbital and rotational motion on the earth.

55. *The English Works*, 1:410–44.

56. "Lubrica res mens est," warns Hobbes at the end of his cosmological poem (edited by Jacquot and Jones, p. 447) and begs his "more alert readers" to ignore whatever error he might have fallen captive to, a request much more appropriate than he suspected.

57. Being the kind of "mechanist" he was, Hobbes could only see a bête noire in the notion of vacuum and he attacked it wherever he found it. His "Dialogus physicus, sive de natura aeris," written in 1661, was a brief but acid attack on Boyle's experiments with vacuum pumps. Boyle replied with dignified firmness in his "An Examen of Mr. T. Hobbes's *Dialogus physicus de natura aeris*, as far as it concerns Mr. Boyle's Book of New Experiments touching the Spring of Air," in *The Works of the Honourable Robert Boyle* (new ed.; London: printed for J. and F. Rivington, 1772), 1:189–244.

58. *The English Works*, 1:426–27. The first supposition is the composition of the universe of stars, atoms, and ether; the second, the heliocentric ordering of the planets; the third, the rotation of all celestial bodies; the fourth, the composite character of the air.

59. Ibid., p. 427.

60. Ibid., p. 312.

61. Ibid.

62. In the form of a "corporeal spirit." See his controversy with Bishop Bramhall in *The English Works*, 4:306.

63. See *Leviathan* (chapter 46): "because the universe is all, that which is no part of it is nothing." *The English Works*, 3:672.

64. "Of the World and of the Stars," in *The English Works*, 1:412. In his "God and Thomas Hobbes" (*Hobbes Studies*, pp. 141–68), W. B. Glover ignores Hobbes's cosmology, and as a result he overlooks Hobbes's strategy to profess his supernatural belief in God in his political, ethical, and theological writings and to advocate materialistic atheism in his philosophical publications.

65. "Of the World and of the Stars," in *The English Works*, 1:414.

66. "In all your geometry there is hardly anything of any consequence which is yours and would also be sane," wrote Wallis in his *Elenchus geometriae Hobbianae* (Oxford: excudebat H. Hall, 1655, p. 134). "I have done enough already, to let the world see, how little 'tis that you understand in Geometry and how much they deceive themselves who expect any great matter from you," concluded Wallis a year later in his *Due Correction for Mr. Hobbes, or Schoole Discipline, for not saying his Lessons right: In answer to his Six Lessons, directed to the*

Professors of Mathematicks by the Professor of Geometry (Oxford: printed by Leonard Lichfield, 1656, p. 128), a work in which Wallis declared that "all or most of what was worth any thing in your Mathematicks, was manifestly stollen from Galilaeo, Robervall, Cartesius, Fermat, etc. And one of them, as I perceive by somewhat but now comes to my hands from him, doth not stick to call you *Plagiarius*, again and again, for so doing" (p. 130). The *Due Correction* had to seem all the more effective as it carried for its motto on the front page Hobbes's boasting in the *Leviathan* (chapter 5): "Who is so stupid as both to mistake in Geometry, and also to persist in it, when another detects his error to him?"

67. Paris: sumptibus Sebastiani Cramoisy, 1623, cols. 25–226. For a discussion of those proofs, see R. Lenoble, *Mersenne; ou la naissance du mécanisme* (Paris: J. Vrin, 1943), pp. 247–59. A year later Mersenne published his *L'impiété des déistes, athées et libertins de ce temps* (Paris: chez Pierre Bilaine, 1624) in which he offered eleven proofs (pp. 72–120). As in the former work, the philosophical proofs were treated briefly, whereas the proof from the orderliness and quantitative aspects of the world was given with profuse illustrations. The ontological argument received special attention, but the argument from contingency was not presented as such. Hobbes, who severely criticized Thomas White for endorsing traditional metaphysics, never reproached Mersenne for upholding metaphysics to the tune of thirty-six and eleven proofs. Such was perhaps Hobbes's way of expressing his gratitude for Mersenne's help in publishing his essay on motion and geometry—which was a set of platitudes. With his enthusiasm for geometry and mechanics Mersenne might have seen a redeeming value in any such essay as a means of combatting magic, cabbala, and animism.

68. *Quaestiones celeberrimae in Genesim*, cols. 35–38.

69. Ibid., col. 213.

70. *La vérité des sciences contre les septiques* [sic] *ou Pyrrhoniens* (Paris: chez Toussainct du Bray, 1625). See also R. H. Popkin, "Father Mersenne's War against Pyrrhonism," *The Modern Schoolman* 34 (1956–57): 61–78.

71. See text in Lenoble, pp. 243–44.

72. In a letter of March 14, 1648, to Hevelius. For further details, see Lenoble, p. 492.

CHAPTER FIVE

1. W. Temple, *Nature, Man and God* (London: Macmillan, 1934), p. 57.

2. As recalled by Descartes in his *Discourse on the Method*. See *The Philosophical Works of Descartes*, rendered into English by Elizabeth S. Haldane and G. R. T. Ross (Cambridge University Press, 1911; reprinted with corrections, 1931; Dover reprint, n.d.), 1:87.

3. *Nature, Man and God*, p. 57. Even though the French original, *poêle*, once meant a room heated by a *poêle de faïence*, as noted by E. Gilson in his *René Descartes: Discours de la méthode: Texte et commentaire*, 3d ed. (Paris: J. Vrin, 1962), p. 157, in English the meaning of "stove" cannot be stretched to "stove-heated room."

4. At the end of the preface to his *Traité de l'équilibre et du mouvement des fluides* (Paris: chez David, l'ainé, 1744), p. xxxii, and in his *Preliminary Discourse to the Encyclopedia of Diderot*, translated by Richard N. Schwab, with the collaboration of Walker E. Rex, with an introduction and notes by Richard N. Schwab (Indianapolis: Bobbs-Merrill, 1963), p. 79.

5. *Pascal's Pensées*, translated by W. F. Trotter, with an introduction by T. S. Eliot (New York: E. P. Dutton, 1958), p. 23.

6. Manuscript note 2791, in *Oeuvres complètes de Christiaan Huygens* (The Hague: Martinus Nijhoff, 1880–1950), 10:403.

7. These details are known from the autobiographical fragments "Olympica," first published by A. Baillet in 1691. See *Oeuvres de Descartes*, edited by C. Adam and P. Tannery (Paris: Cerf, 1897–1913), 10:186.

8. Letter of March 26, 1619, to Beeckman; *Oeuvres*, 10:157–58.

9. *The Philosophical Works of Descartes*, 1:5.

10. *Discourse on the Method*, in *The Philosophical Works*, 1:99.

11. Letter of November 25, 1630, to Mersenne, in *Oeuvres*, 1:181–82. The letter shows something of the age-old misunderstanding about the difference between the intrinsic validity of a philosophical demonstration and its psychological effectiveness. That misunderstanding is, of course, well-nigh insurmountable, if one believes with Descartes that anything genuinely philosophical ought to be reducible to something akin to geometry. It was the "effectiveness" of geometrical demonstrations which made Descartes believe that he had found an "evident demonstration which would make everybody believe that God exists." But he also admitted doubt about his own ability "to make everybody understand the demonstration in the same way" he did. His other remarks were that it was better not to broach a subject unless one handled it perfectly, and that the general agreement about the existence of God was enough to combat the atheists!

12. In his letter of January 1630 to Mersenne he expressed his regret on hearing of Mersenne's sickness and urged him to take care of himself "until I learn whether there is a means of finding a science of medicine based on infallible demonstration, the very thing which I am now looking for" (*Oeuvres*, 1:105–6).

13. See his letter of June 15, 1646, to Chanut (*Oeuvres*, 4:442). The phrase "ut doctus emoriar" expresses the same resignation in his letter of March 6 of the same year (*Oeuvres*, 4:378). Descartes must have read with no aversion in Constantin Huygens's letter to him (May 28, 1639) about a Dutchman who was working on a method of "putting an end one day to that irksome custom of dying" (*Oeuvres*, 2:549–50).

14. *Discourse on the Method*, in *The Philosophical Works*, 1:101.

15. Ibid., p. 104.

16. As pointed out in chapter 4, Mersenne gave a prominent place to the ontological argument in both cases.

17. *Meditations on First Philosophy*, in *The Philosophical Works*, 1:170.

18. This is not to suggest that the traditional proofs had been simply abandoned. Yet any perceptive reader could easily notice their subordinate value in the writings of Arnauld, Bossuet, Malebranche, and Fénelon, who set with their Cartesianism the tone of theological discourse in France for the rest of the seventeenth century and beyond. It was no accident that Fénelon's *Traité de l'existence et des attributs de Dieu* consisted of two parts. The first was a presentation of the proofs from the contemplation of nature, the second a set of proofs drawn "from intellectual ideas." There Fénelon outdid Descartes by offering a "new proof from the nature of ideas" and claimed that man's ideas "have the character of Deity because they are universal and immutable as God is. They exist most really according to a principle which I have already stated: nothing exists except that which is universal and unchangeable. If that which is changeable, transitory, and borrowed really exists, all the more so should exist that which cannot change and is necessary" (*Fénelon: Oeuvres choisies* [new ed.; Paris: Garnier, 1880], p. 144). That the almost elementary rebuttal of Descartes's proof, which rested on the innateness of the idea of God, had to be performed

effectively by an Englishman, John Locke, shows the extent to which Cartesian natural theology had got hold of French minds. Descartes himself was fully aware of the sharp conflict between his and Aquinas's natural theology, a point amply documented by E. Gilson, *René Descartes: Discours de la méthode*, pp. 324–27. In view of the tremendous popularity enjoyed by the proof from teleology in the latter half of the seventeenth century, Descartes's denial of finality even in the mind of the Creator had to appear all the more glaring, and it formed the basis of contemporary accusations that Descartes's method led to atheism. Concerning the latter point within the context of seventeenth-century biology, philosophy, and theology, see the penetrating remarks in *D'Aristôte à Darwin et retour: Essai sur quelques constantes de la biophilosophie* (Paris: J. Vrin, 1971, p. 41), a masterpiece by the almost nonagenarian Gilson.

19. Even if Descartes did not know that his phrase, which earned him much undeserved praise, had a long medieval background reaching back at least as far as Hugh of St. Victor, he should have recalled Genesis 2 and realized his debt to that Christian tradition which he, as a philosopher, systematically tried to overlook. The ineptness of Descartes's physics can easily be gathered from *The Scientific Work of René Descartes (1596–1650)* (London: Taylor and Francis, 1952) by J. F. Scott. The less than a century-long demise of Cartesian physics is (somewhat unwittingly) the topic of *Le développement de la physique cartésienne 1646–1712* (Paris: J. Vrin, 1934) by P. Mouy.

20. "It is at least as certain that God, who is a Being so perfect, is or exists, as any demonstration of geometry can possibly be." *Discourse on the Method*, in *The Philosophical Works*, p. 104.

21. A conviction stated in his letter of March 26, 1619, to Beeckman. See *Oeuvres*, 10:157. Increasingly strengthened in that conviction as time went on, Descartes could but frown on Fermat's innovating efforts opening the way toward infinitesimal calculus.

22. For further details, see my *The Relevance of Physics* (Chicago: University of Chicago Press, 1966), p. 103.

23. Emphatic references to distinctness can be found both in the *Meditations on First Philosophy* and in the *Discourse on the Method*. See *The Philosophical Works*, pp. 105, 140, 153, 165, 176, 196.

24. *Meditations on First Philosophy*, p. 196.

25. Ibid., p. 187.

26. Ibid., pp. 148, 150–51.

27. Ibid., pp. 158–59 and 171.

28. Descartes derived the necessity of linear inertial motion from God's immutability, a procedure which reflected his a priorism in natural theology. Once more wrong premises yielded a correct conclusion, and one that represented a major advance over Galileo, who in distinctly Aristotelian fashion held circular motion to be natural for celestial bodies. Descartes emphatically warned that "no part of matter ever tends to keep moving along curved lines." See *Principes de la philosophie*, 2:39, in *Oeuvres*, 8:85–86. It is the French translation of his *Principia philosophiae*, published three years after the publication in 1644 of the Latin original, and wholly approved by Descartes.

29. *Principes*, 3:45, in *Oeuvres*, 8:124.

30. *Le Monde*, in *Oeuvres*, 11:32–33. Descartes's protestations of his belief in the Creator's freedom with respect to the particular form of the creation first saw print in 1637 in his *Discourse on the Method* and, revealingly enough, in a cryptic reference to *Le Monde*, still in manuscript. See *The Philosophical Works*, p. 107. *Le Monde* was almost completed when Descartes heard of Galileo's condemnation in 1632 and decided to search for an explanation of the earth's motion around

the sun which would satisfy both physics and Scripture. He found that explanation by postulating a vortex around each celestial body. Thus while the earth was carried with its vortex around the sun, it could be viewed as being at rest at the center of its vortex.

31. Letter of April 15, 1630, in *Oeuvres*, 1:145. On the basis of his premises Descartes could argue that his innate ideas did not derogate God's freedom and sovereignty, because he let God put the notion of extension into the thinking mind, an unextended entity. But since the notion of linear extension seemed to Descartes to exclude all other forms of bodily existence, Descartes's reasoning implied that God freely created the only possible world that could be created, namely, the one which embodied Euclidean goemetry. On such a basis God was not really needed, and this was the conclusion drawn by some before long.

32. Ibid.

33. In the *Principes* (3:47; *Oeuvres*, 8:126) Descartes described the original chaos as "the perfect equality" of all particles of matter in every respect, an advance over his accounts of it in *Le Monde* (*Oeuvres*, 11:34) and in the *Discourse on the Method* (*The Philosophical Works*, p. 107) as an agglomeration "as confused as the poets ever feigned." Once that chaos was created by God "in an imaginary space" He could conclude "His work by merely lending His concurrence to Nature in the usual way, leaving her to act in accordance with the laws which He had established" (ibid.). This was an inconsistent effort to safeguard God's creative freedom, because the laws governing the development of chaos into the actual world could only be what they were, once Descartes had derived them from God's immutable perfection.

34. *Principes*, 3:46 (*Oeuvres*, 8:125).

35. Ibid. In the same context Descartes also assigned to the Creator the division of matter into very small particles and the rotational movement of each "around its center."

36. *Pascal's Pensées*, p. 23.

37. For example, R. M. Blake in his "The Role of Experience in Descartes' Theory of Method," in E. H. Madden (ed.), *Theories of Scientific Method: The Renaissance through the Nineteenth Century* (Seattle: University of Washington Press, 1960), pp. 75–103.

38. *Principes*, 4:204 (*Oeuvres*, 8:322): "It is certain that God has an infinity of various means by each of which he might have achieved that all things of this world should appear as they now appear, without its being possible for the human mind to perceive which of those means he wanted to use to make all those things. This is something I have no difficulty whatever in agreeing with."

39. *Principes*, 3:1 (*Oeuvres*, 8:103): "Since pure reason furnished us with enough light to let us discover some principles of material things and since it presented them with so much evidence that we cannot doubt their truth, it must now be seen whether we can derive from those principles alone the explanation of all phenomena." Descartes's elaboration at the end of the *Principes* (4:205–6; *Oeuvres*, 8:323–25) on the difference between moral and metaphysical certainty was offered as a support of his a priori approach to the physical world. In vain did he protest in the *Discourse on the Method* (*The Philosophical Works*, p. 109) that his approach did not do "outrage to the miracle of creation."

40. Letter of May 17, 1638, in *Oeuvres*, 2:143–44.

41. In his letter of June 1645 to Huygens, in *Oeuvres*, 4:224–25.

42. *Discourse on the Method* in *The Philosophical Works*, pp. 123–24. A little later (p. 128) he added, however, that he really had no hope that "the public should to any large degree participate in my interest."

43. Descartes merely gave credit to Harvey for having shown the presence of

"many little tubes at the extremities of the arteries" and for having demonstrated that "certain little membranes or valves... are so arranged in different places along the course of the veins, that they do not permit the blood to pass from the middle of the body towards the extremities, but only to return from the extremities to the heart" (*Discourse on the Method*, in *The Philosophical Works*, pp. 112–13).

44. This point was overlooked by R. M. Blake ("The Role of Experience," pp. 78–79), who emphasized the foregoing distinction to play down the a priori character of Cartesian physics.

45. *Principes* 2:53 (*Oeuvres*, 8:93). The truth of his laws, Descartes noted, presupposes the existence of perfectly hard bodies, but "we never see such bodies in this world."

46. See his letter of July 30, 1640, to Mersenne, in *Oeuvres*, 3:134–35.

47. See the English translation of his *Recherche de la vérité*, entitled *Father Malebranche's Treatise concerning the Search after Truth: The Whole Work Compleat*, by T. Taylor (Oxford: printed by L. Lichfield, 1694), 2:61.

48. Hardly a rash judgment in view of Descartes's admission that his explanation of the various features of the globules rests on principles "the falsity of which by no means prevents what is derived from them from being true" (*Principes* 3:47, in *Oeuvres*, 8:125).

49. Brevity is certainly in order when one reports a fact, however unusual, which God performs. In Descartes's case brevity was due to his tacit admission that the fact in question could not be derived from an a priori plausibility.

50. In battling atoms Descartes insisted that any indivisible entity with some extension, however small, implied contradiction and that his globules were not to be taken for atoms, a request not without some contradiction. See, for instance, *Principes* 4:201 (*Oeuvres*, 8:319), his letter of Jan. 16, 1642, to P. Gibieuf (*Oeuvres*, 3:476) and *Les Météores* (*Oeuvres*, 6:238).

51. For a detailed discussion, see chapter 2, "The Spell of Vortices," in my *Planets and Planetarians: A History of Theories of the Origin of Planetary Systems* (Edinburgh: Scottish Academic Press, 1976). The enormous originality of Descartes in emphasizing the evolutionary view of the cosmos can best be grasped when contrasted with the static viewpoint that wholly dominated Copernicus's and Kepler's thought on the cosmos and nearly as completely that of Galileo.

52. It is hardly an accident that the very first cosmogonical theory with some scientific veneer had been plagued with the question of angular momentum, the Achilles' heel of all subsequent theories of the evolution of the system of planets. The rotation of entire galaxies is not without serious problems for modern astrophysics.

53. A designation largely due to the proponents of the steady-state theory. See my *The Paradox of Olbers' Paradox* (New York: Herder and Herder, 1969), pp. 231–42.

54. Ibid., pp. 72–83. "I have heard urged," was Halley's reference in 1720 to previous discussion of the problem, which had appeared in a rudimentary form in Bentley's correspondence with Newton on the gravitational counterpart of the paradox and in the shell model of the distribution of stars endorsed both by Newton and David Gregory.

55. On Descartes's two references to the Milky Way, see my *The Milky Way: An Elusive Road for Science* (New York: Science History Publications, 1972), p. 119. Tellingly enough, the better of the two references did not find its way from the *Le Monde* into the *Principes*.

56. In *La Dioptrique*, in *Oeuvres*, 6:202.

57. A variation of that claim, made emphatically in his letter of July 27, 1638,

to Mersenne, was the concluding chapter of book 2 of the *Principes* which had for its title: "That I do not accept any principles in physics which are not also accepted in mathematics, so that I may prove by demonstration all that I derive from them, and that these principles are sufficient that all phenomena of nature might be explained by them."

58. In *Les Météores*, in *Oeuvres*, 6:297–304 and 325–44.

59. In *La Géométrie*, in *Oeuvres*, 6:428–30, where a diagram shows an easy method of drawing an ellipse.

60. See his letter of April 20, 1646, to Mersenne, in *Oeuvres*, 4:398–99.

61. As suggested by his remark that the "planets always depart more or less from the circular motion" (*Principes* 3:157, in *Oeuvres*: 8:200).

62. See plate 16 there and his remark that "this vortex ABCD is not exactly round" (*Principes* 4:51, in *Oeuvres*, 8:229).

63. Spinoza pioneered in biblical criticism, wrote an essay on political theory, and volunteered his services as a mediator between the Spanish and Dutch armies, relying for his credentials on his renown as a philosopher. His "Algebraic calculation of the rainbow," available in facsimile edition of the original Dutch text, with an introduction by G. ten Doesschate (Leiden: Nieuwkoop, 1963), runs to a mere twenty-six pages.

64. As is abundantly clear from the sundry propositions of part 2, "Of the Nature and Origin of the Mind," of the *Ethics*. They meant all the more a reversal of Descartes's reasoning as they formed part of a book "demonstrated in the manner of geometry."

65. *The Chief Works of Benedict de Spinoza*, translated from the Latin, with an introduction by R. H. M. Elwes (1893; New York: Dover, 1951), 2:408. For Spinoza's reply, see p. 409.

66. The story is told and used with great force by Gilson in his *The Unity of Philosophical Experience* (New York: Charles Scribner's Sons, 1937), pp. 194–95.

67. See his *Dialogues on Metaphysics and on Religion*, translated by M. Ginsberg (London: G. Allen and Unwin, 1923), p. 165.

68. In one of his essays contributed to the Académie des Sciences he extended the notion of vortex to the atoms. See my *Planets and Planetarians*, p. 51.

69. As to la Mettrie, he extolled in his *L'Homme machine* (1748) Descartes's "complete demonstration" of the purely mechanical nature of all animals as a discovery of crucial importance "demanding so much sagacity" and urged in return an oversight of "all his other errors." La Mettrie was so eager to have Descartes as his ally as to ascribe to him the view that "medicine alone can change minds and morals." See *Man a Machine* (French text with English translation, and with philosophical and historical notes by Gertrude C. Bussey [Chicago: Open Court, 1912], pp. 90 and 142–43.

70. *Pensées sur l'interprétation de la nature* (1753; rev. ed., 1754) in *Oeuvres complètes: Édition chronologique* (Paris: Le Club Français du Livre, 1969–73), 2:717–18.

71. Ibid., p. 718.

72. See his article "Art" in the *Encyclopédie*; in *Oeuvres complètes*, 2:349.

73. See his Prospectus to the *Encyclopédie*; ibid., 2:294.

74. Diderot quickly fell into disrepute in England, where one could only read with dismay his pretence that Saunderson countered the fictitious clergyman, visiting him at his deathbed, with the words: "If you wish me to believe in God you must allow me to touch him" (*Lettre sur les aveugles*, ibid., 2:195). In his role as a sensationist skeptic Saunderson was made to conjure up the primitive condition of the universe, dominated by "aimless and lawless agitations" and subject to cyclic transitions from one chaos to another permitting but a "merely

transitory symmetry and momentary appearance of order" (ibid., 2:199). L. G. Crocker, author of a monograph of this, undoubtedly basic, aspect of Diderot's thought comes to the conclusion that with Diderot chance and order are locked together through a dialectic impervious to ordinary logic. In that dialectic the fall of a die is completely determined but the die can change its shape while falling. Such a dialectic is as useless for science as the conceptual content of Crocker's apt summary of Diderot's world view: "The turbulence of all that is, is governed by the order of law; but that turbulence is a law of disorder" (*Diderot's Chaotic Order: Approach to a Synthesis* [Princeton University Press, 1974], p. 51).

75. *Le rêve de d'Alembert* also shows that at the end of his career Diderot was still as ready to distort facts and personalities as he was in his younger years if the "cause" demanded such strategy. The titles of chapters 2–4 in *Diderot: De l'athéisme à l'anticolonialisme* by Y. Bénot (Paris: François Maspero, 1970) read as follows: "Singularité du personnage: 1. Mensonges, bavardages et lâchetés. 2. Fidélités idéologiques et compromis tactiques. 3. L'insatisfaction."

76. "Cosmologie," *Encyclopédie ou Dictionnaire raisonné des sciences* ... , vol. 4 (Paris: chez Briasson, 1754), p. 294.

77. See *Oeuvres complètes*, 2:302 and 309.

78. Ibid., 2:713–14.

79. Ibid., 2:769.

80. Ibid., 2:770. The question, Diderot added with his consummate cunning, can only be answered by revelation.

81. *Mémoires sur différents sujets de mathématiques* (1748), ibid., 2:114. In the leading study of Diderot's relation to science, *Diderot: L'homme de science* by J. Mayer (Rennes: Imprimerie Bretonne, 1959), the chapter on Diderot's expertise in mathematics has the title "Le mirage mathématique," and ends with the remark that mathematics was for Diderot "a glory of which he kept dreaming and even tried to earn it, but his too intuitive and concrete mind was not made for it" (p. 104). Not surprisingly, Diderot saw his main glory in the fact that he had taught his "fellow citizens to appreciate and read Chancellor Bacon." The phrase is from Diderot's article "Encyclopédie" in the *Encyclopédie*, where he also noted that his fellow citizens "have read the pages of this profound writer [Bacon] more during the past five or six years than they ever did before." See *Oeuvres complètes*, 2:454.

82. *Elémens de la philosophie de Newton*, in *Oeuvres complètes de Voltaire* (Paris: Garnier, 1877–83), 22:404.

83. *Précis du siècle de Louis XV*, in *Oeuvres*, 15:433–34, where Voltaire also deplores the folly of those who, following the example of Descartes, "wanted to put themselves in the place of God and, like him, with a word create a world."

CHAPTER SIX

1. For documentation and further details, see I. B. Cohen, *Introduction to Newton's Principia* (Cambridge University Press, 1971), pp. 267–68.

2. Since Pemberton saw the great novelty of Newton's accomplishment somewhat superficially, he could hardly feel any misgiving in interpreting Newton's method in terms of Bacon's "inductionism" (see the Introduction of his *A View of Sir Isaac Newton's Philosophy* [with an Introduction to the reprint edition by I. B. Cohen; New York: Johnson Reprint, 1972], pp. 24–25). Pemberton saw the foundation of the "method of arguing by induction without which no progress could be made in natural philosophy" (p. 25) in the Baconian precept that "those qualities, which in the same body can neither be lessened nor increased, and which belong to all bodies that are in our power to make trial upon, ought to be accounted the universal properties of all bodies whatever."

Yet, the truth of this precept, which Newton himself espoused, could not be had on the basis of Bacon's empiricism. While Pemberton could write with some justification that "we had before no true knowledge at all" (p. 17), that the moon gravitated toward the sun as well as toward the earth and that comets had well-defined orbits, Newton's scientific achievement meant much more than providing clues to these and similar topics.

3. While in his letter of Dec. 23, 1630, to Mersenne, Descartes first noted in connection with the method of making useful experiments that he had nothing to add to what Bacon had already written on the subject, he rejected in the same breath as useless the observation of anything that was not obvious. Observations of the obvious, such as the observation that "bodies of all animals were composed of three parts, head, chest and abdomen," can be done, Descartes remarked, "without any expense and, far more importantly, they "serve us infallibly in the search for truth." Concerning particular experiments, Descartes's view was that it was impossible not to make many that were "superfluous and even false," and that "even the useful ones cannot be performed if one does not know the truth of the matter before making them" (Oeuvres de Descartes, edited by C. Adam and P. Tannery [Paris: Cerf, 1897–1913), 1:195–96). With that statement Descartes added in fact so much to what Bacon wrote on the subject as to deprive it of any intrinsic merit.

4. Micrographia; or, Some Physiological Descriptions of Minute Bodies Made by Magnifying Glasses, with Observations and Inquiries Thereupon, with a Preface by R. T. Gunther (New York: Dover Publications, 1961), p. 54. In his "General Scheme or Idea of the Present State of Natural Philosophy" Hooke viewed the intellect as "continually to be assisted by some method or engine." About that engine he wrote that it would prevent the tendency of the intellect "to act amiss," that only "the incomparable Verulam had any thoughts" about it, that he "indeed hath promoted it to a very good pitch," and that with the aid of that engine "the business of invention will not be so much the effect of acute wit, as of a serious and industrious prosecution." See The Posthumous Works of Robert Hooke (London, 1705), pp.6–7.

5. The True Intellectual System of the Universe, with the notes and dissertations of J. L. Mosheim (London: Thomas Tegg, 1845), 2:608.

6. Micrographia, p. 16.

7. Ibid., p. 2. The proof was based on the skillful arrangement of countless small parts within a very small space. Only an Author who was omnipotent could do that, Hooke concluded.

8. He did so in the preface (p. 2) of his Museum Regalis Societatis; or A Catalogue & Description of the Natural and Artificial Rarities Belonging to the Royal Society and Preserved at Gresham College (London: printed by W. Rawlins for the Author, 1681).

9. Cosmologia Sacra; or, A Discourse of the Universe As It Is the Creature and Kingdom of God, Chiefly Written to Demonstrate the Truth and Excellency of the Bible, Which Contains the Law of His Kingdom in This Lower World (London: W. Rogers, 1701).

10. Ibid., p. 101: "had all faces been made alike, Phancy having once begot Love; the same Phancy which makes a Man love his Wife, would have made him in Love with all other Women."

11. See chapter 2, "Of the Ends of Providence: And First, in This Life," of book 3 (pp. 92–105), where he said the same of minerals, singling out iron as the most useful and most plentiful, and of plants, noting that "corn, so necessary for all people, is fitted to grow and, to seed, as a free Denison, all over the world."

12. Ibid., p. 99. The most useful animals also excelled by some special virtue,

such as the gentleness of a sheep both "in the field and when she comes to a slaughter." Within such a perspective one could be euphoric about the good effects of bad things and reason that *"cantharides,* taken by some Whores, to distroy their Big-Bellies; and wherewith they commonly kill themselves to boot," or that "Lice oblige us to Cleanlyness in our Bodies, Spiders in our Houses; and the Moth in our Cloathes" (p. 102). Concerning Grew's encomium of the dung of horses it may be noted that its smell was not unqualifiedly sweet for everybody even in Grew's century. A few days before this lecture was delivered, I had the opportunity to tour St. Andrews and found in a leaflet distributed by the Tourist Office that because of the large accumulation of dung and dead fish in the streets, the city almost lost its university.

13. Bentley's sermons were originally printed separately. The phrase, "confutation of atheism," was first the beginning of the general title of sermons 3 to 8. For a facsimile of sermons 7 and 8, which are of most interest for the historian of science, see *Isaac Newton's Papers and Letters on Natural Philosophy and Related Documents,* edited with a general introduction by I. B. Cohen (Cambridge: Harvard University Press, 1958), pp. 313–424.

14. See his *The Vanity of Dogmatizing* (1661), p. 248, and its second edition, *Scepsis scientifica* (1665), p. 182, in the facsimile edition, *The Vanity of Dogmatizing: The Three 'Versions' by Joseph Glanvill,* with a critical introduction by Stephen Medcalf (Hove, Sussex: Harvest Press, 1970). A generation later Bentley decried atheists who "make such a noisy pretence to wit and sagacity" but forebore naming anyone (except Hobbes, and only in a roundabout way) in his Boyle lectures. See *The Works of Richard Bentley,* edited by A. Dyce (London: Macpherson, 1836–38), 3:3, 50, and 113.

15. The work, posthumously published by J. Tillotson (London: printed for T. Basset), consisted of two books, of which the first contained the proofs; these were introduced by a discussion of the various kinds of evidence and assents and by an analysis of the difference between moral and mathematical proofs.

16. The full title of the work, first published in 1688, contains the clause: *wherein is inquired whether and (if at all) with what caution a naturalist should admit them.* See *The Works of the Honourable Robert Boyle* (London: new ed. printed for J. and F. Rivington, 1772), 5:392–451. On Descartes, see pp. 395–402.

17. Ibid., p. 427. A few pages later Boyle sets great store by the skill of spiders and silkworms in fabricating their webs and cocoons.

18. Ibid., pp. 404–9 and 425–27. Some of Boyle's reflections were based on the Jesuit Scheiner's work on the eye, which he mentioned with praise. Boyle's concern for natural theology is discussed in relation to his views on alchemy in H. Fish, "The Scientist As a Priest: A Note on Robert Boyle's Natural Theology," *Isis* 44 (1953): 252–65. Boyle would have been more pleased with the monograph of M. S. Fisher, *Robert Boyle, Devout Naturalist: A Study in Science and Religion in the Seventeenth Century* (Philadelphia: Oshiver Studio Press, 1945).

19. On the failure of the *Principia* to make immediately a great stir, see E. J. Aiton, *The Vortex Theory of Planetary Motions* (London: Macdonald, 1972), pp. 113–14.

20. Another philosopher who wanted professional assurance on the reliability of the mathematical propositions of the *Principia* was Locke, who turned to Huygens for advice. As J. T. Desaguliers, a close associate of Newton, reported in the preface of his *Course of Experimental Philosophy,* 3d ed. (London: A. Millar, 1763), p. viii: "being told he [Locke] might depend upon their Certainty: he took them for granted, and carefully examined the Reasonings and Corollaries drawn from them, became Master of all the Physics."

21. Those letters are reproduced in facsimile from their first printing in 1756 in *Isaac Newton's Papers and Letters on Natural Philosophy*, pp. 279–312. On their relevance to the gravitational paradox, see my *The Paradox of Olders' Paradox* (New York: Herder and Herder, 1969), pp. 60–65.

22. *Isaac Newton's Papers and Letters*, pp. 293–96.

23. See the conclusion of his eighth sermon, *Works*, pp. 351–52.

24. *Opticks* (New York: Dover, 1952), p. 370. See also Query 31 (p. 403) added at the same time. In a more covert manner the same view was also expressed in the General Scholium added to the second edition (1713) of the *Principia*.

25. Most likely such was the character of the "new" proof to which he referred at the end of his first letter to Bentley (*Isaac Newton's Papers and Letters*, p. 290) but which he apparently never wrote down. That Newton's natural theology was taken to be exhausted by the argument from design and by the infinity of space and time is well attested in Pemberton's conclusion to his *A View of Sir Isaac Newton's Philosophy*, pp. 405–6.

26. See Query 22 of the *Opticks*, pp. 352–53 and *Principia*, Bk. 3, Prop. 10, theorem 10 in Motte's translation, revised by F. Cajori (Berkeley: University of California Press, 1962), p. 419.

27. These aspects were: the uniqueness of the sun as a heat- and light-giving body, the motion of planets and satellites in the same direction and plane, the proper adjustment of the distances, masses, and velocities of planets, their rotation on their axes, the measure of the inclination of the earth's axis, and the imparting of the exact amount of angular momentum to each planet. For a brief discussion with documentation, see my *The Relevance of Physics* (Chicago: University of Chicago Press, 1966), pp. 429–30; for more details, see chapter 3, "Gravity and God's Arm," in my *Planets and Planetarians: A History of Theories of the Origin of Planetary Systems* (Edinburgh: Scottish Academic Press, 1977).

28. For this misrepresentation of his own theory the chief responsibility lies with Laplace, who insisted, in the presence of Napoleon and Herschel, that it did not need the hypothesis of a First Cause. See my *Planets and Planetarians*, pp. 127–28.

29. As may be gathered from his insistence in the General Scholium on the demonstrative value of final causes as evident from the "most wise and excellent contrivances of things" *Principia*, p. 546.

30. "All these things being consider'd, it seems probable to me, that God in the Beginning form'd Matter in solid, massy, hard, impenetrable, moveable Particles, of such Sizes and Figures, and with such other Properties, and in such Proportion to Space, as most conduced to the End for which He form'd them and that these primitive Particles being Solids, are incomparably harder than any porous Bodies compounded of them; even so very hard, as never to wear or break in pieces; no ordinary Power being able to divide what God himself made one in the first Creation" (*Opticks*, p. 400 [Query 31]).

31. *Principia*, p. 544.

32. The qualifications, which relate to the role of experiment, mathematics, theory, and certainty in scientific method, are indeed such as to make less surprising D. Brewster's conclusion that Newton "would have enriched science with the same splendid discoveries if the name and the writings of Bacon had never been heard of" (*Memoirs of the Life, Writings, and Discoveries of Sir Isaac Newton* [Edinburgh: Thomas Constable, 1855], 2:403).

33. *Principia*, p. 547 (General Scholium.) As A. Koyré pointed out, the meaning of the phrase related to the surreptitious use of hypotheses by Baconians and Cartesians, a use for which their respective methods provided no justification. *Newtonian Studies* (Cambridge: Harvard University Press, 1965), p. 52.

34. Newton treated force in an increasingly abstract perspective as a "quantitative concept able to enter into a quantitative mechanics," and this meant, as R. S. Westfall noted in his *Force in Newton's Physics: The Science of Dynamics in the Seventeenth Century* (London: Macdonald, 1971), p. 345, a "turning point in the terminology of mechanics."

35. While the anonymous reviewer of the *Principia* admitted in the *Journal des Sçavans* that "the work of Mr. Newton is the most perfect mechanics that we can imagine," he urged Newton to complete his work by giving "us a physics as exact as the mechanics." See E. J. Aiton, *The Vortex Theory of Planetary Motions*, p. 114.

36. The claim has enjoyed much credence through the works of Comte, J. S. Mill, and Mach, and of their rearguard disciples, past and present, but must appear hollow to anyone familiar with Koyré's *Newtonian Studies*, a work which offers powerful (though possibly unintended) support to the contention of this lecture that Newton instinctively endorsed a median position between empiricism and rationalism, and that he did so in virtue of his scientific creativity. Oversight of the import of that epistemological middle road is the most telling though hardly surprising aspect of T. H. Huxley's felicitous remark in his "The Progress of Science" (1887) that "the progress of physical science has been effected neither by Baconians nor by Cartesians, as such, but by men like Galileo and Harvey, Boyle and Newton, who would have done their work just as well if neither Bacon nor Descartes had ever propounded their views respecting the manner in which scientific investigation should be pursued" (*Method and Results* [London: Macmillan, 1894], pp. 48–49). The same oversight is the chief defect of the studies in *The Methodological Heritage of Newton*, ed. R. E. Butts and J. W. Davis (Toronto: University of Toronto Press, 1970), whose authors mostly inject into Newton's way of thinking the logicism and psychologism characteristic of most recent studies of the philosophy of science.

37. *Principia*, p. 5.

38. Ibid., pp. 5–6.

39. Ibid., p. 5.

40. Ibid., p. 568.

41. Ibid., p. 398.

42. In this connection one cannot help thinking of Einstein's candid admission, "the man of science is a poor philosopher," in his "Physics and Reality" (1936) in *Out of My Later Years* (New York: Philosophical Library, 1950), p. 58.

43. *Opticks*, p. 404.

44. See, for instance, *Theories of Scientific Method: The Renaissance through the Nineteenth Century*, ed. E. H. Madden (Seattle: University of Washington Press, 1960), p. 140.

45. *Opticks*, p. 403 (Query 31).

46. Ibid., p. 353 (Query 23).

47. Ibid., pp. 353–54 (Query 24).

48. Such is the obvious thrust of his blunt declaration: "And if at any time I speak of Light and Rays as coloured or endued with Colours, I would be understood to speak not philosophically and properly, but grossly, and accordingly to such Conceptions as vulgar People in seeing all these Experiments would be apt to frame" (ibid., p. 124).

49. *Principia*, p. 399 (Rule III of Reasoning in Philosophy).

50. A memorable remark of R. S. Westfall in his "Newton and the Fudge Factor," *Science* 179 (1973): 753.

51. *A View of Sir Isaac Newton's Philosophy*, p. 23.

52. This is why for Newton natural theology, or a discourse about God "from

the appearances of things, does certainly belong to Natural Philosophy" (*Principia*, p. 546); and this is why he consistently assigned the frame of the world "to the Counsel of an Intelligent Agent" performing the "first Creation," to the "counsel and dominion of an intelligent and powerful Being" (p. 544), and to the "Counsel and Contrivance of a voluntary Agent" (first letter to Bentley, in *Isaac Newton's Papers and Letters*, p. 288). He did so not only consistently but also naturally, because for him "the main Business of natural Philosophy is to argue from Phaenomena without feigning Hypotheses, and to deduce Causes from Effects, till we come to the very first Cause, which certainly is not mechanical" (*Opticks*, p. 369, Query 28).

53. *Newtonian Studies*, pp. 4–5. The claim is hardly reconcilable with what is best there in Koyré's discussion of Newton's relation to Descartes and of the respective roles of concept and experience in Newton's scientific thought. See also note 36 above.

54. *Conjectures and Refutations: The Growth of Scientific Knowledge* (New York: Harper and Row, 1968), pp. 106–7.

55. Dublin: Geo. Ewing and Wil. Smith, 1743.

56. A point which failed to receive justice in E. M. MacKinnon, "Theism and Scientific Explanation," *Continuum*, Winter-Spring, 1967, pp. 70–88.

57. As amply revealed in F. E. Manuel, *Isaac Newton Historian* (Cambridge: Harvard University Press, 1963), and in R. S. Westfall, *Science and Religion in Seventeenth-Century England* (New Haven: Yale University Press, 1958). To make matters worse, Newton approached the facts of history with the mind of a geometer, a pattern in which he was followed by his successor in the Lucasian chair, William Whiston, about whom Warburton aptly remarked: "But the thing is notorious: and it is now no secret that the oldest mathematician in England is the worst reasoner in [history]." See his introduction to *Julian* in *The Works of the Right Reverend William Warburton* (London: new ed. printed by Luke Hansard and Sons, 1811), 8:xvi.

58. In his "Some Motives and Incentives to the Love of God, pathetically discours'd of, in a Letter to a Friend," composed in 1648, but published only in 1660. See *Works*, 1:249.

59. As pointed out in R. S. Westfall, *Science and Religion in Seventeenth-Century England*, pp. 89–91.

60. See on this chapter 11, "The Interlude of 'Re-naissance,'" in my *Science and Creation: From Eternal Cycles to an Oscillating Universe* (Edinburgh: Scottish Academic Press, 1974).

61. D. Stimson, "Puritanism and the New Philosophy in 17th-century England," *Bulletin of the Institute of the History of Medicine*, 3 (1935): 334. Stimson's felicitous remarks have more merit than most publications on the role of Puritans and Puritanism in the rise of science.

62. It was in fact the subtle absence of genuine ontology and metaphysics in Wolff's system which later prompted Kant to espouse the surface truth of Newtonian physics as ultimate verity and jettison in the same act ontology and metaphysics.

63. The subtitle reads: *More Particularly in Answer to Mr. Hobbs, Spinoza, and their Followers*. References are to the seventh edition (London: James and John Kapton, 1728). The printed text, as also stated on the title page, was "the substance of eight sermons preach'd in the Cathedral Church of St. Paul."

64. Ibid., p. 485 (answer to the Fifth Letter).

65. Ibid., p. 487 (answer to the Sixth Letter).

66. Ibid.

67. Ibid., p. 489.

68. Ibid., p. 45.

69. Ibid., p. 40.

70. Ibid., p. 488.

71. Ibid., p. 66.

72. Ibid., p. 24.

73. Ibid., p. 49. A natural invitation for d'Holbach to take a phrase from Clarke's *Demonstration* and write "matter" wherever Clarke wrote "God." See B. Willey, *The Eighteenth Century Background* (London: Chatto and Windus, 1940), p. 161.

74. "The Principles of Nature and of Grace, Based on Reason" (1714), in *Leibniz Selections*, edited by Philip P. Wiener (New York: Charles Scribner's Sons, 1951), p. 527.

75. *Demonstration*, p. 487 (answer to the Sixth Letter).

76. "Suppose a book on the elements of geometry to have been eternal and that others had been successively copied from it, it is evident that, although we might account for the present book by the book which was its model, we could nevertheless never, by assuming any number of books whatever, reach a perfect reason for them; for we may always wonder why such books have existed from all time; that is, why books exist at all and why they are thus written. What is true of books is also true of the different states of the world" ("On the Ultimate Origin of Things" [1697] in *Leibniz Selections*, p. 345).

77. As well illustrated by the twenty impressive studies on Leibniz written for the 250th anniversary of his death and edited by W. Totok and C. Haase, *Leibniz: Sein Leben, sein Wirken, seine Welt* (Hanover: Verlag für Literatur und Zeitgeschehen, 1966). He is discussed there, in connection with science, as a mathematician, a cybernetician, and as an organizer of science, but not as a physicist.

78. *An Essay concerning Human Understanding*, edited with notes by Alexander C. Fraser (New York: Dover reprint, 1959), 2:312.

79. Ibid., p. 307.

80. Ibid., p. 215.

81. Locke's subtle leaning toward nominalism can be seen in his attitude toward the relation between individuals and species, as was aptly noted in A. O. Lovejoy, *The Great Chain of Being* (Cambridge: Harvard University Press, 1936), pp. 228–29.

82. In order to save infinity Halley seemed to opt for an inhomogeneity, that is, for a gradual thinning out of stars with distance. It did not occur to him that he introduced thereby an absolute center in Euclidean space. See on this my *The Paradox of Olbers' Paradox*, pp. 76–83. In connection with the meeting M. Hoskin conjectured ("Dark Skies and Fixed Stars," *Journal of the British Astronomical Association* 83 [1973]: 260) that Newton was asleep while Halley read his papers, but quite possibly Newton still had the same high-handed attitude regarding the difficulties of an infinite universe which he had displayed toward Bentley.

83. *An Essay concerning Human Understanding*, 2:231. The point is emphasized in E. Cassirer, *Das Erkenntnisproblem*, 3d ed. (Berlin: Bruno Cassirer, 1922), 2:255.

84. *An Essay concerning Human Understanding*, 2:311. The declaration (Rom. 1:20) has been quoted in chapter 3.

Chapter Seven

. 1. It did not even reach such distinction, he added, as "to excite a murmur among the zealots." See his "My Own Life" (1776) in *The Philosophical Works of David Hume* (Edinburgh: Adam Black and William Tait, 1826), 1:v.

2. *An Enquiry concerning Human Understanding,* sec. 4, pt. 1, *Philosophical Works,* 4:38.

3. Even if Hume had heard about the lack of rigor which at that time still characterized the theory of limit in infinitesimal calculus, his lack of expertise in it and his insensitivity to its spectacular effectiveness would be betrayed by his deprecating appraisal which, revealingly enough, could but land him in skepticism about skepticism itself: "No priestly *dogmas,* invented on purpose to tame and subdue the rebellious reason of mankind, ever shocked common sense more than the doctrine of the infinite divisibility of extension, with its consequences; as they are pompously displayed by all geometricians and metaphysicians, with a kind of triumph and exultation. A real quantity, infinitely less than any finite quantity, containing qualities [quantities] infinitely less than itself, and so on *in infinitum;* this is an edifice so bold and prodigious, that it is too weighty for any pretended demonstration to support, because it shocks the clearest and most natural principles of human reason ... How any clear, distinct idea, can contain circumstances contradictory to itself, or to any other clear, distinct idea, is absolutely incomprehensible, and is, perhaps, as absurd as any proposition which can be formed. So that nothing can be more sceptical, or more full of doubt and hesitation, than this scepticism itself, which arises from some of the paradoxical conclusions of geometry or the science of quantity" (*Enquiry,* sec. 12, pt. 2; *Philosophical Works,* 4:182–84).

4. Such is at least the implicit thrust of his remark that "moral philosophy is in the same condition as natural, with regard to astronomy before the time of Copernicus" (*Treatise of Human Nature,* bk. 2, pt. 1, sec. 3, *Philosophical Works,* 2:11).

5. The title of essay 4, one of the original fifteen essays published in 1741 under the title, *Essays, Moral and Political* (Edinburgh: A. Kincaid), pp. 27–48.

6. *Treatise,* introduction, *Philosophical Works,* 1:7–8.

7. *Enquiry,* sec. 12, pt. 3, *Philosophical Works,* 4:192.

8. Hume's foremost modern biographer, E. C. Mossner, tried to create the impression in his *The Life of David Hume* (Austin: University of Texas Press, 1954), pp. 43–46 and 73, that Hume became amply aquainted with science and especially with Newton's physics during his student days at the University of Edinburgh, but the evidence merely proves that Newton was held in high regard by some professors there. At any rate Newtonian physics, let alone the *Principia* itself, could hardly be the subject of regular instructions in an institute of learning about which Hume wrote in 1734 in a letter to a physician friend: "Our college education in Scotland, extending little further than the languages, ends commonly when we are about fourteen or fifteen years of age." What Hume added in the same letter written shortly before his departure for France provides no ground for supposing that he read much about the exact sciences after he had left school: "I was after that left to my own choice in my reading, and found it incline me almost equally to books of reasoning and philosophy, and to poetry and the polite authors. Everyone who is acquainted either with the philosophers or critics, knows that there is nothing yet established in either of these two sciences, and that they contain little more than endless disputes, even in the most fundamental articles." The foremost modern student of Hume's philosophy, N. K. Smith, was no more fortunate in his effort to present Hume as one with a proper grasp of Newtonian physics. That physics could not be learned, contrary to Smith's contention, from Locke's *Essay,* and it is a mere guess that Hume attended the classes of Robert Stewart, who taught natural philosophy. At any rate, unless a class of young teen-agers was made up of precocious geniuses, the physics lessons given by Stewart to regularly sched-

uled classes had to be on a very elementary level. On Smith's conjectures, see his *The Philosophy of David Hume: A Critical Study of Its Origins and Central Doctrines* (London: Macmillan, 1941), pp. 53–76. A cryptic evidence of Hume's unfamiliarity with exact science is provided in the collection of essays, *Scienza e filosofia scozzese nell' età di Hume*, ed. A. Santucci (Bologna: Società editrice il Mulino, 1976), which contains no treatment of, not even a reference to, Hume's reflections on science. In the Scottish science of Hume's time Hume had no part even as a philosopher of science.

9. Boswell did so in 1762. See Mossner, *The Life of David Hume*, p. 223.

10. In a letter in which he admitted that he had not read d'Alembert's scientific works. In quoting that letter Mossner also provides the priceless detail that Diderot, the thorough empiricist, was strongly attracted to Hume, no doubt because of the affinities of their minds (*The Life of David Hume*, p. 477). Diderot, a scoffer at theoretical science, could but find congenial a Hume for whom "experimental" was virtually equivalent to "empirical," as Smith was compelled to admit (*The Philosophy of David Hume*, p. 62).

11. See article "Hume" in the 1964 edition, 11:834, col. 2.

12. *The History of England from the Invasion of Julius Caesar to the Revolution in 1688* (New York: Harper and Brothers, 1879), 4:402.

13. Ibid., 6:342–44.

14. Ibid., p. 344.

15. The public character of that knowledge can easily be gathered from *A Portrait of Isaac Newton* by F. E. Manuel (Cambridge: Harvard University Press, 1968), a work which in spite of its heavy reliance on Freudian psychoanalysis provides a welcome antidote to the moral apotheosis of Newton which Pemberton, Desaguliers, and Voltaire initiated and which found its fullest expression in D. Brewster's Newtonian studies. That apotheosis is not wholly absent in L. T. More's still standard monograph, *Isaac Newton: A Biography* (London: Constable, 1934), made widely available through its Dover reprint (1962).

16. Sensations, he wrote, arise "in the soul originally, from unknown causes" (*Treatise*, bk. 1, pt. 1, sec. 2, *Philosophical Works*, 1:22).

17. The essay, which was not among the original fifteen first published in 1741 (see note 5 above) and again in 1742, saw print in the third edition, "corrected with additions" (London: A. Millar . . . and A. Kincaid in Edinburgh, 1748), as one of eleven additional essays. Its thirty-six pages (pp. 156–92) exceeded by a factor of three the length of most other essays, a circumstance striking enough to convey something of the importance Hume attached to it. That importance can also be gathered from the care with which he improved it in the fourth edition (1753) of the *Essays* (pp. 156–93), but with no revisions on what strictly pertained to the question of the origin of science. The more than a dozen further editions of the *Essays* during the remainder of the century made Hume's reflections on the origin of science the most widespread and yet most generally ignored discussion of the topic. Essay 17 is overlooked in most major works on Hume. In the index of Mossner's work twenty-three essays are listed by title, but not the one "Of the Rise and Progress of the Arts and Sciences"! References are to the text in *Essays, Moral, Political, and Literary*, ed. T. H. Green and T. H. Grose (London: Longmans, Green and Co., 1898), 1:174–97.

18. *Essays, Moral, Political, and Literary*, p. 175.

19. Ibid., p. 177.

20. Ibid., p. 187.

21. Ibid., p. 181.

22. Without that new method, wrote Henry Power, a Fellow of the Royal Society, in 1664, man would still be without "the useful Inventions of Guns,

Printing, Navigation, Paper, and Sugar ... Decimal and Symbolical Arithmetick, the Analytical Algebra, the Magnetical Philosophy, the Logarithms, the Hydrargyral Experiments, the glorious Inventions of Dioptrick Glasses, Wind-guns, and the Noble *Boyle's* Pneumatick Engine." With that new method in man's hands, "there is no Truth so abstruse, nor so far elevated out of our reach, but man's wit may raise Engines to Scale and Conquer it." Formulation of that method signaled in Power's eyes the onset of "the Age wherein (me-thinks) Philosophy comes in with a Spring-tide." He certainly voiced the sentiment prevailing among the virtuosi that theirs were "the days ... of a more magnificent Philosophy never to be overthrown." Like Power, none of the others seemed to feel that "it is no Rhetorication to say, that all things are Artificial; for Nature it self is nothing else but the Art of God," the obvious inference being that therefore all problems could be tackled with the wizardry of the new method. *Experimental Philosophy in Three Books: Containing New Experiments, Microscopical, Mercurial, Magnetical* (London: John Martin and James Allestry, 1664), pp. 190–93.

23. *Essays, Moral, Political, and Literary,* p. 195.

24. Ibid., p. 183.

25. Ibid.

26. Ibid.

27. Ibid., p. 177.

28. Ibid.

29. First published in 1757 with three other essays under the title, *Four Dissertations.* Advance word about its contents made Hume believe that he would be declared an infidel by some at the General Assembly of the Church of Scotland in 1756. See Mossner, *Life,* p. 325. The following references are to the text in *The Philosophical Works,* 4:435–513.

30. Hume's comparison of polytheism and monotheism with regard to persecution and toleration, to courage and abasement, to reason and absurdity, to doubt and conviction had it that "the human sacrifices of the Carthaginians, Mexicans, and many barbarous nations, scarcely exceed the inquisition and persecutions of Rome and Madrid" (p. 477–78); that "Brasidas seized a mouse, and being bit by it, let it go ... [whereas] Bellarmine patiently and humbly allowed the fleas and other odious vermin to prey upon him" (p. 480); that "a system becomes more absurd in the end, merely from its being reasonable and philosophical in the beginning" (p. 483); and that "there is no tenet in all paganism which would give so fair a scope to ridicule as this of the *real presence;* for it is so absurd that it eludes the force of all argument" (p. 484). "Upon the whole," Hume concluded, "the greatest and most observable differences between a *traditional, mythological* religion, and a *systematical, scholastic* one, are two: The former is often more reasonable, as consisting only of a multitude of stories, which, however, groundless, imply no express absurdity and demonstrative contradiction; and sits also so easy and light on men's minds, that though it may be as universally received, it happily makes no such deep impression on the affections and understanding" (pp. 497–98). This last remark reveals something of Hume's paramount objective, the achieving of mental comfort. For its sake Hume let his skeptical philosophy undermine religious as well as scientific thought, neither of which can be cultivated with a horror of that intellectual tension which is needed to prevent the collapse of one's mental edifice into a heap of bricks.

31. For further details and documentation, see Mossner, *Life,* pp. 321–22.

32. Will be quoted as *Dialogues,* with references to the edition with introduction and notes by N. K. Smith (Edinburgh: Thomas Nelson and Sons, 1947).

33. For Copernicus, a Christian Neoplatonist, some impressions could only be dull shadows of some crystal-clear ideas.

34. A Christian Neoplatonist like Copernicus could have no problem along these lines.

35. *Treatise,* bk. 1, pt. 1, sec. 3; *Philosophical Works,* 1:26.

36. *Treatise,* bk. 1, pt. 1, sec. 4; ibid., p. 29.

37. *Treatise,* ibid.

38. *Treatise,* bk. 1, pt. 4, sec. 2; ibid., p. 268. Once Hume had shown that the mind was but a series of impressions, he still should have explained how the mind constructed itself to exercise such activities as reflection on impressions.

39. *Treatise,* ibid.

40. *Treatise,* bk. 1, pt. 4, sec. 6; ibid., p. 322.

41. *Treatise,* bk. 1, pt. 4, sec. 7; ibid., p. 335.

42. *Treatise,* ibid., pp. 335 and 341.

43. In the Appendix to the *Treatise; Philosophical Works,* 2:556. A little later Hume wrote: "All my hopes vanish, when I come to explain the principles that unite our successive perceptions in our thought or consciousness" (p. 559).

44. In the *Treatise* (bk. 1, pt. 4, sec. 7; *Philosophical Works,* 1:341) Hume spoke with nostalgia about the hours spent in dining and playing backgammon as contrasted with the hours spent on the clarification of philosophical ideas, which appeared to him at times "so cold, and strained, and ridiculous, that I cannot find in my heart to enter into them any further."

45. The vistas were the ones embodied in the somber Calvinistic sermonizing in vogue in Scotland during Hume's early years, as noted by both Mossner and Smith.

46. Actually, it was a "friend" of Hume who made the speech to which Hume replied with several objections, but in a manner which made it all the more clear that the speech, a rebuttal of transcendental perspectives and a confinement of reasoning to the strictly observable, carried Hume's central message (see *Philosophical Works,* 4:158–73). Hume was certainly not contesting the final remark which his friend made in defense of Epicurus, a remark that could not be more Humean: "All the philosophy, therefore, in the world, and all the religion, which is nothing but a species of philosophy, will never be able to carry us beyond the usual course of experience, or give us measures of conduct and behaviour different from those which are furnished by reflections on common life. No new fact can ever be inferred from the religious hypothesis; no event foreseen or foretold; no reward or punishment expected or dreaded, beyond what is already known by practice and observation" (ibid., p. 171). Hume's turning to Epicurus illustrates a principal feature of the history of philosophy, namely, the instinctive ease with which a thinker recognizes among his predecessors the one most akin to his own frame of mind. Another feature consists in the "rediscovery" of already well-articulated positions and in the spelling out of basic alternatives. Illustrations of the latter points are Hume's endorsement of the notion of eternal cosmic returns and his admission that it is always "the antagonists of Epicurus," in short, theists, who advocate the idea of a fully rational and quite singular universe (ibid., p. 173). What Hume failed in particular to realize was that it was that kind of universe which was constantly presupposed by all great scientists. Not surprisingly, Hume advocated the "Epicurean hypothesis" also in the *Dialogues* (pt. 8, p. 182), a work in which misunderstanding of science was a logical part of the derision of natural theology.

47. *Dialogues,* pt. 2, p. 150.

48. Ibid. The rotation of Venus on its axis became an experimental fact only

in the 1950s through the application of radar techniques. Hume might have taken the phases of Venus as evidence of its rotation, but they merely prove that Venus is an inferior planet.

49. Ibid.

50. As noted and documented in chapter 3.

51. Also a point discussed there.

52. *Dialogues*, pt. 5, p. 167.

53. *Dialogues*, pt. 9, p. 190.

54. *Dialogues*, pt. 2, p. 142.

55. *Dialogues*, pt. 9, p. 189.

56. *Dialogues*, pt. 6, p. 174 and pt. 8, pp. 184–85. As in all other endorsements of the Great Year, the antiscientific character of the stance was apparent in Hume's case as well. That matter may be "susceptible of many and great revolutions, through the endless periods of eternal duration," was voiced by Philo while being forced to admit at the same time that "strong and almost incontestable proofs may be traced over the whole earth that every part of this globe has continued for many ages entirely covered with water," and that "order were supposed inseparable from matter and inherent in it." Hume might have heard from Diderot, another skeptical materialist and scoffer at theoretical science, the idea of eternal returns, but he might very well have been led to it by the inner logic of his basic presuppositions. For an extensive documentation of the clash of the idea of eternal returns with science in any age and culture, see my *Science and Creation: From Eternal Cycles to an Oscillating Universe* (Edinburgh: Scottish Academic Press, 1974).

57. *Dialogues*, pt. 7, p. 180.

58. For details and documentation, see chap. 1, "The World as an Organism," in my *The Relevance of Physics* (Chicago: University of Chicago Press, 1966).

59. *Dialogues*, pt. 7, p. 177.

60. See chap. 2, "The World as a Mechanism," in my *The Relevance of Physics*.

61. *Dialogues*, pt. 7, p. 177.

62. *Dialogues*, pt. 5, pp. 167–69.

63. *The Philosophy of David Hume*, p. 564. Smith did not recall that Hume's principal contention was aimed at showing that the human mind is incapable of learning those features of nature which would reveal her objective rationality and that, therefore, man could live comfortably without being constrained by superior truths. Nor did Smith perceive the significance of Hume's attachment to Epicurus as his intellectual idol, an attachment motivated by the same intellectual and emotional "comfort" that Epicurus sought to achieve by denying intrinsic rationality to the universe.

64. *Dialogues*, pt. 7, p. 178.

65. *Dialogues*, pt. 7, pp. 180–81.

66. Had he known of them, he would have most likely let Philo point out their shortcomings. These were abundant not only in Descartes's cosmogony, out of fashion by Hume's time, but also in Whiston's and Buffon's efforts to explain the origin of the solar system through the collision of a comet with the sun. Hume, however, would hardly have let Philo recall in detail Newton's still valid insistence on the need of specific intervention by God in the formation of the solar system and of the universe of stars.

67. Hume's sundry references to cosmos and cosmology are still in need of a special study. It would show not only the true physiognomy of his whole philosophy within a special topic, but also his incurably and inescapably antiscientific bent of mind. This point wholly escaped Whitehead, who spoke of the *Dialogues* as a "masterpiece" in his *Process and Reality: An Essay in Cosmology*

(New York: Macmillan, 1929, p. 520), a work in which Hume's sharp eyes would have quickly discovered to his great delight Whitehead's subtle advocacy of the idea of a finite God and of cosmic returns.

68. *Dialogues*, pt. 9, p. 189.

69. *Enquiry*, sec. 12, pt. 3, *Philosophical Works*, 4:193.

70. See note 3 above.

71. See chap. 1, note 26.

72. Butler was only one of the many who failed to do so. Not his slighting of Hume, still a beginner in 1740, but the *Analogy*'s impact was the reason for the composition by Hume of his *Dialogues* in such a way as to give some credence to the claim that Cleanthes represented Butler—a claim rejected by A. Jeffner in his *Butler and Hume on Religion: A Comparative Analysis* (Stockholm: Diakonistyrelsens Bokforlag, 1966), pp. 170–71.

73. *Treatise*, bk. 1, pt. 4, sec. 7, *Philosophical Works*, 1:335.

74. If they read him approvingly, they would have also agreed with Hume, who remarked that "whatever may be the reader's opinion at this present moment, ... an hour hence he will be persuaded [that] there is both an external and internal world" (*Treatise*, bk. 1, pt. 4, sec. 2, *Philosophical Works*, 1:281). Those scientists, with perhaps the sole exception of Mach, believed in an external world subject to the consistent interaction of its constituent parts, and did so not on the basis of philosophical "carelessness and inattention," which Hume singled out as the sole justification of such a belief, but on the basis of that sound epistemological instinct which is usually generated by creative work in science.

75. The subsequent reaction was similar to what happened a hundred years earlier to the author of the *Principia*. No less than Newton, Herschel had become a tourist attraction.

76. *Treatise*, bk. 1, pt. 2, sec. 6, *Philosophical Works*, 1:97.

77. In my encounters with two such astronomers of world fame, one hesitated to be consistent to the extent of claiming that not only the stars but also the wall opposite to him existed only as long as he perceived it. The other, a solipsist, was hard put to explain the validity for others of his account of the universe of galaxies which he could observe only through giant telescopes, hardly a part of his own self.

78. In his paper, "On the Utility of Speculative Inquiries," read on April 14, 1780; *The Scientific Papers of Sir William Herschel*, ed. J. L. E. Dreyer (London: Royal Society, 1912), 1:lxxxi.

79. Ibid., pp. lxxxi–lxxxii.

80. In his "Catalogue of a Second Thousand of new Nebulae and Clusters of Stars" (1789), *Scientific Papers*, 1:330.

81. In his "On the Construction of the Heavens," one of his two epoch-making papers; *The Scientific Papers*, 1:223.

CHAPTER EIGHT

1. No sooner had it been printed in 1755 than the publisher, J. F. Peterson, went bankrupt and his holdings were impounded. The book, which did not carry the author's name, was dedicated to Frederick the Great, a move by which Kant hoped to obtain an academic post. Although it was given a brief and favorable review in the *Freye Urtheile* (July 15, 1755, p. 432), only a few copies reached the public. Ten or so years later, Lambert, already a member of the Berlin Academy, was unable to obtain a copy from any of the booksellers in Berlin. German scientists looked askance at Kant's theory of the evolution of the solar system, until Helmholtz gave a favorable, though very superficial, account

of it in 1854 in a lecture which was largely responsible for creating the myth of the Kant-Laplace theory. The introduction written by the theologian W. Hastie to his translation published in 1900 of Kant's work is as uncritical as are the introductions written by G. Whitrow and W. Ley respectively to two recent reprints of Hastie's translation, which will be referred to as *Kant's Cosmogony*. For further details and documentation, see chap. 5, "The Nebulous Advance," in my *Planets and Planetarians: A History of Theories of the Origin of Planetary Systems* (Edinburgh: Scottish Academic Press, 1977), my *The Milky Way: An Elusive Road for Science* (New York: Science History Publications, 1972), p. 235, and my translation with introduction and notes of J. H. Lambert's *Cosmological Letters on the Arrangement of the World-Edifice* (New York: Science History Publications, 1976), p. 26.

2. The conviction was developed naturally by any enthusiast of Kant as can be seen from the anonymous translator's note in Emanuel Kant, *Essays and Treatises on Moral, Political, and Various Philosophical Subjects* (London: printed for the translator and sold by William Richardson, 1798–99, 2:331): "Kant foretold in 1755 (in his *Universal Physiognomy and Theory of the Heavens*) from theoretical grounds what Herschel discovered many years after by the assistance of his gigantic telescope. It cannot but be interesting to compare the structure of the heavens, which one great man has conceived according to Newtonian laws from the original *genesis* of the celestial bodies, with the construction of the heavens as another great man has exhibited it according to observations."

3. These and similar details can easily be gathered from the monograph on Knutzen by B. Erdmann, *Martin Knutzen und seine Zeit: Ein Beitrag zur Geschichte der Wolfischen Schule und insbesondere zur Entwicklungsgeschichte Kants* (Leipzig: Verlag von Leopold Voss, 1876; reprinted, Hildesheim: H. A. Gerstenberg, 1973).

4. A claim made by J. W. Ellington in his article "Kant" in *Dictionary of Scientific Biography* (New York: Charles Scribner's Sons, 1970–), 7:225. Inaccuracy and superficiality are the true features of Ellington's article, for example, that upon entering the University of Königsberg in 1740 Kant "studied mainly mathematics and physics with Martin Knutzen and Johann Teske" (p. 224), that for fifteen years (1755–1770) Kant as a Privatdozent lectured "on physics and nearly all aspects of philosophy" (p. 225), that "Wright gave the first essentially correct interpretation of the Milky Way" (p. 231), and that "in his *Theory of the Heavens*, Kant, by a series of bold strokes, anticipated astronomical facts that were later confirmed ... with the help of relativistic [!] cosmological theory" (p. 231). It is sheer agnostic propaganda and romantic speculation to claim as Ellington does that in spite of his pietistic background Kant "became the one, who, above all others, liberated philosophy and science from theology. His single-minded devotion to both philosophy and science also accounts largely for the fact that he never married" (p. 225). Ellington should rather have focused on the problem that if Kant was truly aware of the relativity of all motion (p. 230) why did he fail to disavow the absolute physical center of the universe he had advocated in his cosmogony?

5. *Kant's Cosmogony*, p. 36. The "degree of thoroughness" did not include mathematical exactness as Kant pointed out rather defensively in the same context. Later, however, he boasted that it was possible "if we cared" to present the evolution of the planetary system with "the parade" of the mathematical method (p. 72). The claim was all the more hollow as he subtly hinted in the same context at his incompetence in mathematics: "I prefer to present my views in the form of a hypothesis ... rather than bring their validity into suspicion by the appearance of a surreptitious [mathematical] demonstration, lest, while

winning the ignorant, I should lose the approval of those who really know the subject." The only notable quantitative detail in Kant's cosmogony, his computation of Saturn's rotation period as 6 hours, 23 minutes, and 53 seconds, a result remarkably close to the value established later by Herschel's observations, was the result of sheer luck. The dynamical basis of his calculations was wholly unsound.

6. Ibid., p. 36. Such minor details were, according to him, "the determination of the relations of eccentricity, the comparison of the masses of the planets, the manifold deviations of the comets, and some other propositions."

7. Ibid., p. 37.

8. In both respects Kant was anticipated by Lambert who, however, did not publish his insights until 1761. Even a quarter of a century later Herschel could make the same discoveries without being aware of Kant's work, an indication of the almost general failure of scientifically informed men to take note of Kant, the cosmologist. For details, see my *The Milky Way*, chaps. 6 and 7.

9. *Kant's Cosmogony*, p. 142. He defined that point in terms of the greatest density. It was there that he located that central body which by its gravitational attraction made "in the infinite sphere of the creation the whole universe into only one single system" (p. 143). Being a very amateur physicist, Kant did not perceive that this central body, playing the role of gravitational fulcrum in an infinite universe, had to be infinitely massive, a circumstance which destroyed his concept of an infinite universe.

10. Ibid., pp. 149–50.

11. See note 66 below.

12. G. Siegmund: *God on Trial: A Brief History of Atheism*, trans. E. C. Briefs (New York: Desclee Company, 1968), p. 185.

13. See especially the introduction and the concluding chapter of part two in his cosmogonical work. In the former he defends himself against the charges that his theory is "Epicurean," in the latter he repeatedly voices a worshipful reverence for the great Designer evidenced by the lawfulness of nature.

14. *Kant's Cosmogony*, p. 151.

15. Ibid., p. 75. The context is also a perfect example of Kant's studied vagueness with the word "infinity." In theory , the range of specific densities could not be limited and, indeed, Kant spoke of gradations "as infinite as possible" (p. 75), stating also that the "kinds of ... elementary matter are undoubtedly infinitely different" (pp. 74–75). The expression "as infinite as possible" needs no comment. The formation of the enormously large body in the center of the Milky Way (p. 137) presupposed an element of a density far exceeding the range specified by Kant, to say nothing of that infinite density implied in the formation of the central body of the entire infinite universe. Instead of facing up to the implications of infinity, Kant described the massiveness of that central body in relation to the Milky Way as the ratio of an insect to the whole earth (p. 151). The comparison was worthy of a poet but not of one parading as another Newton.

16. As emphasized and documented throughout in my *Planets and Planetarians*.

17. "Prüfung der Kantischen Hypothese von dem mechanischen Ursprung des Planetensystems," *Philosophisches Archiv* (Berlin: 1792), Band I, Stück 2, pp. 1–36. A year later the same periodical (Band I, Stück 4, pp. 1–21) carried Schwab's criticism of Kant's theory of the origin of Saturn's ring and of his derivation of the rotation period of Saturn.

18. The letters, originally published in the *Teutsche Merkur* in 1785–86, appeared in a book form in 1792 under the title, *Briefe über die Kantische Philoso-*

phie (Leipzig: bey Georg Joachim Göschen) in two volumes. For Reinhold's discussion of the impact of Kant's philosophy on natural theology, see letter 4 (1:110–44). It is there (p. 111) that Reinhold's sole reference is made to Newtonian physics, namely, to Newton's theory of colors, in uncanny evidence of the very tenuous connection between the *Critique* and science. Reinhold's "unscientific" and uncritical enthusiasm for Kant's *Critique* is well reflected in his claim made to Schiller that "within a century Kant will have the reputation of Jesus Christ." See on this latter point J. H. W. Stuckenberg, *The Life of Immanuel Kant* (London: Macmillan, 1882), p. 376.

19. See *Immanuel Kant's Critique of Pure Reason,* translated by Norman Kemp Smith (London: Macmillan, 1929), p. 20. This translation will be referred to as *Critique.*

20. This third part, not translated by Hastie and passed over in studied silence by all admirers of Kant as cosmologist and critical philosopher, can now be read in my English translation in *Cosmology, History of Science, and Theology,* ed. A. D. Breck and W. Yourgrau (New York: Plenum Press, 1977), pp. 387–403.

21. See Stuckenberg, *The Life of Immanuel Kant,* p. 140. In the same context Stuckenberg quotes Count Purgstall of Bavaria, an admirer of Kant, who recalled that Kant had refused to yield to him on such particulars as the kinds of fowl in Bavaria and the degree of culture of Catholic clergy there.

22. *Der einzig mögliche Beweisgrund zu einer Demonstration des Daseins Gottes.* References are to the text in *Kant's gesammelte Schriften: Kant's Werke* (Berlin: G. Reimer, 1902–55), 2:63–163.

23. Ibid., pp. 155–56. The verdict had to appear rather shattering in view of the length (pp. 137–51, equivalent to almost one-sixth of the entire work) of Kant's summary of his cosmology.

24. Ibid., p. 157. The argument starts with the statement, distinctly Cartesian, that one cannot deny the possibility of existence because any such denial implies thinking, a form of existence. Once, however, the possibility of existence is affirmed, the ground is lost for denying that there is an existent ground of possibility.

25. References are to the translation in *Kant: Selected Pre-Critical Writings and Correspondence with Beck,* translated and introduced by G. B. Kerferd and D. E. Walford, with a contribution by P. G. Lucas (Manchester: University Press, 1968), pp. 5–35.

26. Ibid., p. 14.

27. Ibid., p. 17.

28. Ibid., p. 5.

29. Actually, Warburton stated in his *Julian* (1750) that concentration on geometry "incapacitates the mind for reasoning at large, and especially in the search of moral truth," emphasizing at the same time that the same concentration "habituates the mind to think long and closely." See *The Works of the Right Reverend William Warburton* (new ed.; London: printed by Luke Hansard and Sons, 1811), 8:xiv. It was in sermon 13, "The Influence of Learning on Revelation," in his *The Principles of Natural and Revealed Religion,* originally published in three volumes between 1753 and 1767, that Warburton blamed concentration on geometry for the weakening of one's grasp of philosophical and theological demonstrations. See *Works,* 11:264.

30. "Enquiry" in *Kant: Selected Pre-Critical Writings,* p. 29.

31. Ibid., p. 31.

32. F. S. C. Northrop also credited Kant with the derivation of the eccentricity of planetary and cometary orbits and with the general history of the sun and concluded with words which perfectly illustrate how myths are being made and

perpetuated concerning matters of the history of science: "For brilliance of imaginative conception combined with the rigor prescribed by restriction to the principles of Newtonian mechanics this [work of Kant] is one of the greatest achievements in the history of science." See Northrop's contribution, "Natural Science and the Critical Philosophy of Kant," to *The Heritage of Kant*, ed. G. T. Whitney and D. F. Bowers (Princeton: Princeton University Press, 1939) p. 42.

33. Thus A. N. Whitehead in his *Science and the Modern World* (New York: Macmillan, 1926), p. 199. Later, Whitehead flatly declared that "Kant was a scientist" (p. 225).

34. *Conjectures and Refutations* (New York: Harper and Row, 1968), pp. 175–77. Let the many other examples, that could be added, be limited to the following three: G. Ardley claimed that Kant was "well-versed in the latest scientific developments of his day" and that "Kant's early period was one of considerable scientific activity" (*Aquinas and Kant: The Foundations of the Modern Science* [London: Longmans, Green, 1950], p. 71); according to K. Löwith (*Gott, Mensch und Welt in der Metaphysik von Descartes bis Nietzsche* [Göttingen: Vandenhoeck und Ruprecht, 1967], p. 70), "Kant was and remained a physicist even as a critical metaphysician"; G. Buchdahl presented Kant as "the philosopher of science *par excellence*," a rather meaningless evaluation if no critical appraisal is made of the scientific competence of the philosopher of science. Buchdahl's failure to say anything about the scientific bunglings piled up in Kant's *Universal Natural History* and elsewhere, and especially in the *Opus postumum*, turns his warning, "it would be misleading to think of Kant as a creative scientist," into a device of distraction. See his *Metaphysics and the Philosophy of Science* (Oxford: Basil Blackwell, 1969), pp. 471 and 480.

35. "On the Structure of the Universe" (Hitchcock Lectures at the University of California, April, 1924), *Publications of the Astronomical Society of the Pacific* 37 (April 1925): 63.

36. *Critique*, pp. 52–54. To support one of the proofs Kant declared that his "concept of *straight* [line] contains nothing of quantity, but only of quality"!

37. While N. K. Smith is correct in insisting in his *A Commentary to Kant's "Critique of Pure Reason"*, 2d rev. ed. (New York: Humanities Press, 1962, pp. 22–25), that Kant's aim was to establish an "anthropocentric" metaphysics, it is difficult to see how the implementing of this aim can be characterized by Kant or by others as a Copernican turn, unless the reference to Copernicus is a mere metaphor implying no real connection with the epistemology of Copernicus's science. The most debilitating defect in Smith's benevolent interpretation of Kant's claiming Copernicus to himself is the assertion that for Copernicus the earth's motion was merely a hypothesis that could safely be presented to the Pope. The interpretation, protested by Kepler and Galileo, to say nothing of properly informed historians of science of our times, reveals much the same unfamiliarity on Smith's part with Copernicus's firm endorsement of the reality of the earth's motion, as is revealed by Kant's sundry utterances on Copernicus. On Kant's misunderstanding of Copernicus and on the lack of full explicitness of the parallel he had drawn between his and Copernicus's achievement, see N. R. Hanson, "Copernicus' Role in Kant's Revolution," *Journal of the History of Ideas* 20 (1959): 274–81.

38. See especially the preface to the second edition where Kant recognizes the fatal possibility of landing "in the absurd conclusion that there can be appearance without anything that appears" (*Critique*, p. 27).

39. Or as Kant put it programmatically in the same preface (*Critique*, pp.

20–21), metaphysics had to be reformulated along the "secure path of a science" if it was not to remain a discourse "far above the teachings of experience."

40. See secs. 9–10 in Part I of his first major publication, an appraisal of Leibniz's doctrine of force (1747), *Gesammelte Schriften*, 1:23–24. In referring to these sections, in which Kant asserts the reality of multidimensional worlds, J. R. Lucas pointedly remarks (*A Treatise on Time and Space* [London: Methuen, 1973], p. 161 and note) that Kant "perhaps did allow" alternative geometries "as being at least conceivable."

41. That the "canonization" in question had the overtones of fanaticism was noticed by Kant's contemporaries (see Stuckenberg, *Life of Kant*, p. 268). Kant, who started his philosophical career with postulating multidimensional worlds, separate from ours, did not suspect that a hundred or so years after the publication of the *Critique* the scientific demonstration of the non-Euclidean character of our own world would be imminent. There was indeed an unintended pathetic ring in Kant's remark made in 1797: "I have come with my writings a century too soon; after a hundred years people will begin to understand me rightly, and will then study my books anew and appreciate them." According to R. M. Wenley (*Kant and His Philosophical Revolution* [New York: Charles Scribner's Sons, 1910], p. 93, Kant wrote this to C. F. A. von Stägemann.

42. *Critique*, p. 113.

43. See W. Temple, *Nature, Man, and God* (London: Macmillan), p. 70.

44. *Critique*, pp. 142–43 and 246–47.

45. As will be discussed in the next chapter.

46. See the next chapter.

47. *Kant: Selected Pre-Critical Writings*, p. 14.

48. The first volume appeared in 1785 and the reference there to Kant's cosmogony represented its first printed endorsement. Somewhat earlier, J. E. Bode, the leading German astronomer of the time, began to make generic references in his widely read textbooks on astronomy to the wisdom and inspiration by which Lambert and Kant interpreted the world edifice, though without endorsing Kant's cosmogony as such. See my *The Milky Way*, pp. 201 and 215–16.

49. For the best modern presentation of this, see T. A. Johnston, "A Note on Kant's Criticism of the Arguments for the Existence of God," *Australasian Journal of Philosophy* 21 (1943): 10–16.

50. Although through an article of C. C. Smart ("The Existence of God," first published in 1955 and reprinted in *The Cosmological Arguments: A Spectrum of Opinion*, edited by D. A. Burrill [Garden City, N.Y.: Doubleday, 1967], pp. 255–78, esp. p. 267), Johnston's conclusion received a prominently "positivist" endorsement and therefore wide publicity, belief in the validity of Kant's criticism of the cosmological argument is today still almost as strong as it was around the turn of the century when William James wrote in his *The Varieties of Religious Experience: A Study in Human Nature* (London: Longmans, Green and Co., 1910, p. 437): "I will not discuss these arguments technically. The bare fact that all idealists since Kant have felt entitled either to scout or to neglect them shows that they are not solid enough to serve as religion's all-sufficient foundation." Had James studied carefully at least one of those textbooks on scholastic philosophy that had been published "since Pope Leo's Encyclical recommending the study of Saint Thomas," which he brushed aside almost with contempt, he might have learned that Kant's criticism of the cosmological proof was not valid, and that only a few and hardly the best scholastic philosophers had ever

asserted that those proofs are the "all-sufficient foundations" of one's theistic conviction.

51. *Critique,* pp. 323 and 555–70.

52. There is an ample literature related to the manifold weaknesses of Kant's discussion of the antinomies. Popper's effort to reinterpret it "from the point of view that he saw rightly that mere speculation cannot establish anything where experience cannot help to weed out false theories" (*The Open Society and Its Enemies* [new ed.; Princeton: Princeton University Press, 1950], p. 647) will hardly appear convincing if one considers that the notion of the universe as a whole, though not an object of experience, has an indispensable validity for modern scientific cosmology, a validity unexplainable either on Kantian or Popperian bases.

53. *Philosophy* (New York: W. W. Norton, 1927), p. 80.

54. Thomas Aquinas, author of *De aeternitate mundi contra murmurantes,* would certainly agree on this point with Kant.

55. For further details on that translation (Hamburg, 1715), see A. T. Bartholomew, *Richard Bentley, D.D.: A Bibliography of His Works and of All the Literature Called Forth by His Acts or His Writings,* with an introduction and chronological table, by J. W. Clark (Cambridge: Bowes and Bowes, 1908), pp. 8–9.

56. *Critique,* p. 669.

57. See English translation by P. Carus, *Kant's Prolegomena to any Future Metaphysics* (Chicago: Open Court, 1902), pp. 51 and 64.

58. The contribution of the Hegelian right and left was, of course, important, but the stark voluntarism of Kant's ethical philosophy was powerfully brought into focus in 1911, the year of the long-postponed publication of *Die Philosophie des als ob* by H. Vaihinger, the founder in 1896 of the *Kant-Studien.* The message of Vaihinger's work is amply revealed from its full title: "the philosophy of the AS IF, being a system of the theoretical, practical, and religious fictions of mankind, on the basis of an idealistic positivism." Compared with the incisive unfolding of Kant's ethical philosophy in Vaihinger's work, Popper's summary of the spirit of Kant's ethics, "dare to be free; and respect the freedom of others" (*Conjectures and Refutations,* p. 182), should appear a benevolent apology.

59. See *Religion within the Limits of Reason Alone,* translated by T. M. Greene and H. H. Hudson, with an introduction by T. M. Greene (Chicago: Open Court, 1934), where "revealed" is equated with "historical" (pp. 94–103) and Christian religion is presented as "natural and learned religion" (pp. 145–56).

60. For details, both from the precritical and postcritical writings of Kant, see J. D. McFarland, *Kant's Concept of Teleology* (Edinburgh: University of Edinburgh Press, 1970), pp. 56–68. While Kant could not admit that the black tails of ermines were for the purpose of helping them to see one another on the snow-covered plains of Siberia, he saw purpose in the drifting of wood toward the Northern regions where forests were scarce. That man was the purpose of creation and that the spreading of races throughout the globe was the implementation of that purpose, were such metaphysical claims in the *Critique of Judgment* which the author of the *Critique of Pure Reason* had no logical justification to make.

61. References will be to the edition by A. Buchenau, *Kant's Opus postumum* (Berlin: Walter de Gruyter, 1936–38).

62. "Über die Vulkane im Monde," *Kant's Werke,* 8:69–76. For a somewhat cumbersome English translation, see *Essays and Treatises* (n. 2 above), 2:145–57.

63. *Kant's Werke,* 8:317–24. The title in German has "Witterung," which Kant explains (p. 320) as "temperies aeris." A similarly cumbersome English translation is in *Essays and Treatises,* 2:81–91.

64. *Kant's Werke,* 8:318.

65. The situation, Kant remarked, was similar to one's attitude toward the contents of the catechism. For children all its words are clear, but we understand it less and less as we grow older—a subtle indication that by 1794 Kant certainly did not wish to understand anything about Christianity except that it was not supernatural in origin.

66. *Kant's Opus postumum,* 1:25. Popper's approving remark, that Kant showed that every man makes his own God, should seem very appropriate and also very revealing (*Conjectures and Refutations,* p. 182).

67. E. Adickes, *Kant als Naturforscher* (Berlin: W. De Gruyter, 1925), 2:204. Latter-day admirers of Kant the scientist prefer to decry or simply overlook Adickes's conclusion. The former is illustrated in J. W. Ellington's article "Kant" (n. 4 above) where Adickes's portrayal of Kant as "an armchair scientist" is protested; the latter is the characteristic of the two modern discussions of the physics of the *Opus postumum,* J. Vuillemin, *Physique et métaphysique Kantiennes* (Paris, Presses Universitaires, 1955) and H. Hoppe, *Kants Theorie der Physik: Eine Untersuchung über das Opus postumum von Kant* (Frankfurt am Main: Vittorio Klostermann, 1969). N. K. Smith revealed a thorough unfamiliarity with the history of physics when he stated (*A Commentary to Kant's "Critique of Pure Reason,"* p. 633) that had the *Opus postumum* been published a century earlier, physicists would have received it more favorably.

68. See the Index of Names in the edition by Buchenau, 2:629–31.

69. Quoted by E. Schrödinger, *Nature and the Greeks* (Cambridge University Press, 1954), p. 72.

70. *Critique,* p. 560.

71. *Kant's Prolegomena,* p. 140. This had to be the case if there was any merit in Kant's claim made in the *Critique* (p. 602) that there was henceforth no need for him to open any future book containing proofs of the existence of God in order to find them wrong.

Chapter Nine

1. See his letter of April 1790 to Johanna Rahn in *J. G. Fichte Briefwechsel,* ed. H. Schulz (Leipzig: H. Haessel, 1925), 1:61.

2. "I now heartily believe in the freedom of man," he wrote to H. N. Achelis on November 29, 1790, in a letter (*Briefwechsel,* 1:142) which still reverberates with the liberating and joyous impact which the *Critique* made on Fichte and of which he had already written on September 5 to his fiancée: "My scheming spirit has now found rest, and I thank Providence that, shortly before all my hopes were frustrated, I was placed in a position which enabled me to bear with cheerfulness the disappointment [of not finding a suitable job]. A circumstance, which seemed the result of mere chance, led me to give myself entirely to the study of Kantian philosophy, a philosophy that restrains the imagination, which was always powerful with me, gives understanding the sway and raises the whole spirit to an indescribable elevation above all earthly considerations. I have gained a nobler morality, and instead of occupying myself with what is outside of me, I employ myself more with my own being. This has given me a peace such as I have never before experienced; amid uncertain worldly prospects I have passed my happiest days. I shall devote at least some years of my life to this philosophy; and all that I write, for some years at any rate, shall be on it" (*Briefwechsel,* 1:61.). Quotation is based on the translation in R. Adamson, *Fichte* (Edinburgh: William Blackwood and Son, 1881), pp. 21–22. "I live in a new world since I have read the *Critique,*" wrote Fichte to Weisshuhn about the same time (*Briefwechsel,* 1:123).

3. To F. I. Niethammer (*Briefwechsel*, 1:304); quoted in the translation of W. Smith, *The Popular Works of Johann Gottlieb Fichte*, 4th ed. (London: Trubner & Co., 1889), 1:79.

4. To H. Stephani (*Briefwechsel*, 1:319); quoted in Smith's translation.

5. This hope of Fichte, which brings *The Closed Commercial State* to a close, should not, however, be taken for an advocacy of liberalism based on science: all scientific academies are subjected to strict state control. A good summary of the work is given in H. C. Engelbrecht, *Johann Gottlieb Fichte: A Study of His Political Writings with Special Reference to His Nationalism* (New York: Columbia University Press, 1933), pp. 76–82, and in the Introduction to the excellent French translation by J. Givelin, *L'Etat commercial fermé* (Paris: Libraire générale de Droit et de Jurisprudence, 1940).

6. See Lecture 2, "Closer Definition of the Meaning of the Divine Idea," in *The Popular Works*, 1:231.

7. He did so to an extent which even Coleridge, a champion of German idealism and of Naturphilosophie in England, found unpalatable. Because Fichte's basic idea was "overbuilt with a heavy mass of mere notions and psychological acts of arbitrary reflections ... it degenerated into a crude egoismus, a boastful and hyperstoic hostility to NATURE, as lifeless, godless and altogether unholy," wrote Coleridge (*Biographia Literaria* [1817; London: Oxford University Press, 1907], 1:101–2) who, ironically enough, found in Schelling a guide to nature!

8. See Lecture 2, "General Delineation of the Third Age," in *The Characteristics of the Present Age* in *The Popular Works*, 2:17.

9. Fichte's "Europeanism" is discussed by Engelbrecht, pp. 89–90.

10. See Lecture 7, "Ideal Condition of the Scientific World," in *The Characteristics of the Present Age* in *The Popular Works*, 2:117. He referred disdainfully to the endless experimentation in science, a program supported by "common" opinion, common being opposed to enlightened (ibid., p. 137).

11. "Ueber den Grund unseres Glaubens an eine göttliche Weltregierung" (1798), in *Johann Gottlieb Fichte's sämmtliche Werke*, edited by J. H. Fichte (Berlin: Verlag von Veit, 1845), 5:177–89.

12. See Engelbrecht, p. 23.

13. "Ueber den Grund unseres Glaubens," p. 180. Fichte's proviso, "insofar as truly *the world and its forms* ought to be explained and we should remain in the domain of pure, I say *pure*, natural science," could not mean on his part a tacit endorsement of philosophical demonstrations as distinguished from scientific proofs, because in the next breath he declared: "At any rate, we are not helped a whit by the statement that an Intelligence is the originator of the material world, ... because the statement has not the least intelligibility."

14. Ibid., p. 185.

15. Ibid., p. 181.

16. As can be seen from his essay, "Über Machiavelli als Schriftsteller und Stellen aus seinen Schriften" (1807), of which an informative summary is given by Engelbrecht, pp. 108–11.

17. The year in which Fichte wrote his essay on Machiavelli is also the time of his drafting his "Politische Fragmente: Die Republik der Deutschen zu Anfang des 22. Jahrhunderts," of which startling details are given by Engelbrecht, pp. 103–6.

18. Fichte envisioned the minister laying his hands on the infant while pronouncing the words: "We name you Maria Meyerin ... (repeated by the congregation) as a sign that we, and through us the entire Fatherland of the German nation, recognize you as being *capable of Reason* (repeated by the congregation),

as one who is partaker in all rights of citizenship (repeated by the entire congregation), *as co-heir of eternal life, which also we hope for* (repeated by the entire congregation.)" In quoting this passage Engelbrecht added (p. 106) the apologetic remark: "This astonishing fragment stands alone in Fichte's work. There is nothing in his previous thought to prepare us for it, and he recurred to it but once." It is, of course, understandable that such travesties on traditional Christian rites occur but rarely in Fichte' writings, but the explanation for this is not, as Engelbrecht and most other well-meaning admirers of Fichte would have it, that such details conflict with Fichte's universalism. The conflict was between Fichte's idealistic apotheosis of the will, finding its concrete manifestation in the German race, and the universalism of Christian theism.

19. See Kant's letter of February 2, 1792, to Fichte, quoted in Smith's translation, *The Popular Works*, 1:50. As to Kant's *Religion within the Limits of Reason*, its true spirit and thrust were concisely described in Fichte's remark that "in five years there will be no more Christian religion; reason is our religion" (see J. H. W. Stuckenberg, *The Life of Immanuel Kant* [London: Macmillan, 1882], p. 386). It also casts a revealing light on Kant that he did not mind Fichte's plagiarizing his own rejection of Christianity, which he did not dare to divulge because the Prussian government had forbidden him to touch on topics concerning Christianity. Kant, who meekly complied in clear evidence of his lack of bravery, turned against Fichte only when the latter appropriated Kantian philosophy. Nothing of this is intimated in the denunciation of Fichte by K. R. Popper (*The Open Society and Its Enemies* [Princeton: Princeton University Press, 1950], pp. 653–54), who is wont to portray Kant as the brave herald of a strictly rationalistic Enlightenment.

20. "On the Possibility of a Form for Philosophy in General" (1794) was about equal in length to the dissertation, the two covering about seventy pages in *Schellings Werke*, ed. M. Schröter (Munich: C. H. Beck'sche Verlagsbuchhandlung, 1927), vol. 1, but both were considerably exceeded in length by "Of the Ego as Principle of Philosophy, or on the "Unconditioned" in Human Knowledge" (1795) (ibid., pp. 73–168).

21. As clearly conveyed in the title of the concluding, or sixth, part, "Derivation of a general organ of philosophy, or the chief tenets of the philosophy of art according to the basic propositions of transcendental idealism," *Schellings Werke*, 2:612–29.

22. A work written in 1795 and covering about sixty pages in the *Werke* (1:205–66).

23. Ibid., p. 237.

24. Ibid., p. 238.

25. Such is the thrust of the concluding remark there about the "love of the infinite" in which alone can peace be found (ibid., p. 240).

26. Ibid.

27. *Ideen zu einer Philosophie der Natur als Einleitung in das Studium dieser Wissenschaft*, in *Werke*, 1:653–723.

28. *Von der Weltseele, eine Hypothese der höheren Physik zur Erklärung des allgemeinen Organismus* (1798) in *Werke*, 1:413–652. It should be of no surprise that the "higher physics" was an explanation of the universe in terms of living organism in a manner closely analogous to Aristotle's discourse on physics. It is a major facet of the history of philosophy that any intensive thinker in modern times finds sooner or later his ancient prototype, not, of course, without somewhat distorting him. Just as Hume found *his* Epicurus, so did Schelling find *his* Aristotle, a fact which will be found true of Hegel as well. To see the shocking contrast between a physics based on a "world soul" and a physics purged of it

by Galileo and Newton, it is enough to glance through the lengthy outline provided by Schelling. There he refers to the "negative matter of light" evidenced in the slow and quick warming up of transparent and dark bodies respectively; to light "inasmuch as it loses its negative matter and binds itself to another principle which is, however, present only in the moment of conflict"; to light "inasmuch as it is the first principle of the entire nature and of the general dualism of nature." No wonder that the air too was endowed by Schelling with a duality which in turn made him criticize the "ordinary [or scientific] meteorological notions." That all this was not at all a departure from the foundations laid by Kant can be seen from the curious resemblance between Kant's dicta on the influence of the moon on the weather and Schelling's claim about the influence of "higher (immaterial) forces on our atmosphere."

29. *Werke*, 2:269–326. "Our aim," wrote Schelling almost at the outset (p. 283), "is to separate science and the empirical as soul and body, and, insofar as we do not include in science anything incapable of an a priori demonstration, to divest of all theory the empirical and to restore its pristine nakedness." All this shows not only in its stark "nakedness" the antiscience of Schelling's idealism but also the inner logic that the fallacy of an extreme position (the a priorism of idealism in this case) can but generate the fallacy of the other extreme, in this case the belief that one can discourse of the empirical in such a way as not to convey any conceptual content, which inevitably implies at least a rudimentary form of theory.

30. *Allgemeine Deduktion des dynamischen Prozesses*, in *Werke*, 2:635–712.

31. *Über den wahren Begriff der Naturphilosophie und die richtige Art, ihre Probleme aufzulösen*, in *Werke*, 2:713–37.

32. *Bruno, oder über das göttliche und natürliche Prinzip der Dinge: Ein Gespräch* in *Werke*, 3:109–225.

33. Its printed text fills much (pp. 61–506) of the second supplementary volume of the *Werke*. Typically enough, Naturphilosophie once more started out not with nature but with the Absolute, out of which the idealist expert on nature could derive with ease the totality of things and their patterns. As in Schelling's *Von der Weltseele* the detailed outline given by him of his *System der gesamten Philosophie und der Naturphilosophie insbesondere* provides a revealing glimpse of that counterscience which Naturphilosophie proved itself to be, precisely because of its a priori character. It is this work of Schelling, completed in the year of Kant's death, that proves, especially when compared with the contents of Kant's *Opus postumum*, the validity of Schelling's claim that he had merely unfolded in full Kant's presuppositions.

34. *System der gesamten Philosophie*, p. 196.

35. Ibid., p. 417.

36. *Bruno*, p. 167.

37. *System der gesamten Philosophie*, p. 421.

38. *Bruno*, pp. 169 and 167.

39. For details, see chap. 3.

40. *System der gesamten Philosophie*, p. 491.

41. Ibid.

42. *Philosophie und Religion*, in *Werke*, 4:1–60.

43. Such is the English title of the German original, *Die Weltalter*, translated with an introduction and notes by Frederick de Wolfe Bolman, Jr. (New York: Columbia University Press, 1942). According to Bolman, the *Weltalter* was Schelling's "favorite child" (ibid., p. 67).

44. "Philosophical Investigations on the Essence of Human Freedom" (1809) in *Werke*, 4:278.

45. Especially Augustine in his *De civitate Dei;* see my *Science and Creation: From Eternal Cycles to an Oscillating Universe* (Edinburgh: Scottish Academic Press, 1974), pp. 179–81.

46. As documented in detail in my "Goethe and the Physicists," *American Journal of Physics* 37 (1969): 195–203.

47. See his address, "On the Relation of Natural Science to General Science," in *Popular Lectures on Scientific Subjects,* translated by E. Atkinson (New York: D. Appleton, 1873), p. 7.

48. In a letter of November 1, 1844, to Schumacher; in *Gauss Werke* (Göttingen: Königliche Akademie der Wissenschaften, 1877), 12:63.

49. In a paper written in 1873 on determinism and contingency, published posthumously by L. Campbell and W. Garnett in their *The Life of James Clerk Maxwell* (London: Macmillan, 1882), p. 436.

50. For a German translation facing the original Latin, *Dissertatio philosophica de orbitis planetarum* (Jena: Typis Prageri et Soc., 1801), in *G. W. F. Hegel, Erste Druckschriften,* edited by G. Lasson (Leipzig: Felix Meiner, 1928), pp. 346–401; see especially pp. 398–401. Hegel's reason for his claim was that "the true measure and number of nature cannot differ from reason; nor does the study and knowledge of the laws of nature have a basis in anything else than in our belief in the conformity of nature with reason and in our persuasion about the identity of all laws of nature" (p. 399). It is rarely noted that Hegel's dissertation starts with a rejection of Newtonian physics on the ground that it is merely "mechanics" (p. 353).

51. According to the geometrical progression the relative distances of planets should be as 1, 2, 4, 8, 16, 32, 64, which is approximately the case from Venus (1) to Uranus (64), counting the asteroid belt (8), a pattern which was widely discussed during the last three decades of the eighteenth century and prompted the search for the missing planet between Mars (4) and Jupiter (16). See on this my article, "The Early History of the Titius-Bode Law," *American Journal of Physics* 40 (1972): 1014–23. Since the Pythagorean series, 1, 2, 3, 2^2, 2^3, 3^2, 3^3, or 1, 2, 3, 4, 8, 9, 27, was patently at variance with the relative distances of planets, Hegel changed 8 to 16 and claimed that there was no major gap between 4 and 9, that is, between Mars and Jupiter, and that therefore it was unreasonable to search for a new planet. It was also implied in Hegel's interpretation of planetary distances in terms of the geometrical series that there could be no planet beyond Uranus.

52. See R. Wolf, *Handbuch der Astronomie, ihrer Geschichte und Literatur* (Zurich: Druck und Verlag von F. Schulthess, 1892), 2:455.

53. The latest and truly monumental example of this is the three-volume *Hegel's Philosophy of Nature,* edited and translated with an introduction and explanatory notes by M. J. Petry (London: George Allen & Unwin, 1970). According to Petry, Hegel's mistakes in matters scientific are few and far between (vol. 1, p. 49), historians of science would find Hegel a master of the particularities of the various sciences (p. 21), and Hegel's treatment of science is an antidote to the "irresponsible extravagances of Schellingianism" (p. 12). Petry comes much closer to the heart of the matter, however, in reminding his reader that Hegel's lengthy discourses on science are indispensable for a proper grasp of Hegelianism (p. 18) and that Hegel himself looked at his *Enzyklopädie* as the best means of studying his thought (p. 21). While there is a growing awareness of the need of studying Hegel, the interpreter of science, nothing similar can be noticed in connection with Schelling, who could have hardly made clearer the intimate connection of his philosophy with his sustained criticism and "reformation" of the exact sciences. No justice is given to Schelling by a historian

of philosophy, however eminent, who excuses himself, as F. Copleston does, for not presenting in some detail Schelling's borrowing from the sciences on the ground that they are "more a matter for specialized treatment . . . than for a general history of philosophy" (*A History of Philosophy, vol. 7, Modern Philosophy, pt. 1, "Fichte to Hegel"* [Garden City, N.Y.: Doubleday, 1965], p. 142).

54. In 1817, 1827, and 1830, respectively.

55. The quotation is from the *Phenomenologie des Geistes* and is given in the translation of D. Ainslie (n. 56 below).

56. B. Croce, *What Is Living and What Is Dead in the Philosophy of Hegel,* translated from the third Italian edition (1912) by D. Ainslie (London: Macmillan, 1915), p. 29.

57. Ibid., p. 28.

58. Quoted in the translation of D. Ainslie (p. 28) from Rosmini's *Saggio storico-critico sulle categorie e la dialettica,* published posthumously in 1883.

59. Ibid., p. 191.

60. In his first public address in the United States. For its full text, see *US News and World Report,* July 14, 1975, p. 45.

61. *What Is Living,* p. 27; see also p. xii.

62. Ibid., chap. 9, "The Construction of the False Sciences and the Application of the Dialectic to the Individual and the Empirical," pp. 174–191.

63. Ibid., p. 177.

64. Ibid., p. 178.

65. In a letter of July 30, 1814, to Paulus, in *Briefe von und an Hegel,* edited by J. Hoffmeister (Hamburg: Felix Meiner, 1953), 2:31.

66. For references to this and similar statements of Hegel, see my *The Relevance of Physics* (Chicago: University of Chicago Press, 1966), pp. 48–49.

67. The best illustration of this is provided by Schopenhauer, an acid critic of all proofs of the existence of God, including Kant's proof based on practical reason, but also an advocate of subjectivism, who sought in the physical sciences evidences of a will operative in nature. The logic connecting these two attitudes are unwittingly documented in the joint publication of the English translation by K. Hillebrand of two works of Schopenhauer, *On the Fourfold Root of the Principle of Sufficient Reason* and *On the Will in Nature,* rev. ed. (London: George Bell and Sons, 1907). As in most studies of the main representatives of German idealism, the rejection by Schopenhauer of the proofs is never recalled with a reference to his arbitrary handling of contemporary science. Yet, there should be much food for thought in the fact that Schopenhauer, who extolled gravitation, animal magnetism, and sundry phenomena in physiology as evidences of a cosmic will, hailed Buddhism and held high (ibid., p. 367) the conclusion of the German sinologist, Neumann, who had remarked: "In China, neither Mahometans nor Christians found a Chinese word to express the theological conception of the Deity . . . . The words God, soul, spirit, as independent of Matter and ruling it arbitrarily, are utterly unknown in the Chinese language . . . . This range of ideas has become so completely one with the language itself, that the first verse of the book of Genesis cannot without considerable circumlocution be translated into genuine Chinese." Had Schopenhauer reflected on the stillbirth which science had suffered in China, he might have abstained from providing this unwitting confirmation of the intimate connection between the theism of Genesis and the genesis of science.

68. After reading such boastful assertions one might be struck by the modesty which characterizes official declarations of Christian theism such as that "it is impossible to notice a strong similarity between Creator and creatures without being forced to note an even stronger dissimilarity between them" and that "in

the present condition of humanity, revelation is morally necessary in order that everyone might arrive in fact at the full and certain knowledge of God." The first of those declarations was made by the Fathers of Lateran IV (1215) in the heyday of a scholasticism steeped in the notion of analogy, the second by the Fathers of Vatican I (1870), the time of the first infiltration of idealism into Roman Catholic theology. Only time will tell whether the Fathers of Vatican II should not have been much more outspoken about another, far more pervasive penetration of that very same idealism, including its rank subjectivism, into the thinking of some of their very advisors in matters doctrinal.

69. *Lectures on the Philosophy of Religion together with a Work on the Proofs of the Existence of God*, translated by E. B. Speirs and J. B. Sanderson (London: Kegan Paul, Trench, Trübner and Co., 1895), 3:153–367; see p. 237.

70. Ibid., p. 261.

71. Ibid.

72. Ibid.

73. Ibid., p. 256.

74. Ibid., p. 156.

75. Ibid.

76. Ibid., p. 221.

77. Ibid., pp. 353 and 357.

78. Ibid., p. 221.

79. *Studies in Hegelian Cosmology* (Cambridge: University Press, 1901), p. 250. This statement of McTaggart is all the more telling because it is part of his conclusion to the long chapter 8, "Hegelianism and Christianity," in which much emphasis is given to the importance attributed by Hegel to historic Christianity as a supreme confirmation of his claim that any religion can only approximate the truth but can never give *truth* itself. McTaggart's work also provides a convincing illustration of the fact that Hegelian cosmology has little if anything to do with the factual cosmos, in perfect agreement with McTaggart's opening statement: "By Cosmology I mean the application to subject-matter empirically known, *a priori* conclusions derived from the investigation of the nature of pure thought" (p. 1). Needless to say, within such a cosmology one cannot have a physical motion that would impress one with its gripping concreteness, a circumstance which vitiates such attempts to utilize Hegel's notion of motion for natural theology, as, for instance, part 4, "Hegel," in *Motion and Motion's God: Thematic Variations in Aristotle, Cicero, Newton, and Hegel* by M. J. Buckley (Princeton: Princeton University Press, 1971). It is also well to recall a remark of Schopenhauer, who saw at close range the impact of Hegel on many a young mind: "Should you ever intend to dull the wits of a young man and to incapacitate his brains for any kind of thought whatever, then you cannot do better than give him Hegel to read." Fortunately, the passage and its sequel has reached many readers through K. R. Popper's *The Open Society and Its Enemies* (Princeton: Princeton University Press, 1950), p. 271. It is less fortunate that, in spite of the evidence provided in Schopenhauer's own *The World as Will and Idea*, Popper failed to perceive the inner logic that ties Fichte, Schelling, and Hegel to Kant. That logic is rooted in part in the Kantian proposition, explicitly endorsed in Schopenhauer's rejection of all proofs of the existence of God (see his *On the Fourfold Root of the Principle of Sufficient Reason*, pp. 25 and 51), that the principle of sufficient reason applies only to relations between sensuous entities. With remarkable consistency, Schopenhauer therefore postulated the eternity and uncreatedness of all matter.

80. See translation by J. Sibree with a new introduction by C. J. Friedrich (New York: Dover, 1956), p. 419.

81. See translation with an introduction and notes by J. B. Baillie, with an introduction to the Torchbook edition by G. Lichtheim (New York: Harper, 1967), pp. 351–72.

82. Ibid., p. 372.

83. Ibid., p. 290. In speaking of attractive (chemical) forces, Hegel could find support only in the law proposed by one Winterl, who is little remembered by historians of science, as his law contained little merit.

84. *The Philosophy of History*, p. 440.

85. Ibid.

86. See note 50 above. In another context Hegel inveighed against Newton by referring to the "apple that was present at the onset of the misery of the whole human race, then at that of Troy, and has now become a bad omen for the philosophical sciences" (*Dissertatio philosophica de orbitis planetarum*, p. 378).

87. *The Open Society and Its Enemies*, pp. 217–18.

88. For documentation, see chap. 13, "On Murky Backwaters," in my *Science and Creation*, pp. 308–35.

89. *The Will to Power*, in *The Complete Works of Friedrich Nietzsche*, ed. Oscar Levy (Edinburgh: T. N. Foulis, 1909–11), 14:48–49.

Chapter Ten

1. The calendar was part of the conclusion of his *Catéchisme positiviste*, or a "summary exposition of the universal religion in eleven systematic conversations between a woman and a priest of HUMANITY," according to the subtitle. See edition by P. Arnaud (Paris: Garnier-Flammarion, 1966), pp. [264]–[271].

2. Comte's brief reference to Kant in the *Catéchisme positiviste* (p. 32) is as revealing of his "positivist retrospect" as is his allusion to a small essay published by Kant in 1784 on the general history of the human race. See "Considérations philosophiques sur les sciences et les savants" (1826) in *Auguste Comte: Ecrits de jeunesse, 1816–1828*, ed. P. E. de Berrêdo Carneiro and P. Arnaud (Paris: Mouton, 1970), p. 341.

3. For the French text, see *Ecrits de jeunesse*, pp. 241–322.

4. On the respective measures of Comte's indebtedness to others and of his originality, see H. Gouhier, *La jeunesse d'Auguste Comte et la formation du positivisme*, vol. 3, *Auguste Comte et Saint-Simon* (Paris: J. Vrin, 1941), pp. 395–403.

5. *Ecrits de jeunesse*, p. 259.

6. *Cours de philosophie positive*, vol. 1 (Paris: Bachelier, 1830); see 5th ed. (identical with the first) (Paris: Au Siège de la Société positiviste, 1892), 1:4.

7. *Cours de philosophie positive*, vol. 5 (Paris: Bachelier, 1841), pp. 1–393 (Lectures 52–55).

8. Ibid. p. 590.

9. Ibid., 1:6.

10. Ibid., vol. 3 (Paris: Bachelier, 1838), p. 617.

11. Ibid., p. 623

12. Ibid.

13. Ibid.

14. Ibid., p. 627. There are appreciative references to Gall throughout that long Lesson 45, "General considerations on the positive study of intellectual and moral, or cerebral, functions" (pp. 604–71). Gall's glory was still untarnished in the *Catéchisme positiviste* (pp. 32 and 299).

15. *Catéchisme positiviste*, p. [271].

16. *Cours de philosophie positive,* 3:609. On the preceding page Comte laid the blame for the vagaries of phrenology on Gall's epigones.

17. The most relevant documents on Comte's petitioning Guizot in 1832 are available in *Correspondance générale d'Auguste Comte,* ed. P. Arnaud and P. E. de Berrêdo Carneiro (The Hague: Mouton, 1973–76), 1:244–48 and 406–9, and 2:viii–xi. They cast an equally revealing light on Guizot and Comte. The latter was probably right in claiming that Guizot, once an enthusiast of Comtean positivism, was under "sacerdotal influence" as he shelved Comte's petition. But like many other erstwhile admirers of Comte, Guizot too could after some time see the rank dogmatism of Comte's positivism and suspect something of the hollowness of the history and philosophy of science to be taught by Comte. In a public criticism of Guizot, Comte decried the four chairs for the history of philosophy at the Collège de France as places devoted "entirely to the meticulous study of the dreams and aberrations of the human mind in the course of centuries, whereas there is not a single course, either in France or in all of Europe, for the explanation of the formation and progress of our real knowledge, be it the entirety of natural philosophy or any particular science" (p. 409).

18. See his letter to Valat, September 8, 1824; quoted in L. Lévy-Bruhl, *La philosophie d'Auguste Comte,* 2d ed. (Paris: F. Alcan, 1905), p. 270.

19. *System of Positive Polity,* translated by J. H. Bridges and others (London: Longmans, Green & Co., 1875–77), 1:414. In the *Cours* the Mephistophelic aspect in question was limited to the precept that phenomena of the outer fringes of the solar system need not be given as detailed an analysis as those closer to the earth (2:246). That cosmology was restricted to the study of the earth and of its immediate surroundings was a twice-repeated tenet in the *Catéchisme positiviste* (pp. 98 and 112).

20. *Cours,* 2:22. That Comte had a great stake in the stability of the solar system as established through Laplace's analysis of the mutual perturbations of Jupiter and Saturn is shown by the fact that he was the only man of science in France until 1860 to discuss Laplace's nebular hypothesis, which he tried to bolster with a mathematical argument. See for further details my *Planets and Planetarians: A History of Theories of the Origin of Planetary Systems* (Edinburgh: Scottish Academic Press, 1977), pp. 137–39.

21. *System,* 1:340–41.

22. *Cours,* 2:2 and 4.

23. Only three years before Bessel, Henderson, and Struve established independently of one another the experimental touchstone of Copernicanism, the parallax of stars, Comte ridiculed such efforts and claimed that the independence of the sun and planets of all other stars was "perfectly certain" (*Cours,* 2:282). He could hardly suspect that long before the rotation of the sun and planets around the center of the galaxy was to be established, the list of known elements was to increase through spectroscopical analysis of the sun.

24. For Comte's scorn for suggestions of studies of the physical constitution of the sun, see *Cours,* 2:2.

25. As if willfully closing his eyes to the marvelous discoveries of Herschel on the Milky Way, globular clusters and nebulae, Comte submitted the astonishing claim that "we shall never be able to rise to a true conception of the ensemble of the stars" (*Cours,* 2:7).

26. Quoted with no reference in "Science" by Charles Singer (*Encyclopaedia Britannica* [1964], 20:114). In a private communication to me, P. E. de Berrêdo Carneiro, a leading authority on Comte, expressed his doubts about the

Comtean provenance of the phrase, though not about its Comtean spirit.

27. *Cours*, 2:24.

28. Ibid., p. 280.

29. Ibid., p. 290; see also p. 302.

30. Ibid., p. 9. A revealing example of Comte's technique of evasion concerning obvious problems of cosmology is his handling of the gravitational interaction of all stars and of the effect of that interaction on the earth. The first part was the gravitational paradox of an infinite, homogeneous universe of stars, a paradox which he simply ignored. About the second part he noted that although it would be "absurd to consider" the resultant force of that interaction to be zero, the perturbation caused by it would be imperceptible on the earth because of the great distance of stars. Therefore "the independence of our world [the solar system] was perfectly certain" (*Cours*, 2:265–66).

31. Ibid., pp. 6–8.

32. Ibid., p. 306. Equally disastrous was Comte's legislation in chemistry. For details, see my *The Relevance of Physics* (Chicago: University of Chicago Press, 1966), pp. 473–76.

33. *Catéchisme positiviste*, p. 176. Such odd specifications (for instance, the limiting to thirteen the number of truly great writers from Homer to Walter Scott [p. 169]) show that as other Utopians, Comte had use only for a history with no future.

34. Ibid., p. 241. He also mentioned Belgium and the Netherlands as countries of ideal size. Comte's visionary partitioning of the "Great Western Republic" into sixty states to be financed by two thousand bankers is not without aspects entertaining to readers of our times. He hoped not only for the separation of Scotland and Wales from England but also for the endurance of a vast Russia (pp. 241 and 254).

35. Ibid., p. [97]. The schematic list of the "theoretical hierarchy of human concepts, or synthetic table of universal order," starts in its "dogmatic division" with the "study of the earth or cosmology." The table was drawn up on the tenth day of the month Dante of the year 64 (July 24, 1852).

36. Ibid., pp. 51–55.

37. Ibid., p. 32.

38. Published in 1865, eight years after Comte's death. See reprint by the University of Michigan Press (Ann Arbor, 1961).

39. *Autobiography of John Stuart Mill*, published for the first time without alterations or omissions from the original manuscript in the possession of Columbia University, with a preface by John Jacob Coss (New York: Columbia University Press, 1924), p. 158.

40. *A System of Logic Ratiocinative and Inductive*, bks. 1–3, ed. J. M. Robson (Toronto: University of Toronto Press, 1973), p. 575.

41. Ibid.

42. Ibid., p. 565. The passage must be read in Mill's own words: "I am convinced that anyone accustomed to abstraction and analysis, who will fairly exert his faculties for the purpose, will, when his imagination has once learnt to entertain the notion, find no difficulty in conceiving that in some one, for instance, of the many firmaments into which sidereal astronomy now divides the universe, events may succeed one another at random, without any fixed law; nor can anything in our experience, or in our mental nature, constitute a sufficient, or indeed any, reason for believing that this is nowhere the case."

43. In his *An Examination of Sir W. Hamilton's Philosophy and of the Principal Philosophical Questions Discussed in His Writings* (London: Longman, Green, Longman, Roberts & Green, 1865) Mill first stated that "we should probably

have no difficulty in putting together the two ideas supposed to be incompatible, if our experience had not first inseparably associated one of them with the contradictory of the other" (pp. 68–69). Then in a footnote he quoted at length from "the concluding paper of a recent volume, anonymous, but of known authorship, 'Essays, by a Barrister'": "Consider this case. There is a world in which, whenever two pairs of things are either placed in proximity or are contemplated together, a fifth thing is immediately created and brought within the contemplation of the mind engaged in putting two and two together. This is surely neither inconceivable, for we can readily conceive the result by thinking of common puzzle tricks, nor can it be said to be beyond the power of Omnipotence. Yet in such a world surely two and two would make five." What this proved was that once "Omnipotence" was turned by empiricism into a tricky word, no reasonable word could be raised against worlds teeming with contradictions in terms.

44. The most revealing part of the admission was the inevitable reliance by empiricists on some kind of metaphysics while defending their position: "Each party has been able to urge in its own favour numerous and striking facts, to reconcile which with the opposite theory has required all the metaphysical resources which that theory could command" (*Dissertations and Discussions: Political, Philosophical and Historical* [London: John W. Parker and Son, 1859], 1:409). Equally striking should seem the claim of the antiempiricists, as phrased by Mill, that within empiricism science becomes "a mere enumeration and arrangement of facts, not explaining nor accounting for them: since a fact is only then accounted for, when we are made to see in it the manifestation of laws (p. 406).

45. *A System of Logic*, p. 311. If nothing else, the wisdom of hindsight based on the crucial role of elliptical orbits for Newtonian dynamics should have kept Mill from summing up Kepler's work as follows: "Knowing already that the planets continued to move in the same paths, when he found that an ellipse correctly represented the past path, he knew that it would represent the future path. In finding a compendious expression for the one set of facts, he found one for the other; but he found the expression only, not the inference, nor did he (which is the true test of general truths) add anything to the power of prediction already possessed." For a penetrating analysis of Mill's treatment of Kepler, see N. R. Hanson, "Is there a Logic of Scientific Discovery?" in H. Feigl and G. Maxwell, eds., *Current Issues in the Philosophy of Science* (New York: Holt Rinehart and Winston, 1961), pp. 27–30.

46. *Nature, the Utility of Religion and Theism*, 2d ed. (London: Longmans, Green, Reader and Dyer, 1874), p. 182.

47. Ibid., p. 131.

48. Both points can readily be ascertained from Whewell's *On the Philosophy of Discovery: Chapters Historical and Critical* (London: John W. Parker and Son, 1860). Whewell's most telling point against Mill was that the antimetaphysics of empiricism, which discredited induction, forced Mill to adopt the deductive method, with the consequence of abandoning hope of any major new discovery taking place in the physical sciences (p. 282). Concerning monotheism, see the discussion of Whewell's views on medieval scholasticism in chapter 1, and especially his oversight of the importance of the struggle of leading schoolmen against Averroism.

49. London: Trubner and Co. Romanes was then thirty, doing biological research in Cambridge. Originally he planned to become a clergyman.

50. Ibid., p. 194.

51. The essay is printed as "Notes for a Work on a Candid Examination of

Religion by Metaphysicus" in *Thoughts on Religion*, edited by Charles Gore (London: Longmans Green and Co., 1895), pp. 97–183; for quotation see p. 119.

52. "They that know the entire course of the development of science will, as a matter of course, judge more freely and more correctly of the significance of any present scientific movement than they, who, limited in their views to the age in which their own lives have been spent, contemplate merely the momentary trend that the course of intellectual events takes at the present moment" (*The Science of Mechanics*, trans. T. J. McCormack from the ninth German edition, 6th ed. [La Salle, Ill.: Open Court, 1960], pp. 8–9).

53. Mach's insensitivity on this point was all the more glaring as he must certainly have agreed with the remark of William James, a great admirer of his, that a "permanently existing 'idea' or 'Vorstellung' which makes its appearance before the footlights of consciousness at periodical intervals, is as mythological an entity as the Jack of Spades" (*The Principles of Psychology* [New York: Henry Holt, 1890], 1:236).

54. *Erkenntnis und Irrtum: Skizzen zur Psychologie der Forschung*, 2d rev. ed. (Leipzig: Johann Ambrosius Barth, 1906), p. 27.

55. Mach's heavy dependence on Spencer had been noted by R. Bouvier in his *La pensée d'Ernst Mach: Essai de biographie intellectuelle et critique* (Paris: Librairie au Vélin d'Or, 1923), p. 261, and was presented in great detail by M. Čapek in his "Ernst Mach's Biological Theory of Knowledge," *Synthese* 18 (April 1968): 171–91.

56. "Über den relativen Bildungswert der philosophischen und der mathematisch-naturwissenschaftlichen Unterrichtsfächer der höheren Schulen," a lecture given on April 16, 1886, in Dortmund; *Populär-wissenschaftliche Vorlesungen*, 4th rev. ed. (Leipzig: Johann Ambrosius Barth, 1910), p. 320. Mach's statement proves beyond doubt what should be clear to any perceptive reader of his discourses on the history of science, namely, that even as Mach purportedly writes history he merely offers his own empiricist philosophy. Its basic weakness is, of course, the inability of anyone who utters more than trivia to steer clear of metaphysical statements, a point which matches the conclusion reached by E. N. Hiebert in his "Mach's Philosophical Use of the History of Science" (*Historical and Philosophical Perspectives of Science*, ed. R. H. Stuewer [Minneapolis: University of Minnesota Press, 1970], pp. 184–203). According to Hiebert, "Mach should have learned that antimetaphysical protestations and all that goes with trying to establish an epistemology without overtly recognizing some philosophical presuppositions lead nowhere if not to metaphysics" (p. 203). Hiebert's study far surpasses in value O. Blüh's programmatic and panegyrical essay, "Ernst Mach as an Historian of Physics" (*Centaurus* 13 [1968–69]: 62–83), an essay unfortunately typical of most references to Mach as a historian of science. As. I. B. Cohen showed ("History and the Philosopher of Science," in *The Structure of Scientific Theories*, edited with a critical introduction by F. Suppe [Urbana: University of Illinois Press, 1974], pp. 316–17), it is easy to pick almost at random a set of statements from Mach's *The Science of Mechanics* and show that they are wrong. What is still to be aired in full is the extent to which a student should be informed about the erroneous views of Mach, the historian of science, before it becomes true that a student can learn from Mach's book "an enormous amount" (p. 372).

57. *The Analysis of Sensations and the Relation of the Physical to the Psychical*, translated from the first German edition by C. M. Williams; revised and supplemented from the fifth German edition by S. Waterlow; with a new introduction by T. S. Szasz (New York: Dover, 1959), p. 30.

58. Ibid.

59. Ibid.

60. *History and Root of the Principle of the Conservation of Energy*, translated and annotated by Philip E. B. Jourdain (Chicago: Open Court Publishing Company, 1911), p. 54. The first (1872) and the second (1909) editions of the German original have the same text, but the second has some additional notes.

61. *The Science of Mechanics*, p. 578.

62. As can be seen from the wide and perhaps even wild variety of meanings attached in modern relativistic cosmologies to the expression "Mach's principle," a facet presented with much incisiveness by H. Goenner, "Mach's Principle and Einstein's Theory of Gravitation," in *Ernst Mach: Physicist and Philosopher*, Boston Studies in the Philosophy of Science, vol. 6, ed. by R. S. Cohen and R. J. Seeger (Dordrecht: J. Reidel, 1968), pp. 200–215. In his *Mach's Philosophy of Science* (London: Athlone Press, 1971), J. Bradley is equally categorical: "There is no Mach Principle in Mach's writings. . . . Einstein and other more recent writers have honoured Mach by attributing to him a principle which cannot fairly be found in his writings" (pp. 145 and 157).

63. "Ueber das kosmologische Problem," *Vierteljahrschrift für wissenschaftliche Philosophie* (Leipzig), 1 (1887): 80–136.

64. *The Science of Mechanics*, pp. 287–88. The context was the inertial motion of bodies in the universe, but Mach was reluctant to take our own cosmic neighborhood as a representative sample of more distant regions.

65. Ibid., p. 541. Twenty pages later Mach contradicted himself as he insisted on the privacy of religious beliefs and stated that scientists even in his time entertained the most diverse opinions in matters of religion (pp. 559–60). Not only open-mindedness but scholarship was also betrayed in the fact that the chapter in question remained unchanged during the three decades that stretched between the first (1883) and seventh (1912) editions of *The Science of Mechanics* although other parts of it underwent notable changes.

66. The periodical was the *Stimmen aus Maria Laach*, with K. A. Kneller as the author of its Ergänzungsband 21:84–85 (1903) under the title *Das Christentum und die Vertreter der neueren Naturwissenschaft* (266 pp.), published also as separate volume in the same year (Freiburg i. Br.: Herdersche Verlagsbuchhandlung) and eight years later in the English translation by T. M. Kettle under the title *Christianity and the Leaders of Modern Science* (London: Herder).

67. It was that hatred that blinded Mach, the historian, to the pivotal role of Christianity in cultural progress. Indeed, as John T. Blackmore put it tersely in his magisterial work, *Ernst Mach: His Life, Work, and Influence* (Berkeley: University of California Press, 1972, p. 290): "Mach never tired of abusing the 'Christian' foundation of Western 'superiority.'" Whether Blackmore's objective and massively documented portrayal of Mach will discredit the apotheosis of Mach characterizing much of the Mach literature, an apotheosis casting a curious light on the professed reverence of logical positivists for facts, is still to be seen.

68. For further details and documentation, see Blackmore, *Ernst Mach*, p. 291.

69. *The Science of Mechanics*, p. 551.

70. Ibid., p. 557. He found it, of course, puzzling that, as he put it, the Middle Ages showed remarkable evidences of freedom of thought.

71. Ibid., pp. 556–57.

72. Referring in his *The Science of Mechanics* (pp. 97–103) to Duhem's *Les origines de la statique* as a "mine of stimulating, instructive and enlightening details" and as a "brilliant book," Mach carefully avoided saying that the instructiveness and brilliance of Duhem's book largely consisted in his presentation of *medieval* material. Instead, Mach referred repeatedly to the early Re-

naissance cultivators of statics and of "the intimate connection of modern scientific civilization . . . with ancient scientific civilization."

73. Of the three volumes of Duhem's *Etudes sur Léonard de Vinci, ceux qu'il a lus et ceux qui l'ont lu* (Paris: Hermann) the first appeared in 1906, the second in 1909, and the third, as if by irony of fate, in 1913, a year after the publication of the seventh edition of *The Science of Mechanics*, the last which Mach saw through the press.

74. *The Science of Mechanics*, p. 97.

75. Ibid., p. 559.

76. For details, see Blackmore, *Ernst Mach*, p. 293.

77. Ibid., p. 289.

78. *The Science of Mechanics*, p. 560.

79. *Between Physics and Philosophy* (Cambridge: Harvard University Press, 1941), p. 53.

80. Although much of the publicity became quickly buried in the pages of journals and newspapers, the book *Ernst Mach*, by A. Lampa, a chief advocate of "Machist" physics, should have kept the facts in focus. For quotations from Lampa's book, see Blackmore, *Ernst Mach*, pp. 293–94.

81. Whether this was one of the phases of the history of science "made up" by some philosophers of science, a procedure for which Herbert Feigl, a prominent member of the Vienna circle was to apologize many years later (see chap. 14), is not known, but it would certainly serve as a convincing example.

82. Blackmore, *Ernst Mach*, chap. 18, "Mach and Buddhism."

83. For his offering this not at all flattering evaluation of Mach in his *Between Physics and Philosophy* (p. 37) Philipp Frank can hardly be suspected of any adverse bias.

84. The often quoted remark of Lord Kelvin, made at the Royal Institution on April 27, 1900, referred to the motion of the earth through the ether and to the partition of energy in black-body radiation. See his *Baltimore Lectures on Molecular Dynamics and the Wave Theory of Light* (London: C. J. Clay and Sons, 1904), p. 486.

CHAPTER ELEVEN

1. "Zur Geschichte der Auffindung des physikalischen Wirkungsquantum" (1943), in M. Planck, *Physikalische Abhandlungen und Vorträge* (Braunschweig: Friedr. Vieweg & Sohn, 1958), 3:257.

2. "Wissenschaftliche Selbstbiographie" (1948), *Physikalische Abhandlungen*, 3:375.

3. "Antrittsrede zur Aufnahme in die Akademie vom 28. Juni 1894," *Physikalische Abhandlungen*, 3:4.

4. Jolly's advice was pointedly and prominently recalled by Planck exactly fifty years later in his address given in Munich on December 1, 1924, under the title "Vom Relativen zum Absoluten"; see Planck, *Wege zur physikalischen Erkenntnis: Rede und Vorträge*, 4th ed. (Leipzig: S. Hirzel, 1944), p. 142. Jolly's complacency, as Planck remarked, had its roots in the success of reducing various fields of physics to mechanics through the principle of the conservation of energy, a principle worked out by Mayer, Joule, and Helmholtz.

5. A fine collection of these photographs graces the excellent monograph on Planck by A. Hermann, *Max Planck in Selbstzeugnissen und Bilddokumenten* (Reinbek bei Hamburg: Rowohlt Taschenbuch Verlag, 1973).

6. In a letter of December 14, 1930, to Josef Strasser. Quoted in Hermann, *Max Planck*, p. 11.

7. "Wissenschaftliche Selbstbiographie," p. 376.

8. "Zur Geschichte der Auffindung," p. 258.

9. "Wissenschaftliche Selbstbiographie," p. 378.

10. Such is the theme of A. Hermann's introduction, "Das Suchen nach dem Absoluten," to his edition of the text of Planck's two papers from 1900 containing the exact form of the temperature-dependence of black-body radiation and its theoretical derivation on the basis of the quantum of action: *Die Entdeckung des Wirkungsquantums: Dokumente der Naturwissenschaft: Abteilung Physik*, Band 11 (Munich: Ernst Battenberg Verlag, 1969).

11. "Zur Machschen Theorie der physikalischen Erkenntnis," *Naturwissenschaften* 11 (1910):1187.

12. In the opening paragraph of his "Wissenschaftliche Selbstbiographie," p. 374.

13. Ibid., p. 380.

14. "Antrittsrede," p. 2.

15. Ibid.

16. Ibid., p. 3.

17. Ibid.

18. Ibid., p. 4.

19. Ibid.

20. Ibid.

21. "Gegen die neuere Energetik" (1896), *Physikalische Abhandlungen*, 1:459–65. Planck named Rankine as the particular target of his remarks, adding that he also spoke of the trend Rankine started. In Germany criticism of that trend in 1896 could, however, only mean Ostwald and Mach, the chief spokesmen for "Energetik." Again, while Planck's concluding remarks were directed at Rankine, the whole school of "Energetik" was put on trial by his charge that the school sought its survival through evading critical problems.

22. "Wissenschaftliche Selbstbiographie," pp. 389–90.

23. "Gegen die neuere Energetik," p. 459. As Planck noted in his "Wissenschaftliche Selbstbiographie" (p. 386), his failure to convince Ostwald and Mach of their error was "one of the most painful experiences of my entire scientific career." The following two paragraphs profited much from M. J. Klein's articles, "Thermodynamics and Quanta in Planck's Work," *Physics Today* 19 (Nov. 1966): 23–32, and "Max Planck and the Beginning of the Quantum Theory," *Archives for History of Exact Sciences* 1 (1962): 459–79. The relatively few pages (10–22) on Planck's search for the quantum of action in *The Conceptual Development of Quantum Mechanics*, by M. Jammer (New York: McGraw Hill, 1966), contain little new and do not give justice to the deep philosophical motivation behind that search, let alone to a principal effect of it on Planck, namely, his complete break with the positivism advocated by Mach.

24. "Ueber elektrische Schwingungen, welche durch Resonanz erregt und durch Strahlung gedämpft werden" (1897), in *Physikalische Abhandlungen*, 1:466.

25. It culminated in the vain effort of E. Zermelo, a student of Planck, to answer, on behalf of his teacher, Boltzmann's demonstration that neither the equations of electrodynamics nor those of mechanics justified the assumption of the nonstatistical character of radiation equilibrium. Indeed, Zermelo's paper prompted Boltzmann's sarcastic remark that his work on statistical mechanics had at long last been noticed in Germany, even if not understood ("Entgegnung auf die wärmetheoretischen Betrachtungen des Hrn. E. Zermelo," *Annalen der Physik* 57 [1896]: 773).

26. In his fourth communication to the Berlin Academy on irreversible radiation, in *Physikalische Abhandlungen*, 1:532–59.

27. In his fifth communication, "Ueber irreversible Strahlungsvorgänge" (1899), in *Physikalische Abhandlungen*, 1:560–600.

28. This momentous remark made on May 18, 1899, in the session of the Berlin Academy (see *Physikalische Abhandlungen*, 1:666) was preceded by Planck's remarks on the artificial, culture-conditioned character of units of measurement used in physics. See also *Planck's Original Papers in Quantum Mechanics*, German and English edition annotated by H. Kangro, trans. D. ter Haar and S. G. Brush (London: Taylor and Francis, 1972).

29. "Entropie und Temperatur strahlender Wärme," *Physikalische Abhandlungen*, 1:674.

30. For a lengthy section of that letter, see A. Hermann, *The Genesis of Quantum Theory (1899–1913)*, trans. C. W. Nash (Cambridge, Mass.: MIT Press, 1971), p. 23.

31. In his letter of June 11, 1910, to W. Nernst; quoted in M. Klein, "Thermodynamics and Quanta in Planck's Work," p. 24.

32. A felicitous remark of L. Pierce Williams in his "Normal Science, Scientific Revolutions, and the History of Science," in *Criticism and the Growth of Knowledge*, ed. I. Lakatos and A. Musgrave (Cambridge University Press, 1974), p. 50.

33. As pointed out by Planck in his letter of July 6, 1905, to Ehrenfest; quoted in M. Klein, "Thermodynamics and Quanta in Planck's Work," p. 28.

34. Quoted in Klein's translation, ibid., p. 32.

35. Quoted in Hermann, *The Genesis of Quantum Theory*, p. 24.

36. See his Nobel address given in 1920 on the history of the development of quantum theory, *Physikalische Abhandlungen*, 3:125.

37. One of them was Bernhard Bavink, who earned fame with his book on the philosophy of physics, the other Robert Pohl, physicist in Göttingen. For details, see Hermann, *Max Planck in Selbstzeugnissen und Bilddokumenten*, pp. 29 and 131.

38. The paper read on October 19 was "On an Improvement of Wien's Equation for the Spectrum," as its title reads in English translation in *Planck's Original Papers in Quantum Mechanics* (n. 28 above), which also contains the text of his paper read on December 14, under the title "On the Theory of the Energy Distribution Law of the Normal Spectrum."

39. Ibid., p. 38.

40. Ibid., p. 40.

41. Ibid., p. 45.

42. In his letter to Wood; see Hermann, *The Genesis of Quantum Theory*, p. 23.

43. "Suppose, for instance, someone maintained that there is a minimum magnitude; that man with his minimum would shake the foundations of mathematics" (*On the Heavens* 271b). The upheaval in mathematics would have necessarily cast its shadow on physical science and philosophy even within the Aristotelian context, where a rather isolated existence was carved out for mathematics.

44. In his letter to Wood; see Hermann, *The Genesis of Quantum Theory*, p. 23.

45. That influence is well portrayed in chapter 13, "World Influence: Philosophy," of John T. Blackmore's *Ernst Mach: His Work, Life, and Influence* (Berkeley: University of California Press, 1972).

46. The number of physicists between Faraday and Einstein, who would as physicists be unanimously rated higher than Mach by unbiased historians of physics, would easily run into two or three dozen. An unintended proof of this is the paucity of pages on Mach's contributions to physics in the commemorative volume, *Ernst Mach: Physicist and Philosopher*, ed. R. S. Cohen and R. J. Seeger (Dordrecht: D. Reidel, 1968).

47. As late as April 1908, Lorentz, in a much publicized lecture given in Rome at the Fourth International Congress of Mathematicians, considered Planck's and Jeans's formulas as contenders of equal merit and called for further experiments for a decision betweeen the two. Reaction of the best experimentalists on black-body radiation was immediate, and Lorentz had to concede victory to Planck. See Hermann, *The Genesis of Quantum Theory*, pp. 37–41.

48. The original title, "Die Einheit des physikalischen Weltbildes," is rendered as "The Unity of the Physical Universe" in the widely known English translation, *A Survey of Physics: A Collection of Lectures and Essays by Max Planck*, trans. R. Jones and D. H. Williams (London: Methuen & Co., 1925), reprinted as a Dover paperback under the title *A Survey of Physical Theory* (see pp. 1–26). "Weltbild" in the original title carries a crucially important epistemological connotation which is not conveyed in the translation. Planck later considered this lecture to be one of his "most essential" writings. See his "Geleitwort" to the collection of his lectures and essays, *Wege zur physikalischen Erkenntnis: Reden und Vorträge* (1933), 4th ed. (Leipzig: S. Hirzel, 1944), p. [v].

49. Here Planck mentioned the complementary usefulness of the method advocated by Kirchoff, according to whom mechanics should only aim at a "description of all known motions" (*A Survey of Physical Theory*, p. 2). This descriptive (or rather positivist) method was in Planck's eyes, however, only an auxiliary factor to facilitate conceptual unification of the subject matter of physics.

50. Ibid., p. 15.

51. Ibid., p. 16.

52. Here Planck contrasted artificial units of measurement with units based on universal constants which "are such that the inhabitants of Mars, and indeed all intelligent beings in our universe, must encounter at some time—if they have not already done so" (ibid., p. 18). Planck returned to this theme in the fourth part of his lecture, where he insisted that because of these natural constants the present picture in physics "has certain properties [which] ... no revolution in Nature or Man can obliterate" (p. 24). This passage is still to be mentioned in the writings of those who today keep busy recasting the history of science in the paradigm of revolutions.

53. Ibid., p. 20.

54. Ibid., p. 22. Here Planck referred to Mach's emphatic assertions in his *Beiträge zur Analyse der Empfindungen* (1886) on that genuine reality which is to be accorded only to our sensations. Some of those assertions are worth quoting in Mach's own words: "Bodies do not produce sensations, but complexes of elements (complexes of sensations) make up bodies." But once sensations were declared to be the rockbed of reality, the genuineness of that reality had to appear merely provisional. Or as Mach himself perceived this in the same context: "For us, colors, sounds, spaces, times, ... are provisionally the ultimate elements, whose given connexion it is our business [that is, the business of science] to investigate." See E. Mach, *The Analysis of Sensations and the Relation of the Physical to the Psychical*, translated from the first German edition by C. M. Williams, revised and supplemented from the fifth German edition by S. Waterlow, with a new introduction by T. S. Szasz (New York: Dover, 1959), pp. 29–30.

55. Ibid., p. 23. Planck spoke of "the proud expectations of previous generations associated with special mechanical phenomena following the discovery of the energy principle" (the principle of the conservation of energy), expectations that, according to him, were particularly in evidence in the writings of Emil du Bois-Reymond. Planck's singling out the writings of du Bois-Reymond should

seem odd to anyone familiar with the writings of nineteenth-century physicists, almost all of whom made soaring proclamations concerning physical phenomena about the identity of mechanical explanation and intelligibility. See on this chapter 2, "The World as a Mechanism," in my *The Relevance of Physics* (Chicago: University of Chicago Press, 1966).

56. Mach's mistake was lowering "the standard of the physical world picture to that of the mechanical world picture" (ibid., p. 24). Of course, this "lowering" was of a piece with Mach's sensationism, which ultimately prevented him from anticipating some of Einstein's deepest insights on space and time, although these were precisely the topics that had been at the center of Mach's attention. See on this the penetrating remarks of M. Polanyi in his *Personal Knowledge: Towards a Post-Critical Philosophy*, 2d rev. ed. (Chicago: University of Chicago Press, 1962), p. 12.

57. "The Unity of the Physical Universe," p. 23.

58. Ibid.

59. Ibid.

60. For details, see J. Thiele, "Ein zeitgenossisches Urteil über die Kontroverse zwischen Max Planck und Ernst Mach," *Centaurus* 13 (1968): 85–90. Although the printed repercussions gathered by Thiele were in favor of Mach, their physicist-authors were very insignificant. The absence of first-rate physicists from the fray may be explained by their satisfaction that at long last the authority of Mach, which in Planck's own recollection was "simply above argument" in many circles, had met its well-deserved challenge. On Planck's phrase, see his *The Philosophy of Physics*, translated by W. H. Johnston (New York: Norton & Norton, 1936), p. 96. The contemporary discussion by K. Gerhards of the controversy, "Zur Kontroverse Planck-Mach," (*Vierteljahrschrift für wissenschaftliche Philosophie und Soziologie* 36 [1912]: 19–67) is rather short on physics, but its concluding pages have some relevance. There Gerhards noted that Mach's philosophical position should perhaps be viewed within the perspective of the route that epistemology had taken from Kant through Fichte to Hegel. Obviously, an extreme like Hegel (a most logical and genuine offshoot of Kant), could only generate another extreme, the radical sensationism of Mach.

61. While Mach noted in the preface of his *The Science of Mechanics* his indebtedness to Lagrange's work published in 1788, the measure of his debt— largely ignored by most of Mach's admirers—is still to be presented in full. Even a brief glance at the historical introductions written by Lagrange to each of the four parts of his *Traité* can make it clear that they were a gold mine of information for Mach, who, of course, gave an unjustified twist to the basic standpoint of Lagrange, as if the latter meant to turn the method of mathematical physics into basic epistemology.

62. "The Unity of the Physical Universe," p. 25.

63. Ibid., p. 26.

64. Ibid.

65. "Die Leitfaden meiner naturwissenschaftlichen Erkenntnislehre und ihre Aufnahme durch die Zeitgenossen," *Scientia* 7 (1910): 225–40; for quotation, see p. 233.

66. "Zur Machschen Theorie der physikalischen Erkenntniss: Eine Erwiderung," *Physikalische Zeitschrift* 11 (1910): 1186–90.

67. A point noted by Planck (ibid., p. 1187) but still to be recognized by most admirers of Mach.

68. Ibid., pp. 1189–90. This point too is largely ignored, especially where it should not be, namely, in the sundry endorsements of "Mach's principle."

69. S. G. Brush, "Mach and Atomism," *Synthese* 18 (1968): 208.

70. "Zur Machschen Theorie," p. 1188.

71. Ibid.

72. See Hermann, *Max Planck in Selbstzeugnissen und Bilddokumenten*, p. 98.

73. Planck's letter of June 18, 1947, was addressed to W. Kick, engineer in Regensburg, and first saw publication in an essay of F. Herneck, "Ein Brief Max Plancks über sein Verhältnis zum Gottesglauben" (*Forschungen und Fortschritte* 32 [1958]: 364–66), which also contains excerpts from Kick's letter to Herneck concerning the reasons and occasion of his inquiry to Planck. In that letter Kick refers to the report of the "amerikanische Zeitung *Neue Zeitung*" about Planck's conversion to Catholicism, a report which I have not been able to verify. Herneck's discussion is dominated throughout by the dictates of dialectical materialism. Somewhat less offensive is his second communication on the topic "Bemerkung zur Religiosität Max Plancks," *Physikalische Blätter* 16 (1960): 382–84. Needless to say, Herneck ignored statements of Planck that were indicative of at least a rudimentary belief in God, if not in a Christian God.

74. Hermann, *Max Planck in Selbstzeugnissen und Bilddokumenten*, p. 98.

75. See especially his public lectures given in the 1920s and 1930s, published under the title, *Wege zur physikalischen Erkenntnis*. An often free translation of some of those lectures is widely available in *The Philosophy of Physics*, in *Scientific Autobiography and Other Essays*, translated by F. Gaynor (New York: Philosophical Library, 1949), and in *The New Science* (New York: Meridian Books, 1959).

76. The most incisive and memorable of those phrases is from an interview of Planck with J. Murphy: "Science demands also the believing spirit. Anybody who has been seriously engaged in scientific work of any kind realizes that over the entrance to the gates of the temple of science are written the words: *Ye must have faith*. It is a quality which the scientist cannot dispense with" (*Where Is Science Going?* trans. J. Murphy [New York: W. W. Norton, 1932], p. 214).

77. See chapter 5.

Chapter Twelve

1. The first reached the *Annalen der Physik* on March 18, the second on May 11, the third on June 30. The next year Einstein disclosed ("Das Prinzip von der Erhaltung der Schwerpunktsbewegung und die Trägheit der Energetik," *Annalen der Physik* 20 [1906]: 629) the energy equivalence of rest-mass in the form that to the energy E embodied in mass S there corresponds an inertia E/V^2, where V is the velocity of light. In 1907 Einstein changed the notation by writing μ for S and c for V and wrote that "a mass μ is in relation to an inertia equivalent to an amount of energy of the magnitude μc^2." ("Ueber das Relativitätsprinzip und die aus demselben gezogenen Folgerungen," *Jahrbuch der Radioaktivität und Elektronik* 4 [1907] 442). That the now classic formula $E = mc^2$ was yet to appear in print should be a graphic illustration of the time needed for the gradual emergence and clarification of a great insight in the mind of its discoverer, to say nothing of its acceptance by lesser minds.

2. Its importance appeared to be so great to Planck that in his letter of July 6, 1907, to Einstein he insisted that work be concentrated on special relativity rather than on his own theory of radiation. See A. Hermann, *The Genesis of Quantum Theory (1899–1913)*, trans. C. W. Nash (Cambridge: MIT Press, 1971), p. 66.

3. Planck's words were addressed to A. Lampa, head of the physics department at the University of Prague, who was in charge, on behalf of the Austrian government, of the procedure of filling the vacant chair. See P. Frank, *Einstein: His Life and Times* (New York: A. Knopf, 1947), p. 101.

4. Quoted in A. Hermann, *Max Planck in Selbstzeugnissen und Bilddokumenten* (Reinbek bei Hamburg, Rowohlt, 1973), p. 45.

5. For excerpts from that document, see R. W. Clark: *Einstein: The Life and Times* (New York: Thomas Y. Crowell, 1971), p. 169.

6. The statement was made by J. Petzoldt at the November 11, 1912, meeting of the Gesellschaft für positivistische Philosophie in Berlin and was printed in the first article of the first issue of the *Zeitschrift für positivistische Philosophie*. Einstein should have protested, because the statement attributed special relativity to his alleged concern about the null result of the Michelson-Morley experiment. For details, see G. Holton's essay, "Einstein, Michelson, and the 'Crucial' Experiment" (1969), in his *Thematic Origins of Scientific Thought: Kepler to Einstein* (Cambridge: Harvard University Press, 1973), pp. 275–76.

7. See Clark, *Einstein: The Life and Times*, p. 154.

8. Quoted in Holton's essay, "Mach, Einstein, and the Search for Reality" (1968) in *Thematic Origins of Scientific Thought*, p. 226. It is still to be seen whether this incisive essay will succeed in clearing away that heavy positivist coat of paint imposed on Einstein's portrait through the systematic efforts of logical positivists over several decades.

9. Ibid., p. 227.

10. According to Einstein's own recollection of that meeting communicated to I. B. Cohen shortly before his death. Einstein repeated his statement several times to make it sure that its significance might not be lost on Cohen. See Clark, *Einstein: The Life and Times*, p. 160. According to the same recollection Mach kept insisting that acceptance of atoms was a mere "economy of thought," in clear evidence of his refusal to depart from his sensationist epistemology, for which external reality had but a shadowy existence.

11. The paper, "Entwurf einer verallgemeinerten Relativitätstheorie und einer Theorie der Gravitation" (*Zeitschrift für Mathematik und Physik* 62 [1913]: 225–61), consisted of a physical and a mathematical part of which the former (pp. 225–44) was written by Einstein and the latter by M. Grossman, his advisor in mathematics.

12. Quoted in Holton, "Mach, Einstein, and the Search for Reality," p. 228. Einstein's steps toward the recognition of the specific form of the bending of light in a strong gravitational field will be discussed later.

13. As noted in the preceding chapter.

14. See translation by P. E. B. Jourdain (Chicago: Open Court, 1911), p. 95.

15. *The Principles of Physical Optics: An Historical and Philosophical Treatment*, trans. J. S. Anderson and A. F. A. Young (1926; New York: Dover, n.d.), pp. vii–viii. Mach declined to be seen as a forerunner of relativity, which he found to be "growing more and more dogmatical," and claimed that it may very well turn out to be a "transitory inspiration in the history of science."

16. "Ueber das Relativitätsprinzip und die aus demselben gezogenen Folgerungen," p. 439.

17. "Vom Relativen zum Absoluten," lecture given at the University of Munich on December 1, 1924; see Planck, *Wege zur physikalischen Erkenntnis: Reden und Vorträge*, 4th ed. (Leipzig: S. Hirzel, 1944), pp. 142–55.

18. Ibid., p. 149. The two other evidences offered by Planck were the quantum of action and the reducibility of all matter to fundamental particles.

19. In the words of L. Infeld: "There are no references, no authorities quoted, and the few footnotes are of an explanatory character. The style is simple, and a great part of this article [on special relativity] can be followed without advanced technical knowledge" (*Albert Einstein: His Work and Its Influence on Our World* [New York: Charles Scribner's Sons, 1950], p. 23).

20. As Max Talmey reported it in his *The Relativity Theory Simplified and the Formative Period of Its Invention* (New York: Falcon Press, 1932), p. 164, Einstein read the *Critique* at the age of thirteen and felt that he had understood it. Talmey was a close friend of Einstein for five years prior to the Einstein family's departure to Milan in 1895.

21. See Einstein's "Autobiographical Notes" in P. A. Schilpp, ed., *Albert Einstein: Philosopher-Scientist* (Evanston: Library of Living Philosophers, 1949), 1:53. The same "Notes" also contain the telling information that at the age of four Einstein sensed, on being shown a compass, the need for supposing a reality beneath the phenomena: "I can still remember—or at least believe I can remember—that this experience made a deep and lasting impression upon me. Something deeply hidden had to be behind things" (ibid., p. 9). The same instinctive "meta-physical" sense was in evidence in the sixteen-year-old Einstein's eight-hundred-word essay, which he sent to his uncle, Cesar Koch in Belgium, "on an investigation of the state of the ether in a magnetic field," in which he argued that to understand the "essence" of electric current one must first investigate the surrounding magnetic field by probing it with polarized light. The essay, in the Einstein Archives at Princeton, was written under the inspiration which young Einstein, to quote his words, received from reading Hertz's "genial experiments."

22. Quoted in the translation of Clark, *Einstein: The Life and Times*, p. 53. For the German original, see C. Selig, *Albert Einstein: A Documentary Biography*, translated by M. Savill (London: Staples Press, 1956), p. 53, or *Albert Einstein: Leben und Werk eines Genies unserer Zeit*, 2d enlarged ed. (Zurich: Europa Verlag, 1960), pp. 85–86.

23. For the text of both letters (in photocopy), see Hans-Günther Körber, "Zur Biographie des jungen Albert Einstein, mit zwei unbekannten Briefen Einsteins an Wilhelm Ostwald vom Früjahr 1901," *Forschungen und Fortschritte* 38 (1964): 74–78.

24. See Clark, *Einstein: The Life and Times*, p. 180.

25. After an introductory meeting with French physicists at the Collège de France on March 31, 1922, Einstein held discussions with them on April 3, 5, and 7. His discussion with philosophers took place at the Sorbonne on April 6. Unfortunately, the most detailed and most accessible account of these discussions—that given by the astronomer Charles Nordmann ("Einstein expose et discute sa théorie," *Revue des Deux Mondes* 9 [1922]: 129–66)—is tainted with Nordmann's positivism, already in full evidence in his *Einstein et l'univers* published a year earlier (Paris: Hachette). In his account of the discussions Nordmann claimed that the negative result of the Michelson-Morley experiment was the starting point of Einstein's theory (pp. 134, 141, and 164) and that its chief effect was that it "has freed science of metaphysics" ("démétaphysiqué la science") (p. 137). More reliable is the shorter account of the discussion with philosophers in the July 1922 issue of the *Bulletin de la Société Française de Philosophie*. Its sections containing Einstein's replies to Brunschwicg and Meyerson were printed in *Nature* (112 [1923]: 253) in English translation. For Einstein's reply to Brunschwicg, see *Bulletin* 17 (1922): 101–2. According to Einstein, science needed "arbitrary" concepts in the sense that they were not the direct fruit of observations and experiments, but not concepts that claimed absolute, a priori validity.

26. "En somme, ce qu'a fait Mach, c'est un catalogue et non un système" (ibid., p. 101).

27. Ibid., p. 102.

28. "Ernst Mach," *Physikalische Zeitschrift* 17 (1916): 101–4; see, especially, p.

103. But Einstein's deploring Mach's unfortunate usage of crucial words, such as "Empfindung" (p. 104), was a prophetic sign of his eventual disavowal of Mach's epistemology.

29. Quoted in the translation of Holton, "Einstein, Mach, and the Search for Physical Reality," p. 240.

30. P. Frank, *Einstein: His Life and Times*, p. 215. The physicist, not identified by Frank, began by stating: "I hold to the views of the man who for me is not only the greatest physicist, but also the greatest philosopher, namely, Albert Einstein."

31. Letter of November 28, 1930. Quoted in the translation of Holton, "Einstein, Mach, and the Search for Reality," p. 243.

32. "In all such cases the matter turns on grasping the empirical law as a logical necessity. Once one assumes the basic hypothesis of molecular kinetic theory, one realizes in a sense that God himself could not have established those connections other than as they actually exist, just as it was in no way possible for him to turn four into a prime number" ("Ueber den gegenwärtigen Stand der Feldtheorie" in *Festschrift Prof. Dr. A. Stodola überreicht* [Zurich: Orell Füssli Verlag, 1929], p. 127).

33. The endorsement, drafted in mid-April 1931, was meant to be an introduction to the printed text of Planck's address on positivism and the reality of the external world. For quotation from the draft, now in the Einstein Archives, see Holton, "Mach, Einstein, and the Search for Reality," p. 244.

34. "Positivismus und reale Aussenwelt," address given on November 12, 1930, in the Harnack Haus of the Kaiser Wilhelm Gesellschaft for the Promotion of Science. For its English translation, "Is the External World Real?" see *Where Is Science Going?* translation and biographical notes by J. Murphy (New York: W. W. Norton, 1932), pp. 64–83.

35. "You uncovered an insidious defect in the ether theory of light, as it then existed, and stimulated the ideas of H. A. Lorentz and Fitz Gerald [*sic*], out of which the special theory of relativity developed. These in turn pointed the way to the general theory of relativity, and to the theory of gravitation." See "Professor Einstein at the California Institute of Technology," *Science* 73 (1931): 379.

36. As shown convincingly by Holton in his essay, "Einstein, Michelson, and the 'Crucial Experiment,'" in *Thematic Origins of Scientific Thought*, p. 261.

37. "Clerk Maxwell's Influence on the Evolution of the Idea of Physical Reality," in *The World as I See It* (New York: Covici-Friede, 1934), p. 60.

38. Ibid., p. 63.

39. Ibid., p. 66.

40. "On the Method of Theoretical Physics," in *The World as I See It*, p. 30.

41. Ibid., p. 31.

42. Ibid., p. 32.

43. See pp. vi–xix in *Dialogue Concerning the Two Chief World Systems*, translated with revised notes by Stillman Drake (Berkeley: University of California Press, 1962). It should seem telling that Einstein's sole reference to Plato in that foreword concerned the dialogue form of presentation, but not the Platonists' belief in the absolute perfection of circles and spheres. Einstein's failure to note Galileo's continual references to Archimedes should seem equally revealing. Needless to say, the role of *Christian* Neoplatonism in Galileo's thought was completely lost on Einstein.

44. See pp. 9–13 in Carola Baumgardt, *Johannes Kepler: Life and Letters*, with an introduction by Albert Einstein (London: Victor Golancz, 1952). Einstein clearly indulged in rhetoric in asserting that Kepler's "life work was possible only when he succeeded in freeing himself to a large extent from the spiritual

tradition in which he was born" (p. 13). Einstein's other assertion (ibid.), that Kepler "had to free himself from an animistic, teleologically oriented manner of thinking in scientific research," flies in the face of almost every page written by him.

45. The most startling evidence in that connection was not so much Einstein's obituary of Mach, but his answer given in 1950 to R. S. Shankland to the latter's question whether it was worth writing the history of the Michelson-Morley experiment. "Yes," came Einstein's reply, "by all means, but you must write it as Mach wrote his *Science of Mechanics.*" In the rest of his reply Einstein presented Mach, the historian of science, as one who without really knowing the manner in which early scientists tackled their problems, had the ability to read their minds so that what Mach said "is very likely correct any way." See R. S. Shankland, "Conversations with Albert Einstein," *American Journal of Physics* 31 (1963): 50. Such was a classic case of lack of reverence on the part of a scientist for the facts of scientific history and for the demands of the historical method, an attitude which until very recently failed to elicit criticism, however well-deserved.

46. This point is systematically underplayed in P. Frank's *Relativity: A Richer Truth* (Boston: Beacon Press, 1950). Frank saw in the Copernican revolution only the "relativisation" of up and down (pp. 7–15), and he saw Einstein's world view as wholly devoid of metaphysical elements (pp. 16–22). Indeed, Frank thought that the epistemology of relativity is germane to operationism (pp. 23–28). Since Frank seemed to know only of idealistic metaphysics, he equated assertion of absolute truth with the behavior of totalitarian regimes and of heresy-hunting theologians (pp. 119–22). No wonder that the ethical philosophy which Frank based on Einstein's relativity was equivalent to a pragmatism cultivated in the spirit of an "anti-metaphysical view of science" (pp. 112–18). It is even more regrettable that Einstein provided some support to Frank's interpretation of his thought through a foreword in which he drew a parallel between the free choice of axioms in science and a similar choice in ethics, although it was his well-known belief that one set of scientific axioms is always superior to all others precisely because of an objectively existing world order. In praising man's moral genius (p. vii), Einstein credited our inborn tendencies to avoid pain, hardly a solid ground for any ethics which may inflict great pain on the individual by obliging him to resist his inborn urge to inflict pain on others.

47. Curiously, that singular constancy of light, which makes the universe what it is, is still to become the subject of universal wonderment. The prevalent attitude is a kind of insensitivity, fostered perhaps by the matter-of-fact tone of Einstein's epoch-making statement in 1905 in his paper "On the Electrodynamics of Moving Bodies": "We . . . also introduce another postulate, . . . namely, that light is always propagated in empty space with a definite velocity c which is independent of the state of motion of the emitting body." See *The Principle of Relativity: A Collection of Original Memoirs on the Special and General Theory of Relativity* by H. A. Lorentz, A. Einstein, H. Minkowski, and H. Weyl, with notes by A. Sommerfeld, translated by W. Perrett and G. B. Jeffrey (1923; New York: Dover, n.d.), p. 38.

48. "Ueber die Relativitätsprinzip," p. 461.

49. He stated in 1911 in reference to his paper quoted above that it had now occurred to him that this bending might be observed through the displacement of fixed stars when visually close to the sun's edge, and he gave the displacement as 0.83 seconds of an arc. See "Ueber die Einflusz der Schwerkraft auf die Ausbreitung des Lichtes," *Annalen der Physik* 35 (1911): 898 and 908. Two years later at the annual gathering of German scientists in Vienna Einstein called

attention to the opportunities presented by the total eclipse in 1914, a suggestion which was warmly received but which, because of the outbreak of World War I, could not be implemented.

50. At the end of his memoir, "The Foundation of the General Theory of Relativity," in *The Principle of Relativity*, pp. 162–64.

51. Quoted in Clark, *Einstein: The Life and Times*, p. 200.

52. Ibid.

53. See chapters 5 and 6.

54. Seeliger's efforts to resolve the gravitational paradox are discussed in my *The Paradox of Olbers' Paradox* (New York: Herder and Herder, 1969), pp. 189–98.

55. This is the title of the English translation, in *The Principle of Relativity*, pp. 177–88; see especially pp. 177–78.

56. Ibid., p. 178.

57. Ibid., p. 179.

58. Ibid., p. 181.

59. The formula (ibid., p. 187) as given by Einstein is $M = \varrho \cdot 2\pi^2 R^3 = 4\pi^2(R/\varkappa) = \pi^2\sqrt{(32/\varkappa^2\varrho)}$, where ϱ is the mean density of matter, R the radius of the universe, $\varkappa$ a universal constant, and $\varkappa\varrho/2 = 1/R^2$.

60. Ibid., p. 179.

61. Ibid., p. 188.

62. See his article, "Do Gravitational Fields Play an Essential Part in the Structure of the Elementary Particles of Matter?" (1919), in *The Principles of Relativity*, pp. 191–98.

63. Ibid., p. 193.

64. "Cosmological Considerations," p. 188.

65. *Science and the Modern World* (New York: Macmillan, 1926), p. 15.

66. The occasion was a banquet given in honor of Einstein in the Hotel Savoy in London in 1930. Shaw's improvised speech was recorded by his secretary, Miss B. Patch, and published in her *Thirty Years with G. B. S.* (London: V. Gollancz, 1951), p. 194.

67. As recalled by E. Borel, one of those present at the discussions which Einstein held with French physicists and philosophers in Paris in 1922, in his *Space and Time* (London: Blackie & Son, 1926), pp. 226–27. Borel was willing to admit only the "convenience" of Einstein's insistence on the finiteness of the universe. It was simply ignored by Nordmann, the most prolific reporter of those discussions, although he recalled in detail discussions of the Schwarzschild-singularity and the possible gravitational contraction of the universe which is a consequence of the finiteness of the total mass ("Einstein expose et discute sa théorie," pp. 154–55).

68. In an appendix to the second edition of his *The Meaning of Relativity* (Princeton: Princeton University Press, 1945).

69. On those tactics, as articulated by Schlick and Russell, see my *The Paradox of Olbers' Paradox*, pp. 220–23.

70. "Physics and Reality" (1936), in *Out of My Later Years* (New York: Philosophical Library, 1950), p. 61.

71. See his letter of April 23, 1953, to J. E. Switzer; quoted in D. J. de Solla Price, *Science since Babylon* (New Haven: Yale University Press, 1961), p. 15.

72. "The axiomatic bases of theoretical physics cannot be extracted from experience but must be freely invented," he stated in his Spencer lecture (1933), where he qualified as "doomed to failure" all attempts to derive them from elementary experiments (*The World as I See It*, p. 36). Three years later he specified the basic error of most physicists of the nineteenth century as their

inability to recognize that "there is no inductive method which could lead to the fundamental concepts of physics" (*Out of My Later Years*, p. 78). He had already urged in 1930 the physicist "to give free rein to his fancy, for there is no other way to the goal" (*The World as I See It*, p. 60).

73. *Lettres à Maurice Solovine* (Paris: Gauthier-Villars, 1956), p. 102.

74. Ibid., p. 115. One can only speculate on Einstein's reaction had he lived to read the essay, "The Integration of Form in Natural and in Theological Science" (*Science, Medicine and Man* 1 [1973]: 143–72), by the distinguished theologian Thomas F. Torrance, in which the claim about a substantial identity between the methods of science and theology is largely based on Einstein's own reflections on creative science.

75. See B. Hoffmann, *Albert Einstein: Creator and Rebel*, with the collaboration of Helen Dukas (New York: The Viking Press, 1972), pp. 224 and 228.

76. *Out of My Later Years*, pp. 32–33.

77. Ibid., pp. 26–27.

78. Ibid., pp. 32 and 30.

79. The espousals were certainly well phrased, such as, for instance, that "faith in the possibility that the regulations valid for the world of existence are rational" is rooted in man's religious sense and that he could not "conceive a genuine scientist without that profound faith" (ibid., p. 30). The dismissal was best exemplified in his refusal to pay taxes to the synagogue in Berlin in the 1920s and in his complaint made in 1952 that he now had to play "the role of Jewish saint." See Hoffmann, *Albert Einstein: Creator and Rebel*, pp. 144 and 245.

80. On being told about the positive result of the eclipse observation in 1919 he was asked what would have been his reaction to a negative outcome. His reply was: "Then I would have been very sorry for the dear Lord—the theory is correct." See Holton, "Mach, Einstein, and the Search for Reality," p. 237. Even more revealing is his statement to an assistant, "What really interests me is whether God had any choice in the creation of the world," quoted in Holton's review of Clark's *Einstein: The Life and Times* in the *New York Times Book Review*, September 5, 1971, p. 20, col. 2.

81. The expression is from his letter of March 30, 1954, to M. Mühsam, where he added: "this is assuredly a new kind of religion." Quoted in C. Selig, *Helle Zeit, Dunkel Zeit* (Zurich: Europa Verlag, 1956), p. 28.

82. The most insistent was H. Reichenbach, who in a sense received a firm "rebuke" from Einstein. See Holton, "Einstein, Michelson, and the 'Crucial Experiment'," pp. 278–79.

83. See his "Reply to Criticisms," in Schilpp, *Albert Einstein: Philosopher-Scientist*, p. 673.

84. In his letter of December 9, 1935, to A. Lampa, Einstein disputed the claim that Mach had fallen into oblivion and added: "the philosophical orientation of physicists is rather close to that of Mach." See Holton, "Mach, Einstein, and the Search for Reality," p. 253.

85. "On the Generalized Theory of Gravitation" (1950), in *Ideas and Opinions by Albert Einstein* (New York: Crown, 1954), p. 342.

86. See Clark, *Einstein: The Life and Times*, pp. 611–12.

87. As recalled by A. Sommerfeld, in Schilpp, *Albert Einstein: Philosopher-Scientist*, p. 99.

Chapter Thirteen

1. *Principles of Modern Physics* (New York: McGraw-Hill, 1959), pp. 678–79.

2. Ibid., p. 679.

3. *The Search* (Indianapolis: Bobbs-Merill Company, 1935), p. 179.

4. Ibid. Snow's *Search*, originally published in London a year earlier, prompted Rutherford to ask its author: "Keep off us as much as you can. People are bound to think that you are getting at some of us. And I suppose we've all got things that we don't want anyone to see." Reported by Snow himself in his *Variety of Men* (Harmondsworth: Penguin Books, 1969), p. 19.

5. *Letters on Wave Mechanics: Schrödinger, Planck, Einstein, Lorentz*, ed. K. Przibram, translated with an introduction by M. J. Klein (New York: Philosophical Library, 1967), p. 36. A few years after Planck's death, Einstein wrote to Schrödinger: "You are the only contemporary physicist, besides Laue, who sees that one cannot get around the assumption of reality—if only one is honest" (ibid., p. 39).

6. *What Is Life? And Other Scientific Essays* (Garden City, N.Y.: Doubleday, 1956), pp. 161–62.

7. Quoted as firsthand information by W. E. Hocking in his *Science and the Idea of God* (Chapel Hill: University of North Carolina Press, 1944), p. 96. A generation later the bewilderingly complex world of "elementary" particles provoked a similar feeling in H. Margenau. He characterized his paper on "The Meaning of 'Elementary Particle' " (*American Scientist* 39 [1951]: 422–31) as an attempt "to introduce the reader without too much technical equipment to a place behind the splendid scene of experimental discovery, to the place where theorists, miserable with many failures, invoke by strange cantations even stranger notions to provide the rationale for the findings of the experimenter."

8. From his letter of May 21, 1925, to R. Kronig. See the latter's essay, "The Turning Point," in *Theoretical Physics in the Twentieth Century: A Memorial Volume to Wolfgang Pauli*, ed. M. Fierz and V. F. Weisskopf (New York: Interscience Publishers, 1960), p. 22.

9. Letter of October 9, 1925, to Kronig; ibid., pp. 25–26.

10. See notes 65 and 66 below.

11. In his *Physics and Beyond: Encounters and Conversations*, translated from the German by A. J. Pomerans (New York: Harper & Row, 1971), pp. 62–69.

12. Ibid., p. 67.

13. As reported by G. Hevesy in a letter of October 14, 1913, to Rutherford. Quoted in A. S. Eve, *Rutherford: Being the Life and Letters of the Rt. Hon. Lord Rutherford, O. M.* (Cambridge University Press, 1939), p. 226.

14. As should be clear from a brief glance at pp. 106–10 in vol. 2 of E. T. Whittaker's classic, *A History of the Theories of Aether and Electricity* (London: Thomas Nelson, 1953).

15. The most farfetched of these efforts is undoubtedly the chapter "Niels Bohr and the Ekliptika Circle," in *Einstein and the Generations of Science* by L. S. Feuer (New York: Basic Books, 1974) pp. 109–57.

16. In fact, it was in such a way that Balmer himself reached his famous formula, the derivation of which from Bohr's theory provided its first and signal verification. The grouping by Heisenberg of the energy levels of the hydrogen atom in matrix form illustrates the same instinctive groping. For further examples of this from the history of modern and classical physics, see chapter 3, "The World as a Pattern of Numbers," in my *The Relevance of Physics* (Chicago: University of Chicago Press, 1966).

17. Clearly, if Bohr had been given to philosophizing to any significant degree prior to 1913, the fact would certainly have become well known by the 1960s. Yet, in *Niels Bohr: His Life and Work As Seen by His Friends and Colleagues*, ed. S. Rozental (Amsterdam: North-Holland Publishing Company, 1967), the

two essays dealing with Bohr's early years are conspicuously barren of philosophical connotation. Feuer's efforts (*Einstein and the Generations of Science*, p. 136) to attribute Bohr's advocacy of quantum jumps to Kierkegaard's influence readily reveal their inconsistency: Feuer admits that Harald Höffding, whose philosophy had a distinct appeal for the young Bohr, rejected the Kierkegaardian disjunction 'either-or.'

18. No sooner had Rutherford read Bohr's historic paper in manuscript than he wrote to Bohr, on March 20, 1913, about the "one grave difficulty" in his hypothesis (little suspecting that fourteen years later Dirac and Heisenberg would lock horns about that difficulty with as much naturalness as Rutherford spotted it): "Your ideas as to the mode of origin of spectra in hydrogen are very ingenious and seem to work out well; but the mixture of Planck's ideas with the old mechanics makes it very difficult to form a physical idea of what is the basis of it all. There appears to me one grave difficulty in your hypothesis, which I have no doubt you fully realise, namely, how does an electron decide what frequency it is going to vibrate at when it passes from one stationary state to the other? It seems to me that you would have to assume that the electron knows beforehand where it is going to stop" (A. S. Eve, *Rutherford*, p. 221).

19. *Physics and Beyond*, pp. 62–64.

20. Ibid., p. 63.

21. As already mentioned and documented in the preceding chapter.

22. *Physics and Beyond*, p. 67.

23. Socrates professed to know nothing only when it came to those who, like the Sophists and some materialists, such as Anaxagoras, called in doubt metaphysical and spiritual reality. Socrates was so convinced about having an immortal soul that he chose to die rather than disobey the voice of his conscience, one of the best-known facts of cultural and philosophical history. This fact was divested, in the agnostic style characteristic of most adherents of the Copenhagen school, of its true character when Born commented on Einstein's scathing remark on the "Church of the Atheists," that is, Soviet Communism which mocked his theory of relativity: "He [Einstein] had no belief in the church, but he did not think that religious faith was a sign of stupidity, nor unbelief a sign of intelligence; he knew, as did Socrates, that we know nothing" (*The Born-Einstein Letters*, with commentaries by Max Born, trans. Irene Born [New York: Walker and Company, 1971], p. 203).

24. "The Quantum Postulate and the Recent Development of Atomic Theory," in Niels Bohr, *Atomic Theory and the Description of Nature* (Cambridge University Press, 1934), pp. 52–91. For quotation see p. 90.

25. Ibid., p. 52.

26. Ibid.

27. Ibid., p. 54. Remorseless inner logic of initial assumptions immediately asserted itself as Bohr advocated in the same breath the equivalent of Mach's reduction of reality to sensations: "Ultimately, every observation can, of course, be reduced to our sense perceptions." This is certainly true of observations already severed of the 'observed,' but then the reduction in question turns into a tautology, an obvious trap which Bohr was not always sensitive enough to recognize.

28. Ibid.

29. Ibid., p. 75. Here Bohr spoke of the "irrational element expressed by the quantum postulate."

30. Ibid., p. 91.

31. Ibid.

32. Ibid., p. 77.

33. Ibid., p. 84.

34. Ibid., p. 87.

35. Ibid., pp. 1–24; for quotation, see p. 19.

36. Ibid. Here Bohr should have recalled the astute remark in Rutherford's letter to him about electrons knowing in advance the specific jumps to take. As Bohr's next remark was to show, the alternative to a personification of nature was the admission of a personal external "chooser," or a Creator, an alternative which implied the objectivity of nature, an objectivity already gainsaid by Bohr.

37. Ibid.

38. Ibid., p. 20.

39. He did so in connection with some basic claims of Otto Neurath, to be discussed in detail in the following chapter.

40. Especially through his "Introductory Survey": with an eye on the opposition expressed by a number of physicists to his lecture at Como in 1927, he declared that the "fundamental postulate of the indivisibility of the quantum of action is itself . . . an irrational element which . . . forces us to adopt a new mode of description designated as *complementary* in the sense that any given application of classical concepts precludes the simultaneous use of other classical concepts which in a different connection are equally necessary for the elucidation of the phenomena" and added that "the main purpose of the article is to show that this feature of complementarity is essential for a consistent interpretation of the quantum-theoretical methods" (*Atomic Theory and the Description of Nature*, pp. 10–11).

41. Bohr, "Unity of Knowledge" (1954), in *Atomic Physics and Human Knowledge* (New York: John Wiley & Sons, 1958), p. 81.

42. Ibid. While the picture of that coat of arms could appear quite innocuous and wholly respectable in *Niels Bohr: His Life and Work* (facing p. 305), one wonders what Bohr's feelings would have been on seeing his coat of arms reproduced by the physicist Fritjof Capra in his *The Tao of Physics* (1975), which a year later became widely available in paperback, with the six-limbed Shiva gracing its front cover. A theist, and especially a Christian theist, who is aware of the fact that it is under Christ's impact that the rationality of monotheism has become the cultural matrix of the Western world as the cradle of science, will find revealing Capra's remark (his sole reference to Christ) that "for the Eastern world the Buddhist image in the state of meditation is as significant as the image of the crucified Christ for the West" (p. 100 in Fontana-Collins paperback edition). That West-born science in one of its most incisive forms (fundamental particle theory) can only be understood in terms of thought of the East (where apparently unknown to Capra and certainly to many of his readers disillusioned with their Western Christian heritage science suffered monumental stillbirths), is a claim germane to the conceptual somersaults fostered by the philosophy of complementarity, but it is hardly in tune with the dictates of consistency and with the hard facts of scientific history. The words in which Capra relates the genesis of his "insight" are worth quoting, all the more so as in all likelihood he did not write them under the influence of Mach. The latter's mystical experience that led from sensationism to Buddhism reoccurs with the force of inner logic in Capra's preface: "As I sat on that bench [on the ocean shore one late summer afternoon] my former experiences came to life; I 'saw' cascades of energy coming down from outer space, in which particles were created and destroyed in rhythmic pulses; I 'saw' the atoms of the elements and those of my body participating in this cosmic dance of energy; I felt its rhythm and I 'heard' its sound, and at that moment I *knew* that

this was the Dance of Shiva, the Lord of Dancers worshipped by the Hindus." A perusal of Capra's book can easily show that it is not science that leads from Christ to Shiva, or from Christian monotheism to Buddhist pantheism, but a failure to ponder the historical and philosophical facts of the many still-births and the only birth of science.

43. "Natural Philosophy and Human Cultures" (1938), ibid., p. 31. The plural form "cultures" can be seen as an unintended admission that culture as such had only aspects but no ontological reality.

44. "Discussion with Einstein on Epistemological Problems in Atomic Physics" (1949), ibid., p. 66.

45. "The Quantum of Action and the Description of Nature" (1929), in *Atomic Theory and the Description of Nature*, p. 101.

46. *Electrons et Photons: Rapports et discussions du Cinquième Conseil de Physique tenu à Bruxelles du 24 au 29 Octobre 1927 sous les auspices de l'Institut International de Physique Solvay* (Paris: Gauthier-Villars, 1928), pp. 258–63.

47. In their experiment the coincidence occurred within such a short time and so frequently as to take three hundred years if the Bohr-Kramers-Slater theory had been correct. The theory fared equally badly with respect to the angle of the recoil of electrons as determined by the Compton effect, a result shown immediately by Compton himself. For a brief description of these experiments and for details in their further refinement, see R. S. Shankland, *Atomic and Nuclear Physics*, 2d ed. (New York: Macmillan, 1960), pp. 208–13. On comments of a philosophical character which the experiments provoked from leading contemporary physicists, see R. H. Stuewer, *The Compton Effect: Turning Point in Physics* (New York: Science History Publications, 1975), pp. 299–305.

48. Indeed its authors declared that they had abandoned "any attempt at a causal connexion between the transitions in distant atoms, and especially a direct application of the principles of conservation of energy and momentum" ("The Quantum Theory of Radiation," *Philosophical Magazine* [London] 47 [1924]: 799). For the antecedents of the theory and for its explosive impact on epistemological considerations, see M. Jammer, *The Conceptual Development of Quantum Mechanics* (New York: McGraw-Hill, 1966), pp. 184–85.

49. Of course, the choice, as Dirac hastened to add, was irrevocable and was "to affect the whole future state of the world" (*Electrons et photons*, p. 262). Nature, therefore, already saddled with the burden of making the judicious choice of selecting the coherent pattern corresponding to the formation of a series of condensations in Wilson cloud chambers, was now enjoined by Dirac never to go back on her choice, nay to keep that choice in mind concerning all her future choices. Such was the curious way of a physicist to save a nature consistent for his purposes, an aim that could have been secured without any personification of nature as long as one espoused a realist epistemology. On reading Dirac's explanation of the formation of tracks in cloud chambers one cannot help thinking of nature as similar to a Mexican woman producing her colorful sets of beads held together by a string always carefully hidden from view.

50. *Electrons et photons*, p. 264. There is no reference to this exchange of views between Dirac and Heisenberg in the major study of the philosophy of Heisenberg, *Quantum Mechanics and Objectivity: A Study of the Physical Philosophy of Werner Heisenberg*, by P. A. Heelan (The Hague: Martinus Nijhoff, 1965).

51. See chapter 3 above; and chapter 1, "The World as an Organism," in my *The Relevance of Physics*.

52. See chapter 9.

53. *Electrons et photons*, p. 266.

54. A similar remark of Einstein, "Raffiniert ist der Herrgott, aber boshaft ist er nicht" ("God is subtle but he is not malicious"), made in Princeton during his visit there in 1921, became engraved in marble above the fireplace in the faculty lounge of Fine Hall, until 1972 housing the Department of Mathematics.

55. "Discussion with Einstein," p. 47.

56. See chapter 2.

57. However untraceable, the remark proves the truth of the saying: "se non è vero ma ben trovato!"

58. "Discussion with Einstein," p. 41.

59. In a letter of May 31; see *Letters on Wave Mechanics*, p. 31.

60. In spite of numerous and often ingenious attempts, which are discussed in F. J. Belinfante's classic monograph, *A Survey of Hidden Variable Theories* (Oxford: Pergamon Press, 1973), quantum mechanics is still in no need of a "cryptodeterministic" overhauling.

61. As Born himself recalled in his Nobel Prize address; see Jammer, *The Conceptual Development of Quantum Mechanics*, p. 204. J. Rosanes, who taught Born matrix calculus, did not suspect how prophetic he was in concluding in 1865 his doctoral dissertation on matrices with the words: "The laws of physics cannot be expressed or perceived except with the help of higher mathematics" (ibid.).

62. It was only much later that E. P. Wigner broached the subject in a remarkable essay, "The Unreasonable Effectiveness of Mathematics in the Natural Sciences," *Communications on Pure and Applied Mathematics* 13 (1960): 1–14.

63. See chapter 16, n. 66. Also, the question of mind, creative or not, implied that ontology which Bohr was resolved to keep out of sight.

64. "Discussion with Einstein," p. 52.

65. Schrödinger's timidity was all the more unwarranted as, to recall a remark of Dirac ("The Evolution of the Physicist's Picture of Nature," *Scientific American* 208 [May 1963]: 46), he "got his equation by pure thought, looking for some beautiful generalization . . . and not by keeping close to the experimental developments of the subject."

66. That such was indeed the genesis of Dirac's great feat was strongly intimated by Dirac himself in what he added to his foregoing remark: "I think there is a moral to this story, namely, that it is more important to have beauty in one's equations than to have them fit the experiment. If Schrödinger had been more confident of his work, he could have published it some months earlier, and he could have published a more accurate equation. . . . It seems that if one is working from the point of view of getting beauty in one's equations, and if one has really a sound insight, one is on a sure line of progress. If there is no complete agreement between the results of one's work and experiment, one should not allow oneself to be too discouraged, because the discrepancy may well be due to minor features that are not properly taken into account and that will be cleared up with further developments of the theory" (ibid.).

67. A grouping by M. Gell-Mann of nuclear resonance levels in terms of eight quantum numbers, on the basis of which J. J. Sakurai predicted in late 1962 the existence of ϕ mesons, discovered four months later by groups working at Brookhaven and Berkeley.

68. For these and other similar features of modern physics, see my *The Relevance of Physics*, pp. 180–83.

69. See his words referred to in note 6 above.

70. Or as he put it in his letter of March 3, 1947, to Born: "I am quite convinced that someone will eventually come up with a theory whose objects, connected by laws, are not probabilities but considered facts, as used to be

taken for granted until quite recently. I cannot, however, base this conviction on logical reasons, but can only produce my little finger as my witness, that is, I offer no authority which would be able to command any kind of respect outside of my own hand." Quoted from *The Born-Einstein Letters* with commentaries by Max Born, translated by Irene Born (New York: Walker and Company, 1971), p. 158.

71. See Einstein's letter of August 8, 1939, to Schrödinger, in which he mentions Bohr in connection with the problem of whether a cat is real when actually observed (*Letters on Wave Mechanics*, p. 36).

72. Ibid.

73. "The Nature of Quantum Mechanical Reality: Einstein versus Bohr," in R. G. Colodny (ed.), *Paradigms and Paradoxes: The Philosophical Challenge of the Quantum Domain* (Pittsburgh: University of Pittsburgh Press, 1972), pp. 67–302; for quotation see p. 208. That this categorical and, in my belief, very well-argued rendering of Bohr's refusal to consider questions of ontology is not recalled in M. Jammer's *The Philosophy of Quantum Mechanics: The Intrepretation of Quantum Mechanics in Historical Perspective* (New York: John Wiley, 1974), shows that even a most informative and detailed discussion of a topic is not necessarily an incisive analysis of it. Jammer's book, which comes to an end with the advice of a French moralist that "it is better to debate a question without settling it than to settle a question without debating it," seems to suffer throughout from a lack of willingness to face up to fundamental questions about reality. A historian may, of course, claim to be exempt from settling questions of philosophy, but without a readiness to declare himself on at least the fundamental questions concerning reality he will not perceive the futility of long debates, however learned from the scientific viewpoint, based on the systematic evasion of those very same questions. These questions cannot, of course, be answered without asserting reality, a stance which implies the willingness to accept reality as existing objectively. It is that willingness which is nipped in the bud by the postulates of positivism, empiricism, and sensationism which, in one way or another, underlie the Copenhagen philosophy of quantum mechanics. By submitting to others their arguments on behalf of that philosophy, its spokesmen refute by their very argumentation that solipsism which inevitably follows from their epistemological premises. The inexorability of the inner logic of basic presuppositions is once more shown by the last sections of Jammer's book where we see the inner logic of the solipsism of the Copenhagen interpretation of quantum mechanics being drawn to its next-to-last phase in the many-world theory in which the universe becomes a set of as many worlds as there are observers, nay observations. The very last phase of that logic should be the stance of complete silence, the only stance consistent with solipsism. Only those uninformed about the catastrophe brought upon science in the Muslim world by al-Ashari's occasionalism would feel comfort on finding Jammer see merit in the many-world theory. His reason for this is that the theory saves the consistency of observations equivalent "to a continual splitting of the world into a stupendous number of branches" in a manner analogous to the way in which the Mutakallimuns' "daring assumption of continual dissolution and recreation of the universe reconciled the apparent continuity of macroscopic phenomena with the atomic doctrine of space, time, and matter" (p. 512). Whereas a consistent respect for that assumption played no small part in bringing about a stillbirth of science in the Muslim world (see chapter 9, "Delay in Detour," in my *Science and Creation: From Eternal Cycles to an Oscillating Universe* [Edinburgh: Scottish Academic Press, 1974]), the unwillingness of the devotees of the Copenhagen interpretation of quantum mechanics to be thor-

ough and consistent in matters philosophical is what permits them to use surreptitiously a realist epistemology germane to doing science, be it the science of quantum mechanics.

74. *The Philosophy of Physical Science* (New York: Macmillan Company, 1939), p. 77.

75. "The Nature of Quantum Mechanical Reality," p. 206.

76. See ibid., p. 207, where reference is made to a study dealing specifically with that aspect of Bohr's mental world.

77. *Letters on Wave Mechanics*, p. 36.

78. Ibid., p. 40.

CHAPTER FOURTEEN

1. Their respective authors were J. H. Mädler, A. Clerke, and H. Shapley, each of whom was highly respected in his time for his grasp of the state of art of astronomical research.

2. The history of the Vienna Circle is still to be written. The available accounts are sketchy and tainted with a positivist bias. See, for instance, V. Kraft, *Der Wiener Kreis: Der Ursprung des Neopositivismus: Ein Kapitel der jüngsten Philosophiegeschichte*, 2d rev. ed. (Vienna: Springer Verlag, 1967), pp. 1–10; A. J. Ayer, ed., *Logical Positivismus* (New York: Free Press, 1959), pp. 3–10; H. Feigl, "The Wiener Kreis in America," *Perspectives in American History* 2 (1968): 631–73.

3. The title page of the Manifesto reads as follows: Veröffentlichungen des Vereines Ernst Mach / *Wissenschaftliche Weltauffassung: Der Wiener Kreis* (herausgegeben vom Verein Ernst Mach, 1929; Artur Wolf Verlag: Wien). The Manifesto, written on behalf of the Kreis by Hans Hahn, Otto Neurath, and Rudolf Carnap, comprises in its fifty-nine pages the following sections: a prehistory of the Circle, together with its present setup described as "Der Kreis um Schlick"; an outline of the "Wissenschaftliche Weltauffassung"; a specification of the main areas relating to it under such headings as principal problems of arithmetic, of physics, of geometry, of biology and psychology, of social sciences; a retrospect and prospect; bibliographical references; listing of publications (a) of members of the Circle, among whom Gödel is listed with one publication, (b) of those closely associated with it, among whom the names of Reichenbach and Zilsel are the most noteworthy, (c) of leading representatives of the "wissenschaftliche Weltauffassung," who are named as Einstein, Russell, and Wittgenstein. Under (a) the following were listed: Bergmann, Carnap, Feigl, Frank, Gödel, Hahn, Kraft, Menger, Natkin, Neurath, Hahn-Neurath, Radakovič, Schlick, Waismann. Soon afterwards Gödel ceased to be a regular member of the Circle, possibly under the impact of his discovery of his famed "incompleteness theorem." Einstein's inclusion in the list shows a basic misapprehension about Einstein's maturing views, to which Einstein himself called Frank's attention in 1929, as noted in chapter 12.

4. The official organ for both was *Erkenntnis*, a periodical which until it was taken over by the Circle was known as *Annalen der Philosophie*.

5. For an unabashed reference to the "missionary spirit" of the Circle, see Ayer, *Logical Positivism*, p. 6.

6. See B. Magee, *Karl Popper* (New York: The Viking Press, 1963), p. 3.

7. See the introduction by H. Feigl and A. E. Blumberg in M. Schlick, *General Theory of Knowledge*, translated by A. E. Blumberg (New York: Springer Verlag, 1974), pp. xvii–xxv. Schlick, however, was not pleased with the turning of the Circle into a "movement." See Feigl, "The Wiener Kreis in America," p. 646.

8. Published in 1908, when Schlick was twenty-six, the *Lebensweisheit* struck

W. Ostwald, unaware of the author's youth, as the work of a "wise old Ph.D." See Schlick, *General Theory of Knowledge*, p. xviii. Schlick returned to the theme of "wisdom of life" in 1927 with an essay on "The Meaning of Life" and left behind an unfinished manuscript on "Philosophy of Youth" (ibid.).

9. Berlin: J. Springer.
10. References will be to the translation by Blumberg, see n. 7 above.
11. Ibid., p. 399.
12. Ibid., p. 398. Schlick had, therefore, no choice but to plead for a consistently physicalist psychology in a chapter entitled "Quantitative and Qualitative Knowledge," see especially pp. 287–89.
13. The reference to Planck might have just as well been omitted, because it was a far cry from Planck's widely known views on epistemology.
14. Schlick's discussion of Einstein's cosmology first appeared in the second edition (1919) of his *Raum und Zeit in der gegenwärtigen Physik*, first published in 1917 (Berlin: Springer Verlag). The subtitle of the work was: "for an introduction to the understanding of the theory of relativity and gravitation."
15. See the English translation by H. L. Brose of the third edition (1920): *Space and Time in Contemporary Physics: The Theory of Relativity and Gravitation* (New York: Oxford University Press, 1920), pp. 68 and 74. The incongruity of the reference to Bruno was certainly glaring in a chapter dealing with the "Finitude of the Universe," a consequence of Einstein's cosmological equations, which Schlick in no way disputed. But had not Bruno staked all his message on the infinity of the universe?
16. "Erleben, Erkennen, Metaphysik," *Kantstudien* Band 31, Heft 2/3 (1926): 146–58; see especially p. 146. Schlick had therefore to assert that "all qualitative and inner aspects of our experiences must remain forever private and can in no way be known by several individuals in common" (ibid., p. 149).
17. Ibid., p. 150–51. In the same context Schlick also rejected the warning of the eminent mathematician and philosopher of mathematics, H. Weyl, about the urge to formalize, or "the sickness of mathematicians," as Weyl put it. Schlick had no choice but to disagree with Weyl if it was true that "experience is content, whereas knowledge in its true nature relates to form" (ibid., p. 150).
18. "Physicalism," *The Monist* 41 (1931): 622.
19. *Wissenschaftliche Weltauffassung*, p. 30. Had Hahn, Neurath, and Carnap been consistent, they should have said that "positive knowledge" serves life by leaving it alone, a tenet which matched the Nazi assertion of life through the radical rejection of rational discourse. In epistemology, as elsewhere, extremes have a deeper affinity than usually suspected.
20. "The Turning Point in Philosophy," trans. D. Rynin, in Ayer, *Logical Positivism*, p. 54.
21. Ibid., p. 55.
22. Ibid., p. 56.
23. See entry for August 6, 1763, in any edition of *The Life of Samuel Johnson* by James Boswell. At any rate, neither Schlick nor the other members of the Vienna Circle seem to have realized that all their reasonings, insofar as they were *arguments*, that is, discourses aimed at convincing others, were so many *deeds* implying an assertion of a reality far transcending the level of mere logic, an assertion for which their logicism provided no logical room.
24. "The Turning Point in Philosophy," p. 58.
25. Ibid., p. 59.
26. H. Feigl, "Empiricism at Bay?" in *Methodological and Historical Essays in the Natural and Social Sciences*, ed. R. S. Cohen and M. W. Wartofsky (Dordrecht: D. Reidel, 1974), p. 1. The context of the remark was, to quote Feigl's

words, "the almost hostile vogue of 'beating-up' on the empiricists, a fashion that is still in full swing." His defense of empiricism, or at least of what still appeared salvageable of it, included its modern form, which he should have called logical positivism and not logical empiricism.

27. Hahn defined intuition as a "force of habit rooted in psychological inertia," in concluding his list of examples, which according to him showed that logic and not intuition was the mainspring of great mathematical discoveries. See his "The Crisis of Intuition," in *The World of Mathematics*, ed. J. R. Newman (New York: Simon and Schuster, 1956), p. 1976.

28. In speaking of the impossibility of giving an operational definition of simultaneity Hahn declared: "This most recent and revolutionary development of physics will necessarily come as a shock to most persons—including most physicists—grounded as they are in dogmatic and metaphysical theories; but for the thinker trained in empirical philosophy it contains nothing paradoxical. He will recognize it at once as something familiar and will welcome it as a major step forward along the road toward the 'physicalisation' of physics, toward cleansing physics of metaphysical elements" (ibid., p. 1958).

29. Translated into English by G. Schick, in Ayer, *Logical Positivism*, pp. 165–98.

30. Its English translation by M. Black was published under the title, *The Unity of Science* (London: Kegan Paul, Trench, Trubner and Co., 1934). It contains a new introduction by Carnap written in January 1934.

31. "Psychology in Physical Language," p. 174.

32. Ibid., p. 168.

33. Since Copernicus saw in the heliocentric system evidence of the Creator's wisdom far more convincing than geocentrism could provide, the "dethroning of man" through heliocentrism would have been for him a misleading physicalist inference to be rejected out of hand.

34. "And since confession is (said to be) 'good for the soul,' I will admit that for a long time, I (along with quite a few other philosophers of science of recent times) have been a 'sinner.' Some of us have been satisfied with a 'smattering of ignorance' in regard to the historical development of the sciences, their socioeconomic settings, the psychology of discovery and of the theory of invention, etc. A few of us, though proud of our *empiricism*, for some time rather unashamedly 'made up' some phases of the history of science in a quite 'a priori' manner—at least in public lectures and classroom presentations, if not, even in some of our publications. 'This is the way Galileo, or Newton, or Darwin, or Einstein (for example) must have arrived at their ideas' was not an uncommon way of talking—through our respective hats. Even if the sources were not always complete, and not always accurate, they were available, but we rarely consulted them. Most of us have come to repent this inexcusable conduct." While these words of H. Feigl ("Beyond Peaceful Coexistence," in R. H. Stuewer, ed., *Historical and Philosophical Perspectives of Science* [Minneapolis: University of Minnesota Press, 1970], p. 3) cannot be admired enough for their courageous candor, one wonders whether most empiricists (logical positivists) have lately developed a sincere respect for the facts of history, especially for its facts laden with metaphysical connotation, to say nothing of their alleged repentance for their contempt of historical facts flying in the face of their theorizing.

35. *The Unity of Science*, p. 69.

36. The exclusion of introspection by physicalists as a means to valid knowledge is too well known to be documented here. Carnap's encomiums of graphology ("Psychology in Physical Language," pp. 185–90) deserve special

attention because they form a most graphic evidence of the futility of any effort to interpret one's handwriting without relying, tacitly at least, on introspection.

37. Sir Cyril Burt, "The Concept of Consciousness," *British Journal for Psychology* 53 (1962): 229.

38. For statements of leading modern physicists on the need to transcend, nay to renounce the urge to visualize, see my *The Relevance of Physics* (Chicago: University of Chicago Press, 1966), pp. 90 and 120. Needless to say, what holds true of the use of one sense (vision) holds also true of the other senses, a consequence which Carnap himself recognized when he admitted that the connection between his protocol statements and the basic statements of physics were tenuous, but failed to draw the consequences of his admission. See *The Unity of Science*, p. 81.

39. *The Unity of Science*, p. 44.

40. Mathieu's equation (see E. T. Whittaker and G. N. Watson, *A Course of Modern Analysis* [Cambridge University Press, 1928], chap. 19) handles equally well the vibrations of a stretched elliptical surface and the dynamics of an acrobat balancing himself on the top of a sphere.

41. Mathematics, Whitehead noted, could not even provide the finiteness of the numbers of atoms in an apple. More generally, "there is no valid inference from mere possibility to matter of fact, or, in other words, from mere mathematics to concrete nature" (*Adventures of Ideas* [New York: Macmillan, 1933], p. 161).

42. Ayer, *Logical Positivism*, p. 80.

43. The difference between the numerical relations of notes and the tune itself was for Eddington one of the illustrations of the fact that "in most subjects exact science goes a little way and then stops, not because of the limitations of our ignorance, but because we are dealing with something which includes both metrical and non-metrical aspects." See his "The Domain of Physical Science," in J. Needham, ed., *Science, Religion and Reality* (New York: Macmillan, 1925), p. 201.

44. The story is told by V. E. Frankl in his address, "Reductionism and Nihilism" (*The Alpbach Symposium 1968: Beyond Reductionism: New Perspectives in the Life Sciences*, ed. A. Koestler and J. R. Smythies [London: Hutchinson, 1969], p. 403). Frankl's address, although a frontal attack on reductionism, proves also that without endorsing metaphysics in some sense, it is impossible to give rational guarantee to that higher level of existence for which he and many other antireductionists plead. According to Frankl, all that belongs to that higher level can only be "lived" but not articulated in a rational manner, in line with Schlick's distinction between Erkenntnis and Erlebnis, about which Hegelians would say that it merely constitutes an illogical form of dialectics.

45. *The Psychology of the Emotions* (London: Walter Scott Publishing Company, n.d.), p. 357. The French original, *La psychologie des sentiments*, was published in 1896.

46. *Le rire: Essai sur la signification du comique*, 7th ed. (Paris: Alcan, 1911), p. 204. The book, a collection of three essays, was first published in 1900.

47. *Wit and Its Relation to the Unconscious*, authorized English edition, with introduction by A. A. Brill (New York: Moffat, Yard, and Company, 1916), p. 384.

48. *Laughing and Crying: A Study of the Limits of Human Behavior*, trans. J. S. Churchill and M. Grene (Chapel Hill: University of North Carolina Press, 1970), p. 32. Espousal of equivocation as means of rational explanation will naturally lead to statements which present one with the alternative of laughing or crying: "It was overlooked," Plessner states, "that man has not a univocal but an

equivocal relation to his body, that his existence imposes on him the ambiguity of being an 'embodied' (leibhaften) creature and a creature 'in the body' (im Körper), an ambiguity that means an actual break in his way of existing. It is this brokenness that distinguishes what phenomena like laughter and tears suggest: the impenetrability of man's relation to his body" (ibid.). Such statements should be helpful in restoring respectability to what is between the univocal and the equivocal, namely, the analogous and the epistemology based on it.

49. *Wissenschaftliche Weltauffassung*, p. 15. According to Schlick, "in principle there are no limits to our knowledge. The boundaries which must be acknowledged are of empirical nature and therefore never ultimate; they can be pushed back further and further; there is no unfathomable mystery in the world" ("Meaning and Verification," *Philosophical Review* 45 [1936]: 352). Obviously, a knowledge which deals only with what is on the surface and a knowledge which admits no unfathomable mystery are two sides of the same coin.

50. I wish to thank Nicholas Kremmer, professor of physics at the University of Edinburgh, for this priceless story, of which he was an eyewitness.

51. "Sociology and Physicalism," in Ayer, *Logical Positivism*, pp. 282–317.

52. Chicago: Henry Regnery Company, 1956.

53. London: André Deutsch, 1972. Andreski is entirely right in stating that the social scientist (he refers to C. Lévi-Strauss) offers "hallucinogenic incantations" when using the notation, jaguar = anteater $^{(-1)}$, to register a fight between the two. The notation is a farce on mathematics, for, clearly, no jaguar has ever been equal to that fraction which can only be obtained if an anteater could be divided into 1, or if 1 could be divided by an anteater.

54. Presented at the December 1965 meeting of the American Association for the Advancement of Science. See *The New York Times*, December 29, 1965, p. 16, col. 1.

55. L. Benson of the University of Pennsylvania in a lecture, "Quantification and History," given on May 11, 1967, at Princeon University. See also *The Dimensions of Quantitative Research in History*, ed. W. O. Aydelotte, A. G. Bogue, and R. W. Fogel (Princeton: Princeton University Press, 1972).

56. *The Use of Time: Daily Activities of Urban and Suburban Populations in Twelve Countries*, edited by A. Szalai in collaboration with P. E. Converse and others (The Hague: Mouton, 1972). In all the 868 pages of the book there is only one brief reference to church attendance, with the remark that, like pub attendance, it is cyclic (p. 80). Another tragic aspect of such physicalist sociology, whether Marxist inspired or not, is that it contains no data on time spent on compulsory political indoctrination.

57. In his "Sociology and Physicalism" (in Ayer, *Logical Positivism*, pp. 282–317), Neurath, who participated in the Bolshevik Spartacist government in Munich at the end of World War I (ibid., p. 7), presented Marxism as by far the most advanced form of empiricist sociology and declared with obvious satisfaction that "the most important Marxist theses employed for prediction are either already formulated in a fairly physicalist fashion . . . or they can be so formulated, without the loss of anything essential" (ibid., p. 309).

58. See R. S. Cohen, "Dialectical Materialism and Carnap's Logical Empiricism," in *The Philosophy of Rudolf Carnap*, ed. P. A. Schilpp (La Salle, Ill.: Open Court, 1963), pp. 99–158, together with Carnap's reply (pp. 863–67). Whereas Carnap's philosophy could properly be described as materialistic, it was certainly not the embodiment of that dialectical materialism which prompted Cohen to present the Soviet regime as the true representative of positivism and not of dialectical materialism, a feat in logic that left Carnap wondering, not

without good reason (p. 866).

59. New York: Bantam Books, 1972. A long overdue, systematic criticism of Skinner's reductionism is *The Pseudo-Science of B. F. Skinner* by T. R. Machan (New Rochelle, N.Y.: Arlington House, 1974).

60. *The Unity of Science*, p. 74 note.

61. The importance which Popper attributed to that statement of his can easily be perceived from the fact that it is the third, or concluding sentence, in the brief summary which introduces his essay, "The Demarcation between Science and Metaphysics," in *The Philosophy of Rudolf Carnap*, p. 183.

62. Ibid., p. 201.

63. London: George Allen and Unwin, 1940.

64. Ibid., p. 148.

65. Ibid.

66. "Remarks on Bertrand Russell's Theory of Knowledge," in *The Philosophy of Bertrand Russell*, ed. P. A. Schilpp, 3d ed. (New York: Tudor Publishing Company, 1951), p. 301.

67. *The Unity of Science*, p. 29.

68. "Sociology and Physicalism," p. 282. This programmatic rejection of the term "world" is of a piece with the inability of logical positivism to build a universe with purely logical means, the very aim pursued in Carnap's *Der logische Aufbau der Welt* (Berlin-Schlachtensee: Weltkreisverlag, 1928), his first major publication.

69. In his Vanuxem Lectures delivered in Princeton University under the title *The Nature of Physical Theory* (Princeton: Princeton University Press, 1936); see especially pp. 109–10.

70. Especially through his *The Logic of Modern Physics* (New York: Macmillan, 1927), in which he identified the validity of concepts with their operational feasibility (pp. 5 and 25).

71. The seven volumes of *Collected Experimental Papers* (Cambridge: Harvard University Press, 1964) certainly attest Bridgman's ingenuity in handling technical details and his positivism bent on gathering data but not on probing into their underlying causes.

72. In his "On the Nature and the Limitations of Cosmical Inquiries," *Scientific Monthly* 37 (1933): 385–97.

73. Ibid., pp. 386–87.

74. *The Nature of Physical Theory*, p. 110.

75. J. Wisdom, "Metamorphoses of the Verifiability Theory of Meaning," *Mind* 72 (1963): 335.

76. His lectures were published under the title *The Central Questions of Philosophy* (London: Weidenfeld & Nicolson, 1973). References will be to the text of the concluding lecture, "The Claims of Theology," as published in *The Listener* (August 9, 1973), pp. 165–73.

77. Ibid., p. 165, col. 3. The anecdote was taken from W. H. Mallock's anonymously published satire, *The New Republic; or Culture, Faith, and Philosophy in an English Country House*, 2d ed. (London: Chatto and Windus, 1877), in which a character representing Dr. Jowett is made to admit that any atheist can disprove the existence of God once God's definition has been given. Comfort is taken by Dr. Jowett, however, from the fact that so far no adequate definition of God has been forwarded and that, therefore, the atheist's attack cannot be conclusive, since, as Dr. Jowett puts it in a manner unwittingly but perfectly serving the purposes of logical positivists, "we should be able to define a thing before we can satisfactorily disprove it" (vol. 2, p. 156).

78. "The Claims of Theology," p. 173, col. 1.

79. Ibid., p. 167, col. 2. The inconclusiveness in question was pointed out in chapter 8, together with reference to its being admitted by C. C. Smart.

80. Ibid., p. 169, col. 3: "I do not know that a scientific study has ever been made of this question, but if one were to be made, I doubt if it would reveal any strong correlation either of morally admirable behaviour with religious intolerance and persecution in behavior with its absence." This rather cumbersome phrase reads in the book edition: "... any strong correlation either of morally admirable behaviour with religious belief or of morally reprehensible behaviour with its absence" (p. 225).

81. *The Logic of Scientific Discovery*, rev. ed. (New York: Harper and Row, 1968), p. 32.

82. "The Claims of Theology," p. 173. cols. 2–3.

CHAPTER FIFTEEN

1. Minimal indeed was the immediate impact of the publication in 1935 of *Galileo and the Tower of Pisa* (Ithaca: Cornell University Press) by L. Cooper, a classical scholar, who tackled his topic after physicists had given him sundry and conflicting accounts of the Aristotelian law which Galileo disproved. Few historians of science paid any more attention when a year later Koyré joined the still thin ranks of demythologizers with his "Galilée et l'expérience de Pise: A propos d'une légende," reprinted in his *Etudes d'histoire de la pensée scientifique* (Paris: Presses Universitaires de France, 1966), pp. 192–201.

2. A point not at all unknown prior to 1939 and fairly well known to the few familiar with Duhem's then already more than thirty-year-old work on Leonardo da Vinci, but put forward with great incisiveness and readability by Koyré in the second fascicle, *La loi de la chute des corps: Descartes et Galilée*, of his *Etudes galiléennes* (Paris: Hermann, 1939). The actual publication did not take place until 1940.

3. Ibid., 2:72–73.

4. Ibid., 2:57.

5. For a sample of those variations, see D. Shapere, *Galileo: A Philosphical Study* (Chicago: University of Chicago Press, 1974), pp. 129–30.

6. T. B. Settle, "An Experiment in the History of Science," *Science* 133 (1961): 19–23. No serious objection was made either against the reliability of the reconstruction by Settle, then a graduate student, of Galileo's apparatus, or against the demonstrative value of the experimental data obtained by it.

7. As noted by C. C. Gillispie in his article, "Koyré, Alexandre," in the *Dictionary of Scientific Biography*, vol. 7 (New York: Charles Scribner's Sons, 1973), p. 486. While the length of this article is proportional to the new profession's appreciation of Koyré, not a scientist himself, it also reminds one of Koyré's dictum: "Tout historien, tout biographe surtout, est un peu hagiographe" (*Etudes galiléennes*, 2:3). For similar superlatives on the influence exercised by Koyré, see A. Thackray, "Science: Has Its Present Past a Future?" in R. H. Stuewer, ed., *Historical and Philosophical Perspectives of Science* (Minneapolis: University of Minnesota Press, 1970), p. 116.

8. Gillispie, "Koyré, Alexandre," p. 486. The reservation concerns the expression "stalking horse." Koyré was not only a student but also an apostle of Plato, in a sense which explains his customary slighting of Christian theism, a point which would well repay a special study.

9. *Essai sur l'idée de Dieu et les preuves de son existence chez Descartes* (Paris: Editions Ernest Leroux, 1922). Koyré's study of the Cartesian version of the ontological argument is best seen in the light of his effort to present Descartes as intimately tied to the "great medieval epoch" (p. iv) in opposition to the "im-

NOTES TO PAGE 231

portant works" of Gilson and Blanchet. They, especially Gilson, saw that Descartes's giving a new meaning to scholastic terms was telling evidence of his radical departure from scholastic thought, a point which Koyré himself was to emphasize years later in the *Etudes*.

10. *L'idée de Dieu dans la philosophie de St. Anselme* (Paris: Editions Ernest Leroux, 1923), p. 240.

11. Koyré's *La philosophie de Jacob Boehme* (Paris: J. Vrin, 1929) reveals more sympathy for the invariably obscurantist Boehme than for the not always obscurantist defenders of Lutheran orthodoxy and is also informative on Boehme's influence on Fichte and Schelling, both well known for their pantheistic proclivities.

12. In 1929 Koyré provided another subtle glimpse into his pantheistic sympathies through his warm portrayal of Tchaadaev, who tried to implement Schelling's "positive" Christianity by recourse to Hellenic classicism. See chapter 6 in Koyré's *La philosophie et le problème national en Russie au début du XIX*ᵉ *siècle* (Paris: Librairie Ancienne Honoré Champion, 1929), pp. 174–93. That Tchaadaev knew Spinoza and held a theology not at all orthodox are pointedly noted by Koyré in his lengthy essay "Petr Tchaadaev," in his *Etudes sur l'histoire de la pensée philosophique en Russie* (Paris: J. Vrin, 1950), pp. 19–102; see especially pp. 67 and 85.

13. Koyré's translation with introduction and notes of Spinoza's *De intellectus emendatione (Traité de la réforme de l'entendement et de la meilleure voie à suivre pour parvenir à la vraie connaissance des choses* [Paris: J. Vrin, 1938]) could not be necessitated either by inaccessibility of the original Latin or by lack of French translations. One must not forget that between 1930 and 1934 Koyré published three sympathetic studies on Hegel and Hegelianism! Koyré's sympathy for Hegelianism, his early preoccupation with the ontological proof, and his penchant for pantheism are equally overlooked by P. Redondi in his "Introductory Notes on Epistemology and the History of Science in France," *Scientia* 69 (1975): 171–97; see especially p. 182 and the corresponding bibliography on Koyré, the historian of science, p. 194.

14. Published only in 1945 both in the original French and in English translation, *Discovering Plato* (New York: Columbia University Press) is a series of reflections on the "Socratic" dialogues, but also gives an insight into the extent to which Koyré was able to be "selective" in reading his texts. In referring to Plato's portrayal of the "radiant image of the philosopher condemned to death" as Plato's means to bring us the message of Socrates, Koyré added that the message is not a "doctrinaire lesson" but a "lesson in method" (p. 2). Now, according to Plato, Socrates spent his last hours in sustained argumentation in support of his choice of accepting death precisely because the soul was immortal. If this is not a doctrinaire message, what is it?

15. Although Koyré pointedly notes that for Galileo the theory must agree with the facts (*Etudes galiléennes*, 2:61), he never discusses the extent to which this agreement was important for Galileo. He mentions rather that Galileo's contemporaries found all his figures for acceleration wrong, a fact certainly true. Had Koyré not been averse to the Christian component in Galileo's Neoplatonism, he might have even spotted the Aristotelian strain present to the end in Galileo's scientific reasoning. That strain is now under close scrutiny, and the already published results show a much closer connection of Galileo with the Parisian school of Buridan and Oresme and of their followers, especially in Spain, than would be conceivable in the framework of a sudden and total mental shift advocated by Koyré and others. See A. C. Crombie, "Sources of Galileo's Early Natural Philosophy," in M. L. Righini Bonelli and William R.

419

Shea, eds., *Reason, Experiment, and Mysticism in the Scientific Revolution* (New York: Science History Publications, 1975), pp. 157–75, and W. A. Wallace, "Galileo and the Thomists," in *St. Thomas Aquinas Commemorative Studies, 1274–1974* (Toronto: Pontifical Institute of Medieval Studies, 1974), 2:293–330, and "Galileo and Reasoning *ex suppositione:* The Methodology of the *Two New Sciences,*" in *Philosophy of Science Association 1974 Biennial Meeting,* ed. A. C. Michalos and R. S. Cohen (Dordrecht: Reidel, 1976), pp. 79–104.

16. A point noted with approval by Gillispie on the ground that Koyré "always held the creations of intelligence to be triumphs in the long battle between mind and disorder, not burdens to be lamented" ("Koyré, Alexandre" p. 488). That Pascal lamented intellectual achievements, including his own scientific ones, is still to be demonstrated. It was not with lamenting science but with a deep and prophetic insight into man's frightening ability (for which Platonizing admirers of science are still to account properly) to abuse one of the most powerful products of his intellect that Pascal remarked: "Man is neither angel nor brute, and the unfortunate thing is that he who would act the angel acts the brute," and "Physical science will not console me for the ignorance of morality in the time of affliction. But the science of ethics will always console me for the ignorance of the physical sciences" (*Pascal's Pensées,* trans. W. F. Trotter and with an introduction by T. S. Eliot [New York: E. P. Dutton, 1958], pp. 99 and 15).

17. "In Koyré's view," Gillispie remarks, "geometrization of physical quantity in the Archimedean sense was the crux of the scientific revolution" (p. 487).

18. Indeed, Koyré could show himself astonishingly oblivious to the coming of Greek science to a standstill. Toward the end of his distinguished career he claimed in Oxford in 1961 that it was possible to explain that science could not arise in China and Persia, but not that it did arise in Greece. He conspicuously failed to ask why was there any need for another "rise" of science in the seventeenth century. See A. C. Crombie, ed., *Scientific Change* (New York: Basic Books, 1963), p. 855. In fact the first part of his claim was an unintended endorsement of the Marxist explanation of science which he spiritedly opposed.

19. "In Koyré's view," to quote Gillispie again, "the scientific revolution entailed a more decisive mutation in man's sense of himself in the world than any intellectual event since the beginnings of civilization in ancient Greece" ("Koyré, Alexandre" p. 487).

20. *Science and the Modern World* (New York: Macmillan, 1926), p. 2.

21. See his avant-propos to his translation of Spinoza's *De intellectus emendatione,* p. xx.

22. For the expression, see R. S. Westfall, "Newton and the Fudge Factor," *Science* 179 (1973): 751.

23. There is indeed much food for thought in Gillispie's remark: "Admirers of Koyré's writings in the history of science would do well to read the most considerable of those studies [of Koyré on philosophical thought in Russia], a monograph on Tchaadaev. Although it has nothing to do with their subject, it is one of the finest, most sympathetic and revealing pieces that he wrote" (Koyré, Alexandre" p. 485).

24. See remarks in note 14 above. For a similar distortion of Socrates' philosophy, see also n. 23 in chapter 13.

25. Crombie, *Scientific Change,* p. 852.

26. As plainly pointed out by T. S. Kuhn in his "The History of Science," in *International Encyclopedia of the Social Sciences* (New York: Macmillan, 1968), 14:77 and 79.

27. "En effet, l'étude de l'évolution (et des révolutions) des idées

scientifiques—seule histoire (avec celle, connexe, de la technique) qui donne un sens à la notion, tant glorifiée et tant décriée, de progrès—nous montre l'esprit humain aux prises avec la réalité," a phrase revealing of Koyré's historicism, which invariably leaves questions unanswered about the meaning of reality and of progress. The word "revolution" was used sparingly in the *Etudes*. In one case Koyré spoke of the "révolution scientifique" (1:72), in another (2:45) of "révolution intellectuelle" and called the change undergone by Descartes's thought equivalent to a "révolution" (ibid). The word has already become a household expression among historiographers of science when it graced for the first time the title page of a book written by Koyré, his *La révolution astronomique: Copernic, Kepler, Borelli* (Paris: Hermann, 1961).

28. In spite of Koyré's reference to two works of Bachelard (*Le nouvel esprit scientifique* [Paris: Alcan, 1934] and *La formation de l'esprit scientifique: contribution à une psychanalyse de la connaissance objective* [Paris: J. Vrin, 1938]) Bachelard's views are hardly ever mentioned, let alone discussed to a considerable extent, in the works published by Koyré's admirers and disciples in America, where he first made his influence. It did not carry them, in spite of their master's insistence on studying the sources, to the source of their master.

29. See *Etudes* (1:1), where Koyré speaks of the "fécondité philosophique" of such study and refers to F. Enriques's *Signification de l'histoire de la pensée scientifique* (Paris: Hermann, 1934). Whatever that "fécondité," it did not produce in Koyré's hands that fruit which would have consisted in explaining how science can be the sole justification of progress (*Etudes*, 1:5) if its origin consisted in ideas irreconcilably different from older, apparently related notions (impetus versus acceleration, rest versus inertia; ibid., p. 58) and if science had already undergone another revolution at Einstein's hands, which restored the validity of the notion of the totality of things (ibid., p. 11) dissolved in its first revolution!

30. *Etudes*, 3:131.

31. For an incisive analysis of that feeling, see S. G. Brush, "Should the History of Science Be Rated X?" *Science* 183 (1974): 1164–72.

32. A conclusion reached by Dilthey rather reluctantly at the age of seventy. For further instances of similar admissions by historicist historians, see M. Eliade, *Cosmos and History: The Myth of Eternal Return*, trans. W. R. Trask (New York: Harper and Row, 1959), p. 150. While the role of historicism in general historiography has already invited serious studies, such study is still to take place in the historiography of science.

33. *Cours de philosophie positive*, 5th ed. (identical with the first) (Paris: Au Siège de la Société positiviste, 1892), 1:2.

34. The title of the German original, *Logik der Forschung* (Vienna: Springer Verlag, 1934), was but slightly less of a misnomer in relation to the chief contention of the work.

35. First through his essay, "Science in Flux" (*Boston Studies in the Philosophy of Science*, vol. 3, ed. R. S. Cohen and M. W. Wartofsky [Dordrecht: D. Reidel, 1968], pp. 293–323) and more recently through a collection of his essays published under the title *Science in Flux* (Dordrecht: D. Reidel, 1975) which is graced by a self-contradictory motto characteristic of all that are presumably in radical flux. For if there is no absolute truth and if common sense is ever changing, how can one be sure that the big mistakes (in science or anywhere else) are gradually being replaced by smaller ones?

36. See chapter 3, "Causality," in his *Patterns of Discovery* (Cambridge University Press, 1958) and his "The Logic of Discovery" (*Journal of Philosophy* 55 [1958]: 1073–89).

37. As done by I. Lakatos in his "Falsification and the Methodology of Research Programmes," in I. Lakatos and A. Musgrave, eds., *Criticism and the Growth of Knowledge* (Cambridge University Press, 1970), pp. 91–196; see especially p. 133.

38. The "image" of science at a given time and milieu is obviously the chief of the three factors through which Y. Elkana tried to find the answer to the growth of knowledge. See his "Scientific and Metaphysical Problems: Euler and Kant," in *Criticism and the Growth of Knowledge*, pp. 277–305, especially p. 279.

39. As done by G. Holton in his *Thematic Origins of Scientific Thought: Kepler to Einstein* (Cambridge: Harvard University Press, 1973) and in his "On the Role of Themata in Scientific Thought," *Science* 188 (1975): 328–34.

40. For a fair but firm criticism of this approach mainly advocated by P. K. Feyerabend, see "The History and Philosophy of Science: A Taxonomy," by E. McMullin in *Historical and Philosophical Perspectives of Science*, ed. R. H. Stuewer (Minneapolis: University of Minnesota Press, 1970), pp. 34–40.

41. As done by Elkana, "Scientific and Metaphysical Problems," p. 301.

42. R. K. Merton, "Thematic Analysis in Science: Notes on Holton's Concept," *Science* 188 (1975): 335.

43. Originally published in the *International Encyclopedia of Unified Science*, vol. 2, no. 2 (Chicago: University of Chicago Press, 1962), *The Structure of Scientific Revolutions* contrasted sharply, at a cursory view at least, with other monographs comprising the *Encyclopedia*, an enterprise serving the aim of explaining various aspects of scientific knowledge in terms of logical positivism. But the work was a good attempt, and its author intended it to be one, "to explain to myself and to friends how I happened to be drawn from science to its history in the first place" (p. vii).

44. See especially chapter 4, "Certain Principles of the Tactics and Strategy of Science," in Conant's Terry Lectures given at Yale in 1947 and published under the title *On Understanding Science: An Historical Approach* (New Haven: Yale University Press, 1947). This little book is a proper key to the aim of the eight case studies in *Case Histories in Experimental Science*, ed. James Bryant Conant and Leonard K. Nash (Cambridge: Harvard University Press, 1957).

45. *The Structure of Scientific Revolutions*, p. xiii.

46. Next to Koyré was mentioned (ibid., p. viii) E. Meyerson who, as will be noted in the next chapter, prompted much puzzlement by his truly historicist refusal to consider some obviously philosophical questions arising from his historical research into what constitutes the very core of theories in classical physics. Two others, H. Metzger and A. Maier, earned their scholarly reputations by monographs in which no questions were raised about the relation of a special period to the whole course of science and about philosophical problems implied in that relation. In addition, Kuhn singled out A. O. Lovejoy, certainly a historicist historian of ideas, B. L. Whorf, a linguistic philosopher, and W. V. O. Quine, a logician.

47. Ibid., pp. viii–x.

48. Among the many readers of Kuhn's work, those few persistent spirits who tracked down a copy of Fleck's monograph—this is almost nonexistent in U.S. libraries, and Kuhn mentioned only the title, which was wholly uninformative of the very specific topic of the monograph—could but wonder about the conclusion Kuhn had drawn on reading it, namely, that his very general ideas about the history of science would best be "set in the sociology of the scientific community" (ibid., p. ix).

49. Ibid., p. x.

50. The close alliance of the sociological and psychological perspectives is

best illustrated in the sequence of chapters 9 and 10 devoted respectively to the necessity of scientific revolutions and to their being equivalent to Gestalt switches.

51. See his "The Function of Dogma in Scientific Research," a paper read at the Symposium on the History of Science, University of Oxford, July 9–15, 1961. Published in Crombie, ed., *Scientific Change*, pp. 347–69.

52. *Patterns of Discovery*, p. 1. The claim made by Stephen Toulmin in his *Human Understanding* (Princeton University Press, 1972), p. 107, that "among philosophers of science, the theory of paradigms was explored in the 1930s by Wittgenstein's student, W. H. Watson, in his book *On Understanding Physics* [Cambridge University Press, 1938; Harper Torchbook, 1959], and subsequently by Hanson and myself," is certainly in need of qualification. Whereas, for instance, the distinction between the logic and psychology of perception is clearly present in Watson's book, together with the notion of perceiving images as wholes (though not with reference to Gestalt switches), the word paradigm is not used in these connections. The absence of the word paradigm is just as conspicuous in Watson's *Understanding Physics Today* (Cambridge University Press, 1963) in which Watson could have easily pointed out his use, prior to Kuhn, of the Kuhnian meaning of the paradigm, if not of the word itself. The weaknesses of Toulmin's presentation of the recent prehistory of the use of the word paradigm are matched by his far-fetched attributing in this respect an important role to Georg Christoph Lichtenberg and Ernst Mach. In sum, whatever the intrinsic merits of Kuhn's use of the word paradigm, its entry into philosophical parlance is undoubtedly Kuhn's achievement.

53. In accordance with the definition of "paradigm" in the *Oxford Dictionary of the English Language*, 7:449, where only the grammatical connotation of the word is noted. Obviously, that entry will have to be rewritten in view of the sundry books that carry the word "paradigm" in their title since the publication of Kuhn's work.

54. *The Structure of Scientific Discovery*, p. 10. Kuhn himself noted his departure from the meaning which grammarians attach to the word (p. 23).

55. Ibid., p. 11.

56. For the list of the twenty-one meanings and their reduction to three groups, see "The Nature of a Paradigm," by M. Masterman, in *Criticism and the Growth of Knowledge*, pp. 61–65. On Kuhn's explanation of his paradigms in 1969, F. Suppe still could note with good reason: "As one has come to expect from Kuhn, [his] 'Second Thoughts on Paradigms' is a pregnant paper loaded with original and valuable insights on the nature of the scientific enterprise ... I wish he would stop populating science with new entities [paradigms reified into shared entities] so that we more easily can have access to his insights" (*The Structure of Scientific Theories*, edited with a critical introduction by F. Suppe [Urbana: University of Illinois Press, 1974], p. 499).

57. The three main groups comprise the metaphysical, the sociological, and the construct paradigms (ibid., p. 65).

58. *The Structure of Scientific Revolutions*, p. 93. Oddly enough, Toulmin starts his scathing criticism of Kuhn's use of the word *revolution* (of which he distinguishes five phases in the relatively brief span of ten years) with the declaration that "the two key notions in Kuhn's account—'paradigm' and 'revolution'—are in fact separate and independent, both in their implications and in their historical origins" (*Human Understanding*, p. 106). The application of the word revolution is, of course, much older than the notion of paradigm change as a Gestalt switch, but as the massive evidence gathered by I. B. Cohen shows (see his essay, "The Eighteenth-Century Origins of the Concept of Scientific Revolu-

tion," *Journal of the History of Ideas* 37 [1976]: 257–88), d'Alembert and Diderot, who were chiefly responsible for the popularization of the interpretation of the history of science in terms of revolutions, certainly meant something akin to sudden intellectual changes.

59. Ibid., p. 91.

60. Ibid., p. 93. In addition to nature and logic, Kuhn mentioned the "techniques of persuasive argumentation effective within the quite special groups that constitute the community of scientists," a clear indication of Kuhn's gravitating in this case too toward psychologism.

61. Ibid., p. 4.

62. Ibid., p. 147.

63. Ibid., p. 165.

64. Ibid., p. 158.

65. Ibid., p. 171.

66. Ibid.

67. Ibid.

68. Thus, for instance, D. Shapere in *Philosophical Review* 73 (1964): 391–92; and I. Scheffler in his *Science and Subjectivity* (Indianapolis: Bobbs-Merrill, 1967), p. 77. It should not seem surprising that because of their Popperian leanings most contributors to *Criticism and the Growth of Knowledge* failed even to mention the status of scientific progress within the perspective of Kuhn's work.

69. *The Structure of Scientific Revolutions*, p. 171.

70. As pointedly remarked by D. Shapere in his review of the second edition of Kuhn's work in *Science* 172 (1971): 707.

71. *The Structure of Scientific Revolutions*, p. 172.

72. Ibid.

73. Ibid.

74. Ibid., pp. 110 and 120.

75. Ibid., p. 109.

76. Ibid., chapter 10, "Revolutions as Changes of World View," pp. 110–34.

77. D. Shapere in *Science* 172 (1971): 707.

78. For illustrations of this, see chapter 9 above and pp. 45–49 and 483–85 in my *The Relevance of Physics* (Chicago: University of Chicago Press, 1966).

79. *The Structure of Scientific Revolutions*, pp. 17 and 41.

80. Ibid., p. 143.

81. Ibid., p. 170.

82. Ibid., pp. 100–101.

83. Tellingly enough, Shapere advocated, with an eye on Kuhn's work, a middle course as a cure for certain historians of science: "But until historians of science achieve a more balanced approach to their subject—neither too positivistic nor too relativistic—philosophers must receive such presentations of evidence with extremely critical eyes" (*Philosophical Review* 73 [1964]: 393).

84. This point is illustrated and documented, in addition to what is contained in chapters 3–6, by much of the material in chapters 11 and 12 in my *Science and Creation* and in chapter 10 of my *The Relevance of Physics*.

85. *The Structure of Scientific Revolutions*, p. 167.

86. Ibid.

87. My entire book *Science and Creation* is devoted to that theme.

88. About revolutions, *plus ça change, plus c'est la même chose* is not an inappropriate motto. It is certainly very applicable to the French and American revolutions. Even the fifty some years of Bolshevik revolutions provided plenty of evidence for the tenacious persistence of hallowed traditions and their covert

reaffirmation by the "revolutionary" regimes.

89. The "conversions" refer to Kuhn's characterization of a scientist's intellectual transition from one paradigm to another as a conversion-experience (*The Structure of Scientific Revolutions*, pp. 150–51).

90. In spite of Kuhn's protestation to the contrary (ibid., pp. 8–9), a protestation all the more hollow because it comes to a close with an appeal to the fundamental role of epistemology, for which he then substitutes sociology and psychology.

91. Such was the gist of Polanyi's concluding remark (*Scientific Change*, p. 380) in his appraisal of the preliminary form of Kuhn's theory.

CHAPTER SIXTEEN

1. "The Philosophical Significance of the Theory of Relativity," in *Albert Einstein: Philosopher-Scientist*, ed. P. A. Schilpp (Evanston, Ill.: Library of Living Philosophers, 1949), p. 292. "The gist of scientific method," wrote H. Mehlberg in the same vein, "is therefore verification and proof, not discovery," in his *The Reach of Science* (Toronto: University of Toronto Press, 1958), p. 37. It should therefore be no surprise that massive books on scientific explanation, such as *The Structure of Science* by E. Nagel (New York: Harcourt, Brace and World, 1961), contain no significant reference to the act of discovery, as if that very act did not make the explanation itself possible *and* meaningful.

2. "The Philosophical Significance of the Theory of Relativity," p. 292.

3. *The Structure of Scientific Revolutions* (Chicago: University of Chicago Press, 1962), p. 118.

4. Ibid. As Kuhn notes, in that case the new perceptual possibilities were made available by a "medieval paradigm shift." The shift was the advance from the Aristotelian concept of motion to the impetus theory, a "late medieval paradigm which held that the continuing motion of a heavy body is due to an internal power implanted in it by the projector that initiated its motion." The phrase not only contradicts Koyré, who programmatically insisted in the very preface of *Etudes galiléennes* (Paris: Hermann, 1939) on the essential novelty of Galileo's thought with respect to the Parisian impetus theory, but also weakens Kuhn's claim about the sudden, all-or-nothing kind of emergence of a major scientific insight.

5. As argued notably by G. Ryle in his *The Concept of Mind* (London: Hutchinson, 1949).

6. According to the murmur of some intellectual communities which A. J. Ayer gladly took for the symphony of the academic world in his inaugural lecture at Oxford in 1960: "There is now a fair measure of agreement among philosophers that theirs is what is technically called a second order subject. They do not set out to describe, or even to explain, the world, still less to change it. Their concern is only with the way in which we speak about the world. Philosophy, it has been said, is talk about talk" (*Philosophy and Language* [Oxford: Clarendon Press, 1960], p. 5). By then Russell had already put himself on record about the new philosophy which abandoned the age-old urge of philosophers to understand not only one another (always a noble enterprise) but above all the world. Linguistic philosophy "seems to concern itself, not with the world and our relation to it, but only with the different ways in which silly people can say silly things. If this is all that philosophy has to offer, I cannot think that it is a worthy subject of study" (*My Philosophical Development* [London: Allen, 1959], p. 230).

7. *Philosophy* (New York: W. W. Norton, 1927), p. 14.

8. This is why Einstein warned: "If you want to find out anything from the

theoretical physicists about the methods they use, I advise you to stick closely to one principle: don't listen to their words, fix your attention on their deeds." Such was the opening remark of his famed Herbert Spencer Lecture given on June 10, 1933, in Oxford "On the Method of Theoretical Physics" (*The World as I See It* [New York: Covici, 1934], p. 30).

9. *Conjectures and Refutations: The Growth of Scientific Knowledge* (New York: Harper and Row, 1968), p. 226.

10. Ibid.

11. The various mechanical devices to which recourse (invariably frustrating) was made to explain the workings of the mind make a long list, to which computers are the latest addition. For details, see my *Brain, Mind and Computers* (New York: Herder and Herder, 1969).

12. A variant on an often quoted statement of Archbishop Temple.

13. A chief and amply justified contention of Polanyi's Gifford Lectures, *Personal Knowledge: Towards a Post-Critical Philosophy* (New York: Harper and Row, 1964). Far from advocating subjectivism, idealist or psychologist, Polanyi was overwhelmed by the unfathomable active union which the act of knowledge creates between the knower and the known, a union that cannot be had if the mind creates, à la Descartes, the world, or if the mind, as Locke imagined, is but a rubber-stamp impression of external objects. That union was for Polanyi an "indwelling" which he identified with Heidegger's "being-in-the-world" (ibid., p. x). Whether these and other similar terms helped rather than hampered Polanyi's epistemological message is debatable, but his groping toward the epistemological middle road—he wanted his philosophy to be taken as postcritical, a barb at Kant—was as inevitable as was Heidegger's ultimately casting his vote for the primacy of being as the foundation of knowledge.

14. See his "Tacit Knowing: Its Bearing on Some Problems of Philosophy," *Reviews of Modern Physics* 34 (1962): 601–16, and his Terry Lectures (1962), *The Tacit Dimension* (London: Routledge and Kegan Paul, 1966). As was the case with "personal knowledge", "tacit knowing" too was meaningful only within an epistemology free of rationalist and empiricist extremes. It cannot be emphasized enough that it was a rude distortion of science, Bernal's Marxist presentation of it, which provoked Polanyi, the scientist, to begin making reflections on science which he knew from firsthand experience. It tells something of its genuineness that his reflections on it issued in a philosophy akin to moderate realism. The importance of Polanyi's philosophy in its derivation from a scientific background is brilliantly set forth in T. F. Torrance's essay, "The Place of Michael Polanyi in the Modern Philosophy of Science" (mimeographed), in which Polanyi's thought is related to that of Einstein, Bohr, Gödel, and Popper.

15. "Erinnerungen: Tischrede gehalten bei der Feier des 70. Geburtstages" (1891) in *Vorträge und Reden*, 5th ed. (Braunschweig: F. Vieweg, 1903), 1:14–15.

16. "Notes on the Origin of the General Theory of Relativity" (1933) in *The World As I See It*, p. 108.

17. "Introductory Lecture on Experimental Physics" (1871) in *The Scientific Papers of James Clerk Maxwell*, edited by W. D. Niven (Cambridge University Press, 1890), 2:251.

18. J. A. Wheeler, "A Septet of Sybils: Aids in Search for Truth," *American Scientist* 44 (1956): 360.

19. A statement of J. C. Eccles, used as motto in Popper's *Conjectures and Refutations*, p. [2].

20. As evidenced by his characterization of false conjectures as being approx-

imations of the truth and by emphasis on the attainability of verisimilitude between notions and their objects. He offered in 1966 such points as part of "A Realist View of Logic, Physics, and History" (*Objective Knowledge: An Evolutionary Approach* [Oxford: Clarendon Press, 1974], p. 318), and they certainly imply a commitment to an objectively existing reality. Once, however, knowledge puts man in touch with such a reality, he is confronted with the authority of a truth which patently transcends him. Popper has shown no evidence that he had given up his earlier appraisal of the authority of truth, an appraisal not without a touch of contradictoriness. On the one hand he recognized that without "a truth which is beyond human authority" there can be "no objective standards of inquiry," but on the other hand he rejected the inference that any human knowledge (inspiration) can carry "an authority, divine or otherwise" ("On the Sources of Knowledge and of Ignorance" [1961] in *Conjectures and Refutations*, pp. 29–30). While one should understand a rationalist's uneasiness at the sight of the divine, of which truth is the messenger par excellence, one should beware of taking the rationalist's inconsistency for an act of understanding, be it a conjecture or a mere falsification.

21. That the number in question was "three" might have been an additional reason for Galileo's belief that the three main periods of tides were connected to three motions of the moon (its diurnal parallax and its librations in longitude and latitude), although there was no empirical agreement between the two sets of data. For details, see W. R. Shea, *Galileo's Intellectual Revolution: Middle Period, 1610–1632* (New York: Science History Publications, 1972), pp. 185–86.

22. A trust which demands, it should be noted, a middle course between empiricism and rationalism, a point implicitly recognized in Koyré's study of Newton's attitude toward hypotheses. "The expression 'hypothesis' thus seems to have become, for Newton, toward the end of his life, one of those curious terms, such as "heresy," that we never apply to ourselves, but only to others. As for us, *we* do not feign hypotheses, *we* are not heretics. It is *they*, the Baconians, the Cartesians, Leibniz, Hooke, Cheyne, and others—*they* feign hypotheses and *they* are the heretics" (*Newtonian Studies* [Cambridge: Harvard University Press, 1965], p. 52). This list of "heretics" contains only empiricists and rationalists, a point unfortunately not noted by Koyré.

23. *Space, Time and Creation: Philosophical Aspects of Scientific Cosmology* (Glencoe, Ill.: The Free Press, 1957)), p. 117.

24. *The Logic of Scientific Discovery* (New York: Basic Books, 1959), p. 31.

25. *Discovery in the Physical Sciences* (Notre Dame, Ind.: University of Notre Dame Press, 1969), p. 122.

26. What follows is a summary of pp. 120–54 in Blackwell's work.

27. Ibid., pp. 155–86.

28. *The Rise of Scientific Philosophy* (Berkeley: University of California Press, 1958), p. 231.

29. Popper's account of what happened indicates that Carnap himself was not ready to administer the medicine to himself: "Carnap was the first philosopher who recognized the immense importance of Gödel's discoveries, and he did his best to make them known to the philosophical world. It is the more surprising that Gödel's result did not produce the change which it should have produced in the Vienna Circle's tenets (in my opinion, undoubtedly and obviously metaphysical tenets, all too tenaciously held) concerning the language and the scope of science" (*Conjectures and Refutations*, p. 270).

30. The origin of the expression is the Stoic phrase, *zōon logikòn*, which appears in the dictum of Seneca, himself a Stoic: "rationale animal est homo"

(*Epistulae morales ad Lucilium*, 46:63). The expression has become a byword through Christian usage, in which, however, its meaning has considerably deepened owing to Christian belief in the immortality of rational soul.

31. As aptly noted by E. McMullin in his "Realism in Modern Cosmology," *Proceedings of the American Catholic Philosophical Association* 29 (1955): 142–43.

32. The stark physicalism of basic tenets of the Vienna Circle was an unwitting plagiarization of d'Holbach's dictum, "all errors of man are errors of physics" (*Système de la Nature ou Des loix du monde Physique & du monde Moral*, new ed. [London, 1775], 1:19) and of Condorcet's declaration that "all errors in politics and in ethics are based on philosophical errors which in turn are tied to errors in physical science" (*Esquisse d'un tableau historique des progrès de l'esprit humain* in *Oeuvres de Condorcet*, ed. A. C. O'Connor and F. Arago [Paris: Firmin Didot Frères, 1847], 6:223).

33. Its most articulate proponent is H. Feigl. See especially sec. 5, "Mind-Body Identity: Explications and Supporting Arguments," or pp. 419–65 in his book-length essay, "The 'Mental' and the 'Physical'," in *Minnesota Studies in the Philosophy of Science*, vol. 2, *Concepts, Theories, and the Mind-Body Problem*, ed. H. Feigl, M. Scriven, and G. Maxwell (Minneapolis: University of Minnesota Press, 1958). According to the classic simile of the identity theory, the mind-body duality is like seeing a mass of vapory air from within and from without. From within such air will look like mist (mind), and from without like a cloud (body). And so with man: viewed from within he is rationality, but he is mere materiality when seen from the outside. But where the simile, and the identity theory with it, breaks down is with that mysterious ability of man for getting, so to speak, out of his skin and viewing himself from the outside without losing his sense of rationality and of identity. Mist, which is good, so it is believed, for one's complexion, can do no more than to save face for the identity theory, which, being an unabashedly monistic position by Feigl's own admission (ibid., p. 483), is but a philosophical face-saving. Clearly, there is need for some face-saving when such a prominent physicist as de Broglie states that he does "not see how consciousness can be derived from material things" and adds in the same breath: "I regard consciousness and matter as different aspects of one thing. There is one substance out of which both consciousness and matter are built." Quoted by J. W. N. Sullivan in his collection of interviews with leading representatives of thought in the early 1930s, published under the title *Contemporary Mind: Some Modern Answers* (London: Humphrey Toulmin, 1934), p. 164.

34. Its classic statement is still T. H. Huxley's hundred-year-old essay, "On the Hypothesis That Animals Are Automata, and Its History" (*Method and Results: Essays* [London: Macmillan and Company, 1894], pp. 199–250). Modern epiphenomenalists can merely improve on the scientific vocabulary used by Huxley but hardly on the consistency with which he assigned consciousness to *all* animals precisely because they were automata as man was one. They may even follow him in such mental acrobatics as to disclaim being fatalists and materialists, though not atheists. It would not be unfashionable today to state with him that the concept of necessity is merely a logical construct and that matter is inconceivable without a thinking mind. But where are the epiphenomenalists who would claim with him that the only thing worse than discoursing on the nature of God is the effort to prove that he does not exist? (ibid., p. 245).

35. Various aspects of that theory give unity to Popper's essays published under the title, *Objective Knowledge*, quoted above.

36. He was not even unwilling to be classified as "naive realist" because of his belief that "there are physical worlds and a world of states of consciousness,

and that these two interact" (ibid., p. 107).

37. As programmatically stated in the title of his essay, "Epistemology without a Knowing Subject," (ibid., pp. 106–52).

38. Ibid., p. 108. Popper, therefore, has to frown on traditional epistemology, which by studying knowledge in the subjective sense leads, according to him, to irrelevancies. He also has to state that scientific knowledge is not knowledge in the ordinary sense, which he simply equates with a subjective knowledge lacking objective content. To make palatable these extravagant claims he produces his trump card, a twofold thought experiment. Unfortunately he does not explain the exact meaning of "our capacity to learn," which constitutes the nerve cell of his second thought experiment. It consists in the prediction of a relatively quick recovery of culture were all our machines and our ability to use them destroyed but not our libraries and our capacity to learn. Mere capacity to learn, let it be remarked, would not have enabled a Champollion to decipher the Rosetta stone. In addition, he had to have mastery of two ancient languages, to say nothing of a large number of auxiliary branches of knowledge. The twofold thought experiment of Popper is a classic exercise in inexactitude on the part of a philosopher aiming above all at being exact.

39. Ibid., p. 112, where he presents the "close analogy between the growth of knowledge and biological growth" as the third supporting thesis attached to the three main theses of his epistemology.

40. "People and Other Animals," in *The Understanding of Nature: Essays in the Philosophy of Biology* (Dordrecht: D. Reidel, 1974), p. 354.

41. Ibid., p. 360. Grene's explanation of the mind-body relationship is heavily influenced by H. Plessner's manifestly Hegelian speculations rich in verbal reveling and specious equivocations. (Concerning the latter, reference was made in chapter 14 to Plessner's explanation of laughter on the basis of an equivocal relationship between body and mind.) Thus while Grene "radically" rejects dualism as well as idealism (p. 347), she also claims that "somehow human perception is not just a biological event" (p. 358). The only merit of her theory of the mind is its label "eccentric" (p. 347).

42. See my "The Five Forms of Laplace's Cosmogony," *American Journal of Physics* 44 (1976): 4–11.

43. The passage in the introduction of Laplace's *Théorie analytique des probabilités* (1812) earned fame through its being taken over into his more popular exposition of the same topic, *Essai philosophique sur les probabilités* (1814). The human mind provided, in Laplace's presentation, a feeble outline of a hypothetical intelligence "which would comprehend all the forces by which nature is animated and the respective situation of the beings who compose it—an intelligence sufficiently vast to submit these data to analysis—it would embrace in the same formula the movements of the greatest bodies of the universe and those of the lightest atom; for it, nothing would be uncertain and the future, as the past, would be present to its eyes" (*A Philosophical Essay on Probabilities* trans. F. W. Truscott and F. L. Emory, with an introductory note by E. T. Bell [New York: Dover, 1951], p. 4).

44. M. Grene, "People and Other Animals," p. 359.

45. Ibid., p. 346.

46. The report, buried in a letter to *Nature* for over twenty years, provoked chuckles all around the globe when recalled in M. Polanyi's *The Tacit Dimension* (Garden City, N.Y.: Doubleday, 1967), p. 64. A hundred years ago, however, much respectability was given in the pages of the prestigious *Philosophical Magazine* to speculations on planetary distances, sizes, and masses based in part on a "π-geometrical series." For details, see my *Planets and Planetarians: A*

History of Theories of the Origin of Planetary Systems (Edinburgh: Scottish Academic Press, 1977), p. 165.

47. As done by A. Wyler, a Swiss mathematician. For details and references to his publications, see *Physics Today* 24 (August 1971): 16–18. According to Wyler's calculations, the experimentally known value of the ratio of the mass of the proton to the mass of the electron is equal to $6\pi^5$.

48. His discussion of that "unreasonableness" started, tellingly enough, with a story about the incredulous remark of a statistician's friend over the role of π in studies of population trends usually reflecting a Gaussian distribution. "Well, now you are pushing your joke too far. . . . Surely the population has nothing to do with the circumference of the circle" ("The Unreasonable Effectiveness of Mathematics in the Natural Sciences," *Communications on Pure and Applied Mathematics* 13 [1960]: 1).

49. "The Evolution of the Physicist's Picture of Nature," *Scientific American* 208 (May 1963): 47.

50. This enduring hope was voiced by S. Weinberg in his "Unified Theories of Elementary-Particle Interactions" (*Scientific American* 231 [Jan. 1974]: 56). On receiving the Robert Oppenheimer Memorial Prize in 1972, he defined his own motivation in research as the expectation that "it is in the area of elementary particles and fields (and perhaps also of cosmology) that we will find the ultimate laws of nature, the few simple general principles which determine why *all of nature is the way it is*" (italics added). Quoted by G. Holton in his "The Mainsprings of Discovery: The Great Tradition," *Encounter* 42 (April 1974): 91.

51. The idealist in question is Eddington. For his graphic phrase, see his *Space, Time and Gravitation: An Outline of the General Relativity Theory* (Cambridge University Press, 1920), p. 201.

52. A detail communicated to me by Mr. Vincent Buranelli, author of *Josiah Royce* (New York: Twayne Publishers, 1964).

53. "Physics and Reality" (1936), in *Out of My Later Years* (New York: Philosophical Library, 1950), pp. 60–61.

54. As discussed in chapter 12.

55. *Physics and Microphysics*, translated by M. Davidson (New York: Harper and Brothers, 1960), pp. 208–209.

56. Ibid., p. 209.

57. "En marge d'un texte," in *Louis de Broglie: Physicien et penseur* (Paris: Albin Michel, 1953), p. 156.

58. Ibid., p. 158.

59. "Physics and Reality," p. 60.

60. Essentially a remark of Gilson, "En marge d'un texte," p. 158.

61. As L. A. Steen reported on the latest setbacks of chess-playing computers, the only chess-playing automaton that achieved an enviable record against humans is still the machine "Turk," first presented in Austria by Baron Wolfgang von Kempeler in 1769: "Its *élan vital* was neither minimax algorithms nor smart heuristics, but an intricate series of levers manipulated by a chess master concealed within the machine itself" (*Science News* 108 [1975]: 350).

62. "The Mind-Body Problem," in *Dimensions of Mind: A Symposium*, ed. S. Hook (New York: New York University Press, 1960), p. 3.

63. The claim is usually based on the alleged obliteration through quantum mechanics of the difference between object and observer. But as Schrödinger remarked: "The observing mind is not a physical system, it cannot interact with any physical system. And it might be better to reserve the term 'subject' for the observing mind" (*Science and Humanism: Physics in Our Time* [Cambridge University Press, 1951], p. 53).

64. J. Maritain's caricature of Cartesian dualism in his *Religion and Culture*, trans. J. F. Scanlan (London: Sheed and Ward, 1931), p. 24.

65. G. Ryle's "deliberately abusive" characterization (*The Concept of Mind* [London: Hutchinson, 1949], pp. 15–16) of what he called "Descartes' Myth" and the "official doctrine," to the main articles of which "most philosophers, psychologists and religious teachers subscribe with minor reservations ... although they admit certain theoretical difficulties in it" (ibid., p. 11). Ryle could have learned from Gilson and others that in this connection too Descartes reduced to a mere skeleton the rich philosophical articulation of his medieval predecessors. Ryle, who tried linguistic incantations (ibid., pp. 195–98) to divest the "I" of its elusiveness, was not perceptive enough to match it with that of the "now." In that connection he might have profited from Einstein's remark to Carnap on the inability of physics to cope with the question of "now." See P. A. Schilpp, ed., *The Philosophy of Rudolf Carnap* (La Salle, Ill.: Open Court, 1963), p. 37.

66. For an early emphasis by Einstein of this point, see *The Meaning of Relativity* (Princeton University Press, 1923, pp. 2–3) where he warned, however, in an instinctive endorsement of a need for a middle road in epistemology that "the universe of ideas is just as little independent of the nature of our experiences as clothes are of the form of the human body."

67. A personal recollection of H. Feigl about a lecture which Einstein gave in Prague in 1920 and which he attended as a "very young student." See Feigl, "Beyond Peaceful Coexistence," in R. H. Stuewer, ed., *Historical and Philosophical Perspectives of Science* (Minneapolis: University of Minnesota Press, 1970), p. 9.

68. Pascal's phrase is too well known to be quoted. What is hardly remembered is its immediate sequel, where he prophetically warned against all future physicalists, that "all our dignity consists in thought" and therefore "by it we must elevate ourselves, and not by space and time which we cannot fill." See *Pascal's Pensées*, with an introduction by T. S. Eliot (New York: E. P. Dutton, 1958), p. 97.

69. Thus, for instance, I. Scheffler (*Science and Subjectivity* [Indianapolis: Bobbs-Merrill Company, 1967], pp. 7–8) who commends them for their "upholding of the ideal of responsibility in the sphere of belief as against willfulness, authoritarianism, and inertia."

70. Such is the unintended but true message of Carnap's *Der logische Aufbau der Welt* as pointed out by Popper in *Conjectures and Refutations*, p. 265.

71. Ibid., p. 265.

72. Although no one, in a sense, emphasized those facts and acts more frequently than Popper, he failed to commit himself in an unconditional and ontological sense to the reality of the universe and of the mind, a failure which has its source in his suspicion of essentialism, but which also justified P. K. Feyerabend's evaluation of his contribution as the elimination of "the last element of authoritarianism, the idea that knowledge must have a foundation." See Feyerabend's review of Popper's *Conjectures and Refutations* in *Isis* 56 (1965): 88.

CHAPTER SEVENTEEN

1. It tells something of the not-so-logical frame of mind of logical positivists that Carnap's *Der logische Aufbau der Welt* (1928), which shows logical positivism at its most logical, received but cursory attention by Carnap and by the many other contributors to *The Philosophy of Rudolf Carnap*, ed. P. A. Schilpp (La Salle, Ill.: Open Court, 1963). Not even a brief reference to it

was made by R. S. Cohen, the sole contributor to discuss in detail the problem of solipsism (pp. 111–22). Popper merely noted (p. 196) that the methodological solipsism of the *Aufbau* was soon abandoned by its author. Carnap himself failed to refer to that methodological solipsism which he had once advocated and very logically so, for only the admission of metaphysics can justify transition from strictly personal to interpersonal or universal language, the sole foundation of meaningful discourse about the universe of things.

2. Popper's declaration made in 1958, "all science is cosmology, I believe" (*Conjectures and Refutations* [New York: Harper and Row, 1968], p. 136), would serve as an outstanding example.

3. See, for instance, O. Schmidt, *A Theory of Earth's Origin: Four Lectures* (Moscow: Foreign Languages Publishing House, 1958), pp. 9–10.

4. For details, see chapter 6.

5. *Cosmologia generalis, methodo scientifica pertractata, qua ad solidam, inprimis Dei atque naturae, cognitionem via sternitur* (Frankfurt and Leipzig: Officina Libraria Rengeriana, 1731). The second "improved" edition (1737) is nearly identical to the first. The book, as stated in its subtitle, is a "treatise based on scientific method which lays the road to solid knowledge, especially of God and nature." The English form of *cosmologia*, or cosmology, is noted in 1656 in Blunt's *Glossographia*, but no widespread usage is indicated. Wolff's role in the popularization of "cosmology" in English contexts is attested in 1753 in *Chambers' Cyclopedia, Supplement*. See the *Oxford English Dictionary* (Oxford: Clarendon Press, 1933), 2:1032.

6. As mentioned in chapter 5.

7. A work in the form of twenty letters, exchanged fictitiously between Lambert and a friend, now available in my English translation with introduction and notes, *Cosmological Letters on the Arrangement of the World-Edifice* (New York: Science History Publications, 1976).

8. And republished by Laplace in four more revised editions during the next twenty-eight years. See my article, "The Five Forms of Laplace's Cosmogony," *American Journal of Physics* 44 (1976): 4–11.

9. A point emphasized in "Situation et rôle de l'hypothèse cosmogonique dans la pensée cosmologique de Laplace" (*Revue d'Histoire des Sciences* 29 [1976]: 21–49), by J. Merleau-Ponty who, however, overlooked the fact that Laplace was very superficial in criticizing Newton for his recourse to divine intervention in the establishment of the solar system. Laplace's theory could not (among other things) cope with the distribution of angular momentum, a fact which he could have easily ascertained had he not had undue fondness for his theory, as noted by contemporary scientists. See chapter 5, "The Nebulous Advance," in my *Planets and Planetarians: A History of Theories of the Origin of Planetary Systems* (Edinburgh: Scottish Academic Press, 1977).

10. See *The Measure of the Universe: A History of Modern Cosmology* (Oxford: Clarendon Press, 1965), by J. D. North. According to North, in place of the term "creation" "there are the perfectly adequate expressions 'First Event,' which will cover most cases, and for the steady-state theories, 'spontaneous occurrence.' Both sorts of event may be described without inconsistency, without the language of cause and effect, and without recourse to the supernatural" (p. 406). Whatever the value of sheer verbalization, it is an invaluable witness to the inexorable logic which asserts itself with regard to our understanding of material reality when a systematic avoidance of any reference to the creation of matter is obeyed in cosmological discourse. Thus in the concluding sentence of North's work cosmology appears deprived of contact with the truth of material reality: "The individual theory of cosmology is neither true nor false: like any

other scientific theory, it is merely an instrument of what passes for understanding."

11. J. Merleau-Ponty, *Cosmologie du XXe siècle: Etude épistemologique et historique des théories de la cosmologie contemporaine* (Paris: Gallimard, 1965), p. 457.

12. See chapter 12.

13. A process philosophically codified by Kant but which found its most graphic expression in Lord Kelvin's declaration, "I say *finitude* is incomprehensible, the infinite in the universe *is* comprehensible," in his lecture, "The Wave Theory of Light," delivered in Philadelphia in 1884. See *Popular Lectures and Addresses* (London: Macmillan, 1889–94), 1:314.

14. A summary by Popper; see his *Conjectures and Refutations*, pp. 101 and 149–51.

15. The inexorable and universal working of fire, however, could but produce an endless sequence of that absolute chaos which the universe had to be if Heraclitus was right in claiming that "the cosmos, at best, is like a rubbish heap scattered at random." The claim, well-known to uncounted readers of chapter 2, "Heraclitus," in *The Open Society and Its Enemies* (Princeton: Princeton University Press, 1950), by K. R. Popper, is presented by him as part of the *discovery* made by Heraclitus's genius that the world is not "the sum-total of all *things*, but rather . . . the totality of all events, or changes, or *facts*" (p. 15). This comment of Popper merely proves the old truth that if the existence of *things* is denied, the cosmos is reduced to rubbish, and so is the strict consistency of any discourse about the cosmos, including cosmology, philosophical or scientific. Any admirer of the alleged exclusivity of facts still has to find a logical way of defining a process which is not undergone by something.

16. In spite of modern estimates of the number of protons in the whole universe as being of the order of 10^{79}, the most tellingly modern aspect of Archimedes' reasoning in his "The Sand Reckoner" (*The Works of Archimedes*, edited in modern notation with introductory chapters by T. L. Heath [Cambridge University Press, 1897], pp. 220–32) is not his reckoning that the number of grains of sand of which 10,000 would go into a poppy seed cannot be larger than 10^{63} if they were to fill the sphere of the fixed stars having a radius not larger than 10^{10} stadia. It is Archimedes's concluding remark, which attributes to mathematics the power to establish something quantitatively singular about the whole universe.

17. Alexander of Aphrodisias (fl. A.D. 190), the only one in antiquity to defend Aristotle's theory of the Milky Way, was duly censured by Olympiodorus (fl. A.D. 530). See my *The Milky Way: An Elusive Road for Science* (New York: Science History Publications, 1972), pp. 20–21.

18. An opinion ascribed to Democritus. See *The Milky Way*, pp. 10–11.

19. As reported by Hippolytus, "Democritus holds the same view as Leucippus . . . [that] there are innumerable worlds, which differ in size. In some worlds there is no sun and moon, in others they are larger than in our world, and in others more numerous. The intervals between the worlds are unequal; in some parts there are more worlds, in others fewer." It was also noted in antiquity that unlike Epicurus, who held all atoms to be imperceptibly small, Democritus held that some atoms are very large. See G. S. Kirk and J. E. Raven, *The Presocratic Philosophers: A Critical History with a Selection of Texts* (Cambridge University Press, 1962), pp. 409 and 411.

20. *The Milky Way*, p. 20.

21. See *The Collected Dialogues of Plato, including the Letters*, ed. E. Hamilton and H. Cairns (New York: Pantheon Books, 1961), pp. 542–43.

22. Ibid., p. 544.

23. *Timaeus* 22b; ibid., p. 1157.

24. In chapter 7 of book I of *The Almagest*. See *Great Books of the Western World*, vol. 16, *Ptolemy, Copernicus, Kepler* (Chicago: Encyclopaedia Britannica, 1952), pp. 11–12.

25. Thus, for instance, Popper, *Conjectures and Refutations*, p. 257.

26. A rather modern myopia, of which not even Giordano Bruno wanted to be guilty. The whole thrust of Copernicus's discussion in chapter 6 of book 1 of his *De revolutionibus* of the immensity of the heavens in relation to the size of the earth and of its orbit is quite "Ptolemaic." According to Copernicus, the practically infinite ratio of the distance of fixed stars to the size of the earth, as stated by Ptolemy, is also true in reference to the earth's orbit.

27. This second argument was proposed, tellingly enough, in 1618 in the *Epitome astronomiae copernicanae*, in clear indication of Kepler's firm belief in the finiteness of the Copernican universe. See *The Milky Way*, pp. 107–8.

28. See chap. 5, n. 55.

29. In an entry from 1812 in his *Annalen*. See *Gedenkausgabe der Werke, Briefe und Gespräche* (Zurich: Artemis Verlag, 1949), 11:857.

30. In his *From the Closed World to the Infinite Universe* (New York: Harper and Brothers, 1958), originally published in 1957.

31. See Andrew Motte's translation of the *Principia*, revised and annotated by F. Cajori, *Sir Isaac Newton's Mathematical Principles of Natural Philosophy and His System of the World* (Berkeley: University of California Press, 1962), p. 525.

32. *From the Closed World to the Infinite Universe*, p. 184.

33. This statement of Bentley is from the seventh of his *Eight Sermons Preached at the Honourable Robert Boyle Lectures in the First Year MDCXCII* in London in 1693, the very enterprise that led to the Bentley-Newton correspondence. See *The Works of Richard Bentley*, ed. A. Dyce (London: Francis Macpherson, 1838), 3:171.

34. Indeed, Koyré did not seem, as I noted in my *The Paradox of Olbers' Paradox* (New York: Herder & Herder, 1969), p. 17, to be familiar with other, less conspicuous details of the seventeenth-century history of the optical paradox, although he was known for his attention to and mastery of minute particulars.

35. See Koyré's concluding remark in his *From the Closed World to the Infinite Universe*, p. 276.

36. According to the diary which Herschel kept of his visit of 1802 to Paris, the topic of the vastness of the sidereal heavens made the First Consul remark "in a tone of exclamation or admiration . . . : 'And who is the author of all this!' Mons. De la Place wished to shew that a chain of natural causes would account for the construction and preservation of the wonderful system. This the First Consul rather opposed. Much may be said on the subject; by joining the arguments of both we shall be led to 'Nature and nature's God'." *The Herschel Chronicle: The Life-Story of William Herschel and His Sister Caroline Herschel*, edited by his granddaughter, Constance Lubbock (New York: The Macmillan Company, 1933), p. 310.

37. See his *Astronomy and General Physics Considered with Reference to Natural Theology* (Philadelphia: Carey, Lea & Blanchard, 1833), p. 149.

38. "On the Reconcentration of the Mechanical Energy of the Universe" (1852) in W. J. Macquorn Rankine, *Miscellaneous Scientific Papers*, ed. W. J. Millar (London: Charles Griffin, 1891), pp. 200–202.

39. See chapter 8, "The Myth of One Island," in my *The Milky Way*.

40. "On Ether and Gravitational Matter through Infinite Space," *Philosophical Magazine* 2 (1901): 161–77.

41. As C. F. von Weizsäcker reported in his *The Relevance of Science* (New York: Harper and Row, 1964), p. 151, the reaction of W. Nernst to his calculation of the age of the universe on the basis of radioactive decay: "He said, the view that there might be an age of the universe was not science.... He explained that the infinite duration of time was a basic element of all scientific thought, and to deny this would mean to betray the very foundations of science. I was quite surprised by this idea and I ventured the objection that it was scientific to form hypotheses according to the hints given by experience, and that the idea of an age of the universe was such a hypothesis. He retorted that we could not form a scientific hypothesis which contradicted the very foundations of science."

42. "Cosmological Considerations on the General Theory of Relativity" (1917), in *The Principle of Relativity: A Collection of Original Memoirs on the Special and General Theory of Relativity* by H. A. Lorentz, A. Einstein, H. Minkowski, and H. Weyl, with notes by A. Sommerfeld; translated by W. Perrett and G. B. Jeffrey (London: Methuen, 1923), p. 179.

43. "Discussion on the Evolution of the Universe," in *British Association for the Advancement of Science: Report of the Centenary Meeting: London, 1931, September 23–30* (London: Office of the British Association, 1932), see especially pp. 578 and 594–605.

44. The *locus classicus* is chapter 7, "A Personal View," in his *The Nature of the Universe*, rev. ed. (New York: The New American Library of World Literature, 1963), pp. 117–24. There Hoyle describes religion as a "desperate attempt to find an escape from the truly dreadful situation in which we find ouselves" (p. 121) and Christian hope "as an eternity of frustration" (p. 123). Of course, if the account of creation in Genesis is taken for what it was *not* meant to be, a science, then one may say with Hoyle that it is "the merest daub compared with the sweeping grandeur of the picture revealed by modern science" (p. 121). It will, however, certainly appear in its grandiosely sweeping logic when compared with the idea of continuous creation—in which, according to Hoyle, "matter chases its own tail" (p. 108). One more proof of the age-old logic that consistent dismissal of Creation leads to going around in circles, in more than one sense.

45. See, for instance, H. Bondi, *Cosmology* (Cambridge University Press, 1952), p. 144.

46. This is not to suggest that Hoyle confessed to failure in logic as he described the creation of all matter at once "as an irrational process that cannot be described in scientific terms" (*The Nature of the Universe*, p. 108). But logic and science were certainly absent in his claim that the alleged continuous "creation" of hydrogen atoms was rational and scientific because "it can be represented by mathematical equations whose consequences can be worked out and compared with observations" (pp. 108–9). Perpetual motion machines, it is well to recall, do not become scientific by being presented in the garb of mathematics. As to the logic of the claim that the coming into being of something (be it a hydrogen atom) out of nothing is "observable," it is still to be vindicated.

47. "The steady-state theory was philosophically killed several years ago by M. K. Munitz, *Brit. Jour. Phil. Sci.*, 5, 32 (1954), but apparently this criticism has been as ineffective as Augustine's refutation of astrology in his *Confessions*," mused M. Bunge in his "Cosmology and Magic," *The Monist*, 47 (1962), p. 126.

48. M. K. Munitz, *The Mystery of Existence: An Essay in Philosophical Cosmology* (New York: Appleton-Century-Crofts, 1965), p. 11.

49. J. Monod, *Chance and Necessity* (New York: Vintage Books, 1971), p. 44.

50. *New Pathways in Science* (Cambridge: University Press, 1934), p. 217.

51. In a conversation with Manfred Clynes, a Viennese-born Australian concert pianist as reported in P. Michelmore, *Einstein: Profile of the Man* (New York: Dodd, 1962), p. 253.

52. "Highly Condensed Objects," reprinted in R. J. Seeger and R. S. Cohen, eds., *Philosophical Foundations of Science* (Dordrecht: D. Reidel, 1974), pp. 215–26.

53. As admitted by H. Bondi and T. Gold, "The Steady-State Theory of the Expanding Universe," *Monthly Notices of the Royal Astronomical Society* 108 (1948): 266.

54. "Highly Condensed Objects," p. 222.

55. Ibid.

56. Ibid., p. 224.

57. "Cosmology as a Science," in *Philosophical Foundations of Science*, pp. 181–88; see especially p. 185.

58. Ibid., p. 186.

59. As claimed by Bergmann (ibid., p. 186), but the evidence he offers is slender to say the least.

60. "The Case for a Hierarchical Cosmology," *Science* 167 (1970): 1203–13.

61. E. R. Harrison at a symposium organized by the Center of Astrophysics operated jointly by the Harvard College Observatory and the Smithsonian Astrophysical Observatory, quoted in the *New York Times*, November 2, 1975, p. 56, col. 2.

62. "Physical Processes near Cosmological Singularities," in *Annual Review of Astronomy and Astrophysics* 11 (1973): 387–410.

63. In their paper "Is Physics Legislated by Cosmogony?" in *Quantum Gravity*, ed. C. Isham, R. Penrose, and D. Sciama (Oxford: Clarendon Press, 1975), p. 541.

64. In putting forward the idea of a "self-reference cosmogony," Patton and Wheeler invoke the philosophy of Parmenides and Berkeley in support of their claim "that the 'observer' gives the world the power to come into being, through the very act of giving meaning to that world" (ibid., p. 564).

65. Ibid., p. 558.

66. Ibid., p. 560.

67. S. Hawking and G. F. R. Ellis, *The Large Scale Structure of Space-Time* (Cambridge University Press, 1973), pp. 348–64. Recent papers by leading cosmologists with the word "singularity" in their titles are a commonplace. Nor is it rare to find in them a confusion of scientific and philosophical perspectives. In discussing "naked," that is, observable cosmic singularities, R. Penrose concludes with the baffling phrase: "The initial mystery of creation, therefore, would no longer be able to hide in the obscurity afforded by its supposed uniqueness" ("Naked Singularities," *Annals of the New York Academy of Sciences*, 224 [1973]: 125–34). It takes more than science to grasp the meaning of creation out of nothing, or to sense what is implied in what Penrose calls "cosmic censorship," namely, the inability of "naked singularities" to develop out of an initially nonsingular state. The singularity of the universe is more and more revealed in its stark nakedness by modern cosmology, a "nakedness" which should intimate the ultimate presence of the act of creation behind even such an already partly explored "naked," that is, visible, singularity as a rotating black hole.

68. "Of Atoms, Mountains, and Stars: A Study in Qualitative Physics," *Science* 187 (1975): 605–12.

69. In his presidential address to the 137th meeting of the British Association

for the Advancement of Science, August 27, 1975. An expanded version of the original address ("In the Centre of Immensities") was published under the title "Whence" in the *New York Times Magazine*, November 9, 1975. For quotation, see p. 88.

70. For the French original, see A. O. Lovejoy, *The Great Chain of Being: A Study of the History of an Idea* (Cambridge: Harvard University Press, 1936), p. 150. Pantheist as he was, Hugo could only be upset by the perspective of having been created out of nothing, a perspective that is a source of confidence for the theist.

71. In his doctoral dissertation, *De la contingence des lois de la nature* (Paris: G. Baillière, 1874), Boutroux emphasized the contingency of physical reality in such a way as to cast doubt on the consistency of physical interactions. His aim was to vindicate rationally the existence of freedom, soul, and Creator, but the aim could hardly appear satisfactorily implemented when causality as a basis of metaphysical inference was undermined in the fear that strict physical causality preempted the possibility of nonphysical existence. Boutroux's work went through eight editions before it appeared in authorized English translation, *The Contingency of the Laws of Nature*, trans. F. Rothwell (Chicago: Open Court, 1916). See especially pp. 32 and 180.

72. This is not to suggest that Meyerson approved of the reduction of reality to identity relations. On the contrary, he tacitly kept pressing the classical objection against that reduction, that if it were valid nothing would ever happen. This was the true message of Meyerson's *Identité et réalité*, first published in 1908 and translated into English by K. Loewenberg in 1929 under the title, *Identity and Reality* (Dover reprint, New York, 1962). But as Gilson aptly noted, "few doctrines have been as commonly misunderstood as that of Meyerson" (E. Gilson, T. Langan, A. A. Maurer, *Recent Philosophy: Hegel to the Present* [New York: Random House, 1966], p. 762).

73. A detail, which Gilson most likely reported (ibid., p. 289) from first-hand information.

74. A point emphasized by Gilson in reference to Eddington's effort to replace the "metaphysical concept of real existence" with a "structural concept of existence." See *God and Philosophy* (New Haven: Yale University Press, 1941), p. 138. Physicists who fail to realize the epistemological limitations of their mathematical methods are apt to turn against reality itself, namely, against the irreducible act of existence, by trying to redefine it to suit their method.

75. N. Malcolm, *Ludwig Wittgenstein: A Memoir*, with a biographical sketch by G. H. von Wright (London: Oxford University Press, 1958), p. 70.

76. *Tractatus Logico-Philosophicus*, with an introduction by B. Russell (London: Kegan Paul, Trench, Trubner and Co., 1923), p. 31. The phrase is the second (1.1) of Wittgenstein's aphoristic utterances and is followed by a bewilderingly inconsistent list of statements on world, atomic facts, and things, the last being a glaring contraband in a philosophy of facts.

77. The phrase is the evocative title of his book *The Unexpected Universe* (New York: Harcourt, Brace and World, 1969), which, however, does not offer much food for thought for the cosmologist or the philosopher.

78. "Nature somehow manages to be both relativistic and quantum mechanical: but those two requirements restrict it so much that it has only a limited choice of how to be—hopefully a very limited choice," remarked S. Weinberg in his acceptance speech for the Oppenheimer Memorial Award for 1972. Quoted in G. Holton, "The Mainsprings of Discovery—The Great Tradition," *Encounter* (April 1974): 91.

79. In a letter to the editor, *Nature* 139 (1937): 323.

80. For the text of the debate, see J. Hick, *The Existence of God* (New York: Macmillan, 1964), pp. 167–91.

81. Ibid., pp. 174–75.

82. Such is Popper's translation (*Conjectures and Refutations,* p. 268) of a phrase in the opening section of Carnap's "Psychology in Physical Language" (1932). The same phrase is rendered as "metaphysics would be discarded as meaningless" in *Logical Positivism,* ed. A. J. Ayer (New York: Free Press, 1959), p. 166.

83. The writings of most present-day antipositivist philosophers and historians of science are a good illustration of this predicament.

84. On the crucial impact of this passage of Exodus (3:14) on theistic metaphysics, see Gilson's Gifford Lectures, *The Spirit of Medieval Philosophy,* translated by A. H. C. Downes (New York: Charles Scribner's Sons, 1940), pp. 51 and 433–34.

85. *The Causes of Evolution* (London: Longmans, Green & Co., 1932), p. 169.

86. This sparkling phrase in Whitehead's *Modes of Thought* (New York: Macmillan, 1938), p. 185, refers to efforts to understand Einstein's physics in terms of that of Newton.

87. As aptly put, though in a purely artistic perspective, by A. Huxley, *Point Counter Point* (New York: Harper and Brothers, 1928), p. 293.

88. This phrase, which opens the concluding paragraph in E. A. Burtt's classic, *The Metaphysical Foundations of Modern Science,* 2d rev. ed. (New York: Humanities Press, 1932), leads to statements which illustrate the bewilderment of a perceptive writer on the philosophical history of science unaware of the liberating vistas of moderate realism. Burtt, who better than anyone before him perceived the epistemological middle road that Newton had instinctively chosen and who was fully aware of the need to avoid the pitfalls of empiricism (behaviorism) and of idealism, caught no glimpse of a method to satisfy the just aspirations of those two extremes. But how could anyone see his way out of that dilemma who envied the good fortune of the Greeks of old for not having been tainted yet by "theological superstition," which in Burtt's context can only mean Christian theism.

89. The most recent example of unfolding that alternative is *The Mystery of Existence: An Essay in Philosophical Cosmology* (New York: Appleton-Century-Crofts, 1965), by M. K. Munitz. Its most instructive part is Munitz's concluding admission—which in fact contradicts his main thesis—that the question about the ultimate meaning of existence is unanswerable only in respect "to known rational methods" (p. 262). Wittgenstein was more consistent in stating that "if a question can be put at all, then it *can* also be answered" (*Tractatus Logico-Philosophicus,* 6.5), in obvious warning that the question about the meaning of the world's existence cannot even be asked in a meaningful way if it is true that "not *how* the world is, is the mystical, but *that* it is" (ibid., 6.44). One must first renounce the positivist injunction about "the right method of philosophy"—namely, "to say nothing except . . . the propositions of natural science," if one wants to be free of its ultimate straitjacket tailored by Wittgenstein: "Whereof one cannot speak, thereof one must be silent" (ibid., 7).

Chapter Eighteen

1. See chapter 17, note 49.

2. J. Monod, *Chance and Necessity: An Essay on the Natural Philosophy of*

Modern Biology, trans. A. Wainhouse (New York: Vintage Books, 1971), p. 170.

3. That the task of writing it fell *by chance* to Huxley was curiously Darwinian.

4. The quotation is from the sixth of Huxley's lectures "On Our Knowledge of the Causes of the Phenomena of Organic Nature," in *Darwiniana: Essays* (New York: D. Appleton, 1912), p. 455.

5. Ibid. This second part of Huxley's statement is strangely omitted in *The Wisdom of Evolution* by R. J. Nogar (Garden City, N.Y.: Doubleday, 1963), p. 110.

6. *The Autobiography of Charles Darwin 1809–1882,* with original omissions restored, edited with appendix and notes by his granddaughter, Nora Barlow (New York: W. W. Norton, 1969), pp. 108–9.

7. "The Progress of Science" (1887) in *Method and Results* (London: Macmillan, 1894), pp. 103–4. The passage is another classic example of the workings of inner logic, in this case of radical empiricism, leading to a specific world view that had already been independently discovered and portrayed by others, such as Hume, of the same epistemological persuasion. Whereas Huxley was aware of the intimate connection of that world view with his agnosticism, if not atheism, its incompatibility with creative science remained hidden to him.

8. *The Function of Reason* (Princeton: Princeton University Press, 1929), p. 12.

9. *The Letters and Diaries of John Henry Newman,* edited with notes and introduction by C. S. Dessain and T. Gornall, vol. 25 (Oxford: Clarendon Press, 1973), p. 97. In the same letter of April 13, 1870, to W. R. Brownlow, Newman also points out that his preference for the argument from conscience over that from design is motivated by the fact that although many no longer believe in conscience, it is still remembered by all, and therefore gives a common ground for a demonstration, whereas the general disbelief in design deprives the theist of such ground. Newman also noted that the argument from design leads to a minimal notion of God and reveals nothing of his sanctity, mercy, and of the final judgment, "which three are of the essence of religion." Two months later, in his letter of June 5, 1870, to Pusey, Newman displayed a remarkable calm in connection with the millions of years postulated by Darwin's theory for man's ancestry. If there is no need to take literally the sun's coming to a halt at Joshua's command, he noted, why should one take literally the dust out of which man was formed (*The Letters and Diaries,* 25:137–38). Newman also set a sound pattern for theists in connection with Darwin's theory as he praised St. George Mivart's success (see note 13 below) in laying bare its non sequiturs. "In saying this," he wrote to Mivart on December 9, 1871, "you must not suppose I have personally any great dislike or dread of his theory, but many good people are much troubled at it—and at all events, without any disrespect to him, it is well to show that Catholics may be better reasoners than [natural] philosophers" (p. 446).

10. See *The Origin of Species by Charles Darwin: A Variorum Text,* ed. M. Peckham (Philadelphia: University of Pennsylvania Press, 1959), pp. 758–59. A few pages earlier Darwin made a similar insertion in the second edition (see p. 753).

11. *The Autobiography of Charles Darwin,* pp. 92–93.

12. Ibid., p. 140. This was a long-standing conviction with Darwin, as shown in his letter of June 14, 1859, to his publisher, J. Murray, from whom he begged understanding for his "incredibly bad style," due mainly to his "attention being fixed on the general line of argument, and not on details" (*The Life and Letters of Charles Darwin,* ed. F. Darwin [London: J. Murray, 1888], 2:158).

13. One of them, Loren Eiseley, points out, for instance, the curious ability of a book turned into a classic to conceal its contradictory details from most of its readers (*Darwin's Century: Evolution and the Men Who Discovered It* [1958; Garden City, N.Y.: Doubleday, 1961], p. 242). Another, P. J. Vorzimmer, provides the painstakingly documented evidence (*Charles Darwin: The Years of Controversy: The Origin of Species and Its Critics, 1859–1882* [Philadelphia: Temple University Press, 1970]) concerning Darwin's gradual retreat under the impact of criticism, of which the most incisive was *On the Genesis of Species* (1871) by St. George Mivart.

14. *The Autobiography of Charles Darwin*, p. 119.

15. "But I believe," Darwin wrote in a letter in 1861 after the publication of the second edition of the *Origin*, "in nat. selection, not because I can prove in any single case that it has changed one species into another, but because it groups and explains well (as it seems to me) a lot of facts in classification, embriology, morphology, rudimentary organs, geological succession & distribution." A photocopy of that letter, catalogued in the British Museum as A DD Ms 37725 f6, faces the title page of *L'évolution du monde vivant* by M. P. Vernet (Paris: Plon, 1950).

16. As bluntly stated by C. F. A. Pantin: "The old arguments for evolution were only based on circumstantial evidence. Each new fact made evolution seem more probable. But the core of Darwin's argument was of a different kind. It did not make evolution more probable—it made it a certainty. Given his facts his conclusion *must* follow: like a proposition in geometry: You do not show that any two sides of a triangle are very *probably* greater than the third. You show they *must* be so. Darwin's argument was a *de*ductive one—whereas an argument based on circumstantial evidence is *in*ductive" (*The History of Science: Origins and Results of the Scientific Revolution, A Symposium* [London: Cohen and West, 1951], p. 137).

17. T. Dobzhansky, *Genetics and the Origin of Species*, 3d rev. ed. (New York: Columbia University Press, 1951), p. 75.

18. G. G. Simpson, *The Major Features of Evolution* (New York: Columbia University Press, 1953), p. 271.

19. In his "The Principle of Evolution," a pamphlet written in 1895, Spencer tried to regain for himself credit for the idea of evolution, but by then the word had been firmly identified with Darwin. The basic differences between Darwin's and Spencer's views on evolution are given with full documentation in E. Gilson, *D'Aristôte à Darwin et retour: Essai sur quelques constantes de la biophilosophie* (Paris: J. Vrin, 1971), in sections with titles that deserve to be quoted: "Darwin sans l'Évolution" and "L'Evolution sans Darwin" (pp. 82–121).

20. See, for instance, the defense of Dewey's interpretation of Darwin's doctrine by J. H. Randall Jr. ("The Changing Impact of Darwin on Philosophy," *Journal of the History of Ideas* 22 [1961]: 435–62), and the critique of that defense by M. Grene, who wrote as late as 1974: "The firmest lesson of Darwinism for metaphysics . . . is of course the lesson of our own animal nature, our demotion from supernatural support to a place in nature comparable to that of any other living thing; . . . certainly the attempt to overcome Cartesian dualism, which still remains, alas, the major philosophic task of the waning twentieth century, found its first massive support in the Darwinian theory" (*The Understanding of Nature: Essays in the Philosophy of Biology* [Dordrecht: D. Reidel, 1975], p. 195).

21. The review appeared under the caption, "Genealogy for Mankind," p. 4, col. 6. The reviewer, G. F. Sheddon, regularly wrote reviews of science for the

Manchester Guardian. The heaviness of the dosage in question can be judged by the advice, "Keep away from Himmelfarb." given by some teachers at a prestigious American university to a senior working on a thesis concerned with Darwin (personal communication).

22. *Evolution in Action* (New York: Harper and Brothers, 1953), p. 7.

23. Whatever the intrinsic merit of belief in miracles, some scientifically heuristic value must be accorded to it if it enables a man of science to keep sharply in focus the difficulties of a scientific theory—as done, for instance, in *Evolution and Christians* by P. G. Fothergill (London: Longmans, 1961) and in *Flaws in the Theory of Evolution* by E. Shute (Nutley, N.J.: Craig Press, 1962). Yet, even apart from what belief in miracles can contribute to seeing the difficulties of Darwinism, the ultimate reason for its conflict with belief in miracles or, to be specific, with Christianity, can easily be found in its parading as a basic philosophy of life, as shown in the study of D. Lack, *Evolutionary Theory and Christian Belief: The Unresolved Conflict* (London: Methuen, 1957); see especially pp. 113–16.

24. "If this implies," he wrote to Galton on November 7, 1875, "that many parts are not modified by use and disuse during the life of the individual, I differ widely from you, as every year I come to attribute more and more to such agency" (*More Letters of Charles Darwin: A Record of His Work in a Series of Hitherto Unpublished Letters*, ed. F. Darwin and A. C. Seward [New York: D. Appleton and Company, 1903], 1:360.

25. *The Origin of Species ... A Variorum Text*, p. 60.

26. See letter of July 12, 1865 (1866?), to Huxley in *The Life and Letters of Charles Darwin*, 3:45.

27. Letter of July 11, 1861, to Julia Wedgwood, ibid., 1:313.

28. Ibid., p. 316.

29. *Autobiography*, p. 93. Darwin was not enough of a philosopher to consider the questions of what was the basis of the conclusion that all our knowledge depended on inheritance, and why was it less dangerous to inculcate this in children's minds than to inculcate belief in God, which, he complained in the same breath, "would be as difficult for them to throw off ... as for a monkey to throw off its instinctive fear and hatred of a snake."

30. Darwin reported in his *Autobiography* (p. 57) that in going up to Cambridge to study for the Anglican ministry he did not "in the least doubt the strict and literal truth of every word in the Bible" and that therefore he easily persuaded himself that the Creed "must be fully accepted." Of his time on board the Beagle, he wrote: "I was quite orthodox, and I remember being heartily laughed at by several of the officers (though themselves orthodox) for quoting the Bible as an unanswerable authority on some point of morality" (ibid., p. 85).

31. "Never use the word higher and lower," wrote Darwin on a slip of paper which he kept inserted in his copy of Chambers's *Vestiges of the Natural History of Creation* (see *More Letters*, 1:114).

32. "Scientific Use of the Imagination," in *Fragments of Science* (New York: P. F. Collier, 1901), p. 135.

33. "The Genealogy of Animals" (1869) in *Darwiniana: Essays*, p. 110, and "On the Reception of the *Origin of Species*" (1887) in *The Life and Letters of Charles Darwin*, 2:201.

34. In fact, no sooner had Gray written in his article, "Charles Darwin" (*Nature*, June 4, 1874, p. 81), that in view of "Darwin's great service to Natural Science ... instead of Morphology versus Teleology we shall have Morphology

wedded to Teleology" than Darwin wrote to Gray: "What you say about Teleology pleases me especially, and I do not think any one else has ever noticed the point" (*Life and Letters*, 3:189). A curious remark in view of Huxley's statement of 1869 quoted above.

35. *The Autobiography of Charles Darwin and Selected Letters*, ed. F. Darwin (New York: D. Appleton, 1882), p. 316.

36. *The Influence of Darwin on Philosophy* (New York: H. Holt, 1910), p. 13.

37. "The World into Which Darwin Led Us," *Science* 131 (1960): 972. As to Simpson's inference that "there is no need, at least, to postulate any non-natural or metaphysical intervention in the course of evolution," two remarks may be in order, one scientific and one metaphysical. It is the scientific burden of a proponent of automatic evolution to account for the nonautomatic features in man's behavior in general and for the presumably nonautomatic formulation of theories advocating universal automatism. As for metaphysics, it is indispensable to evolutionary theory not so much in relation to any point during the evolutionary process as in relation to its very start.

38. Eiseley did not voice the majority opinion in stating at the end of his *The Immense Journey* (New York: Vintage Books, 1957): "If 'dead' matter has reared up this curious landscape of fiddling crickets, song sparrows, and wondering men, it must be plain even to the most devoted materialist that the matter of which he speaks contains amazing, if not dreadful powers, and may not impossibly be, as Hardy has suggested, 'but one mask of the many worn by the Great Face behind.'"

39. Nor does science have an answer to Beadle's subsequent question, "Is it any less awe-inspiring to conceive of a universe created of hydrogen with the capacity to evolve into man than it is to accept the creation of man as man?" a question which on a closer look should inspire less awe than perplexity. The alleged turning of hydrogen into thinking and purposive beings is scientifically undemonstrated, to say nothing of its philosophical merit. Beadle's words are quoted from his talk before the Chicago Sunday Evening Club as reported by the *Chicago Daily News*, March 18, 1962.

40. *The View from a Distant Star: Man's Future in the Universe* (New York: Basic Books, 1963), p. 46.

41. On the contrary, it is stated there in connection with a seven-point summary of Darwin's theory: "This is the formal theory of evolution by natural selection, which recent observation and controlled experiment have proved to be correct in all cases" (3:572).

42. *The Origin of Species*, with an introduction by Sir Julian Huxley (New York: The New American Library, 1958), p. xiii.

43. Simpson sounded his warning in connection with his report (*Evolution* 10 [1956]: 333) of the proceedings of an international congress on paleontology held in Sabadell, Spain, in July 1954.

44. *Encyclopédie française, tome 5. Les êtres vivants* (Paris: Société de Gestion de l'Encyclopédie française, 1937), pp. 82–88. The editing of that volume was directed by P. Lemoine, R. Jeannee, and P. Allorge, all professors at the Muséum de Paris.

45. The role of chauvinism is undoubtedly overplayed in Himmelfarb's brief account of the unfavorable reception of Darwin's theory in France (*Darwin and the Darwinian Revolution*, pp. 303–4). For an explanation of it one should rather make use of Duhem's penetrating analysis of the respective ways of thinking of French and British men of science in his *The Aim and Structure of Physical Theory*, trans. Philip P. Wiener (Princeton: Princeton University Press, 1954), chap. 4.

46. *The Reign of Law,* by the duke of Argyll [George Douglas Campbell] (London: Alexander Strahan, 1867), p. 55.

47. The most massive record of those encomiums is provided in the three volumes of *Evolution after Darwin,* ed. Sol Tax (Chicago: University of Chicago Press, 1960). They represent the text of papers read and the panel discussions held at the University of Chicago Darwin centennial.

48. The statement is part of Gray's review of J. Huxley's *Evolution in Action* in *Nature* 173 (1954): 227. In connection with Huxley's admission that "the human species to-day is burdened with many more deleterious mutant genes than can possibly exist in any species of wild creatures" Gray rightly noted: "It seems a great pity that natural selection should have met its Waterloo just when it was most needed." No wonder that Huxley found Gray's comments "of major concern to general biological theory" (*Nature* 174 [1954]:279) and referred to evidence contained in various works, which prompted Gray to make the following rejoinder: "I can only say that none of the works to which Prof. Huxley refers, or appears to have in mind, gives me reason to believe that a 'conclusive demonstration' of the fact that certain things *can* happen is necessarily proof that they *have* happened. . . . Nor does a feeling of disappointment in natural selection as a working hypothesis during the past hundred years prove that biologists— prominent or otherwise—are either vitalists or Lamarckian fellow-travellers."

49. The latest of those data became widely shared public knowledge through the *Nature-Times News Service* (*Times* [London], May 11, 1976, p. 16), less than a week before this lecture was delivered. According to the findings of C. Wills of the University of California, single-celled baker's yeast responds when exposed to favorable and unfavorable light by turning through mutation into a new species which makes better use of the radiation. The report did not serve the "public" interest, however, as it failed to explain what is implied in the fact that in order to produce those mutant cells the geneticist must compress "into a few months the millions of years over which evolution naturally takes place."

50. "Geological Climates and the Origin of Species," *Quarterly Review* 126 (1869): 359–94.

51. "A consideration of the character of the grammar that is acquired, the degenerate quality and narrowly limited extent of the available data, the striking uniformity of the resulting grammars, and their independence of intelligence, motivation, and emotional state, over wide ranges of variation, leave little hope that much of the structure of the language can be learned by an organism initially uninformed as to its general character" (*Aspects of the Theory of Syntax* [Cambridge: M.I.T. Press, 1965], p. 58). But almost in the same breath Chomsky rejected the inference as naive that "man is, apparently, unique among animals in the way in which he acquires knowledge."

52. One such (fairly representative) chart indicating the convergence of the newly assumed four (three extinct) branches of man's family tree appeared in *Newsweek* (July 15, 1974, p. 72) as part of a report, the most telling part of which is the comment of the anatomist, Alan Walker: "Richard [Leakey] has found so many specimens recently that he has devalued the currency, so to speak. Now it is no longer possible to build an elaborate theory on the basis of a couple of teeth and an armbone."

53. *More Letters of Charles Darwin,* 1:450.

54. *The Origin of Species. . . . A Variorum Text,* p. 72.

55. The most careful and convincing study in that respect is still "The Probability of the Existence of a Self-Reproducing Unit," by E. P. Wigner (*The Logic of Personal Knowledge: Essays Presented to Michael Polanyi on His Seventieth Birthday* [London: Routledge and Kegan Paul, 1961], pp. 231–38), who in part

because of that improbability was led to postulate biotonic laws. See also his "Physics and the Explanation of Life," in *Philosophical Foundations of Science,* ed. R. J. Seeger and R. S. Cohen (Dordrecht: Reidel, 1974), pp. 119–32.

56. *Invention et finalité en biologie* (Paris: Flammarion, 1941), pp. 57–58. Cuénot was a biologist who instinctively recognized the presence of finality in nature, but who was unable to perceive that such a recognition was a metaphysical judgment however instinctive and immediate. In place of metaphysics he had to rest his case with ardent protest against attributing to chance the fact that "each type of eye from the most rudimentary to the most developed is complete in itself . . . . When one examines an animal, one does not hesitate for a moment to identify the eyes . . . . How could one assign to chance variations the recurring origin of such complexes with multiple interconnections?" (pp. 192–93). In that ardent protest he went so far as to postulate—in order "to safeguard the notion of universe as a coherent and rational system"—an "irrational factor," which was "irrational" with respect to the "rationality" of mechanism and which he described as "Anti-chance, a Will or Intelligence, which guides nature under the veil of secondary causes" (*Hasard ou finalité: L'inquiétude métaphysique,* Discours de réception à l'Académie Stanislas de Nancy, le 24 mai 1928 [Brussels: Editions du Renouveau, 1946], p. 36). The metaphysical anxiety and perplexity resulting from this pathetic conflict between the rationality of science and a superior irrationality safeguarding the rationality of the universe (and especially of the universe of the living) could but remain unresolvable within that pantheism to which Cuénot subscribed and which, unknown to him, was ultimately responsible for that conflict. Pantheism was endorsed by Cuénot in his capacity as a biologist in the "Conclusion des conclusions" of his *L'évolution biologique: Les faits, les incertitudes* (Paris: Masson, 1951), pp. 568–69.

57. *Creative Evolution,* in the authorized translation by Arthur Mitchell, with a foreword by Irwin Edman (New York: Random House, 1944), pp. 48–49.

58. "On the Hypothesis That Animals Are Automata, and Its History" (1874) in *Method and Results: Essays* (London: Macmillan, 1894), pp. 199–250.

59. For a detailed articulation of some of the following views see M. Polanyi, "Life's Irreducible Structure," *Science* 160 (1968): 1308–12. Polanyi fails to spell out the obvious metaphysical implications of his argument that the purposefulness of life cannot be explained in terms of mechanics. The "emergence" of ever-higher forms of life becomes therefore in Polanyi's presentation a purely phenomenological assertion devoid of precisely that explanatory strength which was his starting point but which he could not in the end vindicate because of his shying away from any reference to a realist metaphysics.

60. *The Autobiography of Charles Darwin,* p. 84.

61. A strong but just remark of P. G. Fothergill in his *Evolution and Christians,* p. 201.

62. *More Letters of Charles Darwin,* 1:321.

63. It made the American botanist Barry Commoner remark that "life is the secret of DNA" rather than the other way around (*Saturday Review,* October 1, 1966, p. 75). What most astonished Commoner was the fact that DNA and RNA molecules appear spontaneously only in living organisms.

64. *More Letters of Charles Darwin,* 1:321.

65. "It is not upon demonstrative evidence that we rely when we champion the doctrine of selection as a scientific truth; we base our argument on quite other grounds," declared Weismann at the centenary of the birth of Darwin, which was also the fiftieth anniversary of the publication of the *Origin.* See his essay, "The Selection Theory," in *Darwin and Modern Science* (Cambridge University Press, 1909), p. 25.

66. *The Causes of Evolution* (London: Longmans, Green & Co., 1932), pp. 5–6.

67. Letter of November 23, 1859, to Darwin; see *The Life and Letters of Charles Darwin*, 2:230.

68. *Darwiniana: Essays*, p. 467.

69. Ibid.

70. See C. E. Raven, *Science, Medicine and Morals* (New York: Harper and Brothers, 1959), p. 72. L. J. Burlingame's assertion in his article "Lamarck" (*Dictionary of Scientific Biography*, 7:593), that "much of Lamarckism has died out," was tellingly enough of a piece with his suggestion that there was only "seemingly purposive biological behavior."

71. Such is the strategy of E. Mayr, "Teleological and Teleonomic, a New Analysis," in *Methodological and Historical Essays in the Natural and Social Sciences*, ed. R. S. Cohen and M. W. Wartofsky (Dordrecht: D. Reidel, 1974), pp. 91–117.

72. As pointed out in detail by M. Grene, *The Understanding of Nature*, p. 174.

73. This delightful though very revealing phrase is attributed (and appropriately so) to Ernst Wilhelm von Brücke (1819–1892), one in the group formed by Müller, Helmholtz, Ludwig, and Du Bois-Reymond, determined to discredit vitalism once and for all. Being as poor philosophers as they were excellent physiologists they contributed much to the effort of throwing out the baby (teleology) with the bathwater (vitalism).

74. The most articulate of these efforts in S. Toulmin's "The Evolutionary Development of Natural Science" (*American Scientist* 55 [1967]: 456–71). Their common characteristic is the inner logic by which their authors are forced to make concepts and theories come alive and do the thinking and choices until recently reserved for the thinking individual.

75. As well exemplified in the concluding pages of T. S. Kuhn's *The Structure of Scientific Revolutions* (Chicago: University of Chicago Press, 1962), where the idea of scientific advance advocated in its pages is traced to the "conceptual transposition" undertaken by the West a century ago through the publication of Darwin's *Origin of Species*, which "recognized no goal set either by God or nature" (p. 171), but which, oddly enough, demanded recognition for the goal set by its author, a point never recalled by Darwinian biologists and historians of science.

76. As already noted in chaps. 3 and 5.

77. See *The Autobiography of Charles Darwin*, pp. 123 and 141.

78. He did so in his last major address, his Romanes Lecture "Evolution and Ethics" (*Evolution and Ethics and Other Essays* [New York: D. Appleton, 1914], pp. 46–86), in which Darwinian theory was unfolded in its ultimate implication: a concept of the universe steeped in the treadmill of eternal returns and void of any and all meaningful ethics. Huxley failed to perceive that the concept in question was the matrix of the stillbirth of science in all great ancient cultures, including the India of old conquered by Buddhism which Huxley endorsed, not without logic, in glowing terms.

CHAPTER NINETEEN

1. "The road ahead," as noted recently by two eminent cosmologists, "can hardly help being strewn with many a mistake. The main point is to get those mistakes made and recognized as fast as possible!" Charles M. Patton and John A. Wheeler, "Is Physics Legislated by Cosmogony?" in C. Isham, R. Penrose, and D. Sciama, *Quantum Gravity* (Oxford: Clarendon Press, 1975), p. 568.

2. F. J. Dyson, who offered this advice, took pains to emphasize that "very

few active scientists are particularly well informed about the history of science, and almost none of them are directly guided in their work by historical analogues." Then he drew a comparison between scientists and politicians: "The greatest politician of our century was probably Lenin, and he operated successfully within a historical viewpoint that was grossly limited and distorted. The only important historian of modern times to achieve high political office was François Guizot, prime minister of France during the 1840s, and all his historical understanding did not save him from mediocrity as a statesman. A good historian is too much committed to the past to be either a creative political leader or a creative scientist." See his "Mathematics in the Physical Sciences," *Scientific American* 211 (September 1964): 131.

3. See his letter of May 22, 1860, to A. Gray in *The Life and Letters of Charles Darwin*, ed. F. Darwin (London: J. Murray, 1888), 2:312. Obviously, if physical pain could not be reconciled with the idea of God, eternal punishment had to be declared that "damnable doctrine" which Darwin thought the Christian creed assigned unqualifiedly to any nonbeliever. See *The Autobiography of Charles Darwin 1809–1882*, with original omissions restored, edited with appendix and notes by his granddaughter, Nora Barlow (New York: W. W. Norton, 1969), pp. 87 and 90.

4. "Evolution and Ethics" (1893) in *Evolution and Ethics and Other Essays* (New York: D. Appleton, 1914), p. 80. No less credit should be given to Huxley for his blunt statement in the same context (p. 83): "Let us understand, once and for all, that the ethical progress of society depends, not on imitating the cosmic process, still less in running away from it, but in combating it." While most advocates of ethics in the teeth of their Darwinistic belief still have to match Huxley's perceptiveness on this point, they are just as unable as he was to explain the strange workings of that cosmic process which issues in a being or species, man, who must contradict that process in order to survive.

5. See his *Human Society in Ethics and Politics* (London: George Allen and Unwin, 1954), especially the chapter on "Sources of Ethical Beliefs and Feelings."

6. Logically enough, Darwin's reflections on ethics followed his recall of his spiritual journey from theism to agnosticism. See *The Autobiography of Charles Darwin*, pp. 93–94.

7. Ibid., p. 94.

8. Ibid.

9. Ibid., pp. 94–95.

10. In his letter of May 22, 1960, to A. Gray, in *The Life and Letters of Charles Darwin*, 2:312.

11. *The Autobiography of Charles Darwin*, p. 140. Of course, a "reasoned" rejection (and Darwin wanted his reasoning to appear as such) of the metaphysical validity of conscience presupposes precisely those qualities of mind which Darwin, in his own candid admission, did not possess: "My power to follow a long and abstract train of thought is very limited; I should, moreover, never have succeeded with metaphysics or mathematics."

12. A. Harrison, *Frederic Harrison: Thoughts and Memories* (London: William Heinemann, 1926), pp. 127–28. The real issue in the conversation was not, of course, traditional sexual morality, but the unconditional validity of morality as such. Harrison's remark, "morality cannot be twisted about to suit people's tastes," conveyed the inconsistency of a positivist unable to see that positivism was at its core pure relativism. Or as the whole dialogue was prefaced by young Harrison: "Positivism is in its very essence individualist, and, strange though this may appear to many people led astray by a French word which signifies the

converse of its meaning in our language, its whole basis is *relativity*, or the very opposite of the absolute, thus according considerable latitude to its interpreter, which my father made wide use of" (p. 126). And all other positivists, if one may add.

13. A recent example of this is a recommendation by a committee of the Swedish government to the parliament to abolish "repressive" laws against incest. The recommendation flies in the face of basic demands of the biological interest of the human species, but is in perfect harmony with biologism, or a philosophy which has its origin in the replacement of metaphysics with biology only to find in the end that the tactic inevitably leads to flouting some of the most vital findings of biology. That the abolition, if granted, may turn all Swedes into "look-alikes" (*National Review*, April 2, 1976, p. 309) may seem a rude sarcasm, but a badly needed one when common sense and decency fail so drastically.

14. R. S. Morison, "Where Is Biology Taking Us?" *Science* 155 (1967): 431.

15. "Mr. Darwin's Critics" (1871) in *Darwiniana: Essays* (New York: D. Appleton, 1912), p. 147. The "critics" were actually but one, St. George Mivart, Darwin's most formidable critic and a Roman Catholic.

16. The passage forms part of the concluding reflections in Spencer's *An Autobiography* (London: Williams and Norgate, 1904), 2:467.

17. The two letters were written on December 19, 1860, and January 16, 1861, respectively, and in both the reference to Darwin begins with an allusion to Marx's recent trials during which he had read "all sorts of books, among them Darwin's"—the "heavy English presentation" of which is deplored in both cases. In the letter to Lassalle Marx credited Darwin for having dealt "a death blow to teleology in natural sciences" and for having explained their rational meaning empirically. See Karl Marx and Frederick Engels, *Selected Correspondence 1846–1895*, with explanatory notes, trans. Dona Torr (New York: International Publishers, 1942), pp. 125–26. Marx's admiration for the *Origin* was so great as to request its author to accept the dedication of the English translation of *Das Kapital*, a request which Darwin declined with thanks.

18. The quality of that light is revealed in what Carnegie added in the next breath: "Not only had I got rid of theology and the supernatural, but I had found the truth of evolution. 'All is well since all grows better' became my motto, my true source of comfort" (*Autobiography of Andrew Carnegie* [Garden City, N.Y.: Doubleday Doran Company, 1933], p. 327). As in countless other cases, the abandonment of the supernatural for the natural meant the espousal of a nature with powers that were vying with the supernatural.

19. "Wealth," *North American Review* 148 (1889): 655.

20. Rockefeller regaled the Y.M.C.A. at Brown University with these ideas in an address given on Wednesday evening, February 5, 1902. Later that year brief quotations from his address, including a reference to the rose "American Beauty" appeared in *Our Benevolent Feudalism* by W. J. Ghent (New York: Macmillan Company, 1902, p. 29), but no sources were given. Ghent's quotations were taken over by R. Hofstadter (*Social Darwinism in American Thought*, 1944, rev. ed. [Boston: Beacon Press, 1955], p. 45), a circumstance which gave them wide publicity. My quotations are from the hundred-word-long outline of the address kindly sent to me by Joseph W. Ernst, director of the Rockefeller Archive Center.

21. It is a telling evidence of the inner weakening of the free enterprise world that the British representative at the United Nations objected to the presence of "political ideology" in the speech by which the American representative denounced the resolution branding Israel with racism.

22. In his letter of June 5, 1861, to A. Gray; *The Life and Letters of Charles Darwin*, 2:374.

23. In his letter of July 3, 1881, to W. Graham; ibid., 1:316.

24. Ibid. That Darwin, who wanted to bring man under the same head as animals, failed to see to the end, in spite of his endorsement of warfare by superior races, the relevance of his theory to social dynamics, is one more instance of his baffling inability to pursue "abstract" reasoning.

25. *The Scientific Origins of National Socialism: Social Darwinism in Ernst Haeckel and the German Monist League* (London: Macdonald, 1971), p. 6.

26. *Freedom in Science and Teaching*, with a prefatory note by T. H. Huxley (London: C. Kegan Paul, 1879), p. 91.

27. Ibid., p. 92.

28. Ibid.

29. Ibid., p. 93.

30. Ibid.

31. Ibid.

32. See Gassman, *The Scientific Origins of National Socialism*, p. 132.

33. *Selections from Treitschke's Lectures on Politics*, trans. Adam L. Gowans (London: Gowans & Gray, 1916), p. 22.

34. Ibid., p. 39.

35. Ibid., p. 11.

36. Ibid.

37. *Germany and the Next War*, trans. A. H. Powles (London: Longmans Green & Co., 1912), pp. 6, 15, 17, 18, 20, 22.

38. One of the officers, as Kellogg recalled it in his *Human Life as the Biologist Sees It* (New York: H. Holt & Company, 1922, p. 51) "was a professional biologist of much repute, a professor of zoology in one of the larger German universities." That admiration for a great scientist can easily blind his devotees to the humanly disturbing aspects of his basic ideas is well evidenced in Kellogg's claim that it is permissible only "from a post-Darwinian point of view that goes much beyond Darwin's own conceptions" to assume "that natural selection is the all-powerful factor, almost the sole really important factor in organic evolution. And that as man as an animal species is subject to the control of the same major evolutionary factors as control the other animal kinds, his evolutionary progress or fate is to be decided on the basis of a rigid, relentless, natural selection" (ibid., p. 54).

39. *Heartbreak House, Great Catherine, and Playlets of the War* (1919; London: Constable and Company, 1925), p. xiii. The "religion" as described by Shaw is best rendered in his own words: "In the middle of the XIX century naturalists and physicists assured the world, in the name of Science, that salvation and damnation are all nonsense, and that predestination is the central truth of religion, inasmuch as human beings are produced by their environment, their sins and good deeds being only a series of chemical and mechanical reactions over which they have no control. Such figments as mind, choice, purpose, conscience, will, and so forth, are, they taught, mere illusions, produced because they are useful in the continual struggle of the human machine to maintain its environment in a favorable condition, a process incidentally involving the ruthless destruction or subjection of its competitors for the supply ... of subsistence available." Shaw did his best to minimize Darwin's role in the rise and spread of that religion. Darwin was merely the great naturalist reacting "against a barbarous pseudo-evangelical teleology intolerably obstructive to all scientific progress." Shaw went on to state—falsely—that teleology had no useful role in scientific investigation and that subsequent "extraordinary dis-

coveries in physics and chemistry" evinced the truth "of that lifeless method of evolution which its investigators called Natural Selection." Such a mixture of keen artistic sensitivity to inhumane falsehood garbed in science and of misinformation about science could only lead to the dejected conclusion: "Howbeit, there was only one result possible in the ethical sphere; and that was the banishment of conscience from human affairs" (p. xiv).

40. In his foreword to *Darwin's Theory Applied to Mankind* by A. Machin (London: Longmans, Green and Co., 1937), p. viii.

41. "I did wish the world to try a new experiment—an experiment that would keep the dogs of war kennelled up for five centuries" (ibid.), the experiment being the turning of the Geneva of the League of Nations into a Jerusalem of Peace for Europe.

42. A claim made in Keith's Conway Memorial Lecture, *The Religion of a Darwinist* (London: Watts & Co., 1925), p. 70.

43. *Evolutionary Ethics* (London: Oxford University Press, 1943), pp. 44–45.

44. See B. Chobuda, *Of Time, Light and Hell: Essays in Interpretation of the Christian Message* (The Hague: Mouton, 1974), p. 72. Quite understandably, L. de Grandmaison, editor of *Etudes* and a confrère of Teilhard, did not accept for publication the evolutionary apotheosis of war ("The Promised Land" in *Writings in Time of War*, trans. R. Hague [New York: Harper and Row, 1968], pp. 278–88) which Teilhard sent him in February 1919.

45. *In the Matter of J. Robert Oppenheimer* (Washington, D.C.: U.S. Government Printing Office, 1954), p. 649.

46. The statement was made in Boston on November 10, 1948.

47. "Science, Ethics and Politics," *Science* 125 (1957): 225–26.

48. *Science and Human Values* (New York: Harper and Row, 1965), p. 84. This smallish book is burdened throughout with sweeping generalizations, with a pseudophilosophy, and with a shallow acquaintance with the history of science coupled with its exploitation on behalf of an agnosticist humanism.

49. The title of Bronowski's much publicized book brought through its video transcript to countless television viewers.

50. *Science and Human Values*, p. 74.

51. *Public Knowledge: An Essay concerning the Social Dimension of Science* (Cambridge University Press, 1968), p. 22.

52. Romans 1:32.

53. Quoted in R. Jungk, *Brighter than a Thousand Suns*, trans. J. Cleugh (New York: Harcourt, 1958), p. 199.

54. *In the Matter of J. Robert Oppenheimer*, p. 81.

55. See *The Opus Majus of Roger Bacon*, edited with introduction and analytical table by J. H. Bridges (Oxford: Clarendon Press, 1897), 2:633. The long section on experimental philosophy is followed by an equally long section on moral philosophy!

56. See *Léonard de Vinci par lui-même*. Textes choisis, traduits et présentés par A. Chastel (Paris: Nagel, 1952), pp. 156–57.

57. This phrase (*New Organon*, bk. 1, aph. 129, in *The Works of Francis Bacon*, ed. J. Spedding, R. L. Ellis, D. D. Heath [New York: Garrett Press, 1968], 4:115) is a variant on the one which completes the preceding quotation from Bacon's "Of the Interpretation of Nature" (1604), in *Works*, 3:218.

58. In his *Essai sur l'application de l'analyse à la probabilité des décisions rendues à la pluralité des voix* (Paris: Imprimerie Royale, 1785) Condorcet contended that miscarriages of justice should be accepted when the chances for it are not greater than the risks of taking a mailboat from Calais to Dover in good weather, or of dying between the age of thirty-seven and forty-seven of a sickness that

lasts less than a week. Since tables of statistics showed that the chances of the latter were approximately equal to 1/150,000, he could easily outline the composition of a tribunal of thirty judges each of whom would make only one wrong judgment out of ten, and nineteen of whom should agree in the sentence. See "Discours préliminaire," pp. cix and clxiv–vii.

59. *Précis du siècle de Louis XV,* in *Oeuvres de Voltaire* (Paris: Garnier Frères, 1877–85), 15:434.

60. The story, perhaps apocryphal, matches the deist Voltaire's ambivalent attitude toward atheism and atheists as evidenced by the many entries under these words in the index of the *Oeuvres.*

61. *Souvenirs d'enfance et de jeunesse* (Paris: Calmann Lévy, 1883), pp. 359–60.

62. The charge, if made within the narrow perspectives of a historian of technology, can only lead to even narrower theologizing. Such is the contrasting by L. White, Jr., of "the Christian axiom that nature has no reason for existence save to serve man" with what "the greatest spiritual revolutionary in Western history, Saint Francis" thought was "an alternative Christian view of nature and man's relation to it," namely, "the idea of the equality of all creatures, including man" ("The Historical Roots of Our Ecologic Crisis" *Science* 155 [1967]: 1207). Such flimsy evaluation of "Christian axiom" and of Saint Francis not only entitles the author to say that "orthodox Christian arrogance toward nature" must first be rejected if the ecologic crisis is to be solved, but also clears the ground for those who like P. Singer, author of *Animal Liberation: A New Ethics for Our Treatment of Animals* (New York: New York Review of Books, 1975), claim that doing an experiment on a dying dog is more objectionable than experimenting with a dying human fetus, because "it is the dog that is the more intelligent, sensitive, and autonomous being" (*New York Review of Books,* August 5, 1976, p. 34). For an unsparing exposure of the fallacies and hypocrisy present in efforts that blame Christianity for the impending disaster in ecology, see R. V. Young, Jr., "Christianity and Ecology," *National Review* 26 (1974): 1454–58, 1477, and 1479.

63. "Science and Ethics," *Science* 86 (1937): 595.

64. *F.A.S. Public Interest Report,* vol. 28, no. 10, see especially pp. 6 and 10.

65. A. Vucinich, "Science and Morality: A Soviet Dilemma," *Science* 159 (1968): 1208–12.

66. On the contrary, they emphasized the irrelevance of physics concerning the subject. See my *The Relevance of Physics* (Chicago: University of Chicago Press, 1966), pp. 381–82.

67. "Our new-found freedom is like that of the mass of 0.001 mg. which is only allowed to stray 1/5000 mm in a thousand years," wrote Eddington in his *The New Pathways in Science* (Cambridge University Press, 1934), p. 88. Five years later he recognized that such an approach to the question of freedom of will was "nonsense" (*The Philosophy of Physical Science* [London: Macmillan, 1939], p. 182).

68. See his remarks in *The Born-Einstein Letters: Correspondence between Albert Einstein and Max and Hedwig Born from 1916 to 1955, with Commentaries by Max Born,* trans. Irene Born (New York: Walker and Company, 1971), p. 154.

69. *The Freedom of Man* (New Haven: Yale University Press, 1935), p. 26.

70. They are as a rule quickly exposed, although more than a decade elapsed before attention was focused on the possible nonexistence of Misses M. Howard and J. Conway, two chief coworkers of Sir Cyril Burt, and on the forged character of his research data from the period 1955–66. See N. Wade, "IQ and Heredity: Suspicion of Fraud Beclouds Classic Experiment," *Science* 194 (1976): 916–19.

71. Quoted in C. A. Coulson, *Science and Christian Belief* (Chapel Hill: University of North Carolina Press, 1955), p. 64.

72. For one such model-making, see G. Basalla, "The Spread of Western Science," *Science* 156 (1967): 611–21.

73. From the flood of comments released by the statement of a committee on genetic engineering of the National Academy of Sciences (see *Science* 185 [1974]: 303) let here be recalled the "harrowing prospect of parents shopping in a genetic supermarket, or of a tyrant specifying the genes in his subjects" raised by Bernard D. Davis in his editorial, *Science*, October 25, 1974.

74. "Evolution and Ethics," pp. 80–81. More generally, as Huxley noted, "social progress means a checking of the cosmic process at every step and the substitution for it of another."

75. *The Ethical Animal* (London: George Allen & Unwin, 1960), pp. 210–11.

76. See R. W. Clark: *Einstein: The Life and Times* (New York: Thomas Y. Crowell, 1971), p. 10.

77. See A. Moszkowski, *Einstein the Searcher: His Work Explained from Dialogues with Einstein*, trans. H. L. Brose (London: Methuen, 1921), p. 99. Contrary to G. Sarton (*The Study of the History of Science* [Cambridge: Harvard University Press, 1936], p. 51), Einstein himself did not make such a claim about Beethoven. But he made it very clear to Moszkowski that in his estimation the novelty in an artistic invention far exceeded that of a scientific discovery.

78. The story told by M. Baring is reported in Norman St. John-Stevas's lecture, "Laws and the Moral Consensus," in *Life or Death: Ethics and Options*, text of six lectures given at a symposium on the sanctity of life held at Reed College, Oregon, March 11–12, 1966, under the sponsorship of Bess Kaiser Hospital and Reed College (Reed College, Oregon, 1968), p. 49.

79. To what has already been pointed out in note 46 of chapter 12, let here only be added the incisive remark made by A. Sommerfeld in connection with Einstein's essay of 1905 on special relativity: "Not the *relativizing* of the perceptions of length and duration are the chief point for him, but the *independence of natural laws*, particularly those of electrodynamics and optics, *of the standpoint of the observer*. The essay has, of course, absolutely nothing whatsoever to do with ethical relativism, with the 'Beyond Good and Evil'" (*Albert Einstein: Philosopher-Scientist*, ed. P. A. Schilpp [Evanston: Library of Living Philosophers, 1949], p. 99).

80. A case in point is J. B. Conant's declaration, "to my mind, there is no escape from the conclusion that ethics cannot be based on science," in his *Scientific Principles and Moral Conduct* (Cambridge University Press, 1967), p. 33.

81. Ibid., p. 37.

82. "The man of education will seek exactness so far in each subject as the nature of the thing admits, it being plainly much the same absurdity to put up with a mathematician who tries to persuade instead of proving, and to demand strict demonstrative reasoning of a rhetorician," as goes the advice in the opening section of the *Nicomachean Ethics* (1094b). Quoted in J. A. Smith's translation, *The Ethics of Aristotle* (London: J. M. Dent and Sons, 1911), p. 3.

83. For an informative survey, see L. J. Brinkley, *Contemporary Ethical Theories* (New York: Philosophical Library, 1961).

84. W. E. H. Lecky, *History of European Morals from Augustus to Charlemagne* (New York: D. Appleton and Company, 1869), 1:91.

85. *The Myth of Sisyphus and Other Essays*, translated from the French by Justin O'Brien (New York: Vintage Books, 1960), p. 42.

86. See L. M. Rieser, "The Role of Science in the Orwellian Decade," *Science* 184 (1974): 486–89.

87. For an endorsement of that "Democritean" ethics, see K. R. Popper, *The Open Society and Its Enemies* (Princeton University Press, 1950), pp. 222 and 641. That the ethics in question is sheer pragmatism can easily be seen from Popper's allying it with Epicurean ethics.

Chapter Twenty

1. *Pascal's Pensées*, trans. W. F. Trotter, with an introduction by T. S. Eliot (New York: E. P. Dutton, 1959), p. 74 (no. 252).

2. Ibid.

3. Ibid., p. 73 (no. 252).

4. Ibid., p. 72 (no. 244).

5. Ibid., p. 70 (no. 242). Pascal possibly had in mind Mersenne's prolific extraction of proofs from every nook and cranny of nature as he remarked in the same context: "[to tell] persons destitute of faith and grace ... that they have only to look at the smallest things which surround them, and they will see God openly ... is to give them ground for believing that the proofs of our religion are very weak."

6. It is rarely remembered that both the first and the last philosophical writings of Voltaire were a series of vitriolic remarks on Pascal's *Pensées*. The former was written in 1728, the latter in 1777 (see *Oeuvres complètes de Voltaire* [Paris: Garnier Frères, 1877–85], 22:27–61 and 31:3–40). The former came to a close with the remark that "it has been customary to present as rules the *pensées* which Pascal probably jotted down as doubts. It is not necessary to believe as demonstrated what he himself would have refuted." The true quality of that remark can easily be grasped from Voltaire's comment—"Is it possible that Pascal should be the one who does not feel himself strong enough to prove the existence of God?"—on Pascal's *pensée*: "I do not intend here to demonstrate by natural reasons either the existence of God or the ... immortality of the soul or anything of the kind; not only because I would not feel myself strong enough to find in nature something by which to convince *hardened* atheists, but also because such knowledge, without Jesus Christ, is useless and sterile" (*Oeuvres*, 22:60–61). The sole objection that could have been made to this *pensée* was its latent Jansenism, hardly an issue with Voltaire.

7. The phrase in the *Elémens de la philosophie de Newton* (1738), "car si selon Newton (et selon la raison) le monde est fini ... " (*Oeuvres*, 22:403), is a subtle indication of the superiority of reason as conceived by Voltaire over the reasoning and, what is even worse, the very dicta of Newton.

8. See his letter of January 8, 1777, to Condorcet, in *Oeuvres*, 50:171.

9. *Pascal's Pensées*, p. 74 (no. 253).

10. What Voltaire said in this connection in his *Essai sur les moeurs* (*Oeuvres de Voltaire*, 11:173) has a genuine ring of modernity, including its evasiveness: "It seems that nature has given to this species of men, so different from ours, faculties adapted for finding with one stroke all that was necessary for them and unable to go beyond. We, however, acquired our notions very late and brought all to perfection very quickly." But Voltaire saw in the superstitiousness, which did not cease plaguing Chinese astronomy, a general human characteristic and merely registered that we in the West had been cured of it lately. Nor did Voltaire enter into the relation of the universality of natural reason to the peculiarity of Chinese writing in which he saw one of the two specific reasons for the backwardness of Chinese science. The other, the proverbial respect of the Chinese for their parents and ancestors, would have also warranted some reflection.

11. *Pascal's Pensées*, p. 163 (no. 592).

12. Ibid.

13. Yet the measure of scholarship evidenced in A. Gaubil's studies of Chinese astronomy, published by E. Souciet between 1729 and 1732, and in J. B. du Halde's massive synthesis of Chinese lore set forth in 1735 in four folio volumes, was as high as one could expect at that time in a field so difficult to survey owing to geographical remoteness and to the unusually high language barrier, to say nothing of the secretiveness of the Chinese about themselves.

14. *Essai sur les moeurs* in *Oeuvres*, 11:230. In letting Jesus Christ appear at long last on the scene of history, Voltaire would not have been himself had he not tried to discredit in the same breath "the Founder of true religion" by contrasting him with his foundation untrue to him.

15. In addition to what he offered on this topic in his *Histoire de l'astronomie ancienne* and in his *Lettres sur l'origine des sciences* (see chap. 1 for details and documentation) he gave it a full treatment in his *Lettres sur l'Atlantide de Platon et sur l'ancienne histoire de l'Asie* (London: M. Elmesly; Paris: Frères Debure, 1779).

16. The topic is still to be aired in full. Glimpses of what may turn out to be a rude awakening for those still seeing in the leaders of the French Enlightenment the fair-minded champions of sheer rationality can be had from reading chapter 4, "The Grand Order," in E. B. Smith's monograph, "Jean-Sylvain Bailly: Astronomer, Mystic, Revolutionary, 1736–1793," *Transactions of the American Philosophical Society* 44, pt. 4 (1954): 427–538; see especially pp. 465–67.

17. In his letter of March 5, 1777, to Voltaire, in *Voltaire's Correspondence,* ed. T. Besterman (Geneva: Institut et Musée Voltaire, 1953–65), 96:100. The epithet matched in thrust Voltaire's reference to Bailly as "Pascal" (ibid., p. 91), a reference which must have been quite familiar in Voltaire's circle, as shown by d'Alembert's description of Bailly as "Condor Pascal" in his letter of March 6, 1777, to Voltaire (ibid., p. 104). That the name of Pascal was chosen as the vehicle for biting sarcasm reveals something of the genuineness of his Christian theism, which indeed cast a long shadow on the deism of Voltaire and even more so on the atheism of some of his most prominent correspondents.

18. A glance at the index of names in Popper's books reveals the drastic character of his write-off of one and a half millennia in the history of philosophy, the epoch stretching from Aristotle to Aquinas, as the age of the unqualified error of essentialism. The procedure can seem rational criticism only to those who had already made up their minds before starting their work of criticism.

19. Thus, for instance, J. Agassi, "Science in Flux: Footnotes to Popper," in *Boston Studies in the Philosophy of Science* (Dordrecht: D. Reidel, 1968), 3:318.

20. See his essay on *The Ecclesiastical and Political History of the Popes* by L. Ranke in *Edinburgh Review* 72 (1841): 230. The remark should be seen in its contrasting light, namely, the indisputable verity which was accorded by Macaulay and his contemporaries to mathematics and physics. They did not suspect that mathematics was soon to divorce itself from the problems of physics, a step which not only provided it with autonomy but also led to Gödel's disclosure of the fundamental lack of consistency in any nontrivial mathematical system.

21. As if by symbolic fate, Leibniz made the suggestion as Newton's *Principia,* which seemed to provide the supreme seal of approval to the truth of a mechanical conception of the world, was being printed and published. In his "Discourse on Metaphysics" (1686) Leibniz emphasized the presence in physical laws of teleology, which he identified with minimum principles, such as the one evident in the path followed by refracted light. His discussion of "the

utility of final causes in physics" reminded him of a "fine disquisition by Socrates in Plato's *Phaedo*, which agrees perfectly with my opinion on this subject and seems to have been uttered expressly for our too materialistic philosophers." A year later, in his essay-letter to Bayle "On a General Principle, Useful for the Explanation of Laws of Nature" he claimed that "very far from excluding final causes and the consideration of a being acting with wisdom, we must from these deduce everything in physics," and again referred to Socrates' discourse in the *Phaedo* on true physics, which, he said, "deserves to be read in its entirety, for it contains very beautiful and solid reflections" (*Leibniz Selections*, ed. Philip P. Wiener [New York: Charles Scribner's Sons, 1951], pp. 320 and 69–70). It wholly escaped Leibniz that Socrates certainly did not mean to cure the shortcomings of mechanism with sinking deeper into it. Nor did it dawn on Leibniz that the "very solid reflections" of Socrates had a very serious flaw, namely, the going from the extreme of mechanism to the extreme of exclusive teleology. It shows something of the irresistible sway of mechanism that Leibniz, a sincere Christian, failed to perceive that a recognition of the respective merits of mechanism and teleology could only be done within a perspective which only Christian theism could provide both historically and philosophically.

22. Quoted in R. C. Batchelder, *The Irreversible Decision: 1939–1950* (Boston: Houghton Mifflin, 1962), p. 46.

23. As reported in *U.S. News & World Report* (July 22, 1974, p. 47), the odor-measuring machine cost $28,361, whereas the tricycle study cost $19,300. In the same report one is informed also of a study of the impact of rural road construction in Poland costing $85,000 and of a study on teaching mothers how to play with their children costing more than half a million dollars.

24. However, since Aristotle emphatically rejected the possibility of a creation out of nothing, he had to restrict the notion of contingency to what he called chance events, in which the consistency of natural processes suffered a breakdown. The insufficient depth of the Aristotelian notion of contingency as having its origin in Aristotle's rejection of the notion of creation out of nothing is overlooked in *Time and Necessity: Studies in Aristotle's Theory of Modality* (Oxford: Clarendon Press, 1973; see especially pp. 93–113), by J. Hintikka, who refers to no scholastic criticism and reinterpretation of Aristotle's thought on this point. The oversight is rather curious, as part of Hintikka's discussion is devoted to the shortcomings of Lovejoy's account of the history of the principle of plenitude from the Stoics to Leibniz.

25. As was admitted by S. Pines in his "What Was Original in Arabic Science?" (*Scientific Change*, ed. A. C. Crombie [New York: Basic Books, 1963], pp. 204–5), criticism of Aristotle in Muslim ambience failed to develop into a trend comparable in impact to criticism of Aristotle in the Christian West.

26. For a criticism of W. Hartner's oversight of this factor in his discussion of the decline of cultural and scientific enterprise among the Arabs ("Quand et comment s'est arrêté l'essor de la culture scientifique dans l'Islam?" in R. Brunschvicg and G. E. von Grunebaum, eds., *Classicisme et déclin culturel dans l'histoire de l'Islam* [Paris: Éditions Besson-Chantemerle, 1957], pp. 319–37), see my *Science and Creation: From Eternal Cycles to an Oscillating Universe* (Edinburgh: Scottish Academic Press, 1974), pp. 212–13.

27. A process even longer if considered, with A. C. Crombie, as stretching from "Augustine to Galileo," the title of the first edition of his now classic *Medieval and Early Modern Science* (Garden City, N.Y.: Doubleday, 1959).

28. *Autobiography of John Stuart Mill*, published for the first time without alterations or omissions from the original manuscript in the possession of Co-

lumbia University, with a preface by J. J. Cross (New York: Columbia University Press, 1924), p. 167. Mill then pointed to the need for a new, merely human religious faith!

29. End of the preface of *Cosmologia Sacra; or, A Discourse of the Universe As It Is the Creature and Kingdom of God* (London: W. Rogers, 1701).

30. In a letter of September 23, 1860, to the Rev. Charles Kingsley, who broached to Huxley the belief in resurrection on learning of the death of his son at the tender age of seven. See L. Huxley, *Life and Letters of Thomas Henry Huxley* (London: Macmillan, 1900), 1:219.

31. *The Openness of Being: Natural Theology Today* (Philadelphia: Westminster Press, 1971).

32. The story first saw print in 1804, in Dieudonné Thiébault's *Mes souveniers de vingt ans de séjour à Berlin* . . . , a work immediately translated into English under the title, *Original Anecdotes of Frederic the Second, King of Prussia, and of His Family, His Court, His Ministers, His Academics, and His Literary Friends; Collected During a Familiar Intercourse of Twenty Years with that Prince* (London: J. Johnson, 1805), 2:4. From there it passed into *A Budget of Paradoxes* (2d ed., D. E. Smith [Chicago: Open Court, 1915], 2:339) by A. De Morgan whose account is reprinted in *The World of Mathematics*, ed. J. R. Newman (New York: Simon and Schuster, 1956), 4:2377–78. *Diderot: L'homme de science* by J. Mayer (Rennes: Imprimerie Bretonne, 1959) contains a review of reasons militating against the authenticity of the story of which the principal is Diderot's well-attested familiarity with elementary algebra (pp. 93–96).

33. Both in *The Two Cultures and the Scientific Revolution: The Rede Lecture 1959* (Cambridge University Press, 1959) and in its second edition, enlarged by an essay, "A Second Look," Snow's reply to his critics, who came mostly from the ranks of humanists. One of the few scientists who strongly disagreed with Snow was F. Hoyle who noted in his *Of Men and Galaxies* (Seattle: University of Washington Press, 1964, p. 24) that "creative spirit cannot be engendered by five-year plans," a remark whose validity was offset by Hoyle's identifying the stimulus of scientific creativity in attention to the needs of society. Hoyle failed to explain in what sense Copernicus, Newton, and Einstein were motivated by awareness of the needs of their times while doing creative work in science. See my *Culture and Science: Two Lectures Delivered at Assumption University, Windsor (Canada) on February 26 and 28, 1975* (Windsor: University of Windsor Press, 1976), p. 26.

34. See *The Two Cultures: And a Second Look* (Cambridge University Press, 1969), pp. 16–21.

35. In addressing in 1966 the Committee of the U.S. House of Representatives on science and astronautics, Snow claimed that men of wisdom who lacked scientific training were preferable to scientists without wisdom when it came to making vital policy decisions, although he stressed at the same time that this was not a realistic alternative. See *Science* 151 (1966): 651.

36. See "La tentation de l'Occident" in his *Antimémoires*, new rev. ed. (Paris: Gallimard, 1972), pp. 265–379.

37. This seems at least to be the thrust of Butterfield's remark that the study of the history of science "is going to be as important to us for the understanding of ourselves as Graeco-Roman antiquity was for Europe during a period of over a thousand years" ("The History of Science and the Study of History," *Harvard Library Bulletin* 13 [1959]: 331). In the same context Butterfield also noted that the study of the history of science "has become something more than a hobby for the ex-scientist or a harmless occupation for a crank." In fact, historians and philosophers of science constitute today an easily identifiable and academically

well-established body of intellectuals ready to challenge sundry statements of leading scientists, past *and* present, and are in the process of taking over from them the culturally crucial role of interpreting science to society at large. They will find, however, that the incompetence of scientists in matters philosophical, the field of interpretation par excellence, will not be remedied by that pseudometaphysics of historicism, sociologism and psychologism, in which most of their numbers are nowadays taking refuge—a point which a theologian attentive to the contributions of science can ignore only at grave peril.

38. Hardly a cause for surprise, since T. S. Warshaw brought to focus the "cultural deprivation" as evidenced by the unfamiliarity of otherwise bright and highly informed college-bound high school juniors and seniors with simple biblical allusions. The report, originally published in the *English Journal*, was given immediate wide publicity in *Time*, March 20, 1964, p. 44.

39. As actually happened at the Eotvös (formerly Pázmány Péter) University in Budapest, Hungary's leading university.

40. Even more curiously, the statement was made in connection with the merits of cosmologies presenting a temporal and an atemporal universe, respectively: "There is little that can be said at this time about why there would be an atemporal universe. The question is a form of the ancient philosophical problem of 'Why is there Being?' and this appears to be one that cannot be very profitably discussed." R. Schlegel, author of the foregoing statement (*Completeness in Science* [New York: Appleton-Century-Crofts, 1967], p. 146), failed to perceive that the atemporal universe of steady-state theory gained a wholly unmerited scientific respectability precisely because so many cosmologists have grown insensitive to the fundamental profit derivable from such questions.

41. The illusion has for its source Gödel's theorem, according to which nontrivial mathematical sytems (and these must of necessity underlie any modern cosmological and elementary-particle theory presented with or without that illusory claim) cannot have their proof of consistency within themselves. The proof of the claim can therefore be had only from empirical data, or rather from the claim that its scientist-proponent knows everything about the universe that can be known about it empirically, a claim which can be the source not only of self-deceit but also of well-merited ridicule. See also my paper, "The 'Chaos' of Scientific Cosmology," read at the Twelfth Nobel Conference (Gustavus Adolphus College, Saint Peter, Minnesota, October 6 and 7, 1976) the topic of which was "The Nature of the Physical Universe." Others who read papers at that conference were M. Gell-Mann, V. F. Weisskopf, H. Putnam, S. Weinberg, and Sir Fred Hoyle, who all participated in the panel discussions. The papers and the substance of the discussions will be published by John Wiley, Inc., New York.

42. The most systematic of them was, undoubtedly, J. B. Cobb, Jr., author of *A Christian Natural Theology Based on the Thought of Alfred North Whitehead* (Philadelphia: Westminster Press, 1965).

43. As aptly noted by E. Gilson in his *D'Aristote à Darwin et retour: Essai sur quelques constantes de la biophilosophie* (Paris: J. Vrin, 1971), p. 189.

44. As set forth convincingly by Gilson in his William James Lectures, *The Unity of Philosophical Experience* (New York: Charles Scribner's Sons, 1937). A reasonable approach to the universals, of course, can be had only on the basis of that moderate realism which Gilson characterized in another context in words that cannot be reprinted often enough: "The first step on the path of realism is to recognize that one has always been a realist; the second is to recognize that, however much one tries to think differently, one will never succeed; the third is

to note that those who claim that they think differently think as realists as soon as they forget to act a part. If they ask themselves why, their conversion is almost complete" (*Le réalisme méthodique* [Paris: Téqui, n.d.], p. 87; quoted in Mascall's translation, *The Openness of Being*, p. 93).

45. This, I believe, is the basic shortcoming of *Method in Theology*, by Bernard Lonergan (London: Darton, Longman and Todd, 1972), the most articulate and persuasive of such efforts. These qualities are not so obvious in *The Relevance of Natural Science to Theology*, by W. H. Austin (London: Unwin Brothers, 1976).

46. In an essay, "Après une visite au Vatican," (*Revue des Deux Mondes* 127 [1895]: 97–118), which created quite a stir and in which Brunetière started with the remark that although science was in the eyes of almost everybody the voice of the future and the true religion, he found it more realistic to speak of the "banqueroute de la science" (p. 98).

47. The phrase is part of his answer to the question how the study of history can make one better and wiser: "I will answer you by quoting what I have read somewhere or other in Dionysius Halicarn. I think that history is philosophy teaching by examples." See his "Letters on the Study and Use of History, Letter 2, Concerning the True Use and Advantages of It," in *The Works of the Right Honourable Henry St. John, Lord Viscount Bolingbroke* (London: David Mallett, 1754–98), 2:266.

48. As done, for instance, by Jean-Théophile Désaguliers, in his *The New-tonian System of the World, the Best Model of Government: An Allegorical Poem* ... (Westminster: J. Roberts, 1728).

49. *Science and Human Values* (New York: Harper and Row, 1959), p. 90, where Bronowski argues that "like the other creative activities which grew from the Renaissance, science has humanized our values." Obviously then, science is not the source of values which, even according to Bronowski's implicit admission, it can only "humanize," an admission that can only be implicit as long as a propagandist of scientism tries to appear a humanist.

50. Quoted in *Time*, May 26, 1967, p. 48.

51. It is again the illustration of the logic connecting monotheism and science that James's endorsement of polytheism in a broad sense in the postscript to his Gifford Lectures delivered in the University of Edinburgh in 1901–2 under the title, *The Varieties of Religious Experience: A Study of Human Nature* (London: Longmans, Green, and Co., 1910), p. 526, goes hand in hand with the suggestion that the universe may not be truly coherent: "If there be different gods, each caring for his part ... [one must admit the possibility] of there being portions of the universe that may irretrievably be lost."

52. *A Pluralistic Universe* (London: Longmans, Green and Co., 1909), p. 198. James once more recognized that parting with strict rationality implied the possibility of incoherence in the cosmos.

53. Ibid., p. 319. The suggestion that rationality be replaced by intimacy may help poets but hardly the cultivators of "hard science," whose mentality was portrayed by James in memorable strokes in the first chapter of his work.

54. Quoted by A. Camus, *The Myth of Sisyphus and Other Essays*, translated from the French by J. O'Brien (New York: Vintage Books, 1960), p. 82.

55. For Tillich's statement, see his *Systematic Theology* (Chicago: University of Chicago Press, 1951), 1:237; for the comment made by J. H. Randall, Jr., see *The Theology of Paul Tillich*, ed. C. W. Kegley and R. W. Bretall (New York: Macmillan, 1956), p. 136.

56. R. W. Hepburn, *Christianity and Paradox* (London: A. & C. Watts, 1958), p. 156.

57. See "Israel in der Wüste" in Noten und Abhandlungen zum *Divan* [*West-östlicher Divan*], in *Gesamtausgabe der Werke und Schriften* (Stuttgart: Cotta, 1956–63), 2:280.

58. *Fear and Trembling: A Dialectical Lyric,* trans. R. Payne, 2d ed. (London: Oxford University Press, 1946), p. 32.

59. *Christianity and Philosophy,* trans. R. MacDonald (New York: Sheed and Ward, 1939), p. 78.

60. T. Gornall, *A Philosophy of God: The Elements of Natural Theology* (New York: Sheed and Ward, 1962), p. 7.

INDEX OF NAMES

Abbott, E. A., 351
Abraham, 34
Abu-Mashar, 338
Achelis, H. N., 381
Adickes, E., 126, 381
Adler, F., 185
Agassi, J., 235, 333, 421, 453
Agathon, 20
Agricola, 56, 353
Aiton, E. J., 364, 366
Alaric, 344
Albertus Magnus, Saint, 43, 344–45
Alcibiades, 20
Alembert, J. d', 10, 37, 65, 68, 77–79, 97, 126, 262–63, 346, 370, 424
Alexander of Aphrodisias, 433
Alexander the Great, 32, 320
Allah, 35, 42
Allorge, P., 442
Anaxagoras, 19–20, 317, 339, 407
Anaximander, 16
Anaximenes, 264
Andreski, S., 224, 416
Anselm, Saint, 36, 62, 121, 140, 231, 345–46
Apollonius, 12
Aquilecchia, G., 348
Aquinas, Thomas, Saint, 23, 36–39, 43, 48, 52, 62, 344–47, 358, 379–80, 453
Archimedes, 12, 17, 19, 24, 48, 232, 279, 305, 350, 402, 433
Ardley, G., 378
Argyll, duke of. See Campbell, G. D.
Aristarchus of Samos, 46, 266
Aristophanes, 265
Aristotle, 21–26, 29, 35–36, 38–39, 43, 48, 53, 55–56, 71, 134, 173, 207, 233, 265, 294, 311, 320, 340–41, 343, 345–46, 349, 352, 383, 433, 451, 453–54
Arnauld, A., 357
Arnold, M., 333
Arnou, R., 345
Asclepius, 24
Ashari, al-, 42, 411
Ashoka, 17
Augustine, Saint, 35, 62, 342, 385

Austin, W. H., 457
Autrecourt, N., 43–44
Avenarius, R., 216
Averroës, 35, 37, 346
Avicenna, 345
Ayer, A. J., 228–29, 412, 417–18, 425

Bachelard, G., 233, 421
Bacon, F., 4, 8, 12, 50–58, 60, 62–63, 80–81, 83, 85, 94, 98, 150, 231, 257, 282, 306, 321, 333, 337, 351–54, 362–63, 365–66, 449
Bacon, R., 38, 43, 82, 87, 305
Bailly, J.-S., 5, 8–11, 18, 316, 334, 336, 453
Balmer, J. J., 406
Baring, M., 451
Basalla, G., 451
Batchelder, R. C., 454
Bauer, G., 166
Baumgardt, C., 402
Baumgarten, A. G., 112
Bavink, B., 396
Bayle, P., 454
Beadle, G., 287, 442
Becker, C. ., 334
Beeckman, I., 357–58
Beer, G. R. de, 287
Beethoven, L. van, 310, 451
Belinfante, F. J., 410
Bellarmine, R., Saint, 371
Benot, Y., 362
Benson, L., 416
Bentham, G., 290
Bentley, R., 81–83, 122, 267, 360, 364–65, 367–68, 434
Bergmann, P. G., 271, 412, 436
Bergson, H., 223, 291
Berkeley, G., 77, 86, 257, 436
Bernal, J. D., 426
Bernard, C., 288
Bernhardi, F. von, 302
Bessel, F. W., 148, 389
Besso, M., 185
Blackmore, J. T., 393, 396
Blackwell, R. J., 252–53, 427
Blake, R. M., 359

Blake, W., 297
Blanchet, L., 419
Blanqui, L. A., 143
Blüh, O., 392
Blumberg, A. E., 412
Boas, G., 343
Bochner, S., 350
Bode, J. E. von, 379
Boehme, J., 140, 231–32, 419
Bohr, N., 171, 195, 198–212, 224, 249, 406–8, 410–12, 426
Bolingbroke, Lord (Henry St. John), 328
Bolman, F. de Wolfe, 384
Boltzmann, L., 170, 172–76, 189, 395
Boman, T., 344
Bonaventure, Saint, 344, 346–47
Bondi, H., 435–36
Borel, E., 404
Born, M., 210, 249, 308, 407, 410–11
Bossuet, J.-J., 357
Boswell, J., 97, 370, 413
Bothe, W., 206
Boutroux, E., 274, 437
Bouvier, R., 392
Boyle, R., 81–82, 89, 98–99, 354, 364, 366, 371, 410–12, 426
Bradley, J., 393
Bradley, O., 303
Bramhall, J., 355
Brasidas, 371
Brewster, D., 365, 370
Bridgman, P. W., 195, 228
Brinkley, L. J., 451
Broglie, L. de, 249, 258, 428
Bronowski, J., 112, 304, 329, 449, 457
Brownlow, W. R., 439
Brücke, E. W. von, 445
Brunetière, F., 328, 457
Bruno, Giordano, 44–45, 134–35, 217, 267, 348–50, 413, 434
Brunschwicg, L., 184, 401
Brush, S. G., 398, 421
Buchdahl, G., 378
Buckley, M. J., 387
Buddha, 15
Buffon, G., 10, 102, 284, 373
Bunge, M., 435
Buranelli, V., 430
Buridan, J., 43, 81, 347, 419
Burlingame, L. J., 445
Burnet, J., 343
Burt, C., 415, 450

Burtt, E. A., 438
Butler, J., 109, 335, 374
Butterfield, H., 325, 455
Byrnes, J. F., 318

Calvin, J., 52–54, 351
Campbell, G. D., 288, 443
Camus, A., 312, 457
Čapek, M., 392
Capra, F., 408–9
Carnap, R., 195, 204, 215–16, 218, 220–23, 225–27, 253, 262, 412–17, 427, 431, 438
Carneades, 28
Carnegie, A., 300, 447
Carneiro, P. E. de Berrêdo, 389
Cassirer, E., 368
Catherine the Great, 324
Cauchy, A. L., 68
Chambers, R., 441
Champollion, J. F., 429
Charleton, W., 94
Charlier, C. V. L., 118
Chenu, M. D., 347
Chesterton, G. K., 262
Cheyne, G., 427
Chobuda, B., 449
Chomsky, N., 289, 443
Christ, Jesus, 35, 136, 337, 345, 408–9, 452–53
Cicero, 29–32, 208, 342
Clagett, M., 350
Clark, R. W., 400
Clarke, S., 91–93, 119, 335, 368
Clausius, R., 165–66, 249
Cleanthes, 28
Clement of Alexandria, 145
Clerke, A., 412
Clynes, M., 436
Cobb, J. B., Jr., 456
Cohen, I. B., 362, 392, 400, 423
Cohen, R. S., 339, 416, 432
Coke, E., 55
Coleridge, S. T., 151–52, 382
Commoner, B., 447
Compton, A. H., 249, 308, 409
Comte, A., 12, 145–50, 152–53, 234, 251, 316–17, 321, 328, 334, 366, 388–90
Conant, J. B., 236, 311, 422, 451
Condorcet, M. J., 5, 97, 218, 254, 306, 314, 334, 344, 428, 449–50, 452
Confucius, 101

Conklin, E., 307
Cooper, L., 418
Copernicus, N., 8, 11, 45–47, 56–57, 96, 100, 103–6, 112, 115, 118, 123, 126, 141–42, 149–50, 152, 172, 177, 181, 220, 227, 241, 249, 266, 282, 316, 338, 349, 353, 360, 369, 372, 378, 414, 434, 455
Copleston, F., 276, 347, 386
Coulomb, C. A., 134
Coulson, C. A., 451
Craig, E., 120
Croce, B., 137–39, 386
Crocker, L. G., 362
Crombie, A. C., 419, 454
Cromwell, O., 100
Crusius, F., 63
Cudworth, R., 80
Cuénot, L., 288, 291, 444

Dalton, F., 123, 134
Dante, A., 325
Darwin, C., 153, 220, 238, 242, 255, 280–96, 298–303, 414, 439–48
Darwin, F., 286
Davis, B. D., 451
Davy, H., 134
De la Mettrie, J. O., 77, 361
Democritus, 25–26, 55, 173, 265, 313, 341, 433
Derham, W., 336
Desaguliers, J. T., 364, 370, 457
Descartes, R., 38, 49, 58, 62, 63, 65–77, 79–80, 82, 84–85, 87, 91–93, 97, 116–17, 134, 156, 192, 218, 231, 254, 260, 266, 280, 306, 317, 321, 354, 356–61, 366–67, 373, 419, 426, 431
Deussen, P., 127
Dewey, J., 215, 286, 440
Dhar, N. R., 16
Diderot, D., 7–8, 77–79, 97, 324, 335, 361–62, 370, 373, 418, 424, 455
Dilthey, W., 234, 421
Diogenes, 219
Dionysius of Halicarnassus, 457
Diophantes, 24
Dirac, P. A. M., 101, 199, 206–8, 211, 249, 257, 276, 407, 409–10
Dobzhansky, T., 440
Dominic, Saint, 344
Dostoevsky, F., 329–30
Drachmann, A. G., 342
Du Bois-Reymond, E., 397, 445

Du Halde, J. B., 453
Duhem, P., 13–14, 158, 233, 337–39, 350, 393–94, 418, 442
Dukas, H., 405
Dyson, F. J., 445

Eberhard, J. A., 114
Eccles, J. C., 426
Eddington, A. S., 212, 222, 257, 270, 308, 326, 415, 430, 437, 450
Ehrenfest, P., 198, 396
Einstein, A., 39, 44, 47, 156, 159–61, 181–201, 205, 207–210, 216–20, 227, 241–42, 249–51, 257–60, 263, 269–72, 309–11, 322, 349, 353, 366, 396, 398–407, 409–14, 421, 425–26, 431, 438, 455
Eiseley, L., 276, 440, 442
Eliade, M., 421
Elizabeth I, 51, 351
Elkana, Y., 422
Ellington, J. W., 375, 381
Ellis, G. F. R., 436
Engelbrecht, H. C., 382–83
Engels, F., 139, 300, 447
Enriques, F., 421
Epictetus, 27–28
Epicurus, 25–27, 31, 105, 341–42, 351, 372–73, 383, 433
Erdmann, B., 375
Ernest of Saxa-Gotha, 137
Ernst, J. W., 447
Euclid, 24, 58, 70, 187
Eudemus, 29
Euler, L., 126, 134, 150, 241, 324
Eve, A. S., 406

Fackenheim, E. L., 345
Farabi, al-, 35
Faraday, M., 101, 150, 178, 241, 249–50, 297, 396
Farrington, B., 352–53
Feigl, H., 394, 412–14, 428, 431
Fellmann, F., 348
Fénelon, F., 357
Fermat, P., 356, 358
Fermi, E., 305
Feuer, L. S., 406–7
Feyerabend, P. K., 422, 431
Fichte, J. G., 120, 128–30, 132, 134, 141–42, 145, 381–83, 387, 398, 419
Ficino, M., 45, 266
Fish, H., 364

Fisher, M. S., 364
Fitzgerald, G. F., 402
Fleck, L., 236, 422
Foster, K., 347
Fothergill, P. G., 441, 444
Francis, Saint, 89, 344, 450
Frank, P., 159, 185, 215, 394, 399, 402–3, 412
Frankl, V. E., 415
Franklin, B., 126
Fraunhofer, J., 148
Frederick the Great, 374
Freud, S., 220, 223, 299

Galileo, 4, 8, 20, 43, 46–48, 56–58, 60, 63, 75, 98, 100, 105–6, 115, 123, 126, 141–42, 147, 150, 172–73, 187, 230–32, 234, 241, 246–47, 249, 251, 254, 266, 279, 316, 320–21, 334, 340, 349–50, 353, 356, 358, 360, 366, 378, 384, 402, 414, 418–19, 425–26
Gall, F. J., 141, 147, 388–89
Galton, F., 441
Gama, Vasco da, 17
Gandhi, M. K., 15
Gassendi, P., 26
Gassman, D., 301
Gaubil, A., 453
Gaunilo, 121
Gauss, K. F., 126, 137
Geach, R. T., 346
Gell-Mann, M., 410, 456
Gerhards, K., 398
Gershenson, D. E., 339
Geymonat, L., 349
Ghent, W. J., 447
Gibieuf, G., 360
Gifford, Adam, Lord, vii, 3, 161, 317
Gilbert, W., 56, 353
Gillispie, C. C., 418, 420
Gilson, E., 258–59, 330, 339, 344, 346–48, 356, 358, 361, 419, 430–31, 437–38, 440, 456–57
Glanvill, J., 81
Glover, W. B., 355
Gödel, K., 253, 319, 412, 426–27, 453, 456
Goenner, H., 393
Goethe, J. W., 136, 267, 325, 330
Gold, T., 436
Gorgias, 31, 217
Gornall, T., 458
Graham, W., 285, 448

Grandmaison, L. de, 449
Gray, A., 286, 441–42, 446, 448
Gray, J., 289, 443
Greenberg, D. A., 339
Gregory of Rimini, 348
Gregory the Great, Saint, 343
Gregory, D., 360
Grene, M., 255, 429, 440, 445
Grew, N., 81, 262, 323, 363–64
Grimsley, R., 346
Grosseteste, R., 47, 320
Grossman, M., 400
Gruner, R., 350
Guerlac, H., 14
Guizot, F., 389, 446

Hack, R. K., 339
Haeckel, E., 301–2
Hahn, H., 218–20, 412–14
Haldane, J. B. S., 277, 294
Halley, E., 75, 94, 267, 360, 368
Hanson, N. R., 235, 237, 378, 391, 423
Hardy, T., 442
Harnack, A., 195
Harrison, A., 299, 446
Harrison, E. R., 436
Harrison, F., 299, 446–47
Hartner, W., 454
Harvey, W., 53, 72, 82, 352, 359, 366
Hastie, W., 375, 377
Hawking, S., 436
Heath, T., 32
Heelan, P. A., 409
Hegel, G. F. W., 12, 120, 128, 137–42, 145, 207, 321, 334, 383, 385–88, 398, 419
Heidegger, M., 426
Heisenberg, W., 198–200, 207–8, 249–50, 406–7, 409
Helmholtz, H., 136, 165, 249, 374, 394, 445
Helvetius, C. A., 77
Henderson, T., 389
Hepburn, R. W., 457
Heraclitus, 19, 264, 342, 433
Herbert of Cherbury, Lord, 89
Herder, J. G., 121
Hermann, A., 394–96, 399–400
Herneck, F., 399
Herschel, J. F. W., 111, 148, 151
Herschel, W., 110–12, 115, 124, 126, 134, 148, 150–51, 268, 365, 374–76, 389, 434

Hertz, H., 168, 249, 401
Hesiod, 23
Hesse, M. B., 338
Hevelius, J., 335, 356
Hevesy, G. von, 406
Hick, J., 438
Hiebert, E. N., 392
Himmelfarb, G., 283, 441–42
Hintikka, J., 454
Hipparchus, 148
Hippolytus, 433
Hitler, A., 301
Hobbes, T., 50, 57–63, 82, 100, 354–56, 364
Hocking, W. E., 406
Höffding, H., 202, 205, 407
Hoffmann, B., 405
Hofstadter, R., 447
Holbach, Baron d', 77, 218, 254, 368, 428
Holkot, Robert, 348
Holton, G., 400, 402, 405, 422, 430
Homer, 101, 325, 390
Hooke, R., 80–81, 94, 98–99, 354, 363, 427
Hooker, C. A., 212
Hooker, J., 293
Hoppe, H., 381
Hoskin, M., 368
Hoyle, F., 263, 269–71, 435, 455–56
Hugh of St. Victor, 49, 295, 358
Hugo, V., 274, 437
Hume, D., 54, 87, 96–112, 116–18, 145, 150, 154, 160, 216, 229, 257–58, 321, 335, 369–74, 383, 439
Huxley, A., 438
Huxley, J., 283, 287, 289, 303, 310, 442–43
Huxley, L., 455
Huxley, T. H., 280–81, 284, 286, 291, 294–95, 298, 300–301, 310, 324, 333, 366, 428, 439, 441–42, 445–46, 451, 455
Huygens, Constantin, 357
Huygens, Christiaan, 65, 126, 178, 359, 364

Ibn Abdallah Naime, 345
Infeld, L., 400
Isaiah, 344

Jacobi, F. H., 132
Jaki, S. L., 5, 333, 338–342, 344, 348,
358, 360–61, 365, 367–68, 373, 375–77, 379, 385–86, 389–90, 398, 404, 406, 409–11, 415, 424, 426, 429, 432–34, 450, 455–56
James I, 51–52, 98
James II, 97–98
James, W., 205, 257, 329, 379, 392, 457
Jammer, M., 395, 409–11
Jeannee, R., 442
Jeans, J., 269
Jeffner, A., 374
Jerome, Saint, 343
John Damascene, Saint, 345
Johnson, S., 219
Johnston, T. A., 379
Jolly, P. von, 166, 394
Jonah, 326
Joule, J., 394
Judas, 136
Julian, Emperor, 117, 343
Jungk, R., 449

Kant, I., 4, 12, 96, 112–29, 131–32, 134, 140–43, 145, 154–55, 159, 166, 177, 184–85, 191, 193–94, 212, 216–18, 229, 231, 257–60, 268, 298, 321–22, 333, 346, 367, 374–81, 383–84, 386–88, 398, 426, 433
Karsten, G., 168
Kaufmann, W., 183
Keith, A., 303, 449
Kellogg, V. L., 302, 448
Kelvin, Lord, 268, 321, 333, 394, 433
Kempeler, W. von, 430
Kenny, A., 37, 346
Kepler, J., 47–48, 60–61, 75, 100, 126, 148, 150, 152–53, 178, 187, 241, 249–50, 266, 337, 350, 354, 360, 378, 391, 403, 434
Kick, W., 399
Kingsley, C., 455
Kirchoff, G., 165–66, 397
Kirkegaard, S., 330, 407
Klein, M. J., 395
Kneller, K. A., 393
Knowles, D., 344
Knutzen, M., 112, 375
Koch, C., 401
Köhler, W., 259
Körber, H.-G., 401
Koyré, A., 14, 88, 230–35, 267–68, 349, 365–67, 418–22, 425, 427, 434
Kraft, V., 412

Kramers, H. A., 206
Kremmer, N., 416
Kronig, R., 406
Kuhn, T., 236–47, 420, 422–25, 445
Kurlbaum, F., 169

Lack, D., 441
Lagrange, J. L., 126, 134, 177, 398
Lakatos, I., 422
Lalande, J. J. L. de, 102
Lamarck, J.-B., 284, 294, 445
Lambert, J. H., 262, 374–76, 379, 432
Lampa, A., 394, 399, 405
Laplace, S. P., 12, 15, 83, 126, 134,
    148, 255, 262–63, 268, 336–37, 365, 389,
    429, 432, 434
Lassalle, F., 300, 447
Laue, M. von, 211, 406
Lavoisier, A. L., 123, 126, 134, 147
Leakey, R., 443
Lecky, W. E. H., 451
Lecomte, L., 6, 8
Leff, G., 347
Leibniz, G. W., 4, 7, 20, 80, 91, 93,
    112, 119, 121, 169, 280, 317, 335, 368,
    427, 453–54
Leighton, R. B., 197
Lemoine, P., 442
Lenin, V. I., 446
Lenoble, R., 356
Leo XIII, 379
Leonardo da Vinci, 4, 13, 158, 306,
    316, 418
Lessing, G. E., 197
Leucippus, 25, 433
Levi-Strauss, C., 416
Ley, W., 375
Lichtenberg, G. C., 125–26, 423
Locke, J., 91, 93–94, 260, 364, 368–69,
    426
Löwith, K., 350, 378
Lohne, J. A., 354
Lonergan, B., 457
Lorentz, H. A., 397, 402
Loschmidt, J., 172
Louis XV, 17
Lovejoy, A. O., 368, 422, 454
Lovell, B., 274
Luc, J. A. de, 125–26
Lucas, J. R., 379
Lucretius, 25–26, 105, 341
Ludwig, K. F. W., 445
Luther, M., 46, 349

Macaulay, T. B., 317
McFarland, J. D., 380
Mach, E., 14, 55, 96, 154–60, 166–67,
    169, 174, 176–79, 182–84, 188, 190,
    192, 195, 200–201, 215–16, 218, 220,
    222, 227, 251, 258, 260, 321–22, 338,
    347, 366, 374, 392–98, 400–403, 405,
    407–8, 412, 423
Machiavelli, N., 131, 382
Machin, A., 449
MacKinnon, E. M., 367
Maclaurin, C., 99
McMullin, E., 350, 422, 428
McTaggart, J. M. E., 141, 387
Mädler, J. H. von, 412
Magee, B., 412
Maier, A., 350, 422
Maimonides, 338, 345
Mairan, J.-J. d'Ortous de, 6–8, 18, 102,
    336
Majumdar, R. C., 16, 339
Malcolm, N., 437
Malebranche, N., 73, 77, 257, 357
Mallock, W. H., 417
Malraux, A., 325
Manuel, F. E., 367, 370
Marcel, G., 303
Marcus Aurelius, 27
Maritain, J., 431
Margenau, H., 406
Marx, K., 220, 300, 447
Mascall, E., 324
Masterman, M., 423
Maupertuis, P. L. M., 113, 156
Maxwell, J. C., 3, 101, 137, 186–88,
    241, 249–50
Mayer, J., 362, 455
Mayer, R., 394
Mayr, E., 445
Mehlberg, H., 425
Menger, K., 412
Merleau-Ponty, J., 432–33
Mersenne, M., 50, 58, 62–64, 66–67,
    70, 72, 81, 356–57, 360–61, 363, 452
Merton, R. K., 422
Metzger, H., 422
Meyerson, E., 185, 274, 275, 401, 422,
    437
Michelson, A., 186
Mill, J. S., 96, 150–54, 312, 323, 366,
    390–91, 454–55
Millikan, R., 269
Mirecourt, John, 43, 44

Mittelstrass, J., 339
Mivart, St. George, 439–40, 447
Moerbeke, William, 48
Monod, J., 270, 279–80, 435, 438
Montaigne, M. E., 44, 348
Montesquieu, C. L., 11, 336
Moore, G. E., 311
More, L. T., 370
Morgan, A. de, 352, 354, 455
Morison, R. S., 447
Moses, 23, 39, 206, 326
Mossner, E. C., 369–70, 372
Moszkowski, A., 451
Mouy, P., 358
Muhammad, 35
Mühsam, M., 405
Müller, J. P., 445
Munitz, M. K., 251, 270, 435, 438
Murdoch, J. E., 351
Murray, G., 343
Murray, J., 439
Murphy, J., 399

Nagel, E., 425
Namer, E., 348
Napoleon, 115, 365
Natkin, E., 412
Nebuchadnezzar, 321
Needham, J., 14, 338
Nehru, J., 15, 20
Nernst, W., 396, 435
Neumann, C., 165
Neumann, J. von, 303
Neumann, K. F., 386
Neurath, O., 195, 215, 218, 224–27,
    408, 412–13, 416
Newman, J. H., 281, 292, 439
Newton, I., 8, 11, 39, 79–80, 82–92,
    94, 97–99, 101–2, 105, 112–14, 116,
    118–20, 123, 126, 134, 136, 141–42,
    147–48, 150, 154, 160, 172–73, 178,
    182, 189–90, 193, 241–42, 249, 251,
    263–64, 267, 299, 314, 321, 328, 338,
    340, 354, 360, 362–70, 373–74, 376–
    77, 384, 388, 414, 427, 432, 438, 452–
    53, 455
Nicholas of Cusa, 44–45
Niethammer, F. I., 382
Nietzsche, F., 137, 143, 220
Nogar, R. J., 439
Nordmann, C., 401, 404
North, J. D., 432

Northrop, F. S. C., 377–78
Novikov, I. D., 272

Oakeshott, M., 354
Oakley, F., 347
Ockham, W., 40–43, 46, 48–49, 244,
    270, 347
O'Connor, D., 344
Oersted, H. C., 249
Olbers, W., 269
Olympiodorus, 433
Oppenheimer, J. R., 43, 305
Oresme, N., 43, 279, 347, 419
Origen, 145, 342
Orwell, G., 312
Ostwald, W., 159, 169–70, 184, 395,
    413

Paley, W., 342
Palmer, R. R., 334
Pantin, C. F. A., 440
Parmenides, 19, 436
Parrenin, D., 6–8, 17, 102, 334–35
Pascal, B., 61, 65, 71, 100, 146, 231–32,
    314–15, 317–18, 420, 431, 452–53
Patton, C. M., 273, 436, 445
Paul, Saint, 36, 94, 305, 345
Pauli, W., 198–99, 208
Pemberton, H., 80, 87, 362–63, 365,
    370
Penrose, R., 436
Penzias, A. A., 274
Pepys, S., 80
Peter Lombard, 36, 365
Peterson, J. F., 374
Petry, M. J., 385
Petzold, J., 182, 400
Philo of Alexandria, 338
Philoponus, John, 39
Pines, S., 454
Pinot, V., 334
Planck, E., 172, 179
Planck, M., 160–61, 165–83, 185–86,
    195, 197–99, 201, 215, 217, 220, 227,
    241, 249, 322, 338, 394–400, 402,
    406–7, 413
Plato, 19–22, 25, 46–48, 55, 134, 231–
    34, 255, 265, 325, 339–40, 343, 345,
    349, 352, 402, 419, 454
Playfere, T., 354
Plessner, H., 223, 415–16, 429
Plotinus, 134, 343, 345
Pohl, R., 396

Polanyi, M., 244, 250, 398, 425–26, 429, 444
Polybius, 32, 343
Pope, A., 99
Popkin, R. H., 356
Popper, K. R., 88, 118, 142, 215, 226, 229, 235, 248, 250–51, 255, 260, 343, 380–81, 383, 387, 417, 426–29, 431–34, 438, 452–53
Porphyry of Tir, 345
Poseidonius, 29
Power, H., 370
Preller, V., 345
Price, D. J. de Solla, 342
Ptolemy, 10, 24, 32, 46, 266, 336, 434
Pusey, E. B., 439
Putnam, H., 456
Pyrrho, 31, 32
Pythagoras, 18, 46, 266, 342

Quine, W. V., 422

Rabi, I. I., 329
Radakovič, T., 412
Rahn, J., 381
Randall, J. H., Jr., 440, 457
Rangnekar, D. K., 15
Ranke, L., 453
Rankine, M., 268, 395
Raven, C. E., 354, 445
Rawley, W., 50, 351
Rayleigh, Lord (R. J. Strutt), 171
Redondi, P., 419
Reichenbach, H., 195, 246, 405, 412
Reinhold, K. L., 115, 120, 129, 377
Renan, E., 306–7
Ribot, T. A., 223
Rieser, L. M., 451
Roberval, G. P. de, 356
Robinson, B., 88
Rockefeller, J. D., Jr., 300, 447
Rohault, J., 91
Romanes, G., 153–54, 391
Rosanes, J., 410
Rosmini, S. A., 138, 386
Rosse, Lord, 151
Rousseau, J.-J., 97, 124, 306
Royce, J., 257
Rubens, H., 169
Russell, B., 14, 37, 122, 195, 204, 226, 247, 276, 298, 338, 346, 404, 412, 425
Rutherford, E., 101, 406–8
Ryle, G., 425, 431

Sabunde, Raymond de, 44, 348
Saint-Simon, C. H., 218
Sakurai, J. J., 410
Salusbury, T., 350
Sambursky, S., 342
Sarton, G., 12–13, 32, 337–38
Saunderson, N., 78, 361
Scheffler, I., 424, 431
Scheiner, C., 364
Schelling, F. W. J., 126, 128, 132–37, 139, 142, 232, 350, 382–85, 387, 419
Schiller, J. C. F., 377
Schlegel, R., 456
Schlick, M., 185, 204, 215–19, 222, 227, 404, 412–13, 415–16
Schmidt, O., 432
Schopenhauer, A., 386–87
Schrödinger, E., 198–99, 209, 211–13, 249, 343, 406, 410–11, 430
Schumacher, H. C., 385
Schwab, J. C., 114, 376
Scott, J. F., 358
Scott, W., 390
Scotus, Duns, 121, 344
Seeliger, H., 189
Selig, C., 401
Seneca, 427
Settle, T. B., 418
Sextus Empiricus, 31, 341–42
Shakespeare, W., 325
Shankland, R. S., 403, 409
Shapere, D., 418, 424
Shapley, H., 287, 412
Shaw, B., 191, 302, 404, 448
Shea, W. R., 427
Sheddon, G. F., 440
Shiva, 409
Shute, E., 441
Siegmund, G., 376
Sighart, J., 348
Sillem, E., 345
Simpson, G. G., 287–88, 440, 442
Singer, D. W., 348
Singer, P., 450
Skinner, B. F., 224, 417
Slater, J. C., 206
Smart, C. C., 379, 418
Smith, E. B., 334, 453
Smith, N. K., 106–8, 369, 370, 372–73, 378
Snow, C. P., 197–98, 325, 406, 455
Socrates, 19–24, 27, 29–30, 207, 233, 312, 317, 407, 419–20, 454

Solomon, 326
Solon, 265
Solovine, M., 192
Solzhenitsyn, A., 138
Sommerfeld, A., 189, 405, 451
Sorokin, P., 224
Souciet, E., 453
Spedding, J., 351–52
Spinoza, B., 76–77, 79, 126, 129, 132–33, 140, 179–80, 231–32, 234, 254, 311, 335, 361, 419
Stägemann, C. F. A. von, 379
Stahl, G. E., 115
Stanhope, Lord (Philip), 102
Steen, L. A., 430
Stegmüller, F., 348
Stewart, R., 369
Stephani, H., 382
Stimson, D., 367
St. John-Stevas, N., 451
Strasser, J., 394
Struve, F. G. W., 389
Stuckenberg, J. H. W., 377
Stuewer, R. H., 409
Sullivan, J. W. N., 428
Suppe, F., 423
Switzer, J. E., 404
Sylla, E. D., 351
Szalai, A., 416
Szent-Gyorgyi, A. von, 304

Talmey, M., 401
Tannery, P., 32
Tchaadaev, P., 231–32, 419–20
Teilhard de Chardin, P., 303, 449
Telesius of Cosenza, 353
Tempier, E., 39
Temple, W., 65, 426
Teske, J., 375
Thackray, A., 418
Thales, 16, 19, 279, 317
Theodoric of Freiberg, 43
Theophrastus, 25, 265
Thiébault, D., 455
Thiele, J., 398
Thiesen, M., 171
Tillich, P., 330, 457
Tindal, M., 7, 335
Toland, J., 89
Torrance, T. F., 352, 405, 426
Torricelli, E., 61
Toulmin, S., 423, 445
Treitschke, H., von, 302

Tschirnhausen, E. W. von, 76
Tyndall, J., 286

Vaihinger, H., 380
Valat, J.-P.-F., 389
Van Leeuwen, H. G., 354
Varro, M. Terentius, 30, 342
Vaucouleurs, G. de, 272
Vernet, M. P., 440
Voltaire, 5, 8–11, 18, 79, 97, 263, 306, 314–16, 318, 354, 362, 370, 450, 452–53
Vorzimmer, P. J., 440
Vucinich, A., 450
Vuillemin, J., 381

Waddington, C. H., 310–11
Wade, N., 450
Waismann, F., 412
Walker, A., 443
Wallace, A. R., 289
Wallace, W. A., 347, 420
Wallerius, J. G., 126
Warburton, W., 117, 367, 377
Warshaw, T. S., 456
Wassermann, A. von, 236
Watson, J. B., 215
Watson, W. H., 423
Webb, C. C. J., 348
Wedgwood, J., 441
Weidler, J. F., 336
Weinberg, S., 430, 437, 456
Weisheipl, J. A., 37, 346–47
Weismann, A., 294
Weisshuhn, 381
Weisskopf, V. F., 274, 456
Weizsäcker, C. F. von, 435
Wenley, R. M., 379
Westfall, R. S., 366–67, 420
Weyl, H., 413
Wheeler, J. A., 273, 426, 436, 445
Whewell, W., 4, 12, 153, 268, 333, 391
Whiston, W., 367, 373
White, L., Jr., 450
White, T., 60, 355–56
Whitehead, A. N., 14, 191, 222, 232, 281, 327, 341, 351, 373–74, 378, 415, 438
Whitrow, G., 375
Whittaker, E. T., 37, 346, 406
Whorf, B. L., 422
Wien, W., 169–70, 396
Wigner, E. P., 257, 410, 443–44

Wilkins, J., 82
Willey, B., 368
Williams, L. P., 337, 396
Wills, C., 443
Winterl, J. J., 388
Wisdom, J., 417
Witelo, 43
Wittgenstein, L., 215–16, 275, 412, 423, 437–38
Wolf, R., 385
Wolff, C., 91, 112, 262, 367, 432
Wood, R. W., 171–72, 396
Wright, G. H. von, 437
Wright, T., 375
Wundt, W., 156
Wyler, A., 430

Xenophanes, 434
Xenophon, 25

Yahweh, 42, 344
Yates, F., 45, 348
Young, R. V., Jr., 450

Zach, F. X. von, 137
Zel'dovich, Ya. B., 272
Zeno of Citium, 25, 27, 30–31
Zeno of Elea, 219, 312
Zermelo, E., 395
Zeus, 24, 28
Zilsel, E., 412
Ziman, J. M., 304–5
Zoroaster, 126

INDEX OF SUBJECTS

Absolute, as embodied in laws of physics, 167, 169–70, 172–73, 183
Absolute center, 113
Absolute ego, 129
Absolute origins, 286
Absolute units, 170
Absolute value of metric, 183
Agnosticism, 47, 311
Algebra, noncommutative, 210
Anagenesis, evolutionary, 310
Analogy, ontological, 54, 387
Analytical geometry, 66, 354
Ancient cultures. See Stillbirths of science
Angular momentum in planetary system, 114, 360, 365, 432
Animals: attributed morality, 146; attributed consciousness, 291, 428; as machines, 361; as superior to human foetus, 450
Animism, attributed to nature, 16, 22, 135, 203, 207, 285, 291, 349, 382–83, 386, 407–9

Antichance, 444
Antimatter, 211
Antinomies, 122–23, 380
A priori approach in science, 21–22, 38, 54, 71–72, 114–15, 118, 135, 137, 186, 193, 256–57, 326, 359, 384, 402, 405, 430
Artisans and science, 78
Artistic experience, as foundation of epistemology, 132
Asteroids, search for, 137
Astronomy: as example of completed science, 148; future of, predicted, 214
Atheism (atheists), 79, 81–82, 193, 324, 326, 351, 355, 357–58, 364, 450
Atomic bomb and ethics, 303–4
Atomism (atoms), 25–26, 55, 122–23, 126, 154, 173, 176–77, 182, 200, 341, 351–52, 365, 396, 400, 433
Atomism, psychological, 154, 392
Averroism, rejection of, 39
Averroists, 35–36

Beauty of equations, 188, 190, 410
Behaviorism, 53, 215, 225
Belief in objective world, 186
Believers and scientists, 157, 393
Bible: notion of universe in, 36, 39–40, 42, 44–46; enjoins mastery of nature, 49, 358; ignorance of, 325–26, 456
Biology: as completed, 148; reductionist, 221
Biotonic laws, 444
Birth of science. See Origin of science
Black-body radiation, 169–70, 290, 394–95, 397
Black holes, 272, 436
Bohr-Kramers-Slater theory, 206–7, 409
Bohr's atom model, 198–200
Boundary conditions: and quantum of action, 290; as evidence of design, 292; hierarchy of, 292
Brain: primitive, and language, 289; as product of survival, 304
Brain-mind relationship, 253–55, 289. See also Mind; Mind-body relation
Buddhism, 15–17, 108, 143–44, 159–60, 386, 408, 445
Byzantine thought, 35

Capitalism and Darwinian evolution, 300–301
Cartesianism: and natural theology, 67, 357–58; and Newton, 85–86
Categories, Kantian, 120, 185, 258–60
Causality, 53–54, 149, 154, 202–3, 207, 274–75
Cause: final, 20, 22–23, 31, 53–54, 80–82, 352–53, 365 (see also Teleology); formal, 53–54; infinite and finite, 133
Certitude, 66, 117
Chance, 279, 281, 293, 439
Chaos, 70, 113, 193, 264, 287, 359, 361–62, 433
China and science, 5–8, 13–15, 101–2, 192, 304, 315, 335, 338, 386, 452
Chinese mind, 8, 335, 452; and ideographic script, 156; and natural theology, 7, 386
Christian God, 179–80, 208
Christian Neoplatonism, 46–47, 104, 232, 402
Christian religion, 32–33, 124, 131,

157, 178–79, 344, 380–81, 383, 393, 437–38, 453
Christian theism and science, 39–40, 47–49, 90–91, 101–2, 138, 147, 153, 156–57, 179–80, 243, 266, 270, 304–8, 315–17, 338, 386, 453–54
Christianity and Hegelianism, 387
Christianity Germanized, 131, 382–83
Circulation of the blood, 72, 359–60
Civil War, American, 301
Class struggle, 300
Classics, teaching of, 325
Classification of sciences, 56, 334
Climate, and origin of science, 5–6, 9–10, 336
Colors, Goethe's theory of, 136
Compassion, and evolutionary theory, 310
Complementarity, principle of, 202, 204–6, 308, 322, 408
Compton effect, 206, 409
Computers, chess-playing, 259, 430
Consciousness, unity of, 105, 120, 221, 261, 372, 428
Consensus: ethical, 298–99, 304–6, 311; of scientists, 237, 240
Consistency: and science, 151, 180, 242–43; and philosophy, 203; of nature and ethics, 309; and cosmology, 456
Constants of physics, their universality, 170, 172–73, 175–76, 180, 396–97
Contingency, 35, 38, 89, 92–93, 102, 105, 135, 149, 153, 258, 270, 278–79, 292, 312, 320, 437, 454
Continuous creation. See Steady-state theory
Copenhagen interpretation of quantum mechanics, 195, 197–213, 411
Copernicanism, 45–46, 103–6, 115, 118–19, 123, 353
Copernican turn, 96, 100, 115, 378
Cosmological argument, 121, 379–80
Cosmological constant, 190
Cosmology (cosmogony): Hindu, 16; Aristotelian, 21–22; a priori, 21–22, 69–71, 73–75, 112–14, 256–57, 456; Epicurean, 26–27; Stoic, 28–29; and Averroism, 39; and Hobbes, 61, 355; Cartesian, 65, 69–71, 73–75; as natural theology, 78, 262; and Hume, 107; Buddhist, 108; Kantian,

112–14, 118; and Comte, 149, 389–90; as basic science, 156, 262, 273, 432; and statistical mechanics, 170; achieves scientific status, 189–90; 263; as study of totality of things, 190, 263, 433; slighted in reductionism, 228; and philosophy of mind, 277–78; Hegelian, 387; truth denied to, 432–33, and consistency, 456; and Gödel's theorems, 456

Creation out of nothing, 31, 33, 39, 70–71, 93, 143, 149, 263, 270, 274, 359, 382, 432, 435, 437, 454

Creativity, scientific, 60, 142, 176, 181, 183, 210, 244, 307–8, 374, 446

Creator, 14, 31, 33–34, 39–40, 44–46, 59, 69, 71–74, 83, 89, 106, 132–33, 138, 142, 180, 242–43, 259, 266–67, 277, 281–82, 285–86, 292, 299, 358–59, 382, 408

Cycles. See Eternal recurrence; Great Year

Darwinian theory of evolution: as growth of science, 238–39, 295; as vision, 283; difficulties of, 283–84, 287–89, 442–43; belief in, 283, 286, 294, 444; and natural theology, 283–84, 447; and belief in God, 285–86; as purely mechanistic, 279–80, 442; as deductive, 282, 440; and teleology, 286, 441–42, 446; basic fallacy of, 294; refractive of morality, 298, 446; and Marxism, 300–301; and capitalism, 300–301; and wars, 301–3, 449; and compassion, 310; as religion, 448

Decimal system, 12, 15

Deism, 10–11, 78–79, 89

Democritean ethics, 313, 452

Design, argument from. See Proof from design

Determinism: psychological, 154; mechanistic, 225

Dialectic, idealist, 120, 137

Dialectical materialism, 416

Dictatorial regimes and science, 309, 336

Ding an sich, 119

Discovery, scientific: as a mechanistic process, 147; complexity of, 152; and logic, 235, 251–53; in logical

positivism, 246, 252, 425; as Gestalt switch, 246; indicative of mind's powers, 249; phases of, 251–53; and artistic invention, 310, 451; history of, 352; in the future, 391

Divinity of the spheres, 23

DNA molecules and life, 444

Dualism, 253–55, 431, 440. See also Mind-body relation

Earth, motion of, 46, 358–59

Eclipses: as cause of mortal disease, 125; as source of superstition, 336; and general relativity, 189, 191, 403–4

Ecology: and ethics, 307; and Christianity, 307, 450

Economy of thought, 161, 176–78, 400

Education: religious, within Darwinian perspective, 285, 441; scientific versus humanistic, 325, 333

Electron spin, 199

Elliptical orbit of planets, 75–76, 135, 152, 391

Empirical investigation. See Experimentation

Empiricism: Baconian, 57, 353, 362–63; Hobbesian, 58–59; Lockean, 93–94; Humean, 98; positivist, 151–52; and the discovering mind, 248–49; and metaphysics, 384, 391–92; and history of science, 414

Energeticism (Energetik), 169–70, 395

Energy, principle of conservation of, 166, 168–69, 394, 397; equivalence to mass, 399

Enlightenment: and origin of science, 7–11; pretensions to full clarity, 91; slighting of historic Christianity, 315–17; mysticism of, 316, 334

Entropy, 166–67

Epicureanism, 25–27, 105, 281

Epiphenomenalism, 254, 428

Epistemological middle road, 87, 90–91, 161, 186, 207, 242, 333, 352–53, 366, 424, 427, 431, 456

Epistemology: and creative advances in science, 39, 90, 175, 178, 180, 192–93; and imagination, 120; and will, 129; and artistic experience, 132; and thought itself, 140, and

pragmatism, 201–2, 205; "scientific," 216; replaced by psychology and sociology, 232, 234–40; as theory of scientific knowledge, 255; and wonderment, 257–59; and possibility of science, 258–59
Erkenntnis versus Erlebnis, 217–19, 325, 415
Errors, making of, 25, 250–51, 254, 297, 341, 428, 445
Essence, 88. *See also* Substance
Essentialism, 453
Eternal recurrence, 16–18, 24, 29, 32, 107, 136, 143, 159, 268, 286, 295, 342, 373, 445
Ether: vortices in, 3, 333; existence of, 90; concave walls of, 268
Ether-drift experiment, 186, 394, 400–401, 403
Ethical consensus: need of, 298–99; and science, 304–6; not demonstrable, 311
Ethical progress and biological evolution, 446, 451
Ethics: of practical reason, 298; as countering evolution, 298, 446; pragmatist, 298–99, 304, 306–7; evolutionary, 298–99, 304, 310; as social custom, 299; positivist, 299, 304, 306–7; sexual, 299–300, 305, 307; and atomic bomb, 303–4; and inventions, 305–6; and statistics, 306, 449–50; agnostic, 311; "scientific," 311; and quantitative exactitude, 311, 451; and happiness, 312; and problem of evil and pain, 312; Democritean, 313, 452; indispensability of, 420; not founded on science, 451
Ethos of science, 308–9
Euclidean geometry, 48, 58, 62, 68, 359; and space, 113; and infinity, 113, 263–64, 267–69
Eugenics, 310
Europe, as cradle of science, 130, 158, 243
European mind. *See* Mind, European
Evil, problem of, 312
Evolution: Spencerian, 283, 440; as a dogma, 288; of man, 289–90, 439. *See also* Darwinian theory of evolution

Evolutinists, American versus European, 290
Existence: mystery of, 270, 278, 438; wonder of, 275; itself or God, 277; queerness of, 277–78; singularity of, 277–81, 283; actuality of, 346; reality versus structurality of, 437; puzzle of, 456
Existentialism, 312
Experience, inner, 413. *See also* Erkenntnis versus Erlebnis
Experiment, crucial, 56, 354
Experimentation, 22, 38, 55–57, 60, 72, 110, 141–42, 309–10, 359–60, 363, 382
Extension versus matter, 69
Extraterrestrial beings, 94, 113, 115, 355

Fact laws, 253
Facts versus theories, 186–87, 260, 352
Faith, role of, in science, 180, 338, 399, 405
Falsification theory of science, 251
Final cause. *See* Cause
Fine structure constant, 326
Finiteness of the universe, 190–91, 263, 404, 413, 433, 452
Five ways, of Aquinas, 23, 37, 292, 346
Formal cause. *See* Cause
Freedom, 225, 284, 307–8, 312
Free fall of bodies, 22, 230, 340
Free will, 24, 26, 39, 57, 122, 128, 136, 308, 341, 450
Fundamental (elementary) particles, 214, 406

Genetic engineering, 309, 451
Genius, role of in science, 9, 57, 100, 247, 253, 363
Geocentrism, epistemological, 118, 135, 149
Geometry: in rise of science, 48, 231–32; as handled by Hobbes, 58, 62, 355–56; analytical, 66; versus historical studies, 117, 367, 377. *See also* Euclidean geometry
Gestalt and Gestalt switch, 237, 423
Gifford lectures, vii, 3, 317
God: biblical notion of, 34, 42, 277; his omnipotence, 40–42, 347, 391;

his "materiality," 63; freedom of, 70, 359; personal, 179–80, 194, 208, 298; Christian, 179, 208; definition of, 229, 417; noncreated being, 273; fainéant, 267; and evil, 312; finite, 374. *See also* Christian theism and science; Creator; Deism; Proofs of the existence of God
Gödel's theorems, 253, 427, 453, 456
Graphology, 221
Gravitational collapse, 272–73. *See also* Black holes
Gravitational paradox of infinite homogeneous universe, 83, 123, 189, 290, 390
Great Year, 106, 113, 136, 143, 338, 340, 373, 374. *See also* Eternal recurrence
Greek science, 19–33, 155, 242; failure of, 13, 25, 32–33, 54, 320, 341; and Christianity, 32–33, 54, 343
Guilt, sense of, 298, 307

Happiness, and ethics, 312
Hegelian dialectic, 137–39, 198
Heliocentrism, 46, 266, 349, 414
Hierarchical universe, 113, 272
"Higher" physics, 136–37. *See also* Naturphilosophie
Historians of science: as new profession, 230–31; internalists versus externalists, 233–34
Historicism, 233–34, 236, 241, 322, 421–22
Historiography: of science, 3, 4, 13, 158, 233–34, 287–88, 316, 318–19; reductionist, 8, 224, 315–16
History: as cycles, 32; as cultural endeavor, 97; as pure will, 130; as thought, 141; as philosophy, 328, 457. *See also* Great Year; Eternal recurrence
History of science: and the Enlightenment, 5–12; and Sarton, 13; and Duhem, 13–14; and Hegel, 141; and Comte, 147; and Mach, 154, 177; and Planck, 175–76; and Einstein, 187–88, 192; and logical positivism, 220–21, 414; as a chain of revolutions, 232–33, 397; as a sequence of

intellectual mutations, 233, 243; as a lesson in philosophy, 233; as a succession of paradigms, 241–42; as supplanting study of classical antiquity, 325, 455–56; real course of, 336–37; as understanding of science, 392
Hydrogen, as ultimate, 287
Hypotheses, 84–85, 367, 427
Hypothetico-deductive theory of science, 244

"I," elusiveness of, in empiricism, 431
Idealism (idealists), 240, 257; German, 3, 128–42, 145, 150, 152, 252, 254, 384, 387
Ideal state, 129
Idea pool, as standard of ethics, 310–11
Impetus theory, 43, 425
Inclined-plane experiment, 230
Incoherent universe, 107–8, 151, 206–7, 390–91, 409, 411
Indeterminacy principle, 209, 308
India and science, 9, 15–16, 304
Induction, 85, 150–52, 177, 247, 362, 391, 405
Inertial motion, 37, 67, 358, 393
Infinite duration of the universe, 435
Infinite number, actually realized, 267, 346
Infinite regress, 273, 292
Infinitesimal calculus, 68, 358, 369
Infinite space, 83, 92
Infinity: Euclidean, 263–64; as foundation of science, 269; as mischief, 270; as catastrophe, 290; as intelligibility, 433
Infinity of the universe, 45, 83, 113, 263, 267–68, 376; optical paradox of, 75, 94, 156, 267, 434; gravitational paradox of, 83, 189, 267; center of, 113, 368, 375–76; as pseudo-deity, 268; as intelligibility itself, 433
Innateness of ideas, 67, 92–93, 357–58
Inquisition, Spanish, 138
Instantia crucis, 56, 354
Instinct, 103–4
Introspection, 221, 414–15
Intuition, 219, 414
Inventions: potential misuse of, 305–6; to be made mechanically, 353,

363, 370–71; a priori approach to, 363
Ionization tracks, 206, 409
Iron Curtain, 224–25

Jesuits, in China, 6–7, 315, 335
Judeo-Christian tradition, 194

Knowledge: as patterned on geometry, 66–67; biological view of, 146, 154, 255, 429, 445; content versus form of, 217–18, 225
Koran, world view of, 35, 42; theism of, 320

Lamarckism, 284, 294, 441, 445
Language: physicalist, 221–22; and meaning, 226–27; and primitive brain, 289, 443
Laughter, 223–24, 416–17
Law of three states, 145–47, 328
Laws of mathematics as matter of conditioning, 391
Laws of physics, noncontingent, 149; nonuniform, 151, 391; objectivity of, 169–70, 175–76; economic adaptations of our ideas, 176; and causality, 274; identity relations, 274, 437; not a grasp of existence, 274–75; contingent, 437
Libido, 220
Life: contingency of, 279; as product of chance and necessity, 279; as product of evolution, 287; as product of antichance, 444; and DNA molecules, 444
Light: and Descartes's universe, 74; as stream of quanta, 181; constancy of its speed, 188, 403; bending of, in gravitational field, 189, 403; duality of, 384
Logic: empiricist, 151; modal, 235
Logical atomism, 215–26
Logical positivism: and history of science, 220–21; and psychology, 220–21; and sociology, 224–25; and Marxist materialism, 225; and cosmology, 228; and natural theology, 228–29; and metaphysics, 276
Logicism, 413

Machines: boundary conditions of, 290–91; examples of scientific method, 353
Mach's principle, 156, 178, 182, 393
Macroevolution, 289
Man: as master of nature, 49, 295, 307; as rational animal, 146, 253, 261, 427–28; evolution of, 289–90, 439, 443; as purposive being, 294; purely animal, 440
Many-world theory, 411
Marriage, 346
Marxism: and logical positivism, 225; and Darwinian evolution, 300–301
Mass: Newtonian and Einsteinian concepts of, 241–42; equivalence of, to energy, 399
Materialism, 77–78
Mathematics: in Cartesian physics, 75, 360–61; and logical positivism, 219; and intuition, 219; and reality, 222, 415; heuristic value of, in physics, 257, 429–30; and ethical theory, 306, 311; and Baconian empiricism, 353–54; in cosmology, 433; and Gödel's theorems, 453
Mathieu's equation, 415
Matrix mechanics, 199, 210
Matter: as extension, 69; Cartesian kinds of, 73
Meaning: restricted to Erkenntnis, 217–19; as study of relations, 219, 225; and protocol sentences, 221–22; and langugage, 226–27; verifiability theory of, 228
Measurements: units of, 170, 396; and reality, 209
Mechanical models, 176; and philosophy, 291
Mechanics: theological origin of laws of, 156–57; inadequacy of, in physics, 168, 290, 317
Melanism, industrial, 289
Metaphysics: idealist, 3, 132–33, 136–37, 257; and empiricism, 53–55; as surveyed and completed by Kant, 116–17, 123; dismissed by Comte, 146–47; equated with idealism, 150; endorsed by Einstein, 195; "scientific," 217; indispensability of, 226–27; excluded, 276, 438; rationalist, 277; and Darwinian theory, 282, 284

Methodology. *See* A priori approach; Empiricism; Epistemological middle road; Epistemology; Idealism; Logical positivism; Positivism; Rationalism; Reductionism

Michelson-Morley experiment. *See* Ether-drift experiment

Microevolution, 289

Middle Ages: and origins of science, 13–14, 48, 158, 304–5, 320, 337; prejudices against, 13, 37, 317, 350, 453; and origins of classical physics, 43, 233; and appreciation of Greek science, 48; and technology, 48, 350

Middle road. *See* Epistemological middle road

Milky Way, 22, 75, 110, 113, 151, 265–68, 340, 360, 375, 433

Mind, European, 8; creativity of, 86–87; and objective truth, 248; and discoveries, 248–49; transcending empiricism, 248–49; mechanical models of, 249, 426; and external nature, 252; as epiphenomenon, 254–55, 428; nonmechanizable, 259; and Darwinian theory, 284–85, 299. *See also* Mind-body relation

Mind-body relation: interpretations of, 253–55; identity theory of, 254, 428; "eccentric" theory of, 255, 429; perennial relevance of, 259–60; and natural theology, 260–61; as equivocation, 415–16. *See also* Dualism

Minimum magnitude, 396

Minimum principle, 453

Miracles, belief in, 283, 351, 441

Moderate realism. *See* Epistemological middle road

Monotheism, 33, 35, 146, 153, 157–58, 337–38, 343, 391, 408

Morality: and religion, 229, 418; of unconditional validity, 446. *See also* Ethics; Paganism, and Christianity

Morphology, 280, 441–42

Motion: natural, 22, 340; inertial, 37; as coming into being, 37, 346

Muslim world and science, 35–36, 411, 454

Mutakallimun, 35

Mutations: intellectual, 233, 243; genetic, 443

Mutazalites, 35

Natural motion, 22, 340

Natural selection, 280, 282–83, 288, 293, 440, 443, 448–49

Natural theology: unpopularity of, 3, 317; and China, 7, 14; and deism, 7, 89, 314; consonance of, with creative science, 9, 49, 87, 95, 179–80, 192–93, 195–96, 241, 261, 273, 278, 293, 307, 313, 318–31; rejection of, and antiscientific reasoning, 14, 16, 33, 57, 64, 76, 79, 93, 95, 107–8, 111, 126–27, 136, 140, 143–45, 149; 151, 158–59, 208, 226, 228–29, 240, 312–13; and Hindu cosmogony, 16; and Plato, 21; and Aristotle, 22–24, 340–41; and Cicero, 29–30; and the Bible, 36; and Scholasticism, 36–38; and Aquinas, 37–38, 358; and Sabunde, 44, 348; and Copernicus, 46–47, 349; and Calvin, 52; and Bacon, 52–53, 351, 354; and Hobbes, 59; and Mersenne, 62–63; and Descartes, 67; and post-Cartesian France, 67, 357–58; and Newton, 83, 365–67, 432; and Clarke, 91–92, 335; and Leibniz, 93, 368; and Locke, 93–94; and Hume, 103–8, 335; and Butler, 109, 335; and Herschel, 111; and Kant, 115–16, 376; and Fichte, 131–32; and Schelling, 132–33; and Hegel, 140–41; and Mill, 150, 152–53; and Comte, 145–46; and Mach, 156–57; and Einstein, 191–95; and Bohr, 202–3, 208; and logical positivism, 214–15; and Popper, 226, 261; and Ayer, 229; and Koyré, 231; and Kuhn, 239–40; and mind-body relation, 260–61; and Newman, 281, 439; and Darwin, 285, 293–94; and Pascal, 314; and Voltaire, 314; its progress, 317, 324; and pluralism, 329; as a harlot, 330; and Roman Catholic declarations, 386–87; and Schopenhauer, 386; and Hegelianism, 387

Nature: as totality of things, 203; and thought, 207; as constituted by observer, 207, 436; as making science possible, 239–40; and paradigms, 240; declared to be unnecessary, 241. *See also* Animism; Objective physical reality

Naturphilosophie, 126, 134–37, 139, 384
Nazism: and evolutionary ethics, 310; ideology of, and Darwinian theory, 301–2
Nebular hypothesis, 389. *See also* Planetary system
Necessitarianism, 25, 35, 59. *See also* Determinism
Neo-Kantianism, 168, 177
Neoplatonism: Christian, 46–47, 231–32; Renaissance, 46–47, 90
Neptune: sighting of, 148; weighing of, 177
Newtonian science, 84–88; and Hume, 98–99; and Kant, 113–14, 118–19, 126
Newtonian synthesis, 88
Nominalism, 41, 222
Normal science, 237, 243–44

Objective physical reality, 169, 172–73, 178, 184, 198, 201, 211–13, 373–74, 406, 427
Observables, and physical theory, 200
Observer, and nature, 207, 430, 436
Occasionalism, 42, 347, 411
Ockham's razor, 41
Olbers' paradox, 75, 156, 267–69, 360, 368. *See also* Infinity of the universe
Omniscient spirit, of Laplace, 256, 429
Ontological proof, 36, 62, 67–68, 73, 91–92, 116, 121, 140, 231, 345, 346, 356–57, 418–19
Ontology, 53–54, 212, 234, 263, 275, 410
Order in universe, 193, 259. *See also* Consistency; Simplicity
Origin of science, 4–6, 9–10, 12–14, 90–102, 147, 158, 160, 192, 242–43, 296, 316, 333–34, 409, 420
Orwellian decade, 312
Oscillating universe, 269, 272

Paganism, and Christianity, 102, 157, 371
Pantheism, 35–36, 44–45, 54, 76, 79, 113, 125–26, 132–33, 140, 231–32, 267, 335, 409, 444
Paradigm theory of science, 236–41; and natural theology, 239–40

Periodic table of elements, 199
Philosophy, and logical positivism, 218–19, 227, 425
Phrenology, 141, 147, 388–89
Physicalism, 136, 217, 221, 225, 227, 428
Physicalist language, 221–22
Physics: Aristotelian, 22, 340; Cartesian, 75–76, 358; Newtonian, 83–85, 116–17, 142, 366, 454; Leibnizian, 93, 453–54; Kantian, 116, 123–27; "higher," 137, 383; Hegelian, 142. *See also* Quantum mechanics; Relativity
Planck's constant, 170–72, 180
Planetary system: formation of, 74, 114, 360, 374–75; unexplained features of, 83, 373, 432; and proofs of God's existence, 83, 373, 432
Planets: as sensitive beings, 32, 45, 135, 149; number determined a priori, 135, 137, 385
Plenitude, principle of, 120
Pluralism and natural theology, 329
Plurality of worlds, 119–20
Pluto, search for, 295
Politics and science, 318, 328
Polytheism, 27, 329, 371, 457
Population question and Catholic Church, 300
Positivism, 84, 145–46, 299, 388–90, 446–47
Positivist calendar, 145, 388
Positivist church, 145, 149–50
Positivist library, 150
Positivists, and relativity, 190–92
Pragmatism, 201–2, 205, 215
Precision, quantitative, 45
Prime mover, 23, 24
Private property, 300, 306
Process philosophy, 327
Proofs of the existence of God: from motion, 22–23, 37, 61, 346, 387; from design, 29–30, 62–63, 81–82, 106–7, 116, 153, 281, 292, 439; as five ways, 37; and psychological difficulties, 38, 345, 357; from gaps of knowledge, 83; and Popper, 142–43; and Pascal, 314, 452; and Voltaire, 314, 452; as skeletons, 330; from nature of ideas, 357; from conscience, 439. *See also* Cosmological argument;

Ontological proof; Natural theology; Boundary conditions; Teleology

Protocol sentences, 221–22, 415

Pseudoproblems, 225

Psychological atomism, 154

Psychological determinism, 154

Psychologism, 232, 240–41, 334

Psychology, reductionist (physicalist), 220–21, 413

Psychophysical causality, 256

Puritans, 90, 367

Purpose: in Greek science and philosophy, 19–30; in nature, 29–30, 62–63, 81, 124, 291, 352, 364, 444; and scientific research, 279, 295; and biological evolution, 279–96; and natural selection, 280; the inconsistency of arguing against, 281; analogous realization in nonconscious living beings, 293; obviated in nature, 297. *See also* Proof from design

Pythagorean series, 385

Qualities, primary and secondary, 86, 88

Quantum mechanics: as final form of physical science, 197; and pragmatism, 202; and natural theology, 202–6, 208; and hidden variables, 209–10; its incompleteness, 210; nonstatistical assumptions in, 210; and complete description of nature, 211–12

Quantum of action, 165, 171

Rationalism (rationalists), 244, 261, 277; Cartesian, 65–79, 86–87, 91–93, 117, 358–63

Rationality: Greek, 19–21, 33; Christian, 34; Hebrew, 344

Realism, epistemological, 177–78, 182, 263, 275, 412, 426, 444, 456–57

Reality: truth of, 205; as equivalent to measurements, 209; commonsense, 212; versus mathematical formalism, 222; and logical positivism, 226

Reductionism, 96, 214, 415; threat to science, 219–22; and music, 222–23; and ethics, 298

Reduplication of living beings, 291, 443–44

Regress, infinite, 273, 292

Relations, as exclusive object of valid knowledge, 219, 225

Relativism of all knowledge, 234, 245, 403; and ethics, 304–5, 311, 446–47, 451; and theory of relativity, 311, 403

Relativity, theory of: special, 181, 183, 188; general, 183, 188, 216, 260, 265, 269, 271–72; and realism, epistemological, 185, 201; absolutist character of, 188, 451; and quantum mechanics, 209, 437; and ethical relativism, 451

Renaissance: and Neoplatonism, 46–47, 90; and science, 47–48

Research, scientific: as organized by Bacon, 57, 354; as purposeful enterprise, 279, 295

Revivalism, utopian, 40

Revolution, astronomical, 47, 421

Revolutions in science, 232–33, 237–39, 420–24. *See also* Gestalt switch; Mutations

Roman practicality and science, 32, 344–43

Rosetta stone, 429

Royal Society, 57, 80

Saving the phenomena, 19, 339

Scholastic philosophy, 34–37, 334, 344, 387

Schwarzschild singularity, 404

Science, genesis of, 4, 333–34; in ancient China, 5–6; in ancient India, 9, 15–16, 304; in ancient Greece (*see* Greek science); and ancient Rome, 32, 344–43; and Muslim world, 35–36, 411; and Middle Ages (*see* Middle Ages); and nominalism, 40–41; and Christian Neoplatonism, 46–48; and Renaissance, 47–48; as technical know-how, 51, 54, 57, 63–64, 77–78, 129–30, 328; and Bacon, 55–56; and Hobbes, 60–61; Cartesian, 72–76; Newtonian, 83–86; as self-sustaining enterprise, 90, 100; and Hume, 98–104, 369–70; and Kant, 112–15, 124–27, 375–78; as mechanistic development, 147, 152, 155; justified by social usefulness,

148; and Comte, 148–49, 389–90; as economy of thought, 161, 176; based on belief in objective world, 186; as completed in quantum mechanics, 197; and logical positivism, 216–18, 228; as chain of revolutions, 232–33, 237–39, 420–24; as set of research programs, 235; as succession of images, 235–36; as succession of themata, 236; as set of myths, 236; as paradigms and paradigm-shifts, 236–44; as Darwinian evolution, 238–39, 295; coherence of, through time, 239; as growth, 243; as two-tiered enterprise, 244; as chain of discoveries, 249; as personal knowledge, 250; and intelligibility of the world, 258–59; as cosmology, 260, 263–64; as purposeful activity, 279, 295; and ethical consensus, 304–6; ethos of, 308–9; spread of, in non-Western cultures, 309; and totalitarian regimes, 309; as making history, 318; and politics, 318, 328; and atheists, 324; bankruptcy of, 328, 457; and human values, 329, 457. See also, Origin of science; Christian theism and science; Naturphilosophie; Positivism; Reductionism; Relativity; Scientism, Stillbirths of science; Universe

Scientific theories: and facts, 186–87, 260, 352; discovery of, 253; as free creations, 260; convergence of, 338

Scientism, 3–4, 218, 279, 303, 329, 333, 457

Scientists: and theism, 157, 393; as ethical children, 303–4; as ethically neutral, 305

Selection, natural. See Natural selection

Sensationism, 78, 103, 155, 158–59, 176, 182, 397–98, 407–8, 411

Simplicity, 46, 193, 228, 349

Simultaneity, 217, 414

Singularities in nature, 44, 75, 262–74, 276–81, 433, 436

Singularity of existence, 277–81, 283

Skepticism, 31–32, 43–44, 62, 69, 108, 293

Sociology, 224–25, 416

Solar system, stability of, 83, 148, 389. See also Planetary system

Solipsism, 262, 374, 411, 432

Sophists, 31–32

Soul, immortality of, 20–21, 30, 39, 407, 419. See also Mind-body relation

Soviet scientists and freedom, 308

Soviet slave labor camps, 303

Space, 45, 83, 113, 190, 349

Species, biological, 282, 287

Stars, parallax of, 389. See also Milky Way; Olbers' paradox

Statistical character of physical interactions, 206

Statistical mechanics and cosmology, 175–76

Statistics as standard of ethics, 306, 449–50

Steady-state theory, 269–71, 435

Stillbirths of science, 9–10, 99–100, 107, 147, 160, 242–43, 295–96, 304, 309, 319, 409

Stoics, science of the, 27–29

Subconscious, 221

Subjectivism, 128, 139, 142

Substance, 54, 346, 433. See also Essence

Suffering, 298

Sufficient reason, principle of, 387

Supernatural, the, and science, 47

Survival of the fittest, 298, 300–303

Symmetry, 211, 257

Taoism, 15, 408

Technology: and the Middle Ages, 48, 350; as science, 51, 54, 57, 63–64, 77–78, 129–30, 328–29

Teleology, 19–23, 80–81, 83, 106–7, 207, 286, 294–95, 352, 363–64, 380, 441–42. See also Causes; Purpose

Teleonomy, 294

Theism, 328–30. See also Christian theism and science; Natural theology; Proofs of the existence of God

Theology, mythological, 23–24

Theology, natural. See Natural theology

Theories. See Scientific theories

Thermodynamics, 166, 168–69, 338

Thinking machines, 259

Thought experiments, 209, 230

Three-Worlds theory of mind-body relation, 255, 429
Tides, 251, 355, 427
Time, perspective of, 295–96
Totalitarian regimes and science, 309
Totality of things, 276, 421, 433
Transcendental perspectives, elimination of, 372
Truth: and relevant community, 237; authority of, 427, 431
Two cultures, 325, 455
Two-tiered theory of science, 244

Unified field theory, 193, 257
Universals, 41, 327, 456
Universe: necessary, 25, 35–36, 59; a clockwork, 30, 91, 342; incoherent, 42, 151, 281, 411, 457; simple, 46; richly variegated, 76; aborted, 108; of imagination, 110; hierarchically organized, 113, 272; multidimensional, 119, 379; notion of, invalid, 121–22; evolving in time, 122, 268, 276; of causation, 150–51; oneness of, 176; wholeness of, 189; expanding, 190, 272; notion of, valid, 191, 248, 275–76; givenness of, 193; order of, 193; a purely regulative principle, 248; embodiment of objective truths, 248; notion of, indispensable for science, 251; totality of things, 261, 269, 276; coherent, 263, 276, 309, 311; end of, 272; coming into being of, 272–73; beginning of, 274; totality of facts, 275. See also Contingency; Cosmology; Finiteness of the universe; Gravitational collapse; Infinity of the universe; Oscillating universe; Singularities in nature; Steady-state theory
Uranus, discovery of, 148

Vacuum, 61, 354, 355
Variety of things, 76–77, 280
Venus, rotation of, 106, 372–73
Verein Ernst Mach. See Vienna Circle
Verifiability theory of meaning, 228
Vienna Circle, 215, 218, 224–27, 412
Vitalism, 291, 445
Vortices, 3, 27, 72–73, 333, 359, 361

War, 138, 301–3
Wave mechanics, 199
Wien's law, 169–70
Will, 129, 131, 383, 386. See also Animism, attributed to nature; Free will
Wonderment, 257–58
World, comprehensibility of, 192–93, 258

Yin and yang, 204